
VOLUME XIV/2

EU Law and the Welfare State

The Collected Courses of the Academy of European Law
Edited by Professor Philip Alston, Professor Gráinne de Búrca, and Professor Bruno de Witte

This series brings together the Collected Courses of the Academy of European Law in Florence. The Academy's mission is to produce scholarly analyses which are at the cutting edge of the two fields in which it works: European Union law and human rights law. A 'general course' is given each year in each field, by a distinguished scholar and/or practitioner, who either examines the field as a whole through a particular thematic, conceptual, or philosophical lens, or who looks at a particular theme in the context of the overall body of law in the field. The Academy also publishes each year a volume of collected essays with a specific theme in each of the two fields.

EU Law and the Welfare State

In Search of Solidarity

Edited by
GRÁINNE DE BÚRCA

Academy of European Law
European University Institute

OXFORD
UNIVERSITY PRESS

OXFORD
UNIVERSITY PRESS

Great Clarendon Street, Oxford OX2 6DP

Oxford University Press is a department of the University of Oxford.
It furthers the University's objective of excellence in research, scholarship,
and education by publishing worldwide in

Oxford New York

Auckland Cape Town Dar es Salaam Hong Kong Karachi
Kuala Lumpur Madrid Melbourne Mexico City Nairobi
New Delhi Shanghai Taipei Toronto

With offices in

Argentina Austria Brazil Chile Czech Republic France Greece
Guatemala Hungary Italy Japan Poland Portugal Singapore
South Korea Switzerland Thailand Turkey Ukraine Vietnam

Oxford is a registered trade mark of Oxford University Press
in the UK and in certain other countries

Published in the United States
by Oxford University Press Inc., New York

First published 2005

British Library Cataloguing in Publication Data
Data available

Library of Congress Cataloging in Publication Data

EU law and the welfare state: in search of solidarity / edited by Gráinne de Búrca.
p. cm.
Includes bibliographical references and index.
ISBN 0–19–928740–6 (hardback: alk. paper)—ISBN 0–19–928741–4
(pbk.: alk. paper) 1. Public welfare—Law and legislation—European Union
countries. 2. Welfare state—European Union countries. I. Title: European
Union law and the welfare state. II. De Búrca, G. (Gráinne)
KJE3431.E9 2005
344.2403′165—dc22 2005021915

Typeset by Newgen Imaging Systems (P) Ltd., Chennai, India
Printed in Great Britain
on acid-free paper by
Biddles Ltd., King's Lynn

ISBN 0–19–928740–6 (Hbk.)
ISBN 0–19–928741–4 (Pbk.)

1 3 5 7 9 10 8 6 4 2

Contents

Table of Cases

European Court of Justice (alphabetical order)

European Court of Justice (numerical order)

Opinions

Court of First Instance (alphabetical order)

Court of First Instance (numerical order)

EFTA Court

France

United Kingdom

Table of Legislation and Treaties

European Legislation

Regulations

Directives

Decisions

Commission Decisions in Competition Proceedings

International Treaties and Conventions

National Legislation

Notes on Contributors

Julio Baquero Cruz is a Marie Curie Fellow at the Robert Schuman Centre for Advanced Studies, European University Institute, Florence. He holds a Ph.D. from the European University Institute (2001), an LL.M. from the College of Europe (Bruges, 1996), and a Spanish Law degree (Madrid, 1994). From December 2000 to September 2004 he was a référendaire at the Court of Justice of the European Communities, first in the chambers of President Rodríguez Iglesias (2000–2003), then in those of Advocate General Poiares Maduro (2003–2004). His legal publications include *Between Competition and Free Movement: The Economic Constitutional Law of the European Community* (Hart, Oxford, 2002; Spanish translation published by Civitas, Madrid, 2002); 'Constitutional Gaps in European Community Law', in *Mélanges en hommage á Jean-Victor Louis* (Éditions de l'Université de Bruxelles, Brussels, 2003); and 'The Economic Values of the European Union: Past, Present and Future', in M. Aziz and S. Millns (eds.), *Locating Common Values in the Constitution of Europe* (Ashgate, Aldershot, 2005).

Gráinne de Búrca is Professor of European Union Law at the European University Institute and a member of New York University's Global Law Faculty. She has been Co-Director of the EUI's Academy of European Law since 1998 and is Series Co-Editor of two Oxford University Press book series: *Oxford Studies in European Law*, and the *Collected Courses of the Academy of European Law*. She is co-author with Paul Craig of the textbook *EU Law*, currently in its third edition.

Maurizio Ferrera is Professor of Social and Labour Market Policy at the State University of Milan. He also directs the Research Unit on European Governance (URGE), Moncalieri, Turin and the Center for Comparative Political Studies ('Poleis') at the Bocconi University of Milan. He formerly taught at the University of Pavia and has been Visiting Professor in several foreign universities, including the University of California–Berkeley, the London School of Economics, McGill, the Juan March Institute, and the European University Institute, where he co-directed a Forum on the welfare state in 1998/99. He is a member of several academic and editorial boards, including the Research Council of the European University Institute (IUE) and the Executive Committee of the ECPR. He has consulted for the European Commission, the ILO, and the OECD on several occasions. His field of research is comparative social policy. He is the author of many books and journal articles. In English he has recently published *Welfare State Reform in Southern Europe* (editor, Routledge, London, 2005), *Rescued by Europe? Social and Labour Market Reforms from Maastricht to Berlusconi* (with E. Gualmini, Amsterdam University Press, 2004), and 'European Integration and National Social Sovereignty' (appeared in *Comparative Political Studies*, August 2003).

Síofra O'Leary (B.C.L., University College Dublin; Ph.D., European University Institute) is currently an Administrator at the Court of Justice of the European Communities, a Lecturer in EC Employment and Social Law and Policy at the College of Europe, Bruges and a Visiting Fellow at University College Dublin. She has worked for several years as a legal secretary at the Court of Justice and previously at the Universities of Cambridge (UK) and Cádiz (Spain). She is the author of two books, entitled *The Evolving Concept of Community Citizenship* (Kluwer, Amsterdam, 1996) and *Employment Law at the European Court of Justice* (Hart, Oxford, 2001). She has published extensively in academic journals on the protection of fundamental rights in the EU, the free movement of persons and services, and EU citizenship generally.

Vassilis Hatzopoulos is a full-time Assistant Professor at the Democritus University of Thrace and teaches EC Law, as a visitor, in the University of Athens and the National School for Public Administration, Athens. He also teaches a seminar on the 'Area of Freedom Security and Justice' at the College of Europe, Bruges. He has been practising as a lawyer at the Athens Bar since 1995 and has advised the Secretary General of Commerce (2000–2001), on behalf of which he represented the Greek Government at the OECD Regulatory Reform Assessment (2001) and at the EC Commission SMEs initiative (2002). Until the end of 2004 he was a consultant for the Greek Rail (OSE) on issues of market deregulation. His Ph.D. (Strasbourg) has been published as *Free Movement of Services and the Principle of Equivalence and Mutual Recognition* by Bruylant (Brussels)/Sakkoulas (Athens) (1999). He is a regular contributor to the *Common Market Law Review*, where he has published case notes, articles, and book reviews. Recently he published an article on the impact of the free movement and competition rules on healthcare services ('Killing National Health and Insurance Systems but Healing Patients? The European Market for Health Care Services after the Judgments of the ECJ in Vanbraekel and Peerbooms', 4 *CMLRev.* (2002) 683–729) and, in Greek, a monograph on the doctrine of essential facilities (Sakkoulas, Athens, 2002).

Dorte Sindbjerg Martinsen is Assistant Professor at University of Copenhagen, Institute of Political Science. She holds a Ph.D. from the European University Institute, Florence and M.Sc. from University of Copenhagen as well as from the London School of Economics. Her forthcoming and recent publications include 'The Europeanisation of Welfare: The Domestic Impact of Intra-European Social Security' (forthcoming 2005/2006) in *Journal of Common Market Studies*; 'With the European Court Towards an Internal Health Market' (forthcoming 2005/2006) in *West European Politics*; and 'European Institutionalization of Social Security Rights: A Two-layered Process of Integration' (2004), Ph.D. thesis from the European University Institute, Florence.

Jonathan Zeitlin is Professor of Sociology, Public Affairs, Political Science, and History at the University of Wisconsin–Madison, where he is also Director of the Center for World Affairs and the Global Economy (WAGE) and Founding Director of the European Union Center. His current research focuses on experimental governance, Europeanization, and the reform of national welfare states. He edits the online Research Forum on the Open Method of Coordination, http://eucenter.wisc.edu/OMC/index.htm, and has presented his policy research to numerous committee hearings and conferences organized by EU institutions. Among his recent publications are: *The Open Method of Co-ordination in Action: The European Employment and Social Inclusion Strategies* (co-edited with Philippe Pochet and Lars Magnusson, P.I.E.-Peter Lang, Brussels, 2005); *Governing Work and Welfare in a New Economy: European and American Experiments* (co-edited with David Trubek, Oxford University Press, 2003); and *Local Players in Global Games: The Strategic Constitution of a Multinational Corporation* (co-authored with Peer Hull Kristensen, Oxford University Press, 2004).

1

Towards European Welfare?

GRÁINNE DE BÚRCA

The story of the European Union has been one of steadily expanding powers, of an incremental extension of policy capacity across many aspects of economic, political, and social life. And yet there are areas—even if they cannot be described as a 'nucleus of (national) sovereignty'[1]—in which the states retain primary competence and the EU's influence is indirect or relatively minor. The regulation of social welfare is often described as one of this kind, in which responsibility for the regulation and delivery of welfare lies largely with each state. Thus the argument is made that even though the EC for many years has had legal power to regulate aspects of employment, the remit of the EU's social policy remains closely tied to labour-market participation, leaving the broader field of welfare provision and regulation essentially to the states.

One of the aims of this volume is to revisit and to question this perception by investigating the various ways in which the EU, and EU law in particular, is having a significant impact on the laws and practices of the Member States in the area of welfare more broadly conceived. There are two main aspects to the claim that the EU has an important impact in this field. The first relates to the impact that EU economic law and policy have on existing national laws and policies in the area of social welfare and the second relates to the gradual emergence of elements, albeit still in fragmented form, of a distinctive EU welfare dimension.

As far as the first is concerned, there are a number of ways in which EU law has an effect on national welfare laws and policies. The most obvious of these concern the direct and indirect effects of EC internal market and competition law. The core commitment of the European project to the creation of an internal market free of barriers to the movement of goods, persons, services, and capital, and to a system of 'undistorted competition', has translated into a dense body of law created over the years through the interaction of the European Court of Justice (ECJ) and the EU legislature. And gradually, but in particular in recent years, the effect of the treaty provisions on the free movement of workers and services, and of EC competition and state aids law on the provision of important national services, have exposed the vulnerability of national welfare institutions to the varying influence of

[1] K. Lenaerts, 'Constitutionalism and the Many Faces of Federalism', 38 *AJCL* (1990) 205 at 220.

a range of European norms. In some cases, that influence is direct and disruptive, in others—as for example in the context of the disciplines imposed by economic and monetary union—it operates indirectly to create pressures and incentives for national welfare institutions and practices to adapt and change. It has long been evident to those familiar with EU law that the potential reach and impact of internal market and competition law is powerful and transverse, to enter and disrupt not only the obvious areas of inter-state trade in goods and commercial services, but also aspects of life which—although they may have an economic dimension—are not normally conceived of primarily in commercial terms. High-profile examples have included the regulation of the transfer of football players,[2] access to information on abortion,[3] access to higher education,[4] and most recently access to cross-border medical assistance.[5]

In relation to the second dimension, elements of an EU welfare law and policy, alongside the conventionally defined field of EU employment law, can be seen emerging through deliberate action in this field at the European level and not only in the impact of other EU policies on national welfare institutions. In the first instance, it can be seen to arise from the provisions on EU citizenship and more specifically from the ECJ case which has evolved around them. Secondly, it can be detected—even if only faintly so far, given the limited justiciability of some of the most relevant provisions—in parts of the EU Charter on Fundamental Rights, particularly in the titles on 'Solidarity', 'Equality', and 'Citizens' Rights'. Thirdly, it can be seen in the complicated body of EC legislation regulating the coordination of social security benefits. While this legislation was adopted mainly in the context of the internal market, in order to facilitate the free movement of labour, it has in substance become a partial guarantor of welfare rights for EU citizens. Fourthly, the large and expanding body of EC equality law, which originated in the provisions on equal pay and the general nationality non-discrimination clause of the Treaty, may also be seen as an element of the developing EU welfare law and policy. Finally and importantly, it can arguably be seen in some of the 'softer' attempts to coordinate across the EU a range of national social policies in areas such as employment, anti-poverty, pensions, and health.

More generally, EU organs and institutions themselves deliberately invoke a language that suggests the existence of a conscious European welfare dimension. While the 'European social model' is a term normally used to refer to the existence of common principles and features characterizing the range of different national

[2] Case C-415/93, *URBSFA v. Bosman* [1995] ECR I-4921.

[3] Case C-159/90, *SPUC v. Grogan* [1991] ECR I-4685.

[4] Case 293/83, *Gravier v. City of Liège* [1985] ECR 593.

[5] Cases C-120/95 *Decker* [1998] ECR I-1831, C-158/96 *Kohll v. Union des Caisses de Maladie* [1998] ECR I-1931, C-368/98 *Vanbraekel v. ANMC* [2001] ECR I-5363, C-157/99 *Geraets-Smits v. Stichting Ziekenfonds, Peerbooms v. Stichting CZ Groep Zorgverzekeringen* [2001] ECR I-5473, and C-385/99 *Müller-Fauré* [2003] ECR I-4509.

welfare systems in Europe, rather than to a collective or single model promoted at European level, the EU has also built on this discourse and has arguably exploited the ambiguity of the term. Indeed the renewal and 'modernization' of the European social model has been a theme of EU social policy over the last decade in particular. Even if the notion of the European social model is thus rather vague and diffuse, it suggests something which is simultaneously based on and drawn from various national welfare systems, but which is also promoted by the EU and independently shaped by developments at transnational and supranational level.

Simply to recognize the fact of these two distinct aspects of the EU's emerging welfare dimension, however, leaves open the question whether such a development is desirable. Indeed, profound divisions over both the current nature and the possible future of 'social Europe' emerged clearly during the recent Convention on the Future of Europe, which led to the drafting of the ill-fated EU Constitution. Deep disputes within the working group on Economic Governance led to the establishment of a separate working group on 'Social Europe', which in turn struggled to reach consensus or to come up with a significant set of proposals. And the final result—the settlement which was eventually embodied in the EU Constitution—has been described from one end of the political spectrum as a charter for economic neo-liberalism, and from the other as the blueprint for a socialist super-state.

More specifically, the question whether the emergence of an EU welfare policy, both through the impact of EU economic law on national policy and through the emergence of a specific welfare dimension at European level, is a desirable development is a question on which observers are sharply divided, for a range of different reasons. In the *first* place, at one ideological extreme, there are those who oppose the active development of a welfare policy at any level of government, whether national, federal or supranational, and which see the market as the appropriate provider of public welfare. *Secondly*, however, even for the great many who consider that the role of government in shaping a system premised on social solidarity is essential, views on the proper role of the EU in this respect are quite divided.

(1) Again, at one extreme of the federalism spectrum there are those who reject a significant role for the EU in the delivery or shaping of public policy, including social welfare, and who consider that the nation–state remains the proper social and political unit for the making and delivery of policy.

(2) Then there are those who, while supporting a role for the EU in other aspects of cooperation and integration, including market regulation, consider that the EU is not the appropriate locus for the creation of a social welfare system. The range of reasons given for opposing this include the weakness of 'transnational majoritarian democracy', the difficulty of conducting redistributive politics beyond the state, the lack of a strong European demos and the insufficient bonds of social solidarity amongst citizens of different states particularly in a much enlarged EU, as well as the constitutional pre-commitment of the EU to certain core economic

policies which limit the choices and possibilities for pursuing particular welfare policies.[6]

(3) Finally, there are those who, while favouring the development of a strong EU social welfare dimension, are critical about the way in which that dimension has so far been developed, and who perceive the need for significant institutional and constitutional reform before the EU could properly be entrusted with the development of welfare policy.

The essays in this book demonstrate a shared belief that the EU does indeed have a significant impact on the provision of welfare within and across its Member States. Each essay also reflects an assumption—implicit or otherwise—that some degree of deliberate intervention by the EU in the field of welfare provision and regulation is necessary due to the challenges posed to national welfare systems both by EU economic rules and by many other socio-economic changes. Each of the essays also points, in different ways, to the range of political, social, legal, and economic obstacles to the creation of a coherent and significant EU welfare dimension. There are six essays altogether, each of which addresses a different dimension of the impact of EU law and policy on social welfare policy. Maurizio Ferrera's contribution begins with the fundamental question of how the notion of social citizenship in Europe has been transformed by the process of European integration. Three of the chapters—those by Síofra O'Leary, Dorte Martinsen, and Jonathan Zeitlin—most directly address the emergent elements of an EU welfare law and policy. The chapters of Julio Baquero Cruz and Vassilis Hatzopoulos, on the other hand, focus more on the effect of EU economic law on particular national welfare laws and institutions.

The book begins with Ferrera's essay, which examines how European integration has challenged the boundaries of welfare, interfering with the rules of inclusion and exclusion set by national citizenship, and weakening the capacity of states to control the resources and actors within their own 'social space and jurisdiction'. Ferrera questions whether some form of post-state solidarity is possible, and in so doing explores both the impact of European integration on the boundaries of social protection at the national level, as well as the emerging 'spatial architecture of social rights in the EU'. He describes the decoupling of EU social rights from national citizenship alongside the gradual construction of what he terms a new 'EU space for the exercise of social citizenship'. And while recognizing the limits of the EU's contribution towards shaping a transnational solidarity, he argues that EC law has nonetheless invoked the existence of 'a new pan-European solidarity space', restricting the discretion of states and challenging their tactics of closure.

Building on the conceptual foundation laid by Ferrera, Síofra O'Leary's chapter explores a specific dimension of this new 'solidarity space' in more concrete terms,

[6] Two prominent commentators of this kind are F. Scharpf, 'The European Social Model: Coping with the Challenge of Diversity' 40 *JCMS* (2002) 645, and G. Majone, *Regulating Europe* (1996) who in their different ways and for different reasons are sceptical about the possibility or desirability of a strong EU social policy.

by examining the provisions of the Charter of Fundamental Rights which can be categorized as solidarity and citizenship rights, and considering their potential impact—crucially via the interpretative role of the European Court of Justice—on the EU's embryonic body of welfare law. Of the latter, she suggests that 'the result of [the] symbiotic relationship between EC and national law is a developing multi-level system of social welfare entitlement, with welfare conditions subject to governance on two and perhaps more levels, depending on the internal organization of welfare and social policies in the Member State concerned'. More specifically on the issue of solidarity and citizenship rights, O'Leary examines and analyses the Charter provisions and the existing ECJ case law concerning three key categories of rights: those of free movement and residence, those of fair working conditions, and those concerning the reconciliation of family and working life. On the third category, she notes that the contribution so far of the EU, and of the ECJ in particular, has been minimal or non-existent, and suggests that the hope that the Charter might change this situation is very faint. As against this however, she argues (in a similar vein to Ferrera) that the rights conferred by EU citizenship—expanded in cases such as *Martínez Sala*,[7] *Grzelczyk*,[8] and *Baumbast*[9]—are clearly underpinned by an element of European social solidarity, which may well conflict with national welfare laws premised on bounded principles of territoriality, solidarity, and membership. Further, the impact of such case law may well be significant, in cumulative terms, on the medium- and long-term planning and financing of welfare benefits by Member States. Indeed O'Leary suggests that it may already have played a role in encouraging several Member States to restrict the conditions under which EU migrants from the newer Member States are entitled to welfare benefits. Similarly, the ECJ's strong rulings on the Working Time Directive, provisions of which are echoed in some of the social rights contained in the Charter, have arguably moved Member States to use various derogations under the legislation and to adopt a more cautious approach to the drafting of social legislation in the future. In this sense, her chapter demonstrates that the impact of the emergent EU welfare law—and not only its internal market law—on national law may well at times be perverse or counter-effective in the short term.

Continuing on this theme, Dorte Martinsen's chapter analyses the EC's regulation of social security for migrant workers. While this rather technical and detailed area of EU law is one often neglected by academics, Martinsen describes 'the mutual responsibility for welfare undertaken by the Member States of the Union' in this field as 'an extraordinary piece of "social Europe" ', albeit one 'patched up by judicial activism and political compromises'. Her chapter depicts the denationalization and (partial) deterritorialization of welfare brought about by the Social Security

[7] Case C-85/96, *Maria Martínez Sala v. Freistaat Bayern* [1998] ECR I-2691.

[8] Case C-184/99, *Rudy Grzelczyk v. Centre Public D'Aide Sociale d'Ottignes-Louvain-la-Neuve (CPAS)* [2001] ECR I-6193.

[9] Case C-413/99, *Baumbast, R v. Secretary of State for the Home Department* [2002] ECR I-7091.

Regulation (originally Regulation 1408/71, now 883/2004), and the evolution of free movement and cross-border welfare rights from rights held by workers to rights held by non-economically active persons, and more recently also by non-EU nationals albeit under restricted conditions. The account she provides of the origins and evolution of the social security legislation emphasizes the fact that although welfare policies were always regarded as a field of national competence, they were also from the outset subject to direct and intensive European legal regulation insofar as they could constitute an obstacle to the free movement of labour. Martinsen describes the close interplay between legislator and court in this field, showing how recent legislation such as the 2004 Residence Directive has consolidated the movement towards extensive residence rights for all EU citizens, guaranteeing full welfare equality after five years of residence in a Member State. The legislation demonstrates, in her view, 'that the Member States have approved a much greater social responsibility for each others' citizens'. However, she also notes that the principle of denationalization (making welfare rights available on the basis of residence rather than nationality) has taken stronger hold than that of deterritorialization (making welfare rights 'exportable', so that they can be claimed from one Member State while resident in another), with the Court's activism in relation to the latter having been politically curbed through amending legislation. Finally, she speculates as to whether the recent enlargement of the EU is likely to change the relationship between law (represented in particular by the Court) and politics (as represented in the legislative process) in this sensitive and politicized field of policy-making.

The two chapters which follow, by Vassilos Hatzopoulos and Julio Baquero Cruz respectively, look in detail at two particular aspects of the way in which EC economic law affects aspects of national welfare law and policy. Hatzopoulos looks specifically at national healthcare policy, and considers the impact of various aspects of EC internal market and competition law on this field. He begins by noting that although there are many varieties of national European healthcare systems, there can nonetheless be said to be a core principle of solidarity underlying them which is specifically manifested in the (guiding) idea of universal coverage—an idea that indeed found its way into the EU constitution. Outlining what might be called the EU's limited 'positive' policy powers in the field of health, including some indirect regulation in secondary legislative instruments such as Regulation 1408/71 (the topic of Martinsen's chapter), he points out that the real impact of EU law on national healthcare has come about not through these but rather through the relatively recent impact of internal market law, and the unfolding implications of the categorization of healthcare as a commercial 'service' under the treaty. Competition law, too, is very likely to have an impact on this field of policy although there is as yet considerably less case law than on the free movement of services. The flood of litigation triggered by the *Decker/Kohll* cases[10] demonstrates in part the significance of the differences between various national healthcare systems, since each factual

[10] Cases *Decker* and *Kohll v. Union des Caisses de Maladie, supra* n. 5.

situation has generated a different and detailed ruling by the ECJ, rather than simply an answer directing the national court to apply the same broad principle to the case. It also demonstrates the central role which the ECJ has created for itself in policing case-by-case the details of national healthcare systems under the Free Movement of Services chapter of the Treaty. An interplay of legislator and court in this field, as was seen in the area of social security benefits under Regulation 1408 discussed by Martinsen, is so far strangely absent, and judicial intervention—in such a complex, important, and nationally embedded field—dominates. The principle of solidarity appears, alongside those of protecting public health, and protecting the financial cohesion of national social security systems, as an exception to the application of the free movement rules, in a partial narrowing of the earlier *Sodemare* judgment which appeared to shelter national solidarity-based systems from a disruptive application of internal market rules,[11] and a significant degree of solidarity is one of the factors that may shield health insurance funds or other from the application of the competition law rules. Hatzopoulos' ultimate conclusion is that solidarity is a 'fundamentally national concept' and that, apart from some kind of legislative or open coordination, the Community lacks the legitimacy to pursue any significant degree of 'positive integration' in the field of healthcare.

In his treatment of the topic of EC involvement in regulating the provision of 'services of general interest', Julio Baquero Cruz adopts a rather different perspective. He argues that the EU's impact on a range of fundamental social institutions of this kind is such that it can be seen as 'contributing to the basic structure of a society of societies', even if the EU's social model for now is only a partial one. The specific issue of the organization and provision of services of general interest, however, like that of healthcare systems, varies enormously from state to state. His chapter is essentially a study of how one particular provision of the EC Treaty, Article 86(2), regulates the manner and the extent to which entities providing services of general economic interest are subject to the other treaty rules, in particular the competition law rules. One of his key questions—a question of considerable political salience given the importance to particular European states of the notion of services of general interest—is whether the EC Treaty in this provision effectively prioritizes the economic over the social, and his ultimate answer is that it does not. Rather he concludes that it establishes a mechanism for balancing the different concerns, and gives to the judiciary (national as well as European) the power to conduct this balancing exercise in specific cases. The ECJ in his view has properly used an intermediate 'objective necessity' test rather than a stricter and more intrusive proportionality test when engaging in this balancing. On the other hand, he notes that the EC's political institutions in specific legislative measures regulating particular sectors such as postal services have given greater priority to the interests of economic operators—who seem to have been successful in capturing EU political processes—than to broader welfare or consumer concerns. This is a deeply disturbing dimension

[11] Case C-70/95, *Sodemare* [1997] ECR I-3395.

of EU law- and policy-making, and one which, if true, undermines in an invidious way the possibilities of shaping a European welfare dimension that genuinely reflects the notion of solidarity.

In the final chapter of the book, Jonathan Zeitlin examines the emergence and the constitutional future of the new coordination processes—and in particular the Open Method of Coordination (OMC)—which have been tried out in recent years within the EU in various fields of social and employment policy, amongst others. He presents these various developments as a possible 'new compromise regarding social Europe', in the context of which the states, in an apparent recognition of common and in many cases related challenges, relax their resistance to EU intervention into the regulation and provision of social welfare. He describes a shift away on the part both of individual states and of the EU as a whole from the aspiration towards a single 'Social Europe' model to counterbalance the single European market, in favour of an approach that embraces but links the diverse national welfare systems within the European Social Model through coordination of policy and mutual learning. His chapter sketches the functioning of the OMC and suggests responses to some of the familiar critiques: that it is too intrusive, that it marginalizes other forms of law- or policy-making, and that it exacerbates the EU's democratic legitimacy problems. While acknowledging many of the 'actually existing' shortcomings, he emphasizes the experimentalism and the commitment of this new approach—at least in principle—to open participation and to transparency. As for the most familiar and probably the most persuasive critique, i.e. that the OMC is largely a paper exercise which lacks real impact or effectiveness on social welfare, Zeitlin points to the methodological difficulties of demonstrating impact in this context. However, he also argues that recent empirical research points to the cognitive influence of OMC processes in both raising the salience of particular issues at national level and in incorporating EU concepts and categories into domestic debate, as well as in the introduction of specific changes within particular national programmes, and more generally in the introduction of different domestic governance arrangements. Ultimately, he suggests that the OMC has its greatest value as a framework for considering and appraising potential solutions to common Europe-wide problems, and as a potential vehicle for reflexive learning—if the commitment to participation and openness were more fully realized—rather than for 'direct policy transfer'.

Four common themes can be identified that unite the otherwise diverse contributions on the changing welfare dimension of the EU. *Firstly*, that despite the absence of a legally or politically agreed basis on which an EU welfare policy might be built, the existence and functioning of the EU has, in part by disturbing the boundedness and integrity of national welfare systems, nonetheless shaped a novel 'spatial architecture' and a distinctive new arena within which issues of European welfare arise and are being addressed. *Secondly*, while the authors are not in agreement as to the merits of the existing elements (see e.g. Baquero's critique of EU sectoral legislation regulating services of general interest, and O'Leary's observation of the perverse effects of certain ECJ rulings intended to protect social rights) and as to the legitimacy of a possible future and stronger EU welfare system (contrast Ferrera's, Martinsen's and O'Leary's cautious optimism, and Baquero's and Zeitlin's positive vision of the possibilities offered by the EU for enabling its Member States to address social welfare collectively, with the scepticism expressed by Hatzopoulos) they share the perception that an EU response to the disruption of national systems and to the trans-European welfare space created by increased personal mobility, immigration, and economic integration is necessary. *Thirdly*, the authors collectively depict an EU welfare dimension which is *ad hoc*, partial, and lacking in design or coherence. In the absence of any clear legal competence, political consensus, or overall vision, the EU's welfare dimension has emerged as an unplanned collage. The diverse instruments and elements include binding rules and rights such as those created by the social security regulation, legally ambiguous entitlements such as those articulated in the Charter of Fundamental Rights, and soft political coordination mechanisms such as the guidelines, strategies, and action plans of the OMC. Most of these elements have emerged over time, as a consequence of particular conflicts, controversies, or challenges, and in several instances have been triggered by litigation and judicial activism. *Fourthly*, with the exception of the final chapter which concentrates on the open coordination processes, all of the contributions emphasize the significant part so far accorded to itself by the Court of Justice in relation to both the disruptive negative-integration aspect and the rights-creation aspect of the EU's welfare dimension. The weak political impetus for any kind of comprehensive or coherent EU social welfare regulation is, on the other hand, striking and it reflects the lack of consensus both between and within states on these issues. It is in the field of experimentalist policy coordination, rather than rights-creation or other legal forms of welfare regulation that political energy and imagination has so far been directed.

The central question which ultimately remains is whether the kind of social solidarity needed to underpin a collective welfare system—even a system, such as the EU's must necessarily be, that engages with and complements rather than replaces or supersedes national welfare systems—is possible within the EU. While the lack of such transnational solidarity is frequently cited as a reason for the absence of and indeed the undesirability of an EU welfare policy, this argument underestimates the constructive potential of the experiment in economic, political, and social cooperation exemplified by the EU. As the various chapters in this collection show, the new 'welfare space' opened up by the process of European integration, in part by its disruption of various national institutions, laws, and policies relevant to the provision of welfare, brings neither a policy vacuum nor a comprehensive policy field. Instead, the growing patchwork of interventions in areas such as access to healthcare, social security regulation, and citizenship rights, are both premised on and arguably also serve gradually to promote a degree of solidarity and mutual responsibility—however tentative and limited at first—between states, citizens, and other residents within the enlarging European space.

2

Towards an 'Open' Social Citizenship? The New Boundaries of Welfare in the European Union

MAURIZIO FERRERA

INTRODUCTION

Since the last decades of the nineteenth century, the social rights of citizenship have played a crucial role for the process of state- and nation-building in Europe. The European nation–state is typically a *welfare state*; the social components of citizenship are no less important than its civil and political components; the right to decide about the forms and substance of social citizenship has always been considered in its turn a crucial aspect of national sovereignty.

The dynamics of European integration have been gradually challenging this institutional configuration. The right to decide on social policy matters of each individual state has become less comprehensive and 'ultimate' than it used to be. By interfering with the rules of inclusion and exclusion set by domestic citizenship spaces, the integration process has been gradually weakening two essential traits of social sovereignty in its traditional meaning: (1) the capacity of a state to 'lock in' and exert coercive rule on actors and resources which are crucial for the stability of redistributive institutions within the national territory and (2) the capacity of a state to bar external authority structures from interfering into their own social space and jurisdiction.[1] In other words, integration has launched a direct challenge to the *boundaries* of welfare, *qua* institutional foundations of its solidaristic mission.

[1] I am well aware of the ambiguities inherent in the concept of 'sovereignty'. As highlighted by recent debates in both international relations and comparative politics theory (T. Biersteker and C. Weber, *State Sovereignty as a Social Construct* (1996); D. Elkins, *Beyond Sovereignty* (1995); S. D. Krasner, *Sovereignty: Organized Hypocrisy* (1999); A. Osiander, 'Sovereignty, International Relations and the Westphalian Myth', 55 *International Organization* (2001) 251), such ambiguities concern both the connotation of the concept (many different meanings) and its denotation (various discrepancies between meanings and observed phenomena). But treated with due caution, the concept remains pertinent and useful, I believe, for capturing the logic of ongoing developments at the interface between Member States and EU institutions. A detailed discussion of what we mean by 'social sovereignty' will be offered below.

Boundaries are quintessential components of modern citizenship. Let us remember Marshall's famous definition of citizenship as 'a status bestowed on those who are full members of a community'.[2] It is clear from this definition that citizenship rests on boundaries that separate insiders from outsiders. The salience of boundaries has always been particularly high in the case of *social* citizenship, which touches delicate issues of material redistributions and raises thorny dilemmas of equity, justice, and reciprocity. Originally drawn between the end of the nineteenth and the first half of the twentieth centuries, the boundaries of social citizenship have witnessed several changes with the passing of time. But these changes were almost entirely internal to the nation–state container, e.g. adding category after category (private employees, agricultural workers, the self-employed, etc.) within the reach of social insurance. The community that Marshall had in mind was the nation, and the citizenship whose history he so effectively traced was 'by definition national'.[3] Only with the deepening of European integration has the issue of boundaries started to affect the container itself, i.e. the nation–state and its 'sovereign' capacity to bound not only internally, but also externally, i.e. in respect of the outside environment.

The process of boundary redrawing with respect to social citizenship raises some fundamental questions. In what way and in which areas, exactly, are boundaries being redrawn? What are the implications of such developments for the politico-institutional stability and sustainability of social protection? Are new forms of post-state and post-national solidarities, possibly anchored to the EU level, feasible and desirable?

I believe these are important questions for both the welfare state and for Europe. A focus on the 'spatial' challenges to national welfare and its link to territory can cast new light on its increased vulnerability as an institution geared to securing individual life chances and fostering appropriate redistributions. An accurate diagnosis of such vulnerability can bolster the identification of remedies capable of reconciling the traditional and important objectives of this institution with the transformations of its external environment.

A focus on the boundaries of social rights and their ongoing reconfiguration can in its turn contribute to a better understanding of the EU as a polity-in-the-making and thus to identifying a profile and a substance for a distinct EU citizenship capable of strengthening its current 'anaemic content' and unclear functions.[4] The institution of citizenship (in its various components) can play a major role in constituting and consolidating the EU as a single polity or political community. And the consolidation of the EU as a relatively cohesive political community is in its turn a prerequisite for its functioning according to satisfactory standards of legitimacy and performance.[5]

[2] T. H. Marshall, *Citizenship and Social Class* (1992) at 18.

[3] *Ibid.* at 9.

[4] A. Follesdal, 'Union Citizenship: Unpacking the Beast of Burden', 20 *Law and Philosophy* (2001) 313.

[5] For an articulated discussion of the legitimacy and performance dilemmas of the EU, see F. Scharpf, *Governing in Europe* (1999).

Starting from this general thematic (and problematic) background, the chapter will be organized as follows. In the first part I will revisit the classical notion of citizenship, in order to offer both an adequate conceptualization and an historical perspective to my discussion. The second part will develop an argument about the way in which European integration is redefining and challenging the established boundaries of social protection, in its national configuration. The third part will illustrate in some detail the new spatial architecture of social rights in the EU, as originated from EC law and jurisprudence. The final part will discuss emerging trends and future options for post-national and 'open' forms of social citizenship.

1. MODERN CITIZENSHIP AS A BASIC FORM OF SPATIAL CLOSURE

In order to understand the ongoing process of reconfiguration of social rights and their boundaries in Europe, one has to start by revisiting the classical notion of citizenship. Political theorists look at citizenship as a salient, if not the most salient, space of social interaction.[6] Citizenship is a space, in that boundaries separating insiders (the community of citizens) from outsiders (foreigners or aliens) are a constituent element of this institution. Citizenship affects interaction, because its substance disciplines and orients individual and group behaviours within those boundaries. Finally, citizenship has become very salient also because it often operates as a filtering mechanism for other, more specialized spaces of domestic interaction (from the market to the tax system; from social benefits to the military draft).

Citizenship's boundaries incorporate two dimensions: a territorial dimension and a social dimension. A basic purpose of contemporary citizenship is that of allocating persons to states.[7] Besides being a 'territorial filing' device, citizenship operates however also as 'social marking' device, providing persons with rights and obligations,[8] as well as roles and identities.[9]

In his pathbreaking historical sketch of this institution, T. H. Marshall suggests that the evolution of modern citizenship involved a double process: of fusion and separation.[10] The fusion was geographical and entailed the dismantlement of local

[6] R. Brubaker, *Citizenship and Nationhood in France and Germany* (1992); Marshall, *supra* n. 2; P. Flora, S. Kuhnle, and D. Urwin (eds.), *State Formation, Nation Building and Mass Politics in Europe: The Theory of Stein Rokkan* (1999); C. Tilly, 'Citizenship, Identity and Social History', in C. Tilly (ed.), *Citizenship: Identity and Social History* (1996) 1; G. Zincone, 'Cittadinanza: trasformazioni in corso', 15 *Filosofia Politica* (2000) 71.

[7] Brubaker, *supra* n. 6; D. Heater, *Citizenship: The Civic Ideal in World History, Politics and Education* (1990).

[8] Marshall, *supra* n. 2.

[9] Tilly, *supra* n. 6.

[10] Marshall, *supra* n. 2 at 9.

privileges and immunities, the harmonization of rights and obligations throughout the national territory, and the establishment of a level playing field (the equal status of citizen) within state borders. The separation was functional and it entailed the creation of new sources of nationwide authority and jurisdiction as well as new specialized institutions for the implementation of that authority and that jurisdiction at the decentralized level. As is well known, Marshall had essentially in mind the British experience, where this double process unfolded itself slowly and smoothly over the centuries and where the building of solid and secure territorial boundaries was achieved very early in history.[11] This is why Marshall concentrated his pioneering analysis on the three internal components of citizenship (civil, political, and social) and neglected the external side of it (what separates citizens from non-citizens), taking for granted that the territorial filing device was in place—or perhaps that it was not even pertinent for his analysis.

In other European contexts (and especially in the continental lands), however, the double process of fusion and separation encountered much greater difficulties. State borders remained rather vague and fluctuating, with no univocal and clear-cut implications apart from the military ones, well into the early nineteenth century. In much of continental Europe the territorial dimension of citizenship remained rather confused and contested for a long period of time and it took the cement of nationalism between the nineteenth and the twentieth centuries to uphold effectively both the geographical fusion of pre-existing institutional spaces and the emergence and concrete functioning of specialized organizations with a nationwide scope.

The nationalization of citizenship (emblematized by the creation of the nineteenth-century synonym 'nationality') weaved a *fil rouge* across the various rights and obligations bestowed on all the inhabitants of a state territory and promoted the formal separation between the container (the status of citizen *per se*, conferring a sort of 'right to have rights') and the content (the specific rights and obligations of citizenship). The two sides remained closely related in symbolic terms, at least in Europe; but this separation produced a gradual problematization of the criteria defining 'insiderhood' as such—the *jus sanguinis* and the *jus soli* being the two opposite poles of various possible empirical combinations.[12]

Reasoning from a slightly different perspective than that of Marshall—a perspective more attentive to the territorial dimension of citizenship—the Norwegian social scientist Stein Rokkan identified two kinds of rights typically associated with citizenship: *rights to roots* and *rights to options*.[13] The right to roots can be understood as a right (freedom or faculty) to belong to a community, to plant and/or

[11] In Finer's reconstruction, the Kingdom of England may be considered as having achieved territorial unification as early as in AD 975. Even adopting stricter criteria on the meaning of 'territorial unification', by the second half of the eleventh century 'no peripheral elites within the well-defined borders of the kingdom ever aspired to its division or tried to secede from it' (S. Finer, 'State-Building, State Boundaries and Border Control', 13 *Social Science Information* (1974) 79 at 116).

[12] Heater, *supra* n. 7.

[13] Flora, Kuhnle, and Urwin, *supra* n. 6.

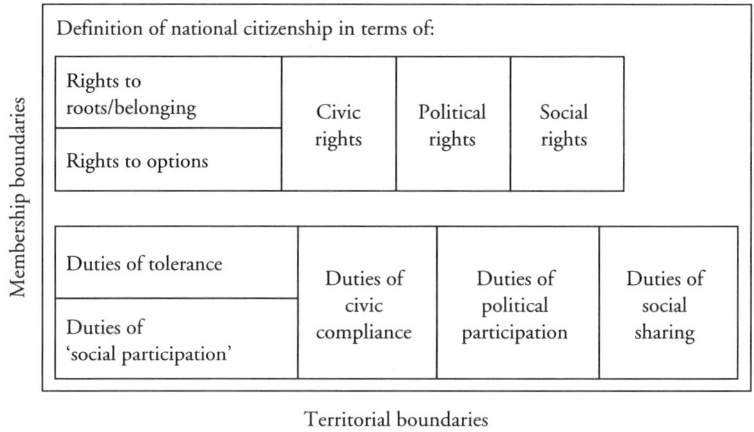

Figure One *The boundaries and content of citizenship.*

cultivate one's roots on a portion of space. The rights to options provide you with opportunities and choices in the surrounding territorial network, with chances to better your life—and even deroot or reroot yourself if that suits you. Exactly what options are provided depends on the civil, political, and social rights that are in force in a given nation–state. Civil, political, and social rights in turn give additional substance to people's roots, to their belonging to a community and—more importantly still—supply powerful procedural and material resources for obtaining respect for these roots and belonging.[14]

Figure One summarizes my discussion of modern citizenship as a form of spatial closure. The space of citizenship is demarcated by both territorial boundaries—which identify the geographical reach of the citizen's status—and by membership boundaries, which specify the criteria for insiderhood. Within this container, we find the actual substance of citizenship: not only Marshall's classical trio (civil, political, and social rights), but also Rokkan's more basic duo: roots (belonging) and options. Civil, political, and social rights are placed transversally with respect to the rights to roots and the rights to options because, as mentioned, the former provide resources for the exercise of the latter. In turn, the rights to roots and the rights to options are placed at the beginning of the figure, since they may be considered as the underlying, ultimate purposes of citizenship (and thus normatively prior to the three sets of more instrumental rights). The figure also includes the symmetrical

[14] The 'exclusionary' nature of citizenship as a membership space raises, of course, delicate normative issues. What ethical principles can justify the construction of boundaries between 'equal persons', who just happen to be born or to find themselves on different sides of borders? Such boundaries generate disparities of treatment and often huge inequalities in terms of life chances that have extremely shaky normative foundations. For a discussion of such thorny issues, see, among others, C. McKinnon and I. Hampsher-Monk (eds.), *The Demands of Citizenship* (2000).

counterparts of rights. The duty of tolerance is associated with the rights to roots and belonging. The rights to options must be backed by duties (essentially moral duties) to participate in some way to the life of the community.[15] Civic compliance (e.g. essentially respect for the law), political participation and readiness to share are in their turn the prime counterparts of civil, political and social rights.

In Europe, the twentieth century has marked the apex of national citizenship as a powerful machine for the production and maintenance of rights and the forging of cultural identities. But the last decades of the same century have also witnessed the emergence of a seemingly contradictory trend: the content of citizenship has continued to thicken up, while the container has started to thin out. New rights have been added and the old ones have been specified. Adopting the language of the EU Charter of Fundamental Rights, let us think of the explicit clarification of the 'rights to dignity',[16] the addition of new 'freedoms from' (e.g. the protection of personal data and privacy, or the protection in the event of removal, expulsion, or extradition), of new rights of equal or even preferential treatment (e.g. for children, the elderly, or the disabled), and of course new (or better defined) rights in the field of solidarity (see Table One). The substantial catalogue of rights becomes wider and thicker.

But at the same time the territorial boundaries of citizenship have become more permeable, while the possession of national roots (the sharing of a distinctive cultural and symbolic heritage or the pledge to doing so) has become less important as marker of insiderhood, and in particular as filter for the exercise of many rights.

The process of European integration has been a major driving force of this double development: the thickening of the content and the thinning out of the container of citizenship. Not only has the Union introduced a distinct EU citizenship superimposed on national ones, but it has also—and especially—promoted a creeping, but constant decoupling of rights from national territories. The europeanization of options through the 'four freedoms' and accompanying measures has entailed a gradual opening up of the distinct citizenship spaces of the Member States. A new political figure has emerged on the stage: the *denizen*, i.e. an outsider who can enter (and of course re-exit), stay inside, voice and even 'share', even if under certain conditions.[17]

[15] Social participation is of course a vague concept, as was Marshall's idea of 'a general obligation to live the life of a good citizen, giving such service as one can to promote the welfare of the community', starting with the duty to work (Marshall, *supra* n. 2 at 45). Recent debates on the basic income have addressed squarely the issue of citizen's obligations *vis-à-vis* the options they enjoy by living in a political community.

[16] Right to human dignity (Art. 1), right to life (Art. 2), right to the integrity of the person (Art. 3), prohibition of torture and inhuman or degrading treatment or punishment (Art. 4), prohibition of slavery and forced labour (Art. 5) (Chapter 1 of the Charter).

[17] T. Hammar, *Democracy and the Nation–State: Aliens, Denizens and Citizens in a World of International Migration* (1990). The term comes from the old French *denzein* and ultimately from the Latin *de intus*, i.e. being inside. The Romans were the first to invent different forms of citizenship based on the external association and partial incorporation of the outsiders (e.g. peripheral populations). Such forms of partial citizenship were used as a political instrument and significantly contributed to securing the long-term viability of the Empire (M. Doyle, *Empires* (1996); H. Spruyt, 'The Origins, Development and Possible Decline of the Modern State', 5 *Annual Review of Political Science* (2002) 127).

Table One *The Nice Charter: rights in the field of solidarity.*

Article	Content
Article 27 Workers' right to information and consultation within the undertaking	Workers or their representatives must, at the appropriate levels, be guaranteed information and consultation in good time in the cases and under the conditions provided for by Community law and national laws and practices.
Article 28 Right of collective bargaining and action	Workers and employers, or their respective organisations, have, in accordance with Community law and national laws and practices, the right to negotiate and conclude collective agreements at the appropriate levels and, in cases of conflicts of interest, to take collective action to defend their interests, including strike action.
Article 29 Right of access to placement services	Everyone has the right of access to a free placement service.
Article 30 Protection in the event of unjustified dismissal	Every worker has the right to protection against unjustified dismissal, in accordance with Community law and national laws and practices.
Article 31 Fair and just working conditions	1. Every worker has the right to working conditions which respect his or her health, safety, and dignity. 2. Every worker has the right to limitation of maximum working hours, to daily and weekly rest periods, and to an annual period of paid leave.
Article 32 Prohibition of child labour and protection of young people at work	The employment of children is prohibited. The minimum age of admission to employment may not be lower than the minimum school-leaving age, without prejudice to such rules as may be more favourable to young people and except for limited derogations. Young people admitted to work must have working conditions appropriate to their age and be protected against economic exploitation and any work likely to harm their safety, health, or physical, mental, moral or social development or to interfere with their education.
Article 33 Family and professional life	1. The family shall enjoy legal, economic, and social protection. 2. To reconcile family and professional life, everyone shall have the right to protection from dismissal for a reason connected with maternity and the right to paid maternity leave and to parental leave following the birth or adoption of a child.
Article 34 Social security and social assistance	1. The Union recognizes and respects the entitlement to social security benefits and social services providing protection in cases such as maternity, illness, industrial accidents, dependency or old age, and in the case of loss of employment, in accordance with the rules laid down by Community law and national laws and practices.

Table One (*Continued*)

Article	Content
	2. Everyone residing and moving legally within the European Union is entitled to social security benefits and social advantages in accordance with Community law and national laws and practices. 3. In order to combat social exclusion and poverty, the Union recognizes and respects the right to social and housing assistance so as to ensure a decent existence for all those who lack sufficient resources, in accordance with the rules laid down by Community law and national laws and practices.
Article 35 Healthcare	Everyone has the right of access to preventive healthcare and the right to benefit from medical treatment under the conditions established by national laws and practices. A high level of human health protection shall be ensured in the definition and implementation of all Union policies and activities.

Source: *European Union Charter of fundamental Rights*, Chapter IV—Solidarity. (This chapter includes three more articles, which respectively refer to access to services of general economic interest (Art. 36), environmental protection (Art. 37), and consumer protection (Art. 38).)

Since the early 1970s, an increasingly detailed regulatory framework (Council Regulation 1408 of 1971) has been in place in the EU which basically allows all EU citizens (and since May 2003, virtually all legal residents) to take advantage of domestic social protection schemes and even to export their benefits when they leave the country. This body of rules specifies the conditions under which entitlements matured in a given national system can be exported or converted into the system of another Member State.[18]

Again echoing Marshall, we could look at the development of EU citizenship as a new process of 'fusion and separation': fusion in terms of legal integration; separation in terms of the appearance of new authority structures capable of producing and protecting citizenship rights—in particular the ECJ.[19]

However, while this way of seeing things may capture the logic of developments in the sphere of civil and to some extent political rights, in the sphere of social rights the question is much more problematic. In nineteenth-century Europe, social rights emerged out of a *tabula rasa*: there was not much to 'fuse' and a lot to create *ex novo* in terms of institutions. In today's Europe, not only is the institutional material to be fused very thick and very solid, but *closure* has become a quintessential element for the stability and proper functioning of social rights. These rights rest on *ties*, which are both more delicate and more sticky than civil ties and to some extent even than political participation ties.[20] What are the implications of the growing opening of boundaries for the sphere of social rights? This is a crucial point, which deserves a detailed discussion.

2. THE COMPLEX STRUCTURING OF SOCIAL RIGHTS

Solidarity is a rather elusive concept and a complex social good. On the one hand, it connotes a trait of whole social aggregates, i.e. a high degree of 'fusion' or internal union, cohesion and commonality of purpose of a given group (the term 'solidarity' comes from the Latin *solidus*—a firm and compact body). On the other hand, it connotes a particular set of ties among the members of such group: *sharing ties*,

[18] P. A. Van der Mei, *Free Movement of Persons within the European Community* (2003).

[19] Given the still low degree of 'polity-ness' of the EU, the membership dimension of these two processes remains somewhat vague. What kind of 'community' serves as a marking base for the emerging EU citizenship space? In the words of James Caporaso (J. Caporaso, 'Citizenship and Equality: A Long and Winding Road', paper presented at the International Studies Association Meeting, Chicago, 22–25 February 2001, at 23), we might ask: is this community merely a transnational market, an aggregate of those affected by trans-border externalities, an authoritative civic proto-space? And what kind of authority is backing EU citizenship rights? Is it 'technical authority, the authority of the expert, or legitimate authority deriving from the people'?

[20] It is true that national voting rights are still a sacred cow and remain strictly restricted to citizens. But, while there exists a supranational political body (the European Parliament) formed through direct elections of all EU citizens, no supranational redistributive scheme targeted to individuals has been created at the EU level so far—and for vast numbers of commentators this is a desirable state of affairs.

i.e. transactions aimed at pooling (a part of) each member's resources for some common purpose (we might call this the 'brotherhood' side of solidarity). As is well known, modern welfare state programmes pool resources (primarily financial) with the aim of contrasting typical risks and adversities of the life cycle: from sickness to old age, from work accidents to unemployment. Such risks are contrasted by redistributing pooled resources both horizontally (from the damaged to the non-damaged) and vertically (from the better off to the worse off). Looked at from this perspective, the welfare state can be considered as a highly articulated and specialized form of institutionalized solidarity, serving both efficiency and social justice objectives.[21]

The institutionalization of solidarity slowly unfolded itself during the last two centuries in the wider context of state- and nation-building.[22] The incorporation of social rights into the space of citizenship was no easy task. Social rights are more demanding political products than civil and political rights. All rights have costs: enablement costs, to create the conditions for their actual exercise (e.g. free legal counsel for those people who cannot afford it) and enforcement costs.[23] But—resting as they do on material transfers and services—social rights originate 'substance' costs as well. They require the availability of significant amounts of material resources that are not easy to extract from society and of moral commitments to 'sharing with others' that are not easy to activate at the individual and primary group levels.[24] The definition of boundaries plays a critical role in the production of these rights. In the first place, boundaries are essential for constructing new 'special-purpose communities' ready to pool certain risks. For welfare state builders, boundary setting was a delicate balancing act between indulgence *vis-à-vis* the particularistic inclinations of pre-existing social categories and self-defeating ambitions of redistributive 'stretching', i.e. pushing the scope of solidarity beyond the limits that could be sustained by available material and moral resources.

In the second place, boundaries are essential for enforcing affiliation to a sharing community. Now, compulsion is a prime component of citizenship in all its aspects, a fundamental instrument for assuring a correspondence between rights and duties. But in the sphere of social rights—which have precise, quantifiable costs—the matching between rights (entitlements) and duties (obligations to pay taxes and contributions) must be particularly accurate and stringent, if fiscal bankruptcy is to be avoided. At least some civil and political rights can survive even without the full and constant exercise of the corresponding duties (contemporary democracy often

[21] A. B. Atkinson, *Poverty and Social Security* (1989); N. Barr, *The Economics of the Welfare State* (1993).

[22] M. Ferrera, 'European Integration and National Social Citizenship: Changing Boundaries, New Structuring?', 36 *Comparative Political Studies* (2003) 611.

[23] S. Holmes and C. R. Sunstein, *The Cost of Rights* (1999).

[24] K. Offe, 'Politica sociale, solidarietà e stato sociale', in M. Ferrera (ed.), *Stato sociale e mercato mondiale* (1993) 169. For an interesting discussion of social rights as qualitatively different from civil and political rights, see J. Klausen, 'Social Rights Advocacy and State Building: T. H. Marshall in the Hands of Social Reformers', 47 *World Politics* (1995) 244.

functions with voting turnouts closer to 50% than to 100%). But social rights must be sustained by unrelenting sharing acts. This is why they rest on a specialized organizational form: that of compulsory social insurance. In most countries, the establishment of social rights meant the establishment of compulsory insurance schemes: against old age and disability, work injuries and sickness, maternity and unemployment. And, especially in the field of old age, the first implication for the members of such schemes was the payment of contributions (i.e. the exercise of the duty), with benefits only arriving after long 'vesting' periods.

Defining and enforcing closure (under the form of obligatory affiliation and compulsory payments) remained a balancing act politically, but it allowed several economic advantages: a less costly protection per insured (thanks to the large, predictable, and reliable size of the sharing pool), the possibility of charging 'contributions' (i.e. flat rate or proportional payments) rather than premiums (i.e. payments differentiated according to individual risk profiles, as in private insurance schemes), and the possibility of granting special treatment (e.g. lower or credited contributions, or minimum benefits) to categories of disadvantaged members. In contrast to private or voluntary insurance, compulsory (and public) social insurance could thus cover 'difficult' risks such as unemployment or family breakdowns,[25] and also produce not only horizontal redistributions—from the healthy to the sick, from the employed to the unemployed, etc.—but also vertical ones, from rich to poor. In this way, social citizenship could bring that 'general enrichment of the concrete substance of civilized life' through an 'equalization between the more and the less fortunate at all levels' that Marshall saw as its fundamental mission.[26]

Boundaries and closure matter, then, for social rights: probably in a more direct and intense way than for the other rights of citizenship. Historically the *territorial* dimension of closure was important, but it essentially worked to align the boundaries of social rights with those of the nation–state. The establishment of compulsory social insurance entailed a nationalization of redistribution, even if in many countries such nationalization remained based on categorical differentiations (private vs. public employees, employees vs. the self-employed, etc.). Between the nineteenth century and the first half of the twentieth, most European countries introduced codes specifying the criteria for acquiring citizenship, thus putting in place more or less effective 'filing' filters to guard their territorial spaces of redistribution. The turning point in this process was the inter-war period, during which most European countries started to link rights with nationality and to strictly police their borders.[27]

[25] As demonstrated by welfare economics, the private market can only insure those risks where the following conditions obtain: the probability of risk incurrence for each insured must be independent of the probability of any other insured; such probability must be lower than 100%; it must be known or estimable; there must be no adverse selection; there must be no moral hazard (Barr, *supra* n. 21).

[26] Marshall, *supra* n. 2 at 33.

[27] C. Strikwerda, 'Reinterpreting the History of European Integration: Business, Labour and Social Citizenship in Twentieth-Century Europe', in J. Klausen and C. Tilly (eds.), *European Integration in Social and Theoretical Perspective: From 1850 to the Present* (1997) 51.

The membership dimension of closure was much more controversial and required much heavier political investment than the territorial dimension. Until the 1970s, the 'who' question (i.e. who is included, which categories are protected and how) regarded essentially domestic actors and the definition of internal boundaries for redistribution. However problematic and contentious, the drawing of internal membership boundaries gave rise to a web of redistributive collectivities and arrangements, which got gradually 'crystallized' through dynamics of institutionalization. If observed from the angle of social citizenship *circa* 1970, the European landscape appeared as a dense forest of compulsory spaces of affiliation, covering virtually 100% of national populations, with very limited 'exit' opportunities (e.g. under the form of exemption from insurance) and very stringent 'entry' rules for aliens crossing state borders.

Since the early 1970s the process of European integration has worked to thin out gradually the national boundaries of citizenship, with specific and significant implications for social rights. Through binding regulations and court rulings, social rights (and the corresponding obligations) have been decoupled from national citizenship within the EU and linked merely to work or residence status. As I mentioned before, the adoption of the 1971 regulation on the coordination of social security regimes was the starting-point of this snowballing process, which witnessed a marked acceleration after the Single European Act of 1987. The citizens (and, in most cases, more simply the denizens, i.e. legal residents) of any Member State who move in another Member State cannot be discriminated against as 'foreigners' and must receive the same treatment in terms of social rights that is reserved to nationals. While residence is still partly a matter of national sovereignty, the freedom to work anywhere in the territory of the Union is protected by the Treaties and attentively policed by supranational authorities (especially the ECJ).[28]

On this front, it is clear that European integration has promoted an almost complete cross-local 'fusion' of what Marshall considered the basic civil right in the economic sphere: 'the right to follow the occupation of one's choice in the place of one's choice, subject only to legitimate demands for preliminary technical training'.[29] To be sure, the Member States still retain very substantial prerogatives over the definition and operation of social rights within their borders. But the underlying and ultimate filtering function performed by national citizenship *qua* overall and solid container of rights and basic instrument of closure is no longer there. European integration has opened up unprecedented opportunities of entry into 'foreign' redistributive spaces, and unprecedented opportunities of challenging the authority of domestic social institutions by appealing to external actors. Let us typically think of the possibility of accessing the ECJ in order to enforce rights (freedoms or entitlements) denied by domestic authorities—an opportunity that can be resorted to both by the direct bearers of social rights (e.g. an unemployed person or a pensioner) or by a wider set of stakeholders, such as for instance service

[28] Van der Mei, *supra* n. 18.

[29] Marshall, *supra* n. 2 at 10.

providers (e.g. insurance companies) trying to break national monopolies over social insurance. During the 1990s the French system of *monopoles sociaux* (compulsory social insurance schemes) was challenged before the ECJ, both on the side of individual insured wishing to elude the obligation to affiliate and by private insurers interested in breaking into (or creating *ex novo*) a potentially very lucrative market. The ECJ ruled in favour of the *monopoles* as far as first-pillar schemes are concerned (i.e. compulsory schemes offering basic benefits), but established that on top of this first pillar domestic social protection schemes are only partially immune from EC norms on competition (cf. below).

Building on the contrast between 'negative' and 'positive' integration, recent debates have already highlighted the destabilizing effects of all these developments on national 'social contracts'.[30] The main preoccupation in such debates has to do with the increased power of markets and market actors to the detriment of long-established redistributive arrangements and their supporting coalitions, laboriously built through domestic political channels and resting on territorially bounded balances of power. Using spatial metaphors, we could say that the main line of argument found in the literature connects vertical pressures from above (EU directives and rulings) to horizontal rebalancing between markets and rights in clear favour of the former. In general terms, both the preoccupation and the argument are well grounded. But I contend that they need to be qualified 'horizontally' and developed 'vertically'. Let me explain.

The institutionalization of solidarity through social rights has effectively contrasted the disintegrative tendency of the nineteenth century's greatest social utopia: that of a market entirely capable of self-regulation.[31] Societies have mobilized in search of protection; states have responded with the production of rights. But not all the buffers against market expansionism have served their declared 'emancipatory' objectives and some buffers have gone too far.

In some moments and in some contexts, the progressive thrust of social reformism has been hijacked by petty interests, sectional lobbies, circumscribed groups defending their privileges. Social closure has been used to serve 'usurpative' rather than emancipatory objectives. Contemporary rational-choice theories (in both economics and political science) have unveiled the dynamics that may lead to such undesirable outcomes.[32] But both the awareness and the preoccupation about such dynamics were clearly present already in the early and classical debates about social citizenship.

Commenting on the increase in unofficial strikes at the time while he was writing his famous essay, Marshall lamented that an attempt had been made 'to claim the rights of both status and contract while repudiating the duties under both these heads'.[33] In his turn, Bendix warned that a fundamental civil right and precondition

[30] For a discussion of such debates, see M. Ferrera, A. Hemerijck, and M. Rhodes, *The Future of Social Europe* (2000).

[31] K. Polanyi, *The Great Transformation: The Political and Economic Origins of Our Time* (1957).

[32] The classical references are M. Olson, *The Logic of Collective Action* (1965) and J. Buchanan and R. Wagner, *Democracy in Deficit* (1977).

[33] Marshall, *supra* n. 2 at 42.

of voice, the freedom of association or 'right to combine', can be used 'to enforce claims to a share of income and benefits at the expenses of the unorganized and the consumers'.[34] Economically inefficient and normatively unjustifiable forms of rights-based closure must be singled out with care and precision, context by context. But to the extent that the vertical and market-oriented pressures of European integration are (or can be) targeted at such forms of closure, then 'destructuring' might serve functionally useful and normatively desirable purposes. The challenge on this front is how to single out and how to target correctly.

This brings us to the vertical deepening of mainstream arguments about European integration and national welfare systems. European integration has the potential of prompting changes that are more far-reaching than 'just' a mutual reproportioning of markets vs. states in responding to social needs. What is at stake is the basic spatial architecture of social citizenship, i.e. the territorial reach of solidarity, the identity of its constituent communities, and, last but not least, the ultimate source of legitimate authority for the production and the enforcement of rights. National social citizenship, backed by state authority, has played a crucial integrative role in domestic polities not only as a mechanism of (efficient and equitable) redistribution, but also as a kernel for group formation and group persistence, for voice structuring and loyalty generation. By challenging national boundaries and by redrawing these boundaries along different geographical, socio-economic and institutional lines (EU vs. non-EU citizens, workers vs. non-workers, insurance vs. assistance schemes, first-pillar vs. second-pillar insurance, and so on) European integration can undermine—and thus *destructure*—deep-seated social and political equilibriums, with social and political consequences that are not fully predictable, but which may also be of a negative sign. In order to explore and discuss these points further, we must however build a more detailed map of the new institutional scaffolding of social citizenship in the EU, focusing (and to some extent 'unpacking') the box relative to social rights in Figure One above.

3. THE NEW SPATIAL ARCHITECTURE OF SOCIAL CITIZENSHIP IN THE EU

As stated, the modern welfare state is essentially centred on compulsory social insurance schemes. A map aimed at identifying the state of the art of the spatial architecture of social citizenship in the EU must obviously start from these schemes and capture the impact that European integration has had on them and in particular on their degree of closure, both under the territorial viewpoint (who is allowed to enter and to exit, in terms of geographical mobility?) and under the membership viewpoint (who is subject to the obligation to insure when this person legally resides in a given national territory?). In contemporary Europe, however, social protection

[34] R. Bendix, *Nation-Building and Citizenship* (1964).

can no longer be reduced to the level of compulsory social insurance: there are other 'sharing' and redistributive spaces both below and above this level—and punctuated by rights of their own—which must be seriously considered in order to build a full map.

The space that finds itself below compulsory social insurance is that of social assistance. Between the 1960s and 1970s a new generation of non-contributory schemes and benefits made their appearance, with two main objectives: filling the coverage gaps at the margins of the extant social-insurance programmes, in particular for some categories of people and for some (new) types of need, and establishing a safety net of last resort for the whole citizenry, below which nobody would be allowed to fall.

These 'new' assistance schemes do share some traits with social insurance. Claimants have subjective rights, disciplined by codified legislation. Benefit agencies (which in some cases can coincide with the agencies administering social insurance) can exert discretion only within the limits set by laws, and administrative decisions are justiciable in courts. On the other hand, contrary to social insurance, such schemes are typically tax-based, there is no explicit link between their fruition and (past) actual financial contributions, they rest on some verification of economic need—through the so-called means test—and, especially in recent years, they are accompanied by some degree of behavioural conditionally for those who are able to work and/or participate in 'activation' programmes.

The economic significance of needs-based, means-tested, non-contributory and tax-funded transfers has been increasing in all EU countries throughout the 1980s and 1990s. According to Eurostat calculations, means-tested benefits have come to absorb 10% of social protection.[35]

The space above compulsory social insurance is that of supplementary schemes. Starting, again, from the 1960s, a significant second pillar of supplementary insurance has emerged, offering additional benefits and coverage to selected occupational categories. Some countries have maintained the principle of compulsory membership also within the second pillar: in the field of pensions, this is most notably the case of the Nordic countries, France, and Greece. Many countries have however adopted a softer approach: membership rules (including obligatory cover) can be set by collective agreements, which may in turn be backed by national legislative provisions (e.g. the Netherlands); in some cases, membership is instead voluntary, but encouraged and subsidized by the state (e.g. Ireland or the Iberian countries). Even if not (always) formally compulsory, this second pillar still tends to retain a 'collective' nature, in that it rests on group insurance principles and categorical agreements, thus allowing for many of the redistributive and solidaristic effects typically linked to compulsory social insurance. On top of this second tier of provision, a third pillar has in its turn developed, essentially based on individual choice and market criteria. Here there is no compulsion and the distance from

[35] Eurostat, *The Social Situation in the European Union* (1999).

solidarity principles is much higher; but also at this level public regulation plays a role on both efficiency and equity grounds.

In the field of pensions, the second pillar of supplementary provision had already developed by the 1970s in most EU countries. During the 1980s and 1990s it further consolidated, not only in the wake of institutional inertia or self-propulsion, but also following deliberate policies of encouragement on the part of national authorities.[36] The increasing strains of public pension programmes due to demographic ageing, system maturation, budgetary constraints, and the new competitive imperatives have in fact induced governments (as well as the European Commission) to look at supplementary schemes as a promising instrument for relieving the pressure on first-pillar schemes—and thus partly on labour costs. Favourable regulatory and especially tax frameworks have been introduced in order to induce both workers and enterprises to earmark resources for supplementary pensions. A corollary objective of such initiatives has been that of promoting capital accumulation within the economy and of supporting and enlarging domestic financial markets. Even though it is not wholly uncommon for supplementary pensions to rest on pay-as-you-go financing and defined-benefit formulas, they typically rest on defined-contribution formulas and pre-funding, i.e. on large-scale accumulation of financial assets to match future liabilities. Against this background, by the early 1990s a fairly substantial 'market' for second- (and third-) pillar pensions had developed in several EU Member States: a significant share of the income and security of a growing number of EU pensioners depends on the solidity and reliability of these two new pillars of provision, directly or indirectly regulated and guaranteed by the state (EC 1997 and 1999).[37]

Considering the hierarchy of spaces just illustrated, we can now proceed to draw our map. Figure Two must be read as a specification of Figure One as far as social rights are concerned. Like Figure One, Figure Two is also generated by the combination of two distinct dimensions:

- A territorial dimension, on which geographical movements occur, physical borders between systems are located, and rules defining what can pass through such borders are of prime importance. On this dimension, the main novelty in respect of the past is the formation of a new space, the EU, next to (or better: underneath) the traditional space occupied by national systems. Through the four freedoms and the coordination regime, the EU can now legitimately encroach into national social citizenships; this new space is in turn increasingly demarcated by its own external borders, set against foreign

[36] J. Myles and P. Pierson, 'The Comparative Political Economy of Pension Reform', in P. Pierson (ed.), *The New Politics of the Welfare State* (2001) 305.

[37] European Commission, *Supplementary Pensions in the Single Market: A Green Paper* (COM[97]283), *Commission Communication: Towards a Single Market for Supplementary Pensions* (COM[99]134), *Commission Communication: The Elimination of Tax Obstacles to the Cross-Border Provision of Occupational Pensions* (COM[2001]214).

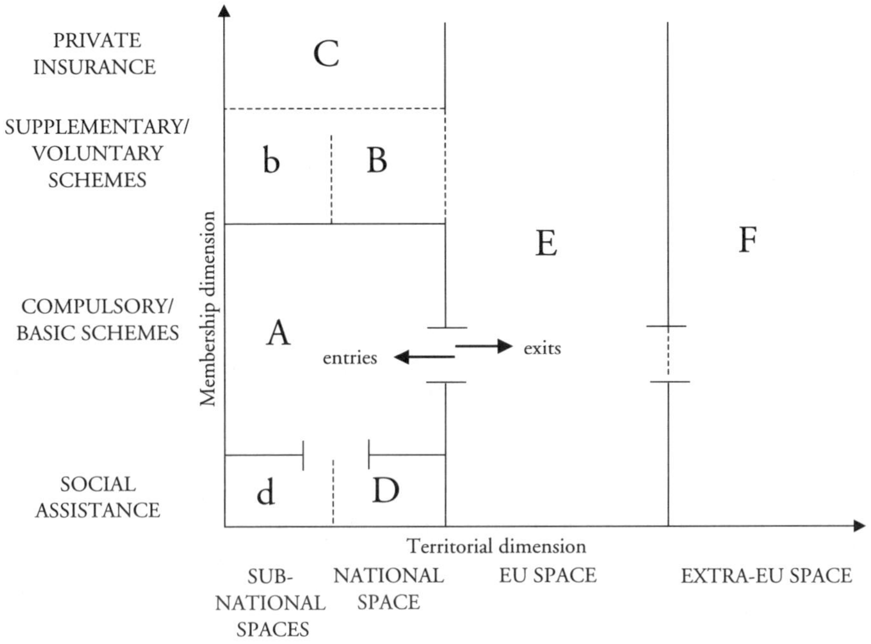

Figure Two *The new configuration of boundaries for social sharing.*

territorial units and 'third-country nationals': the *extra-comunitari* (as this group is called in the Italian language).

- A membership dimension, on which 'movements' across the various layers or pillars of social sharing occur, institutional boundaries between schemes are defined and rules over who is eligible to what benefits and over who can provide such benefits are of prime importance. On this dimension, the main novelty is the 'cap' posed on statutory, first-pillar schemes and the emergence of an increasingly salient space occupied by supplementary (second-pillar) and private (third-pillar) schemes: a space which extends beyond the reach of obligatory affiliation and public monopoly on provision.

The intersection between the two dimensions and of their internal partitions generates a number of different sub-spaces, characterized by different kinds of boundaries. Space 'A' is the historical core of social sharing systems: it includes those compulsory and public insurance schemes that still constitute the fundamental pillars of national welfare—as well as a prime source of domestic legitimation for the Member States. This space remains relatively protected from external encroachments as far as its internal structuring is concerned. The EU regulatory framework (essentially, Regulation 1408/71[38]) rests on the *lex loci laboris* principle: it is the

[38] Council Regulation 1408/71 of 14 June 1971 on the application of social security schemes to employed persons and their families moving within the Community, OJ 1971 L 149/2.

social security law of the country of employment that applies to whoever works (and, more generally, legally resides) in that country. In a long series of 'social insurance cases'[39] the ECJ has so far upheld the principle of compulsory affiliation and public monopoly as a prerequisite for social solidarity: national authorities remain 'sovereign' in setting affiliation and eligibility rules. The novelty of this particular space is the opening of a relatively wide gate, through which workers, some other social categories, and certain providers from other EU Member States can enter and exit, according to the rules set by the coordination regime, constantly monitored (and often reinterpreted) by the ECJ.

In April 2004 a new Regulation on 'the coordination of social security regimes' (883/2004) was adopted by the European Parliament and the Council, replacing the old Regulation 1408, taking into account all the amendments, ECJ rulings, and changes in national legislation that have been introduced since 1971.[40] This new regulation is now the fundamental text setting the rules for entries and exits of persons through the two gates of space 'A'. The personal scope of 883 is very wide and covers all 'nationals of a Member State, stateless persons and refugees residing in Member State who are or have been subject to the legislation of one or more Member States, as well as to the members of their families and to their survivors' (Art. 2, para. 1). As to the material scope, the regulation applies to social security legislation, defined as all laws and regulations which establish an obligatory cover or insurance obligation for the whole range of social protection benefits, i.e.: (a) sickness benefits; (b) maternity or equivalent paternity benefits; (c) invalidity benefits; (d) old-age benefits; (e) survivors' benefits; (f) benefits in respect of accidents at work and occupational diseases; (g) death grants; (h) unemployment benefits; (i) pre-retirement benefits; (j) family benefits. The new Regulation is still based on the four principles of its predecessor, i.e. equal treatment, *lex loci laboris*, cumulability, and exportability, but it is simpler and internally more coherent. It includes new provisions on civil servants, pre-retirement benefits, long-term care benefits, and unemployment benefits, and is generally in line with the previous EU jurisprudence in this field, with the exception of healthcare, for which the situation is still in flux.[41]

Space 'B' is the new area of second-pillar schemes—particularly important in the field of pensions. In its take-off phase (1960s and 1970s) this space was characterized by a relatively high territorial closure. Regulation 1408/71 did not cover supplementary pensions and thus national authorities could discriminate both *vis-à-vis* non-national workers and *vis-à-vis* nationals who left their domestic territory and

[39] S. Giubboni, *Diritti sociali e mercato; La dimensione sociale dell'integrazione europea* (2003).

[40] Regulation 883/2004 of the European Parliament and of the Council of 29 April 2004 on the coordination of social security systems, OJ 2004 L 166/1.

[41] The Regulation does cover access to benefits in kind in case of sickness, but it still maintains the authorization regime that has been challenged several times by ECJ rulings. In the recent Communication *Follow-Up to the High Level Reflection Process on Patient Mobility and Healthcare Developments in the European Union*, the Commission has formulated some general principles that should inspire the regulatory framework on healthcare services (see COM [2004] 301 final).

moved abroad: benefits were not portable and contributions could not be cumulated. The degree of closure of second-pillar schemes remained weaker from the very beginning along the membership dimension. As was said above, several countries opted for voluntary affiliations, even if encouraged and subsidized by the state. The more constraining approach adopted by France and the Netherlands originated, however, a strand of litigation before the ECJ, which in this field took a much less protective orientation in respect of national prerogatives and domestic forms of closure than it had taken for first-pillar schemes. The Luxembourg judges found that the predominance of funding as a system of financing and the delicate nature of investment decisions (on the side of both the insured and fund managers) bring this tier of provision closer to the market and thus make it partially liable to EC competition law. In the wake of this strand of litigation the French *régimes légaux supplémentaires* have had to 'recycle' themselves as first-pillar schemes so as not to lose their privileges of *monopoles sociaux*, while the principle of compulsory affiliation could be maintained within certain Dutch pension funds only based on their contractual origin, on the judicial status of collective agreements in the Netherlands, and on the new provisions of the Amsterdam Treaty on the relationship between management and labour.[42]

Increased litigation, transnational lobbying on the side of business and pension funds,[43] and Commission activism prompted steps in the legislative arena for arriving at a common and coherent regulatory framework. In 1998 a Directive (98/49) established basic criteria for safeguarding supplementary pension rights: acquired rights must be maintained in case of cross-border worker movements, all EU nationals must be equally treated, benefits are exportable to the territory of other member states.[44] In 2000 the Commission put forward a draft directive on pension funds, which, after lengthy negotiations, was formally adopted in 2003 (Directive 2003/41/EC).[45] This Directive regulates the activities and supervision of all 'institutions for occupational retirement provisions' (IORP), including pension funds and superannuation schemes. The text contains detailed 'prudential' rules on both the operation and the investment strategies of IORPs. It also sets a regulatory framework on cross-border activities aimed at liberalizing the provision of second-pillar benefits across the EU: paragraph 5 of the preamble explicitly states that the Directive is 'a first step on the way to an internal market for occupational

[42] Giubboni, *supra* n. 39.

[43] A European Association of Paritary Institutions (AIEP), linking most second-pillar pension providers, was established in 1996.

[44] Council Directive 98/49 of 29 June 1998 on safeguarding the supplementary pension rights of employed and self-employed persons moving within the Community, OJ 1998 L 209/46. The framework for coordination of supplementary pensions remains however only partially complete and in 2002 the Commission issued a new communication on the portability of supplementary pension rights.

[45] Directive 2003/41 of the European Parliament and of the Council of 3 June 2003 on the activities and supervision of institutions for occupational retirement provision, OJ 2003 L 235/10.

retirement provision organised on a European scale'. And paragraph 33 specifies the core elements of the regulatory strategy that will make this possible:

> Without prejudice to national social and labour legislation on the organisation of pension systems, including compulsory membership and the outcomes of collective bargaining agreements, institutions should have the possibility to provide their services in other Member States. They should be allowed to accept sponsorship from undertakings located in other Member States and to operate pension schemes with members in more than one Member State. This would potentially lead to significant economies of scale for these institutions, improve the competitiveness of the Community industry and facilitate labour mobility [. . .]

The underlying rationale seems in other words that of reconciling national prerogatives and practices on compulsory affiliation and on scheme profiles with an EU market of competing providers, abiding by detailed prudential rules and subject to supervision (the IORPs). The Directive explicitly excludes from its scope of application both first-pillar schemes ('social security schemes which are covered by Regulation no. 1408/71') and in general institutions that operate on a pay-as-you-go basis. It also lists a number of specific national exceptions. Nevertheless this Directive opens up an enormous space for dynamics of social protection 'europeanization': the institutions affected by the Directive cover about 25% of the EU labour force and manage assets worth €2500 billion, or about 29% of the EU GDP. The Directive's provisions on cross-border activities are very complex and envisage various national filters (authorizations, information, consultations, etc.). Based on past regulatory experiences of this kind at the EU level, we can expect that the emergence of pan-European pension funds will not be a rapid and uncontroversial process—and the legislative text appropriately speaks of 'a first step', as mentioned above. But there is no question that a novel institutional dynamics has been unleashed, which might lead to a significant reconfiguration of European pension systems in the years to come, along both the membership and the territorial dimensions.

Space 'D' is that of means-tested benefits and services. Here the external wall of national systems is still buffered by Member State prerogatives on rules of residence. The gate opened in space 'A' does allow non-nationals to access social assistance benefits 'from above' (through the horizontal gate in the figure): a worker from another EU country can for example claim means-tested non-contributory benefits if he or she meets the requirements set by the host country for its own nationals. But 'lateral' accesses are still barred. In this respect, the EU is not (yet) like the USA or other federal polities, whose citizens are free to settle where they choose.[46]

[46] This freedom tends to originate 'welfare magnet effects', i.e. incentives on the side of 'the poor' to shop around for those sub-federal units that offer more generous benefits. For a discussion of these issues, see D. Mabbet and H. Bolderson, 'Non-Discrimination, Free Movement and Social Citizenship in Europe: Contrasting Provisions for the EU Nationals and Asylum-Seekers', paper presented at the International Social Security Association conference in Helsinki, September 2000; see also ISSA, *Social Security in the Global Village* (2002).

Moreover, access is limited to a predefined list of benefits, set by Regulation 1247 of 1992;[47] benefits are not portable and are paid only if the claimant is legally resident in the country. Now, while the Treaties protect the free circulation of workers, Member States have maintained important competencies regarding who can legally reside within their territory, especially if this person is not a worker. It is true that a number of directives have extended the right to free circulation to several categories other than workers (family dependents, students, pensioners, etc.).[48] But all such directives rest on the principle that those who aspire to reside in a Member State different from that of nationality must have 'sufficient' economic resources, so as not to originate 'unreasonable burdens' for the public purse of the host country. In order to obtain the right of residence in a Member State other than one's own, one has in other words to pass a sort of reverse means test (or affluence test), demonstrating economic self-sufficiency. Non-contributive social assistance is typically the realm of 'a-symmetric' solidarity: the realm of those sharing ties that, being based on needs rather than contributions, presuppose high degrees of 'we-feelingness', a strong sense of membership to a community of equals. Thus it is not surprising to find heavy resistance in this sector to the opening of borders and the admission of non-nationals.

In Figure Two, space 'D' and space 'B' are crossed by (incomplete) dotted lines that give rise to internal sub-spaces ('d' and 'b'). These lines are meant to signal the emergence, within many domestic systems, of some internal differentiations based on territory rather than (or on top of) categorical membership. Regional and even municipal responsibilities in the area of social assistance and services are growing everywhere in Europe. In some countries (e.g. Italy) regions may soon become the most active level of government for the regulation and even the creation of region-specific supplementary pension and health funds. Decentralization trends are (re-)creating infranational boundaries which—though much weaker than cross-national ones—could lead to new forms of fragmentation and may thus represent a threat *from within* to the maintenance of nationally bounded (standardized and integrated) social rights. In a few countries (e.g. Italy, Belgium, or Spain) this trend is affecting healthcare systems as a whole. In these cases, the dotted line of boundary 'infranationalization' cuts across space 'A' as well—to the extent that the latter includes compulsory sickness insurance.

Space 'E' corresponds to the 'near abroad' of national welfare systems: i.e the EU space from which entries and exits are legitimized either by rights of free movement (especially of workers and services) or by portability rules. The figure visualizes this space at the same level as the national space. In reality, what we find next to the latter are all the other EU national spaces. The EU space as such should be considered as an underlying floor on which national spaces rest. The formation of this

[47] Council Regulation 1247/92 of 30 April 1992 amending Regulation 1408/71 on the application of social security schemes to employed persons, to self-employed persons and to members of their families moving within the Community, OJ 1992 L 136/1.

[48] Van der Mei, *supra* n. 18.

space has been primarily regarded in terms of 'market-making' and therefore as a source of disturbance and erosion for national solidarity. The ability of the EU to engage in 'activist social policy' (i.e of affirming itself as a source of 'market-breaking' social rights) is limited by those inherent obstacles of 'positive' integration that have been identified and analysed by a vast literature.[49] In our perspective, however, in the midst of its negative and positive rule-making, the EU has slowly started to perform two tasks with at least some degree of 'structuring' potential. Along the membership axis, it has started to point towards the existence of possible pan-European solidarity publics. EC law has indeed attenuated or even eliminated many boundaries between the Member States in the sphere of social protection, but in many cases it has done so by invoking the existence (at least in terms of normative desirability) of a new pan-European solidarity space. Especially in the field of social assistance (the *sanctum sanctorum* of national welfare, under the symbolic profile), the orientation of the ECJ has been very clear: its jurisprudence has tended to restrict the scope of discretionality of the Member States, contrasting their 'closure' tactics by appealing not only to the principle of non-discrimination, but often by referring also to the need to promote transnational solidarity flows at the individual level.[50]

The EU has not only played, in other words, a role of market-making, but also a role of 'solidarity-making'. Moreover, it has also started to perform another important function of spatial structuring: that of building a single (or at least more homogeneous) boundary *vis-à-vis* third countries and their nationals. For this reason our map identifies a space 'F' (extra-EU) in respect of which the EU is increasingly affirming itself as the legitimate authority for defining and guarding the borders of citizenship—and not only social citizenship. As is known, the Amsterdam Treaty has paved the way for a gradual communitarization of immigration and asylum policy within the EU.[51] If it is true that one of the main external objectives of communitarization is the containment/control of entry flows (and thus the construction of recognizable EU boundaries along both the territorial and membership dimensions), among the internal objectives we find that of legal assimilation: i.e. non-discrimination of third-country nationals in terms of rights, starting from social rights.[52] It is not by chance that the Nice Charter (now included in the Constitutional Treaty adopted by the Dublin European Council in June 2004) speaks of 'individuals' and not of EU citizens. The principle of non-discrimination on the grounds of social rights was eventually introduced for third-country nationals

[49] On the concept of 'negative' and 'positive' integration and their application to the analysis of the process of European integration, see: J. Tinbergen, *International Economic Integration* (1965); F. Scharpf, 'Negative and Positive Integration in the Political Economy of European Welfare States', in G. Marks *et al.* (eds.), *Governance in the European Union* (1996) 15; S. Leibfried and P. Pierson, 'Social Policy', in H. Wallace and W. Wallace (eds.), *Policy-Making in the European Union* (2000) 267.

[50] Van der Mei, *supra* n. 18.

[51] A. Geddes, *Immigration and European Integration: Towards Fortress Europe*? (2000).

[52] European Commission, *Communication on Immigration, Integration and Employment* (COM [2003] 336).

in May 2003, through an amendment of Regulation 1408/71. Thus as far as employment and social protection are concerned, the *c.*13 million third-country nationals who find themselves within the EU now enjoy the same rights (and obligations, of course) that are recognized to EU nationals—as long as they are legally resident in one of the Member States. It is to be noted, however, that third-country nationals do not enjoy the right of free circulation: they cannot be discriminated against in the hosting country, but they cannot freely move for employment purposes from one Member State to another as can EU nationals. Member States are still in full control of the rules of residence on their own territory as regards third-country nationals (as was said above, discretionarity on this ground still exists also as regards other EU nationals, but has been significantly limited by the ECJ jurisprudence). Third-country nationals remain in other words second-class denizens: the EU has become an important source of external boundary-building, but the nation–state still retains important prerogatives as to who can establish roots within its territory.

If our mapping is correct, it is plausible to conclude that the process of European integration has significantly altered the spatial architecture of social citizenship. Confirming the hypothesis put forward at the end of the second part, we can say that this change has extended the scope of solidarity along the territorial dimension and along the membership dimension, has posed the basis for the formation of new sharing collectivities (especially at the level of supplementary pensions), and has transferred onto the EU certain important boundary-control prerogatives—with all the 'structuring' potential that such prerogatives always carry with them.[53] Far from being a mere question of 'transnationalization' of rights, the construction of a new EU space for the exercise of social citizenship has rested on distinct and salient dynamics of supranationalization: not only the elaboration of common definitions of old and new rights, but also the codification of jurisdictional protection of such rights. The EU certainly does not have (and perhaps will never have) its own social protection budget, fed by autonomous taxing powers, through which direct interpersonal flows of redistributions can be financed. But it has gradually equipped itself with regulatory competences that are able to discipline the sharing spaces of the Member States—and thus to orient their distributive outcomes.

How stable is the new spatial architecture mapped in Figure Two? Are there symptoms of strain, signals of change, margins for institutional fine-tunings? These are the questions that will be addressed in the concluding section.

4. OPEN CITIZENSHIP: DILEMMAS AND PERSPECTIVES

As we have suggested, the redrawing of the boundaries for social citizenship, induced by European integration, works as a destructuring factor in respect of traditional redistributive arrangements at the national level. At the same time it tends however

[53] S. Bartolini, *Exit Options, Boundary Building, Political Structuring*, EUI Working Paper SPN 98/1 (1998).

to create incentives for forms of 'restructuring' at the supranational level, i.e. the definition of institutional frameworks that are more coherent with the changed spatial coordinates. Both hypotheses rest upon the well-known insights of Stein Rokkan on the structuring and destructuring processes of politico-institutional spaces, when boundaries are redrawn. An increase of exit/entry options (i.e. changes towards a greater opening) tends to disturb the *status quo* of a given space, as this emerged in the wake of long and complex historical dynamics of political and ideological confrontations, in which both voice and loyalty components have intertwined with each other. In its turn, the construction of new external boundaries aimed at demarcating wider spaces reactivates, at least potentially, the process of structuring, creating opportunity frameworks for the emergence of new institutions.[54]

Which forms can 'destructuring' take and which effects can it have in the sphere that interests us, i.e. social protection? We can plausibly hypothesize that the ongoing trends towards an opening of social citizenship may have four main destructuring effects. The first one is of a financial nature and has to do with the balance of single national schemes and programmes. The production and maintenance of social rights are very demanding operations in terms of the symmetry between entitlements and obligations, benefits and contributions. The 1971 and 1992 Regulations were designed in order to contain as much as possible the disturbing effects inevitably connected with growing cross-border movements. But there are legal gaps and objective difficulties, which may transform the free circulation of workers and beneficiaries, the portability of benefits, and the cumulability of contributions into a potentially destabilizing factor for the final balance sheets of national programmes[55] and, more generally, for the planning and rationing policies adopted by the Member States with a view to containing the costs of their welfare states. So far, cross-border flows (of migrant workers, pensioners, patients, etc.) have remained relatively modest. But the deepening of economic integration is deemed to promote an acceleration of such flows, which have been constantly growing since the 1970s in any case. And the Eastern enlargement will add a potent engine to such growth starting from 2007, when the moratorium on the free circulation of workers envisaged by the accession Treaties will expire. According to recent estimates, in the next twenty-five years 3–4 million workers are likely to migrate from the new Eastern Member States, attracted not only by better job opportunities, but also by more generous social benefits.[56] It is true that the entry of foreign workers into national sharing spaces will imply new contributions and not only new outlays. Much will depend (as it already depends today) on the actual patterns of migrations (into which jobs on the part of which kind of workers, with what kind of demographic profiles and family backgrounds, etc.). But it is plausible to think that the final

[54] For a discussion of Rokkan's theory and its application to welfare state questions, see M. Ferrera, 'European Integration and National Social Citizenship: Changing Boundaries, New Structuring?', in 36 *Comparative Political Studies* (2003) 611.

[55] Van der Mei, *supra* n. 18.

[56] *The Economist*, 17 January 2004.

balance sheets will be negative for many countries or at least for important schemes within them.

The second effect is also of an economic nature, but has far reaching socio-political implications. The process of opening of social citizenship does not only affect, as stated, the territorial dimension, but also the membership dimension, through a weakening of the public monopoly on social insurance. The legitimacy of such monopoly in respect of first pillars has been confirmed in that strand of social insurance cases that was mentioned above. But the rulings of the ECJ on these issues rest upon a 'benevolent' interpretation of Treaties which—as is well known—place a predominant emphasis on the internal market and competition rules. As was briefly illustrated, both EC law and jurisprudence have promoted the market and upheld competition rules at the level of second and third pillars, with a view to developing a big European space for occupational and private pensions. The destructuring effects of such developments is threefold: weakening (or at least 'bounding') of the scope of operation of public monopolies in the field of solidarity and redistribution; possible erosion of the consensus around redistribution *qua* salient and legitimate function of the state; potential dualization of social protection, with a private/occupational channel catering to the aspirations of wealthier categories and a public channel devoted to the more vulnerable social groups. Such scenarios have been frequently evoked in debates over 'negative integration' and its implications for 'Social Europe'.[57] In the second paragraph above I argued that the destructuring of certain domestic redistributive arrangements may be a good thing to the extent that such arrangements are inequitable and inefficient—less a response to genuinely solidaristic than to 'usurpative' logics. The problem remains, however, of how to favour desirable restructurings—i.e. those that promote equity and efficiency—and of how to neutralize undesirable ones.

The other two effects connected with an opening of social citizenship are essentially of a politico-institutional nature and have to do with the survival of the nation–state both as a space and as an actor (source, guarantee) of redistribution. The map drawn in Figure Two indicates the emergence of new subnational spaces of solidarity, not only within space 'D' (social assistance), but also within space 'B' (supplementary pensions) and even within space 'A' (basic social insurance, especially health insurance). These developments are the product of complex dynamics, but may be at least partly interpreted as a direct or indirect consequence of European integration:[58] direct consequences, in that European integration has been promoting since the 1970s a greater protagonism of the regions and local authorities in the social policy sphere: indirect consequences, in that economic integration, the deepening of the internal market (and of globalization), and the intensification of territorial competition encourages forms of particularistic contraction of solidarity, a scenario that

[57] Leibfried and Pierson *supra* n. 49.

[58] M. Keating, *The New Regionalism in Western Europe: Territorial Restructuring and Political Change* (1998).

Wolfgang Streeck has dubbed the emergence of 'competitive solidarities' on a subnational basis.[59] But there is a second cluster of dynamics that can undermine the survival of the nation–state as the fulcrum of solidarity: the process of solidarity 'trans-nationalization', i.e. the formation of redistributive collectivities that cut across traditional state borders. Let us think of the emergence of inter-regional associations (also promoted and encouraged by specific EU policies), which often include among their objectives the strengthening of cooperation and exchanges in the field of social policy. Or let us think of the establishment of new transnational IORPs, made possible by the recently approved EU pension fund directive. Transnationalization dynamics are so far less pronounced than subnationalization dynamics. But to the extent that they will be able to develop their own institutional momentum, they too are likely to work in a destructuring direction in respect of the *status quo*, providing important social groups (or territorial units) with new, tangible, and appealing exit options from the more traditional and national redistributive schemes.

The effects of boundary opening than we have just discussed are already something more than mere hypotheses: to a great extent they are already observable in actual dynamics, which need to be carefully monitored and investigated in the near future in order to understand and interpret the evolution of European welfare states. But let us come to the counter-trends, i.e. to signs, options, possible scenarios of restructuring within the new and wider spatial coordinates of the Union.

Despite the obstacles encountered by positive integration, the Union has already developed through time a distinctive social policy, essentially of a regulatory type: in many of the spheres listed in Table One there exist regulations and directives that establish minimum standards or that have harmonized national legislations based on common principles.[60] The Treaties of Amsterdam and, especially, Amsterdam and Nice have in their turn strengthened the constitutional rank of social protection as a fundamental objective of the Union.[61] Moreover, the ECJ has often operated as a balancing actor between market and solidarity principles.[62] In the perspective of this chapter: some degree of 'restructuring' has already taken place, in the wake of an EU change in the spatial boundaries of the welfare sphere and the market linked to European integration. But there are in particular two new and promising trends.

The first trend is linked to the process of full constitutionalisation of citizenship rights. A catalogue of social rights recognized by the EU has been included within the Charter of Fundamental Rights, first proclaimed by the European Council at

[59] W. Streeck, 'Competitive Solidarity: Rethinking the 'European Social Model', in K. Hinrichs *et al.* (eds.), *Kontingenz und Krise: Institutionenpolitik in kapitalistischen und postsozialistischen Gesellschaften* (2000) 245.

[60] Leibfried and Pierson, *supra* n. 49.

[61] Giubboni, *supra* n. 39; S. Sciarra, 'From Strasbourg to Amsterdam: Prospects for the Convergence of European Social Rights Policy', in P. Alston (ed.), *The EU and Human Rights* (1999) 473.

[62] M. Poaires Maduro, *We, The Court: The European Court of Justice and the European Economic Constitution* (1998).

the Nice summit of 2000 and subsequently included as Part II of the Treaty Establishing a Constitution for Europe adopted by the Dublin Council in 2004. As can be seen from Table One, the rights listed under Title IV (devoted to 'Solidarity') are nothing new in respect of what already exists in the Member States. Moreover, in strictly legal terms, the recognition of such rights in the new Treaty does not amount to them becoming directly enforceable rights: they have rather the status of 'programmatic principles' or 'aspirational rights', thus endowed with a much less binding character than other civic or political rights (such as free movement or non-discrimination).[63] Looked at from a perfectionist angle, the social dimension of EU citizenship thus remains conspicuously thin, even in the wake of constitutional reform. But perfectionism is seldom an appropriate yardstick for assessing the nature and especially the structuring potential of a new institution. The sheer fact that something akin to a bill of rights—including social rights—has been codified in the Constitutional Treaty must be regarded as a very significant (some have said 'spectacular'[64]) innovation: an innovation that operates a normative and symbolic rebalancing of the Union's overall mission and thus promises to redress gradually the asymmetry between economic and social dimensions of integration. The ECJ may soon start to make reference to fundamental rights in its jurisprudence. So far the Court has not yet used directly the Charter for its case law, considering the 'aspirational' character of its provisions: but according to many commentators, the weaker enforceability of constitutional 'principles' is very controversial from a legal point of view and it may reasonably be expected that the ECJ will sooner or later change its orientation,[65] thus attributing to EU (social) citizenship a denser and more authoritative status, and turning it into a potential magnet for both voice and loyalty dynamics.

The second novelty is the launch of the Open Method of Coordination (OMC) as a new instrument of multi-level governance in the social policy sphere.[66] Initially inaugurated in the field of employment, starting from 1997, such an instrument has been subsequently extended to the field of social inclusion, pensions, and—more timidly—healthcare. In our perspective, the OMC is promising both from a procedural and substantive point of view. Centred as it is on the identification of

[63] S. Giubboni, *Lavoro e diritti sociali nella 'nuova' Costituzione Europea. Spunti Comparatistici*, Working Paper No. 5 (2004), available online at http://www.urge.it. The Treaty establishing a Constitution for Europe adopted in Dublin in June 2004 treats most of the social provisions of the Charter of Fundamental Rights as 'principles'. In Art. II-112.5 it specifies that 'The provisions of the Charter which contain principles may be implemented by legislative and executive acts taken by institutions, bodies, offices and agencies of the Union, and by acts of Member States when they are implementing Union law, in the exercise of their respective powers. *They shall be judicially cognizable only in the interpretation of such acts and in the ruling on their legality*' (emphasis added). This article (and in particular the italicized passages) confers to social rights a weaker binding character, subject to the mediation of other law-making bodies.

[64] J. Ziller, *La nuova Costituzione europea* (2003).

[65] See the debate illustrated in Giubboni, *supra* n. 63.

[66] S. Regent, 'The Open Method of Coordination: A New Supranational Form of Governance?', 9 *European Law Journal* (2003) 190.

grand strategic objectives for each sector of intervention, on the monitoring and evaluation of national institutions and practices through benchmarking exercises, this method can play an important 'restructuring' role in respect of both the symbolic and the substantive components of welfare policies. The OMC can contribute to an 'opening' of national systems of social citizenship from the point of view of normative and cognitive frames, it can invite them to puzzle over the issue of new boundaries and their implications, to identify new ways for reconciling the need to respond to common challenges and priorities with the desire to maintain different traditions and identities,[67] to select—to get back to an earlier remark—desirable from undesirable institutional destructurings. At the procedural level, the OMC can work (as it is already working) as a fulcrum for a gradual and at least partial restructuration of domestic political games around welfare reform.[68] In other words—and concluding—the OMC can provide stimuli and opportunities for remodelling loyalty dynamics and reorienting voice dynamics in the direction of greater europeanization.

It will not be easy for the EU to find in the coming years a stable equilibrium between openness and closure, membership and options, solidarity and market, cohesion and competition. In the developmental juncture which Europe is now crossing (widening with a highly problematic deepening), the signs and risks of destructuring seem higher that the signs and opportunities of restructuring. For this reason, the journey of institutional reform must go ahead: there is no tenable *status quo*.

[67] F. Scharpf, *European Governance: Common Concerns vs. the Challenge of Diversity*, Jean Monnet Working Paper (2004), available online at http://www.iue.it/RSC/Governance.

[68] M. Ferrera, M. Matsaganis, and S. Sacchi, 'L'Unione Europea contro la povertà: Coordinamento aperto e processo di inclusione sociale', 5 *Italianieuropei* (2002) 173.

3

Solidarity and Citizenship Rights in the Charter of Fundamental Rights of the European Union

SÍOFRA O'LEARY

INTRODUCTION

If history remarks on the fashion ushered in by the new millennium for the Member States of the European Union (EU) to proceed by way of convention when discussions of weighty constitutional importance are called for, time alone will tell whether it will also record the outcome of the EU's early experience of the genre as disappointing.

Whether they are intended to proclaim the fundamental rights which the founding fathers omitted from the original EC Treaties or designed to produce a constitutional text prior to the big bang made inevitable by the accession of ten new Member States, conventions, it appears, are an appealing forum. With the EU and its Member States increasingly concerned about the general public's apathy, even disenchantment, with the integration process, the convention which drafted the Charter of Fundamental Rights of the European Union (hereinafter 'the Charter')[1] enabled numerous and disparate elements of civil society to exchange views about the need for the 'constitutional charter of a Community based on the rule of law'[2] to be finally underpinned by a catalogued commitment to fundamental rights; and all this in an atmosphere of apparent openness and transparency.[3] In addition, like latter-day intergovernmental conferences (hereinafter 'IGCs'), both the Charter

The views expressed in this essay are entirely personal. I would like to thank Drs. José María Fernández Martín and Julio Baquero Cruz for their time and invaluable comments. Any errors and weaknesses are the responsibility of the author.

[1] OJ 2000 C 364/8.

[2] See Case 294/83, *Les Verts* [1986] ECR 1339, para. 23 and Opinion 1/91 (EEA) [1991] ECR I-6079, para. 21.

[3] On the question whether the drafting of the Charter was a truly open and participatory process see, *inter alia*, De Búrca, 'The Drafting of the European Union Charter of Fundamental Rights', 26 *ELR* (2001) 126; De Schutter, 'Civil Society in the Constitution for Europe', in E. O. Eriksen *et al.* (eds.), *The Chartering of Europe* (2003) 133; and the House of Lords Select Committee on the European Union, *EU Charter of Fundamental Rights*, Session 1999–2000, 8th Report 14.

convention and the constitutional convention which proceeded it[4] highlighted the EU's predilection for the notions of citizenship and solidarity.

The rights conferred by the status of EU citizenship have become an increasingly frequent point of discussion before the European Court of Justice (ECJ). Although somewhat derided as a public-relations exercise when it first made its appearance in the Maastricht Treaty, the humble bundle of rights (no apparent duties) inserted in Articles 17–22 of the Treaty on European Union (TEU), and little changed to date,[5] have become a source of considerable legal and indeed economic value to migrating EU citizens. The latter have been quick to rely on their new, complementary status in disputes with the national authorities of the Member States which host them, or which they are simply visiting, more often than not over their alleged entitlement to social benefits on an equal footing with that state's own nationals. Although the Charter is less exclusive than the EC Treaty provisions on free movement and citizenship, in that it confers rights on a variety of beneficiaries—EU citizens, migrant workers, and EU residents, including third-country nationals—it was felt that it would be incomplete were reference to the rights of EU citizens not also to be included in the first attempt of the millennium at drafting a comprehensive catalogue of fundamental rights.

As for the notion of solidarity, following a rather modest appearance in early Treaty preambles,[6] it has, of late, been increasingly in vogue. The Member States' continued resolve to create an ever-closer union among the peoples of Europe has now been supplemented in more recent versions of the TEU by their desire to deepen the solidarity between their peoples. The Charter was not immune to this

[4] The intention to establish the convention which drafted the Charter was announced at the Cologne European Council in June 1999 and the details were worked out at the Tampere and Helsinki European Councils of October and December 1999. Declaration No. 23 of the Treaty of Nice stated that the debate on the future of the Union and the following IGC would relate, *inter alia*, to the status of the Charter. The Laeken declaration establishing a convention with a view to considering the future of the EU (hereinafter 'constitutional convention') asked that thought be given to incorporation of the Charter into the basic Treaty, as well as to the question of accession by the ECs to the European Convention on Human Rights and Fundamental Freedoms (hereinafter 'ECHR').

[5] Since the introduction of EU citizenship at Maastricht, subsequent amendments of the EC Treaty have underlined its complementary nature and included a right to write to any EU institution or body in one of the official languages and receive an answer in the same language. The Treaty of Nice specifically amended Article 18 EC to the effect that legislation adopted to facilitate rights of free movement shall not apply to national systems of social security and social protection.

[6] Explicit references to solidarity in the preamble of the original EEC Treaty were confined to confirmation of the solidarity 'which binds Europe and the overseas countries'. Admittedly, the aim to ensure economic and social progress by common action to eliminate barriers between Member States was founded on something akin to solidarity in that the Member States were showing a willingness to cooperate with each other, albeit principally in economic spheres. The preamble to the Treaty of Paris which established the European Coal and Steel Community specifically spoke of the resolve 'to create, by establishing an economic community, the basis for a broader and deeper community among peoples long divided by bloody conflicts'. In addition, one of the essential objectives of the EEC/ECs/TEU has always been to lay the foundations for 'an ever closer union' among the peoples of Europe and to provide for the constant improvement of the living and working conditions of those peoples.

new trend and in it too solidarity features strongly. According to the preamble of the Charter, which refers, inexorably, to the 'ever closer union', the EU is founded on the indivisible universal values of human dignity, freedom, equality, and solidarity. The 'rights, freedoms and principles' that it sets out include a disparate and sometimes puzzling category of social and economic rights grouped together principally in Chapter IV under the title 'Solidarity'. Not to be outdone, the most recent EU product of undetermined legal status to issue from a convention—the Draft Treaty Establishing a Constitution for Europe—is peppered with references to solidarity.[7] In it, the latter no longer features simply in the preamble as a value upon which the EU is founded but appears both as an objective and as what might be described as a characteristic of European society, the others being pluralism, tolerance, justice, and non-discrimination.[8] As regards the EU's objectives under the draft, it shall, *inter alia*, promote social justice and protection, equality between women and men, solidarity between generations and protection of children's rights, economic, social and territorial cohesion, and solidarity among Member States.[9]

With the fate of the Draft Constitution hanging in the balance and, as a result, the question of the legal status of the Charter unresolved by the Member States and, it would seem, deliberately untouched in decisions of the Court,[10] this essay examines the Charter's solidarity and citizenship rights and analyses their impact, actual or potential, on the EU's embryonic welfare law.[11] What may the effect of these provisions be on the diverse obligations which EC law in the social sphere imposes on Member States and on the rights that individuals derive therefrom? The issues that will be addressed, in greater or lesser detail, in the pursuit of this inquiry are several and varied:

- the legal status of the Charter and its legally binding effect, if any, in the absence of agreement on the Draft Constitution;
- the justiciability of the solidarity and citizenship rights in the Charter—whether in terms of access to justice or their substantive content—particularly given proposed changes in the Draft Constitution;

[7] Adopted by consensus by the European Convention on 13 June and 10 July 2003. The latest version (which appears to be that of 6 August 2004) was signed in Rome by the Member States on 29 October 2004. It must now be submitted for ratification by the different Member States.

[8] See, for example, Article I-2 of the Draft Constitution.

[9] Article I-2(3) of the Draft Constitution. The Draft Constitution also provides for a somewhat different type of solidarity in a clause stating that the Union and its Member States shall act jointly in a spirit of solidarity if a Member State is the victim of terrorist attack or natural or man-made disaster (Articles I-43(1) and III-329 as regards the implementation of this solidarity clause).

[10] As opposed to the references to the Charter by the Court's Advocates General and the Court of First of Instance. See Section 4A *infra* for details.

[11] What this embryonic EU welfare law entails is of course open to question. For the purposes of this essay, it is used loosely to describe those aspects of EU law which most resemble or which touch, directly or indirectly, the central core of welfare provision at national level, i.e. essentially national social policies, including social security and social protection, health, education, and housing provision.

- the interrelationship between the substantive rights in the Charter and the *acquis communautaire*;
- the potential, even of the most 'programmatic' rights that figure in the Charter, for unexpected, even far-reaching, developments resulting from interpretations of the Charter's solidarity and citizenship provisions by the ECJ;
- the question of what constitutes EU welfare law—what it entails, what rights and obligations it encompasses, and what, for a favourable verdict regarding impact, must the Charter achieve in its respect.

1. THE PROTECTION OF FUNDAMENTAL RIGHTS IN THE EU PRIOR TO THE PROCLAMATION OF THE CHARTER

The initiative launched at the Cologne European Council in 1999, which culminated in the drafting and solemn proclamation of the Charter, followed many years of discussion about whether the EU should have its own bill of rights and, if so, what that bill should include; whether it should, or indeed could, accede to the ECHR and, for a brief heretical period, whether fundamental rights, which form part of the general principles of EC law, were being taken seriously by the very court that was entrusted to ensure their protection.[12]

To understand the added value, if any, of the Charter as regards the protection of fundamental rights in the EU, never mind its impact on so-called EU welfare law, it is useful to recall briefly the evolution of fundamental rights protection in the EU prior to the adoption of the Charter. It is well known that there was no mention of fundamental rights and, more importantly, the need for their protection and respect, in the original treaties. The genesis of the protection of fundamental rights in the EC/EU can be attributed to two sources. On the one hand, the key doctrines of supremacy and direct effect arguably presupposed a commitment to some level of fundamental rights protection and indicated a central role for the individual in the vindication of those rights. On the other, confronted by the first major constitutional crisis since its existence—with some Member States refusing to recognize those key doctrines if constitutionally protected national norms were to be subordinated to a supranational legal order itself lacking in fundamental rights guarantees—the Court recognized that fundamental rights form part of the general principles that it is entrusted to ensure by virtue of Article 220 EC.[13] In subsequent cases, it elaborated on this commitment: 'respect for fundamental rights forms an integral part of the general principles of law protected by the Court of Justice. The protection of

[12] For a taste of academic debate during the aforementioned heretical period, as well as fundamentally opposed perspectives on the Court's record in protecting fundamental rights see Coppel and O'Neill, 'The European Court of Justice: Taking Rights Seriously?', 29 *CMLRev.* (1992) 669 and Lockhart and Weiler, 'Taking Rights Seriously 'Seriously': The European Court and its Fundamental Rights Jurisprudence', 32 *CMLRev.* (1995) 51 and 579.

[13] Case 29/69, *Stauder* [1969] ECR 419.

such rights, whilst inspired by the constitutional traditions common to the Member States, must be ensured within the framework of the structure and objectives of the Community.'[14] In the absence of a bill of rights specific to the Community and Union and, in the absence for many years of any specific reference to fundamental rights in the Treaties, the Court drew inspiration from constitutional traditions common to the Member States and from guidelines supplied by international treaties for the protection of human rights on which the Member States have collaborated or to which they are signatories.[15] However, the requirements flowing from the respect for fundamental rights in the EC legal order primarily concern its institutions and bodies. They are only binding on Member States, and hence subject to judicial review by the ECJ, when they are acting within the scope of EC law—i.e. both when they are implementing EC law and derogating from their Treaty obligations.[16] The Court has no power to examine the compatibility with its fundamental rights requirements of national rules that do not fall within the scope of EC law.[17]

The Maastricht Treaty recognized the EU's commitment to fundamental rights with the inclusion of Article 6(2) TEU. The latter confirmed the Court's existing case law and explicitly required the EU to respect as general principles of EC law fundamental rights guaranteed by the ECHR and by constitutional traditions common to the Member States. The jurisdiction of the Court in this context was limited, however, with the protection afforded by these general principles essentially being limited to areas in which the EC had competence to act. However, not everyone was

[14] Case 11/70, *Internationale Handelsgesellschaft* [1970] ECR 1125 at 1134.

[15] See, in particular, Cases 4/73, *Nold* [1974] ECR 491, para. 12 and 46/87; 227/88, *Hoechst AG v. Commission* [1989] ECR 2859, para. 13; and C-94/00, *Roquette Frères* [2002] ECR I-9011, paras. 23–24, where the ECHR was first expressly mentioned by the Court and then accorded particular or special significance. The preferential status of the ECHR amongst international fundamental rights texts has been carried over in Article 52(3) of the Charter (Article II-112(3) of the Draft Constitution). Reference to the ECHR was of course important, not only because the ECHR may be regarded as the 'epicentre of human rights protection on Europe', but also because, in the absence of a clear indication to the effect that the principles of the ECHR had been incorporated into the EC legal order, the risk was that the Strasbourg institutions would assume human rights jurisdiction over matters falling within the scope of EC law. See further Curtin, 'The "EU Human Rights Charter" and the Union Legal Order: The "Banns" Before the Marriage?', in D. O'Keeffe *et al.* (eds.), *Liber Amicorum Lord Slynn of Hadley* (2000) 303, at 308. For the examples of the other sources of fundamental rights inspiration see, *inter alia*: Cases 44/79, *Hauer* [1979] ECR 3727, paras. 10 *et seq.* (common constitutional traditions); 149/77, *Defrenne* [1978] ECR 1365, para. 27 and 24/86; *Blaizot* [1988] ECR 379 (the European Social Charter, hereinafter 'ESC'); C-173/99, *BECTU* [2001] ECR I-4881 (Social Charter); and C-249/96, *Grant* [1998] ECR I-621 (International Covenant for Civil and Political Rights).

[16] See Cases 5/88, *Wachauf* [1989] ECR 2609, para. 19; C-292/97, *Karlsson* [2000] ECR I-2737, para. 37; and C-260/89, *ERT* [1991] ECR I-2925. The precise parameters of the Court's jurisdiction in this regard are controversial and it is questionable whether the Charter has clarified matters. Article 51(1) of the Charter (Article II-111(1) of the Draft Constitution) simply states that its provisions are addressed to Member States only when they are implementing Union law. See Carruthers, 'Beware of Lawyers Bearing Gifts: A Critical Evaluation of the Proposals on Fundamental Rights in the EU Constitutional Treaty', *EHRLR* (2004) 424 at 431, on the possible limiting effects of this formulation.

[17] Case C-12/86, *Demirel* [1987] ECR 3719, para. 28.

happy with the open-ended discretion which even this limited reference mechanism conferred on the Court in terms of the fundamental rights that were to be protected, their substantive content, or the limits thereto. The Treaty of Amsterdam, which saw the integration of the Schengen *acquis* into the first pillar, also brought Article 6(2) TEU within the jurisdiction of the Court.[18] Meanwhile, activity on the political front by the other EC institutions resulted in a variety of European Parliament resolutions and other soft law initiatives and premature attempts at Draft Constitutions and legal instruments such as the Community Social Charter, which were themselves essentially lacking in legally binding effect.[19]

As regards fundamental social rights, the core of the original Treaty provisions on social policy, the former Articles 117 and 118 EEC, contained some high-sounding objectives—*inter alia*, the promotion of improved working conditions and a raised standard of living—but these provisions were regarded as being of a purely programmatic nature.[20] Only Article 119 EEC (now Article 141 EC, as amended), which provided that Member States should ensure the application of the principle of equal pay for male and female workers, proved to be an exception to this rule. As a result of the indefatigable efforts of a Belgian lawyer defending her client's claims of discrimination on grounds of sex as regards pay, pension entitlements, and the termination of her contract of employment at the tender age of 40, the Court established the direct effect of this provision and held that the elimination of discrimination based on sex forms part of the fundamental rights which the Court is bound to ensure.[21] Over time, the social provisions of the Treaty were upgraded to include, as EC objectives, a high level of employment and social protection, equality between men and women, and the raising of the standard of living and quality of life and social cohesion and solidarity among Member States. At the same time, EC competence, albeit limited, has been extended in a variety of fields, not least employment, education, and vocational training.

Thus, at least until the adoption of the Charter, and indeed pending clarification of its legal status, the protection of fundamental rights, including fundamental social

[18] Article 46 TEU. For details of these changes in the Treaty of Amsterdam see A. Arnull, *The European Union and its Court of Justice* (1999) Ch. 2. With this extension of EU competence, recognition of fundamental rights was viewed in some quarters no longer as a question of long-term policy, but more one of short-term necessity. See the introduction to the Report of the Expert Group on Fundamental Rights, chaired by S. Simitis, *Affirming Fundamental Rights in the European Union: Time to Act* (1999) at 5 (hereinafter 'Simitis Report').

[19] On the protection of fundamental rights in the EU generally see P. Alston (ed.), *The EU and Human Rights* (1999); Oliver, 'Fundamental Rights in European Union Law after the Treaty of Amsterdam' in O'Keeffe *et al.* (eds.), *supra* n. 15 at 319; K. Feus (ed.), *An EU Charter of Fundamental Rights* (2000) 77; on the Social Charter, see Watson, 'The Community Social Charter', 28 *CMLRev.* (1991) 37 at 45, who points out that it could be used in conjunction with the EC's general law-making powers and as a means of interpreting both EC and national implementing legislation. See Section 4A *infra* for comparable suggestions as regards the impact of the Charter.

[20] See, for example, Case 126/86, *Zaera* [1987] ECR 3697, paras. 11 and 13.

[21] Cases 43/75, *Defrenne* [1976] ECR 455, para. 24 and 149/77, *Defrenne*, para. 27.

rights, in the EU, was to a great extent left to the ECJ, with the latter drawing inspiration from a fluid, unenumerated, open-ended category of general and constitutional principles common to the Member States and international conventions for the protection of fundamental rights.

2. ESTABLISHING THE CHARTER

Regardless of the objectives and interests which the drafting of the Charter were intended to serve,[22] it is important to remember that the mandate of the convention was limited. It was simply charged with consolidating and rendering more visible the EU's existing obligation to respect fundamental rights rather than embarking on the creation of a new body of such rights. The Charter was not intended to alter the system of rights conferred by the Treaties, nor was it intended to extend EU/EC competences.[23] It was also clear from the outset that decisions as regards the Charter's legal status and/or its integration into the Treaties were to be left in abeyance. Some of the sources from which the Charter's rights were to be drawn were specified—not least the ECHR, the revised ESC, and the Social Charter. However, account was to be taken of the economic and social rights in these instruments only 'insofar as they do not merely establish objectives for action by the Union'.

The importance that rights discourse has played in the legislative and decision-making processes of the EU's political and judicial institutions has frequently been

[22] Arguments in support of a written catalogue of rights refer to the need to compensate for the expansion of EC/EU competence into new non-economic areas; the importance of a reinforcement of the EU's commitment to fundamental rights prior to the 2004 accessions; the development of EU citizenship; the need to clarify the legal basis of the rights already protected by the Court; the need for greater transparency and predictability than that provided by the existing reference mechanism used by the Court; and the need to subject the EU's legislative and administrative activities to greater scrutiny. See, for example, the arguments discussed in C. McCrudden, *The Future of the EU Charter of Fundamental Rights*, Jean Monnet Working Paper 01/10 (2001) 8; and by the House of Lords Select Committee, *supra* n. 3 at 15–18. Arguments against the need for a Charter of rights are perhaps most pithily summed up by Weiler, 'Editorial: Does the European Union Need a Charter of Rights?', 6 *ELJ* (2000) 95: EU citizens enjoy a surfeit of judicial protection of their rights; the creation of a competing written catalogue of rights may provoke rather than resolve tension with the ECHR; the proclamation of a Charter without binding legal effect creates a negative perception of the EU and suggests a refusal to take rights seriously; the magisterial language used to draft such catalogues of rights adds to, rather than resolves, confusion; the 'organic living laboratory of human rights protection' that is Article 6(2) TEU may be put at risk; and, finally, of greater importance would be the insertion of a provision making the protection of fundamental rights within the sphere of application of EC law one of the policies of the EC.

[23] See Articles 51(2) and 52(2) of the Charter (now, in an amended form, Articles II-111(2) and II-112(2) of the Draft Constitution) and the discussion in Foubert and Lenaerts, 'Social Rights in the Case-Law of the Court of Justice: The Impact of the Charter of Fundamental Rights of the European Union on Standing Case-Law', 28 *LIEI* (2001) 267 at 293; Lenaerts and De Smijter, 'A "Bill of Rights" for the European Union', 38 *CMLRev.* (2001) 273; and J. Dutheil de la Rochère, *The Future of the EU Charter of Fundamental Rights*, Jean Monnet Working Paper 01/10 (2001) at 2.

identified with efforts to legitimize the constant expansion of EC competence and with attempts to foster a set of common values to underpin the integration process.[24] The drafting of a Charter of fundamental rights seems to be no exception in this respect. Like the People's Europe debate which preceded the Maastricht Treaty and the efforts to create an EU citizenry, the drafting and proclamation of the Charter was intended as a visible sign that the EU, a contested and somewhat opaque organization occupying ever-wider fields of what previously constituted exclusively Member State competence, was doing something concrete for EU citizens by rendering their rights more visible.[25] A report compiled for the European Commission in 1999—the Simitis Report—highlighted the need for the EU's citizens to identify with the ever-changing project which is European integration: '[c]learly ascertainable fundamental rights stimulate the readiness to accept the European Union and to identify with its growing intensification and expanding remits'.[26] In addition, like the introduction of citizenship, the drafting of the Charter was yet another indication, however symbolic, of the ongoing 'constitutionalization' of the EU and its Treaties and, as such, it was of considerable ideological importance.[27] The constitution of a bill of rights would legitimize the Union and aid in its transformation into a wider entity for economic, political, and social integration in the eyes of its citizens. It would, as one commentator has suggested, represent a 'significant constitutional moment',[28] in the same way perhaps that the recognition of direct effect and the principle of supremacy, or even the introduction of EU citizenship,

[24] See, for example, De Búrca, 'The Language of Rights and European Integration,' in J. Shaw and G. More (eds.), *New Legal Dynamics of European Union* (1995) 29 at 30.

[25] According to a Commission communication published as the drafting process came to a close (COM [2000] 559), the task of the Charter convention had been one 'of revelation rather than creation, of compilation rather than innovation'. See also the explanatory memorandum which accompanied the Charter (Charte 4473/00, Convent 49); and the content of its general provisions, particularly Articles 51(2) and 52(2). The European Parliament Working Paper, *What Form of Constitution for the European Union?* (1999) at 15, identified the following as the effects of the establishment of a catalogue of human rights: reinforce the constitutional character of the Treaties; be a point of reference for EU institutions and national authorities when planning and implementing Union measures and enhance the image of the EU so that it would no longer appear simply an economic organization.

[26] See the Simitis Report, *supra* n. 18 at 11.

[27] See also De Búrca, *supra* n. 24 at 43; Pernice, 'The Charter of Fundamental Rights in the Constitution of the European Union', in D. Curtin *et al.* (eds.), *The Emerging Constitution of the European Union* (2003) 3, who observes that fundamental rights are both subjective rights and objective elements of the constitutional order; and Eriksen 'Why a Constitutionalised Bill of Rights?', in Eriksen, *et al.* (eds.), *supra* n. 3, 48, at 57–9.

[28] See A. J. Menéndez, *Chartering Europe: The Charter of Fundamental Rights of the EU*, Arena Working Papers WP 01/13 (2001) 13. See also in this respect De Búrca and Aschenbrenner, 'The Development of European Constitutionalism and the Role of the EU Charter of Fundamental Rights', 9 *CJEL* (2002) 355, who regard 'constitutionalism' in the EU as covering both recognition of the EU's shift from an international to a constitutional legal order as well as signs of the development of a set of beliefs and attitudes on the part of members of the polity as to how law should both constrain and empower government.

were regarded or, more importantly, came to be regarded, as significant constitutional moments in the history of European integration.

3. THE DISPUTED NATURE OF THE RIGHTS GUARANTEED BY THE CHARTER: LEGAL STATUS AND JUSTICIABILITY

Any consideration of the relationship between the Charter's solidarity and citizenship rights, freedoms and principles and the existing *acquis communautaire* and their impact on EU welfare law must also be prefaced by a reference to two related issues—the legal status of the Charter and the justiciability of the rights which it contains.

A. The Legal Status of the Charter

The Cologne European Council having specifically left undecided the question of the Charter's legal status, it is perhaps surprising that agreement was reached at an early stage to the effect that the Charter would be drafted *as if* it were eventually to be incorporated into the Treaties. Given the ideological significance of the proclamation of a Charter of rights, inevitably enhanced by the apparently open, deliberative forum in which it was being drafted, this was a calculating manoeuvre by at least some of the delegates. However, while the decision to draft the Charter as if it would be binding may have allowed the convention to concentrate on the issue of the substantive rights that it would feature, as several commentators have remarked, it did not prevent and probably contributed to a certain ambiguity pervading the text.[29] A document was essentially being drafted as if it would have legal effect with no unanimity and indeed little clarity regarding what it was for or, moreover, whether it contributed anything (apart from greater visibility) to the protection of fundamental rights over and above the existing mechanisms in the Treaty.[30]

In the event, the Draft Constitution incorporates the text of the Charter with the insertion of a provision to the effect that the 'Union shall recognise the rights, freedoms and principles set out in the Charter of Fundamental Rights which constitutes Part II.'[31] Pending resolution of the fate of the Draft Constitution, considerable attention has been paid to the reaction of the Court of Justice and Court of First Instance to the Charter. It has been repeatedly mentioned in Opinions of Advocates General who, while recognizing its lack of autonomous binding effect,

[29] See McCrudden, *supra* n. 22; De Búrca, *supra* n. 3 at 128.

[30] See McCrudden, *supra* n. 22 at 10; Lenaerts and de Smijter, *supra* n. 23 at 281–2.

[31] Article I-9(1) of the Draft Constitution. For discussion of problems which such full incorporation will entail, resulting mainly from the fact that the Charter was drafted as a separate entity with its own internal coherence and without reference to possible overlap and duplication with existing Treaty provisions see De Búrca, 'Fundamental Rights and Union Citizenship', in B. de Witte *et al.* (eds.), *Ten Reflections on the Constitutional Treaty for Europe* (2003) 11.

regard it as 'a substantive point of reference for all those involved in the Community context'[32] or as 'the most valuable evidence on the common denominator of the basic legal values shared by Member States'.[33] While the Court of First Instance has referred expressly to the Charter in support of its legal reasoning, the Court of Justice has avoided such references or referred to the Charter sparingly and with as little fanfare as possible.[34] Indeed in one case the Court responded to a reference by its Advocate General to one of the solidarity rights in the Charter with a reference instead to a similar provision in the Social Charter.[35] Whether one favours the Court's prudence in avoiding reference to the Charter or the contrasting eagerness of the Court of First Instance, the former was clearly influenced by a belief that, at least pending the culmination of the IGC assigned the task of reviewing the Charter's legal status, it was unwise to provide legal interpretations of a document whose status remained open to question.

However, the operation of the reference mechanism in Article 6(2) TEU, which characterizes the Court's development of its fundamental rights jurisprudence to date, suggests that it is unlikely, regardless even of the fate of the Draft Constitution, that the Court will be able to resist the pressure (or even the temptation, in appropriate circumstances) to refer to the Charter or, at the very least, those of its provisions that mirror the *acquis communautaire*.[36] The Social Charter is not a

[32] Opinion of Advocate General Ruiz-Jarabo Colomer in Case C-466/00, *Kaba II* [2003] ECR I-2219, para. 73.

[33] Opinion of Advocate General Ruiz-Jarabo Colomer in Case C-208/00, *Überseering* [2003] ECR I-9919, para. 59. See also the Opinion of Advocate General Mischo of 20 September 2001 in Cases C-21/00 and C-64/00, *Booker Aquaculture* [2003] ECR I-7411, para. 126: '[The Charter] constitutes the expression, at the highest level, of a democratically established consensus on what must today be considered as the catalogue of fundamental rights guaranteed by the Community legal order.'

[34] See the decisions of the Court of First Instance in Cases T-54/99, M*ax.mobil* [2002] ECR II-313; T-112/98, *Mannesmannröhren-Werker AG v. Commission* [2001] ECR II-729, para. 76; and T-177/01, *Jégo-Quéré v. Commission* [2002] ECR II-2365. The Court's reference to the Charter seems to be limited to an order in the context of an application for interim measures—Case C-232/02 P-R, *Commission v. Technische Glaswerke Ilmenau GmbH* [2002] ECR I-8977, para. 85, where it cited and drew legal conclusions from the provisions of Article 41(1) of the Charter (Article II-101(1) of the Draft Constitution).

[35] Case C-173/99, *BECTU*, para. 28 of the Opinion and para. 39 of the judgment. The Social Charter had of course been referred to in the preamble of the Working Time Directive (Directive 93/104/EC of 23 November 1993 concerning certain aspects of the organization of working time, OJ 1993 L 307/18) at issue in that case, which could justify the Court's preference for that Charter as a source of inspiration/confirmation for its interpretation of the Directive's provisions relating to the right to paid annual leave. See further, Ryan, 'The Charter and Collective Labour Law', in T. Hervey and J. Kenner (eds.), *Economic and Social Rights under the European Union Charter of Fundamental Rights* (2003) 77.

[36] See the *Communication of the Commission on the Charter* (COM [2000] 644 final) at 5; De Witte, 'The Legal Status of the Charter: Vital Question or Non-Issue?', 8 *MJ* (2001) 81 at 86; Eeckhout, 'The Proposed EU Charter of Fundamental Rights: Some Reflections on its Effects in the Legal Systems of the EU and its Member States', in Feus (ed.), *supra* n. 19, 97, at 104; and La Torre, 'The Law Beneath Rights' Feet', in Eriksen *et al.* (eds.), *supra* n. 3, 71 at 89, who considers that the Charter might be considered binding indirectly, as a minimum common denominator of the fundamental rights doctrines already in force and operational in the Member States.

binding legal instrument and the Court has no jurisdiction to enforce it directly but that has not prevented it from referring to that Charter to bolster a particular interpretation of a right or principle that figures amongst those which the Court is, pursuant to some other provision of EC law, entrusted to respect.[37] The reasoning of the Advocate General and Court in *BECTU* which is examined in Section 6B, albeit they chose to refer to two different Charters, is illustrative of this point. In addition, the Social Charter inspired a whole Commission action programme containing legislative proposals, many of which did subsequently see the light of day.[38] The Charter will no doubt, in accordance with the Court's well-established case law, act as a source of values and norms that will influence the interpretation of EC legislation and policy-making more generally.[39] Furthermore, although a legally binding Charter would obviously have a stronger impact, the Charter nevertheless calls upon the EU and its Member States to promote the fundamental rights which it contains, some of which at least extend beyond the existing *acquis judiciaire* or *communautaire*. As such, there will inevitably be, as commentators have remarked, some degree of reappraisal or redefinition of the EU's powers and competences and a further rebalancing of its social and economic goals.[40] Article 118a EEC (now Article 137 EC, as amended) referred simply to the adoption of minimum requirements for gradual implementation as regards improvement of the working environment to protect workers' health and safety. Yet the Court's interpretation of the scope of this legal basis in an annulment action against one of the first directives adopted thereunder, in which reference was specifically made to the Social Charter, was unexpectedly broad.[41] The idea therefore that the Charter, whether fully incorporated or not, makes no difference to existing fundamental (social) rights protection is difficult to maintain. Inevitably, the existence of the Charter, regardless of the question of incorporation and the countervailing safeguards in its general provisions, will influence the interpretation by the Court of the nature and consequences of the EU's and, where appropriate, the Member States', objectives, tasks, powers, and obligations. Indeed, it is unlikely that the one

[37] See the references to the Social Charter in Cases C-84/94, *United Kingdom v. Council* [1996] ECR I-5755; C-67/96, *Albany* [1999] ECR I-5751; and C-173/99, *BECTU*.

[38] COM (89) 568 final. See also Watson, *supra* n. 19.

[39] See Foubert and Lenaerts, *supra* n. 23 at 271; De Búrca, *supra* n. 31 at 21 and 24; Pernice, *supra* n. 27 at 5; and De Witte, *supra* n. 36. Since March 2001, Commission proposals for legislative or regulatory acts are the subject of a prior compatibility check with the Charter and a new recital testifying to this compatibility check is inserted into legislative proposals or regulatory acts which have a connection with fundamental rights (see CONV 116/02, at 4). See, for example, Directive 2002/73 of 23 September 2002 amending Council Directive 76/207/EEC on the implementation of the principle of equal treatment for men and women as regards access to employment, vocational training and promotion and working conditions, OJ 2002 L 269/15, para. 3.

[40] See De Búrca, *Human Rights: The Charter and Beyond*, Jean Monnet Working Paper WP 01/10 (2001) 12. See also De Witte, *supra* n. 36 at 86, who admits that the impact of the 'new' social rights which do extend beyond the exisiting *acquis judiciaire* is more uncertain in this respect.

[41] Case C-84/94, *United Kingdom v. Council*, para. 76.

institution which played such a fundamental role in 'constitutionalizing' the Treaties will refrain from resorting to a Charter whose very existence underscores the continued evolution of that constitutionalization process.

B. Justiciability

Put simply, a provision is justiciable only where it is capable of being interpreted and applied by the Courts.[42] It is important to distinguish in this respect between discussion of the substantive nature of the rights concerned, which is of particular importance as regards the social and economic rights figuring in the 'Solidarity' Chapter of the Charter, and more general questions concerning their effective judicial protection.

A distinction between rights, freedoms, and principles is drawn in both the preamble and later in the Charter's general provisions.[43] At least some delegates intended that this distinction would ensure that some provisions of the Charter do not establish subjective rights that can be invoked by the individual directly but rather set out principles that must be respected by and can only be enforced against Community or national authorities in the performance of their legislative and executive functions.[44] Thus, the solidarity rights, whose inclusion in the Charter was the subject of particularly heated debate, were to be recognized as principles that, whilst common to Member States, are implemented differently according to their national laws and practices.[45] The idea was that these principles would only give rise to rights to the extent that they are implemented by national law or, in those areas where there is such competence, by EC law.[46] Nevertheless, many of these hotly contested solidarity provisions—on, for example, social security, social protection, social and housing assistance, access to preventive healthcare and medical treatment—are formulated, not in terms of objectives and principles, but in terms of entitlement, rights, and obligations.[47] Despite this, it is generally accepted that

[42] House of Lords Select Committee, *supra* n. 3 at 37.

[43] Article 51(1) of the Charter (Article II-111(1) of the Draft Constitution) provides that the EU and Member States will respect the rights, observe the principles and promote the application thereof.

[44] See Heringa and Verhey, 'The EU Charter: Text and Structure' 8 *MJ* (2001) 11 at 14; and Goldsmith, 'A Charter of Rights, Freedoms and Principles', 38 *CMLRev.* (2001) 1201.

[45] This is reflected in the reference, in several provisions of the Charter, to the enjoyment of rights under the conditions provided by EC and national law and/or practices. See, for example, in Chapter IV, Articles 27, 28, 30, and 34 (Articles II-87, II-88, II-90, and II-94, respectively, of the Draft Constitution).

[46] Goldsmith, *supra* n. 44 at 1212–13. See also Menéndez, ' "Rights to Solidarity": Balancing Solidarity and Economic Freedoms', in Eriksen *et al.* (eds.), *supra* n. 3, 179, who observes that while most of the work based rights to solidarity are granted the status of fundamental rights, most universalistic rights to solidarity are formulated as ordinary rights, dependent on national law, or as policy clauses.

[47] See Heringa and Verhey, *supra* n. 44 at 15; Peers, 'Taking Rights Away? Limitations and Derogations', in S. Peers and A. Ward (eds.), *The European Union Charter of Fundamental Rights* (2004) 141 at 175. In addition, the drafters of the Charter took some fairly clear fundamental policy principles and drafted them as if they were justiciable rights. Contrast the formulation of Article 29 of the Charter (Article II-89 of the Draft Constitution) and the clear and precise statement to the effect that everyone

the intention was that while some of the solidarity rights are justiciable, others were simply intended as 'fundamental policy purposes' or 'programmatic' rights.[48] The latter require appropriate policies, programmes, and measures to ensure their promotion, access, enforcement, and effectiveness and, in contrast to civil and political acts, which generally operate as limitations on legislative or executive power, they may require legislative action and, in addition, involve a charge on public funds.[49]

Of particular importance as regards this aspect of the justiciability debate as it applies, in particular, to the solidarity rights in the Charter rights, is the insertion in Part II of the Draft Constitution of a general provision to the following effect:

> The provisions of this Charter which contain principles may be implemented by legislative and executive acts taken by institutions, bodies, offices and agencies of the Union, and by acts of Member States when they are implementing Union law, in the exercise of their respective powers. They shall be judicially cognisable only in the interpretation of such acts and in the ruling on their legality.[50]

This amendment seeks to ensure that certain rights or principles listed in the Charter, particularly socio-economic ones, are not transformed into directly effective fundamental rights requiring perhaps positive action and expenditure on the part of Member States.[51]

The problem, of course, with such a distinction between principles and rights or social/economic rights versus civil/political ones, is that these categories are far from watertight. It is, as De Búrca explains, extremely difficult to distinguish between those rights which will require positive action and entail expenditure and those which simply require non-interference for their protection.[52] Take, for example, the right of EU citizens to free movement and residence (discussed in Section 6A). The latter may be regarded as a civil or political right and it figures in the EC, the Charter and thus the Draft Constitution as a right of EU citizens. Yet, as we shall

has a right of access to a free placement service with the formulation of a similar policy principle in Article 1(3) of the revised ESC, on which that provision of the Charter is partly based, which provides that the contracting parties undertake to establish or maintain free employment services for all workers.

48 See the Simitis Report, *supra* n. 18 at 11.

49 See the submissions to the House of Lords Select Committee, *supra* n. 3 at 25; and Goldsmith, *supra* n. 44 at 1212–13: 'it is to be doubted that judges have any mandate or special expertise to determine how national resources should be allocated between different priorities. These are decisions to be made by government chosen through the ballot box.'

50 Article 52(5) Charter or II-112(5) of the Draft Constitution. Note, furthermore, that Article II-112(7) of the Draft Constitution provides that '[T]he explanations drawn up as a way of providing guidance in the interpretation of the Charter of Fundamental Rights shall be given due regard by the Courts of the Union and of the Member States.'

51 De Búrca, *supra* n. 31 at 23. See also Schulte, 'The Welfare State and European Integration' 1 *European Journal of Social Security* (1999) 7 at 28–9, who envisaged that the inclusion of social rights in any EU charter would meet with strong resistance from some Member States due to the possibility of the Court according them direct effect.

52 De Búrca, *supra* n. 31 at 23.

see, while the exercise of a right to free movement and residence by the EU's citizens may require non-interference (specifically non-discrimination) on the part of the host Member State, recognition of its direct effect and the resulting obligation on Member States to respect the substance of this right and protect its *effet utile* mean that its exercise may also give rise to (considerable) expenditure on the part of the Member State which hosts the migrant citizens in question.[53] In fact, as we shall see, the Court has read into the Treaty provision on the free movement and residence of EU citizens and the secondary legislation which implements it a degree of 'financial solidarity' (whose extent is as yet untested) which the Member States when adopting that secondary legislation would no doubt have regarded as unthinkable.[54]

Furthermore, the inclusion of a provision along the lines of Article II-112(5) of the Draft Constitution may undermine principles, fundamental and otherwise, that have already been recognized and enforced by the Court. Take, for example, the direct effect of the *principle* of equal pay in Article 141 EC, which was recognized by the Court in the *Defrenne* cases. The upshot of the insertion of Article II-112(5) in the Draft Constitution would arguably be to undermine the justiciability of such a principle. This would surely fall foul of the existing *acquis*, which the Charter may not have been intended to extend but was equally not intended to limit.[55] As a number of commentators have maintained, there seems to be no good reason for altering the position presently pertaining in the EU, by virtue of which the Court decides, on a case-by-case basis, the extent to which any given right is justiciable.[56] In addition, any attempt to exclude the Court's jurisdiction in this respect misunderstands the fact, as De Búrca points out, that the Court has only on rare occasions used fundamental rights as weapons to trump EC and/or Member State legislation and it is questionable whether it would change its practice wholesale in this respect simply because of the existence of the Charter.[57] In any event, both justiciable rights and fundamental policy purposes require the EU and Member

[53] The right of free movement and residence is also particularly apt when it comes to discussion of the justiciability of the principles in the Charter because, as regards the original EEC Treaty, the Court famously did not consider the absence of legislative implementing acts in the field of the provision of services as a bar to the direct effect of the rights thereunder: Case 33/74, *Van Binsbergen* [1974] ECR I-1299, para. 26: 'As regards at least the specific requirement of nationality or residence, Articles [49] and [50] impose a well-defined obligation, the fulfilment of which by the Member States cannot be delayed or jeopardized by the absence of provisions which were to be adopted in pursuance of powers conferred under Articles [52] and [55].'

[54] For the legislative background to the adoption of the 1990 Residence Directives (references provided *infra* n. 112) see S. O'Leary, *The Evolving Concept of Community Citizenship* (1996), Ch. 4.

[55] Thus Article 53 of the Charter (Article II-113 of the Draft Constitution) provides: 'Nothing in this Charter shall be interpreted as restricting or adversely affecting human rights and fundamental freedoms as recognised . . . by Union law.'

[56] See *Making It our Own: A Trans-European Proposal on Amending the Draft Constitutional Treaty for the European Union*, at 22, available online at http://www.users.ox.ac.uk/~ssfc0041/making_it_our_own_2.0.pdf.

[57] See De Búrca, *supra* n. 31 at 24.

States to provide the necessary framework for their implementation. Despite the abstract nature of many of the various social policy objectives to be found in the EC Treaty (and, for that matter, in the Social Charter) the EC legislator has nevertheless succeeded in adopting directives—such as the Directive on Working Time—to achieve those abstract social policy objectives.[58]

The other aspect of the justiciability debate that cannot be forgotten, particularly if the Charter is incorporated into the Draft Constitution, is the question of the enforceability of the rights that it contains. It is generally, albeit not universally, agreed that the case law of the Court on the standing requirements under Article 230(4) EC, which restricts the right to seek judicial review of general acts of EC legislation to those directly and individually concerned by that legislation, is excessively restrictive.[59] As the law stands, challenges to EC legislation on the grounds of breach of fundamental rights protected in the Charter would be almost certain to be deemed inadmissible, with the result, in certain cases, that the individual would be left without a judicial remedy. Can this be countenanced in a Union subject to the principle of respect for fundamental rights and the rule of law? The constitutional convention which addressed this problem was aware of the friction between the Court of Justice and Court of First Instance on the exact requirements of the principle of effective judicial protection to which both Courts adhere.[60] However, it too ran into difficulties when the issue of standing under Article 230(4) EC (Article III-365(4) of the Draft Constitution) was discussed in one of the working groups and subsequently in the discussion circle on the Court

[58] See the Simitis Report, *supra* n. 18 and the discussion of the Working Time Directive *infra* Section 6B. With reference to the effect of programmatic social rights see, once again, Case 126/86, *Zaera*, para. 14: 'the fact that the objectives of social policy laid down in Article 117 [EEC] are in the nature of a programme does not mean that they are deprived of any legal effect. They constitute an important aid, in particular for the interpretation of other provisions of the Treaty and of secondary Community legislation in the social field.'

[59] See, for example, Barav, 'Direct and Individual Concern: An Almost Insurmountable Barrier to the Admissibility of Individual Appeal to the EEC Court', 11 *CMLRev.* (1974) 191 and the Opinion of Advocate General Jacobs in Case C-50/00 P, *Unión de Pequeños Agricultores (UPA) v. Council* [2002] ECR I-6677. In a document submitted in 1995 to the IGC preceding the Treaty of Amsterdam, the Court itself raised the question whether restrictive standing was compatible with the effective judicial protection of (fundamental) rights which it was charged with ensuring. The Charter convention made no proposal in this respect since it considered the question to fall outside its narrow remit.

[60] Compare Case T-177/01, *Jégo-Quéré*, paras. 42–51 (in the absence of an implementing national act capable of forming the basis of an action before national courts, existing provisions of the Treaty on the jurisdiction of the Court could no longer be regarded, in the light of Articles 6 and 13 of the ECHR and Article 47 of the Charter, as guaranteeing persons the right to an effective remedy enabling them to contest the legality of Community measures of general application which directly affect their legal situation) with Case C-50/00 P, *UPA* (it is for the Member States to establish a system of legal remedies and procedures which ensure respect for the right to effective judicial protection. Consideration of the individual circumstances of an applicant when interpreting the direct and individual concern condition cannot have the effect of setting aside that condition, which is expressly laid down in the Treaty, without going beyond the jurisdiction conferred by the Treaty on the Community Courts).

of Justice.[61] In the end, the wording of Article 230(4) EC has more or less been maintained, subject to the proviso that natural or legal persons can also institute proceedings against 'a regulatory act which is of direct concern to him or her and does not entail implementing measures'. But what, as the commentators already frustratedly cry, are regulatory acts and does this amendment, on the one hand, really remedy the problem when it comes to the protection of the fundamental rights which the Draft Constitution proposes to incorporate?[62] On the other hand, although it is clearly desirable for individuals to be able to invoke their fundamental rights before the Courts, are we, as McCrudden points out, prepared for the effect that such a paramount shift in the EU's judicial structure might have on the relationship between the Member States and the EC institutions and also on the relationship between those institutions themselves?[63] An enumerated catalogue of fundamental rights was called for partly as a means to rein in what appeared to be the Court's excessive discretion when it came to the 'which, why, and how far' of fundamental rights protection in the EU.[64] In these circumstances, are the Member States and other EU institutions likely to relish the prospect of a revised Article 230(4) providing that same Court, at the suit of individual litigants, with the opportunity, this time on the basis of an avowedly constitutional Treaty, to challenge legislation of their own making?

4. THE ESSENCE OF TRADITIONAL NATIONAL WELFARE PROVISION AND THE EMBRYONIC STATE OF EU WELFARE LAW

In T. H. Marshall's classic modern treatise on citizenship, the latter is taken to mean full membership of the community and is based on a triad of civil, political, and social rights. Social citizenship entails 'the right to a modicum of economic welfare and security and the right to share to the full the social heritage and to live the life of a civilised being according to the standards prevailing in society'.[65] Such rights to a minimum standard of welfare and income are intimately linked with the provision of benefits by the welfare state and the notions of solidarity and/or the social contract which have traditionally underpinned that provision. Regardless of the various classifications of the diverse welfare state institutional structures to be found in the EU, not to mention the diversity of the normative aspirations that

[61] For details of the discussion of this issue during the course of the constitutional convention see Barents, 'The Court of Justice in the Draft Constitution', 11 *MJ* (2004) 121–141; and Iglesias and Baquero Cruz, 'The Convention and the Court,' in M. Hoskins *et al.* (eds.), *A True European: Essays for Judge David Edward* (2003) 69.

[62] See Dougan, 'The Convention's Draft Constitutional Treaty: Bringing Europe Closer to its Lawyers', 28 *ELR* (2003) 763 and Barents, *supra* n. 61.

[63] See McCrudden, *supra* n. 22 at 16.

[64] See Menéndez, *supra* n. 28 at 14; Goldsmith, *supra* n. 44 at 1204.

[65] See T. H. Marshall, *Citizenship and Social Class* (1950) and *Social Policy* (1975) at 11.

underpin them,[66] the benefits typically provided by the welfare state include old age pensions, sickness and invalidity allowances, unemployment benefits, minimum subsistence benefits, educational grants, the provision of healthcare, and maternity and child-raising allowances. These benefits may be provided on a contributory or non-contributory basis. The former schemes are insurance-based and usually oblige the insured party to pay premiums and entitle them to benefits when insured risks, such as unemployment, sickness, disability, or retirement, materialize.[67] Non-contributory schemes have a stronger redistributive quality and the benefits provided thereunder are usually funded exclusively out of tax revenue, with the enjoyment of or entitlement to such benefits not conditional upon the actual payment of tax-contributions. As Van der Mei observes, through insurance contributions and tax-generated revenue the welfare state partly displaces normal market rules about the distribution of resources according to economic performance and replaces them with some form of redistribution in accordance with principles of human need, solidarity, mutual aid, and social justice.[68] Solidarity in this context refers both to the interdependency of people as a basis for social cohesion and also to diffuse solidarity in large aggregates (territorial or community groupings, states, insurance schemes, etc.) in which members of one social group are willing to subsidize another.[69]

But even in the most generous of welfare states, indeed perhaps particularly in such states, these notions of solidarity, social justice, and redistribution are not intended to work to the advantage of everyone. As Walzer observes: 'the idea of redistributive justice presupposes a bounded world; a group of people committed

[66] See the excellent book by A. Van der Mei, *Free Movement of Persons within the European Communities: Cross-border Access to Public Benefits* (2003), which includes a summary, at 4–5, of the different possible systems of classification applicable to EU welfare states; Scharpf, 'The European Social Model: Coping with the Challenges of Diversity', 40 *JCMS* (2002) 645 at 650–652; and Schulte, *supra* n. 51 at 8 *et seq.*, where he describes some of the common features of EC welfare states, as well as variations in national expenditure on social protection. Majone, 'The EC Between Social Policy and Social Regulation', 31 *JCMS* (1993) 153 at 161 and 167, observes that national social policies are the result of past struggles rooted in peculiar historical and political traditions which differed widely from one state to the next. As such 'the delicate value judgments about the appropriate balance of efficiency and equity, which social policies express, can only be made legitimately and efficiently within homogeneous communities'.

[67] Van der Mei, *supra* n. 66 at 3; see also Steiner, 'The Right to Welfare: Equality and Equity under Community Law', 10 *ELR* (1985) 21: 'The term social welfare has been chosen to embrace the many benefits in cash or in kind, however financed, which are made available usually, but not necessarily, by a State to its citizens, either in the form of social security provision or 'social aid' in the form of supplementary benefits in cash or kind, concessionary rates and rebates, loans, grants, or other benefits'; and Schulte, *supra* n. 51 at 13.

[68] Van der Mei, *supra* n. 66 at 4–5.

[69] See Tinga and Verbraak, 'Solidarity: An Indispensable Concept in Social Security', in J. P. A. Van Vugt *et al.* (eds.), *Social Security and Solidarity in the European Union: Facts, Evaluations and Perspectives* (2000) 254; Faist, 'Social Citizenship in the European Union: Nested Membership' 39 *JCMS* (2001) 37 at 40; Opinion of Advocate General Fennelly in Case C-70/95, *Sodemare* [1997] ECR I-3395; and Hervey, 'Social Solidarity: A Buttress Against Internal Market Law?', in J. Shaw (ed.), *Social Law and Policy in an Evolving European Union* (2000) 31 at 45, who regards subsidization as the key common factor in social solidarity systems.

to dividing, exchanging and sharing social goods, first of all among themselves'.[70] To benefit from the provision of welfare one must belong in some sense to the society or polity conferring the benefits. In addition, the corollary of a right to benefits is a duty to contribute to the financing of the benefit system. As Van der Mei also observes, the fact that welfare states were developed by and within the legal political framework of the nation–state, with the latter claiming a specific bond with and holding specific responsibility for its own nationals or citizens, compounded this sense of the inclusion and exclusion of members and non-members, respectively.[71] While nationality may be irrelevant when it comes to contributory schemes in which entitlement depends on the payment of taxes or insurance premiums, entitlement to non-contributory benefits is more often than not the subject of nationality or habitual-residence conditions, the latter imposed, in particular, on non-nationals. The reasoning behind this is simple: the more redistributive and therefore morally demanding the nature of the social right or policy concerned, the more necessary it is thought for the basis of entitlement to be reflected in reciprocal ties of citizenship or some other form of diffuse solidarity.[72] Thus, where the benefits of a particular scheme are not restricted to a state's own nationals, residence conditions may be relied upon, reflecting not just the fact of residence, but also its length and quality. The imposition of such conditions is clearly intended to prove the existence of a real and effective link between the society granting the benefit and the benefit applicant, such as to justify an extension, beyond the normal parameters of national membership upon which modern welfare states have developed, of social solidarity in their favour. In terms of the organization and funding of national welfare systems, such conditions are unsurprising. In order to ensure that their social welfare systems function effectively, national authorities understandably seek to predict and control expenditure and ensure that tax receipts and other sources of state funds are sufficient to cover the costs generated by their social security and welfare systems. The bounded world which national welfare states require may be intimately linked with the forging of national identities and social cohesion, but it was also largely dictated by such economic considerations.

It is commonplace that the EC's origins as an organization dedicated almost entirely to economic integration meant that the development of EC social policy was at best spasmodic, at worst dogged by constant arguments about the existence of, or limits to, EC competence in the social field. The EU has no tax-raising powers of its own and no, or at least limited, provision for competence as regards the central core of social policy, namely social insurance, public assistance, health, education, housing, and welfare provision.[73] EC social legislation has, for the most part, concentrated on employment-related rights and issues, and legislation adopted in

[70] M. Walzer, *Spheres of Justice* (1983) at 31, cited in Van der Mei, *supra* n. 66 at 5.

[71] Van der Mei, *ibid.* at 6. See also Faist, *supra* n. 69 at 51, who suggests that nation states have not always been such an important solidarity collective: 'the history of social policy in Europe suggests that welfare state institutions developed first and then collective identities around [the welfare state]'.

[72] See Faist, *ibid.* at 41 and 51.

[73] See generally C. Barnard, *EC Employment Law* (2000), Ch. 1.

this field was, because of a lack of specific social competence, originally justified with reference to the need to remove obstacles to economic integration in the internal market.[74] Although a very large part of the EU's budget is spent on policies that may have indirect effects on Member State social policies (in particular the Common Agricultural Policy or European Structural and Social Funds), only a very small part is specifically aimed at social policy itself.[75] The Member States have referred, of course, since the early Treaty texts, to the need for the 'constant improvement of the living and working conditions of their peoples' but they included little by way of legal basis and, therefore, substantive provisions on social protection, to ensure that this aspiration could actually be achieved.[76] It is tempting therefore to conclude that EU welfare law, as such, does not exist. After all, Regulation 1408/71, the EC's principal incursion into the social security field, merely seeks to coordinate Member State rules on the social security entitlement of migrant workers but it neither harmonizes the benefits available at national level nor interferes with their substantive content. Similarly, although, as we shall see, Regulation 1612/68 has served as the basis for the assimilation of migrant workers and their families into host Member State welfare systems, once again the substantive content of the rights they enjoy is determined at national level, with EC law simply requiring application of the principle of non-discrimination on grounds of nationality with respect to those coming within its personal scope.

Nevertheless, although the EU is not a direct source of welfare provision, the gradual extension of its competence in the social policy field has led to the imposition of an increasing number of positive social obligations on Member States. Take, for example, another minimum-standards directive adopted in the field of health and safety, this time providing for a minimum floor of rights for pregnant workers and those on maternity leave.[77] Although Member States remained free to adopt higher standards of protection than those dictated by Directive 92/85 (and most had already done so or did so subsequently), its adoption was nevertheless an important sign of the construction by the Community legislature of positive, albeit minimal, elements of a European social contract of sorts. Furthermore, national welfare law and policy, although largely remaining within Member State sovereignty, are nevertheless subject to the basic tenets of EC law, not least the provisions of the Treaty relating to the fundamental freedoms, or those on competition, state aids,

[74] See Faist, *supra* n. 69 at 38; and Menéndez, in Eriksen *et al.* (eds.), *supra* n. 3 at 179, who remarks that the imbalance between market-making and market-redressing mechanisms in the EU is particularly striking given that all the existing Member States are mature welfare states, characterized by a balance of these two forces at the core of their socio-economic structures.

[75] Faist, *supra* n. 69 at 44.

[76] See further Barnard, 'EC "Social" Policy', in P. Craig and G. de Búrca (eds.), *The Evolution of EU Law* (1999), 479 on the intended social spillover from the creation of a common market and the evolution of EC social policy.

[77] Directive 92/85/EEC of 19 October 1992 on the introduction of measures to encourage improvement in the safety and health at work of pregnant workers and workers who have recently given birth or are breastfeeding , OJ 1992 L 348/11.

and employment equality between men and women.[78] In the field of social welfare, the result of this symbiotic relationship between EC and national law is a developing multi-level system of social welfare entitlement, with welfare conditions subject to governance on two and perhaps more levels, depending on the internal organization of welfare and social policies in the Member State concerned.[79] The darlings of recent IGCs and conventions—the related notions of citizenship and solidarity—are proving to be of key importance as regards the development of this multi-tier system of entitlement.

Initially, the notion of solidarity proved a useful shorthand for Member States in free movement cases where they sought to draw, with reference to the special bond of nationality, a distinction between their own nationals and nationals of other Member States when it came, in particular, to entitlement to certain social benefits.[80] The *Cowan* case, a precursor of EU citizenship if ever there was one, is perhaps the best example.[81] A British national, the victim of a violent assault while on holiday in France, claimed that to exclude him from entitlement to benefit from a scheme which provided compensation to French nationals and residents who were victims of assault would restrict his EC right to free movement. The French government argued that its rules on compensation did not create any barrier to freedom of movement and reflected the principle of national solidarity. The right to compensation, in their view, presupposed a closer bond with the state than that of a recipient of services such as Mr. Cowan.[82] Famously, the Court refused to accept this argument and held that Article 12 EC requires that persons in a situation governed by EC law be placed on a completely equal footing with nationals of the Member State being visited. Similar arguments based on national solidarity and the particular obligations of Member States towards their own nationals were fairly summarily dismissed by the Court in *Gravier*. The case involved the imposition by Belgium of higher tuition fees for vocational training on Community nationals from other Member States. Albeit not explicitly mentioning solidarity, the Member States considered that they had special responsibilities, in the field of education, towards

[78] See also Hervey, *supra* n. 69 at 3; and Scharpf, *supra* n. 66 at 647: 'When [direct effect and supremacy were] ensured, all employment and welfare-state policies at the national level had to be designed in the shadow of "constitutional" European law.'

[79] See also Faist, *supra* n. 69; Dougan and Spaventa, 'Wish You Weren't Here: New Models of Social Solidarity in the European Union', paper presented to a conference on Social Welfare and EU Law, University of Cambridge, 13–14 June 2003, soon to be published in M. Dougan and E. Spaventa (eds.), *Social Welfare and EU Law* (2004); and Hervey, *supra* n. 69 at 34.

[80] In the context of the EC Treaty provisions on the free movement of persons and services and the exclusion of public service posts from their scope, see the definition of the special bond of nationality provided by the Court: 'Such [public service] posts in fact presume on the part of those occupying them *the existence of a special relationship of allegiance to the State and reciprocity of rights and duties which form the foundation of the bond of nationality.*' Case 149/79, *Commission v. Belgium* [1980] ECR 3881, para. 10 (emphasis added).

[81] Case 186/87, *Cowan* [1989] ECR 195.

[82] See also Schockweiler, 'La Portée du principe de non-discrimination de l'article 7 du Traité CEE', 3 *Rivista di Diritto Europeo* (1991) 24.

their own nationals.[83] However, since the cost of higher education was not being borne by Belgian students, while those from other Member States were being asked to bear part of that cost, the Court held that there was inequality of treatment based on nationality. Regardless of the fact that educational organization and policy did not come within the scope of Community competence, and that a requirement of equal treatment regarding tuition fees would clearly have repercussions on the cost and organization of national vocational training policies,[84] the Court was unwilling to countenance such unequal treatment based on Member State nationality. This case law suggested, as early as the 1980s, a reduction of Member State sovereignty in the social welfare field, as well as increased tension between migration in the EC and the protected sphere of national citizenship.[85]

That EC law cuts across Member State social welfare competence, with the result that even matters that do not fall within the scope of application of EC law must not interfere with the fundamental freedoms, is also evident in a series of cases on the free movement of goods and services and EC competition law, where the solidarity underpinning aspects of Member States' social protection, welfare, and healthcare systems has been at issue. The key issue in this context has been, as Baquero Cruz underlines elsewhere in this volume (Chapter 6), the question whether the undertakings charged with the provision of the social welfare services in question were engaged in an economic activity,[86] whether they fulfilled an exclusively social function, founded on the principle of national solidarity, or whether their activities combined elements of both. Non-contributory and non-profit-making sickness funds and redistributive pension schemes have been regarded as fulfilling an exclusively social function as their activities are based on the principle of national solidarity, with the result that the competition rules were held not to apply to them.[87] The principle of solidarity in this context is reflected in the fact that contribution to these schemes is compulsory and in their redistributive quality.

[83] Case 293/83, *Gravier* [1985] ECR 593, para. 16. In the view of the intervening Member States, Article 12 EC did not prevent them from treating their own nationals more favourably in the area of education, particularly as regards access to education, scholarships, and grants and the contribution of students to the cost of education.

[84] The Court itself admitted as much in Case 24/86, *Blaizot* [1989] ECR 379. In the aftermath of Case 293/83, *Gravier*, the *Blaizot* case concerned the question whether certain university studies came within the definition of vocational training with the result that access to such courses would also be subject to Article 12 EC. Since the case constituted a development of EC law in this respect, the Court was willing to impose a temporal limitation on its effects: 'Pressing considerations of legal certainty preclude any reopening of the question of past legal relationships where that would retroactively throw the financing of university education into confusion and might have unforeseeable consequences for the proper functioning of universities.' See also the Opinion of Advocate General Slynn in Case 293/87, *Commission v. Belgium* [1988] ECR 305, at 331, where he regarded *Gravier* as a complete reversal of Belgian educational policy.

[85] Faist, *supra* n. 69 at 47.

[86] See, in this respect, Joined Cases C-159/91 and C-160/91, *Poucet and Pistre* [1993] ECR I-637 and Case C-364/92, *Eurocontrol* [1994] ECR I-43.

[87] Joined Cases *Poucet and Pistre*, paras. 15 and 18.

National schemes founded upon or promoting such social solidarity are not regarded as carrying out an economic activity. Similarly, it was not contrary to the EC Treaty provisions on establishment and services for the subsidization through public funds of residential care homes in Italy to be made subject to a non-profit-making condition, even if this meant non-Italian companies were less likely to qualify.[88] The social welfare provision in question was, according to the Court, based on the principle of solidarity, as reflected by the fact that it was designed as a matter of priority to assist those who were in a state of need owing to insufficient, family income, total or partial lack of independence, or the risk of being marginalized. In contrast, other bodies managing statutory social security systems that were non-profit-making, of social character, and subject to state rules which included solidarity requirements have been found by the Court to be undertakings engaging in economic activity.[89] Similarly, while the Court emphasizes that EC law does not detract from the power of the Member States to organize their social security systems,[90] this has not prevented it from exposing national health insurance systems to the rigours of EC law on the free movement of goods and the free provision of services.[91]

5. SOLIDARITY AND CITIZENSHIP RIGHTS IN THE CHARTER: AN EXAMINATION OF THEIR IMPACT ON EU WELFARE LAW

The substantive content of the solidarity rights in the Charter can best be described as a heterogeneous mishmash of the predictable and the unexpected.[92] While provisions on the rights of workers to fair and just working conditions or to

[88] Case C-70/95, *Sodemare.*

[89] See, for example, Case C-244/94, *Fédération française des sociétés d'assurance and Others* [1995] ECR I-4013.

[90] See, for example, Case 238/82, *Duphar v. Netherlands* [1984] ECR 523, para. 16. Note that Article 137(4) also provides that: 'The provisions adopted pursuant to this article shall not affect the right of Member States to define the fundamental principles of their social security systems and must not *significantly* affect the financial equilibrium thereof' (emphasis added).

[91] See, *inter alia*, Cases C-158/96, *Kohll* [1998] ECR I-1931; C-157/99, *Smits and Peerbooms* [2001] ECR I-5473; and C-385/99, *Müller-Fauré* [2003] ECR I-4509 and the essay by Hatzopoulos in this volume (chapter 5).

[92] The articles in Chapter IV, many of which relate to aspects of employment, social security and social protection, are entitled as follows:

- Workers' right to information and consultation within the undertaking (Article 27/II-87 of the Draft Constitution);
- Right of collective bargaining and action (Article 28/II-88 of the Draft Constitution);
- Right of access to placement services (Article 29/II-89 of the Draft Constitution);
- Protection in the event of unjustified dismissal (Article 30/II-90 of the Draft Constitution);
- Fair and just working conditions (Article 31/II-91 of the Draft Constitution);

information and consultation within the undertaking for which they work echo existing EC provisions of primary and secondary legislation on collective labour law,[93] who would have expected provisions referring to the Union's commitment to a high level of consumer and environmental protection or the right of access to placement services to have appeared in a document dedicated to fundamental rights? Was the guiding principle for inclusion, as some have suggested, the fact that such issues already found some reference, albeit perhaps not a legal basis for legislative action, in the EC Treaty?[94] Perhaps even more surprisingly, the Chapter also includes provisions relating to matters explicitly excluded from the scope of EC competence. While Article 28 of the Charter (Article II-88 of the Draft Constitution) recognizes the right to engage in strike action, collectively decided, as an EU right, Article 137(5) EC expressly excludes EC legislative competence in this field.[95] Thus, some rights may have found a place in the Charter, but they lack the legislative backing essential to render their enjoyment meaningful, particularly in the event that the Charter's current legal status remains unaltered. And what of the various rights whose enjoyment is subject to 'the conditions established by national laws and practices'? Article 30 (Article II-90 of the Draft Constitution), for example, establishes the right of every worker to protection against unjustified dismissal subject to such a proviso. Can national laws and practices regulate or condition the enjoyment of a right to such an extent that they deprive it of its very substance or *effet utile*?[96]

- Prohibition of child labour and protection of young people at work (Article 32/II-92 of the Draft Constitution);
- Family and professional life (Article 33/II-93 of the Draft Constitution);
- Social security and social assistance (Article 34/II-94 of the Draft Constitution);
- Healthcare (Article 35/II-95 of the Draft Constitution);
- Access to services of general economic interest (Article 36/II-96 of the Draft Constitution);
- Environmental protection (Article 37/II-97 of the Draft Constitution);
- Consumer protection (Article 38/II-98 of the Draft Constitution).

For an overview of the solidarity rights in the Charter see Gijzen, 'The Charter: A Milestone for Social Protection in Europe?', 8 *MJ* (2001) 33; and Menéndez, ' "Rights to Solidarity": Balancing Solidarity and Economic Freedoms', in Eriksen *et al.* (eds.), *supra* n. 3, 179. Social rights fall under different headings in the Charter due, as we have seen, to the traditional differences between the treatment of social rights which can be considered civil and political rights and other social rights of a more programmatic nature. See further Betten, 'The EU Charter of Fundamental Rights: A Trojan Horse or a Mouse?', 17 *International Journal of Comparative Labour Law and Industrial Relations* (2001) 151 at 155.

[93] See Articles 137 and 138 EC; the various EC Directives on Collective Redundancies, Transfers of Undertakings and European Works Councils mentioned in the explanatory note to the Charter, Charte 4473/00, at 27; and the Working Time Directive *infra* Section 6B.

[94] Heringa and Verhey, *supra* n. 44 at 29.

[95] For discussion of the potential impact of the Charter in this respect see Ryan, *supra* n. 35.

[96] See further Eeckhout in Feus (ed.), *supra* n. 19 at 109, who questions the sense of including Article 30 unless it is binding on the Member States. Apart from limited potential utility in the EU's own staff cases, Article 30 of the Charter will only apply in the Member States where a dismissed employee can show that his or her dismissal was in the context of implementation of EC law.

The rights conferred on EU citizens in the Maastricht TEU are well known and in need of little explanation.[97] They are reiterated in Chapter V of the Charter, entitled 'Citizens' Rights', albeit bolstered by the addition of a right to good administration (Article 41 Charter/II-101 of the Draft Constitution) and a right of access to European Parliament, Commission, and Council documents (Article 42 Charter/II-102 of the Draft Constitution). Not all the rights listed in Chapter V are reserved for EU citizens, but a precedent for this curious fusion of the rights of EU citizenship with the rights conferred on EU residents generally can be found in the existing provisions of the EC Treaty on citizenship.[98] The EC treaty refers, without enumerating them, to duties to which EU citizens may be subject. The Charter, in contrast, enumerates citizens' rights but reminds beneficiaries only in the preamble that the enjoyment of the rights in the Charter entails responsibilities and duties with regard to other persons, to the human community and to future generations.

So how might these provisions impact on EU welfare law or, as we have seen from the preceding discussion, more particularly on the interaction between EC social law and policy and the provision of welfare and organization of social policy at national level? Given the heterogeneity of the rights concerned, it is proposed to illustrate the potential impact of the Charter concretely with reference to three very different solidarity and citizens' rights which reflect the diversity of the Charter itself:

- the right of free movement and residence of EU citizens (Article 45 of the Charter/Article II-105 of the Draft Constitution);
- the right to fair and just working conditions (Article 31 of the Charter/Article II-91 of the Draft Constitution);
- the need to reconcile family and professional life (Article 33 of the Charter/Article II-93 of the Draft Constitution);

A. EU Citizenship, Free Movement, and Non-Discrimination

Prior to the introduction of EU citizenship in the Maastricht Treaty, the enjoyment of rights of free movement and residence directly conferred by the EC Treaty was limited to those Member State nationals who performed or were involved, to some extent, in the performance of an economic activity. The Court's jurisprudence recognized the right of Member State nationals to enter and reside in the territory of other Member States, but only for the purposes intended by the Treaty.[99] Migrant

[97] EU citizens enjoy rights of free movement and residence (subject to limitations and conditions) (Article 18 EC); they can vote and stand for election in the Member State in which they reside in European Parliament and municipal elections (Article 19 EC); they have the right to diplomatic and consular protection in third states in which their Member State of nationality is not represented (Article 20 EC); and they have the right to petition the European Parliament, apply to the Ombudsman, and write to the EC institutions and receive an answer in one of the official languages of the EC (Article 21 EC).

[98] See, for example, the rights to petition the European Parliament and apply to the Ombudsman in cases of maladministration pursuant to Articles 21, 194, and 195 EC.

[99] See Case 43/75, *Royer* [1976] ECR 497, para. 31.

workers, the self-employed, providers and recipients of services, students, and job-seekers were, over time, all declared to come within the personal scope of EC law and were thus the beneficiaries of EC rights to free movement and non-discrimination on grounds of nationality, subject, admittedly, in some cases, to temporal[100] or other limitations.[101]

The impact on national welfare provision of the Treaty provisions on the free movement of persons and the Court's early case law can best be summed up with reference to two important developments, both largely Court-driven. On the one hand, the Court insisted that although the Community may not have powers in a particular field of social policy (education or demographic policy, for example), that does not mean that the EC exceeds the limits of its jurisdiction solely because the exercise of its jurisdiction in the field of free movement affects measures adopted in pursuance of those Member State policies in those fields.[102] Thus, even where Member States retain social policy competence, they must nevertheless comply with EC law when exercising their powers. On the other hand, with reference to the principle of non-discrimination on grounds of nationality, the Court interpreted widely the range of substantive social benefits to which those entitled to free movement could be entitled in the host Member State. In particular, pursuant to Article 7(2) Regulation 1612/68, migrant workers and, as it subsequently transpired, in certain circumstances their family members,[103] were entitled to 'those [social] advantages by means of which the migrant worker is guaranteed . . . the possibility of improving his living and working conditions and promoting his social advancement'.[104] The Court's rationale for this broad interpretation of the Regulation's

[100] See, as regards job-seekers, the sanctioning of temporal limitations in Case C-292/89, *Antonissen* [1997] ECR I-745, para. 21—a period of six months did not seem insufficient to enable job-seekers to apprise themselves, in the host Member State, of offers of employment corresponding to their occupational qualifications.

[101] See, as regards students, recognition of a right of residence to pursue vocational studies subject, however, to the legitimate interests of the Member States: Case C-357/98, *Raulin* [1992] ECR I-1027, para. 39.

[102] See, for examples, Cases 9/74, *Casagrande* (national education policy) [1975] ECR 773; 65/81, *Reina* (national demographic policy) [1982] ECR 33, para. 15; and C-224/02, *Pusa* (national rules on the attachment of income for the recovery of debt).

[103] Compare Cases 76/72, *Michel S* [1973] ECR 457, para. 9 (the benefits referred to by Article 7(2) Regulation No. 1612/68 are to benefit the workers themselves) and 32/75, *Cristini* [1975] ECR 1085, para. 13 (in view of the equality of treatment which the provision seeks to achieve, the substantive area of application must be delineated so as to include all social and tax advantages, whether or not attached to the contract of employment, such as reductions in fares for large families).

[104] Case 39/86, *Lair* [1988] ECR 3161, para. 20. The classic definition of social advantages are those which, whether or not linked to a contract of employment, are generally granted to national workers primarily because of their objective status as workers or by virtue of the mere fact of residence on the national territory and the extension of which to workers who are nationals of other Member States therefore seems suitable to facilitate their mobility within the Community: Case 207/78, *Even* [1979] ECR 2019, para. 22. Travel reductions for large families (Case 32/75, *Cristini*), social security allowances for handicapped dependent adults (Case 63/76, *Inzirillo* [1976] ECR 2057), state pensions guaranteed to old persons (Case 261/83, *Castelli* [1984] ECR 3199), unemployment benefit (Case 94/84,

material scope, based on its purpose and spirit, was to ensure that Member State nationals were not dissuaded from exercising their free movement by the prospect of being excluded from welfare provisions in the host Member State and, furthermore, to encourage and facilitate the inclusion of migrant workers into the host Member State precisely by providing them with the same benefits available to that Member State's own nationals.

Thus, prior even to the introduction of EU citizenship, the impact of EC law on the free movement of persons on welfare provision by Member States was considerable. Indeed, before the Single European Act (SEA) and long before Maastricht, Amsterdam, Nice, and the Charter, it was suggested that 'discrimination, whether direct or indirect, with regard to any welfare benefit, against an EC national lawfully resident in a host Member State would be regarded as unlawful by the Court, unless the purpose of the benefit was wholly exceptional and inextricably connected in some way with nationality'.[105] The Court was regarded as having extended Member States' and perhaps individuals' obligations towards migrant workers and their families far beyond the limits originally agreed. It was argued in response to such judicial developments that if Member States were to be required to provide unanticipated and costly benefits, whether in the form of educational grants or long-term social assistance, for all legitimately resident migrant workers and their families, equity required some sharing of the burden.[106]

Faced with this Court-driven breach of their welfare systems, Member States defended the imposition of minimum threshold periods of employment and/or residence before entitlement to welfare benefits kicked in or argued for temporal limitations of Court judgments extending social welfare entitlement. The Court's response was uncompromising—nationality or residence conditions or conditions relating to a minimum duration of employment could not be imposed exclusively on nationals of other Member States, and even habitual-residence tests applicable to nationals and non-nationals alike were, in some instances, suspect.[107] As for

Deak [1985] ECR 1873), minimum subsistence allowances (Case 249/83, *Hoeckx* [1985] ECR 973), maintenance grants and tuition fees (Case 39/86, *Lair* [1988] ECR 3161), study finance (Case C-337/97, *Meeusen* [1999] ECR I-3289), child-raising allowances (Joined Cases C-245/94 and C-312/94, *Hoever* and *Zachow* [1996] ECR I-4895) and state-subsidized childbirth loans to low-income families (Case 65/81, *Reina*), to name but a few, all constitute social advantages to which migrant workers and their family members are entitled subject to the same conditions as nationals of the host Member State.

[105] See Steiner, *supra* n. 67 at 41. For examples of such exceptional cases see Case 207/78, *Even*, which involved a scheme providing additional pension benefits for former soldiers who had served in the allied forces in the Second World War and, subsequently, Case C-315/94, *De Vos* [1996] ECR I-1417, regarding the payment of supplementary retirement contributions for those engaged in compulsory military service.

[106] Steiner, *ibid.* at 41; N. Green *et al.* (eds.), *The Legal Foundations of the Single Market* (1991) at 175–93, in the specific context of the free movement of students.

[107] See, for example, Case 249/83, *Hoeckx*, where the Court held that a minimum subsistence allowance constituted a social advantage within the meaning of Article 7(2) Regulation No. 1612/68 and that an additional residence requirement for non-nationals was discriminatory. It took an infringement

temporal limitations, they were possible only in exceptional cases and were not justifiable simply with reference to the financial consequences that might ensue for a Member State from a preliminary ruling.[108] Despite this, there seemed little real resistance to the Court's view of the Member States' obligations towards the beneficiaries of economic free movement. There was, after all, no equivalent of the *Barber* protocol in the field of the free movement of persons.[109] Reasons for this lack of resistance may have been, firstly, that, from the point of view of the numbers migrating, the situation was far from critical at the time. It is estimated that around 4.7 million Member State nationals are resident in a Member State other than their own. Secondly, apart from students, of those who did exercise their rights to free movement and residence, the vast majority were either contributing to the host economy in some way, through the provision or receipt of services or were contributing tax revenue in the host Member State as a result of the economic activities in which they were engaged as employed or self-employed persons.[110] As a result, they were, in the main, net contributors to the welfare systems in which they were claiming or might claim entitlement to benefits. The right of residence of job-seekers was subject to a temporal limitation and the Court ensured that even during that limited period their right to equal treatment did not extend to costly social welfare benefits.[111] The rationale behind these restrictions and limitations was the need to guard against what was at least the perceived threat of benefit tourism. Economically inactive Member State nationals had no right to free movement and residence until the adoption of three Residence Directives in 1990.[112] Even then, the enjoyment of such rights was subject to two important conditions, namely the

action (Case C-326/90, *Commission v. Belgium* [1992] ECR I-5517) to secure the removal of this residence condition from Belgium law. See also Case C-185/96, *Commission v. Greece* [1998] ECR I-6601 (benefits for large families); Case C-299/01, *Commission v. Luxembourg* [2002] ECR I-5899 (guaranteed minimum income); and Case C-90/97, *Swaddling* [1999] ECR 1075, on the legality of a habitual-residence condition for entitlement to income support in the context of Regulation 1408/71.

108 Case 309/85, *Barra* [1988] ECR 355, paras. 13 and 14 and, subsequently, in the context of Articles 18 and 12 EC, Case C-184/99, *Grzelczyk* [2001] ECR I-6193, para. 52.

109 On the insertion of a protocol in the EC Treaty designed to limit the effect of the judgment of the Court in Case C-262/88, *Barber* [1990] ECR I-1889 see Hervey, 'Legal Issues concerning the *Barber* Protocol', in D. O'Keeffe and P. Twomey (eds.), *Legal Issues of the Maastricht Treaty* (1994) 329.

110 If one reads the case law on students and trainees, it is clear that their inclusion within the personal scope of application of the EC Treaty was based, at least partly, on their role as future economic actors and, therefore, future contributors of tax and social insurance. See, for example, Case 66/85, *Lawrie-Blum* [1986] ECR 2121, paras. 18–19.

111 Case 316/85, *Lebon* [1987] ECR 2811, para. 26. Cf. Case C-85/96, *Martínez Sala* [1998] ECR I-2709, para. 32, where the Court seemed to overrule this aspect of *Lebon* by considering a job-seeker to be a worker within the meaning of Article 39 EC and Regulation 1612/68. See further Dougan, 'The Workseeker as Citizen', 4 *Cambridge Yearbook of European Legal Studies* (2001) 93.

112 Directives 90/364 on the right of residence, OJ 1990 L 180/26; 90/365 on the right of residence for employees and self-employed persons who have ceased their occupational activity, OJ 1990 L 180/28; and 90/366 on the right of residence of students, OJ 1990 L 180/30, annulled and readopted as Directive 93/96, OJ 1993 L 317/54.

possession by the resident applicant of medical coverage in respect of all risks in the host Member State and sufficient resources to prevent him and/or his family becoming a burden on public funds in the host Member State.

It is this right of economically inactive EU citizens to move and reside freely within the territory of the Member States, which features in Article 18 EC and is now mirrored in Article 45(1) of the Charter (Article II-105 of the Draft Constitution), which has proved key to the Court's development of the status of EU citizenship and the rights it entails. It is also this provision which is providing the focus for discussion of the impact of EU citizenship on national welfare provision and the steady dilution of Member State sovereignty when it comes to such provision.[113] In recent years, the Court has overcome its initial reluctance to resolve free movement questions with reference to Article 18 EC and has begun to detail, sometimes with considerable gusto, the import of the status of EU citizenship which, in its own words, is 'destined to be the fundamental status of nationals of the Member States'.[114] It is difficult to identify the truly revolutionary case on EU citizenship and, specifically, the right of free movement and residence that it entails. What is unquestionable, however, is that, just as it had previously done with reference to the free movement of persons and services, the Court has incrementally constructed a line of jurisprudence which widens both the personal and material scope of application of the Treaty provisions on the free movement, residence, and non-discrimination entitlements of EU citizens.

The necessarily reactive and piecemeal operation of the Article 234 reference procedure means that the Court has no say in the preliminary references that come before it nor the order in which they appear. In these circumstances, it was fortunate for migrating EU citizens that the interrelationship between their rights of residence and their rights not to be discriminated against on grounds of nationality were first seriously addressed by the Court in the case of *Martínez Sala*. It was fortunate, firstly, because the case involved an application for a child-raising allowance in Germany which the Court had already had occasion to state fell within the material scope of Regulation 1408/71, at least as regards migrant workers coming within the personal scope of that Regulation.[115] Secondly, and more importantly,

[113] For discussion of the development of the Court's case law on Article 18 EC and the potential impact of that provision on national welfare provision see, variously, Steiner, 'Social Security for EC Migrants', 14 *Journal of Social Welfare and Family Law* (1992) 33 at 46; O'Leary, 'The Principle of Equal Treatment on Grounds of Nationality in Article 6 EC: A Lucrative Source of Rights for Member State Nationals', in A. Dashwood and S. O'Leary (eds.), *The Principle of Equal Treatment in EC Law* (1997) 105; Shaw and Fries, 'Citizenship of the Union: First Steps in the European Court of Justice', 35 *European Public Law* (1998) 533; and Dougan and Spaventa, 'Educating Rudy and the (Non) English Patient: A Double-Bill on Residency Rights Under Article 18 EC', 28 *ELR* (2003) 699.

[114] Case C-184/99, *Grzelczyk*.

[115] As regards Regulation 1408/71 see Joined Cases C-245/94 and C-312/94, *Hoever* and *Zachow*. As regards Regulation 1612/68, there was little doubt, as the Court said, that such an allowance came within the scope of application of the generously defined category of social advantages in Article 7(2), Case C-85/96, *Martínez Sala*, paras. 25–26.

although it was unclear whether the applicant, who was not in possession of a formal residence permit, qualified as a migrant worker within the meaning of Article 39 EC, it was generally accepted that she was legally authorized to reside in the host Member State.[116] As a result, the Court was able to leave unanswered the question whether a Member State national who, like Mrs. Martínez Sala, sought to reside in a Member State and support themselves with recourse to that state's social welfare provisions, derived a right of residence from Article 18 EC, the 1990 Residence Directives, or national law. According to the Court, the unequal treatment of lawfully resident EC nationals from other Member States constituted, in the absence of any justification, discrimination prohibited by Article 12 EC. The Court could have limited the circumstances in which EU citizens could rely on the principle of non-discrimination to those situations coming within the scope of application of the EC Treaty provisions on citizenship. It chose instead to allow EU citizens to rely on that principle with respect to all those benefits falling within the Treaty's material scope; in other words, the range of benefits covered by Regulation 1408/71 and, logically, those covered by Regulation 1612/68, not least the enjoyment of social and tax advantages pursuant to Article 7(2). Remarkably, the Court extended the scope of application of these pieces of secondary legislation to lawfully resident but economically inactive EU citizens without addressing the fact that the other conditions for eligibility (e.g. status as a migrant worker or family member of a worker) to the rights and benefits covered by this legislation were not, arguably, met by such EU citizens.

As regards the questions left unanswered by the *Martínez Sala* case, concerning whether Article 18 EC had direct effect, the effect, in the event that it did, of the limitations and conditions on the exercise of that right contained, principally, in the 1990 Residence Directives, and the consequences for national social welfare law of the combined use of Articles 12 and 18 EC, the answers were not long in coming. The *Grzelczyk* case concerned the effect on an EU citizen's right of residence of an application for a social assistance benefit which was funded by the host Member State and normally available to that state's own nationals and lawfully resident EU nationals. There was no doubt that the applicant had resided lawfully in Belgium prior to his application for the minimum subsistence allowance, known in Belgium as the minimex.[117] The question which arose was whether, following his minimex application, the host Member State was entitled not only to refuse him entitlement to the benefit in question but also to revoke his right of residence.

[116] Due to the referring Court's interpretation of Germany's obligations under the European Convention on Social and Medical Assistance of 11 December 1953. See Shaw and Fries, *supra* n. 113 at 538, on the possibility that this was an erroneous conclusion to draw from the Convention.

[117] He had, in fact, supported his studies through part-time work and credit facilities. Directive 93/96 provides that students simply have to assure the national authorities, by means of a declaration or similar, that they have sufficient resources and medical coverage to avoid becoming a burden on the host Member State and the applicant had presented the necessary declaration to this effect when he first applied for residence.

In *Grzelczyk*, the Court reiterated its decision in *Martínez Sala* to the effect that all those lawfully resident in a Member State can rely on Article 12 EC in situations that fall within the material scope of the Treaty. The minimum subsistence allowance in question constituted a social advantage within the meaning of Article 7(2) Regulation 1612/68. A Member State which considers that a student who has recourse to social assistance no longer fulfils the conditions of his right of residence may, according to the Court, take measures, within the limits imposed by Community law, either to withdraw his residence permit or not to renew it. But, in no case may such measures become the automatic consequence of a student who is a national of another Member State having recourse to the host Member State's social assistance system. Yet the Court still had to overcome what was arguably a rather large hurdle to the applicant's claim to continued lawful residence in Article 4 of Directive 93/96. The latter provides that the student's right of residence is to exist only for so long as beneficiaries of that right fulfil the conditions laid down in Article 1 relating to medical coverage and the possession of sufficient resources. By claiming the minimex, did the applicant not indicate that he no longer fulfilled these conditions? Reasoning *a contrario*, the Court stated that the Students' Directive had not established a right to payment of maintenance grants by the host Member State but, on the other hand, it contained no provision precluding entitlement to other social security benefits.[118] The Court then seized upon the reference in the sixth recital of the Directive to the effect that beneficiaries of the right of residence must not become an *unreasonable* burden on the public finances of the host Member State only to conclude that those Directives accept *a certain degree of financial solidarity between nationals of a host Member State and nationals of other Member States*, particularly if the difficulties which a beneficiary of the right of residence encounters are temporary.[119] Articles 12 and 18 EC therefore preclude entitlement to a non-contributory social benefit from being made conditional, in the case of nationals of Member States other than the host State where they are legally resident, on their falling within the scope of Regulation 1612/68 when no such condition applies to nationals of the host Member State.

Several essential issues remained for the Court to address—the question of the direct effect of Article 18 EC and its relationship with the 1990 Residence Directives, the question of what might constitute an unreasonable burden on public

[118] Case C-184/99, *Grzelczyk*, para. 39. This paragraph of the judgment is particularly confusing given that, on the one hand, the Court had already found in Case 249/83, *Hoeckx*, that the minimex is not a social security benefit, at least not one within the meaning of Regulation 1408/71. On the other hand, as regards the exclusion of maintenance grants from the scope of the Directive, the Court all but overruled Case 197/86, *Brown* [1988] ECR 3205 (where it had previously excluded such grants from the scope of application of the Treaty and Article 12) and in doing so pointed to the possible incompatibility of Article 3 of the Directive with Articles 17–18 and 12 EC (see, in particular, paras. 34–36 of the judgment). See further Case C-209/03, *Bidar* for a possible resolution of this issue in the context of a request by an EU citizen for a favourable student loan on the basis of Articles 17–18 and 12 EC.

[119] Case C-184/99, *Grzelczyk*, para. 44.

funds and the question of the legitimate restrictions which Member States might impose on the enjoyment by EU citizens of social welfare provisions. The Court's partial answer in *Baumbast*[120] to the effect that Article 18 EC did confer a right of residence directly on EU citizens would have been unthinkable when EU citizenship was first established and indeed had been contested by several national courts and, on occasion, by the Commission.[121] However, its decision on Article 18 EC had become the logical conclusion of its preceding citizenship case law and it was depicted as all the more inevitable when the Court framed its answer with reference to the well-established judicial reasoning on the nature of the rights of free movement and residence pursuant to Articles 39, 43, and 49 EC.[122] Thus, the right of nationals of one Member State to enter the territory of another Member State and to reside there is conferred directly on every citizen of the Union by a clear and precise provision of the EC Treaty.[123] Purely as a national of a Member State, and consequently a citizen of the Union, Member State nationals have the right to rely on Article 18(1) EC. Any limitations and conditions imposed on the exercise of the right of free movement and residence of EU citizens do not prevent the provisions of Article 18(1) EC from conferring on individuals rights which are enforceable by them and which the national courts must protect. Although such limitations and conditions are based on the idea that the exercise of the right of residence of citizens of the Union can be subordinated to the legitimate interests of the Member States, their application is subject to judicial review and must be in compliance with the limits imposed by Community law and in accordance with the general principles of that law, in particular the principle of proportionality.

Given the particular circumstances of the *Baumbast* case,[124] it was not difficult for the Court to conclude that to refuse a right of residence to such an applicant, on the ground that his sickness insurance did not cover the hypothetical possibility of emergency treatment in the host Member State, would amount to a disproportionate interference with the exercise of his directly conferred Treaty right of residence. The upshot of the Court's judgment, however, is that all EU citizens can

[120] Case C-413/99, *Baumbast* [2002] ECR I-7091.

[121] See, for example, *R. v. Secretary of State for the Home Department, ex p. Vitale* [1996] All E.R. (EC) 461 and 941, at 955 and the contradictory submissions of the Commission in Cases C-378/97, *Wijsenbeek* [1999] ECR I-6207 and C-413/99, *Baumbast*, where it first supported and then opposed the respective applicants' arguments to the effect that Article 18 EC was directly effective.

[122] However, as Shaw and Fries, *supra* n. 113 at 542, point out, reliance on Case 48/75, *Royer* is only valid if it is assumed that the applicant is lawfully resident in the host Member State pursuant to EC law and that was precisely the question being resolved in these early citizenship residence cases.

[123] Case C-413/99, *Baumbast*, para. 80, relying, in particular, on Case 48/75, *Royer*, para. 31.

[124] *Inter alia*, the fact that Mr. Baumbast was in possession of sufficient resources within the meaning of Directive 90/364; the fact that he had worked and lawfully resided in the host Member State for several years; the fact that during that period his family also resided in the host Member State and remained there even after his activities as an employed and self-employed person in that State came to an end; and the fact that neither the applicant nor members of his family had become burdens on the public finances of the host Member State and that they had comprehensive sickness insurance in another Member State of the EU.

rely on the direct effect of Article 18 EC to trump Member States' attempts to limit, condition, or even exclude the right which that provision of the Treaty confers with reference to provisions of secondary legislation adopted with the specific purpose of ensuring that the right of residence enjoyed by EU nationals independent of the exercise of an economic activity would not result in financial outlay in terms of social welfare provision in the host Member States.[125] The limitations and conditions in the 1990 Residence Directives are no longer conditions constitutive of the right of residence of EU citizens but merely act as conditions, even criteria, to be applied proportionately by Member States to the individual circumstances of the non-national resident or resident applicant.[126] The rights conferred by EU citizenship are thus underpinned by elements of social solidarity but, unlike national citizenship, where such solidarity is essentially the expression of the specific bond between the state and its citizens, this solidarity must be extended by the nationals of one Member State to those from another by virtue of their status as residing, or even visiting, EU citizens.

With Article 18 EC creating directly effective rights enforceable at the suit of individuals, reliance on that provision in conjunction with Article 12 EC is likely to reveal that various aspects of national welfare law and policy, traditionally based, as we have seen, on principles of territoriality, solidarity, and membership based principally on nationality, may be found to be inconsistent with EC law.[127] This appears to be the pattern in citizenship questions coming before the Court at present.[128] The Court, in response to preliminary references from national courts, is having to figure out the implications of its case law on Articles 18 and 12 EC as regards entitlement to key welfare state benefits. First and foremost, are the limitations and conditions in the 1990 Residence Directives compatible with the constitutional provisions in Articles 17, 18, and 12 EC? If so, when will the application by the host Member State of the limitations and conditions in those Directives be proportionate? What other general principles of EC law may apply when assessing the lawfulness of residence and/or welfare claims and the host Member State's refusal of such claims? What is the extent of the financial solidarity now owed to EU citizens—for example, must they first establish lawful residence before being able to rely on a combination of Articles 18 and 12 EC or do the latter open the possibility of automatic residence rights and contingent welfare entitlement when the EU citizen first enters the prospective host Member

[125] Indeed, in the case of students, the financial solidarity referred to by the Court in Case C-184/99, *Grzelczyk*, seems to have been specifically ruled out by Member States when negotiating the 1990 Directive. A proposal for a Community fund paid for by the EC and individual Member States to foot the bill for migrating EC students was, at the time, rejected. See O'Leary, *supra* n. 113 at 126–7.

[126] See also Dougan and Spaventa, *supra* n. 113 at 706.

[127] See also in this respect Hervey, *supra* n. 69 at 32 and 34; Shaw and Fries, *supra* n. 113 at 558.

[128] See, in particular, Cases C-456/02, *Trojani* and C-138/02, *Collins*, Opinions of Advocates General Geelhoed and Ruiz-Jarabo Colomer of 19 February 2004 and 10 July 2003, respectively, judgments of the Court of 7 September 2004 and 23 March 2004, respectively.

State? What might the impact of 'cumulative claims upon the long-term planning and financing of welfare benefits' be?[129]

The Court's case law has thus far considerably eroded much of the previously protected sphere of national citizenship and the 'exclusive' social solidarity between a Member State and its own nationals which underpinned that protective sphere, at least in the welfare context. Yet, aware of the legitimate concerns of Member States as regards the organization, financing, and political and even moral philosophy underpinning their welfare systems, the signs are that the Court is replacing old forms of social solidarity with new ones, albeit detached from Member State nationality and even from the individual's economic contribution to society. Member State nationals may, by virtue of their status as EU citizens, have a *prima facie* entitlement to residence and/or equal treatment with respect to a whole range of social benefits but it is legitimate for the Member State providing the benefit in question to demand proof, at least as regards indirectly discriminatory conditions for entitlement to welfare provision, of a real and effective link with the territory in which the social benefit in question is being claimed.[130] Thus, in *D'Hoop*, the Court held that Belgian legislation which made the grant of a tideover allowance for school-leaving job-seekers conditional on their having obtained the required secondary education diploma in Belgium placed at a disadvantage Belgian nationals who had exercised their freedom to move in order to pursue education in another Member State.[131] Since this indirect discrimination was contrary to the guarantee of the same treatment in law in the exercise of the citizens' freedom to move, the Court examined whether it could be justified with reference to objective considerations independent of nationality which were proportionate to the legitimate aim pursued.[132] According to the Court, it was legitimate for the national legislature to wish to ensure that there is a real link between the applicant for the tideover allowance and the geographical employment market concerned. Conditions may be imposed which, when fulfilled, demonstrate a real and effective degree of connection between the applicant for the allowance and that geographical market.[133] However, the condition in the instant case relating to the completion of secondary education in Belgium was too general and exclusive and went beyond what was necessary to attain the objective pursued. Although the Court identified the latter

[129] See also Dougan and Spaventa, *supra* n. 113 at 707.

[130] Advocate General Jacobs, Case C-224/02, *Pusa*, para. 22, has suggested that Article 18 EC is not limited to cases of discrimination and that no unjustified burden may be imposed on any citizen of the EU seeking to exercise their right of free movement and residence.

[131] Case C-224/98, *D'Hoop* [2002] ECR I-6191.

[132] *Ibid.* paras. 34–36.

[133] *Ibid.* paras. 38–39. For similar reasoning on the establishment of an effective link see, in the context of the rights of family members to remain in the host Member State following the death of a migrant worker, Case C-257/00, *Nani Givane* [2003] ECR I-345, para. 46: 'That condition [imposed by Regulation 1251/70 regarding the length of continuous residence of the migrant worker prior to his death] is intended to establish a significant connection between, on the one hand, the Member State, and on the other hand, that worker and his family, and to ensure a certain level of their integration in the society of that State.'

as the need to establish a link between the job-seekers seeking the benefit and the employment market with reference to which she was seeking it, the real objective must surely have been to ensure that the financial solidarity recognized by the Court in *Grzelczyk* was not, from the Member State's point of view, stretched beyond acceptable limits.

Since *D'Hoop* involved an EU citizen returning to her Member State of origin, it would not, in any event, have been difficult to prove the requisite link, particularly since she had been absent for a short period of time and her centre of interests had remained in Belgium. Similarly, as we saw in *Grzelczyk* and *Baumbast*, the stronger the links between the individual seeking residence and/or welfare benefits and the desired host Member State, the more likely the Court will find any interference (in terms of refusal of the benefit requested or indeed residence) with the individual's right of residence to be disproportionate.[134] But these were, in one sense, the easy cases. The EU citizens in question had been resident in the host Member States concerned for some time, either as students or former workers or by virtue of their nationality of origin. What about the rights of the job-seeker on first entering the host Member State—does he or she have a right of residence *qua* EU citizen and a corresponding right not to be discriminated against as regards access to job-seekers' allowances and income support, or does the old logic of limited rights subject to temporal limitations pursuant to *Antonissen* and *Lebon* still apply? The Court must now resolve the relationship between the fundamental status of EU citizen and the pre-existing one of economic migrant. Consider too the position of the non-resident visitor who finds himself temporarily in another Member State. What access to non-contributory social benefits will his status *qua* EU citizen, in conjunction with Article 12 EC, confer?[135] If the recent Opinions of Advocates General and decisions of the Court are anything to go by, the Court is adrift, proud of its achievements as regards the vindication of the rights of EU citizens, but unsure where to go from here. In the *Collins* case, which involved a claim for income support by an EU citizen on his first arriving in the United Kingdom, the Advocate General responded to claims that the Court's citizenship case law amounts to a charter for benefit tourists, by distinguishing the existing case law with reference to the particular circumstances of each case—in other words, with reference to the temporary and limited nature of the burden on Belgian public funds created by a student such as Mr. Grzelczyk and the length and lawfulness of Mrs. Martínez Sala's

[134] In Case C-413/99, *Baumbast* the Court arguably interfered with the normal division of competence between it and the national court when it detailed the various circumstances surrounding the applicant's residence which indicated that a decision to refuse him continued residence would be unreasonable or a disproportionate interference with the right he derives from Article 18 EC.

[135] See Case C-274/96, *Bickel and Franz* [1998] ECR I-7637, for the Court's strict scrutiny of indirectly discriminatory criteria imposed as regards the enjoyment of a non-welfare benefit (the right to use their own language in judicial proceedings) by visitors.

residence in Germany.[136] In his view, Mr. Collins failed to demonstrate the necessary connection with the host Member State or its employment market, as evidenced by prior residence during an appreciable period, such as to justify entitlement to the benefit in question.[137] A condition of residence designed to ascertain or require the existence of a specific degree of connection with the host Member State may therefore be justified in order to avoid benefit tourism. The Court similarly found that it is legitimate for a Member State to grant a job-seeker's allowance only after it has been possible to establish a genuine link, such as a reasonable period of residence, between the person seeking work and the employment market of the host Member State.[138] The applicant in *Trojani* only fared better because of an indication by the national court that, due to a decision by the Belgian authorities (on an unspecified basis), he was actually lawfully resident in Belgium when he applied for minimum subsistence, with the result that the logic of cases like *Martínez Sala* and *Grzelczyk* inexorably applied.[139]

It is trite but perhaps necessary to remind oneself of the importance, in the context, in particular, of preliminary references, for judicial decision-making at the Court to remain rational, coherent, in terms of the fundamental principles of free movement and non-discrimination, and accessible, something which the aforementioned Opinions and judgments arguably are not. If, as has been the case as regards economically active EU citizens, particularly those whose economic activity has been minimal (for example, students, *stagiaires*, or part-time workers with reduced hours), the Court has been hostile to residence conditions or requirements as regards the duration of employment or the extent of income, it will have to articulate very clearly why such conditions are legitimate when it comes to welfare claims by other EU citizens. Vague references to Member States' legitimate concerns or to nebulous concepts centred on real and effective links with the host Member State are insufficient to justify, or even explain, a departure from the principles held dear by the Court when dealing with the rights to free movement and non-discrimination of the economically active. In this respect, the Court's decision in *Collins* disappoints. On the one hand, it has now made explicit the fact that the establishment of EU citizenship does warrant a departure, but a departure in a positive sense, from previous case law, extending to EU citizens the benefits formerly

[136] Opinion of Advocate General Geelhoed in Case C-138/02, *Collins*. The applicant was a dual Irish/American national who had never resided in Ireland or any other Member State and who had only briefly resided and worked in the United Kingdom when he was a student.

[137] *Ibid.* para. 68.

[138] See the judgment of the Court in Case C-138/02, *Collins*, paras. 68–69. Similar views were expressed by the same Advocate General in Case C-456/02, *Trojani*, a case involving an EU citizen lodged with the Salvation Army in the host Member State, providing that organization with a considerable number of hours of service in return for bed and board, but seeking to supplement the very modest allowance received in return with social assistance.

[139] See the judgment of the Court in Case C-456/02 *Trojani*, para. 37.

reserved to the economically active. Thus, the restrictive position towards the social welfare entitlements of job-seekers established in *Lebon*, and called into question in *Baumbast*, is explicitly overruled in *Collins*. In view of the establishment of EU citizenship and, interestingly, 'the interpretation in the case-law of the right to equal treatment enjoyed by citizens of the Union', the Court held that it was no longer possible to exclude from the scope of Article 39(2) EC a benefit of a financial nature intended to facilitate access to employment of the labour market of a Member State. Since the habitual-residence requirement for the enjoyment of the job-seeker's allowance in question was more easily met by UK nationals than by those from other Member States, that requirement had to be justified by objective considerations which were unrelated to nationality and proportionate. It was regarded as legitimate for the UK to grant the allowance only after it was established that a genuine link existed between the person seeking work and the employment market of that state. Moreover, the Court held that the existence of such a link may be determined by establishing that the person concerned has, for a reasonable period, genuinely sought work in the Member State in question, albeit that period must not exceed that which is necessary for the national authorities to be able to satisfy themselves that the person concerned is genuinely seeking work. The Court did not, however, indicate what a reasonable period might be, as it had previously done in *Antonissen*, with reference to the duration of the right of residence of job-seekers, nor did it specify what might constitute sufficient proof of genuine attempts to seek work, such as registration as a person seeking employment or making oneself available to the employment authorities.[140] In addition, although the aim pursued by the UK legislation, albeit vaguely and imprecisely identified by the Court, may have been legitimate, were the means chosen to achieve that aim necessary and requisite? The disputed legislation clearly provided that a 'person from abroad', who was entitled therefore to no job-seeker's allowance, was to be defined as 'a claimant who is not habitually resident in the UK, the Channel Islands, the Isle of Man or the Republic of Ireland'. If an individual habitually resident in the Republic of Ireland is automatically entitled to a job-seeker's allowance, one must ask where is the genuine link with the UK employment market legitimately required of Member State nationals by virtue of *Collins* and whether the case did not throw up questions as to the discriminatory nature of the UK regime or, at the very least, as to the fact that it provided an advantage to, in the vast majority, the nationals of two Member States, such that the legitimacy, necessity, and suitability of the habitual-residence requirement (at least as applied in the UK legislation to date) was

[140] See, in this respect, Case C-171/95, *Tetik* [1997] ECR I-329, para. 41. In Case C-209/03 *Bidar*, Advocate General Geelhoed (Opinion of 11 November 2004) has finally explored what a genuine link with the host Member State might actually look like. Instead of simply referring to a genuine link or a reasonable period of residence, he explained, in the context of a request by an EU citizen for equal access to student loans, that the host Member State must look at the degree of affinity of the claimant with its educational system, the degree of integration in the host society, the circumstances which led him to seek access to third-level education in the host Member State in the first place, and the possibility of his continuing in employment in that State once his education is complete (paras. 60, 62–63).

undermined. Persons who enjoy a right of residence in the UK pursuant to Directive 68/360 were also considered to be regarded as habitually resident under the UK job-seekers legislation. Yet the Court, having found, in answer to the second question in the *Collins* case, that the claimant's right of residence was not solely based on this Directive, seemed to regard this as sufficient to exclude his claim to habitual residence for the purpose of entitlement to the allowance. It is argued, on the one hand, that the logic of the Court's reasoning is flawed and, on the other, given that *Collins* was a seminal case as regards the right of residence of EU citizens and their resulting rights to social benefits, the judgment touches too superficially on the subject of the genuine links which can be required to establish entitlement to such benefits.

What does this case law tell us about the potential impact of the Charter on EU welfare law or, more particularly, on the multi-tiered system conditioning welfare entitlement now emerging in the EU? First and foremost, it is clear that, in the absence of a catalogue of fundamental rights, whether legally binding or not, the EU and, in particular, its Court of Justice, has breathed more life into the provisions on citizenship than perhaps anyone dared to imagine. Whatever the Court decides in the new citizenship cases making their way to Luxembourg, it follows from the original trilogy explained above—*Martínez Sala, Grzelczyk*, and *Baumbast*—that by virtue of lawful residence in a Member State other than their Member State of origin, EU citizens are entitled, *qua* EU citizens, to be treated equally as regards all matters coming within the material scope of application of EC law. In addition, their right to reside in the host Member State does not automatically become unlawful by virtue of the fact that they have recourse to public benefits there. Although Member States may impose conditions regulating entitlement to social benefits, those conditions, if indirectly discriminatory (or even perhaps when they constitute burdens on the right of residence) must be justified and proportionate. The imposition of conditions which allow too much discretion to national authorities, which fail to take into consideration individual circumstances, which do not rest on clear criteria, or which are not subject to judicial redress are likely to be deemed disproportionate.[141] The elevation of the directly conferred right of residence in Article 18 EC to a fundamental right, further reinforced by a fundamental right to equality in the Charter, can only bolster this trend.

There are two, at least, possible outcomes of the development of the rights of EU citizenship in this way. On the one hand, the gradual extension of social solidarity between Member States and their citizens may serve as the basis for the further development of common and institutionalized ties between them.[142] Some commentators may regret the rights-centred bias of citizenship discourse in the EU and, further, the focus specifically on the right of residence to the detriment, in particular, of political rights. This is regrettable given, in particular, the important political element of the concept of citizenship and in view of the democratic deficit

[141] See also Shaw and Fries, *supra* n. 113 at 552.

[142] Faist, *supra* n. 69 at 55.

which the introduction of EU citizenship was also meant to tackle. However, there is no denying the powerful symbolism at play when the Court begins to speak of social solidarity between EU citizens detached from Member State nationality. On the other hand, faced with even the spectre of untold numbers of EU benefit tourists moving across borders proclaiming their equal rights to a host of social benefits, the Member States may seek to tighten the legislative criteria governing such entitlement, with the result that the Court may yet see another *Barber* type protocol, this time as regards the social benefit entitlements of EU citizens. As Dougan points out, when it comes to policy formation, popular perception often counts for more than empirical reality. It is arguably such popular perception which has led to almost all existing Member States abruptly bringing down the shutters on the free movement rights and resulting welfare entitlement of future EU migrants from the acceding Member States.[143] In the alternative, and more radically, Member States may re-examine the scope and level of welfare entitlements which their systems provide.[144] In some Member States, a commitment to high levels of social protection may be so deeply entrenched in the national psyche that any radical departure would be unthinkable. However, it will be interesting to see how those Member States will accommodate and respect their new Community social solidarity obligations and square them with their hitherto dominance in the welfare field. The Charter and perhaps in future the Constitution's impact in this respect is intriguing but, as the aforementioned discussion of the development of EC law in this field suggests, its adoption was far from indispensable as regards the extension of these social solidarity obligations.

B. Fair and Just Working Conditions: Working Time

Article 31 of the Charter (Article II-91 of the Draft Constitution) provides that every worker has a right to working conditions that respect his or her health, safety, and dignity. Paragraph 2 of this Article provides that every worker has the right to limitation of maximum working hours, to daily and weekly rest periods, and to four weeks' paid annual leave. While Article 31 draws inspiration from both the International Covenant on Economic and Social Rights and the revised ESC,[145] the

[143] See, for example, in this respect, the introduction in March 2004 of a two-year habitual-residence test by the Irish government for entitlement to social assistance, child benefit and other welfare payments by non-Irish EU nationals (*Irish Times*, 3 March 2004). This change in Irish government policy followed similar new restrictions in the United Kingdom in the run-up to accession. Irish and UK legislation poses a particular problem because habitual-residence conditions are, as we saw in the above discussion of Case C-138/02, *Collins*, satisfied by the required period of residence in one or other state. This reciprocal arrangement, attributable to a degree of historical, social, and even political solidarity, as well as to the existence of a common travel area between the two countries, raises questions as regards the discrimination of nationals from other Member States.

[144] See also Shaw and Fries, *supra* n. 113 at 558; Dougan, *supra* n. 111 at 107.

[145] Articles 7, 8, and 19 and 2, respectively, of the revised ESC.

main source of inspiration as regards existing EC law was clearly Directive 93/104 on Working Time.[146] The latter provides for minimum health and safety requirements for the organization of working time in the public and private sector (Arts. 1 and 2). Member States are obliged to take the necessary measures to ensure that every worker is entitled to a minimum daily rest period of eleven consecutive hours per twenty-four-hour period (Art. 3); a rest break where the working day is longer than six hours (Art. 4); a minimum uninterrupted rest period of twenty-four hours in each seven-day period (Art. 5, first sentence); and four weeks' paid annual leave (Art. 7). The average working time for each seven-day period, including overtime, must not exceed forty-eight hours (Art. 6). Several derogations and opt-outs allow Member States to apply these provisions, flexibly, at a later date, or even not at all.

The Court has already had occasion to interpret the provisions of the Directive. In the first place, it sanctioned the choice of the former Article 118a EC as the appropriate legal basis for the adoption of the Directive.[147] According to the Court, the scope for Community legislative action regarding the health and safety of workers provided by that provision of the Treaty must be widely interpreted. Community action designed to provide such protection could comprise measures that are of general application and not merely measures specific to certain categories of workers. In addition, in conferring on the Community legislature the power to lay down minimum requirements, the Treaty did not prejudge the extent of the action which the Council may consider necessary in order to carry out the task which Article 118a EEC and now Article 137 EC has assigned to it. The reference to minimum requirements merely confirms that Member States remain free to adopt more stringent measures than those that are the subject matter of Community action.[148]

With the Working Time Directive in force, its legal basis and proportionality sanctioned by the Court, and the organization of working time in sectors of activity originally excluded from its scope gradually being regulated, how, one might wonder, could such an issue be of interest as regards an exploration of the possible impact

[146] The Working Time Directive was adopted on the basis of the former Article 118a EC (Article 137 EC, as amended) which provided that Member States shall pay particular attention to encouraging improvements, especially in the working environment, as regards the health and safety of workers, and shall set as their objective the harmonization of conditions in this area. In order to help achieve these objectives, the Council was to adopt minimum-standards directives which were to avoid imposing administrative, financial, and legal constraints in a way that would hold back the creation and development of small and medium-sized undertakings. For the subsequent development of EC secondary legislation on the organization of working time see also Directive 2000/34/EC of 22 June 2000, amending Council Directive 93/194/EC covering certain aspects of the organization of working time to cover sectors of activities excluded from that Directive, OJ 2000 L 195/41; Directive 2002/15/EC of 11 March 2002, on the organization of the working time of persons performing mobile road transport activities, OJ 2002 L 80/35; Directive 2000/79 of 27 November 2000 concerning the European Agreement on the Organization of Working Time of Mobile Workers in Civil Aviation concluded by AEA, ETF, ECA, ERA, and IACA, OJ 2000 L 302/57; and Directive 2003/88/EC of 4 November 2003, concerning certain aspects of the organization of working time, OJ 2003 L 299/9.

[147] See Case C-84/94, *United Kingdom v. Council*.

[148] *Ibid.* para. 17.

of the Charter's solidarity rights on EU welfare law? Ironically, the answer may be found tucked away in a decision on the right to paid annual leave in which the Court deliberately ignored, or so it seemed, the Advocate General's reliance on the Charter and opted instead for a reference to the Social Charter which, until then, had made but rare appearances in its case law. Article 7 of Directive 93/104 provides that Member States shall take the measures necessary to ensure that 'every worker is entitled to paid annual leave of at least four weeks *in accordance with the conditions for entitlement to, and granting of, such leave laid down by national legislation and/or practice*' (emphasis added). Article 18(1)(b)(ii) of the Directive provides that Member States are to have the option, as regards the application of Article 7, of making use of a transitional period of not more than three years from the date of transposition of the Directive. During the additional period, every worker must receive three weeks' paid annual leave and the latter may not be replaced by an allowance in lieu, except where the employment relationship is terminated. The United Kingdom availed itself of the temporary derogation granted by Article 18(1)(b)(ii) of the Directive. At issue in the *BECTU* case was a provision of the UK regulations implementing the Working Time Directive which provided that workers could accrue rights to paid annual leave only after completion of a qualifying period of thirteen weeks' continuous employment with the same employer. The effect of this implementing provision was to limit the scope of application of the Directive, particularly as regards workers engaged on short-term contracts. Most of the members of BECTU, a trade union in the field of broadcasting, were engaged on short-term contracts, frequently for less than thirteen weeks with the same employer, so that many of them did not satisfy the condition in the UK regulations. They claimed that these provisions of the national implementing regulations were incompatible with the Directive as regards the right to paid annual leave.

The Court concurred—a national rule such as that at issue in *BECTU* violated Article 7 of the Working Time Directive. Having referred to the Social Charter, the Court stated that the right to paid annual leave is a particularly important principle of Community social law from which there can be no derogations and whose implementation by national authorities must be confined within the limits expressly laid down in Directive 93/104.[149] In this regard, the Court's reasoning is significant in two respects. Firstly, it clearly felt unable to qualify the right in Article 7 as a fundamental social right as the Advocate General had done with reference to Article 31(2) of the Charter. Nevertheless, its characterization of the right contained in that provision of the Directive was unequivocal—it constituted a social right directly conferred by Directive 93/104 on every worker.[150] According to the Court,

[149] Case C-173/99, *BECTU*, para. 43.

[150] The importance of Case C-173/99, *BECTU* for the restriction in EC law of horizontal and vertical direct effect to provisions of the Treaty has, arguably, yet to be realized. The Court's language is uncompromising and no distinction is drawn between the rights directly conferred by Article 7 of the Directive on private and public sector employees. Such distinctions may have been unnecessary in *BECTU* (because of the judicial review nature of the action at national level which led to the preliminary reference)

Member State legislation which imposes a precondition for *entitlement* to paid annual leave which has the effect of preventing certain workers from any such entitlement negates an individual right expressly granted by Directive 93/104 and is contrary to its objective.[151] Secondly, the reference in Articles 7 and 18(1)(b)(ii) to the fact that every Member State should ensure that every worker is entitled to the right 'in accordance with the conditions for entitlement to, and granting of, such leave laid down by national legislation and/or practice' must simply be construed as referring only to the conditions for the exercise of the right in question and do not indicate the possibility of conditioning the *existence* of that right, which derives directly from Directive 93/104.[152]

As regards the potential impact of the Charter on EU welfare law, admittedly writ large, this case is important in three distinct ways. In the first place, the Advocate General's Opinion, and indeed the decision of the Court, confirm that the use of the Charter can aid in the interpretation of existing EC and national implementing legislation. A right conferred by a provision of secondary legislation is thus transformed into a directly effective social right, entitlement to which cannot be made the subject of additional conditions. Second, the Court's language and reasoning in the social field appear to be becoming increasingly uniform. Just as in *Baumbast*, where the 1990 Residence Directives were said not to negate the *existence* of a right of residence but simply conditioned the *exercise* of such a right (and even then not to such an extent as to deprive the right of its substance), so too the margin of appreciation for Member States when working out the detailed arrangements for the enjoyment of rights conferred by minimum-standards directives is to be kept within strict limits. They can prescribe the specific circumstances in which workers may exercise their rights but they are not entitled to make the existence of those rights subject to any preconditions. The transposition by the Court of similar reasoning from one area of social law to another is not new or indeed surprising, given the Court's readiness to accept teleological forms of interpretation and its general reliance, when aiming for broad legislative interpretations, on the spirit and purpose of the legislation it is entrusted to interpret. As Steiner remarked with reference to the broad interpretation of the material scope of Regulations 1612/68 and 1408/71: 'the Court remedies the deficiencies of each Regulation by arguing by analogy from one to the other, reinforcing its case by reference to the worker's right

and it may have proved unnecessary in Cases C-303/98, *SIMAP* [2000] ECR I-7963 and C-151/02, *Jaeger*, judgment of 9 September 2003, not yet published in the ECR (because of the involvement of public sector healthcare employers in both cases). Clearly it was at the heart of the Court's decision in Case C-397/01, *Pfeiffer*, judgment of the Court of 5 October 2004, not yet published in the ECR. In that judgment the Court regarded the forty-eight-hour upper limit on average weekly working time as 'a rule of Community social law of particular importance from which every worker must benefit'. However, it went on to recall that the Working Time Directive could not of itself apply in proceedings exclusively between private parties (para. 109).

151 Case C-173/99, *BECTU*, para. 48.

152 *Ibid.* para. 53.

[. . .] and building imperceptibly on its own case-law'.[153] Such expansive reasoning bodes well for the impact of the Charter and, in its place, the Draft Constitution, if only as an aid for the interpretation of secondary and implementing legislation. Finally, the Charter, particularly the solidarity provisions, were carefully and restrictively drafted, with references to the enjoyment of rights by workers or EU citizens 'in accordance with national laws and practices' scattered throughout the text. *BECTU* suggests that, in appropriate circumstances, the Court may come up with some surprises when it comes to the interpretation of such provisos and the nature of the rights conferred by the Charter provisions that contain them. If the Court continues to regard the provisions of EC law regulating working time as Community social rights of particular importance, their elevation in the Charter and Draft Constitution may mean that attempts to curtail the Court's jurisdiction with reference to Article II-112(5) of the Draft Constitution will prove insufficient to curtail its fervour.

To those who doubt the impact of rights relating to the organization of working time on national welfare law, look no further than the Spanish and German cases on on-call doctors and the Court's definition of working time therein. In both cases, the Working Time Directive had been transposed into national law on the basis that on-call periods for such workers must, in accordance with national laws and practices, be regarded as rest periods.[154] However, according to the Court, a period of duty spent by a doctor on call, where presence in the hospital is required, must be regarded as constituting in its entirety working time, and, where appropriate, overtime, for the purposes of the Directive.[155] This apparently modest finding has turned the organization of working time in some Member States' public hospitals on its head. According to submissions by the German government in the *Jaeger* case, the decision of the Court will mean a 24% increase in staffing requirements in public hospitals, involving between 15,000 and 27,000 additional doctors at an estimated cost of €1.75 billion.[156] Faced with such costs it is expected, and indeed has already been seen, that Member States will have greater recourse to some of the

[153] Steiner, *supra* n. 67 at 39.

[154] Article 2 of Directive 93/104 provides that, for the purposes of the Directive, working time shall mean any period during which the worker is working, at the employer's disposal and carrying out his activities or duties, in accordance with national laws and/or practices. Rest periods shall mean any period which is not working time. The Court regards the two periods as mutually exclusive (see Cases C-303/98, *SIMAP* and C-151/02, *Jaeger*, paras. 47 and 48, respectively).

[155] Once again, the fact that the definition of the concept of working time refers to national law does not mean that the Member States may unilaterally determine the scope of that concept. Despite the proviso in Article 2 of the Directive, Member States may not make subject to any condition the right of employees to have working periods and corresponding rest periods duly taken into account, since that right stems directly from the provisions of the Directive (see, for example, Case C-151/02, *Jaeger*, paras. 58 and 59).

[156] Case C-151/02, *Jaeger*, Opinion of Advocate General Ruiz-Jarabo Colomer, para. 44. For details of preliminary estimates of the cost from other Member States, see the *Commission Communication concerning the Re-examination of Directive 93/104*, (COM [2003] 843 final), at 20.

derogations provided by the Directive, particularly the possibility of opt-outs, pursuant to Article 18(b)(i) of the Directive, from the application of Article 6 on the maximum number of weekly working hours if the individual employee consents.[157] Alternatively, doctors may increasingly be on call but may no longer be required to be present on hospital premises, with the inevitable consequences that that may have for the quality of emergency healthcare.[158] Should the Court have paid greater heed to the need to ensure a high level of human health protection, itself a solidarity 'principle' enumerated in the Charter, or the need to avoid upsetting the financial equilibrium of national healthcare systems?[159] Time alone will tell whether the Court's already robust approach regarding the interpretation of the scope and effect of the Working Time Directive will be further strengthened with reference to Article 31(2) of the Charter, whether or not the Draft Constitution is ratified. What is perhaps more certain is that Member States are unlikely to forget unexpected jurisprudential surprises like *Jaeger*. The Court's judgment, although unimpeachable from the perspective of legislative interpretation and the purpose and spirit of the particular Directive in question, may actually influence the negotiation of minimum-standards social legislation in future, with some Member States very conscious of the need to include extremely flexible derogating provisions to allow them to absorb, or even avoid, the effect of future robust judgments from Luxembourg.[160]

Indeed, the Commission's current proposal for a new directive on working time suggests that Member States' and employers' fears about the cost of those robust judgments are winning the day.[161] The individual opt-out from the forty-eight-hour average weekly working time limit has been supplemented by the possibility of an opt-out agreed by the social partners. The reference period for the calculation of the maximum weekly working time can be extended to one year, thus allowing businesses to deal with more or less regular fluctuations in demand. In addition, it is proposed that the inactive part of on-call time will not be considered working time within the meaning of the Directive, unless national legislation, collective

[157] *Ibid.* at 15 and 20. In both Cases C-303/98, *SIMAP*, and C-151/02, *Jaeger*, the Court did not regard as working time on-call periods where there was no obligation to remain on the employer's premises. Note that Article 18(b)(i) of Directive 93/104 provides that the Council shall, on the basis of a Commission proposal, re-examine this opt-out provision.

[158] One is forcefully reminded of the warning by Hervey, *supra* n. 69 at 41: 'the application of Community internal market and competition law, through individual litigation, may have not insignificant effects on the organisation, financing, delivery and even content of social welfare in the Member States of the EU'.

[159] See Articles 152(1) EC and Article 35 of the Charter (Article II-95 of the Draft Constitution); or the imperative requirements recognized in its case law on the free provision of medical services (see, for example, Case C-158/96, *Kohll*, para. 41).

[160] There is evidence that this is already happening, with Germany backing the UK's attempts to ensure that the Article 18(b)(i) opt-out from the forty-eight-hour working rule remains in the Directive, as well as its opposition to the Commission proposal for a directive on temporary workers, see 'Germany backs Britain's attempts to ensure that provision for the Article 18(b)(i) opt-out from the 48-hours working week', *Financial Times*, 29 March 2004.

[161] COM (2004) 607 final.

agreements, or agreements between the social partners decide otherwise. Not only are the controversial aspects of the Court's jurisprudence in danger of being overruled, despite the objections of employees' representatives, but the very fundamental nature of the social rights of which the Court spoke in its Working Time jurisprudence are being called into question.

C. Family and Professional Life

Despite the heterogeneity and ambiguity underpinning the solidarity rights in the Charter, closer examination reveals further scope for reliance on these provisions, at the very least to reinforce or clarify aspects of the *acquis communautaire* or *judiciaire*.

Article 33(1) of the Charter (Article II-93(1) of the Draft Constitution) provides that the family shall enjoy legal, economic, and social protection. In addition, to reconcile family and professional life, the Charter provides in Article 33(2) (Article II-93(2) of the Draft Constitution) that *everyone* shall have the right to protection from dismissal for a reason connected with maternity and the right to paid maternity leave and to parental leave following the birth or adoption of a child. Clearly the attribution of rights to 'everyone' is novel when compared to the traditional approach of the Court and indeed Directive 92/85, which confine the enjoyment of rights during pregnancy and maternity to mothers.[162] As regards the 'right to paid maternity leave', the Directive's limited provision for merely an adequate payment or allowance during maternity leave makes it extremely unlikely that the Court would, with reference to the Charter, reopen the debate on the question of entitlement to full pay during that period.[163] In addition, it is noticeable that whereas Article 33(2) refers to the right to paid maternity leave, Article 34(1) of the Charter (Article II-94(1) of the Draft Constitution) refers simply to an arguably weaker entitlement to social security benefits in cases such as maternity, in accordance, moreover, with the rules laid down by Union law and national laws and practices.

However, the insertion into the Charter of a fundamental right to paid maternity leave may provoke questions relating to the adequacy of maternity allowances at

[162] See Case 184/83, *Hofmann v. Barmer Ersatzkasse* [1984] ECR 3047, para. 26: 'A measure such as maternity leave granted to a woman on expiry of the statutory protective period falls within the scope of Article 2(3) of Directive 76/207, inasmuch as it seeks to protect a woman in connection with the effects of pregnancy and motherhood. That being so, such leave may legitimately be reserved to the mother to the exclusion of any other person, in view of the fact that it is only the mother who may find herself subject to undesirable pressures to return to work prematurely'; and Article 2 of Directive 92/85 similarly restricts enjoyment of the rights it provides to future mothers, those on maternity leave or those breastfeeding. See, however, Lenaerts and De Smijter, *supra* n. 23 at 83, who argue that, even if a statement of rights in the Charter sometimes seems broader than the original text, those rights that correspond with the rights expressly mentioned in the EC Treaty or TEU (or, presumably, the secondary legislation adopted thereunder) do not enjoy broader protection than the original rights.

[163] See Cases C-342/93, *Gillespie* [1996] ECR I-475 and C-147/02, *Alabaster*, judgment of the Court of 30 March 2004, not yet published to the ECR.

national level. Similarly, questions may be raised about the scope and content of the now fundamental right to parental leave, with regard to which reference to pay is noticeably absent. Clearly, fundamental rights may be subject to restrictions corresponding to legitimate Member State aims or objectives, provided of course that those restrictions do not constitute a disproportionate or unreasonable interference undermining the very substance of the rights in question. Could it be argued that the exclusion of any provision for paid parental leave in Directive 94/45 undermines the very substance of the right to parental leave which the Charter now deems fundamental?[164] If one were to extend the logic of the Court's case law on the free movement of students and access to vocational training,[165] the answer to this question, leaving aside the issue of cost, would surely be in the affirmative. Like Article 33 of the Charter, the objective of Directive 96/34 was to reconcile work and family life and to promote equal opportunities and equal treatment between men and women. As regards the need to reconcile family and professional life, the Court has emphasized that 'Community policy in this area is to encourage and, if possible, adapt working conditions to family responsibilities. Protection of women within family life and in the course of their professional activities is, in the same way as for men, a principle which is widely regarded in the legal systems of the Member States as being the natural corollary of the equality between men and women, and which is recognised by Community law.'[166] But what substance does an individual non-transferable statutory right to parental leave have if individual workers cannot afford to avail themselves of it or if, by availing themselves of their right to such leave, they risk losing out on the enjoyment of employment rights that they would otherwise have been entitled to? It would certainly seem incompatible with the *effet utile* of the fundamental right to parental leave now enumerated in the Charter and the Draft Constitution for Member States to be left freely to determine the status of the employment contract or relationship during the period of parental leave. In the absence of Community strictures as

[164] Directive 96/34/EC of 3 June 1996 on the framework agreement on parental leave concluded by UNICE, CEEP, and the ETUC (OJ 1996 L 145/4) makes no provision for pay during the course of parental leave. See, in addition, Case C-333/97, *Lewen* [1999] ECR I-7243, para. 32, where the Court favoured a narrow interpretation of one of the clauses of the Parental Leave Directive with the result that a Christmas bonus was not considered as constituting a right acquired or in the process of being acquired by the worker on the date on which parental leave started since it was paid voluntarily after the start of that leave. See, however, Article II-112(1) of the Draft Constitution, which provides that any limitation of the exercise of the rights and freedoms recognized in the Charter must respect the essence of these rights and freedoms.

[165] In Cases 293/83, *Gravier* and C-357/89, *Raulin*, the Court first held that access to vocational training comes within the scope of EC law, with the result that EU nationals cannot be discriminated against as regards tuition fees and then concluded that this right of non-discriminatory access *presupposed* a right of residence for the duration of the vocational training course. In this respect the Court in *Raulin*, para. 32, observed that: 'a student admitted to a course of vocational training might be unable to attend the course if he did not have a right of residence in the Member State where the course takes place'.

[166] Case C-243/95, *Hill and Stapleton* [1998] ECR I-3739, para. 42.

regards that status, a period of parental leave may, for example, be excluded for the purposes of calculating insolvency pay because the working relationship, used as the basis for such a calculation, is deemed to be suspended for the duration of parental leave.[167]

At the present stage of development of EC law, the Court's jurisprudence on the reconciliation of family responsibilities and professional life is riddled with confusion and contradiction. In a series of cases on childcare and the effect which childcare responsibilities may have on the access of mainly female workers to the employment market, the Court revealed itself to be uncertain about the purpose and scope of application of EC sex equality legislation. Thus, in one case it considered that, despite the fact that the failure to deduct childminding expenses when calculating income support for low income families would affect, to a far greater extent, the ability of mothers to take up vocational training courses or part-time employment, this did not bring the applicant's claim of indirect sex discrimination within the scope of application of the Equal Treatment Directive.[168] The Court concentrated on the intended purpose of the national scheme, namely the provision of income support for persons with insufficient means to meet their needs, and ignored the effects of its application in terms of access to employment. In contrast, in a case involving the deduction of childminding expenses from overall income with a view to calculating claimants' entitlements to family credit, the Court held that compliance with the fundamental principle of equal treatment under Directive 76/207 presupposed that such a benefit constitutes a working condition within the meaning of that Directive. Failure to deduct such costs from the applicant's income was regarded as indirectly discriminatory against single parents, the majority of whom are women.[169] It is difficult to discern the differences between the two benefits meriting such a diverse judicial approach and outcome.

Similarly, although the concept of indirect discrimination has proved helpful in tackling some of the structural obstacles that stand in the way of women at work or those who seek access to employment, the Court's case law, several decades on, still demonstrates a considerable degree of uncertainty in the application of this concept. To determine whether detrimental or disadvantageous treatment can amount to unlawful indirect sex discrimination, it is necessary, first, to determine whether the group that claims the disadvantage is in a position similar or comparable to that of a second group which acts as a comparator. Second, the source of the detrimental treatment, whether an employer or legislature, must prove that any difference in treatment is objectively justified with reference to factors unrelated to discrimination on grounds of sex. However, the Court has never clearly defined the criteria on which groups are to be selected for the purposes of comparison. It has been

[167] Case C-160/01, *Mau* [2003] ECR I-4791. See also the disappointing interpretation of the Parental Leave Directive in Case C-333/97, *Lewen*.

[168] Joined Cases C-63/91 and C-64/91, *Jackson* and *Cresswell* [1992] ECR I-4736; and the Equal Treatment Directive (Directive 76/207, OJ 1976 L 39/40).

[169] Case C-116/94, *Meyers* [1995] ECR I-2131.

suggested that the appropriate comparison is between the allegedly discriminatory situation or measure and another situation or measure having a similar *purpose* and arising from a similar *cause*.[170] Yet, a female employee who resigned from her job because of a lack of childcare facilities, but who qualified for only half of the termination payment paid to other employees who resigned for 'important' reasons did not succeed in her indirect sex discrimination claim (based on the fact that the majority of employees forced to resign for the former reason are female). The Court simply found that the situation in which workers who resign in order to take care of their children find themselves is, in substance and origin, not similar to that of employees who resign for important reasons.[171] However, it is arguable that both groups of employees were placed in circumstances such that it was not only unreasonable to require them to continue work but it was impossible for them to do so. The cause of the termination of their employment was thus similar. In addition, the purpose of the termination payment—to compensate them given the aforementioned impossibility to continue working—was also the same. How then could the Court conclude that it was in effect legitimate for the legislature not to regard lack of childcare facilities as comparable to an important reason for an employee involuntarily terminating his contract of employment?

Will the Charter hammer home the message in Luxembourg that it is now a fundamental principle of EC law and policy that reconciliation of family and professional responsibilities is essential if the equal opportunities which the Treaty professes a commitment to respect and promote are to be ensured? This is perhaps the area where the present writer is most pessimistic, at least in the medium term, about the impact of the Charter and, in future, the Draft Constitution, on the interpretation of existing EC law and the formulation of future legislation. As regards the former, indirect sex discrimination cases of the *Gruber* type mentioned above normally involve the identification of a comparator and the existence of a *prima facie* case of discrimination and then treatment of the issue of objective justification. *Gruber* was unusual because the Court never made it to the latter stage. As numerous commentators have pointed out with reference to indirect sex discrimination, the latter is only as effective as the Court which polices it is sympathetic or attuned to the problems and structural obstacles that it seeks to tackle.[172] A Court that

170 See the Opinion of Advocate General Léger in Case C-249/97, *Gruber* [1999] ECR I-5295, para. 40 (emphasis added).

171 *Ibid.* para. 33. According to the Court, the common characteristic of the important reasons listed in the national legislation for the termination of the contract was that they were related to working conditions in the undertaking or to the conduct of the employer such that continued work was impossible. The Court paid no attention to another arguably discriminatory aspect of the national legislation to the effect that parents who resigned for childcare reasons were, in any event, only entitled to the reduced termination payment after five years' continuous employment, as compared to a three-year requirement for those who resigned for important reasons. See also Case C-220/02, *Österreichischer Gewerkschaftsbund*, judgment of the Court of 8 June 2004, not yet published in the ECR.

172 See, *inter alia*, Hepple, 'Equality and Discrimination', in P. Davies *et al.* (eds.), *EC Labour Law: Principles and Perspectives. Liber Amicorum Lord Wedderburn* (1996) 237 at 250.

displays more sympathy for the alleged social or employment policy concerns of the legislature (without properly examining their proportionality and/or reasonableness), or for the business needs of employers, or worse still, that fails to register the disadvantageous treatment complained of,[173] will be unlikely to be swayed by the magisterial tone of a Charter or indeed a Constitution expounding improvement of work/life balances. There has always been concern that the economic cost of redressing unequal treatment led to undue consideration being given to the economic and business concerns of the legislature and employers. It is only if the Court rebalances such economic considerations and the reconfirmed and extended fundamental right to equality, in all its guises, in the Charter and secondary legislation, that the former will be said to have had a real impact. As regards the influence of a provision like Article 33 of the Charter on the formulation of legislative policy, in this field, as in that of health and safety discussed above, there remains the possibility that Member States' experience of robust and potentially costly judicial decisions will put them on their guard when it comes to the formulation and negotiation of future social and equality legislation.

CONCLUSIONS

With the Charter described as an 'elegantly conceived, beautifully drafted, and . . . masterly combination of pastiche, compromise and studied ambiguity',[174] it is unsurprising that any attempt to assess its impact may prove elusive. When the purported impact is to be assessed with reference to the equally slippery notion of EU welfare law, the task is well-nigh impossible. In addition, divining the direction and future scope of EC legislative and judicial developments is a risky business. As the Court, in particular, has demonstrated, not least with reference to the rights of EU citizens, legislative provisions and Treaty articles may easily acquire a far-reaching constitutional significance beyond the original intentions and plans of the governments who designed them.

The choice made in this essay has been to place the negotiation and adoption of the Charter in its political and legal context, chart the rough seas of legal status and justiciability which the Charter and the Draft Constitution, if ratified, have still to navigate, and examine in concrete detail the potential impact of some citizenship and solidarity rights. The Charter will, no doubt, find its place amongst the sources of law relied upon by the Court when protecting fundamental rights, while at the same time tightening the framework within which the Court presently operates. Similarly, it will, over time, influence and sometimes expand the interpretation of primary and secondary EC law. Just as the Court has gone beyond the wording of

[173] See, in this respect, Cases C-249/97, *Gruber*; C-256/01, *Allonby*, judgment of the Court of 13 January 2004, not yet published in the ECR; and C-218/98, *Abdoulaye* [1999] ECR I-5723.

[174] See McCrudden, *supra* n. 22 at 7.

directives and regulations and relied on their purpose and nature when seeking to expand their scope of application, so too the Charter or the future Constitution may be used in a similar vein in future. In the social field, in particular, this may contribute to a rebalancing of the relative importance of economic and social considerations when interpreting and applying the law. In addition, it may have a 'standstill' effect in the social field, preventing any regression from the level of social rights protection already achieved. Beyond these general statements as to its impact, what more can be said at this stage, with the future of the Draft Constitution and the incorporated Charter hanging in the balance? An examination of the existing state of EC law as regards the concrete rights examined in Section 6 reveals that the proclamation of the Charter was to some extent unnecessary. EU citizens do enjoy, as Weiler suggests, a surfeit of rights and reasonable means for their vindication. Even in the absence of the constitutionalization of the social and solidarity rights in the Charter and Draft Constitution, the Court had gone some considerable distance already in ensuring that the rights and guarantees provided in the Treaty and secondary legislation were not without bite.

The introduction to this essay pointed out that history alone will be able to judge the success of the recent spate of conventions and their legal produce. To sound a pessimistic but at the same time challenging note in conclusion, it is suggested that no amount of conventions and enumerated catalogues of rights will compensate in future for the lack of the modern political and judicial equivalents of the far-sighted Monnets, Schumans, Adenauers, Lecourts, Pescatores, and Delors of the past.

4

Social Security Regulation in the EU: The De-Territorialization of Welfare?

DORTE SINDBJERG MARTINSEN

Although the European Union (EU) has not formally been assigned welfare policy competence, it has for decades regulated social benefits between the Member States. The social rights and obligations of the European migrant have for long been safeguarded by the EU, and the mutual responsibility for welfare undertaken by the Member States of the Union constitutes an extraordinary piece of 'Social Europe'.

This chapter examines the integration of national social security schemes that has taken place in the European Union through Community Regulation 1408/71,[1] which has recently been substantially reformed with the adoption of Regulation 883/2004.[2] The chapter seeks to demonstrate that a dimension of European social security has for long been a material fact, patched up by judicial activism and political compromises. A more general description will be drawn of how intra-European welfare has been extended to *all citizens* of the Union in parallel with the extension of the free movement principle to *persons*. The focus of the chapter is, however, on the question of *exportable welfare* between Member States; it describes how the tension between the Community principle of exportability and national principles of territoriality has over time intensified, been reconciled, and reappeared.

The chapter falls into five main parts. *First*, the European dimension of welfare as established through social security coordination will be introduced. *Second*, historical recourse will be taken to describe the europeanization process of migration control and access to national welfare. The *third* part asks to whom intra-European social security applies. The *fourth* part analyses in greater detail the extent to which welfare has been de-territorialized in the EU. *Finally*, the chapter provides some concluding remarks on the evolution of the European dimension of social security, and the relation between law and politics in the course of welfare integration.

[1] Regulation (EEC) No. 1408/71 of the Council of 14 June 1971 on the application of social security schemes to employed persons, to self-employed persons, and to members of their families moving within the Community.

[2] Regulation (EC) 883/2004 of the European Parliament and of the Council of 29 April 2004 on the coordination of social security systems. OJ L 166, 30.04.2004, p. 0001–0123.

1. THE EUROPEAN DIMENSION OF WELFARE

Regulation 1408/71 was adopted as a social complement to the free movement of workers and has developed in parallel with the gradually extended right of free movement. Both the right to free movement for persons within Europe and the right to transnational welfare are from an empirical as well as a theoretical point of view remarkable examples of integration, where rights are gradually decoupled from a person's status as a worker, and where complexes of rules intervene fundamentally with the national competence to decide on the access to and the reach of welfare.

The general purpose of the Regulation is to promote intra-European migration by ensuring that someone who moves and settles in another Member State will not lose their social security entitlements or jeopardize them. The Regulation prescribes that the European migrant has social security rights *equal* to the settling state's own nationals, as well as having a right to *export* acquired welfare entitlements, should one live in a different Member State than the one of social affiliation. The implementation of these Community prescriptions means that the Regulation prohibits national legislation that discriminates against a migrant from another Member State, as well as partly prohibiting the territorialization of national benefits through residence clauses.

The Regulation is based on Article 42 of the Treaty (ex. Art. 51), which obliges the Council to adopt the necessary measures regarding social security to provide freedom of movement for *workers*. Since 1981, when the Regulation was extended to cover self-employed persons, amendments have also been adopted through the use of Article 308 of the Treaty (ex. Art. 235), this constituting the legal basis in conjunction with Article 42.[3] The continuous use, since 1981, of Article 308 has been fundamental to the development of Regulation 1408/71 and has allowed for this social instrument to be extended beyond a literal interpretation of its Treaty basis. The flexibility provided by Article 308 has, however, been rather controversial, raising questions about the scope and limits of Community competencies.

Regulation 883/2004, formerly 1408/71, is organized around a set of main principles, of which two are to be emphasized here.[4] The *principle of equal treatment* applies without exception and sets aside provisions in national legislation which reserve certain benefits for own nationals or long-term residents. The *principle of exportability* stipulates that acquired rights are exportable within the geographical scope of the Regulation. Exportability challenges the traditional territorial boundedness of social security as laid down in national law and policy. However, unlike the principle

[3] D. Pieters, 'Towards a Radical Simplification of the Social Security Co-ordination', in P. Schoukens (ed.), *Prospects of Social Security Co-ordination* (1997) at 182–3.

[4] Other ruling principles are, *inter alia, the principle of aggregation*, meaning that social security rights acquired in one state are added to rights earned by working or residing in another state, and *the principle of lex loci laboris*, meaning that the applicable legislation is, in general, that of the state where the work is carried out.

of equal treatment, exportability is not an absolute principle. Benefits-in-kind can still be demarcated within the national territory without contradicting Community law.[5] The case law of the European Court of Justice (ECJ), clarifying the scope of exportability, has, however, been criticized for eroding the principle of territoriality on a general basis—which will be examined in more detail below.[6] The subsequent analysis suggests that the Community mobilization of social services and benefits has conflicted with the traditional geographical reach of welfare, the latter being nation–state bound.

The recent amendment of the Regulation has updated and extended its material scope,[7] so that today it covers a very extensive range of material benefits, applying to all national *social security* legislation on: (a) sickness benefits; (b) maternity and equivalent paternity benefits; (c) invalidity benefits; (d) old-age benefits; (e) survivors' benefits; (f) benefits in respect of accidents at work and occupational diseases; (g) death grants; (h) unemployment benefits; (i) pre-retirement benefits; and (j) family benefits. At the same time, *social assistance* is explicitly placed outside the Regulation.[8] Much of the political, legal, and administrative dispute on the material scope of the Regulation has concerned the definition of the boundaries between *social security* on the one hand and *social assistance* on the other, and thus the definition of the scope and limits of intra-European welfare.

A. Social Security versus Social Assistance

The boundary set between social security and social assistance dictates the benefits to which the principles of equal treatment and exportability apply.

When Regulation 1408/71 was adopted, its substantive scope seemed reasonably clear. On the one hand social security benefits were included, exhaustively listed in the Regulation. The prime characteristics of national *social security* schemes again seemed fairly obvious. The general characteristic of social security was, and still is, that security from social risks is offered by public schemes through which specific categories of persons are, compulsory or voluntarily, insured against defined social risks. The schemes are generally financed by collectively paid contributions. The beneficiary of social security schemes is entitled to benefits according to a legally defined position, which mirror the individual contributions paid. The level of benefits is likewise legally specified and is independent of income.[9]

[5] G. Haverkate and S. Huster, *Europäisches Sozialrecht* (1999) at 123.

[6] P. Altmaier, 'Europäisches koordinerende Sozialrecht—Ende des Territorialitätsprinzip?' in E. Eichenhofer and M. Zuleeg (eds.), *Die Rechtsprechung des Europäischen Gerichtshofs zum Arbeits- und Sozialrecht im Streit* (1995) 71–93 at 71.

[7] Before the adoption of Regulation 883/2004, 1408/71 covered: (a) illness and maternity; (b) invalidity benefits; (c) old-age pensions; (d) survivors' benefits; (e) occupation-related accidents and disease; (f) death grants; (g) unemployment benefits; (h) family benefits.

[8] As laid down by Art. 3(5) of Regulation 883/2004.

[9] A. P. Van der Mei, 'Regulation 1408/71 and Coordination of special Non-Contributory Benefit Schemes', 27 *European Law Journal* (2002) 551–6.

On the other hand, it excluded *social assistance* benefits as laid down in Article 4(4). Social assistance was, and is, different in nature, consisting in what the state offers its citizens or long-term residents who are not able to provide for themselves, and have no alternative financial means. Social assistance is usually granted on a discretionary basis, within which a means test is likely to play a part. In contrast to social security, social assistance schemes are non-contributory, financed by tax revenues. However, previous tax payment is not a criterion for entitlement.[10] Social assistance policies have traditionally been based on the principle of territoriality.

The distinction between the two types of benefit has become increasingly blurred over the years. As national welfare systems have developed, they have increasingly combined aspects of the two types of benefit. The new mixed nature of some benefits means that, today, social security may be granted on the basis of a means test, while social assistance may increasingly be a legally enforceable right.[11] The right of the European migrant to be eligible for or to export those benefits which may be defined as, or resemble, *social assistance* has been one of the most controversial issues in the history of the coordination system and continues to be so to date, as will be demonstrated below.

2. EUROPEANIZING MIGRATION CONTROL AND ACCESS TO NATIONAL WELFARE

The Community objective of free movement of workers as well as the coordination of their social security rights were introduced from a strictly economic point of view. Both the right to settle in another Member State and also the right to access the social security rights of the host state were linked to the person's status as a worker. Against this historical background, the recent extension of the right to free movement and cross-border welfare to *persons*, irrespective of their economic activity, stands out even more starkly as an example of integration.

Long before the existence of the European Coal and Steel Community, the conditions of European labour migration and the social entitlements of migrants were negotiated between European states.[12] Bilateral agreements between individual countries became the early regulatory modus, where rights and obligations in general favoured the labour-importing country. In this context of 'bilaterally organized interdependence',[13] the Treaty of Paris became the potential frame in which to

[10] A. P. Van der Mei, 'Regulation 1408/71 and Coordination of special Non-Contributory Benefit Schemes', 27 *European Law Journal* (2002) 551–6.

[11] Pieters, *supra* n. 3 at 207.

[12] See J. Holloway, *Social Policy Harmonization in the European Community* (1981); F. Pennings, *Introduction to Social Security Law* (1998); E. Eichenhofer, *Sozialrecht der Europäischen Union* (2001).

[13] See F. Romero, 'Migration as an Issue in European Interdependence and Integration: The Case of Italy', in A. Milward *et al.* (eds.), *The Frontier of National Sovereignty: History and Theory 1945–1992* (1993) 35–59, for his discussion of the era of 'bilaterally organised interdependence'.

negotiate new multilateral provisions. Article 69 of the Paris Treaty became the first, quite reluctant, step taken at Community level to allow for worker mobility. The right, however, was only conferred on workers of 'proven qualifications' and thus from early on reflected the economic purpose of free movement. It was agreed that the limited circulation of workers of 'proven qualifications' should be complemented by a Community provision on their social security situation.[14] Social protection as attached to labour mobility was initiated by Article 69(4) of the Paris Treaty.

Article 48 of the Treaty of Rome went one step further. The founders of the European Economic Community had agreed to grant free movement for workers, and obliged one another to remove those aspects of national legislation that discriminated on the basis of nationality within a twelve-year transition period. With Regulation 1612/68 and Directive 68/360,[15] actual free movement for workers was institutionalized in 1968.[16] In the early 1970s, workers and their families were granted the right to remain in a host state[17] and free movement was equally extended to the self-employed person and his/her family members. Article 51 of the Treaty of Rome supplemented Article 48 and laid down the social security measures to be taken in order to achieve labour mobility. On behalf of the Treaty provision on the coordination of social security, Regulation 1408/71's predecessor, Regulation 3/58, was adopted in the same year that the Treaty of Rome entered into force. Regulation 3/58 became the first major piece of legislation in the European Community.[18] This substantiates the centrality of social security coordination and affirms that although welfare policies were—and are—formally regarded as national competencies, their impediment to the free movement of labour as a production factor was addressed from the very start and in a very intensive way. When Regulation 1408/71 was adopted, it inherited the provisions of its predecessor, but improved some of the regulatory gaps and unclear definitions, as had been pointed out in the early litigation in the ECJ.

The year 1990 witnessed the next landmark on the path to free movement of persons within the Community. With the Council's adoption of the three residence directives in June 1990,[19] the right to reside culminated in the extension of free movement to all Member State citizens, granting the right of free movement to

[14] Haverkate and Huster, *supra* n. 5 at 88.

[15] Council Regulation (EEC) No. 1612/68 of 15 October 1968 on freedom of movement of workers within the Community (OJ L 257, 19.10.1968, p. 2); Council Directive 68/360/EEC of 15 October 1968 on the abolition of restrictions on movement and residence within the Community for workers of Member States and their families.

[16] J.-Y. Carlier and M. Verwilghen, 'Foreword', in J.-Y. Carlier and M. Verwilghen (eds.), *Thirty Years of Free Movement of Workers in Europe* (2000) at 7–9.

[17] Regulation (EEC) No. 1251/70 of the Commission of 29 June 1970 on the right of workers to remain in the territory of a Member State after having been employed in that State.

[18] Holloway, *supra* n. 12 at 260.

[19] Council Directive 90/364/EEC of 28 June on the right of residence (OJ L 180, 13.7.1990, p. 26); Council Directive 90/365/EEC of 28 June 1990 on the right of residence for employees and self-employed persons who have ceased their occupational activity (OJ L 180, 13.7.1990, p. 28) and 93/96/EEC of 29 October 1993 on the right of residence for students (OJ L 317, of 18.12.1993, p. 59).

the respective categories of students, retired persons, and economically inactive persons. Although apparently decoupling the right to reside in other Member States from the exercise of economic activity, the extension was made on condition that the three categories of non-workers and their families were covered by health insurance and had sufficient resources to avoid becoming a burden on the social assistance system of the host Member State. In practical terms a residence permit, issued by the host state, ensured that ultimately it was still a national matter to control the immigration of European citizens. Union citizenship, introduced by the Maastricht Treaty in 1992, and the right conferred on every Union citizen to move and reside freely merely codified the right which had already been adopted by the residence directives. Nevertheless, Union citizenship became the future reference point from which to consolidate the rights of the non-active person.

For those who thought that the residence directives and the largely formalistic notion of Union citizenship in the Maastricht Treaty were as far as Europe could go in terms of europeanizing the competence to decide who resides on national territory, the content of the recently adopted residence Directive 2004/38/EC[20] must be another upset. The Directive eliminates the obligation for EU citizens to obtain a residence permit. It introduces a permanent right of residence after five years of continuous residence. Furthermore, it restricts the scope for national authorities to refuse or terminate the residence of EU citizens. Finally, the new residence rights for all EU citizens, including non-active persons, mean that the social assistance schemes of another Member State become accessible to a greater extent. The Directive stipulates that entitlement to the social assistance of another Member State in the future will depend on the residence status of the EU citizen rather than on more discretionary conditions as set out in the residence directives and national legislation.

Those who have resided for less than five years in a host Member State, will enjoy the right of residence as long as they do not become an unreasonable burden on the social assistance system of the new state of residence and are covered by health insurance in the host Member State. So far the conditions echo those found in the three residence directives. However, the administrative discretion to expel an EU citizen due to his need for social assistance is clearly limited by the new Directive:

> . . . an expulsion measure should not be the automatic consequence of the recourse to the social assistance system. The host Member State should examine whether it is a case of temporary difficulties and take into account the duration of residence, the personal circumstances and the amount of aid granted in order to consider whether the beneficiary has become an unreasonable burden on its social assistance system and to proceed to his expulsion.[21]

[20] Directive 2004/38/EC of the European Parliament and of the Council of 29 April 2004 on the right of citizens of the Union and their family members to move and reside freely within the territory of the Member States amending Regulation (EEC) No. 1612/68 and repealing Directives 64/221/EEC, 68/360/EEC, 72/194/EEC, 73/148/EEC, 75/34/EEC, 75/35/EEC, 90/364/EEC, 90/365/EEC, and 93/96/EEC (OJ L 158, 30.4.2004).

[21] Directive 2004/58/EC, Para. 16; see also Art. 14.3 of the Directive.

When it comes to the EU citizen who has been granted permanent residence after five years of residence, he/she will enjoy full social protection in the new Member State and thus also be entitled to social assistance. The Directive stipulates that the right to permanent residence shall not be subjected to conditions of sufficient resources to provide for oneself. That also applies to family members from non-community countries:

> Union citizens who have resided legally for a continuous period of five years in the host Member State shall have the right of permanent residence there. This right shall not be subject to the conditions provided for in chapter III.[22]

How the new residence rights and the extended right to access of the welfare protection of another Member State will be transformed into the practical politics of each Member State essentially depends on the national implementation of the Directive which is set to take place within two years from its adoption. The scope of the new material rights subsequently depends on the ECJ's interpretation of such implementation. However, the literal reading of the Directive makes clear that the Member States have approved a much greater social responsibility for each others' citizens.

3. INTRA-EUROPEAN SOCIAL SECURITY—FOR WHOM?

The personal scope of Regulation 1408/71 has undergone a gradual, but continual development. From entitling only the worker *sensu stricto*, i.e., the market citizen,[23] to cross-border welfare, its personal scope has been incrementally expanded to the point where by 29 April 2004 the Regulation has been extended to all European citizens and where, recently, legally residing third-country nationals have been included in its personal scope. The development is thus a specific reflection of the general development from economic community to political union. The current personal scope of the Regulation has been settled through a detailed legal–political dialogue, consisting of piecemeal judicial interpretations, Commission proposals, and the Council's codification.[24]

[22] *Ibid.* Art. 16.1.

[23] The concept of 'market citizen', as it is used here, refers to someone who exercises economic activity and the worker *sensu stricto* refers to someone with a contract of employment; see J. Shaw, 'European Citizenship: The IGC and Beyond', 1 *European Integration online Papers* (1997), available online at http://eiop.or.at/eiop/texte/1997-003a.htm; M. Everson, 'The Legacy of the Market Citizen', in J. Shaw and G. More (eds.), *New Legal Dynamics of European Union* (1995) 73–90.

[24] For a more detailed description of the gradual process see, among others, Holloway, *supra* n. 12; B. Schulte, *Europäische Sozialpolitik und die Zukunft des Sozialstaats in Europa: Herausforderungen und Chancen* (1998); G. Igl, 'Pflegerversicherung als neuer Gegenstand sozialrechtlicher Regulierung', in K. Sieveking (ed.), *Soziale Sicherung bei Pflegebedürftigkeit in der Europäischen Union* (1998) 19–37; Haverkate and Huster, *supra* n. 5; A. Christensen and A. Malmstedt, 'Lex Loci Latoris versus Lex Loci Domicilii: An Inquiry into the Normative Foundations of European Social Security Law', 2 *European Journal of Social Security* (2000) 69–111; F. Pennings, 'The European Commission Proposal to simplify

April 2004 perhaps marks the most remarkable extension of Regulation 1408/71's personal scope, and thus temporarily closes the long-running history of defining those with a right to cross-border social security. With the adoption of Regulation 883/2004, the right to coordinated social security has been extended to *all nationals* of Member States covered by the social security legislation of any Member State. This means that not only employed workers, self-employed workers, civil servants, students, and pensioners but also *non-active persons* are to be protected from the coordination rules. Furthermore, as of 1 June 2003, *nationals from third countries* as well as their family members and survivors, provided that they are legal residents in the territory of a Member State and that they have moved between Member States, are covered by the Regulation.[25] Although, on the face of it the inclusion of third-country nationals marks another, significant, step towards a generalized personal scope irrespective of nationality, the practicable rights of third-country nationals are much more restricted, since they lack the underlying right of free movement.

The inclusion of non-active persons and third-country nationals marks the provisional conclusion of a 'long-running saga'.[26] Traditionally, the Regulation has entailed a criterion of Community nationality, waived only for refugees, stateless persons, and family members. This meant that a *third-country national* would not enjoy any rights according to Regulation 1408/71, unless he or she was a family member of a Community national—in which case nationality became irrelevant—or else he or she was a refugee or a stateless person. The Regulation thus clearly discriminated against third-country workers despite their possibly considerable contributions to a Member State's economy. Apparently, the amendment adopted in 2003 put an end to an intense debate between the Commission, Council, Parliament, and Court on the status of third-country nationals, and finally granted equal rights to a previously deprived group. However radical such an extension may seem, it should be noted that in practice it is not of much use. Third-country nationals legally residing in Member States have no right to free movement, but they can *only* invoke the rights under Regulation 1408/71 if they *do move* between Member States. Furthermore, Denmark is not bound by the recent amendment, due to its exemption from the Treaty's Title IV on 'Visas, Asylum, Immigration and Other Policies related to the Free Movement of Persons'. Third-country nationals

Regulation 1408/71', 3 *European Journal of Social Security* (2001) 45–60; D. S. Martinsen, *Who Has the Right to Intra European Social Security? From Market Citizens to European Citizens and Beyond*, EUI Working Paper, Department of Law (2003) 13, 1–48.

[25] As laid down by Council Regulation (EC) No. 859/2003 of 14 May 2003 extending the provisions of Regulation (EEC) No. 1408/71 and Regulation (EEC) No. 574/72 to nationals of third countries who are not already covered by those provisions solely on the ground of their nationality.

[26] S. Peers, 'Joined Cases C-95/99 to 98/99, *Mervett Khalil and others v. Bundesanstalt für Arbeit and Landeshauptsadt Stuttgart* and Case C-180/99, *Meriem Addou v. Land Nordrhein-Westfalen*, judgment of the Full Court of 11 October 2001 [2001] ECR I-7413', 39 *Common Market Law Review* (2002) 1395–406 at 1395.

who enter Danish territory from another Member State or leave the Danish territory bound for another Member State thus continue to have variable protection levels.

Another long-running dispute has been whether the Regulation should include *non-active persons* and thus definitively break the link with the exercise of an economic activity. Over the years, the case law of the ECJ has compromised the link between work activity and rights according to the Regulation, by extending rights to those no longer in active employment, but still enjoying the status of 'employed persons';[27] by clarifying that movement motivated by leisure may generate rights;[28] by extending the rights of family members;[29] and by denying that employment status depends on the hours spent on the work activity.[30] Through successive case law, the Court has declared that the migrant's family has an individual right to equal treatment,[31] that the meanings of employed[32] and self-employed[33] are extensive, and that the number of hours spent working does not influence one's status as a worker in any way. The legal reasoning has thus approached a practical recognition of European citizenship.

The Court's interpretative line has been seconded by the Commission. Since the adoption of the general right of residence in 1990 with the three residence directives, the Commission has persistently used the soft-law tool of recommendations to emphasize how 'the peoples of Europe' merit equal rights, and has brought in European citizenship as the new dimension of European integration.

The Council and the Parliament have recently adopted Regulation 883/2004, on the agenda since the early 1990s, which definitively extends the right to intra-European social security to all 'nationals of a Member State, stateless persons and refugees residing in a Member State who are or have been subject to the legislation of one or more Member States, as well as to the members of their families and to their survivors'.[34] The extension of intra-European social security rights to all Community nationals adds substantial rights to the skeleton of European citizenship, since cross-border social rights are, finally, granted irrespective of economic activity. However, as long as the right to move and reside within the Community is, for the first five years of foreign settlement, conditioned by the ability to provide for oneself, the 'social self' of Europe will still ultimately be subordinated to

[27] Case 75/63, *Mrs. Hoekstra (née Unger) v. Bestuur der Cont. Bedrijfsvereniging voor Detailhandel en Ambachten*, 19 March 1964, ECR 1964, p. 177.

[28] Case 44/65, *Hessische Knappschaft v. Maison Singer et Fils*, 9 December 1965, ECR 1965, p. 1191.

[29] Case 7/75, *Mr. and Mrs. Fracas v. Belgian State*, 17 June 1975, ECR 1975, p. 679.

[30] Case C-2/89, *Bestuur van de Sociale Verzekeringsbank v. G. J. Kits van Heijningen*, 3 May 1990, ECR 1990, p. 1755.

[31] Case C-308/93, *Bestuur van de Sociale Verzekeringsbank v. J. M. Cabanis-Issarte*, 30 April 1996, ECR 1996, p. I-2097.

[32] Case 17/76, *M. L. E. Brack, widow of R. J. Brack v. Insurance Officer*, 29 September 1976, ECR 1976, p. 1429.

[33] Case 300/84, *A. J. M. van Roosmalen v. Bestuur van de Bedrijfsvereniging voor de Gezondheid, Geestelijke en Maatschappelijke Belangen*, 23 October 1986, ECR 1986, p. 3097.

[34] Regulation 883/2004, Art. 2.

economic imperatives.[35] In reality, 'work' or 'economic status' will continue to be the entry point into another Member State for the majority of European migrants, and still constitute the basic condition upon which foreign social rights are granted.

For the time being, the Community Regulation on coordinated social security, through its confirmed link with the provision on the free movement of workers,[36] is essentially legitimated by market integration. However, since the path to social security integration has proven to be incremental, albeit dynamic, and with a high degree of issue linkage between different economic, legal, and political rationales, the substance and reach of future cross-border social security rights are difficult to predict. There can be no doubt that, with the historical development and contemporary achievements, we have witnessed the formation of a key part of Europe's social identity.

4. THE DE-TERRITORIALIZATION OF WELFARE?

The formation and consolidation of modern social policies took place within the territorial borders of the nation–state. Welfare policy was, and remains, closely related to the idea of the nation–state.[37] The welfare state inherited the nation–state method of defining those entitled and its strong emphasis on territoriality. The welfare state has traditionally been in a sovereign position to exercise spatial control, insisting that social benefits and services should be consumed within its own territory.[38] Alongside social citizenship,[39] the principle of territoriality has demarcated the reach of European welfare.

[35] For a description of Europe's social self, see M. P. Maduro, 'Europe's Social Self: The Sickness unto Death', in J. Shaw (ed.), *Social Law and Policy in an Evolving European Union* (2000) 325–49.

[36] That Regulation 1408/71 has not yet achieved status as an independent instrument of social protection was confirmed by the dispute between the Commission and the Member States on the extension of the Regulation to third-country nationals and whether this extension could be based on Art. 42 of the Treaty, as held by the Commission, or should be based on the Treaty's Art. 63(4), as argued by individual Member States. According to a minority of the Member States, an extension of the Regulation to third-country nationals could not be based on Art. 42 since they saw this provision inextricably bound to Art. 39 of the Treaty, the objective of which is to promote the free movement of workers, who are *nationals* of one of the Member States. The Commission, on the other hand, argued that Regulation 1408/71 had become an instrument of social protection in itself and not only a means to achieve the free movement of workers. For a more detailed description of the dispute, see D. S. Martinsen, *European Institutionalization of Social Security Rights: A Two-Layered Process of Integration* (2004), Ph.D. thesis, European University Institute, and *supra* n. 24.

[37] Eichenhofer, *supra* n. 12 at 55.

[38] S. Liebfried and P. Pierson, 'Semisovereign Welfare States: Social Policy in a Multitiered Europe', in S. Liebfried and P. Pierson (eds.), *European Social Policy: Between Fragmentation and Integration* (1995) 43–77.

[39] Social citizens were traditionally those who were members of the nation. Concepts such as equality and solidarity were not unlimited, but restricted to members of the nation. T. H. Marshall's depiction of 'social citizenship' stands to date as perhaps the most often referred to. He wrote: 'Citizenship is a status bestowed on those who are full members of a community. All who possess the status are equal with respect to the rights and duties with which the status is endowed' (T. H. Marshall,

Social legislation in the EU Member States largely remains based on the principle of territoriality, defining the spatial application of welfare.[40] Even in a globalized world, the principle still finds its justification in practical politics. Social benefits and services are designed to fulfil domestic policy aims and correspond to domestic living conditions and costs.[41] Above all, the principle serves as an effective means of national control:

- It ensures budgetary control, by entitling only those residing and consuming within the national borders to the benefits and services supplied.
- It ensures that the intended policy and its objective are actually pursued. To ensure, for example that long-term care benefits are used for actual care and that supplied family benefits meet policy intentions.
- It serves as a means of controlling the quality of supplied services, since standards are nationally defined.
- It facilitates capacity planning, since when services can only be consumed within national borders, consumption is nationally controlled and foreign supply does not have to be integrated.

Whereas, by the adoption of Regulation 1408/71, Member States applied the principle of exportability to *social security benefits* at least for those supplied in cash, an intense dispute has taken place between the ECJ, individual states, and the Council as to: (a) whether those benefits, characterized as *special non-contributory benefits*, due to their affinities with both social security and social assistance, are exportable; (b) whether Community law extends welfare policy objectives, such as those embedded in certain *family benefits*, beyond national borders; and (c) whether Community law prescribes the exportability of more recently accepted social responsibilities such as those undertaken by *long-term care benefits*. On the one hand, the dispute, exercised through legal requests, ECJ case law, and Council responses, mirrors the intervention of an internal market principle into the national organization of welfare. On the other hand, the dispute also mirrors how politics and national preferences may overrule judicial activism undertaken by the ECJ. However, more contemporary developments suggest that such restraints are not ultimate. Recent ECJ decisions have questioned anew the territorialization of certain welfare benefits. The sections below will examine in turn the exportability of special non-contributory benefits, family benefits, and long-term care.

Citizenship and Social Class and Other Essays (1992) at 18). The European integration of social security rights has indeed transformed, or even eroded, this traditional notion of social citizenship, as is clear from the extension of Regulation 1408/71's personal scope depicted above.

[40] Haverkate and Huster, *supra* n. 5 at 115.

[41] W. Tegtmeier, 'Wechselwirkungen zwischen dem Europäischen Sozialrecht und dem Sozialrecht der Bundesrepublik Deutschland: Erfahrungen und Vorstellungen auf deutscher Sicht', in B. Schulte and H. F. Zacher (eds.), *Wechselwirkungen zwischen dem Europäischen Sozialrecht und dem Sozialrecht der Bundesrepublik Deutschland* (1990) 27–47; P. Clever, 'Soziale Sicherheit im Rahmen der europäischen Integration: Perspektiven nach dem Maastrichter Gipfel', 39 *Die Angestelltenversicherung* (1992) 296–304.

A. Special Non-Contributory Benefits within National Borders

One of the first cases examining the spatial reach of 'special non-contributory benefits' was that of *Piscitello*, concerning the Italian social aid pension.[42] Despite the opinions submitted by Member States, which argued that the social aid pension had strong affinities with social assistance, the Court ruled that the benefit was exportable according to Community law.

The legal–political confrontation over the nature of 'special non-contributory' benefits culminated with the assessment of the French supplementary allowance, expressed in Joined Cases 379 to 381/85 and 93/86 *Giletti et al.*[43]

The French government argued in its observations that the nature of the benefit was that of assistance. The supplementary allowance could not be classified as social security, because (1) it was not financed by contributions, but by public funds, (2) it was not related to occupation, but was a matter of national solidarity, and (3) the objective of the national allowance was to alleviate a state of need and, therefore, took the personal income of the receiver into consideration.

The ECJ, however, disregarded the national observations. The Court stated that, although the benefit was financed out of tax revenue and aimed to provide a minimum level of income for the recipient, it was an old-age benefit within the meaning of Regulation 1408/71, since it was granted as a legally protected right. The Court furthermore overruled the French residence clause, holding that in accordance with Community law the supplementary allowance was exportable.

However, despite the Court's conclusions, France still refused to comply, and the dispute on the supplementary allowance went on. Against this background, the Commission issued an infringement procedure, Case C-236/88 *against France*, against the French residence clause for the supplementary allowance. The Court again concluded that the French authorities were obliged to allow for the exportability of its old-age benefit.

The legally imposed exportability of the French supplementary allowance did not, however, last long. On the 30 April 1992, the Council of Ministers unanimously adopted Regulation 1247/92,[44] which overruled the Court's extension of exportability. The collective political response stood out clearly. The interpretations of the Court exceeded political intentions. The Council managed to overcome the significant

[42] Case 139/82, *Paola Piscitello v. Instituto Nazionale della Previdenza Sociale (INPS)*, 5 May 1983, ECR 1983, p. 1427.

[43] Joined Cases 379 to 381/85 and 93/86, *Caisse régionale d'assurance maladie Rhone-Alpes v. Anna Giletti, Directeur régional des affaires sanitaires et sociales de Lorraine v. Domenico Giardini, Caisse régionale d'assurance maladie du Nord-Est v. Federico Tampan and Severino Severini v. Caisse primaire centrale d'assurance maladie*, 24 February 1987, ECR 1987, p. 955. See also Eichenhofer, *supra* n. 12 at 80; Christensen and Malmstedt, *supra* n. 24 at 82.

[44] Council Regulation (EEC) No. 1247/92 of 30 April 1992 amending Regulation (EEC) No. 1408/71 on the application of social security schemes to employed persons, to self-employed persons, and to members of their families moving within the Community.

threshold of unanimous political action, and the unintended case law development was halted.

Regulation 1247/92 amended 1408/71, and added a 'special rule' to the coordination system. The 'special rule' meant that special non-contributory benefits were included in the material scope of Regulation 1408/71, and rights awarded between Member States could thus be aggregated, but that the benefits remained bound to the territory of the competent state and could not be exported. For a benefit to be coordinated according to the 'special rule', it should be listed in Annex IIa of the Regulation. Among other benefit types, Annex IIa came to list the French supplementary allowance from the National Solidarity Fund;[45] the Italian social pensions for persons without means;[46] the British attendance allowance,[47] disability living allowance,[48] and family credit. The Member States thus retained control over the spatial reach of these benefits.

The amendment corrected the expansionary course taken by the Court, and adopted a system within the system allowing for 'special non-contributory benefits' to be territorialized anew. In the subsequent case of C-20/96 *Snares*,[49] the Court was requested to interpret the compatibility of the special rule with Article 51 of primary law. The case questioned whether the territorial binding of the British disability living allowance was not contrary to the essence and purpose of Article 51, namely to promote the free movement of migrant workers. The ECJ, however, chose to accept the political derogation over its previous judgments, codified by Regulation 1247/92, and decided that British legislation did not violate Community law, since 'the principle of the exportability of social security benefits applies so long as derogating provisions have not been adopted by the Community legislature'.[50] Case C-297/97 *Partridge*[51] followed up on the *Snares* case, questioning the nature of another British disability allowance, the attendance allowance, which is a benefit awarded to care-dependent persons. The preliminary reference concerned whether the answer given by the Court in the case of *Snares* also applied to a benefit type such as the attendance allowance. Concretely the case treated the situation of Mrs. Partridge, whose attendance allowance had been withdrawn when she went to live with her son in France. The judgment of the Court reaffirmed the standpoint taken in *Snares*. The attendance allowance was a special non-contributory benefit, exclusively governed by the rules laid down in Article 10a, and was therefore not exportable outside the territory of the UK.

With the adoption of Regulation 1247/92 and the legal approval thereof in the cases of *Snares* and *Partridge*, 'special non-contributory' benefits seemed to have

45 Law of 30 June 1956.

46 Law no. 153 of 30 April 1969.

47 Both as formulated in the Social Security Act 1975, sects. 37A and 35.

48 Disability Living Allowance and Disability Working Allowance Act 1991.

49 Case C-20/96, *Kelvin Albert Snares v. Adjudication Officer*, 4 November 1997, ECR 1997, p. I-6057.

50 *Ibid.* Para. 41 of the Judgment.

51 Case C-297/96, *Vera A. Partridge v. Adjudication Officer*, 11 June 1998, ECR 1998, p. I-3467.

been definitively re-territorialized. Together the Commission, Court, and Council institutionalized the position that the regulatory text can permit new deviations from the general—but not absolute—principle of exportability. Nevertheless, more recent case law has redrawn our attention to 'the special rule'—and especially to the political administration thereof—as will be demonstrated below with the cases of *Jauch* and *Leclere*. On this later date, the ECJ has not acted deferentially to individual political interests.

B. Policy Objectives beyond National Borders: Family Benefits

Whereas national decision-makers formally decide on the objectives, means, and content of their welfare policies, the lesson taught by the ECJ is that their decisions have to take the scope and limits of European law into account. That welfare policy autonomy has been compromised as a consequence of the dynamic interpretation of Community law is well exemplified by the case of family benefits.

Due to their non-contributory character, different policy objectives, and territorial demarcation, family benefits have been the subject of frequent policy conflict for the coordination system. For the politicians it has not been evident why policies with national demographic aims should equally aim beyond national borders.[52]

Case C-78/91 *Hughes*[53] concerned British family credit, and the extent to which it should be categorized as social assistance or rather as a social security benefit. The case considered whether Mrs. Hughes had a right to the British family credit, despite her residence in Ireland, but due to her husband's work in Britain. Since the entitlement to family credit depended on residence in the UK, Mrs. Hughes did not qualify for the benefit. Before the ECJ, both the British and the German government defended the residence clause, arguing that family credit was a social assistance type of benefit.[54] That national classification was, however, overruled by the judgment. The Court pointed to how it had consistently held that a benefit was a social security benefit if it was granted without discretionary assessment of personal needs, but on the basis of a legally defined position.[55] The conclusion was that the

[52] See, among others, Case 41/84, *Pietro Pinna v. Caisse d'allocations familiales de la Savoie*, 15 January 1986, ECR, p. 1 and Case C-185/96, *Commission of the European Communities v. Hellenic Republic*, 29 October 1996, ECR 1998, p. 6601. See also S. Van Raepenbusch, 'Persons covered by Regulation (EEC) no. 1408/71 and European Citizenship: From Migrant Worker to European Citizen', in *25 Years of Regulation (EEC) no. 1408/71 on Social Security for Migrant Workers: Post Experiences, Present Problems and Future Perspectives* (1997) 71–88.

[53] Case C-78/91, *Rose Hughes v. Chief Adjudication Officer, Belfast*, 16 July 1992, ECR 1992, p. I-4839.

[54] The British government clarified that the main purpose of the family credit, a weekly non-contributory cash benefit, was to supplement the incomes of low-paid workers whose income would otherwise be lower than if they were unemployed. The aim of the benefit was to keep low-paid workers in employment, for which reason the government did not find that it was a social security benefit.

[55] Case C-78/91, *Hughes, supra* n. 53, Para. 15 of the judgment.

principle of exportability in Community law entitled Mrs. Hughes to the family credit, and the Court set aside the residence requirement of British law.

During the 1980s, several Member States introduced different types of 'child-raising' allowances as a new family benefit. A general aim of the benefit was to make it possible for one parent to stay at home with the child during its first years. However, neither national nor community law specified the relationship between the new social benefit and Regulation 1408/71.[56] Joined cases C-245/94 and C-312/94 *Hoever and Zachow*[57] concerned the German child-raising allowance, i.e. *Erziehungsgeld*, adopted in December 1985. This type of childcare benefit differed from the traditional German family benefit, i.e. *Kindergeld*, in its objective and qualifying conditions.[58] From a German legal, political and administrative perspective, *Kindergeld* had traditionally been regarded as the only German family benefit within the meaning of Regulation 1408/71.[59] The child-raising allowance had, on the other hand, been regarded as outside the regulatory scope of Regulation 1408/71. That point of view was challenged and corrected by the case law of the Court.

The cases of *Hoever and Zachow* concerned two migrant families, residing in the Netherlands, but with the husbands working full-time in Germany. The wives applied for the German child-raising allowance, without personally being affiliated to the German social security system. Based on the principle of territoriality, the German law on childcare benefit denied Mrs. Hoever and Mrs. Zachow any right to child-raising allowance. Among other criteria, the national law specifies that to qualify for the childcare benefit one must reside in Germany,[60] or, if not residing there, have worked at least fifteen hours a week in Germany.

In its reasoning, the ECJ referred in particular to the case of *Hughes*, and restated that it was the constituent elements of each benefit that decided its classification.[61] Since the German *Erziehungsgeld* was granted automatically to persons fulfilling objective criteria without any individual or discretionary assessment of needs, it was a family benefit within the meaning of Article 4(1)(h).[62]

[56] Altmaier, *supra* n. 6 at 86.

[57] Joined Cases C-245/94 and C-312/94, *Ingrid Hoever and Iris Zachow v. Land Nordrhein-Westfalen*, 10 October 1996, ECR 1996, p. I-4895. The *Erziehungsgeld* is governed by the German *Bundesgesetz über die Gewährung von Erziehungsgeld und Erziehungsurlaub*.

[58] G. Igl, 'Co-ordination and New Forms of Social Protection', in *25 Years of Regulation (EEC) No. 1408/71 on Social Security for Migrant Workers: Past Experiences, Present Problems and Future Perspectives* (1997) 91–111 at 97.

[59] E. Eichenhofer, 'Deutsches Erziehungsgeld und Europäisches Sozialrecht: zur Entscheidung des Europäischen Gerichtshofes vom 10.10.1996–verbundene Rechtsache C-245/94 und C-312/94 Ingrid Hoever und Iris Zachow/Land Nordrhein-Westfalen', in 10 *Die Sozialgerichtsbarkeit* (1997) 449–55.

[60] *Bundesgesetz über die Gewährung von Erziehungsgeld und Erziehungsurlaub*, Para. 1(1).

[61] Joined Cases C-245/94 and C-312/94, *Hoever and Zachow supra* n. 57, Paras. 17 and 18 of the Judgment.

[62] *Ibid.* Para. 27 of the Judgment.

The second question concerned whether a family member who did not reside in the country where her husband was employed and where the competent institution was situated, and also who was not personally subject to German social insurance, was entitled to the benefit. According to national law, the plaintiff must be personally eligible for the allowance, i.e. must *personally* fulfil the conditions. In the observations given by the German, Spanish, and French governments, they all referred to the *Kermaschek* line of case law,[63] and against this background emphasized that the family member only had a derived right.[64] However, the Court opposed the stated opinions by restating its conclusions from case *Cabanis-Issarte*.[65] The scope of the rule laid down in *Kermaschek* was limited by *Cabanis-Issarte* to provisions that were only applicable to workers, and not to family members, such as unemployment benefit.[66] The Court concluded that the distinction between a personal and a derived right thus did not apply to family benefits, and Mrs. Hoever and Mrs. Zachow were therefore entitled to the childcare allowance.[67]

The joined *Hoever and Zachow* cases demonstrate a Court that is both willing and in a position to contradict national opinions and the formulated criteria of national law. In the cases, the Court overruled both the territorial principle of German law, and the criterion that one has to be personally eligible for the childcare allowance. It demonstrates a Court that is willing to rule against national preferences, despite the financial implications. By extending *Erziehungsgeld* beyond German borders, the ability to ensure budgetary control for the specific item of expenditure has been reduced. The litigation furthermore exemplifies how past and future case law relate, establishing different authoritative lines of reasoning, which can be pieced together to formulate new concrete rights for the migrant. The case

[63] Case 40/76, *Kermaschek v. Bundesanstalt für Arbeit*, 23 November 1976, ECR 1976, p. 1669. In the case of *Kermaschek*, the Court established a restrictive view on the rights of the family member and drew a sharp distinction between, on the one hand, the rights of the worker and, on the other hand, the rights of their families. The family member only had 'derived rights', meaning those acquired by national law through his/her status as a family member. The family member could therefore not rely personally on the principle of equal treatment. The Court maintained the distinction for more than twenty years, confirming it in a line of judgments known as the *Kermaschek* case law. This line of cases included, among others, the Case 157/84, *Maria Frascogna v. Caisse des depots et consignations*, 6 June 1985, ECR 1985, p. 1739; Case 94/84, *Office national de l'emploi v. Joszef Deak*, 20 June 1985, ECR 1985, p. 1873; Case C-243/91, *Belgian State v. Noushin Taghavi*, 8 July 1992, ECR 1992, p. I-4401; Case C-310/91, *Hugo Schmid v. Belgian State, represented by the Minister van Sociale Voorz*, 27 May 1993, ECR 1993, p. I-3011.

[64] Joined Cases C-245/94 and C-312/94, *Hoever and Zachow*, *supra* n. 57, Para. 31 of the Judgment.

[65] Case C-308/93, *Cabanis-Issarte*, *supra* n. 31. In the *Cabanis-Issarte* judgement, the Court reconsidered the scope of Regulation 1408/71's equal treatment provision and its application to the family member, and revised the interpretive path of established case law, which had been confirmed through more than twenty years of legal interpretation in the *Kermaschek* line of case law (Martinsen, *supra* n. 36 at 120–5).

[66] Joined Cases C-245/94 and C-312/94, *Hoever and Zachow*, *supra* n. 57, Para. 32 of the Judgment.

[67] *Ibid.* Para. 33.

of *Hughes* was a reference point for the Court when incorporating *Erziehungsgeld* into the material scope of Regulation 1408/71. Another reference was *Cabanis-Issarte*, which extended the principle of equal treatment to family members. Furthermore, the *Hoever and Zachow* cases were referred to by the Court in the much-discussed case of *Martínez Sala*, when concluding that the non-active Martínez Sala also had a right to *Erziehungsgeld*, despite the fact that she had no residence permit to stay in Germany.[68] Both the *Hughes* and the *Hoever and Zachow* cases were replicated in the recent case C-333/00 *Maaheimo*, in which the Court considered whether Finnish 'home childcare allowance' should be paid out abroad.[69] Previous case law formed the basis of the line of reasoning upon which the Court found that the Finnish residence requirement in its home childcare policy was inconsistent with Community law. Once again, the Court set aside the national principle of territoriality.

This cluster of case law has made it increasingly difficult for Member States to disregard Community law, as interpreted by the Court, when trying to tie policy objectives to national territory. On the basis of a patchwork of litigation, principles and aims are applied uniformly to different cases concerning different social security schemes and welfare traditions. The outcomes are, however, similar. The autonomy to define welfare policy means and objectives is compromised by Community law.

C. Exportability of 'New' Social Responsibilities: Long-Term Care Benefits

Long-term care benefit represents a benefit that could not easily have been appreciated back when the material scope of Regulation 1408/71 was first laid down. As a matter of fact, long-term care has taken some time to find its name. Although 'reliance on care' has always existed as a social phenomenon, long-term care did not figure as an independent or conceptualized social security risk in European or international conventions at the end of the 1970s.[70] Although by no means a 'new'

[68] Case C-85/96, *Maria Martínez Sala v. Freistaat Bayern*, 12 May 1998, ECR 1998, p. I-2691. For an in depth discussion of the *Sala* case, see, among others: G. More, 'The Principle of Equal Treatment: From Market Unifier to Fundamental Right', in P. Craig and G. De Búrca (eds.), *The Evolution of EU Law* (1999) 517–55; S. O'Leary, 'European Communities and EEA: Putting Flesh on the Bones of European Union Citizenship', 24 *European Law Review* (1999) 68–79; R. Langer, 'Der Beitrag des Europäischen Gerichtshofüber gemeinschaftsrechtlichen Gestaltungsvorgaben für das Sozialrecht', in I. Ebsen (ed.), *Europarechtliche Gestaltungsvorgaben für das deutsche Sozialrecht: Freizügigkeit, wirtschaftliche Grundfreiheiten und Europöisches Wettbewerbsrecht als Grenzen sozialstaatlicher Suveränität* (1999) 43–56; C. Tomuschat, 'Case C-85/96, *Maria Martínez Sala v. Freistaat Bayern*, Judgment of 12 May 1998, Full Court [1998] ECR I-2691', in 37 *Common Market Law Review* (2000) 449–57.

[69] Case C-333/00, *Eila Päivikki Maaheimo*, 7 November 2002, ECR 2002, p. I-10087, Paras. 22, 32, and 33 of the Judgment.

[70] Igl, *supra* n. 58; opinion of Advocate General Cosmas in Case C-160/96, *Manfred Molenaar and Barbara Fath-Molenaar v. Allgemeine Ortskrankenkasse Baden-Württemberg*, 5 March 1998, ECR 1998, p. I-880.

social risk, it is a risk which, in some Member States, has only lately become a part of public welfare, and has been institutionalized beyond the more immediate care provided by the family.

Germany adopted its *Pflegeversicherungsgesetz* as late as 1995, thereby recognizing long-term care as an independent social risk. Before the adoption of the care insurance law, long-term care was publicly granted as a social assistance benefit, or privately provided and financed.[71] Today any person insured against sickness in Germany is also compulsorily insured in the long-term care scheme. The social insurance is funded from contributions from both worker and employer, and entitles a member[72] reliant on care to care in a nursing home or in one's own home. If one should desire home care, it is possible to choose care either as a benefit in kind, or as a monthly allowance, i.e. *Pflegegeld*, where one purchases the care oneself.

The monthly cash allowance has turned out to be the preferred form of home care. From the outset, 80% of those in home care chose the cash benefit.[73] However, according to national legislation, the entitlement to the German *Pflegegeld* is suspended if one takes up residence abroad.[74] The *Pflegegeld* thus relies on the territorial principle.

Whether the territorial restriction of the German *Pflegegeld* contradicts Community law was examined in case C-160/96 *Molenaar.*[75] The case discussed the right to *Pflegegeld* of Mr. and Mrs. Molenaar, a Dutch–German couple, working in Germany but living in France. They were both voluntarily insured against sickness in Germany and were, from January 1995, required to pay care insurance contributions, which they did. However, on application, they were informed by the competent German social security fund that they were not entitled to care insurance benefits due to their French residence.

The ECJ initiated its legal reasoning by referring to previous case law, stating that a benefit was to be regarded as a social security benefit if granted 'on the basis of a legally defined position and provided that it concerns one of the risks expressly listed in Article 4(1)' of Regulation 1408/71.[76] It added that the list in Article 4(1)

[71] G. Igl and F. Stadelmann, 'Die Pflegeversicherung in Deutschland', in K. Sieveking (ed.), *Soziale Sicherung bei Pflegebedürftigkeit in der Europäischen Union* (1998) 37–51 at 37.

[72] The member has to complete an insurance period, which from the outset was one year, but then increased in stages to five years in 2000.

[73] Igl, *supra* n. 24 at 23.

[74] The residence clause is laid down by §34(1)(1) of the German Sozialgesetzbuch (Social Security Code) XI.

[75] *Molenaar, supra* n. 70.

[76] The Court referred on this point to Case 249/83, *Vera Hoeckx v. Openbaar Centrum voor Maatschappelijk Welzijn, Kalmthont*, 27 March 1985, ECR 1985, p. 973, Paras. 12–14; Case 122/84, *Kenneth Scrivner and Carol Cole v. Centre public d'aide sociale de Chastre*, 27 March 1985, ECR 1985, p. 1027, Paras. 19–21; Case C-356/89 *Roger Stanton Newton v. Chief Adjudication Officer*, 20 June 1991, p. I-3017, Case C-78/91, *Hughes, supra* n. 53, Para. 15.

was exhaustive, meaning that a branch of social security not mentioned there was not part of the regulatory scope.[77] Long-term care, such as the German *Pflegeversicherung*, was to be regarded as a sickness benefit within the meaning of Article 4(1)(a) of Regulation 1408/71. Having thus included the care allowance within the material scope of 1408/71, the Court continued by examining whether the residence clause of German law could be justified against the Community principle of exportability.

Article 19(1)(a) and (b)[78] of the Regulation obliged the competent institution to export sickness benefits in cash, but not equally sickness benefits in kind.[79] However, the monthly cash allowance, *Pflegegeld*, was defined as a benefit in kind in German law. More specifically, the drafter of the *Pflegeversicherungsgesetz* defended the point of view that the care allowance constituted a 'benefit in kind-substitute', a *Sachleistungssurrogat*.[80] The ECJ did not accept the national classification, but ruled that the German care allowance was indeed a benefit in cash.[81] As a consequence, the Court concluded that the residence clause in German law conflicted with the principle of exportability of Regulation 1408/71.[82]

The *Molenaar* case is another among the later jurisprudence in which the Court corrected the way in which national politics had classified a benefit. The obvious attempt by the German government to restrict long-term care benefit to its own territory, by classifying it as a 'benefit-in-kind substitute' failed. The *Molenaar* case illustrates the Court's position in the social security field in the late 1990s. It demonstrates a Court capable of expanding the material and exportable rights of the migrant, despite national preferences and despite the financial implications that it may have for the litigating Member State. The legal activism in which the Court engaged in the *Molenaar* case updated the material scope of Regulation 1408/71, and extended its provision of exportability.

[77] On this point, the ECJ referred here to Case C-25/95, *Siegfried Otte v. Bundesrepublik Deutschland*, 11 June 1996, ECR 1996, p. I-3745.

[78] Art. 19(1) of Regulation 1408/71 stated: 'Residence in a Member State other than the competent State—General rules [. . .]:

(a) *benefits in kind* provided on behalf of the competent institution by the institution of the place of residence in accordance with the provisions of the legislation administered by that institution as though he was insured with it

(b) *cash benefits* provided by the competent institution in accordance with the legislation which it administers [. . .].' (emphasis added)

[79] S. Huster, 'Grundfragen der Exportpflicht im europäischen Sozialrecht', in *Neue Zeitschrift für Sozialrecht* (1999) 10–17.

[80] BT-Drucks (Bundestag Drucks) 12/5262, p. 82; M. Zuleeg, 'Die Einwirkung des Europäischen Gemeinschaftsrechts auf die deutsche Pflegeversicherung', in H. Sieveking (ed.), *Soziale Sicherung bei Pflegebedürftigkeit in der Europäischen Union* (1998) 159–79 at 172.

[81] Case C-160/96, *Molenaar, supra* n. 70, Para. 36 of the Judgment.

[82] As laid down by Art. 19(1)(b) of Regulation 1408/71.

D. Territorialization Re-Questioned

The legal–political dispute on the territorialization of those benefits with dual characteristics of social security and social assistance, with policy objectives tied to the national territory and those that resemble benefits-in-kind, has had two different results. On the one hand, the adoption of Regulation 1247/92, and its subsequent legal approval, seemed to have definitively re-territorialized 'special non-contributory' benefits. On the other hand, the Court's expansive interpretations have made different types of family benefits exportable, for family members as well, and have lifted the residence clause for long-term care benefits granted as benefits in cash.

Recent developments demonstrate further that the limits and the scope of Community law are indeed dynamically interpreted. The recent cases of *Jauch*[83] and *Leclere*[84] show that a legal–political reconciliation such as the one on special non-contributory benefits may only last until a new request is formulated against a Community law background which has meanwhile evolved.

In the cases of *Jauch* and *Leclere*, the Court was requested to clarify the scope of Annex IIa. The case of *Jauch* concerned a German national, residing in Germany, but who had worked in Austria where he was affiliated to the social security scheme. The competent Austrian institution had denied him long-term care, since he was not a habitual resident in Austria, and since the care allowance was listed in Annex IIa of 1408/71 and thus non-exportable. The Austrian government argued before the Court that because the benefit had been admitted in Annex IIa, the residence clause of Austrian law did not contravene Community law. The government supported its view by referring to the previous cases of *Snares* and *Partridge*. The Court's judgment, however, followed another established reasoning, laid down in the case of *Molenaar*:

> . . . while care allowance may possibly have a different legal regime at the national level, it nevertheless remains of the same kind as the German care insurance benefits at issue in Molenaar, and is likewise granted objectively on the basis of a legally defined situation.[85]

The Court thus ruled that the character of the Austrian care allowance was no different from the German *Pflegegeld*. The Austrian care allowance was therefore to be classified as another sickness benefit in cash, for which reason it was exportable and had invalidly been listed in Annex IIa. In the case of *Jauch*, the Court set aside not only the Austrian government's definition of its benefit, but it also overruled the praxis of the Council, which had unanimously agreed to list the care allowance in Annex IIa.

[83] Case C-215/99, *Frederich Jauch v. Pensionsversicherungsanstalt der Arbeiter*, 8 March 2001, ECR 2001, p. I-1901.

[84] Case C-43/99, *Ghislain Leclere and Alina Deaconescu v. Caisse nationale des prestations familiales*, 31 May 2001, ECR 2001, p. I-4265.

[85] Case C-160/96, *Molenaar, supra* n. 70, Para. 26 of the Jauch Judgment.

Furthermore, the *Leclere* case also delimited the scope of Annex IIa. The case interpreted the rights of Mrs. Leclere, whose husband had formerly worked in Luxembourg, although the couple resided in Belgium. The husband was the victim of an accident at work in 1981, and thereafter received an invalidity pension paid by the Luxembourg social security services. With the birth of their child, they applied for various allowances in Luxembourg, among which was the maternity allowance. The application was turned down, since the couple did not fulfil the residence requirement for the benefit, which was one of the benefits explicitly listed in Regulation 1408/71's Annex IIa. Again the Court ruled that the maternity allowance had been invalidly placed in the Annex and, contrary to the opinion of the Luxembourg government, that its maternity benefit had to be exported according to Article 19(1)(b) of Regulation 1408/71.

The rulings in *Hoever and Zachow, Molenaar, Jauch,* and *Leclere* all extend the right to social security entitlements beyond the borders where the competent institution is situated. The cases of *Hoever and Zachow* and *Molenaar* show that social benefits cannot be insulated from the principles of Community law as a consequence of the way their purposes and means are defined nationally. The rulings of *Jauch* and *Leclere* demonstrate that although the social ministers of the Member States have collectively decided to tie certain benefits to national territory and although it is a political decision to which benefits this special rule applies, the political autonomy to administer according to that special rule is not free from judicial supervision.

In the new Regulation 883/2004, the principle of exportability has been given a more prominent position, advanced as Article 7.[86] Whereas the Regulation does not ignore that special benefits may be linked to the place of residence, it is clear that national justification for maintaining residence rules for such benefits will be under closer supranational surveillance in the future.[87] Against this new regulatory context, it seems obvious that the role of the Court will become even more central when the right balance between national principles of territoriality and the Community principle of exportability has to be decided.

CONCLUDING REMARKS

Furthered by cross-border movements of the people inhabiting the EU, their cases before the national courts and the ECJ, the Commission's recommendations and

[86] That is against the former Art. 10.

[87] Notable is that Para. 16 of Regulation 883/2004 mentions that the place of residence *could* be taken into account, instead of *should* be taken into account: 'Within the Community there is in principle no justification for making social security rights dependent on the place of residence of the person concerned; nevertheless, in specific cases, in particular as regards special benefits linked to the economic and social context of the person involved, the place of residence *could* be taken into account.' (emphasis added)

proposals, and the Council's codification, a social security dimension in the EU has emerged and been consolidated.

The European dimension of welfare has come to cover all citizens of the Union, irrespective of their economic status. Attached as the social security dimension is to the free movement of persons, it confirms that European citizenship has indeed been ascribed a substantial content. When the newly adopted Residence Directive is implemented, European citizens will finally be able to settle freely in each others' states without the restrictive obligation to obtain a residence permit. Furthermore, their temporary access to the full scope of welfare has been widened and after five years of residence European citizens will be entitled to full social protection in any Member State of the Union. Against the historical background, where welfare constituted the social contract between the (nation) state and its citizens, the progressive extension of intra-European welfare is an extraordinary example of how the bits and pieces of integration redefine competencies and intervene in virtually all areas of national law and policy.

Whereas de-nationalization of welfare in the EU has largely been achieved, de-territorialization has to date remained controversial. The legal–political dispute on the Community principle of exportability versus national principles of territoriality highlights litigation as a central part of decision-making as well as highlighting the ability of politics to react against such judicial decision-making. It thus exemplifies what may be the scope and limits of integration through law. In the case of special non-contributory benefits, politics managed to overturn law and overcame the institutional barrier of unanimity. The Court subsequently reacted in a receptive way, approving the special rule adopted by the Council. On the face of it, this collective restraint supports an argument of the priority of political power in the relation between law and politics, as for example advanced by Garret and others.[88] However, the very recent litigation as well as the recent legislative reform suggest that territorial principles as effective means to demarcate welfare are subject to further challenge by Community law. When speculating about the future course of welfare integration in the EU, the ability of politicians to restrain the Court must be said to have been reduced significantly with enlargement. In an enlarged Union, it only takes one Member State out of twenty-five to agree with the interpretations of the Court and politics will not be in a collective position to act. The autonomy and authoritative position of the Court has been extended as a consequence of enlargement. The practical impact on the European dimension of welfare remains to be seen.

[88] G. Garrett, D. Keleman, and H. Schultz, 'The European Court of Justice, National Governments, and Legal Integration in the European Union', 52 *International Organization*, 1988, 147–76.

5

Health Law and Policy: The Impact of the EU

VASSILIS HATZOPOULOS

INTRODUCTION

The place of healthcare in European law is increasingly unclear. Already before the creation of the European Community in 1957, each Member State had established a singular model for financing and delivering healthcare services to its population. These models eventually led to a diversity of systems all having in common universal coverage, a feature which sharply distinguishes them from the American and Asian models. Today, after (a) the Treaty of Maastricht, which, for the first time, included a Title on Public Health and (b) the Treaty of Amsterdam, which further enhanced Community action in this field, the core competence for the organization of healthcare still lies with the Member States. This position has been formally confirmed by the European Union Charter of Fundamental Rights, now forming part of the EU Constitutional Treaty, which establishes a right to medical care 'under the conditions established by national laws and practices'.

However, healthcare does not only involve the distribution of funds and the building of hospitals. It also involves people, whether as staff or patients, both of whom are increasingly mobile, as well as goods, such as pharmaceutical goods and technology, which have always been traded internationally. Most importantly, it involves the provision of services the nature of which is evolving under the pressure both of scientific and technological advance and of structural developments which blur the border between the public and the private sector.

Therefore, if the design of Member States' healthcare systems is a matter of national competence, the everyday operation of such systems may be subject to the Treaty rules on the Internal Market and on competition. This is clearly recognized in an important series of judgments given by the European Court of Justice (ECJ) in the last five years, culminating in the *Vanbraekel, Smits and Peerbooms*, and *Müller-Fauré* judgments.[1] After these 'foundation' cases, others have followed which have further clarified the interplay of the EU rules with national healthcare systems.[2]

As illustrated by these cases, the fact that the design and implementation of healthcare systems are (still) a matter for (divergent) regulation by Member States (Section 1), may lead to strain and legal uncertainty when combined with the application of EC rules on the Internal Market on the one hand (Section 2) and on competition, state aids, and public procurement, on the other (Section 3).

1. ELEMENTS OF NATIONAL AND COMMUNITY HEALTHCARE LAW

A. General Facts about Healthcare

Healthcare is only a single, limited, aspect of *health policy*, which, in turn, is only one aspect of *social policy* (See Figure One).

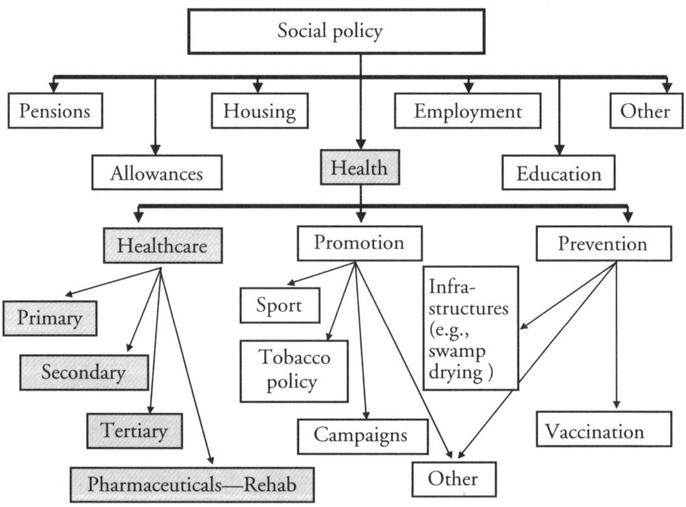

Figure One

[1] On the two former cases and on the general problems linked to the application of internal market and competition rules see among others, Hatzopoulos, '*Killing* National Health and Insurance Systems but *Healing* Patients? The European Market for Health Care Services after the Judgments of the ECJ in *Vanbraekel* and *Peerbooms*', 39 *CMLRev.* (2002) 683 and the select bibliography quoted therein.

[2] This chapter was written just after the *Müller-Fauré* judgment (Autumn 2003) but was last updated in December 2004; the cases of this intermediate period have been integrated into the analysis, but have not been fully exploited.

Social policy covers various areas, such as:

- pensions: for the elderly, incapacitated, widowed, etc.
- aid for the economically disadvantaged: unemployed, young, single parents, etc.
- housing: where/how to develop, to the expense/benefit of whom, etc.
- employment: what jobs, for whom, what level of protection/flexibility, how to deal with the unemployed
- education: primary/secondary/tertiary, geographic coverage, general orientation, links with work, etc.
- health: see below
- other: policies in favour of specific categories of people, e.g. gypsies, those of restricted mobility, the blind, etc.

Health policy, in turn, covers three main fields:[3]

- Prevention: construction of adequate infrastructures (i.e. swamp drying to prevent malaria, etc.), preventive vaccination, communication of preventive methods to the public, etc.
- Promotion: sports' policy, tobacco policy, public awareness campaigns, etc.
- Healthcare: organization of health services, according to various specializations and geographic coverage. For the purposes of this chapter, healthcare also covers the provision of pharmaceuticals and the organization of rehabilitation services.[4]

Despite the fact that health policy is, indeed, one limited aspect of social policy, it accounts for an average of between 4.3% and 10% of GDP in most Western countries.[5]

Healthcare is traditionally organized on a three-tier basis and is divided into the primary, secondary, and tertiary. These three levels of healthcare differ in at least three ways: (a) geographical coverage, (b) population coverage, and (c) the degree of specialization/type of service provided.

Primary healthcare is organized at the level of the local community and is intended to cover not more than 50,000 people. It is administered through general practitioners, ambulant doctors, family doctors, and other non-specialized personnel.

Secondary healthcare is organized at the municipality (or equivalent) level and is intended to cover a population of 50,000 to 500,000. It is administered through small/medium-size general hospitals and through specialized practitioners.

Tertiary healthcare is organized at the department, regional, or national level and is intended to cover populations of at least 500,000. It is administered through large general hospitals, medium-size specialized hospitals, and university clinics or hospitals.

[3] Health was defined by the WHO Founding Convention, in 1948, as 'a state of complete physical, mental and social well being and not merely an absence of disease'.

[4] It is also possible to view these two categories separately as the fourth and fifth components of health policy.

[5] See Palm, 'Voluntary Health Insurance and EU Insurance Directives: Between Solidarity and the Market', in M. McKee *et al.* (eds.), *The Impact of EU Law on Health Care Systems* (2002) 195 at 202.

Primary healthcare is supposed to be the first contact-point of patients with the healthcare system, while secondary and tertiary healthcare should only be made available to patients following a system of devolution: the general practitioner or other primary healthcare contact should direct the patient to the competent secondary or tertiary healthcare specialized person, hospital, or clinic.

It is clear from the above that each one of the three levels of healthcare is aimed at servicing the distinct needs of the population and requires different organizational skills and priorities. Nevertheless, the healthcare system as a whole—and, to the relevant degree, each one of its three tiers—should fulfil some minimal requirements of coverage and accessibility, as guaranteed in general terms by many national Constitutions and international Charters/Conventions on human rights.[6] The three main requirements that any healthcare system should satisfy are:

(1) full territorial coverage;
(2) full personal coverage; and
(3) equal terms of access for all.

The fulfilment of these objectives, in turn, requires some detailed planning concerning:

- the availability of the necessary infrastructure (fixed and consumable) duly scattered around the relevant territory
- the maintenance of an adequate ratio between the available facilities and health practitioners and the population to be covered
- the existence of a full scope of specializations within the relevant territory.

The above requirements may not be fully satisfied without some degree of state financing, as private initiative would tend to concentrate on urban zones and on highly profitable diseases/cures. The answers given by the state to these requirements are linked to the geographic and climatic characteristics to the particular health trends of the population, to budgetary constraints, and to the degree of disease and suffering that is socially accepted in each state. What is clear however, is that:

- some state planning of healthcare is indispensable (in order to ensure universal coverage, etc.)
- planning normally takes place at the national level (in order to cover national population, according to national needs)
- state planning may not rely exclusively upon private initiative for its implementation (i.e., some measure of state financing is required).

It becomes clear, therefore, that traditionally the setting up, administering, and financing of a healthcare system is a national/state issue and that any external interference may only be a source of perturbations thereto. (*Conclusion 1*)

[6] For a very interesting discussion about the existence of a generally recognized 'right to health' and the effects thereof, see Hervey, 'The "Right to Health" in European Union Law', in T. Hervey & J. Kenner (eds.), *Economic and Social Rights under the EU Charter of Fundamental Rights* (2003) 193.

B. Social Coverage of Healthcare

A healthcare system theoretically available to all is of no avail if it is financially inaccessible to portions of the population. This is the reason why the healthcare system is intrinsically linked to the system of social coverage applicable in every state. The extent to which any given person has access to the healthcare system of a state in the form of a social benefit is conveniently called 'social healthcare'.

The scope of social healthcare varies greatly from state to state, but it is commonly defined by the variables of three main parameters (See Figure Two):[7]

(1) The *personal scope*, i.e., who is covered? Here the starting-point is universal coverage, but it may be subject to some exceptions, essentially in favour of the wealthier segments of society (such as the self-employed and civil servants in Germany or high-earners and the self-employed in the Netherlands).[8]

(2) The *scope of treatment*, i.e., what is/is not covered? In this respect there are important differences between the various states. For example some treatments and/or surgeries that may be covered in some states might be considered illegal or simply be unknown in others; e.g., abortions, cosmetic surgeries, sex modification operations, etc. The same applies for drugs and pharmaceuticals, for which some social healthcare systems have specific black/white lists, while others cover them all without distinction.

(3) The *scope of implementation*, i.e., who may provide health services covered by the social healthcare system? In this respect the crucial distinction is between outpatient treatment, on the one hand, and hospital treatment, on the other. Both are in principle covered, but under different conditions

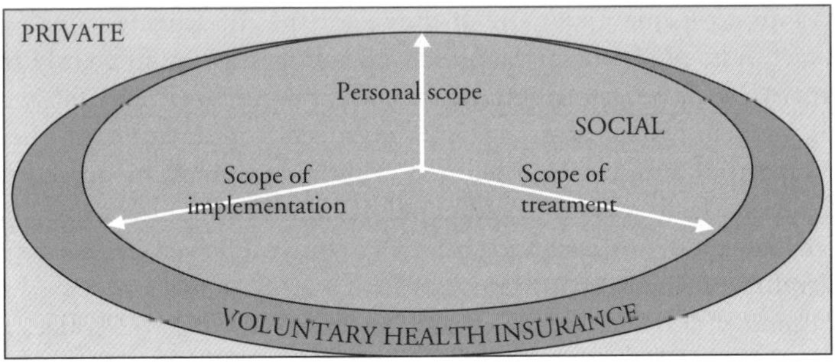

Figure Two *The scope of social insurance.*

[7] The presentation of the three variables defining the scope of social healthcare is essentially due to Nickless, 'The Internal Market and the Social Nature of Health Care', in M. McKee *et al.*, *supra* n. 5, 57, to which the reader is encouraged to refer for further details.

[8] See Palm, *supra* n. 5, at 197–200. The percentage of those not covered by the compulsory social healthcare scheme is estimated at 9% and 31% in Germany and the Netherlands, respectively.

(e.g., application of the devolution principle, according to which specialized laboratory tests or surgery are not paid for unless prescribed by a general practitioner).

For health services or patients who fall outside the scope of social healthcare (or decide to opt out), as defined by the interplay of the three variables mentioned above, coverage may be offered by voluntary or additional health insurance schemes, typically offered by mutual funds and private insurers.

Finally, for those who are not covered by the above, the private sector offers a variety of tailor-made healthcare coverage.

As far as social healthcare is involved, the European standard is universal coverage (3). Except for this essential feature, however, the Member States' systems have very little in common. Indeed, a survey of the social healthcare systems of the Member States (restricted to the fifteen pre-enlargement states) shows as many distinct systems as there are states.[9] All these systems, nevertheless, may be seen as the specific emanations of the two broad models of social healthcare: the *Bismarckian* model or *Insurance Health System* and the *Beveridgeian* model or *National Health System* (1). Moreover, all of the national systems may be classified into two broad categories depending on whether they ensure patients' treatment for free or require reimbursement (2).

I. Contribution v. tax-based systems

The first (chronologically) model of social insurance system was established in Germany during the 1870s by Chancellor Bismarck. It follows a participative pattern, inspired by the middle-age professional corporations. People are insured because of their participation in some professional group, organization, industry, or firm. Complementary schemes are put into place to cover those (essentially inactive people) who do not come under any of the sector-specific schemes. The result is a multitude of funds, public or private, each operating slightly differently from the other, financed by direct contributions of both the employer and the employee. Under this model, global planning and advanced coordination of the overall healthcare capacities are quite complicated. Hospitals, clinics, or other healthcare establishments and facilities may be either public or private (contracted by the state). The Bismarckian model of insurance health system is followed in Austria, France, Germany, and the Benelux countries.

As the Second World War started coming to a close in 1942, Beveridge, a British technocrat, submitted his report (the famous *Beveridge Report* on Social Insurance and Allied Services) to the British Ministry of Health. The starting-point of the Beveridge model is universal coverage. People are insured not because of some sort of direct or indirect participation in a profession or other category, but by virtue of their citizenship and/or physical presence on national territory (this is the reason

[9] See, for a general but comprehensive overview, Jorens, 'The Right to Healthcare across Borders', in M. McKee *et al., supra* n. 5, 83.

why it is called 'national' health system as opposed to the 'insurance' health system). There is one single fund (or, indeed, no fund at all), which is financed directly by the state through tax and other direct or indirect contributions. The existence of a single fund allows for more detailed planning and coordination of healthcare facilities (notably with a strict division of the three levels of healthcare and a consistent application of the devolution principle), which are essentially public. The Beveridge model of national health system is followed in the UK, Ireland, Denmark, Finland, Sweden, and in the 'Mediterranean' countries: Spain, Portugal, Italy, and Greece.[10]

II. Refund v. benefits-in-kind systems

From the point of view of benefits accruing to patients, European social healthcare systems may be classified into two broad categories.

(1) The refund system: it allows patients to receive treatment by any practitioner/institution of their choice and then offers reimbursement (complete or partial) of the expenses incurred. In this system, the patient has a wide choice since he/she may opt for any practitioner and/or hospital, irrespective of its public or private nature and of the prices and techniques practised.

(2) The benefits-in-kind system: patients are directed to specific practitioners or hospitals/clinics—either public or private but contracted into the social healthcare system—where they are treated 'for free'. Where treatment is offered by public undertakings, the expenses are directly covered by the state budget. Contracted private undertakings, on the other hand, usually receive a flat annual fee (calculated *inter alia* on the number of people they are intended to cover) and a fee per capita of patient treated, plus actual expenses incurred. In this system the choice of patients is more restricted, especially where their only choice is public doctors and hospitals. Healthcare under this system is seen more as a public good to which access should be ensured in all circumstances and less as a commodity or good for which the consumer/patient may have a say.

The dichotomy between the reimbursement and the benefits-in-kind system does not coincide with the distinction between the Bismarck and the Beveridge models. While all of the countries following the latter model operate a system of benefits-in-kind, the same is true for some of the countries following the Bismarck model as well, such as Austria, Germany, and the Netherlands, where contracted private hospitals and practitioners treat patients without them incurring out-of-pocket expenses. The refund system is followed in France, Belgium, and Luxembourg.

[10] Whether there is, indeed, such a thing as a 'Mediterranean' model for the organization of social welfare is a highly debated issue, see recently G. Katrougalos and G. Lazaridis, *Southern European Welfare States, Problems, Challenges and Prospects* (2003). Before that see Ferrera, 'The Southern Model of Welfare in Social Europe', 6 *JESP* (1996) 17 and Mossialos, 'Citizens' Views on Health Care Systems in the 15 Member States of the EU', 6 *Health Economics* (1997) 109.

III. Convergence point: the principle of solidarity

The development of all the above systems, and of numerous variations thereof, should not mask the existence of a core principle governing social healthcare which sharply distinguishes Europe from the other continents: universal coverage. Universal coverage has served more as a guiding principle rather than a tangible reality. In many 'advanced' countries (such as in France) it has only been achieved fairly recently,[11] while in the Mediterranean countries it is not clear whether it has been fully achieved at all[12] (the continuing migration from third countries, which is essentially illegal, also adds a new dimension to the issue of universal coverage).

Universal coverage itself is a manifestation of the principle of solidarity, one of the great values inherited by the French Revolution. In the organization of social healthcare in Europe, the principle of solidarity is pervasive. It may be located on, at least, three levels:[13]

(1) In terms of the *integration into the system*, three main characteristics talk of solidarity:
- universality, i.e., the inclusion of all people into the system
- mandatory affiliation, i.e., the fact that opting out is, in principle, prohibited (subject to specific exceptions)[14]
- mandatory acceptance, i.e., the fact that the fund(s) may not exclude some categories of persons or of risk.

(2) In terms of the *funding of the system*, another three characteristics are inspired by solidarity:
- contributions are income-related, so that the wealthy contribute more
- moreover, contributions are independent of individual risk factors, such as age, sex, health history, habits, occupation, etc.
- finally, some permanently loss-making schemes (especially those covering high-risk or low-income activities) are maintained through cross-subsidization by others.

(3) In terms of *benefits* ensured by the system, the principle of solidarity is embodied in, at least, two manifestations:
- all patients receive equal treatment irrespective of their personal, financial, professional etc, situation (and irrespective of how much they have contributed into the system)
- coverage is progressive according to the medical needs of each patient.

[11] For instance, in France Art. 3 of Act 99-641 of 27 July 1999, JORF 28 July 1999, institutes the 'Couverture Maladie Universelle' with the same characteristics, while in Belgium the Royal Decree extending statutory health insurance to all people legally residing in the country and not entitled to coverage under any other Belgian or foreign system, was adopted on 25 April 1998, *Moniteur Belge*, 19 June 1997 (in effect since 1 January 1998); in both schemes contributions are due only from people exceeding a certain level of income.

[12] See *supra* n. 10.

[13] For these three levels of analysis of the principle of solidarity see Palm, *supra* n. 5, at 196–197.

[14] See *supra* n. 8.

The fact that solidarity is the core concept underlying any system of social healthcare stresses the *national character* of social healthcare: it is difficult to expect people from one state to feel solidarity (and to give away part of their income) for people from other states with whom they share very little. (*Conclusion 2*)

C. Healthcare and EU Law

One could ask whether healthcare *is* an issue for EC law at all or whether it *should* be. In order to answer these questions reference should be made to the relevant legal basis in primary and secondary legislation in this field.[15]

I. Primary legislation

In the EC Treaty there has been some important evolution concerning the inclusion of healthcare within the competences of the Community.

The founding Treaties made no direct reference whatsoever to health issues. The only related provision which could be found in the Rome Treaties was Article 2 EC where the aim of 'raising the standard of living' is mentioned as one of the objectives of the EC. The generality of this aim and its unclear legal value (due to the fact that it is part of the 'preamble' of the EC Treaty) has not precluded the Community institutions from using it in conjunction with Article 308 EC (then Article 235), in order to adopt some common programmes in the field of health. Hence the adoption, as far back as 1989, of the first 'Europe against Cancer' programme and, in 1991, of the 'Europe against AIDS' programme.[16]

The 1992 Maastricht Treaty broke new waters in the field of health. Among the activities to be pursued by the EC (Article 3.p EC) was the 'contribution to the attainment of a high level of health protection'. More importantly, the Maastricht Treaty introduced, for the first time, Title X on Health Policy, consisting of a single Article (Article 129). This provision recognized some Community competence to complement and coordinate national policies in the field of health. However, the wording of Article 129 was ambiguous and its precise content difficult to decipher.[17] Therefore, an effort was made to clarify the scope of application of Article 129 by the Council Resolution on Future Action in the Field of Public Health.[18] This Resolution established four criteria which should be satisfied in order for Community action to be justified in the field of public health:

(1) A significant health problem should exist for which preventative actions are necessary.

[15] In relation to the issue of the legal basis for health issues see the excellent article by Hervey, 'The Legal Basis of EC Public Health Policy', in M. McKee *et al.*, *supra* n. 5, 23.

[16] It is worth noting that, despite the fact that in the preamble of Decision 88/351 establishing the former programme the legal basis referred to is 'the Treaty establishing the EEC', no state or EC institution has sought to annul it. See in this respect Hervey, *ibid.*, at 25.

[17] See on this issue E. Mossialos and M. McKee, *EU Law and the Social Character of Health Care* (2002) at 56–68.

[18] Resolution of the Council of 13 December 1993, OJ 1994 C 15/1.

(2) Community actions in the field of health should also supplement or promote other Community policies.
(3) They should also be consistent with actions of other international organizations.
(4) Finally, they should respect the principle of subsidiarity.

In the 1997 Treaty of Amsterdam an effort was made to clarify and enhance the Community competences in the field of health. Hence, Title XIII as it now stands has five paragraphs:

(1) Article 152§1 includes two principles: The first paragraph contains a 'strong mainstreaming' clause inspired by the precautionary principle,[19] according to which 'a high level of human health protection shall be ensured in the definition and implementation of all Community policies and activities'.[20] The second and third paragraphs recognize some Community competences, of strictly complementary nature, in the field of *prevention* and *promotion* of health—*not healthcare*.[21]
(2) Article 152§2 entitles the Commission to encourage and support the cooperation between Member States in the field of public health.
(3) Article 152§3 states that both the Community and Member States should foster cooperation with third countries and international organizations in the field of public health.
(4) Article 152§4 states that there are two instruments for Community action: 'measures' adopted according to the co-decision procedure,[22] and Council Recommendations adopted by a qualified majority upon proposal by the Commission.
(5) Finally, Article 152§5 constitutes a specific application of the principle of subsidiarity as it clearly states that Community action 'shall fully respect the responsibilities of the Member States for the organisation and delivery of health services and medical care'.[23]

The Treaty of Nice did not touch upon the Community competences in the field of health.

[19] See in general for this principle, De Sadeleer, 'Le Statut juridique du principe de précaution en droit communautaire: du slogan à la règle', *CDE* (2001) 91, where, in footnote 13 extensive bibliographic references are to be found, and Salomon, 'A European Perspective on the Precautionary Principle, Food Safety and the Free Trade Imperative of the WTO', 27 *ELRev.* (2002) 138.

[20] The very same clause has been introduced in the EU Charter of Fundamental Rights, now Article II-35, last para. of the draft EU Constitution.

[21] It should be remembered that prevention, promotion, and healthcare are the three distinct aspects of health policy; see 1.A and Figure One.

[22] It is not clear, however, what kind of measures these may be.

[23] It should be noted that Article 137 EC, on social policy, is also a quite limited 'legal basis', since it only allows for action which supports or completes that of Member States, specifically as regards the 'improvement of the working environment to protect workers'.

The EU Constitutional Treaty contains rules on health in all three parts of its substantive provisions. In Part I of the Treaty where competences are allocated between the EU and Member States, public health appears to be both a shared competence (Article I-14) to the extent provided for in Part III of the Constitutional Treaty and an area for support/complementary competence (Article I-17) for the remaining issues. In Article III-278, it is foreseen that the common action should remain complementary to that of Member States and focus more on prevention and promotion rather than healthcare itself. However, paragraph 4 of the aforementioned Article completely innovates by introducing an important derogation: EU laws and framework laws, which may go as far as harmonization, may be adopted in respect to (a) human organs and substances, (b) veterinary and phytosanitary issues, (c) medicaments and medical devices, and (d) transfrontier health menaces. According to paragraph 5 of the same Treaty provision, EU laws and framework laws, which do not harmonize but 'encourage' common action, may also be adopted in the field of prevention of cross-border health scourges and in the development of tobacco and alcohol policies.[24] Further, Article II-94 recognizes as a fundamental right the entitlement to social protection for illness. More importantly, Article II-95 sets universal coverage, both to prevention and to healthcare, as a constitutional standard; at the same time it states that this is to be achieved 'under the conditions established by national laws and practices'.

From the above presentation of the evolution of the legal basis for community action in the field of healthcare, five conclusions may be drawn (*Conclusion 3*):

(1) Community action in the field of health, even after the entry into force of the EU Constitutional Treaty, will mainly be complementary and supportive to action by Member States.
(2) Community action is admitted in the field of *promotion* and *prevention*, but barely tolerated in the field of *healthcare*.
(3) Community measures in the field of health may only exceptionally proceed to harmonization.
(4) Finally, action by the Community should have some added value in relation to action pursued at national level.
(5) Community action should respect the principle of subsidiarity.

Concerning the application of the principle of subsidiarity in the field of health, several arguments point against action at the Community level:[25]

- Member States have acquired the experience of setting up and implementing national policies in the field of health over the years; why change now?

[24] It is interesting to note that between the text submitted by the Convention and the one finally adopted by the Rome European Council, there has been an important increase of the EU's competences in the field of health, both in Part I and in Part III of the Treaty.

[25] On this issue see more in detail Nickless, *supra* n. 7.

- financing is mainly secured through national resources (tax, contributions, etc.), over which the EU has no direct influence
- health needs vary and Member States are in a better position to respond to the pattern of disease in their territory
- the related ethical framework is different in the various Member States and treatment that is considered common in some is not accepted—or may even be illegal—in others (abortion, organ donation, sex transformation, etc.).

Of course, these arguments may be offset, to some extent, by the need to secure economies of scale and greater specialization in the field of health, especially in relation to healthcare. Moreover, the application of common market rules may lead to a strong community grip on health issues.[26] Finally, the impact of other Treaty provisions on heath (such as the ones on the Common Agricultural Policy (Article 37 EC), on social policy (Article 137§1.a), and on the environment (Articles 174 *et seq.*)) should not be underestimated.

II. Secondary legislation

Despite the absence in the EC Treaty of some specific legal basis allowing for the adoption of binding measures in the field of health, there is secondary legislation, dating as far back as the early 1960s, directly or indirectly touching on the way national healthcare systems are organized. These texts, mainly directives and Regulations, may be classified into three broad categories.

Measures adopted in view of the achievement of the free movement of workers, free provision of services, and the freedom of establishment The legal basis of these measures is to be found in Title III of the Treaty (Articles 39 *et seq.*), occasionally strengthened by Article 308 (ex 235). They have been provided for by the General Programmes[27] and may be classified into two broad categories: on the one hand, instruments that aim to secure that workers moving within the Community continue to receive social and healthcare benefits and, on the other hand, instruments that organize the equivalence and mutual recognition of diplomas and other qualifications for the cross-border provision of healthcare services.

In the *first sub-category* the main text is Regulation 1408/71 as it now stands.[28] This Regulation corresponds to an early, limited attempt by the Community

[26] On this see Section 2 below.

[27] Programmes of 18 December 1961, OJ 1962 L 62/32 and 62/36.

[28] Council Regulation (EEC) 1408/71 of 14 June 1971 on the application of social security schemes to employed persons, to self-employed persons and to members of their families moving within the Community, OJ 1971 L 149/2. This Regulation has been modified at least thirty times, the last important modification extending its personal scope to cover nationals of non Member States legally residing within the EU; see Council Regulation (EC) 859/2003 of 14 May 2003, OJ 2003 L 124/1. It has recently been codified and repealed by Regulation (EC) 883/2004 of 29 April 2004, OJ 2004 L 166/1. Since all the legislative and judicial developments of the present contribution relate to Regulation 1408/71, references will be made to this legislative instrument.

Institutions to comply with their obligations under Article 42 (ex 51) of the Treaty. It falls short of achieving any substantial degree of harmonization and limits its ambit to the coordination of basic national rules on the field of social and welfare benefits.[29] The Regulation follows the principle, confirmed time and again by the ECJ,[30] that social security remains a domain reserved to Member States' competence. It therefore does not touch upon the core of the national rules, but only establishes some degree of coordination whereby fundamentally different systems may work together in order to secure minimal social and healthcare benefits.[31]

The provisions of the Regulation which are more specifically concerned with healthcare services are Articles 22 and 36. The basic mechanism established by the said provisions is that any person wishing to receive healthcare services in another Member State has to obtain an authorization by the competent fund in his home state, except for in the case of emergencies; once this authorization is given, the beneficiary is entitled to benefits in kind and to cash benefits.[32]

The *second sub-category* of these measures is aimed at the free movement of health professionals and tends to harmonize the access to and exercise of six main professions related to the provision of health services. The method used is that of substantial harmonization,[33] based on pairs of directives, whereby the first directive harmonizes the content, duration, etc. of studies while the second establishes the equivalence between diplomas or qualifications thus obtained. The harmonized professions include: general practitioners and doctors,[34] nurses,[35] dentists,[36]

[29] On the qualification of this regulation as an instrument of coordination rather than as a means of harmonization see the first recitals of the Regulation.

[30] Clearly in Joined Cases C-159 and 160/91, *Poucet and Pistre* [1993] ECR I-637, and constantly thereafter.

[31] See on this issue, the ECJ judgment in Case 100/78, *Rossi* [1979] ECR 831, para. 13, where the Court expressly acknowledges that 'the regulations did not set up a common scheme of social security, but allowed different schemes to exist, creating different claims on different institutions'.

[32] For more extensive developments on the scope and application of these provisions, see Section 2 below.

[33] Although described as 'partial' or 'minimal' within the texts of the directives, subsequent experience showed that the degree of harmonization achieved in these directives is the highest ever achieved on the recognition of professional qualifications. It is significant to note that only the health professions have been regulated by pairs of directives, while other profession-specific harmonization (i.e., for lawyers and architects) has been restricted to single directives. See for the various techniques and the different degrees of harmonization, V. Hatzopoulos, *Le Principe communautaire d'équivalence et de reconnaissance mutuelle dans la libre prestation de services* (1999) at 327 *et seq.*

[34] Initially regulated by Directives 75/362/EEC, OJ 1975 L 167/1 and 75/363/EEC, OJ 1975 L 167/14. These Directives have been modified by Directive 86/457/EEC, OJ 1986 L 267/26. The two Directives and their modifications have been consolidated (and thus replaced) by Directive 93/16/EC, OJ 1993 L 165/1, which, in its turn, has been modified by Directive 97/50/EC, OJ 1997 L 291/35 and Directive 98/63/EC, OJ 1998 L 119/15.

[35] Directives 77/452/EEC and 77/453/EEC, OJ 1977 L 176/1 and 176/8, respectively.

[36] Directives 78/686/EEC and 78/687/EEC, OJ 1978 L 233/1 and 233/10, respectively.

practitioners of veterinary medicine,[37] midwives,[38] and pharmacists.[39] Professionals who have obtained their qualifications in accordance with the harmonization directives [40] may freely exercise their profession in any Member State, paying due respect to the local professional rules.[41] The other peripheral professions fall under the catch-all umbrella of the 'general systems' for the recognition of professional qualifications[42] or the case law of the Court on professional recognition.[43]

Measures aimed at ensuring the free movement of goods, especially drugs, medical devices, etc.[44] These include Community measures concerning general safety rules, labelling, etc.[45]

Measures ensuing from other policy fields of the EU Measures from other policy fields may be directly related to health. It should be remembered, in this respect, that the precautionary principle, which aims specifically at the protection of health, was recognized as having the status of a general principle of EC law in a series of cases related to the application of the CAP;[46] it also applies to environment policy. Moreover, measures adopted for the implementation of Title IV of the EC Treaty (immigration policy, etc.) or those of third-pillar policies may also relate to health protection.[47]

[37] Directives 78/1026/EEC and 78/1027/EEC, OJ 1978 L 362/1 and 362/7, respectively.

[38] Directives 80/154/EEC and 80/155/EEC, OJ 1980 L 33/1 and 33/8, respectively.

[39] Directives 85/432/EEC and 85/433/EEC, OJ 1985 L 253/34 and 253/37, respectively.

[40] It is interesting to note that out of a total of eight professions whose exercise is specifically harmonized, six concern healthcare services; the other two concern lawyers and architects.

[41] See in this respect, Berman, 'Mobility of Health Professionals', paper delivered in the high-level two-day conference organized by the Belgian Presidency of the EU on *European Integration and National Health Care Systems: A Challenge for Social Policy*, Gent, 7–8 December 2001.

[42] Mainly Council Directive 89/48 of 21 December 1988 (First General System), OJ 1989 L 19/16, as completed by the Council Directive 92/51/EC of 18 June 1992 (Second General System), OJ 1992 L 209/51. For the modification and unification in one single text of the 'general systems', see the proposed directive by the Commission, OJ 2002 C 181/183.

[43] See the leading case on this matter Case C-340/89, *Vlassopoulou* [1991] ECR I–2357, according to which qualifications and experience of the interested person shall be taken into due consideration by the authorities of the host Member State. On the creation and the application of the principle of equivalence and mutual recognition by the judge, see Hatzopoulos, *supra* n. 33, at 114. See recently, for the application of these general principles to the employment conditions of a Portuguese national in a public hospital in France, Case C-285/01, *Burbaud* [2003] ECR I-8219.

[44] For which see Hancher, 'The Pharmaceuticals Market: Competition and Free Movement Actively Seeking Compromises' and Altenstetter, 'Regulation of Medical Devices in the EU', in M. McKee *et al.*, *supra* n. 5, 235 and 277, respectively.

[45] For a brief overview of these measures, in relation to healthcare, see Altenstetter, *ibid.*

[46] See for the Court Case C-180/96R, *UK v. Commission, ESB* [1996] ECR I-3903 (Order of the President) upheld in C-180/96 [1998] ECR I-2265 and for the CFI Case T-76/98, *National Farmers' Union v. Commission* [1996] ECR II-815 (Order of the President) upheld on appeal in Case C-157/96, *National Farmers' Union v. Commission* [1998] ECR I-2211.

[47] See, in this respect, the extension of the personal scope of Regulation 1408/71 to cover third-country nationals by Council Regulation (EC) 859/2003, *supra* n. 28.

It follows from the above that, notwithstanding the fact that the Community lacks the competence to intervene directly in the field of healthcare services, there are a number of specific measures which either coordinate or harmonize issues directly linked to the administration of such services. However, there is no way in which these texts may account for the actual impact of EC law on national healthcare systems. The decisive factor in this direction has been the direct application by the ECJ of the general Treaty rules on the internal market to the provision of healthcare services.

2. INTERNAL MARKET RULES AND HEALTHCARE

The ECJ has extended the scope of application of the Treaty rules on services (and establishment) so as to cover the provision of healthcare services (A) while allowing for important exceptions (B). This, in turn, makes it possible for people affiliated to the social healthcare system of a Member State to receive some healthcare services in any other EU Member State, by bypassing the prior authorization procedure established by Regulation 1408/71 (C). The increased mobility of patients thus recognized is likely to affect all existing national healthcare systems, presumably bringing benefits-in-kind systems closer to refund systems (D).

From a terminological point of view it is worth noting that in Regulation 1408/71 the terms 'state of residence' and 'state of stay' are used instead of the terms more commonly used in the internal market jargon: 'home state' and 'host state', respectively. The 'state of residence' or 'home state' is the state where the patient is insured and where the 'competent institution' is seated, while the 'state of stay' or 'host state' is the state in which the patient receives treatment. These terms will be used interchangeably.

A. Extending the Scope of Application of the Treaty Rules

As stated above,[48] Regulation 1408/71 only performs some limited coordination between Member States' social security and healthcare systems. Further harmonization never ensued, however, as some Member States opposed it. Against this background the Court, in several instances, interpreted the Regulation in an extensive manner so as to cover lacunae not directly covered under the provisions of the Regulation. The activist approach of the Court has led the Council to amend the Regulation on several occasions, thus reversing and restricting previous judicial interpretations. This, in turn, led the Court, in its more recent case law, to pay lip-service to the provisions of Regulation 1408/71 and base its judgments directly on the Treaty provisions on free movement, which are beyond the reach of the legislator.

[48] See Section 1.C.II.

One of the very first occasions on which the Court proceeded on a remarkably extensive interpretation of the provisions of Regulation 1408/71 concerning health was in the *Pierik* cases.[49] These cases concerned a pensioner entitled to benefits in accordance with Dutch legislation, who asked for reimbursement of costs incurred in the course of hydrotherapy dispensed in Germany. This case could not be brought within the terms of Article 31 of Regulation 1408/71, which applies specifically to pensioners who face an urgent need for treatment while staying in another Member State, as Mr. Pierik was not *staying* in Germany when hydrotherapy became necessary, but *moved there* for the specific purpose of receiving it. Therefore, one of the questions that the Court had to answer was whether a pensioner could qualify as a 'worker', in the sense of Article 22(1)c of Regulation 1408/71, and ask for an authorization to move to another Member State. The Court found that 'even if they do not pursue a professional or trade activity, pensioners entitled to draw pensions under the legislation of one or more Member States come within the provisions of the Regulation concerning "workers" by virtue of their insurance under a social security scheme, unless they are subject to special provisions laid down regarding them'.[50] Therefore, the rule was set that while pensioners do qualify under the general system of Regulation 1408/71 (i.e., Article 22) to move within the Common Market in order to receive healthcare services, under the appropriate factual circumstances the more specific rules of the Regulation may apply to them.

A further issue addressed by the Court in the *Pierik* cases was whether the competent (home) institution could refuse the Article 22(1)c authorization for treatment abroad when such treatment was excluded from the benefits provided or reimbursed within the home state. The Court concluded that 'when the competent institution [. . .] acknowledges that the treatment in question constitutes an effective treatment of the sickness or disease from which the person concerned suffers, its power of decision is thus bound by the obligation clearly and unequivocally imposed upon it by the second subparagraph of Article 22(2) of the Regulation not to refuse in that case the authorization required under Article 22(1)c.'[51]

However, the above rulings, which were general in scope, were subsequently disavowed by the Council which, two years later, amended twice the relevant provisions of Regulation 1408/71. Member States sought to restrict both the personal and the material scope of the above provisions. Therefore, Regulation 1390/81[52] replaced the term 'worker' with the more precise terms 'employed or self-employed

[49] Case 117/77, *Pierik I* [1978] ECR 825 and, on the same facts, Case 182/78, *Pierik II* [1979] ECR 1977.

[50] *Pierik II*, para. 4. See also for the idea that the definition of 'worker' for the purpose of applying Regulation 1408/71 is wider than for that of applying other community legislation (such as, e.g., Regulation 1612/68) more recently Case C-85/96, *Martínez Sala* [1998] ECR I-2691.

[51] *Pierik II*, para. 11.

[52] Council Regulation 1390/81 of 12 May 1981, OJ 1981 L 143/32.

person'.[53] Some months later, Regulation 2793/81[54] made the conditions under which the competent institutions may not refuse patients the authorization to go to other Member States much stricter and almost exceptional. Notably, Article 22(2) now makes the authorization compulsory only in regards to treatments that *are* covered by the competent institution, provided that they cannot be offered in the home state within reasonable time.[55]

Subsequently, the Court followed a different track and oriented itself directly to the interpretation of the relevant Treaty provisions. The relevant case law may be categorized into *five (plus one) successive stages.*[56]

I. Healthcare services are 'services' within the meaning of the Treaty

It was acknowledged for the first time by the ECJ in the *Luisi and Carbone* case[57] that health services are deemed to fall within the ambit of the economic 'fundamental freedoms' of the EC. In this early case[58] the Court recognized, for the first time, not only that cross-border provision of health services is governed by Articles 49 (then 59) *et seq.*, but also that recipients of such services have the same rights as providers thereof. This was a breakthrough case and did not go into too many details. Thereafter, the finding that health services do fall within the ambit of Article 49 EC was reiterated in the *Grogan* case.[59] However, this case did not provide any further clarification on the issue since the relevant Treaty provision was found inapplicable on the facts before the Court due to the lack of an economic link between the students invoking Article 49 EC and the hospitals offering the contested health services.

[53] This, however, has not prevented the Court from using the broad interpretation of the term 'worker' followed in *Pierik* in more recent cases, which occurred under the new text of the Regulation; see recently Case C-326/00, *Ioannidis v. IKA* [2003] ECR I-1703, and for a thorough presentation of this case the comment by Hatzopoulos in 40 *CMLRev.* (2003) 1251.

[54] Council Regulation 2793/81 of 17 September 1981, OJ 1981 L 275/1.

[55] What constitutes reasonable time has been discussed by the Court in its recent judgment C-385/99, *Müller-Fauré* [2003] ECR I- 4509 for which see Section 2.A.I.iv below.

[56] The term 'generations', although more evocative, is consciously avoided, since there is linear continuity—and no 'gap' whatsoever—between the four stages described below. Also some of the stages were reached at a time when the previous stage had not yet attained maturity and the overall time of development of the relevant case law (which is less than twenty years) makes the use of the term 'generation' inappropriate.

[57] Joined Cases 286/82 and 26/83, *Luisi and Carbone* [1984] ECR 377, para. 16.

[58] This is an 'early' case in the field of services which, contrary to the case law of the Court in the field of goods, only developed considerably during the last fifteen years, starting with the 'tourist guide cases', Cases C-154/89, C-180/89, and C-189/89, respectively *Commission v. France, Italy, and Greece* [1991] ECR I-659 *et seq.*, the 'TV cases', Cases C-260/89, *ERT* [1991] ECR I-2925, C-288/89, *Gouda* [1991] ECR I-4007, and C-353/89, *Commission v. The Netherlands, Mediawet* [1991] ECR I-4069 and, most importantly, Case C-76/90, Säger [1991] ECR I-4221. For a comprehensive overview of this agitated field of the case law of the ECJ, see Hatzopoulos, 'Recent Developments of the Case Law of the ECJ in the Field of Services', in 37 *CMLRev.* (2000) 43.

[59] Case C-159/90, *Society for the Protection of Unborn Children Ireland* [1991] ECR I-4685, para. 18.

II. Applicability even when treatment is provided in the framework of a social security scheme

The *Kohll* case[60] followed, sending shivers through all social security and healthcare funds.[61] Mr. Kohll, a national of Luxembourg, was seeking reimbursement for a dental treatment received (by his daughter) in Germany without prior authorization from his home institution. Here the Court made it clear that Articles 49 *et seq.* do apply to health services even when they are provided in the context of a social security scheme. Or, as the Court put it: 'the special nature of certain services does not remove them from the ambit of the fundamental principle of freedom of movement'.[62] Then, the Court circumvented Regulation 1408/71 by stating that 'article 22 of Regulation No 1408/71 [. . .] is not intended to regulate and hence does not in any way prevent the reimbursement by Member States, at the tariffs in force in the competent state, of costs incurred in connection with treatment provided in another Member State, even without prior authorization' and went on to examine 'the compatibility of national rules such as those at issue in the main proceedings with the Treaty provisions on freedom to provide services'.[63] The Court concluded that the requirement of prior authorization did, indeed, constitute a violation of Article 49 (then 59) of the Treaty. Such a violation could be justified by the public health exception contained in Article 46 (then 56) of the Treaty to the extent that the national measure served 'the objective of maintaining a balanced medical and hospital service open to all'.[64] The national measure could also be upheld if it were deemed necessary to ensure the financial balance of the social security scheme, an overriding reason in the general interest.[65] However, none of the above justifications was valid in the case under scrutiny since refund at the tariffs of the home state (Luxembourg) could in no way endanger the financial balance of the affected scheme or the quality of medical service in this same state.[66]

Kohll was delivered the same day and based on the same opinion by Advocate General Tesauro as the judgment in *Decker*.[67] In *Decker* the Court affirmed that national security and healthcare schemes should also respect Article 28 (ex 30) EC on free movement of goods. This case came as a confirmation and extension of the rule already set in the *Duphar* case.[68] Therefore, it would seem that *Kohll* is the

60 Case C-158/96, *Kohll* [1998] ECR I-1931.

61 For some comments on this case, see Mavoridis, in *RMUE* (1988) 145; Van Raepenbusch, *CDE* (1988) 683; and Huglo in *RTDEur* (1988) 584.

62 Para. 20 of the judgment. This passage of the judgment has been repeatedly cited by the Court in its more recent judgments, see the developments further down in this para.

63 Paras. 27 and 28 of the judgment.

64 Para. 50 of the judgment.

65 Paras. 41 and 42 of the judgment.

66 Paras. 42 and 52 of the judgment.

67 Case C-120/95, *Decker* [1998] ECR I-1831.

68 Case 238/82, *Duphar* [1984] ECR 523. This case concerned the compatibility with Art. 28 EC of lists enumerating the pharmaceuticals which qualify for reimbursement under Member States'

logical transposition, to the field of services, of the *Duphar/Decker* case law in accordance with the findings of the Court in *Luisi and Carbone* and *Grogan*.[69]

However, the judgment in *Kohll* was not easy to reconcile with the previous judgments of the Court in *Poucet and Pistre*[70] and in *Sodemare*[71] and, more importantly, with the 'trilogy' judgments rendered some months after *Kohll* by the plenary Court, in cases *Albany*, *Brentjens*, and *Drijvende*.[72] Moreover, the judgment in *Kohll* had two peculiarities which left open two crucial questions. First, it left in doubt whether it extended to treatment offered in a hospital infrastructure as this case only concerned a dentist acting alone.[73] Second, the findings of the Court in *Kohll* related to a social healthcare system based on refund, leaving it obscure whether they could also apply to benefits-in-kind systems.

III. Applicability even if the said treatment is offered within a hospital infrastructure

Then the twin judgments of 12 July 2001 in *Vanbraekel*[74] and *Peerbooms*[75] confirmed and extended the ambit of the *Kohll* judgment in a double way.

The *Vanbraekel* case concerned a Belgian national trying to obtain reimbursement from her social security fund for treatment received in a French hospital. According to Article 22(1) and (2) of the Regulation 1408/71, any person who has obtained prior authorization by his institution to receive treatment in another Member State is entitled to do so 'as though he were insured with [the competent institution of this state]'. In practice this means that whenever treatment is not provided for free (benefit-in-kind) and the patient has to undergo medical expenses, he may recover them in accordance with the tariffs applicable in the state of the treatment. However, in the case under discussion benefits provided for by the French (host) legislation were lower than those offered by the Belgian fund for the same treatment administered within Belgium. Therefore, the question arose as to whether the rule of Regulation 1408/71 entitled beneficiaries to recover the higher benefits

healthcare systems. The Court confirmed that the listing system was subject to scrutiny under the relevant provisions of the EC Treaty, but did not infringe such provisions, provided that the choice of qualifying pharmaceuticals was made in an objective way and without any discrimination concerning the origin of the products.

[69] Cases cited *supra* nn. 57 and 59.

[70] Case cited *supra* n. 30.

[71] Case C-70/95, *Sodemare* [1997] ECR I-3395. In the meantime some uncertainty had been created by the judgment of the Court in Case C-238/94, *FFSA* [1995] ECR I-4013.

[72] Case C-67/96, *Albany* [1999] ECR I-5751, Case C-155–157/97, *Brentjens* [1999] ECR I-6025, and C-219/97, *Drijvende* [1999] ECR I-6121, respectively. On these three cases, see Idot, 'Droit social et droit de la concurrence: confrontation ou cohabitation (A propos de quelques développements récents)', 9 *Europe* (1999) 4. For all these cases, concerning primarily the application of the competition rules and the concept of solidarity, see Section 3.A. below.

[73] Cf. para. 11 of AG Saggio's opinion of 18 May 2000, in Case C-368/98, *Vanbraekel* [2001] ECR I-5363.

[74] Case C-368/98, *Vanbraekel* [2001] ECR I-5363.

[75] Case C-157/99, *Smits and Peerbooms* [2001] ECR I-5473.

stipulated by the legislation of their home state or whether the refund was limited to the level stipulated for by the host state legislation.

In the *Peerbooms* case the very requirement of prior authorization, as implemented by the Dutch legislation, was challenged under the Treaty rules on services. Under the Dutch social security scheme patients are treated 'for free' by care-providers, mostly Dutch, who have made an agreement with the social security fund. Authorization to be treated by a care-provider with whom no agreement has been concluded is only given by the fund if two conditions are met: (a) the treatment for which authorization is required should be considered as '*normal* in the professional circles concerned' and (b) it should be *necessary*—both in terms of time and of quality—for the particular patient. In the light of the *Kohll* and *Decker* case law the question arose as to whether such a requirement of prior authorization was compatible with the Treaty rules on services.

In both cases the majority of the ten intervening Member States contended that healthcare services provided in the context of a benefits-in-kind social healthcare scheme do not fall within the ambit of Article 49 EC for lack of remuneration. Moreover, Advocate General Saggio clearly distinguished healthcare services offered within a hospital infrastructure from outpatient treatment and found that the former fall outside the scope of Articles 49 *et seq.* because 'on the one hand, [they] are an integral part of the public health-care system, in the sense that they are established and organised by the state, and, on the other hand, [they]are financed by public funds'.[76]

The Court, however, in two very comprehensive sentences phrased identically in both judgments dismissed all the above arguments. Recalling the *Luisi and Carbone, Grogan*, and *Kohll* case law, the Court affirmed that 'it is settled case-law that medical activities fall within the scope of Article 60 of the Treaty, *there being no need to distinguish in that regard between care provided in a hospital environment and care provided outside such an environment*'.[77] In this respect the Court reiterated the statement already made in *Kohll*[78] that 'the fact that the national rules at issue in the main proceedings are social security rules cannot exclude application of Articles 59 and 60 (now 49 and 50) of the Treaty'.[79]

Thereafter, the Court's findings followed naturally. In the *Vanbraekel* case the Court, referring itself to the judgments in *Luisi and Carbone, Bachmann*,[80] and *Kohll*, found that 'the fact that a person has a lower level of cover when he receives hospital treatment in another Member State than when he undergoes the same treatment in the Member State in which he is insured may deter, or even prevent, that person from applying to providers of medical services established in other Member States and constitutes, both for insured persons and for service providers, a barrier

[76] Opinion of AG Saggio, *supra* n. 73 para. 21.

[77] *Vanbraekel*, para. 41, *Peerbooms*, para. 53, emphasis added.

[78] *Kohll*, para. 21.

[79] *Vanbraekel*, para. 42, *Peerbooms*, para. 54.

[80] Case C-204/90, *Bachmann v. Belgium* [1992] ECR I-249.

to freedom to provide services'. Hence, 'additional reimbursement covering that difference must be granted to the insured person by the competent institution'.[81] In this way the Court further reduced the role of the prior authorization procedure: after having established, in *Kohll*, that patients may receive refunds even when they have not received prior authorization, in *Vanbraekel* the Court stated that even when prior authorization has been obtained the refund mechanism attached thereto may be replaced by more favourable refund conditions.

However, the very requirement of prior authorization has been upheld, albeit strictly circumscribed, by the Court in the *Peerbooms* case. The Court found that the national rule—and hence the Regulation—may 'deter, or even prevent, insured persons from applying to providers of medical services established in another Member State and constitute, both for insured persons and service providers, a barrier to freedom to provide services'.[82] It went on to state, however, that such a restriction may be justified by 'overriding considerations'[83] relating to the control of costs and to the maintenance of high-quality hospital treatments within a Member State and upheld the measure. Hence, the very requirement of a prior authorization stipulated for by the Regulation is qualified *prima facie* as a restriction to the fundamental Treaty freedoms. Such a restriction may only be upheld, according to the Court, by virtue of some mandatory requirement, provided it satisfies the four-tier test unequivocally stated by the Court in the *Gebhard* case.[84]

In particular, the Court held that 'authorisation to receive treatment in another Member State may be refused on that ground [of the mandatory requirement of maintaining the financial balance of the healthcare system] only if treatment which is the same or equally effective for the patient can be obtained without *undue delay* from an establishment with which the insured person's insurance fund has an agreement'.[85] Moreover, the Court held that the 'prior administrative authorisation scheme must likewise be based on a procedural system which is easily accessible and capable of ensuring that the request for authorisation will be dealt with objectively and impartially within a reasonable time, and refusals to grant authorisation must also be capable of being challenged in judicial or quasi-judicial proceedings'.[86]

[81] *Vanbraekel*, para. 51.

[82] *Peerbooms*, para. 69; in the same sense see also *Vanbraekel*, para. 45.

[83] On the various judge-made justifications to restrictions to the fundamental freedoms, see Hatzopoulos, 'Exigences essentielles, impératives ou impérieuses: une théorie, des théories ou pas de théorie du tout?' 34 *RTDEur.* (1998) 191.

[84] Case C-55/94, *Gebhard* [1995] ECR I-4165. For justifications to restrictions to the free movement of healthcare services see Section 2.B. below.

[85] *Peerbooms*, para. 103, as paraphrased by the Court in *Müller-Fauré*, para. 90. Emphasis has been added to the terms 'undue delay', as the Court has had to come back and give further explanations about them in *Müller-Fauré*, see below, under (IV).

[86] *Peerbooms*, para. 90. This requirement of easy access to and the possibility of appeal against the decisions of the competent authority is a manifestation of the general principle that all acts, which pertain to the application of EC law should be subject to (quasi-)judicial control or, to use the term introduced by AG Darmon in his opinion in Case 222/84, *Johnston* [1986] ECR 1651, this *droit au juge* constitutes a general principle of EC law.

IV. Applicability even if refund is asked for by an institution operating a benefits-in-kind scheme

The judgment in *Müller-Fauré*[87] confirmed and refined the previous case law. This case concerned two Dutch patients asking their respective funds for a refund: Mrs. Müller-Fauré received dental treatment from a private practitioner in Germany without having received prior authorization, while Mrs. Van Riet received both hospital and non-hospital treatment in Belgium despite being refused authorization by her home fund. Some of the eleven intervening Member States and, indeed, some members of the Court, thought that all the issues of this case had been resolved by the previous case law. The referring Court, however, followed by the full Court, found that there was still some ground for clarification.

First, the Court confirmed *Kohll* and made it clear that prior authorization may not be required for the reimbursement of medical expenses incurred in other Member States for outpatient treatment and that it is only restricted to hospital treatment according to the conditions and limitations set out in *Smits and Peerbooms* and in *Vanbraekel.*

Second, the Court refused to draw any difference between systems operating a refund system (as was the case in *Kohll*) and systems based on a benefits-in-kind scheme (as is the case for the Dutch healthcare system); it considered that the latter, like the former, should (next to their contracting-in system of practitioners and hospitals) establish a system of reimbursement of medical expenses incurred in other Member States. The Court also refused to accept as an overriding reason of general interest the preservation of the essential characteristics (i.e., the benefits-in-kind nature) of the Netherlands' sickness insurance scheme.[88]

Third, the Court further reduced the cases in which authorization may be refused by setting the criteria by which the existence of 'undue delay' is to be assessed. In this respect, some of the intervening parties submitted that the assessment of whether the delay caused by waiting lists is 'undue' should be determined only by reference to the objective medical condition of the patient. The Court, however, found that account should be taken 'not only of the patient's medical condition . . . and, where appropriate, of the degree of pain or the nature of the patient's disability which might, for example, make it impossible or extremely difficult for him to carry out a professional activity, but also of his medical history'.[89]

The above principles began to be followed by the national jurisdictions of Member States, which refer themselves directly to the case law of the ECJ.[90] The

[87] Case C-385/99, *Müller-Fauré* [2003] ECR I-4509.

[88] Para. 99 *et seq.* of the judgment. It is interesting to note that the Court only very rarely refuses to recognize the status of 'overriding reason' to reasons put forward by the Member States while, on the other hand, it applies stringently the proportionality criterion to the national measures adopted for the achievement of the said 'overriding reason'; see Hatzopoulos, *supra* n. 83. Here, however, is one of the rare cases where the Court refuses to acknowledge the existence of an 'overriding reason'.

[89] *Müller-Fauré*, para. 90.

[90] See *i.a.* the UK Administrative Court, *R (on the application of Watts) v. Bedford Primary Care Trust* [2003] All ER (D) 20 (Oct). This case has subsequently been appealed and the Court of Appeal decided to address a preliminary question to the ECJ, see *The Financial Times*, 21 February 2004, 4.

same principles, however, have led some governments to introduce stricter rules for the admission of non-nationals to their healthcare systems.[91]

V. More recent judgments

One could think that the above judgments settle once and for all the way in which Article 49 EC affects the provision of healthcare services within Member States. It was believed that the principles thus derived could be transposed in a mechanistic way, by means of Orders of the President of the Court, to subsequent cases.[92] This, however, has proved impossible—tangible proof of the great scope of difference between the various healthcare systems of Member States. Hence, a series of more recent judgments apply and refine the principles of the above 'foundation' cases.

Inizan[93] concerned a French national who received multidisciplinary pain treatment in Germany without having received the authorization provided for under French law. This authorization was given under conditions similar to the ones pertaining for Article 22 of Regulation 1408/71. The Court first upheld the requirement of a prior authorization, although it stated that Member States may grant authorization in a more extensive way than the one contemplated by the above-mentioned Regulation provision. However, the Court made clear that such an authorization may only be required where the patient seeks to receive in the host state (a) benefits-in-kind or (b) refund according to the tariffs and conditions there applicable. If, on the other hand, the patient only claims refund according to the legislation of his state of affiliation, then the requirement of a prior authorization violates Article 49 EC. Such a requirement, however, may be justified in relation to hospital treatment.[94] In any event, the authorization procedure should operate according to objective criteria within reasonable time and should be subject to (quasi-)judicial control by courts or other bodies capable of adducing independent medical expertise. Authorization may be refused 'only if treatment which is the same or equally effective for the patient can be obtained without undue delay within the territory of the member state in which the insured person's sickness fund is established'.[95] This judgment is very important in that it completes *Müller-Fauré* by stating that authorization is necessary for hospital treatment abroad, even if the healthcare system in which the patient is affiliated does not operate on a benefits-in-kind (as is the case with the Dutch system), but on a refund basis (as the French system).[96] Moreover, the requirement that review bodies or tribunals be

[91] See in the UK, at the web page of the Prime Minister, article dated 30 December 2003, 'Crackdown on Health Cheats', where Health Minister J. Hutton is reported to be stating that 'NHS resources [must be] used to meet the health care needs of people living in the UK, not those who just happen to be passing through the UK'; see http://www.pm.gov.uk/Page5105.asp.

[92] The question of issuing a mere Order of the President was already lengthily debated in the context of the *Müller-Fauré* preliminary ruling.

[93] Case C-56/2001, *Inizan*, judgment of 23 October 2003, not yet published.

[94] See *Müller-Fauré, supra* n. 87.

[95] *Inizan*, para. 59.

[96] This explains why no fewer than four Member States intervened in this case before the Court.

capable of adducing medical expertise seems to indicate that full-scale judicial review is required, not one that is merely limited to legal issues.

In *Leichte*[97] a German national moved to Italy in order to receive a thermal cure, despite the fact that he had been refused the authorization required under German law. Mr. Leichte received a refund of the expenses strictly linked to the cure itself and was seeking to recover other 'collateral' expenses, such as transport, hotel, boarding, tax, etc. Such expenses qualified for refund only if a medical expert testified that treatment abroad offered 'greatly increased prospects of success'. This requirement was justified, according to the German government, by the need to maintain the financial equilibrium of treatment institutions and competence within the national territory. The Court refused to follow this line of argument since the German government did not offer any 'analysis concerning the appropriateness and proportionality of the restrictive measure'.[98] The Court added, however, that nothing precludes the state from fixing a maximum 'ceiling' of reimbursement for expenses abroad at a level equal to what the cost of the same treatment would be within the national territory. Further, the German legislation made refund conditional upon (a) the finding by a medical expert that such treatment was necessary and (b) that the spa concerned was listed in a national list. Both these requirements were found compatible with Article 49 EC, to the extent that they were applied in an objective and non-discriminatory way. Finally, the Court held that a patient who has appealed against the refusal of the competent institution to grant authorization to receive treatment abroad need not wait for the outcome of the appeal procedure: most patients' state does not allow for long waiting periods and such a requirement would impair the direct effect of the Treaty provisions. This judgment is important because it seems to be assimilating rehabilitation—even if it is dispensed within organized facilities and infrastructures—to outpatient treatment, not to hospital treatment: no prior authorization, specifically covering facilities in other member states, may be required.

The very recent *Bosch* case[99] concerned the practice followed by a federal health insurance fund to fully reimburse to its affiliates, without any authorization procedure, health expenditures incurred in other member states up to a certain amount (DM 200). This practice was challenged by the national supervisory body as violating the authorization procedure provided for in Regulation 1408/71 (Article 22). The Court found no violation of the above rules because (a) these provisions tend to ensure that the interested patient be assimilated to locals and receive benefits-in-kind or refund according the conditions and tariffs applicable in the host state, (b) these provisions are made to facilitate mobility but they do not govern reimbursement according to tariffs fixed by the home state (or according to a flat rate), and (c) the national practice ensures *full* reimbursement of expenses up

[97] Case C-8/02, *Leichte*, judgment of 18 March 2004, not yet published.

[98] *Ibid.*, para. 45.

[99] Case C-193/03, *Bosch*, judgment of 14 October 2004, not yet published.

to the ceiling, hence patients receive at least as much as they would if the formal procedures were followed.

The basic input of the above cases may be identified at, at least, six levels. They seem to:

(1) Uphold the system of prior authorization in respect of hospital treatment abroad, irrespective of whether the healthcare system in which the patient is affiliated offers benefits-in-kind or refund. However, they refuse to assimilate rehabilitation, even when offered within organized facilities and infrastructures, to hospital treatment.

(2) Establish two types of prior authorization: (i) the Article 22 Regulation 1408/71 authorization, which can virtually lead to the assimilation of its holder to patients of the host state and (ii) the Article 49 EC authorization, required only for hospital treatment and allowing for refund at the rates and tariffs applicable in the home state of the holder. Both authorizations are delivered under similar conditions and subject to the same kind of review under the principle of proportionality. Patients, however, may opt for the Article 49 authorization when the refund under their national system is higher than in the host state, thus avoiding extra claims under the *Vanbraekel* case law.

(3) Describe extremely strict conditions (concerning the criteria, time-frame, and control of authorizations) which should be satisfied by national authorization procedures. In particular, they seem to impose fully fledged judicial control of the procedure, not just one limited to points of law.

(4) Make clear that Member States may choose to apply more flexible conditions and/or procedures than those described in Article 22 of Regulation 1408/71, for granting refund of medical (and collateral) expenses incurred in other Member States.

(5) Recognize that expenses that qualify for refund are not only those strictly needed for the payment of a specific treatment/cure, but also other 'collateral' expenses such as travel, boarding, accommodation, etc.

(6) Rationalize the grounds for exceptions to Article 49 EC in the field of health, by reducing all the arguments put forward by the Member States to the single criterion of the financial coherence of healthcare systems.

VI. Case law concerning pensioners

The dramatic evolution of the ECJ's case law in the field of healthcare described above has recently been completed by a couple of cases concerning healthcare rights of the specific category of pensioners.[100]

[100] It should be remembered that the *Pierik cases, supra* n. 49, also concerned a pensioner, but the factual situation was such that he could not claim the more favourable status provided for pensioners by Art. 31 of Regulation 1408/71; therefore the Court interpreted extensively Art. 22 of the same Regulation; see Section 2.A.

The first and more important of the two cases arose from a dispute between a Greek national, Mr. Ioannidis, and the Greek Social Security Fund, IKA.[101] This judgment sheds light on to the relationship between Articles 22 and 31 of Regulation 1408/71. The former provision concerns workers in general (and has given rise to all the case law described above), while the latter specifically targets pensioners. The rights of patients recognized by each of the above provisions differ greatly: Article 22 of the Regulation allows only for benefits (a) which become immediately necessary during a stay in the territory of another member state (upon the presentation of Form E111) and (b) after prior authorization delivered by the competent home institution (in the form of Form E112). On the contrary, Article 31 which recognizes rights of pensioners (and members of their families) 'staying in the territory of a Member State other than the one in which they reside' contains no reference to any urgency requirement and makes no mention of any authorization procedure (benefits are offered upon presentation of Form E111).

Mr. Ioannidis who was affiliated to the IKA as a retired worker received hospital treatment while visiting his son and wife in Germany. He then asked the German fund, according to Regulation 1408/71, to pay for this treatment. His claim was based on the fact that he was in possession of a Form E111, certifying his affiliation to the Greek fund. However, the German fund refused payment and asked the IKA to issue a Form E112 for this patient. According to the Greek legislation in force at the relevant date, an *ex post* authorization of hospital treatment delivered abroad, in the form of a Form E112, could only be delivered exceptionally, where (a) illness manifested itself suddenly while the patient was staying in another country or (b) he had to be transferred urgently in order to avert real risk to his life. Greek legislation did not make any distinction between a worker and a pensioner in this respect. Accordingly, the IKA, considering the fact that the patient's illness was chronic and that deterioration was not sudden, refused Form E112 to Mr. Ioannidis.

The Court distinguished the factual situation of this case from the one pertaining in the *Pierik* cases and found Article 31 alone to be applicable, since Mr. Ioannidis, contrary to Mr. Pierik, did not move to another Member State *in order to* receive treatment (in which case Article 22 would apply), but was *already there* when the need for such a treatment became apparent. Therefore, no reference whatsoever to Article 22 was justified and any authorization procedure for pensioners was ruled out.

More recently, in the *Van der Duin* judgment,[102] the Court confirmed that authorization was indeed required by pensioners (and members of their families) who moved to another Member State for the purpose of receiving treatment. This case concerned two Dutch pensioners who had taken residence in other Member States and had 'moved' their healthcare rights to the institutions of the place of their residence, according to Article 28 of Regulation 1408/71. This provision allows

[101] *Ioannidis*, annotated by the present author, *supra* n. 53 at 1251.

[102] Case C-156/01, *Van der Duin* [2003] ECR I-7045.

pensioners who obtain Form 121 from their home institution to receive benefits-in-kind by the institution of the state of their residence and at its own expenses as if they were pensioners in this latter state. Therefore, during their (long-term) residence in another Member State, the institution of this state is led to act as the 'home institution'. In the course of this period if the pensioner (or a member of his family) decides to go to another Member State—including his country of origin—in order to receive treatment he has to receive prior authorization by the institution of the place of his residence. Therefore, in the *Van der Duin* case the two pensioners who resided in France and Spain, respectively, and moved back to the Netherlands in order to receive healthcare services should have asked for prior authorization by their respective institutions.

B. Exceptions to the Application of the Rules on Free Movement

From the above, it appears clearly that the application of the Internal Market rules on healthcare is far from uncontroversial. Moreover, it is subject to important exceptions. Solidarity (1), financial cohesion of the social security systems (2), and the protection of public health (3) are the main reasons justifying exceptions to the application of the Treaty rules.

I. Solidarity as an 'overriding reason of general interest'?[103]

The *Sodemare*[104] case concerned the organization of old peoples' homes in Italy. The Italian legislation excluded from the refund system establishments that were profit-oriented. Therefore, it created an obstacle to the establishment, in Italy, of pension houses from other Member States where such a restriction did not exist. However, the Court was ready to refrain from the application of the Internal Market rules over a 'system of social welfare [. . .] based on the principle of solidarity'.[105] In an era where, in the vast majority of Internal Market cases, the Court immediately identifies restrictions and only then looks for eventual justifications,[106] the reasoning in this judgment is striking. The Court stopped at an earlier stage of its reasoning and did not examine whether the contested measure was restrictive (which it clearly was). The Court instead reasoned in two stages. First, it found that 'a Member State may, in the exercise of the powers it retains to organise its social security system, consider [what] a social welfare system necessarily implies'.[107] Then

[103] The argument about solidarity is developed in more detail further below, as an exception to the application of the competition rules, the application of which it systematically shields, see Section 3.A.II.

[104] *Sodemare, supra* n. 71.

[105] *Sodemare*, para. 29.

[106] On the single interpretation, by the Court, of all four fundamental freedoms and of justifications thereto, see Hatzopoulos, *supra* n. 83. See, more recently, Hatzopoulos, 'Trente ans après les arrêts fondamentaux de 1974, les quatre, libertés: quatre?', in P. Demaret *et al.* (eds.), *30 Years of European Legal Studies at the College of Europe—30 ans d'études juridiques européennes au Collège d'Europe: Liber Professorum 1973/74–2003/04* (2004).

[107] Para. 32 of the judgment.

it was satisfied that the contested measure did not entail any discrimination on the basis of the place of establishment of the various companies.[108] Hence, the Court concluded that there was no infringement of Articles 43 and 48 (then 52 and 58).

The judgment of the Court in *Sodemare* should be read in conjunction with the more recent judgments of the Court where it has consistently held that 'the special nature of certain services does not remove them from the ambit of the fundamental principle of freedom of movement, so that the fact that the national rules at issue in the main proceedings are social security rules cannot exclude application of Articles 59 and 60 (now 49 and 50) of the Treaty'.[109] The same conclusion has been reached by the Court in relation to the applicability of Article 28 (then 30).[110]

One way of reading the two series of cases is to accept that the most recent judgments have overturned or partially invalidated the earlier *Sodemare* judgment. A more plausible reading is that when in the presence of core solidarity activities, restrictively defined,[111] the Internal Market rules are only infringed by discriminatory measures and not mere hindrances. If this second view were accepted, then the existence of core solidarity activities would have the function of yet another 'overriding reason' justifying non-discriminatory measures. The only difference would be that the existence of core solidarity activities is taken into account at an earlier stage of the reasoning, before any restrictions are identified.

II. The mandatory requirement of 'cohesion'

Except for solidarity, the main mandatory requirement put forward by the states as a possible justification to barriers to the fundamental freedoms is that of maintaining the 'social security system's balance'.[112] This is directly based on the 'coherence of the fiscal system' justification introduced by the Court in the *Bachmann* cases.[113] Both obey the same logic and satisfy the same need: that factors disturbing the difficult equation between contributions received and moneys paid are circumscribed. However, in more recent tax cases the 'coherence' argument has been given less weight in comparison with other more precise reasons for exceptions.[114]

[108] Para. 33 of the judgment.

[109] In *Kohll*, para. 21, *Vanbraekel*, para. 42, and *Peerbooms*, para. 54.

[110] In *Decker*, para. 25.

[111] Following the judgments of the Court in the *FFSA*, the 'trilogy' and the *Pavlov* cases, see Section 3.A.I below.

[112] *Kohll*, para. 41, *Peerbooms*, para. 73 and *Vanbraekel*, para. 47.

[113] Cases C-204/90, *Bachmann* [1992] ECR I-249 and C-300/90, *Commission v. Belgium* [1992] ECR I-305.

[114] See e.g. Case C-250/95, *Futura Participations* [1997] ECR I-2471 and its annotation by the present author in 35 *CMLRev.* (1998) 493. For a more general overview, see Hatzopoulos, 'L'Impact de la fiscalité directe des Etats membres sur les libertés "personnelles" ', *RMUE* (1995) 121; Nguyen, 'Bachmann, Warner, Schumacker Wielockx et les autres . . . ou quand la Cour de Justice harmonise la fiscalité européenne', *Europe* (1995); and more recently Berlin, 'Chronique de jurisprudence fiscale européenne', 36 *RTDEur.* (2000) 548.

In the field of social security, the Court follows a quite balanced approach. For one thing, the Court seems to be paying attention to the argument of 'balance and coherence' since it acknowledges that 'any wastage of financial, technical and human resources [should be prevented]. Such wastage is all the more damaging because it is generally recognised that the hospital care sector generates considerable costs and must satisfy increasing needs, while the financial resources which may be available for health care are not unlimited.'[115] Moreover, the Court declares itself ready to support national efforts not to 'undermine all the planning and rationalisation carried out in this vital sector in an effort to avoid the phenomena of hospital overcapacity, imbalance in the supply of hospital medical care and logistical and financial wastage'.[116]

However, such efforts should fulfil the requirement of proportionality[117] and they should be carried out according to objective and non-discriminatory criteria.[118] At any rate, reimbursement of hospital expenses incurred by a patient in another Member State cannot disturb the aforesaid 'coherence' when it is calculated in accordance with, and does not exceed, the amount payable under the national system. This is why, according to the Court, refund under Articles 49 *et seq.* EC, where no prior authorization has been obtained, is not 'liable to have a significant effect on the financing of the social security system'.[119]

Moreover, the scope of the 'coherence' mandatory requirement is limited only to hospital treatment. The Court in *Müller-Fauré* recognized that 'the distinction between hospital services and non-hospital services may sometimes prove difficult to draw'.[120] This, however, did not preclude the Court from establishing a clear distinction between the two. In recitals 76 to 92 of its judgment (under the general title 'Findings of the Court' and the subtitle 'Hospital Services') the Court extensively acknowledges that all the imperatives mentioned above (planning, avoiding wastage, etc.) do indeed apply to hospital services. On the contrary, in recitals 93 to 98 of the judgment (under the sub-title 'Non-Hospital Services') the Court gives reasons why the same is not true of services of this kind. The Court holds that there are a number of reasons, practical and psychological, that limit the mobility of patients across the borders. Practical barriers include (a) linguistic differences, (b) geographic distance, (c) cost of staying abroad, and (d) lack of information about treatment facilities in other Member States.[121] Psychological factors limiting mobility are related to (a) the proximity to the residence and the home environment of

115 *Peerbooms*, para. 79.

116 *Ibid.*, para. 106. See also paras. 77–81 of *Müller-Fauré*.

117 *Ibid.*, para. 82.

118 *Ibid.*, para. 89.

119 *Vanbraekel*, para. 52 and *Kohll*, para. 42.

120 *Müller-Fauré*, para. 75. It is interesting to note that in this very case the Commission was suggesting a different distinction, placing care provided in a surgery on the same footing as outpatient treatment within a hospital environment and distinguishing them from hospital treatment as such (para. 63 of the judgment). The Court did not seem to follow such a delicate (although economically more sound) distinction.

121 *Müller-Fauré*, para. 95.

the patient, (b) cultural affinities, and, as a consequence thereof, (c) the possibility of building up a relationship of trust with the treating doctor.[122]

A *second* overriding reason of general interest that was put forward by the Member States in the *Müller-Fauré* case but which was rejected by the Court relates to the maintenance of the 'essential characteristics of the sickness insurance scheme' of each Member State. This argument, which has been dismissed by the Court in a thin, pragmatic, and functional way, raises the real problem behind all the case law of the Court here reported: is it possible for the Court, by means of pure negative integration and divestiture, to intervene actively in a field as complex as the organization of healthcare systems?[123]

III. Public health

A *third* overriding reason put forward by the Member States is the need to 'maintain a balanced medical and hospital service open to all'. In relation to this argument the reasoning of the Court has been somehow inconsistent. In *Kohll, Vanbraekel,* and *Smits and Peerbooms* the Court acknowledged that this was a valid objective but denied that it might constitute an overriding reason of general interest. The Court reasoned that this objective is intrinsically linked to the method of financing the social security system and (implicitly) reminded that economic aims may not constitute overriding reasons of general interest.[124] Nevertheless, the Court considered that this objective 'may *also* fall within the derogations on grounds of public health under Article 56 (now 46) of the Treaty in so far as it contributes to the attainment of a high level of health protection'.[125] However, in *Müller-Fauré* the Court abandoned the Article 46 line of reasoning and stated that 'the objective of maintaining a balanced medical and hospital system open to all is inextricably linked to the way the social security system is financed'. Therefore it referred itself back to the 'coherence' mandatory requirement. Recent cases seem to confirm this tendency.[126]

The *fourth* justification put forward by the Member States relating to 'the maintenance of treatment capacity or medical competence on national territory' has had an even more ephemeral fate. The Court in *Vanbraekel* and *Smits and Peerbooms*[127] opted for an extensive reading of the Treaty exception concerning public health (Article 46 EC) and stated that 'the maintenance of treatment capacity or medical competence on national territory is essential for the public health and even for the survival of the population'. In *Müller-Fauré*, however, the Court completely abandoned this justification by stating that 'no specific evidence has been adduced

[122] *Müller-Fauré*, para. 96.

[123] For some elements of answer to this question see below, Section 'Conclusion'.

[124] See, e.g., Case C-398/95, *SETTG v. Ypourgos Ergasias* [1997] ECR I-3091 and its annotation (in Greek) by the present author in 46 *Nomiko Vima* (1998) 421.

[125] *Kohll*, para. 50, *Peerbooms*, para. 73, and *Vanbraekel*, para. 48. Emphasis is given to the word 'also', since it is a source of uncertainty as to the existence of an overriding reason of general interest.

[126] See the cases referred to in Section 2.A.5 above.

[127] Paras. 49 and 74, respectively.

in support of [the] argument [. . .] that the actual competence of practitioners, working in surgeries or in hospital environment, would be undermined because of numerous journeys abroad for medical purposes'.[128] On analogous grounds the Court also dismissed a similar argument raised by the German government in *Leichte*.[129] It is unclear whether this attitude of the Court is effectively linked to the insufficient evidence submitted by the parties in the main proceedings (which would mean that the burden of proof is a heavy one) or whether the Court distances itself from the idea that all medical specializations should be available in all Member States.

The *fifth* justification put forward by the Member States, directly related to public health, has already been completely rebutted by the Court, in its judgment in *Kohll* (and *Decker*). The Court has been unwilling to follow the Member States in considering that receiving healthcare services (or goods) in another Member State may entail dangers for public health as such. The Court gave an excellent illustration of how harmonization of the legislation may enhance the functioning of the Internal Market. It considered that where the medical professions have been harmonized,[130] professionals 'established in other Member States must be afforded all guarantees equivalent to those accorded to [professionals] established on national territory'.[131] It becomes, therefore, apparent that the harmonization directives, aimed at achieving the free movement and establishment of professionals, may also be used to enhance the free provision of cross-border services.[132]

Hence, in *Müller-Fauré* the Court definitively abandoned the extensive reading of the public-health justification contained in Article 46 EC, which had been qualified as 'alternative' and even 'unorthodox'[133] and rejected altogether public health as a ground for justification for restrictions to the free movement of healthcare services within the EC. This is also the case with subsequent cases, where reference to Article 46 is altogether omitted. It is suggested that the solution thus reached by the Court presents both a psychological and a legal advantage.

From a psychological point of view, it bars any insinuation that healthcare services offered in other Member States may be of inferior quality. Therefore, it establishes the idea that healthcare in the whole of the Community is of a comparable level.

From a legal point of view, it contributes towards the objectives of transparency and coherence since it gives to each Treaty provision its proper meaning. It is reminded that, in certain circumstances, derogations from the Internal Market rules may also originate in the application of Article 86(2) of the Treaty.[134] This provision allows for derogations from the application of the Treaty rules where their

[128] *Müller-Fauré*, para. 70.

[129] *Supra* n. 97.

[130] On this issue see briefly 1.C.

[131] *Kohll*, para. 48.

[132] This point is quite controversial; see for some criticisms Jorens, *supra* n. 9, at para. IV(C)1a, where he doubts that it is correct for the Court to assume that the harmonization of the requirements for *access* to some activities necessarily guarantees equally satisfactory *practice* in all Member States.

[133] See Hatzopoulos, *supra* n. 1, at 725–726.

[134] Case C-266/96, *Corsica Ferries III* [1998] ECR I-3949.

application could 'obstruct the performance, in law or in fact, of the particular tasks assigned to [undertakings entrusted with the operation of services of general economic interest]'.[135] There is no doubt whatsoever that the preservation of 'a balanced medical and hospital service open to all' and 'the maintenance of treatment capacity or medical competence on national territory' do constitute a mission of general economic interest.[136] Hence, Article 86(2) allows taking into account strictly economic considerations when assessing the compatibility of national measures with the Treaty. Further, it allows the justification of measures of a (non-arbitrarily) discriminatory nature. Therefore, in conjunction with the more macroeconomic 'coherence' overriding reason, Article 86(2) allows for the safeguard of the national healthcare systems, leaving Article 46 EC to its well-established interpretation, restricted to the prevention or combat of disease.[137]

C. Receiving Healthcare Services without Prior Authorization?

Despite all the exceptions stated above it becomes clear that the intersection of healthcare and market principles is increasingly intense. One consequence of this is that patients may freely move to other Member States, receive non-hospital treatment, and then ask for refund from their home institution. 'Freely' implies the absence of any procedural requirement, prior or subsequent to receiving treatment and, more particularly, the circumvention of the authorization procedure provided for in Article 21 of Regulation 1408/71. However, this 'freedom' is far from absolute.

From the above, it becomes clear that patients seeking outpatient treatment have the choice of either obtaining prior authorization under Article 22 of Regulation 1408/71, or going directly to the practitioner of their choice in any Member State and then asking for a refund from their fund (Figure Three). These two options have considerable differences and yet retain some points in common.

I. Differences

(a) The personal scope Regulation 1408/71 has a more limited personal scope than Article 49 of the EC Treaty. The former text only applies to the categories of

[135] There is much more in Art. 86(2) and there is an important body of case law and doctrine on this issue. For an article which is considered to be a 'classic'—although not the most recent one—in the field, where the most important cases of the Court are discussed, see Kovar, 'Droit communautaire et service public, esprit d'orthodoxie ou pensée laicisée?', *RTDEur.* (1996) 215 and 493.

[136] This directly refers to the extremely vivid debate of what is a service of general interest and how it can be assured in times of divestiture of the state and generalized deregulation. On this issue the French literature is extremely rich; see, among others a multidimensional analysis of the issue in R. Kovar & D. Simon, *Service public et Communauté Européenne: entre l'intérêt général et le marché* (1998); Kovar, 'La Cour de justice et les entreprises chargées de la gestion d'un service d'intérêt économique général: un pas dans le bon sens vers une dérégulation réglée', *Europe* (1994); Kovar, *supra* n. 135.

[137] For the content given to the public health exception, see Council Directive 64/221/EEC of 25 February 1964 on the coordination of special measures concerning the movement and residence of foreign nationals which are justified on grounds of public policy, public security, or public health, OJ 1964 L 56/850; now replaced by Arts 27–34 of Directive 2004/38/EC of 29 April 2004, on 'European Citizenship', OJ 2004 L 158/77.

<table>
<tr><td colspan="2"></td><td></td><td>Hospital treatment</td><td>Outpatient treatment</td></tr>
<tr><td rowspan="2">Art. 22</td><td rowspan="2">Workers
+
Pensioners moving to another MS (Pierik)</td><td>Benefits-in-kind system</td><td>YES Peerbooms + Müller-Fauré</td><td>NO Müller-Fauré</td></tr>
<tr><td>Refund system</td><td>YES Inizan</td><td>NO Kohll</td></tr>
<tr><td>Art. 31</td><td>Pensioners residing in another MS</td><td>Both systems</td><td colspan="2">NO Ioannidis v. IKA</td></tr>
</table>

Figure Three *Is prior authorization required?*

people described in Article 2 thereof, i.e. workers, pensioners, students, refugees, . . . , and members of their families. It is true that the concept of a worker is a community concept[138] that it is generally widely interpreted[139] and even more so for the purposes of Regulation 1408/71.[140] However, Article 49 EC has a much wider personal scope since it covers all community nationals when they act as service providers and, even more importantly, all recipients of services, independently of their nationality, provided that they are established within Community territory.[141]

(b) The material scope As stated above, patients not having received the authorization of Article 22(1)c of Regulation 1408/71 may only be refunded for outpatient treatment and not for hospital treatment.

(c) Level of reimbursement Under Regulation 1408/71, patients may receive a refund according to the tariffs applicable in the state where they received treatment, except where these are lower than the ones applicable in their home state, in which case they should receive additional money according to the *Vanbraekel* rule. On the other hand, if patients have received no prior authorization but, instead, make use of the Article 49 EC freedom to receive services, they may only be reimbursed at the tariffs applicable in their home state.

(d) Out-of-pocket expenses Patients having received the Article 22(1)c prior authorization may, depending on the social healthcare system applicable in the host

[138] Case 53/81, *Levin* [1982] ECR 1035.

[139] See *i.a. ibid.* for part-time occupations, Case 36/74, *Walrave* [1974] ECR 1405 for sports activities, Joined Cases 115–116/81, *Adoui and Cornuaille* [1982] ECR 1665 for the activity of prostitution, Case 196/87, *Steymann* [1988] ECR 6159 for the activities accomplished within a religious community, Case C-292/89, *Antonissen* [1991] ECR I-745 for an unemployed job-seeker.

[140] Case C-118/96, *Jessica Safir* [1998] ECR I-1919.

[141] See Case C-484/93, *Gustavsson and Svensson* [1995] ECR I-3955, annotated by Hatzopoulos in 33 *CMLRev.* (1996) 569. This difference, however, loses importance after the recent extension of the personal scope of Regulation 1408/71 to cover third-country nationals legally residing in the EU by Council Regulation (EC) 859/2003 of 14 May 2003, OJ L 124/1.

Member State, either receive treatment for free (in the benefits-in-kind systems) or pay for their treatment and then ask for refund (in the refund systems) from their home institution. The latter option is the only one applicable for patients who have not received the Regulation 1408/71 authorization. That is, the prior authorization procedure may still be the only solution for patients who may not be able to afford to pay in advance for treatment received in other Member States.

II. Points in common

(a) Access to other Member States' treatment facilities No matter whether the patient requires treatment in another Member State under Article 49 alone or under the more specific rules of the Regulation, the healthcare institutions of other Member States—to the extent that they are bound by EC law—may not discriminate against non-nationals and may not refuse treatment. This has been expressly stated, in relation to patients having obtained the Regulation authorization, in the *Pierik II* case;[142] it is also a general duty arising directly under Article 49 EC.

(b) Cost of the treatment According to the judgment of the Court in *Ferlini*,[143] hospitals and doctors of Member States may not alter their tariffs depending on the status of the patient. Therefore, patients may not be charged differently by the host state's treating facilities, depending on whether they have or have not received prior authorization.

(c) Kind of treatment It is for the patient's home institution to determine which treatments are covered by the social insurance scheme. This is clearly so under Article 22 of Regulation 1408/71 since the home institution has discretion over the issuance of the prior authorization. Also paragraph 2 of the said provision[144] clearly states that the only circumstance in which such authorization may not be refused is 'where the treatment in question *is* among the benefits provided for by the legislation of the [home] Member State'. This also seems to be the case when a patient moves to another Member State without prior authorization, since the Court in *Müller-Fauré* held that 'the conditions on which benefits are granted [. . .] remain enforceable where treatment is provided in a Member State other than that of affiliation. That is particularly so in the case of the requirement that a general practitioner should be consulted prior to consulting a specialist.'[145] If the requirement of a prior consultation may be enforced, *ad minus majorem*, the complete exclusion of a treatment from the scope of the social healthcare system of the home Member State should also constitute a limit to treatment received abroad.

[142] *Pierik II, supra* n. 49 para. 15.

[143] Case C-411/98, *Ferlini* [2000] ECR I-8081.

[144] As modified following to the *Pierik* judgments; see *supra* nn. 49–56 and relevant text.

[145] *Müller-Fauré*, para. 106 *in fine*.

(d) Healthcare model The fact that the home Member State follows a benefits-in-kind or a refund model makes no difference to the application of the rules above.[146]

D. Are the Various Healthcare Models Affected in a Different Way by the Treaty Rules?

All the above rules and exceptions on the application of the Treaty rules beg the question of whether the application of the Treaty rules, and especially Article 49 EC, affect in the same way the various healthcare systems. The answer seems to be a qualified no.

I. National v. insurance healthcare systems

The finding of the Court in *Kohll* to the effect that 'the special nature of certain services does not remove them from the ambit of [. . .] the Treaty'[147] seems to indicate that the same principles apply to all healthcare services irrespectively of the system under which they are provided. The same finding is corroborated by the judgment in *Ferlini*, where the Court acknowledged that private hospitals bear no less burden in discharging the obligations accruing from Article 49 EC than public hospitals. Therefore, the fact that in national health systems (unlike insurance health systems) treatment is essentially provided by public hospitals (and practitioners) does not affect the application of the Treaty rules. This conclusion, however, should be watered down by the findings of the Court in the *Sodemare* case,[148] where it was held that 'a system of social welfare [. . .] is based on the principle of solidarity'[149] and is not to be judged strictly for its compatibility with the Treaty rules. The exact scope of the *Sodemare* judgment[150] is far from clear. It would seem, however, that the closer a system is to a pure national healthcare system, the more likely that it be treated leniently under the Treaty rules. This view was confirmed by the recent judgment of the Court in the *Freskot* case.[151] This case concerned the Greek scheme for compulsory insurance of farmers and agricultural undertakings against natural disasters. The compatibility of the said scheme was tested *inter alia* with Article 49 EC. The Court found that this compulsory insurance scheme could not qualify as a service in the sense of the Treaty since 'the contribution is essentially in the nature of a charge imposed by the legislature and it is levied by the tax authority. The characteristics of that charge, including its rate, are also determined by the legislature. It is for the competent ministers to decide any variation of the rate.'[152] All the above characteristics are mostly true for tax-based national health systems.

[146] *Ibid.*, para. 99 *et seq.*

[147] *Kohll, supra* n. 60, para. 20.

[148] *Sodemare, supra* n. 71.

[149] *Ibid.*, paras. 30 and 34, emphasis added.

[150] And of the subsequent judgements of the ECJ concerning various types of Funds, for which see Section 3.A.I below.

[151] Case C-355/00, *Freskot v. Elliniko Dimosio* [2003] ECR I-5263.

[152] *Freskot*, para. 57.

II. Tax-based v. contributions-based systems

The existence of remuneration, and thus of services in the sense of Article 50 EC, is to be appreciated in relation to the nature of benefits accruing for patients. Three cases may be distinguished:

(1) In refund systems, patients pay for treatment and receive refund: the element of remuneration is clear even if the amount paid by the patients is not strictly proportional to the cost of the treatment received.
(2) In some benefits-in-kind systems (essentially contributions-based ones), patients receive treatment by contracted providers (hospitals, clinics, and practitioners); there is remuneration even though it is not paid by the patient himself (but by the competent fund) and even if the amount paid is not exact consideration for the service received.[153]
(3) In other benefits-in-kind systems (essentially tax-based ones), patients receive treatment by public hospitals and by practitioners directly financed by tax. In this case the existence of remuneration is not clear, although for the sake of coherence it should be inferred in some way.[154]

III. Benefits-in-kind v. refund systems

As already stated, both systems are, in theory, affected in the same way by the application of the Treaty rules. In practice, however, benefits-in-kind systems bear a greater burden in order to comply with the rules, since it was clearly ruled in *Müller-Fauré* that, next to benefits in nature, they have to set up a system of reimbursement for healthcare services provided to affiliated patients in other Member States.[155]

IV. Systems with clear three-tier healthcare organization

In *Müller-Fauré* the Court recognized that the home Member State may impose its own conditions, and notably 'the requirement that a general practitioner should be consulted prior to consulting a specialist'[156] for the reimbursement of treatment received abroad. It is clear, however, that the possibility of having recourse to practitioners in other Member States will appeal more to patients coming from a rigid three-tier system based on strict devolution rules entailing bigger delays. Therefore, these systems are more likely to suffer 'depopulation' from the opening up of the markets for outpatient treatment.

Moreover, outpatient treatment grossly corresponds to the primary level of healthcare. If, as it seems, this level of healthcare is opened up and patients may have

[153] *Smits and Peerbooms*, paras. 56–58.

[154] See, however, the observations *supra*, n. 151 and text above, concerning the judgment of the Court in *Freskot* and its implications for tax-based systems.

[155] *Müller-Fauré*, para. 99 *et seq.*

[156] *Müller-Fauré*, para. 106.

recourse to practitioners in other Member States, the whole logic of a three-tier healthcare system based on devolution may collapse.

From the above, it follows that (a) the Court has not clearly ruled whether the Treaty rules apply in the same manner to all healthcare systems, and in particular to tax-based ones and (b) even if it did so, the effects would not be identical to all, since each healthcare system has different characteristics of its own. (*Conclusion 4*)

3. COMPETITION, STATE AID, AND PUBLIC PROCUREMENT

The rules on competition, state aid, and public procurement are examined together because they are complementary. Articles 81 to 86 EC seek to avoid the conclusion that the functioning of the common market and free competition are fettered from action by private undertakings. Articles 87 to 89 EC (together with Article 86(2) EC) are supposed to prevent Member States from intervening *directly* in favour of specific undertakings or sectors of the industry, thus affecting the trade and competition patterns. Finally, the rules on public procurement, ensuing from secondary legislation adopted under the Internal Market programme, seek to deter *indirect* subsidies and state aids through the arbitrary award of public contracts.

Adapted to fit into the pattern of the provision of healthcare services these rules could apply as follows:

(1) If all the entities involved in the provision of healthcare services (hospitals, clinics, practitioners, insurance funds, etc.) were to qualify as undertakings, *first*, any agreement between them would be caught by the prohibition of Article 81 EC and, *second*, any one of them occupying a dominant position in the relevant market would be compelled to avoid any conduct that could be deemed abusive.

(2) If some of the entities involved were to qualify as undertakings and others as public authorities, any transfer of funds from the latter (e.g., a public find) to the former (e.g., a private hospital) would fall foul of the prohibition of state aids.

(3) In the same hypothesis, any direct award of contract (e.g., the contracting-in of private practitioners and hospitals by a public fund) without a due tendering procedure would violate the public procurement rules.

The applicability of the above rules to healthcare services is all but evident. For, as stated in the introduction to this chapter, the organization of national healthcare systems relies, first, on various systems of cross-subsidies between different public, semi-public, and private bodies and, second, on a network of agreements and contracts between such bodies. These subsidies and the interrelated agreements obey primarily to the requirement of solidarity, not to market principles. Therefore, all of the above rules seem *prima facie* not to be adapted to the operation of healthcare systems.[157]

In other words, by the application of the above rules, any entity involved in the provision of healthcare services may, if a private undertaking, either breach the competition rules or be a state-aid recipient, or if a public authority, either be a state-aid donor or a contracting authority which has violated the rules on public procurement.

Each set of rules merits individual examination.

A. The Competition Rules

I. The application of competition rules

When the issue was first put to it in the *Poucet and Pistre* case, the Court held that 'sickness funds and the organizations involved in the management of the public social security system, fulfil an exclusively social function [. . .] based on the principle of national solidarity' and therefore, their operation is not an economic activity.[158] Hence, the Court found that the organizations entrusted with the above activities are not undertakings and therefore the Treaty rules on competition do not apply to them.

However, in subsequent cases the Court qualified, or overturned, this conclusion by finding that not all, and indeed very few, bodies involved in the organization of healthcare systems are not to be considered as undertakings. In a series of judgments the Court has come up with various criteria according to which the economic nature of an activity and, hence, the qualification of an entity as an undertaking are to be assessed.

The term 'undertaking' has been defined by the Court as 'a single organisation of personal, tangible and intangible elements, attached to an autonomous legal entity and pursuing a given long term economic aim'.[159] More recently, the Court widened its definition of an undertaking, stating that it includes 'any entity engaged in an economic activity regardless of its legal status and the way in which it is financed'.[160] Further the Court has held that undertakings 'bear the financial risks attaching to the performance of those activities since, if there should be an imbalance between expenditure and receipts, they must bear the deficit themselves'.[161]

[157] For a case study see Akyurek-Kievits, 'The Dutch Health Insurance Sector and EU Competition Law', paper delivered in the high-level two-day conference organized by the Belgian Presidency of the EU on *European Integration and National Health Care Systems: A Challenge for Social Policy*, Gent, 7–8 December 2001.

[158] *Poucet and Pistre, supra* n. 30 paras. 18 and 19.

[159] See, e.g., Case 19/61, *Mannesman v. High Authority of the ECSC* [1962] ECR 357.

[160] Case C-41/90, *Höfner and Elser* [1991] ECR I-1979, para. 21; *Poucet and Pistre, supra* n. 30 para. 17; *FFSA, supra* n. 71, para. 14.

[161] Cases C-35/96, *Commission v. Italy, CNSD* [1998] ECR I-3851, para. 37 and C-309/99, *Price Waterhouse* [2002] ECR I-1577, para. 48.

From the *broad* and *functional* definitions given by the Court,[162] it is clear that the crucial element is the pursuance of an independent economic activity bearing economic risk.[163] Therefore, the EC Commission has treated as undertakings an inventor who exploits commercially his invention[164] as well as opera singers.[165] Moreover, the Court has held that, despite the occasional exercise of official authority and other public functions, both customs officers[166] and lawyers,[167] as well as their professional associations, may qualify as undertakings.

(a) Doctors and other health professionals It seems clear that doctors and, more generally, healthcare providers are undertakings in the sense of Articles 81 *et seq.* The Court had the occasion to express its view to this effect in the *Pavlov* case.[168] There, the decision of the Dutch authorities to render compulsory the membership of all doctors to an occupational pension fund at the request of the representative professional body (of doctors) was scrutinized under the competition rules. In order to reply to the questions of the referring jurisdiction, the Court had to examine whether the representative body may be qualified as an 'association of undertakings' and, hence, whether doctors are themselves undertakings. In this respect the judgment of the Court is exempt of any ambiguity. Having found that self-employed medical specialists offer services in the market of medical services for remuneration and that they bear the financial risks attached to their activity, the Court held that they clearly constitute undertakings. It further specified that 'the complexity and technical nature of the services they provide and the fact that the practice of their profession is regulated cannot alter that conclusion'.[169] More recently, the Court held exactly the same reasoning and reached the very same conclusion in relation to lawyers.[170]

(b) Hospitals and clinics There is no doubt that clinics or semi-private hospitals are undertakings in the sense of Articles 81 *et seq.* EC. These are economic entities providing health services for consideration. The fact that they are contracted into a social security scheme whereby patients may recover part or all of the expenses incurred has no bearing whatsoever on the economic nature of the activity pursued.[171]

162 For the notion of undertaking in relation with health services see Pieters, 'The Consequences of European Competition law for National Health Policies', in *Rechtsdogmatik und Rechtspolitik im Arbeits- und Sozialrecht, Festschrift Theodor Tomandl* (1998) 603, at 604 *et seq.* The characteristics of the Court's definition of undertakings as *broad and functional* are his.

163 Hence the case law of the Court on the application of Arts. 49 *et seq.* EC, which is expressly linked to the pursuance of an economic activity provided for remuneration, is also relevant.

164 *Reuter/BASF* [1976], 2 *CMLR* 44.

165 *RAI/Unitel* [1978], 3 *CMLR* 306.

166 *Commission v. Italy, CNSD, supra* n. 161.

167 *Price Waterhouse, supra* n. 161.

168 Joined Cases C-180-184/98, *Pavlov a.o.* [2000] ECR I-6451.

169 *Pavlov*, para. 77 *in fine.*

170 Case C-35/95, *Arduino* [2002] ECR I-1529 and *Price Waterhouse, supra* n. 161.

171 See the underlying reasoning of the Court in *Kohll* (*supra* n. 60) as it has been broadened to include treatment in hospitals by the judgments of the Court in Cases *Peerbooms* (*supra* n. 75) and *Vanbraekel* (*supra* n. 74), where it has been held that there is 'no need to distinguish [. . .] between care provided in a hospital environment and care provided outside such an environment' (see Section 2.A).

A slightly different question arises where the clinics or hospitals are contracted-in in a social security scheme whereby expenses are not paid directly by the patient but by the fund. In the *Peerbooms* and the *Vanbraekel* cases, the Court found that the fact that the expenses were paid by a third party (i.e., the fund) and that they were only indirectly linked to the actual value of services provided did not affect the economic nature of the services offered.

The position is less clear with regard to public hospitals being financed directly from the state budget and where the personnel has the status of civil servants. According to the broad definition of 'undertaking' put forward by the Court whereby any activity pursued or susceptible of being pursued for profit is to be considered as an economic activity,[172] even these public hospitals should be treated as undertakings. This is not an unquestionable conclusion, however. In his opinion in *Smits and Peerbooms*, Advocate General Colomer took the clear position that 'the systems operated in certain Member States where the social security institutions have their own resources and staff which they engage directly for a pre-set number of hours and a given salary'[173] are outside the scope of the Treaty. Although Advocate General Colomer was not followed by the Court in *Smits and Peerbooms*, the validity of his opinion on this issue is corroborated by the subsequent judgments of the Court in the 'lawyers' cases[174] and in *FENIN*.[175] In the former cases the Court stated clearly that a body would not qualify as an undertaking where (a) it pursues aims genuinely linked to the public interest and (b) representatives of the public authorities participate in its board of directors.[176] The *FENIN* case concerned the allegation, by the association of the undertakings which market medical goods in Spain, that the 26 bodies and organizations (including three ministries of the Spanish government) which run the Spanish national health system abuse their dominant position in the relevant market by being systematically late in paying their debts. The Commission held that the bodies in question could not qualify as undertakings and rejected the claim. The Court of First Instance (CFI) upheld the Commission's findings and retained that the health system in question 'operates according to the principle of solidarity in that it is funded from social security contributors and other state funding and in that it provides services free of charge to its members on the basis of universal cover'.[177] Further, the Court stated that the above finding is not altered by the fact that non-members, such as foreign patients, are charged for the same services.

[172] See on this issue *Albany*, para. 84, *Brentjens*, para. 84 and *Drijvende*, para. 74 (*supra* n. 72).

[173] Opinion of AG Colomer *Peerbooms*, *supra* n. 73, para. 30.

[174] See *supra* n. 170.

[175] Case T-319/99, *FENIN v. Commission* [2003] ECR II-357.

[176] The same criteria had already been used, albeit in a less clear way, in the *Pavlov* case in relation to a medical association as well as in case *CNSD*, *supra* n. 161, in relation to an association of custom agents. It should be noted, however, that, despite the negative formulation of the criterion, in all these cases the Court did, indeed, find all the relevant associations to be undertakings.

[177] *FENIN*, para. 39.

The combined reading of the above case law does not allow for easy conclusions, but it would seem that the more integrated into a national health system a hospital or a practitioner is, the less likely it is to be considered as an undertaking.[178]

A different question is whether hospitals which qualify as undertakings may, nevertheless, be exempted from the application of competition rules by virtue of Article 86(2), as engaged in the pursuit of some service of public interest.[179]

(c) Medical aid associations The same logic prevails in relation to medical aid associations. In the *Glöckner* case[180] the Court was called to examine the compatibility of the German legislation concerning ambulance services with the competition rules. According to this legislation, private undertakings wishing to engage in this activity should obtain an authorization. This was granted by the public authorities of the Länder after consultation with the medical aid associations, which were already present in the market for ambulance services.

One of the first issues that the Court had to settle was whether the medical aid associations (which (a) were organized as non-profit associations, (b) had been entrusted by the law with the operation of the public ambulance service and had set up staff, central control units, and ambulance stations to this effect, and (c) were financed partly through direct public funding (for the infrastructure) and partly through user charges (for the operational costs)) were undertakings in the sense of the Treaty. The Court, taking into consideration that 'such activities have not always been, and are not necessarily, carried on by such organisations or by public authorities',[181] found to the affirmative. The Court further reasoned that 'public service obligations may, of course, render the services provided by a given medical aid organisation less competitive than comparable services rendered by other operators not bound by such obligations, but that fact cannot prevent the activities in question from being regarded as economic activities'.[182]

(d) Professional associations In the *Royal Pharmaceutical Society* case[183] it was established that under certain circumstances professional associations may be considered as exercising public authority and, therefore, subject to the Treaty rules on

[178] The preliminary judgment of the Court in the pending *Watts* case (see *supra* n. 90) is expected to shed light on the issue of the qualification of NHS hospitals under the Treaty rules.

[179] For which see Section 3.A.II below. In this respect AG Leger's opinion in the *Price Waterhouse* case is directly relevant, since he follows the same logic: the AG refuses to limit the scope of Art. 81(1) by applying some 'rule of reason' encompassing extra-competitive criteria, while he relegates this function to Art. 86(2). It would seem, however, that in its judgment the Court declined to follow this part of the AG's analysis.

[180] Case C-475/99, *Glöckner* [2001] ECR I-8089.

[181] *Glöckner*, para. 20.

[182] *Ibid.*, para. 21. The Court finally concluded to the compatibility of the contested legislation with Art. 82 of the Treaty, precisely on grounds of securing the financial viability of public service obligations, by virtue of Art. 86(2).

[183] Joined Cases 266 and 267/87, *The Queen v. Royal Pharmaceutical Society of Great Britain, ex parte Association of Pharmaceutical Importers a.o.* [1989] ECR 1295.

the Internal Market. This was also implicitly admitted in the *Klopp* case,[184] where the incriminated single-practice rule for lawyers was stipulated by the internal rules of the Paris Bar.[185]

It is a different question whether professional associations may be viewed as undertakings under Article 81 and 82 of the Treaty or, in the alternative, as associations of undertakings under Article 81 alone. For one thing, the professional association may not be considered as an undertaking itself unless it is engaged in an economic activity distinct from that of its members.[186] This being easily ascertainable, the most delicate issue is whether a professional association which is not itself an undertaking is nevertheless an association of undertakings in the sense of Article 81.

The Commission has on several occasions treated professional associations under the rules in Article 81.[187] In the same line of reasoning, the Court in *CNSD*[188] identified two criteria as to whether an association of professional custom agents in Italy should be dealt with as an association of undertakings: one pertaining to the *composition* and the other to the *legal framework* of the organization's activities. Where the members of the association are the representatives of the professionals concerned and there is nothing in the national legislation preventing them from acting in the exclusive interest of the profession, then Article 81 applies. Or, as Advocate General Léger put it in his opinion in the *Price Waterhouse* case:[189] 'a body will not be classified as an association of undertakings within the meaning of Article 85(1) (now 81(1)) of the Treaty where, on the one hand, it is composed of a majority of representatives of the public authorities and, on the other, it is required by national legislation to observe various public interest criteria when taking its decisions'.

Applying and further clarifying the above criteria, Advocate General Léger, followed by the Court, found that the Dutch Bar Association is to be considered an association of undertakings. According to the learned Advocate General the existence of regulatory powers does not preclude the association from being treated as an association of undertakings. Moreover, the existence of a vague, unenforceable obligation to act in the general interest does not alter the above qualification.

Following the above criteria, the Court specifically gave judgment in relation to the Dutch professional body of medical specialists in the *Pavlov* case.[190] In a very laconic recital, the Court held that the professional body was not to be exempted

[184] Case 107/83, *Klopp* [1984] ECR 653.

[185] Although the same rule also resulted from a ministerial decree.

[186] See Joined Cases 209–215 and 218/78, *Van Landewyck v. Commission* [1980] ECR 3125, paras. 87 and 88; Joined Cases 96–102, 104, 105, 108, and 110/82, *IAZ v. Commission* [1983] ECR 3369, paras. 19 and 20.

[187] See Decision 93/438/EEC of 30 June 1993 (IV/33.407—CNSD), OJ 1993 L 203/27; Decision 95/188/EC of 30 January 1995 (IV/33.686—COAPI), OJ 1995 L 122/37; Decision 1999/267 of 7 April 1999 (IV.36.147—EPI Code of Conduct), OJ 1999 L 106/14.

[188] *Commission v. Italy, CNSD*, *supra* n. 161.

[189] Opinion of the AG Léger delivered on 10 July 2001, para. 70.

[190] Joined Cases *Pavlov*, *supra* n. 168.

from the rules on competition since 'it was composed exclusively of self-employed medical specialists, whose economic interests it defended'.[191]

However, in the recent 'lawyers' cases the Court seems to go beyond the mere examination of the characteristics (composition, aim) of the association. It seems that where the association qualifies *prima facie* as an undertaking, the Court will further examine the nature of every specific measure it adopts. The aim of the Court is to ascertain whether, when adopting the contested measure, the association has acted as an economic agent promoting the interests of the profession or as an independent expert for the state. In order to ascertain this, the Court will take into consideration (a) the very object (economic or other) of the measure and (b) the extent to which the association, when adopting the measure, was bound by public-interest considerations.

The above criteria do not offer hard-and-fast solutions. Therefore, a case-by-case examination of every specific measure is to be carried out, in order to ascertain whether a particular association will be subject to competition rules.

(e) Health insurance funds Whether health insurance funds are to be considered as undertakings has been lengthily debated by the Court, in a series of cases. In the famous *Poucet and Pistre* cases[192] the Court held that a compulsory sickness and old-age insurance scheme, pursuing a social objective and embodying the principle of solidarity, does not fall within the ambit of the competition rules of the Treaty. In this judgment the Court gave some criteria concerning the existence of 'solidarity', which have been subsequently narrowed down by the judgments in the *FFSA* case and, later on, in the 'trilogy' judgments in cases *Albany, Brentjens*, and *Drijvende*. Thereafter, the *Pavlov* case came as a consolidation of the above case law. More recently, however, in the *Batisttello* case,[193] the Court, reversing its previous tendency, found that the Italian fund for occupational accidents and diseases embodies 'enough' solidarity and does not fall under the competition rules. The same restrictive approach was followed by the Court in the *Freskot* case,[194] where the Greek insurance scheme for farmers was found not to constitute an undertaking.

From these cases it appears that not just a single criterion but a set thereof (*faisceau d'indices*) are to be used in order to ascertain, on a case-by-case basis, whether a health insurance fund is an undertaking.[195]

(i) The objective pursued by the scheme In order to avoid the qualification as an undertaking, the objective pursued by the organization should be of a social nature. This was established in *Poucet and Pistre* but was found inadequate in subsequent cases.[196]

191 *Pavlov*, para. 88 *in fine*.

192 *Poucet, supra* n. 30.

193 Case C-281/00, *Battistello* [2002] ECR I-691 and its brief commentary by Idot, 'Nouvelle prise de position de la Cour sur la notion d'entreprise dans la ligne de l'arrêt *Poucet*', 12 *Europe* (2002).

194 *Freskot, supra* n. 151.

195 For a slightly different—and more authoritative—enumeration of the relevant criteria see the remarkable opinion of AG Jacobs in the 'trilogy' cases, *supra* n. 72, para. 333 *et seq*.

196 See e.g. *FFSA*, para. 20.

However, in the more recent case *Freskot*,[197] the Court did again refer to the social objective pursued by the fund there examined, in order to conclude to its public (non-undertaking) nature. The non-profit-making character of the activity and/or the body pursuing it could be used as an indication pointing towards the pursuance of a social objective but is in no way conclusive and may even be considered as irrelevant.[198]

(ii) The compulsory character of the scheme In *Poucet and Pistre* this was considered to be an important factor pointing towards a 'non undertaking', while in *FFSA* the Court pointed to the lack of such a character in order to conclude on the existence of an undertaking. This criterion, however, was not conclusive in the *Albany, Brentjens*, and *Drijvende* judgments, where the Court found that, notwithstanding the mandatory character of the scheme, the funds were undertakings. In *Freskot*, again, the compulsory character of the Greek insurance scheme for farmers was an element taken up by the Court in order hold that the fund in question did not constitute an undertaking.

(iii) The way in which the amount of contributions is calculated In *Poucet and Pistre* and *Batistello* the Court considered, as factors pointing against the qualification of undertaking the fact that 'the funds apply the law and thus cannot influence the amount of the contributions'[199] which is 'in the last resort, fixed by the state'.[200] Similarly, in *Freskot* the Court accorded conclusive weight to the fact that 'the contribution is essentially in the nature of a charge imposed by the state [. . . which] also determines the characteristics of that charge, including the rate'.[201] To the contrary, in *Drijvende* one of the elements that led the Court to the conclusion that the fund concerned was an undertaking was, precisely, that the amounts of contributions and benefits were determined by the fund itself.[202] Also, in *Poucet and Pistre* an important element pointing towards the existence of solidarity was the fact that contributions were proportional to the income from the occupation[203] and not related to the person-specific risks of each insured person, linked to age, sex, health history, etc.

(iv) The way in which the amount of benefits is calculated In the same line of reasoning the Court identifies solidarity elements, where the amount of benefits accruing to each insured person is determined by law and not by the fund itself[204] and where such benefits are 'identical for all those who received them'.[205] Solidarity is even more apparent where benefits are given to insured people notwithstanding

197 See *Freskot*, para. 76.

198 See in that sense AG Jacobs in his opinion in the 'trilogy' cases, para. 336. The learned AG thinks that also the social aim is irrelevant.

199 *Poucet*, para. 15.

200 *Batistello*, para. 43.

201 *Freskot*, para. 78.

202 *Drijvende*, para. 71.

203 *Poucet*, para. 10.

204 *Poucet*, para. 15, *Freskot*, para. 78.

205 *Poucet*, para. 10.

the fact that their payments to the fund are overdue or interrupted.[206] In a more general way, where benefits are not related to the contributions but, rather, to the personal needs of the insured person, this is likely to be dictated by solidarity, not economic considerations. In this respect, the judgments in *FFSA* and the *Albany, Brentjens*, and *Drijvende* cases, as well as in *Batistello* are relevant.[207]

(v) The overall degree of state control The degree of state control that is exercised on the fund, both on the decision-making level[208] and on the discharge of its obligations[209] is to be taken into account. The more closely monitored by the state, the less likely that it be considered as an undertaking.

(vi) Capitalisation—redistribution A quite decisive criterion is whether the organization operates according to the principle of capitalization and is involved in some active management of the funds received, or whether it is limited to the redistribution of the contributions received. In other words, where the amount of benefits distributed depends on the financial results of the organization, we are clearly in the presence of economic activity. In this respect the *FFSA* and the *Albany, Brentjens*, and *Drijvende* cases, as well as *Pavlov*, are explicit.

(vii) Cross-subsidization The pursuance of some activities, even if they are loss-making and receive cross-subsidies by other, profitable ones, corresponds to the redistribution of welfare and is a feature inherent to the implementation of the principle of solidarity. In *Poucet and Pistre* the Court identified cross-subsidization at two levels: *first*, within the framework of the sickness and maternity scheme, from those contributing more to those contributing less, and *second*, between the profitable sickness and maternity scheme, on the one hand, and the loss-making old-age insurance scheme, on the other.[210]

(viii) Competitive schemes The existence of competitive schemes offered by private insurance companies would point towards the pursuance of economic activity and, thus, the existence of an undertaking.[211] Further, it could be that schemes that are economically self-sufficient may be considered to engage in economic activity liable of being pursued by an undertaking, while schemes that need to be (cross-) subsidized, as was the case in *Poucet and Pistre*, stand for the principle of solidarity.[212]

[206] *Poucet*, paras. 10 and 11, *Batistello*, para. 36.

[207] It is interesting to note that in *Batistello* the Court used a more qualified formula, stating in para. 40 that 'the amount of benefits paid is not *necessarily* proportionate to the insured person's earnings', emphasis added.

[208] See *Poucet*, para. 14 in comparison/contradiction with *Pavlov*, para. 114.

[209] See, e.g., *Batistello*, para. 43.

[210] *Poucet*, paras. 10 and 11.

[211] See, e.g., *Brentjens*, para. 84. See also *Pavlov*, para. 115.

[212] See Kessler, 'Droit de la concurrence et régimes de protection sociale: un bilan provisoire', in R. Kovar and D. Simon (eds.), *Service public et Communauté Européenne: entre l'intérêt général et le marché* (1998) 421 at 430, where reference is made to other critical commentators.

(f) Health authorities of the central/decentralized government The central or regional health authorities (ministries, secretariats, etc.) of any state will *prima facie* not be considered as undertakings. Where the public authorities are themselves involved in the pursuance of some economic activity, they will qualify as undertakings in this respect, but still fall outside the scope of the competition rules in as much as they exercise official authority. As Advocate General Jacobs has put it, 'the notion of undertaking is a relative concept in the sense that a given entity might be regarded as an undertaking for one part of its activities while the rest fall outside the competition rules'.[213] Official authorities may, however, be subject to competition rules by virtue of the combined application of Articles 3, 10, and 81 (ex 3, 5, 85) EC.[214]

None of the above criteria is conclusive by itself, but the combination is decisive. The most recent case law of the Court points towards recognizing a restrictive scope to the principle of solidarity and treating most funds as undertakings. In the *FENIN* case the Court confirmed that the test followed is a 'functional' not a 'structural' one[215] and the judgment of the Court may depend directly on the activity examined, not merely on the structure of the organization.[216] Moreover, once the public (i.e., non-undertaking) nature of the activity/organization has been established, the fact that the very exercise of the activity is being carried out by private undertakings contracted by the social security fund does not alter the qualifications.[217] This means that a private undertaking which carries out specific activities of non-economic nature on behalf of a social fund will not be considered as an undertaking, in respect to these very activities. In addition, all agreements and contracts entered into by the organization in relation to the non-economic activity are treated in the same way, irrespective of whether they are central or ancillary to the pursuit of that activity.[218]

II. Exceptions to the application of the competition rules

(a) Solidarity

(i) General Despite all the developments presented above, the principle that 'Community law does not detract from the powers of the Member States to organize

213 Opinion of AG Jacobs in Case C-475/99, *Glöckner* [2001] ECR I-8089, para. 72.

214 See Case C-2/91, *Meng* [1993] ECR I-5751, Case C-185/91, *Reiff* [1993] ECR I-5801, Case C-245/91, *Ohra* [1993] ECR I-5851, and Case C-266/96, *Corsica Ferries France* [1998] ECR I-3949; and more recently *Glöckner, supra* n. 180.

215 See *FENIN*, para. 16, where the Court admitted that 'it is the nature of the activity, not of the body, which decides whether the body is to be regarded as an undertaking'. Such a functional approach had been advocated, among others, by the present author in *supra* n. 1, at 712.

216 See the opinion of AG Jacobs in *Albany, Brentjens,* and *Drijvende* cases, *supra* n.72, paras. 207 and 311 *et seq.* and Pieters, *supra* n. 162 at 605; on a more critical tone Kessler, *supra* n. 212 at 430.

217 See, by analogy, Case C-222/98, *Van der Woude* [2000] ECR I-7111, para. 26, concerning the inapplicability of competition rules on a private undertaking managing a healthcare insurance scheme established within the framework of collective bargaining between employers and employees and, more importantly, *FENIN.*

218 See *FENIN*, para. 37.

their social security systems'[219] remains. These systems account for the principle of solidarity and embody the state's choices in the field of social policy.

This is why the Court in *Poucet and Pistre* and, before that in *Duphar* [220] and *Sodemare*,[221] has avoided the application of free market and/or competition principles on issues that obey a completely different logic. In this respect, one should keep in mind that the very aim of social and healthcare policy is to balance the extreme inequalities produced by free markets and competition.[222] In all subsequent cases, the social security schemes scrutinized by the Court, both under the Internal Market and the competition rules, have been examined as to the degree of solidarity they embody. Hence, in *Poucet and Pistre* and *Garcia*[223] the Court found the competition rules to be inapplicable to the organization of some compulsory insurance schemes, while in the *FFSA, Albany, Brentjens, Drijvende*, and *Pavlov* cases the Court found to the contrary, since in the schemes examined 'the principle of solidarity is extremely limited in scope'.[224]

From the above, it becomes clear that the existence of some 'core' solidarity activity creates a *prima facie* exception to the application of the Treaty rules, both on competition (including state aids) and on the Internal Market (including public Procurement).[225]

(ii) What is solidarity? At the outset, it has to be stressed that it is very difficult to know what exactly constitutes a 'core' solidarity activity. As seen above, the Court makes use of a series of different criteria, many of them tailor-made to the case under examination, to which it attaches variable importance.[226] Therefore, it is almost impossible for an entity involved in the provision of healthcare services to know whether or not it should abide by the aforementioned until before its case is actually judged by the ECJ.

It may be argued that the Court's case law on the existence of solidarity constitutes yet another manifestation of the Court's unwillingness to meddle with the exercise of genuine 'official authority' by the state or the emanations thereof.[227] More convincingly, however, Advocate General Jacobs argues that the exercise of official authority is one of the two reasons that may shelter an entity from the

[219] *Poucet*, para. 6. See also the introduction to the present chapter.

[220] *Duphar, supra* n. 68.

[221] For which see section 2.B.

[222] On the apparent antinomy between competition rules and social security rules see Kessler, *supra* n. 212.

[223] Case C-238/1994, *Garcia* [1996] ECR I-1673, an extremely 'laconic' judgment.

[224] See e.g. *FFSA*, para. 19. For the criteria embodying the principle of solidarity which, in turn, exclude the qualification of an entity as undertaking, see section 3.A.I.

[225] For which see section 3.B.II below.

[226] See section 3.A on the application of the competition rules.

[227] See also Karl, 'EU Competition Law and Health Care Systems' in M. McKee *et al., supra* n. 5, 161 at 163–170.

application of competition rules.[228] The second reason, according to the learned Advocate General, is the pursuance by the said entity of activities that have *always* been and are *necessarily* carried out by public (or assimilated) bodies.[229] Such activities are only indirectly linked to the exercise of official authority and include the coordination of air-traffic control,[230] the operation of a body entrusted with preventive anti-pollution surveillance,[231] and the organization of communal funeral services.[232] The pursuance of 'core' solidarity activities, such as the organization of a healthcare system, may, depending on the role one wants to assign to the state, fulfil either or both of the above criteria.

(iii) Effects of solidarity Where the existence of some 'core' solidarity activity is established, this will affect the application of the aforementioned rules in a different way. Competition rules will be altogether inapplicable. Entities involved in such an activity will freely enter into agreements with other entities[233] and with their employees.[234] Moreover, they will not be liable for the abuse of dominant position and will enjoy unfettered legal or factual monopolies.[235] The issue of cross-subsidization or of receiving public funds will not be raised. All the above situations will be inherent to—and necessary for—the pursuance of the 'core' solidarity activity. However, as it has been made clear from the analysis above, very rare are the cases where the Court will allow for so much discretion to be exercised by Member States. Yet, the fact that a 'core' solidarity activity is not present does not necessarily mean that all the competition rules become applicable since Article 86(2) may provide a valid exception thereto.

(b) Article 86(2) Article 86(2) on the pursuance of 'services of general interest' may be usefully invoked in order to set aside the application of the competition rules. This may be the case when the activity in question does not fulfil all the stringent conditions in order to qualify as a 'core' solidarity activity, but is still crucial to the pursuance of some activity of public interest. This will almost always be the case for activities related to the provision of healthcare services. If Article 86(2) is the Treaty provision securing 'universal service'[236] within the EU, healthcare services accessible to all, under reasonable conditions of time and price, certainly come within it's ambit.

[228] See the conclusions of AG Jacobs in *Albany, Brentjens*, and *Drijvende, supra* n. 216, para. 314.

[229] 'Always' and 'necessarily' are the two criteria set out by the Court in *Höfner and Elser* (*supra* n. 160) in order to ascertain whether any activity is public.

[230] Case C-364/92, *Eurocontrol* [1994] ECR I-43.

[231] Case C-343/95, *Cali e Figli* [1997] ECR I-1547.

[232] Case 30/87, *Bodson* [1988] ECR 2479.

[233] See *Bodson*.

[234] See the *Albany, Brentjens*, and *Drijvende* cases, *supra* n. 72.

[235] See *Bodson* and *Poucet*.

[236] On the highly controversial issue of 'universal service' and how to ensure it in a deregulated environment, see the two volumes edited by R. Kovar and D. Simon, *supra* n. 212.

It would seem, therefore, that Article 86(2) offers yet a second ground for exempting certain activities from the application of the competition rules. The two series of exceptions, however, remain distinct, both in respect of the conditions of their application and of their effects. The existence of a core solidarity activity is linked to the exercise of public authority and it is based on a series of economic, social, societal, and other criteria. On the other hand, the application of Article 86(2) is mainly based on a case-by-case identification of a service of general interest and on a purely economic assessment of its viability. Moreover, the presence of a core solidarity activity is an 'external' exception, rendering inapplicable the competition rules altogether. Article 86(2), however, is an inherent limitation to the application of competition rules, affecting each activity separately, provided that this activity serves the general interest and may be compromised in a competitive environment. The existence of two sets of exceptions is clearly set out by Advocate General Jacobs in his opinion in the *Albany, Brentjens*, and *Drijvende* cases. There, the learned Advocate General *first* qualified the sectoral pension funds as being undertakings, thus rejecting that they were pursuing 'core' solidarity activities and *then* went on to examine, under Article 86(2), whether the various restrictions imposed were necessary for the fulfilment by the funds of their special mission.[237]

In *Albany, Brentjens*, and *Drijvende* the Court introduced a further restriction to the scope of the application of competition rules, in particular Article 81 EC. There, the Court found that some agreements concluded by undertakings may, nevertheless, fall outside the scope of Article 81(1) EC in view of their *nature* and *purpose*.[238] In this case the Court had to appreciate the legality of a collective agreement making compulsory the affiliation to some scheme for supplementary pension. The agreement was found not merely plurilateral, between undertakings, but the fruit of collective negotiations between organizations representing employers and workers (*nature*). Further, the *purpose* of the agreement was of a social nature and not of the sort contemplated by Article 81 EC. In view of these two considerations, the Court held that the agreement in question did not fall within the scope of Article 81(1) EC.

Therefore, in order to ascertain whether an agreement in the field of healthcare falls within the ambit of the competition rules, three successive questions should receive a positive reply:

- Are the entities involved undertakings, or is solidarity predominant? The answer to this question depends from the combined criteria set out above in Section. 3.A.I.e.
- Is there an agreement in the sense of Article 81(1), or are we in the presence of an arrangement of a social nature? This is to be appraised by reference to the nature and purpose of the agreement.

237 See conclusions of AG Jacobs in cases *Albany, Brentjens*, and *Drijvende, supra* n. 216, paras. 306 *et seq*.

238 See e.g. *Brentjens*, paras. 45–62, *Drijvende*, paras. 47–51.

- Is the service provided a commercial one or, rather, is it a service of general interest in the sense of Article 86(2) EC? This will depend on a fine economic analysis following the *Corbeau* line of case law.[239]

Whether an entity involved in the provision of healthcare is to be considered as an undertaking depends on the relative weighing of all the criteria stated under (A) and from the application of the exceptions under (B) above. Such an assessment may only take place on a case-by-case basis, making it almost impossible to know in advance with any degree of certainty whether the competition rules will apply at all, and if so, between which entities and to what degree. A further conclusion which may be drawn from the developments above is that the eventual application of the competition rules on the provision of healthcare services would leave almost intact vertically integrated national health systems and, to a lesser extent, refund systems. On the contrary, it would have a considerable impact on insurance based benefits-in-kind systems (like the ones of Austria, Germany, and the Netherlands) requiring multiple contracts (= agreements) between the various entities. Such agreements should be notified for exemption or else fall in the ambit of Article 81 EC as randomly applied by decentralized authorities and courts of the Member States.[240] The same is true for agreements between hospitals and independent doctors. Such an eventuality would introduce a great deal of legal uncertainty for the operation of benefits-in-kind systems, like the ones of Austria, Germany, and the Netherlands, where the healthcare system is based upon such agreements.[241] (*Conclusion 5*)

B. The Rules on State Aids and Public Procurement

Both the rules on state aids and on public procurement have as recipients the public authorities of Member States. The common aim of these rules is to ensure that governments may neither foreclose national markets nor falsify the competition between undertakings operating within the Internal Market. Therefore, both direct state action, through the allocation of subsidies and indirect action or through the preferential award of procurement contracts is prohibited.

However, the Member States, in order to ensure the proper functioning of their healthcare systems and to promote general social policy objectives, need to inject moneys to entities operating in the relevant sector. In order to ascertain whether

[239] See Case C-320/91, *Corbeau* [1993] ECR I-2562 and for an analysis of the relevant case law Wachsmann and Berrod, 'Les Critères de justification des monopoles: un premier bilan après l'affaire *Corbeau*', *RTDEur.* (1994) 39. See recently on the same topic, in the field of healthcare services, *Glöckner, supra* n. 180.

[240] On the decentralized application of the EC competition rules by national authorities and courts, see, among many: Venit, 'Brave New World: The Modernization and Decentralization of Enforcement under Articles 81 and 82 of the EC Treaty', 40 *CMLRev.* (2003) 569; Gerber, 'Modernizing European Competition Law: A Development Perspective', 22 *ECLR* (2001) 126; and Ehlermann, 'The Modernization of EC Antitrust Policy: A Legal and Cultural Revolution', 37 *CMLRev.* (2000) 537.

[241] Briefly on the various health care systems see Section 1.B.

this is compatible with the rules on procurement and on state aids, the legal qualification of the entities concerned is of crucial importance.[242]

I. State aids

According to the qualifications above, the rules on state aids could, under specific circumstances, stand as an obstacle to money transfers between the entities involved in the provision of healthcare services.

In this respect, some of the traditional aspects of the Commission's and the Court's case law on state aids is of particular importance. *First*, it has to be reminded that the notion of state aid is extensively interpreted. Thus, 'measures which, in various forms, mitigate the charges which are normally included in the budget of an undertaking and which, without therefore being subsidies in the strict meaning of the word, are similar in character and have the same effect are considered to constitute aid'.[243] Therefore, not only direct fund transfers but also alleviations of debts or of charges due by undertakings are to be considered as aids. What is necessary is that the relevant funds be public and that they confer an unjustified advantage to a specific (category of) undertaking(s).

Second, the test in order to ascertain whether the advantage conferred with public moneys is unjustified, is that of the 'private investor'[244] or, if the aid consists of the alleviation of a debt, that of the 'private creditor'.[245] This test consists of the examination, in each set of circumstances, of whether a private investor would reasonably have invested money, or a private creditor would have granted more generous payment facilities, to the undertaking under scrutiny. If under normal market conditions the undertaking were unlikely to obtain such benefits, then we are in the presence of an aid.

Third, the assessment of the above issues has to be made by reference to purely economic criteria, which may include the pursuance of a structural policy, guided by prospects of profitability in the medium or longer term. To the contrary, considerations of social policy may not justify the selective attribution of money benefits. As the Court itself has repeatedly held 'the social character of such state measures is not sufficient to exclude them outright from classification as aid for the purposes of Art. 92 [now 87] of the Treaty'.[246]

Applying the above well-established principles, the ECJ has given two important judgments touching upon the organization of the national welfare and

[242] Therefore, the developments above, at section 3.A.I., concerning the qualification of the various entities as undertakings or as public authorities are extremely relevant.

[243] Case C-200/97, *Ecotrade* [1998] ECR I-7907, para. 34 and Case C-75/97, *Belgium v. Commission, Maribel* [1999] ECR I-3671, para. 23.

[244] See, for instance, Case C-42/93, *Spain v. Commission* [1994] ECR I-4175, para. 14.

[245] *Ibid.*, para. 46.

[246] See Case C-241/94, *France v. Commission* [1996] ECR I-4551, para. 21; Case C-342/96, *Spain v. Commission* [1999] ECR I-2459; *Belgium v. Commission, Maribel, supra* n. 243.

healthcare systems. The *DMT* case[247] concerned the qualification as a state aid of the very important payment facilities (deferral for eight years) granted by the Belgian National Social Security Office (ONSS) to a Belgian removals company that was going bankrupt. The Court found that 'where a public body with responsibility for collecting social security contributions tolerates late payment of such contributions, its conduct undoubtedly gives the recipient undertaking a significant commercial advantage by mitigating, for that undertaking, the burden associated with normal application of the social security system'.[248] Moreover, the Court found that the eventual 'interest or penalties for late payment [. . .] cannot wholly undo the advantage gained by that undertaking'.[249] The same solution seems valid for the late payment of contributions to a contributory healthcare scheme. It is unclear, however, what the position would be in relation, say, to a mutual system of healthcare services, where no state expenditure is involved.

In *Belgium v. Commission, Maribel*, the Court confirmed the Commission's decision in finding that the Belgian system of applying reduced tariffs of social security contributions to selected industrial sectors 'exposed to fierce international competition' constituted a state aid. The Court was ready to accept that such a measure was deemed to foster employment, but held that it should, nevertheless, be regarded as state aid since it distinguished arbitrarily between beneficiaries and non-beneficiaries and 'it [was] not justified by the nature or general scheme of the social welfare system'.[250]

The same logic was followed by the EFTA Court in the *Norway v. EFTA Surveillance Authority* case.[251] According to the Norwegian National Insurance Act, undertakings were subject to social security contributions according to five different tariff scales corresponding to five different geographical zones. The EFTA Court acknowledged that 'the Norwegian scheme is purposeful, effective and proportionate when assessed in relation to its objectives'.[252] This did not prevent the Court, however, from considering that 'the system of regionally differentiated social security contributions must be seen as favouring certain undertakings [. . .] unless it can be shown that the selective effect of the measures is justified by the nature or general scheme of the system itself'. The Court further added that any such justification 'must derive from the inherent logic of the general system and result from objective conditions within that general system'.[253]

[247] Case C-256/97, *Déménagements-Manutention Transport SA (DMT)* [1999] ECR I-3913.

[248] *Belgium v. Commission, Maribel, supra* n. 243, para. 19.

[249] *Ibid.*, para. 21.

[250] *Maribel*, para. 34 *in fine*.

[251] Case E-6/98 *Norway v. EFTA Surveillance Authority*, published in www.efta.int/docs/court/Publications/Decision/1999/E-98-06.html.

[252] *Ibid.*, para. 30.

[253] *Ibid.*, para. 38.

From the above cases, a very fine line is to be drawn between fund transfers or other facilities that form part of a general and coherent system of social benefits, and measures that are aimed at some arbitrarily determined sectors or undertakings. The former will be compatible with the rules on state aids while the latter will, in principle, be illegal. This means that a coherent system of social benefits will not face censorship by the Community institutions. Moreover, the very existence of 'coherence' and the maintenance thereof, will constitute an overriding reason of general interest, justifying the non-application of the Treaty rules on the Internal Market.[254] Further, states are not precluded from invoking policy considerations in order to uphold such illegal measures under Article 87(3)e EC.[255] This, however, would necessitate that the Council, acting by qualified majority, adopts a proposal by the Commission to the effect that aids connected to the functioning of national health systems are exempted from the prohibitions.

II. Public procurement

As far as the application of public procurement rules is concerned, there are no hard-and-fast solutions covering all of the entities involved in the provision and funding of healthcare services.[256] It would seem, however, that doctors, practitioners, and private hospitals or clinics fall outside the scope of the relevant directives, while the public hospitals and national authorities are in principle covered by them. Doubt subsists, therefore, in relation to the social funds and the hospitals, which, although not public, rely heavily on public funds for their survival.

In this respect, it must be remembered that addressees of the directives, i.e., 'contracting authorities', are not only the state, regional, and local authorities but also 'bodies governed by public law'. The latter's legal form (public scheme, company, etc.) is irrelevant[257] as long as three conditions are met: they need (a) to have legal personality, (b) to be financed or controlled by the state (or an emanation thereof), and (c) to have been 'established for the specific purpose of meeting needs in the general interest, not having an industrial or commercial character'. The Court has made it clear that these are cumulative conditions.[258] Member States have been invited to enumerate in Annex I of the Directive 93/37, now

[254] On the general grounds for exceptions to the application of the Treaty rules on health care services cf. section 2.B. More specifically for the argument of 'coherence' see section 2.B.II.

[255] See in that sense the EFTA Court's judgment, *supra* n. 251, para. 39 *in fine*.

[256] For a case study see Sveman, 'Procurement of Health Care Services in Sweden in General' and Essinger, 'The Example of Procurement of Acute Care in the Stockholm Region', joint paper delivered in the high-level two-day conference organized by the Belgian Presidency of the EU on *European Integration and National Health Care Systems: A Challenge for Social Policy*, Gent, 7–8 December 2001.

[257] Case C-360/96, *BFI Holding* [1998] ECR I-6821, para. 53.

[258] See e.g. Case C-44/96, *Mannesmann Anlangebau Austria* [1998] ECR I-73 and Case C-360/96, *Gemeente Arnhem* [1998] ECR I-6821.

replaced by Annex IV of Directive 2004/18,[259] national 'bodies' that fall in the above category.

However, this enumeration is not exhaustive and the Court has been called upon on several occasions to interpret the above three conditions. Unsurprisingly, the most controversial condition has been the one related to the opposition between activities in the pursuance of general interest and activities of an industrial or commercial character. Following the judgments of the Court in the *Mannesmann*, the *BFI Holding*, and, more recently, the *Agora and Excelsior* cases[260] two series of conclusions may be drawn.

First, that the fact that some activity serves the general interest does not, in itself, exclude the industrial or commercial character of that very activity. Or, to use the Court's wording, there is 'a distinction between needs in the general interest not having an industrial or commercial character and needs in the general interest having an industrial or commercial character'.[261]

Second, in order to ascertain in which of the above categories an activity falls, the Court uses a set of criteria (*faisceau d'indices*) which may be summarized as follows: (a) the absence of considerable competition in providing the same activity, (b) the existence of decisive state control over the said activity,[262] (c) the pursuance of the activity and the satisfaction of the relevant needs in a way different from what is offered in the market place, and (d) the absence of financial risk. These are all factors which point towards the absence of industrial and commercial character.[263]

These criteria are very similar to the ones used by the Court in order to ascertain whether social security, pension and healthcare funds are to be viewed as 'undertakings'.[264] Therefore, it would seem that, to the extent that the two series of criteria are applied consistently, the coordination of the two sets of rules is perfectly workable:[265] an entity that is not an undertaking will, more often than not, be considered to be a contracting authority. Hence, any entity operating in the field of healthcare services will be subject either to the competition or to the public procurement rules—but not both. This is a satisfactory result, both from a legal/systematic point of view, since the EC rules are applied in a coherent and complementary way, and from an economic point of view, since the same entities

[259] Directive 2004/18/EC of the European Parliament and the Council of 31 March 2004, OJ 2004 L 134/114.

[260] For the two first cases see *supra* n. 257 and 258; see also Case C-223 and 260/99, *Agora and Excelsior* [2001] ECR I-3605.

[261] *Agora*, para. 32.

[262] Not the entity providing it, this is a distinct condition directly enumerated in the Directives.

[263] H. Synodinos, *Application of the Competition Rules during the Conclusion and Execution of Public Procurement Contracts* (in Greek) (2001) at 72 *et seq.*

[264] See Section 3.A.I.

[265] However, such a consistent approach is lacking. See, below, the two last paragraphs of the present section.

are not simultaneously subject to the restrictive rules on procurement and to competition from other undertakings.

However, this idyllic view collapses if one turns to Annex IV of Directive 2004/18 on public procurement, where an extensive enumeration of entities considered, by the states, to be falling within the meaning of 'contracting authorities', is to be found. In this Annex many states, like Belgium and France, have included a multitude of social funds, some of which are likely to constitute 'undertakings' under the criteria set out above (under 13.A.I.e). Needless to say, the fact that they are enumerated in this Annex does not preclude them from being judged under the basic Treaty provisions and held to be subject to the competition rules.

In this respect, it should be kept in mind that an entity which is listed in Annex IV of Directive 2004/18 or any other entity that fulfils the criteria set out above and is considered to be a contracting authority will be dealt with as such even in respect of auxiliary activities which are of a commercial nature and may be offered within a competitive environment.[266] This is also true in the field of healthcare services, as it is clearly illustrated in the *Tögel* case.[267] The Sickness Insurance Fund for Lower Austria had concluded contracts for the provision of ambulance services in Austria with two private undertakings. Under the terms of these contracts the fund would reimburse to insured persons fees paid to the two undertakings for any sort of emergency transport. A third ambulance operator, Mr. Tögel, who asked to enter into a similar contract was turned down by the fund. Mr. Tögel brought an action before the Austrian courts alleging the direct effect and the violation of Directive 92/50, on the procurement of services. The Court ruled that most of the Directive's provisions are sufficiently clear to be directly effective, but specified that the direct application thereof is possible only after the expiration of the transposition period. Therefore, the Court concluded that the Directive could not be invoked in order to challenge the validity of agreements concluded before that date—not to mention agreements, as the ones at stake, concluded before the accession of Austria to the EU. All these findings are perfectly in line with previous case law. What is interesting, however, is the fact that nowhere in its judgment does the Court pay any attention to the nature of the transport activities and to the fact that they could be offered—and indeed were offered—by private undertakings within a competitive environment. Despite the fact that Annex IV of Directive 2004/18 does not contain any list of Austrian 'contracting authorities', the Court takes it that the fund is such an authority and does not distinguish between the various activities it undertakes. Therefore, *Tögel* stands for the finding that healthcare entities remain subject to the rules on public procurement (a) even where they offer benefits in nature and (b) even when such benefits include auxiliary services of a commercial nature.

[266] Case *Mannesmann, supra* n. 258, and Case C-360/9,6 *Gemeente Arnhem v. BFI Holding BV* [1996] ECR I-6821.

[267] Case C-76/97, *Tögel* [1998] ECR-5357.

Moreover, the eventual existence of solidarity elements is completely irrelevant to the applicability of the rules on public procurement.[268]

This case should be compared with the more recent case on ambulance services decided by the Court. In the *Glöckner* case [269] the Court had to judge on the compatibility of the German legislation on ambulance services with the EC competition rules and Directive 92/50/EC on the procurement of services.[270] The legislation at issue made the taking up of the activity of ambulance services subject to a prior authorization by the local authorities. No system of public tendering was set up. The plaintiff, Glöckner, whose authorization was not renewed, complained that the system of prior authorization was contrary both to the rules on competition and the ones on public procurement. The Court, following the terms of the preliminary question and the opinion of Advocate General Jacobs, limited its answer solely to the applicability of the competition rules. It found that ambulance services did constitute economic activity and, therefore, the entities offering them did qualify as undertakings for the application of the competition rules. On the other hand, the authorities giving the relevant authorization did not constitute undertakings, since they were exercising official authority.

Despite the arguments put forward by the parties, both the Advocate General and the Court avoided the difficult question of whether the absence of a tendering system was altogether compatible with the Treaty rules on free movement of services and the procurement directives.[271] The Advocate General, followed implicitly by the Court, contended that 'the procedure for obtaining such an administrative authorisation is very different from the award of a public service contract and is therefore not covered by the rules on public procurement'.[272]

It is not very easy to reconcile this case with the judgment in *Tögel*. In the earlier case the Court seemed to imply that ambulance services should be awarded to undertakings by public tendering according to Directive 92/50/EC. In the *Glöckner* case, however, the Court took it for granted that such a public tendering system was out of the question. One way of reading the two cases together is to accept that the Court does not intervene directly in the precise way the states organize healthcare services, but rather oversees that the system chosen by each state is applied in accordance with the Treaty rules.

Seen from a slightly different perspective, the difference of approach followed by the Court in the cases above, may be seen as an indication that the same set of

[268] Which is logical, since the rules on public procurement, by definition, are supposed to apply to public authorities which, contrary to undertakings, quite often pursue objectives dictated by solidarity.

[269] *Glöckner, supra* n. 180.

[270] Council Directive 92/50/EC of 18 June 1992 OJ 1992 L 209/1; now repealed and replaced by Directive 2004/18, *supra* n. 259.

[271] The decision keeps, nevertheless, its importance, since it gives a number of precisions to the application of Art. 86(2) on services of general economic interest, thus enriching the *Corbeau* case law; see in this respect Idot, 'De l'application de l'article 82 CE à un service public de santé', 11 *Europe* (2001).

[272] Opinion of AG Jacobs, *supra* n. 213, para. 99 *in fine*.

rules may have completely different outcomes when applied to the legal relationships pertaining to the various healthcare systems. Moreover, it shows that under some circumstances, similar entities, or even the very same entity, operating in the provision of healthcare services may be treated simultaneously as an undertaking for the application of the competition rules, all the same being subject to the restrictive public procurement rules.[273]

CONCLUSION

The conclusion to the present chapter may be reached by combining the interim conclusions drawn at the various stages of the analysis, from which it can be seen that a great *flou juridique* is being designed.

The social healthcare systems of Member States vary greatly and are organized, both materially and financially, on a national basis. The great idea underlying them, solidarity, is also a fundamentally national concept. Furthermore, the Community lacks both experience and, more importantly, legitimacy, in the form of an express legal basis, for it to proceed with substantial positive integration, through harmonization, in the field of healthcare.

Negative integration pursued by the ECJ through the piecemeal application of the Internal Market principles is, by definition, casuistic and may not ensure a coherent and smooth coordination of the various systems. The relevant case law of the Court is neither complete nor entirely coherent and, even if it were, it would affect in distinct ways each healthcare system.[274] Furthermore, both the application of the competition rules and exceptions thereto depend on a series of considerations with innumerate variables. In such a situation legal certainty appears merely as a remote eventuality. The situation becomes even more complicated when the eventual (cumulative, at cases) application of the rules on state aid and public procurement is contemplated.[275]

Therefore, the current situation is not completely satisfactory. It is believed that free movement of both professionals and patients is an irreversible *acquis*, which should be further encouraged. This necessitates the adoption of secondary legislation, which will coordinate, on the lines set by the recent case law of the Court, the conditions under which healthcare services are to be organized within Member States. Such legislation should run parallel to the rules of Regulation 1408/71. It is questionable whether such legislation could have as its sole legal basis the Internal Market rules, or whether recourse should also be made to the provisions of Title XI

[273] However, this is not necessarily an insurmountable constraint for the entity concerned, since the specific nature of medical goods and services and the great 'asymmetry of information', which prevails in this field, will often allow for recourse to be made to the 'closed procedure', thus giving more leeway to the entity.

[274] Putting some more strain on benefits-in-kind systems.

[275] In any event, the applicability of competition and state aid rules is more likely to strain the operation of insurance rather than national health systems.

of the Treaty on social policy, etc.[276] Or, whether, indeed, some more 'valiant' legal basis should be introduced into the Treaty. In this respect, the impact of the Charter of Fundamental Rights of the EC, and its eventual ratification as part of the Constitutional Treaty, remains to be ascertained.[277]

Moreover, the application of the general competition rules to entities administering social security schemes may not be satisfactory. The Court itself has shown great caution in this respect, by excluding altogether from the scope of the said rules specific categories of entities and agreements. However, in an era of deregulation and 'privatization' of activities that were traditionally reserved for the state, the respect of competition principles by entities involved in administering the social security system may be useful. These rules, however, should be clear, known in advance, and sector-specific. Therefore, the adoption of some text of secondary legislation, which could eventually take the form of a block exemption regulation, seems necessary. From the judgments of the Court in the *Albany, Brentjens*, and *Drijvende* cases it seems that such an action would necessitate recourse, except from Article 81 itself, to Article 134 EC. Likewise, a decision by the Council, according to Article 87(3)e, could set the conditions under which social and healthcare systems could be lawfully financed. Moreover, the Commission could, in a text of 'soft law', clarify whether and in what way the notion of 'service of general interest' may be relevant in the field of healthcare services.

Lastly, entities caught by the rules on competition should unequivocally be exempted from observance of the rules on public procurement, while some guidelines should be drawn in order to avoid a rigid and counter-productive application of the rules on state aids on the organization and functioning of national healthcare systems.

From all the above, one final conclusion may be drawn. All Member States are currently contemplating and/or carrying out reform of their healthcare systems. In this context, there is a major political choice to be made: either states continue on a purely national logic which, however, is likely to prove complex and unsatisfactory, or the Community is given the express aim and the relevant competences (in the form of a sufficient legal basis) to coordinate Member States' healthcare policies in a coherent manner. It remains to be seen whether the application of the Open Method of Coordination in the field of health, foreseen in Article III-278 of the Constitutional Treaty, will lead to further convergence or if, to the contrary, it will constitute a mere bureaucratic stalemate.

[276] It should be remembered that Title XIII on Public Health recognizes very limited legislative powers to the Community. Moreover, it should be borne in mind that even if a double legal basis were required, the measures would be adopted according to the procedures laid down in Title III, on free movement, since they provide for a fuller participation of the European Parliament than mere 'consultation' and they do not require unanimity like Art. 137, for the adoption of measures in the field of social security. On the issue of the double legal basis see Case 45/86, *Commission v. Council (generalized preferences)* [1987] ECR 1493 and Case 242/87, *European Parliament v. Council (Erasmus)* [1989] ECR 1425.

[277] 2000/C 364/01 OJ 2000 C 364/1. See also the Commission Communication on the legal nature of the Charter, COM (2000) 644 *final*.

6

Beyond Competition: Services of General Interest and European Community Law

JULIO BAQUERO CRUZ

INTRODUCTION

Does Community law give priority to competition over services of general interest? Does it prejudice the provision of those services? These are the central questions of this chapter, which deals with issues that are as important as they are difficult.

They are important because they touch upon 'the basic structure of society', which is 'the primary subject of justice'.[1] The services of general interest provided in a given society have a bearing upon its cohesion and stability. Other factors may be more important, but the influence of services of general interest can be far-reaching. First, since their provision may involve redistribution through the equalization of tariffs or cross-subsidies, they can be used to complement more traditional instruments of social policy. Second, economic and social policies are so closely linked that decisions concerning services of general interest will probably be reflected in decisions in other fields. Thus, the provision of those services is important as one of the elements giving shape to a society and as an indicator of its general state.

The European Union has such an influence on major social institutions like the level of public expenditure, economic, social and monetary policies, market regulation, and the provision of services of general interest, that one may see it as contributing to the basic structure of a society of societies. The growth of Community legislation concerning services of general interest bears witness to the fact that their vast political potential has not passed unnoticed by the institutions of the Union. In its reports on services of general interest, the Commission always emphasizes that they constitute 'a key element in the European model of society'.[2]

I am grateful to Silvia Acierno, Loïc Azoulai, Gráinne de Búrca, Josh Holmes, Síofra O'Leary, Miguel Poiares Maduro, Daniel Sarmiento, and Stephan Wernicke, for comments, suggestions, and criticism. The text of this chapter was completed on 30 June 2004.

[1] J. Rawls, *A Theory of Justice* (1973), at 7 and 54.

[2] *Communication on Services of General Interest in Europe*, OJ 2001 C 17/4. See also *Services of General Interest in Europe*, OJ 1996 C 281/3: 'general interest services are *at the heart* of the European

As a result of the limited scope of the Treaty and of the competences enshrined in it, however, the Union may only provide a partial social model for the Member States, which can correct it and add to it.

Another reason accounting for the importance of the topic is that it concerns constitutional law. In contrast with the position in most Member States, in which the issue of services of general interest is left to public authorities with wide discretion or no constitutional limits, the Community legal order includes in this field, as in other economic fields, a judicially enforceable constitutional norm.[3] This norm—the normative heart of our inquiry—is Article 86(2) of the Treaty establishing the European Community, according to which undertakings entrusted with the provision of services of general *economic* interest are subject to the rules of that Treaty in so far as they do not obstruct the provision of those services.

Finally, the importance of our topic is also due to the nature of services of general interest. They are generally provided through the public sphere or by private undertakings that have been entrusted with that task. Their mixed character lies in the fact that they are economic and social, private and public. The undertakings that provide them have a special public calling and are used as instruments of the political community. Their main objective is not that of making profits, but that of carrying out activities which are essential for the functioning of a society. And if they collapse, many other activities may collapse (the clearest example being the provision of electricity). In the law of the Member States, this fundamental character is clear in the possibility to restrict the exercise of fundamental rights such as the right to strike in view of the need to provide essential services.[4] Under the international law of war an occupying power is also bound 'to permit and not to prejudice activities related to the maintenance of the essential public utility services'.[5]

Our topic is difficult for various reasons.

First, the jurist is confronted with unclear texts such as Articles 16 or 86(2) of the Treaty. Their obscurity is generally shared by legislation in the field.

A second reason is related to the differences between the legal orders of the Member States concerning services of general interest, which make it difficult to find a common approach. This is not the place for a comparative account, but even

model of society'; *Report to the Laeken European Council: Services of General Interest (Presented by the Commission)*, COM(2001) 598, at 3: 'services of general interest remain *an essential building block* of the European model of society'; *Green Paper on Services of General Interest*, COM(2003) 270, at 3: '[services of general interest] are part of the values shared by all European societies and form *an essential element* of the European model of society'; *White Paper on Services of General Interest*, COM(2004) 374, at 4: '*one of the pillars* of the European model of society' (emphasis added).

[3] See J. Baquero Cruz, *Between Competition and Free Movement: The Economic Constitutional Law of the European Community* (2002), at 29–38 and 76–80.

[4] See, for example, the case law of the French Conseil Constitutionnel, judgment 79-105 of 25 July 1979, *Recueil* (1979) 33, and Article 28(2) of the Spanish Constitution.

[5] Article 63 of the Geneva Convention Relative to the Protection of Civilian Persons in Time of War of 12 August 1949, *United Nations—Treaty Series*, 1950, at 287.

a cursory examination shows major differences. In French public law, services of general interest are very entrenched, legally, institutionally, and culturally. In other Member States, such as Germany, Spain, or Italy, equivalent categories also exist in administrative law, but they are not so entrenched. In a third category of legal orders, such as that of the United Kingdom, there is no legal notion of services of general interest and few or no limits affecting the processes of privatization and liberalization. Differences among the legal orders of the Member States abound in the Union, to be sure, but they do not always make it so hard to find common approaches. In our field, however, the position of certain Member States—in particular that of France—has usually been one of resistance to the 'competition-centred' model propounded by other Member States. This resistance has shaped the law in our field as a fragile and evolving compromise that accommodates but never resolves the tension between services of general interest and competition.

A third difficulty is due to the fact that the solution to the economic issue of how much competition is compatible with the provision of services of general interest has traditionally been left to the political institutions to decide on political and economic grounds. When judges were first confronted with Article 86(2), a provision unprecedented in other legal systems, it was certainly difficult to find operational and predictable legal tests that reflected the economic ideas underlying that provision. And it remains difficult, at present, to devise a legal test that grants the necessary margin of action to political institutions without leaving the rules underenforced or unenforced.

Our topic is therefore important, difficult, and conflictive. It is a topic about limits, blurred areas, and tensions: between the public and the private spheres, the State and the market, cooperative and competitive conceptions of society, market failures and State failures, the social and liberal elements of constitutionalism. It is a difficult legal topic that has to do with the limits of the Community legal order and of the competences of the Union. It could also be seen as an internal test of the flexibility of the predominantly liberal economic constitutional law of the Community, in addition to the external tests provided by its interaction with the sometimes more socially oriented laws and policies of the Member States. Article 86(2) of the Treaty may thus offer an opportunity to enrich Community constitutional law with non-market values, without necessarily abandoning the values of the market. However, this provision is not the magical solution to overcome 'the political decoupling of economic integration and social protection issues which', according to Fritz Scharpf, 'has characterized the real process of European integration from Rome to Maastricht'.[6] It may offer at most a limited correction.

The issues are not insoluble, however. Our task is to trace the constitutional limits that the Treaty imposes on public and private action with regard to services of general interest. Tracing them involves the establishment of tools and criteria to decide whether the advantages given to undertakings entrusted with the provision

[6] Scharpf, 'The European Social Model', 40 *JCMS* (2002) 645, at 646.

of such services are in the public interest or rather aim at improving their own competitive position. The analysis presented here will focus on the general constitutional framework. Legislation, increasingly important as it is, will be examined only in one section and not exhaustively. Among the various constitutional themes only those of direct relevance to the central questions of this chapter are examined: the structure of Article 86(2) and its place in the system of the Treaty, the concept of economic activities, the substantive test of Article 86(2), and the framework for the adoption of legislation. Thus, other important issues such as the relation between services of general interest and State aid law[7] or the precise extent of the direct effect of Article 86(2) are not examined.

1. ARTICLE 86(2) AND THE PRIORITY PROBLEM

Article 86(2) of the Treaty, the normative heart of our enquiry, should be seen in the context of other Treaty provisions and of the ever-growing Community legislation in this field, but it retains its central character both *vis-à-vis* legislation—in view of its constitutional character—and *vis-à-vis* other provisions of the Treaty—in view of its direct effect,[8] its general scope, and its development in the case law.

The context of Article 86(2) of the Treaty is, first of all, that of paragraphs (1) and (3). The first thing to acknowledge is that Article 86(1) and (2) are not self-contained norms.[9] Both refer 'to the rules contained in this Treaty' and, in particular, to certain provisions thereof. Their normative substance will thus partly depend on that of those other provisions to which they refer. Article 86(1) of the Treaty enshrines the principle of equality of treatment between public and private companies, which for all its rhetorical importance has little normative substance in itself: since public undertakings are undertakings, the competition rules would have applied to them in any event. Its added value lies in the fact that it expressly obliges the Member States to respect the Treaty in their relationship with the categories of undertakings mentioned in it. Without Article 86(1), those rules of the Treaty

[7] This issue was at the heart of the judgment of 24 July 2003 in *Altmark* (Case C-280/00 [2003] ECR I-7747). On this judgment, see Acierno and Baquero Cruz, 'La sentencia *Altmark* sobre ayudas de Estado y servicios públicos', *Revista Española de Derecho Europeo* (2004) 169.

[8] From an initial denial of direct effect (Case 10/71, *Ministère Public Luxembourg* v *Muller (Port de Mertert)* [1971] ECR 723), the Court came to recognize it (Case 155/73, *Sacchi* [1974] ECR 409 or Case 66/86, *Ahmed Saeed* [1989] ECR 803). The question of whether Article 86(2) remains directly effective when applied with a provision that is not directly effective has not yet been decided, but *Almelo* (Case C-393/92, [1994] ECR I-1477) seems to imply that a national court may apply Article 86(2) in the context of an agreement in breach of Article 81(1), which at that time could only be exempted by the Commission pursuant to Article 81(3), a non-directly applicable provision. See, in favour of the direct effect of Article 86(2) in such cases, paras. 78–81 of the Opinion of Advocate General Tizzano in *Ferring* (Case C-53/00, [2001] ECR I-6891).

[9] See Buendía Sierra, 'Article 86: Exclusive Rights and Other Anti-Competitive State Measures', in J. Faull and A. Nikpay (eds.), *The EC Law of Competition* (1999) 273, at 277.

addressed to the Member States, such as the free movement rules, would also apply to them regarding their relationship with such undertakings, but one would need to apply Article 10 together with the competition rules addressed to undertakings in order to oblige the Member States not to detract from their effectiveness. Indeed, the Court of Justice of the European Communities (hereinafter 'the Court') has considered Article 86 to be 'only a particular application of certain general principles which bind the Member States',[10] a holding which should be limited to the first paragraph of that provision. Finally, Article 86(3) mandates the Commission to 'ensure the application of the provision of this Article' and, 'where necessary, [to] address appropriate directives or decisions to the Member States'.

According to the second paragraph of Article 86 of the Treaty, '[u]ndertakings entrusted with the operation of services of general economic interest or having the character of a revenue-producing monopoly shall be subject to the rules contained in this Treaty, in particular to the rules on competition, in so far as the application of such rules does not obstruct the performance, in law or in fact, of the particular tasks assigned to them. The development of trade must not be affected to such an extent as would be contrary to the interests of the Community.'

This is a very complex provision. Without it the situation in Community law would be quite different.

Three concentric circles define the scope of Article 86(2). The first coincides with the outer limits of the notion of 'economic activities', the most general condition for its application. The second is defined by the concept of an 'undertaking entrusted with the operation of services of general economic interest'. The third area is defined by the notion of 'obstruction' of the performance of the tasks of general interest assigned to those undertakings, in which case the provision or provisions of the Treaty that obstruct performance of the tasks would not be applicable. It is debatable whether the final sentence of Article 86(2) (development of trade) constitutes an autonomous criterion or a mere qualification of the third criterion, but the latter option seems to me correct.

The concept of an 'undertaking entrusted with the operation of services of general economic interest' does not define the personal scope of Article 86(2) of the Treaty, but only its subject matter. Once we are certain to be in a situation involving such an undertaking, this provision will not only apply to its behaviour, but also to that of public actors in their relationships with it. This broad definition of the personal scope of application of Article 86(2) is essential in view of the hybrid character of those undertakings. Regardless of their public or private status, they take decisions which are commercial in nature. At the same time, they are subject to direct or indirect public influence. It is thus indispensable to allow both undertakings and Member States to benefit from Article 86(2). This applicability is sometimes justified by the systematic connection with Article 86(1), whose addressees

[10] See Case 13/77, *GB-Inno-BM* [1977] ECR 2115, para. 42. On the State action doctrine in Community competition law, see Baquero Cruz, *supra* n. 3, at 127–161.

are the Member States.[11] But even if Article 86(2) is seen as a more autonomous provision, one could defend its application to the Member States in view of the need to assess the relevant situation as a whole.

The substantive scope of the provision is the key to its social and economic effects. It traces the contours of the regime applicable to services of general economic interest, different from the 'common law' of competition and free movement, and justified by the special charges inherent in the provision of those services.[12] For all their importance, the concepts of 'economic activity' and of 'obstruction in law or in fact' are extremely vague. Their gradual definition in the case law will be analysed below.

It may be interesting at this juncture to elaborate further on the 'priority problem'. The very text of Article 86(2) invites us to reflect on whether it establishes a priority between competition and services of general interest. The issue is linked to that of whether the Treaty as a whole gives priority to economic over social matters.

The idea of the 'priority problem' is taken from section 8 of *A Theory of Justice*, in which John Rawls tried to limit the role of intuition in the theory of justice by proposing to find principles which could be put in what he calls 'a serial or lexical order', 'an order which requires us to satisfy the first principle in the ordering before we can move on to the second, the second before we consider the third, and so on. A principle does not come into play until those previous to it are either fully met or do not apply. A serial ordering avoids, then, having to balance principles at all; those earlier in the ordering have an absolute weight, so to speak, with respect to later ones, and hold without exception.'[13] This could be a way of reducing intuitionism in the theory of justice by positing, as a matter of constitutional law, a 'lexical order' between the basic political and civil liberties and social rights and policies. Such an ordering may be questionable in itself, but it may even be more delicate to establish constitutional priorities between policy objectives.

Echoing Rawls, Fritz Scharpf has contended that in the Community context there is a priority of economic over social policy. 'At the national level', he has argued, 'economic policy and social-protection policy had and still have the same constitutional status—with the consequence that any conflict between these two types of interests could only be resolved politically'.[14] In the European Union, however, such conflicts are also resolved judicially. Once such an issue 'reaches the ECJ, the outcome is at best *uncertain*. In principle, at any rate, the Commission and the ECJ have been treating such conflicts by *the logic of a lexicographic ordering*: in consequence of the doctrines of "supremacy" and "direct effect", any requirement deduced from primary or secondary European law will override any national policy

[11] See Case C-320/91, *Corbeau* [1993] ECR I-2533, paras. 12–14. See also Mestmäcker, in U. Immenga and E.-J. Mestmäcker, *EG-Wettbewerbsrecht Kommentar* (1997) 1516, at 1583–1584.

[12] Kovar, 'Droit communautaire et service public, esprit d'orthodoxie ou pensée laïcisée?', *RTDE* (1996) 215, at 236–237.

[13] Rawls, *supra* n. 1, at 42–43.

[14] Scharpf, *supra* n. 6, at 647 and 665.

purposes, no matter how substantively important or politically salient in the national context.'[15] To overcome this situation, Scharpf would favour 'a balancing of market-enhancing and market-correcting concerns at the European level, instead of the lexicographic ordering that presently prevails'.[16]

A complete appraisal of Scharpf's argument would require an examination of Community case law on directly applicable rules of the Treaty and also of Community legislation. The present chapter, however, is limited to the issue of whether Article 86(2) of the Treaty and Community legislation on services of general interest give an absolute or a relative priority to competition over those services.

Since the text of Article 86(2) lends itself to different readings, the point of departure could not be more open. In choosing an interpretative route one will also be guided by one's political conceptions and understanding of competition law. Perhaps a competition law exclusively aimed at economic efficiency is less important than the adequate provision of services of general interest, but a competition law that also aims at taming private economic power and guaranteeing economic liberty may be as important, socially and constitutionally, as the provision of those services. One could even argue that the maintenance of a free and competitive economic system constitutes an important service of general interest.

An absolute priority of competition over services of general interest has never existed in Community constitutional law. Such an option is excluded by the very wording of Article 86(2). Neither the Court nor the Commission have ever contended that services of general interest could only be provided once the goals of competition were realized. The legal dispute has rather been focused on whether there should be a *relative* priority of competition over those services. This depends, first of all, on the characterization of Article 86(2): is it an exception to Article 86(1), an exception to other Treaty rules, or a special regime applying to services of general interest?

The comparison of Article 86(2) with other provisions of the Treaty bears witness to its uniqueness. Its structure and wording are so different from those of Articles 28 to 30 of the Treaty and the other free movement rules that the characterization of Article 86(1) and (2) as respectively being a rule and an exception seems to be unwarranted. The structure of Article 86(2) is also quite different from that of Article 81 (prohibition, sanction, and exemption).

On the other end of the spectrum, the comparison with Article 36 rules out a reading of Article 86(2) that would give precedence to services of general interest over competition and other economic objectives of the Treaty. The Court of Justice has repeatedly held that Article 36 'gives precedence to the objectives of the common agricultural policy over those in relation to competition policy'.[17] This is due to the fact that it makes the application of the competition rules in the agricultural

[15] *Ibid.*, at 657–658 (emphases added).

[16] *Ibid.*, at 658.

[17] Case C-137/00, *Milk Marque* [2003] ECR I-7975, para. 81; see also Case 139/79, *Maizena* v *Council* [1980] ECR 3393, para. 23; Case C-311/94, *IJssel-Vliet* [1996] ECR I-5023.

field subject to a decision of the Council. Unlike Article 36, Article 86(2) does not make the application of the competition and other Treaty rules subject to any political decision. Thus, Article 86(2) does not seem to establish any such precedence of services of general interest over competition.

In sum, Article 86(2) appears not to be a justification nor an exception, but rather a binary- or switch-rule that establishes the conditions for the application or non-application of the Treaty with regard to situations involving undertakings entrusted with the operation of services of general economic interest. This characterization will not be without consequences for its interpretation. The description of Article 86(2) that best accords with this conception is found in *IGAV*: Article 86 'lays down *a particular system* [*un régime particulier*] in favour of undertakings entrusted with the operation of services of general economic interest'.[18] This judgment remains, nonetheless, an isolated precedent. The characterization of this provision rather as an exception, with the attendant strict interpretation, predominates in the legal literature.[19] In the case law the strict interpretation was traditionally limited to the definition of an undertaking entrusted with the performance of those services[20]—an element of Article 86(2) for which a strict interpretation is indeed justified as it obliges public authorities to be transparent in their decisions—but it was extended to the provision as a whole in a judgment of 1997,[21] even though in that judgment the interpretation—as will be shown below—was anything but strict.

Beyond Article 86, Article 16 of the EC Treaty, Article 36 of the Charter of Fundamental Rights of the European Union, and the Treaty establishing a Constitution for Europe should also be taken into account.[22]

Article 16 EC, which was introduced by the Treaty of Amsterdam, provides: '[w]ithout prejudice to Articles 73, 86 and 87, and given the place occupied by services of general economic interest in the shared values of the Union as well as their role in promoting social and territorial cohesion, the Community and the

[18] Case 94/74, *IGAV* v *ENCC* [1975] ECR 699, para. 34 (emphasis added).

[19] See, for example, Mestmäcker, 'Daseinvorsorge und Universaldienst im europäischen Kontext: Ein Beitrag zur Funktion von Art. 90 Abs. 2 EGV', in F. Ruland, B. Baron von Maydell, and H.-J. Papier (eds.), *Verfassung, Theorie und Praxis des Sozialstaats: Festschrift für Hans F. Zacher zum 70. Geburtstag* (1998) 635, at 641.

[20] Case 127/73, *BRT* v *SABAM* (II) [1974] ECR 313, para. 19: since Article 86(2) 'permits, in certain circumstances, derogation from the rules of the Treaty, there must be *a strict definition of those undertakings which can take advantage of it*' (emphasis added).

[21] Case C-157/94, *Commission* v *Netherlands* [1997] ECR I-5699, para. 37: 'Being a provision permitting derogation from the Treaty rules, Article [86](2) must be interpreted strictly.' No reason was given for this extension.

[22] After long discussions and various changes, the draft Treaty establishing a Constitution for Europe elaborated by the European Convention and submitted to the European Council in the summer of 2003 (CONV 820/03 of 20 June 2003 and CONV 850/03 of 18 July 2003) has been agreed upon by the intergovernmental conference on 18 June 2004 and signed in Rome on 29 October 2004. It presently requires ratification by all the Member States in order to enter into force (see the final text of the Constitutional Treaty in document CIG 87/2/04 REV 2 of 29 October 2004; also published in OJ 2004 C 310/1).

Member States, each within their respective powers and within the scope of application of this Treaty, shall take care that such services operate on the basis of principles and conditions which enable them to fulfil their missions'. Declaration 13 annexed to the Final Act of the Treaty of Amsterdam made clear that Article 16 'shall be implemented with full respect for the jurisprudence of the Court of Justice, inter alia as regards the principles of equality of treatment, quality and continuity of such services'.

Different authors have assessed the introduction of this provision in different ways. Mestmäcker has argued that taking into account the aforementioned declaration we can disregard it.[23] Buendía Sierra has argued that Article 16 'does not modify Article 86(2) but rather reaffirms the logic behind the provision'.[24] For Pernice and Wernicke, Article 16 should exclude the interpretation of Article 86(2) as rule and exception, favouring a more balanced approach.[25] A telling appraisal on the part of the French Sénat maintained that Article 16, a declaratory provision that does not change the case law, was no more than 'une consolation' in comparison with the more ambitious French proposals made during the intergovernmental conference.[26]

The case law has not given much weight to changes of a comparable kind in other Treaty contexts. In *Echirolles*, for example, a national court was calling into question previous case law because of a subsequent amendment to the general part of the Treaty. The Court of Justice made clear that new provisions defining general objectives of the Community 'must be read in conjunction with the provisions of the Treaty designed to implement those objectives'. It added that if the directly applicable provisions 'have not been amended' the Court's interpretation thereof 'cannot be called in question'.[27] This could be transposed to the field of services of general interest: the introduction of Article 16 would not affect the interpretation of Article 86(2), which has not been amended, or the relationship between competition and services of general interest under Community law. Thus, the most we can do is to use it as an element in the interpretation of Article 86(2). Article 16 actually supports the interpretation defended in this chapter, but one could reach that interpretation without using it.

The Charter of Fundamental Rights of the European Union, which will become binding law as Part II of the Treaty establishing a Constitution for Europe if the latter comes into force, includes a provision on services of general interest: Article 36 of the Charter (Article II-96 in the final version of the Constitutional Treaty), according to which the Union 'recognises and respects access to services of general economic interest as provided for by national laws and practices, in accordance with

[23] Mestmäcker, *supra* n. 19, at 651.

[24] Buendía Sierra, *supra* n. 9, at 313.

[25] Pernice and Wernicke, commentary to Article 86 of the Treaty, in E. Grabitz and M. Hilf (eds.), *Das Recht der Europäischen Union* (2003), para. 33.

[26] *Rapport d'information fait au nom de la délégation pour l'Union européenne sur les services d'intérêt general en Europe* (No. 82, 2000–2001 of 16 November 2000, rapporteur Hubert Haenel), at 20.

[27] Case C-9/99, *Echirolles* [2000] ECR I-8207, para. 24.

the Constitution in order to promote the social and territorial cohesion of the Union'. The introduction of this provision would not change much. In accordance with both its preamble and Article II-112(7), the Charter 'will be interpreted by the courts of the Union and the Member States with due regard to the explanations', which make quite clear that Article 36 is a programmatic provision and 'does not create any new right'.[28] The aforementioned report of the French Sénat emphasises that this provision would not change the balance between competition and services of general interest.[29]

Will the Treaty establishing a Constitution for Europe modify that balance if it eventually comes into force? The most significant changes proposed are the following. First, the addition to a slightly modified Article 16 (Article III-122 in the Constitutional Treaty) of a sentence according to which 'European laws shall define [the principles and conditions on the basis of which services of general interest operate], without prejudice to the competence of the Member States, in compliance with the Constitution, to provide, to commission and to fund such services'.[30] Second, the proposed Article III-166(3) (equivalent to the current Article 86(3)) would now make clear that the Commission does not have the power to enact legislation under this provision, but only administrative measures of a general or an individual nature—which is just a consequence of the limits imposed by the Court on those powers of the Commission. These changes do not seem capable of altering the current balance between competition and services of general interest in Community law.[31]

If it comes into force, however, the interpretative consequences of *other* textual and structural changes due to the Treaty establishing a Constitution for Europe could be significant, especially since different revision procedures would apply to the various parts of the Constitution, making some of them 'more constitutional' than others. The 'pre-constitutional' case law could change as a result, regardless of the requirement of legal certainty and in spite of the continuity clause enshrined in

[28] CHARTE 4473/00 of 11 October 2000, at 33. This interpretation was not modified by the European Convention in the updated explanations on the Charter (CONV 828/1/03 of 18 July 2003, at 34). In the very last round of negotiations of the 2004 intergovernmental conference, that unfortunate rule of original interpretation ('due regard to the explanations'), which is quite at odds with the dynamic character of fundamental rights, was reinforced through its inclusion as Article II-112(7) of the Treaty establishing a Constitution for Europe (see CIG 87/2/04 REV 2 of 29 October 2004).

[29] *Supra* n. 26, at 25.

[30] As proposed by the Working Group on Social Europe (CONV 516/1/03 of 4 February 2003, para. 32).

[31] A third change mysteriously disappeared from the final text of the Constitutional Treaty. It would have entailed the insertion of a new provision (Article III-17 in document CONV 850/03 of 18 July 2003) which would have enabled the Commission to take action, including the direct initiation of infringement proceedings, if measures based on Article III-122 had the effect of distorting the conditions of competition in the internal market. On this unborn provision, see Rodrigues, 'Vers une loi européenne des services publics', *Revue du Marché commun et de l'Union européenne* (2003) 503.

Article IV-438(4) of the Constitutional Treaty.[32] These are difficult and open questions for Community law as a whole and cannot be pursued here. The analyses contained in this chapter could nonetheless be affected as a result of such changes.

2. THE SCOPE OF APPLICATION OF ARTICLE 86 OF THE TREATY: ECONOMIC ACTIVITIES

The notion of 'economic activities' constitutes a limit to the application of both Article 86 of the Treaty and other economic provisions thereof, in particular the competition and free movement rules. This notion originally defined the scope of the Treaty establishing the European *Economic* Community, and it still defines the scope of many provisions of the basic Treaty of a Community no longer limited to economic matters. Its importance therefore goes well beyond our field, but it is essential to know how it limits the scope of Article 86(2).

A service of general interest which does not constitute an economic activity will not be subject to the economic provisions of the Treaty and it will not need to be shielded from them by Article 86(2). However, the presence of the word 'economic' in Article 86(2) may not be completely redundant. If a non-economic service of general interest is provided in breach of provisions of the Treaty which go beyond the economic field (for example, Article 12, on non-discrimination on the basis of nationality, or Article 18, on citizenship of the Union), no special regime is foreseen in the Treaty and those rules will apply as such.

The notion of economic activity in the context of Article 86(2) will be examined in three judgments that are taken as the point of departure for a wider reflection.

In *Höfner*,[33] a company of recruitment consultants was claiming fees from another company pursuant to a contract. The latter company argued that the contract was void because German law reserved employment procurement activities

[32] Article IV-445, introduced by the 2004 intergovernmental conference, allows to be revised the provisions of Title III of Part III of the Constitutional Treaty (internal policies, including *inter alia* the rules on competition and free movement) through a unanimous decision of the European Council approved by the Member States in accordance with their respective constitutional requirements, as long as it does not increase the competences of the Union (CIG 87/2/04 REV 2 of 29 October 2004). The revision of all other parts of the Treaty requires the common accord of an intergovernmental conference and a Convention shall normally be convened beforehand (Article IV-443). To be sure, the difference between the revision procedures is slight, but it implies that Title III of Part III of the Treaty is somewhat less important and less entrenched than the rest. Concerning the clause on the continuity of the case law, which suffered several changes before it reached its current version (compare CONV 850/03 of 18 July 2003, according to which the case law was to be maintained 'as *a* source of interpretation of Union law'; CIG 4/1/03 of 6 October 2003, for which it provided an '*authentic* interpretation' (*sic*); and the final version in CIG 87/2/04 REV 2 of 29 October 2004, according to which 'pre-constitutional' case law shall 'remain, *mutatis mutandis, the* source of interpretation of Union law and in particular of the comparable provisions of the Constitution' (emphases added)), see J. Baquero Cruz, 'What Prospects for Free Movement Law?: A Review of Peter Oliver, assisted by Malcolm Jarvis, *Free Movement of Goods in the European Community*', reviewed online at http://www.europeanbooks.org.

[33] Case C-41/90, *Höfner and Elser* [1991] ECR I-1979.

to the federal office for employment. Before the national court the question arose of whether that monopoly was compatible with Community law and a preliminary reference was sent to the Court of Justice. The substance of the judgment is discussed below. This section focuses on the issue of whether the federal office for employment carried out an economic activity.

The German government argued that employment procurement services do not fall within the scope of the competition rules if they are carried out by a public undertaking, insofar as they are provided free of charge and the contributions from employers and employees to finance the service are general and have no link with each specific service provided.[34] In contrast, the Court held that employment procurement services constituted an economic activity and the federal office for employment was an undertaking within the meaning of Articles 81 and 82 of the Treaty. The ground was the following: '[t]he fact that employment procurement activities are normally entrusted to public agencies cannot affect the economic nature of such activities. Employment procurement has not always been, and is not necessarily, carried out by public entities. That finding applies in particular to executive recruitment.'[35]

This language suggests a very wide concept of economic activities, although the way in which the paragraph is drafted is not that of a general proposition, but rather that of a dictum limited to the case in hand. If it were understood as a general proposition, the mere possibility for an activity to be carried out by private entities would mean that it is economic. This would be the case if such an activity has not always been carried out by public entities or if there is no objective need to reserve it to them. The decisions of the Member States about the limits of the market would play no role whatsoever in the definition of the Community concept of economic activities. This would amount to an excessively strong presumption in favour of the applicability of the economic rules of the Treaty.

In *Eurocontrol*,[36] the Court of Justice had to consider whether Eurocontrol, an organization established by an international agreement and entrusted with the control of air navigation among its Contracting States, constituted an undertaking carrying out economic activities. Among its various activities, Eurocontrol had to establish and levy certain charges on users of air navigation services. An airline company refused to pay those charges, arguing that in establishing them Eurocontrol had infringed Articles 82 and 86 of the Treaty.

The Court first held that Eurocontrol 'carries out, on behalf of the Contracting States, tasks in the public interest aimed at contributing to the maintenance and improvement of air navigation safety'.[37] Its activity of collecting route charges 'cannot be separated from the organization's other activities. Those charges are merely the consideration, payable by users, for the obligatory and exclusive use of air navigation control facilities and services.'[38] The Court mentioned that Eurocontrol

[34] Case C-41/90, *Höfner and Elser* [1991] ECR I-1979, para. 19.

[35] *Ibid.*, para. 22.

[36] Case C-364/92, *SAT Fluggesellschaft* v *Eurocontrol* [1994] ECR I-43.

[37] *Ibid.*, para. 27.

[38] *Ibid.*, para. 28.

did not have any influence over the amount of the charges, which are fixed by applying a common formula which was established by the Contracting States.[39] It concluded that, '*[t]aken as a whole*, Eurocontrol's activities, by their *nature*, their *aim* and *the rules to which they are subject*, are connected with the exercise of powers relating to the control and supervision of air space which are typically *those of a public authority*. They are not of an economic nature justifying the application of the Treaty rules of competition.'[40]

In comparison with *Höfner*, this judgment introduces a more elaborate approach to the concept of economic activity. It sets out three criteria to assess the existence of an economic activity (nature, aim, rules to which the activity is subject) and accepts that public authorities have a legitimate role to play in the definition of the scope of the market. The inclusion of the expression 'taken as a whole' means that the activities of Eurocontrol were not dissociable. In other cases, however, the Court could draw a difference between activities pertaining to the public sphere and those having an economic character.[41]

In *Albany*,[42] a very important judgment on more than one account, Albany refused to contribute to a supplementary pension fund set up by a collective agreement between employers and workers in the textile sector and to which affiliation was made compulsory by public authorities. It argued that compulsory contributions were contrary to Community competition law. This section focuses on the part of the judgment in which the Court considered whether the pension fund was an undertaking pursuing an economic activity.

The Court started its analysis by recalling that the concept of an undertaking encompasses every entity engaged in an economic activity, regardless of the legal status of the entity and the way in which it is financed.[43] It also recalled the judgment in *Poucet and Pistre* to the effect that the concept of undertaking does not encompass organisations charged with the management of certain compulsory social security schemes, based on the principle of solidarity.[44] The activities were not seen as economic because the benefits were the same for all beneficiaries even though contributions were proportional to income, retirement pensions were funded by workers in employment, pension entitlements were not proportional to contributions paid, etc. Such elements of solidarity required the schemes to be managed by a single organization and for affiliation to them to be compulsory.[45] In contrast, in another judgment the Court held that a non-profit-making organization that managed a supplementary pension scheme as an optional scheme and according to the principle of capitalization (that is, benefits depended solely on the

[39] *Ibid.*, para. 29.

[40] *Ibid.*, para. 30 (my emphases).

[41] See Kovar, *supra* n. 12, at 224.

[42] Case C-67/96, *Albany* v *Stichting Bedrijfspensioenfonds Textielindustrie* [1999] ECR I-5751.

[43] *Ibid.*, para. 77.

[44] *Ibid.*, para. 78 (referring to Joined Cases C-159/91 and C-160/91, *Poucet and Pistre* [1993] ECR I-637).

[45] *Ibid.*

amounts of contributions) was carrying out an economic activity in competition with life assurance companies and constituted an undertaking.[46]

The Court then applied these criteria to the case in hand, recalling first that the pension fund operated in accordance with the principle of capitalization, so that 'the amount of the benefits provided by the Fund depends on the financial results of the investments made by it'.[47] In addition, legislation provided for exemptions from affiliation.[48] The Court concluded that it engaged in an economic activity in competition with insurance companies.[49] The fact that the fund was non-profit-making, and certain manifestations of solidarity within it, were held not to be sufficient to deprive the fund of its status as an undertaking. They were to be taken into account under Article 86(2).[50]

The Court thus examines once again the aim and nature of the activity and the rules to which it is subject. It concludes that it is an economic activity with a degree of solidarity which is not intense enough to exclude it from the purview of the competition rules. The division between social and economic activities is even less clear-cut than that between the latter and activities of public authority. In such cases, the Court balances the different elements and decides whether the activity is predominantly economic or social. The decision depends, to a large extent, on the legal framework regulating the activity. The potential competition of the services provided with services provided by private companies seems to be a consequence of, and not a condition for, the finding of an economic activity.[51] It should not be confused with the *Höfner* test, which referred to the potential economic character of the services provided, that is, to the objective suitability of a given activity to be carried out by private entities. The Court has generally applied a more elaborate test since *Eurocontrol*. In other words, the activity is not rendered economic simply by virtue of the fact that it may be carried out by private actors. It is economic because the rules to which it is subject do not completely shield it from competition on the part of private undertakings. It would not be economic, however, if those rules were framed in such a way that no private undertaking would pursue it under those conditions. Finally, the social aspects of the activity may be relevant

[46] Case C-244/94, *Fédération Française des Sociétés d'Assurance and Others* v *Ministère de l'Agriculture et de la Pêche* [1995] ECR I-4013.

[47] *Albany, supra* n. 42, para. 82.

[48] *Ibid.*, para. 83.

[49] *Ibid.*, para. 84.

[50] *Ibid.*, paras. 85–86.

[51] See, however, the Opinion of Advocate General Jacobs in Joined Cases C-264/01, C-306/01, C-354/01, and C-355/01, *AOK Bundesverband*, of 22 May 2003 (paras. 37–42, in which the finding of an economic activity is said to be linked to the ability of sickness funds to compete with each other). The Court gave its judgment on 16 March 2004 (not yet published), finding, in contrast to its Advocate General, that the sickness funds were not undertakings in spite of their limited ability to compete with each other. The judgment suggests that, as it is argued in the text, the ability to compete is not a condition but simply a consequence, and that limited competition in aspects unrelated to the conduct or measure in hand is not sufficient to conclude that the entity is an undertaking with regard to that conduct or measure.

under Article 86(2), since they may render the services provided 'less competitive than comparable services' offered by private companies that are unconstrained by the requirements of public regulation.[52]

The analysis of these judgments leads us to a general reflection on the notion of economic activity. This notion may apply differently in different situations and in the context of the various Treaty provisions. Similar activities may be held not to constitute an economic activity carried out by an undertaking for the purposes of the application of the competition rules (for example, a health service provided by a public hospital or by a hospital participating in a national social security scheme presenting sufficiently strong elements of solidarity) and yet they may be qualified as an economic activity in the context of the free movement rules (for example, where a national of another Member State who receives health services from the same hospital may have to pay for the service received and then seek reimbursement; she or he is not protected by the national social security scheme; the service received may thus constitute an 'economic activity' for the purpose of the application of the free movement rules).[53] Since Article 86(2) is not a self-contained provision, the existence of an economic activity and of a service of general economic interest will depend on the assessment of this condition in the context of the provisions which are applied with it.

The importance of the notion of economic activity should not be exaggerated, however. In most cases it is crystal clear whether we are dealing with an undertaking carrying out an economic activity within the meaning of the competition rules or with an economic transaction to which the free movement rules apply. The concept only becomes crucial in borderline cases.

It is a desperate enterprise to try to define with precision, by reference to a single criterion, what constitutes an economic activity. This is the simple reason why the test in *Höfner* has been impracticable in borderline cases and why the Court adopted the more complex analysis set out in *Eurocontrol* or *Albany*. While the economic or non-economic character of many activities will be quite clear, in so far as an economic activity implies the offering of goods and services in the market,[54] for a given price, and generally but not necessarily with the aim of obtaining a profit, and non-economic activities are normally non-profit-making activities which will

[52] *Albany, supra* n. 42, para. 86.

[53] As long as they remain *de minimis*, these particular instances of economic activities for the purpose of the application of the free movement rules would not be subject to the competition rules. Thus, the finding of an economic activity in the context of the free movement of services in connection with health services provided through a social security scheme in Case C-368/98, *Vanbraekel* [2001] ECR I-5363 and Case C-157/99, *Smits and Peerbooms* [2001] ECR I-5473 does not necessarily entail that the activity as a whole constitutes an economic activity for the purpose of the application of the competition rules. See, on this issue, the chapter by V. Hatzopoulos in this volume and by the same author: '*Killing* National Health and Insurance Systems but *Healing* Patients? The European Market for Health Care Services after the Judgments of the ECJ in *Vanbraekel* and *Peerbooms*', 39 *Common Market Law Review* (2002) 683, at 707–708.

[54] See Joined Cases C-180/98 to C-184/98, *Pavlov and Others* [2000] ECR I-6451, para. 75, and Case C-475/99, *Ambulanz Glöckner* v *Landkreis Südwestpfalz* [2001] ECR I-8089, para. 19.

not be undertaken by private actors under market conditions, there is a grey area in which it is difficult to decide whether activities are economic or not.

In this grey area, the essentialism of *Höfner*, which points to the definition of an ideal sphere of economic activities that *must* be open to competition and to which the market rules should apply, would be as dangerous as it would be misguided. The very notion of economic activity is indeed misguided, for in hard cases one should actually decide whether it is the economic aspects or the non-economic aspects of an activity that prevail. This is, indeed, what the Court tries to do with the aid of a set of criteria, none of which will alone be determinant. In addition, the predominantly economic character of an activity does not mean that its non-economic aspects will play no role. They will be taken into account under Article 86(2).

The question boils down to the issue of the degree of deference that has to be paid to the decisions of the Member States that trace the line between market and non-market activities. At the preliminary stage of the identification of an economic activity, it is important to take into account the legal framework to which the activity is subject, but only as one among other elements. The competent authorities of a Member State may therefore reject the economic character of an activity in the general interest by excluding it from the operation of the market, but their decision should be complete and transparent. If there is some room left for the market in the regulatory framework, Community economic law will apply, but only to that extent and with regard to conduct in that limited field. Where the market is completely excluded, control by the Court should be minimal. Only in very extreme cases will the Court hold that an activity is economic in spite of a national decision to exclude it from the market.[55]

The more recent judgment in *AOK Bundesverband*,[56] on the German sickness funds, tends to confirm this analysis. It shows that the Court does not apply the potential-economic-activity test of *Höfner*.[57] The Court takes into account the nature of the activity, to be sure, but also its aim and the legal framework to which it is subject. And that legal framework may rule out the existence of an economic activity if the legislator has decided to exclude competition or to impose anticompetitive conduct in the general interest.

One may wonder, finally, about the relationship between the concept of economic activity and Article 86(2) of the Treaty. The effects of Article 86(2) and of the finding of a non-economic activity are equivalent insofar as both may render the

[55] Besides the judgment in *Höfner*, see Case C-18/88, *RTT* v *GB-Inno-BM* [1991] ECR I-5941, paras. 19–22: '[t]he production and sale of terminals, and in particular of telephones, *is an activity that should be open to any undertaking*' (emphasis added; this holding did not concern the notion of economic activity, but the language used by the Court implies that those activities cannot be excluded from the market).

[56] Joined Cases C-264/01, C-306/01, C-354/01, and C-355/01, judgment of 16 March 2004 (not yet published), paras. 46–64.

[57] In contrast, in his Opinion in *AOK Bundesverband* Advocate General Jacobs argued that *Höfner* remains the basic test (para. 27 of the Opinion); see, for another exception, the judgment of the Fifth Chamber of the Court in *Glöckner, supra* n. 54, para. 20 (applying the *Höfner* formula but not citing the judgment).

economic provisions of the Treaty inapplicable. In the case of the finding of a non-economic activity, the inapplicability is unconditional, because those rules are designed to apply only to economic activities. In the case of Article 86(2), the non-application of the Treaty is conditional. This truncated approach explains the relatively large interpretation of the concept of economic activity. A narrow approach to the concept of economic activity would reduce the scope of application of Article 86(2), which was designed to be the normative locus for the balancing of market and non-market values when services of general economic interest are involved. Hence the wide interpretation of the notion of economic activity and the availability of an exclusion of application of the Treaty if the conditions of Article 86(2) are fulfilled.

Therefore, the finding of an economic activity constitutes the first but not the most important hurdle in the application of Article 86(2). The wide interpretation of the concept of economic activity does not make the economic prevail over the social, because the finding of such an activity simply transfers the priority problem to Article 86(2). It is this provision that will give a constitutional answer to the priority problem.

3. OBSTRUCTION TO THE PERFORMANCE OF THE SERVICE: PROPORTIONALITY? WHAT KIND OF PROPORTIONALITY?

The key element of Article 86(2), once we are certain that we are dealing with a service of general economic interest entrusted to an undertaking, is the absence or existence of an obstruction to the performance of a general interest task, which will respectively trigger or exclude the application of the relevant Treaty rules. The interpretation of this condition is thus decisive for the priority question and to determine whether Community law endangers the provision of services of general interest.

The text, context and aim of the provision do not clearly point to a given interpretation of the 'obstruction' element.

The text is indecisive, particularly in view of the differences between linguistic versions.[58] The French version contains strong language that supports a strict interpretation. '*Faire échec*'[59] could be translated as 'make impossible', language that would mean that as a rule the Treaty would apply, and that only in very exceptional cases would it not be applicable. However, the softer language found in other versions of the Treaty supports a more balanced interpretation.[60]

[58] Already noted by Franceschelli, 'La nozione di servizio di interesse economico generale di cui al § 2 dell'art 90 del Trattato institutivo del mercato comune europeo', in *Il Colloquio di Bruxelles sulla Concorrenza tra Settore Pubblico e Privato nella C.E.E.* (1964) 81, at 83.

[59] '[. . .] dans les limites où l'application de ces règles ne fait pas échec à l'accomplissement en droit ou en fait de la mission particulière qui leur a été impartie'.

[60] English: 'obstruct'; German and Dutch: 'verhindert'; Italian: 'osti'; Portuguese: 'não constitua obstáculo'; Spanish: 'impida'.

The place of Article 86(2) in the Treaty would warrant a competition-oriented interpretation, but there are important reasons against this structural argument. Paragraph 2 of Article 86 cannot be seen as an exception to paragraph 1, since it is autonomous and its substance surpasses the scope of paragraph 1.[61] Moreover, the open reference to 'the rules contained in this Treaty' suggests that Article 86(2) is not simply a 'competition' provision, that in spite of its being in the section of the rules on competition applicable to undertakings its wide scope takes it well beyond competition.[62]

Being the result of a compromise, the aim of Article 86(2) is not decisive either. Article 86(2) could be seen as providing for a sort of 'neutrality' of the Treaty with regard to services of general economic interest, but it may also be seen as providing for a very limited derogation from the Treaty rules. Stretching the words a little, it could even be seen as giving priority to services of general interest over competition.

For all the large leeway given to the interpreter, when the 'obstruction' element of the provision has to be applied our general questions become more precise: what kind of test should be used in the context of Article 86(2)? A proportionality test? Why and what kind of proportionality? Should one rather seek a balance between equivalent values and principles? Or should one apply a test of manifest disregard of competition?

A large majority of authors favour a 'competition' approach that they consider to be inscribed in the text and structure of the Treaty, even if some would like to see it changed.[63] We can take the important work of Buendía Sierra on Article 86 as representative of the 'competition' approach. For him, Article 86(2) is an exception to Article 86(1) that should be strictly interpreted. Thus, 'the exception will only apply if the *proportionate* character of the restriction can be proved'. 'The proportionality test contained in Article 86(2) is *no different from those existing in other areas of EC law*. The proportionality test is to be fulfilled when the following three elements are proven: 1) that a causal link exists between the measure and the objective of general interest, 2) that the restrictions caused by the measure are balanced by the benefits for the general interest, and 3) that the objective of general interest *cannot be achieved through other less restrictive means*.'[64]

[61] But see Buendía Sierra, *supra* n. 9, at 312.

[62] See, however, in relation to Article 86(3), Case T-17/96, *TF1* v *Commission* [1999] ECR II-1757, para. 50: 'owing to its position in the general structure of the Treaty and of its purpose, Article [86](3) of the Treaty figures among the rules whose object is to ensure freedom to compete, and is therefore intended to protect economic operators against measures whereby a Member State might frustrate the fundamental economic freedoms enshrined in the Treaty' (this holding was neither confirmed nor infirmed by the Court on appeal in Joined Cases C-302/99 P and C-308/99 P, *Commission and France* v *TF1* [2001] ECR I-5603).

[63] See Kovar, *supra* n. 12, at 514.

[64] Buendía Sierra, *supra* n. 9, at 315 (emphases added) and also by the same author: *Exclusive Rights and State Monopolies under EC Law: Article 86 (Formerly Article 90) of the EC Treaty* (translated by A. Read 1999), at 300–336. See also Lenaerts, 'Les services d'intérêt économique général et le droit

This approach could be problematic in view of its third element, which gives a relative priority to competition over services of general interest. This section tries to prove two points: that the Court has never followed such an approach but a milder approach that entails a softer test; that the case law cannot be classified in temporal periods according to the supposed changes in the weight given to competition. For many authors, indeed, there was a 'passive' period; a second 'aggressive' competition period; a third, more balanced, period after *Corbeau* and *Almelo*.[65] Our examination of the leading cases will try to show that the case law has evolved, but that its evolution has more to do with the gradual elaboration of Article 86(2) than with the priority problem. Thus, *Corbeau* and *Almelo* will not be seen as 'turning points' but as more sophisticated elaborations of the normative elements of Article 86(2).

The Court first ruled on the 'obstruction' element in *Sacchi*, which concerned the Italian television monopoly. The Court held that '[t]he fact that an undertaking to which a Member State grants exclusive rights has a monopoly is not as such incompatible with Article 86'. If a Member State treats it as an undertaking entrusted with the operation of services of general economic interest, 'the same prohibitions [those against discrimination and competition rules] apply, as regards their behaviour within the market, by reason of Article [86(2)], so long as it is not shown that the said prohibitions are incompatible with the performance of their tasks'.[66]

A proportionality test was clearly not applied in *Sacchi*. This is shown by the fact that in the judgment the Court mentioned a rudimentary form of proportionality with regard to the free movement of goods: a measure governing the marketing of products would be a measure having an effect equivalent to quantitative restrictions 'where the restrictive effects are *out of proportion* to their purpose'.[67] In contrast, in the context of Article 86(2) the Court simply refers to 'incompatibility'.

Sacchi is sometimes taken as an example of a strict 'competition' approach, because of its wording, but 'incompatible' is a vague word and everything depends on its interpretation. It could be that obstruction and incompatibility refer to the same idea, that the word 'incompatible' does not actually entail a preference for competition over services of general interest. What is clear is that the Court does not elaborate the concept of 'obstruction' and just glosses over it, without adding to what the Treaty says.

communautaire', in Conseil d'État, *Rapport public 2002: Collectivités publiques et concurrence* (2002) 425, at 425–426; and Van der Woude, 'Article 90: Competing for Competence', *ELR: Competition Law Checklist 1991* (1992) 60, at 62.

[65] See, for example, Simon, 'Les mutations des services publics du fait des contraintes du droit communautaire', in R. Kovar and D. Simon (eds.), *Service public et Communauté européenne: entre l'intérêt général et le marché* (1998), at 69–72.

[66] Case 155/73, *Sacchi* [1974] ECR 409, paras. 14–18.

[67] *Ibid.*, para. 8. The Court referred to Commission Directive of 22 December 1969 on the abolition of measures having an effect equivalent to quantitative restrictions (OJ 1970 L 13/29).

Thinness is also the mark of two judgments rendered after *Sacchi*. *Ahmed Saeed* uses 'indispensable for the performance of a task' instead of 'incompatible' with such performance and adds a requirement of transparency, without which national administrative or judicial authorities would not be in a position to establish whether the violations of the competition rules were indeed indispensable for the performance of a task of general interest.[68] The test of 'indispensability' may seem tougher than that of 'incompatibility', but no further elaboration was provided in that judgment. *Höfner* comes back to the 'incompatibility' test of *Sacchi* and provides guidance about what it meant for the case in hand: 'the application of Article [82] of the Treaty cannot obstruct the performance of the particular task assigned to [a recruiting] agency in so far as the latter is manifestly not in a position to satisfy demand in that area of the market and in fact allows its exclusive rights to be encroached on by those companies'.[69]

The true relevance of these cases is in the fact that they take competition seriously, as a value as important as services of general interest.

At the time this approach may have clashed with the situation in some Member States. *Höfner* should be compared with a judgment of the German Constitutional Court on a challenge of unconstitutionality brought against the same legislation on the ground that the monopoly given to the public employment agency was in breach of Article 12(1) of the basic law (*Grundgesetz*), which confers on all German citizens the freedom to choose their trade or profession. In its judgment, the Constitutional Court held that the monopoly was not contrary to German constitutional law, since it was justified by the public interest because the needs of the labour market could more efficiently be satisfied by a single entity. The Constitutional Court examined the question whether the monopoly was justified in relation to executive recruitment, and concluded that the legislator was not obliged to exclude it from the monopoly because that would damage its effectiveness.[70] This did not mean that their exclusion would have been unconstitutional: the legislator could have done both things. This shows that in this field Community constitutional law has reduced the margin that national legislators had in the national constitutional context, as the competition and free movement rules generally have stronger bite than comparable rules in the Member States.

What would have been the solution in classic French administrative law, for example? Most probably the public agency would have had an obligation to provide the recruitment service according to its *cahier de charges*. An individual may have thus only claimed the provision of the due service before the administrative courts or responsibility for the damages caused by the failure of the agency to provide the service.

[68] Case 66/86, *Ahmed Saeed Flugreisen and Others* v *Zentrale zur Bekämpfung unlauteren Wettbewerbs* [1989] ECR 803, paras. 55–58.

[69] Case C-41/90, *Höfner* [1991] ECR I-1979, para. 25.

[70] BVerfGE, 21, 245 (as reported by Advocate General Jacobs in para. 13 of his Opinion).

Community law substantially changes the situation. Does this mean that *Höfner* gives priority to market values over non-market considerations, as it has been argued?[71] Not really. This judgment considers competition at the same level as the provision of public services, but not superior to it. The decision of a public authority in itself is not sufficient to exclude the rules on competition or free movement: convincing reasons of general interest must be given. And there is no good reason to exclude it when those services are not actually provided and there is an informal toleration of private competitors. Indeed, in such a case an opening to competition would not only be compatible but would actually help in the performance of the service. This deficient situation may only be acceptable in a legal system that gives priority to the decisions of public authorities over services of general interest, regardless of competition considerations, but not in a legal system, such as that of the Community, in which competition is equally worthy of protection.

Corbeau[72] constitutes a step forward in the interpretation of Article 86(2). A reference for a preliminary ruling was sent to the Court in the context of criminal proceedings against Mr. Corbeau, a businessman who was infringing the Belgian postal monopoly. A law had conferred on the Régie des Postes an exclusive right to collect, carry, and distribute all correspondence, laying down penalties for any infringement. Mr. Corbeau provided a special service consisting in collecting mail from the address of the sender and distributing it by noon of the following day if the addressee was within the district concerned. Mr. Corbeau forwarded other correspondence by normal post. The national court wanted to ascertain whether the postal monopoly was in breach of Community law, in which case no penal sanctions could be imposed on Mr. Corbeau.

The Court began by emphasizing that Article 86(2) 'permits the Member States to confer on undertakings to which they entrust the operation of services of general economic interest, exclusive rights which may hinder the application of the rules of the Treaty on competition in so far as restrictions on competition, or even the exclusion of all competition, by other economic operators are *necessary* to ensure the performance of the particular tasks assigned to the undertakings possessed of the exclusive rights'.[73] Second, the Court held that it was beyond dispute that the Régie des Postes was entrusted with 'a service of general economic interest consisting in the obligation to collect, carry and distribute mail on behalf of all users throughout the territory of the Member State concerned, at uniform tariffs and on similar quality conditions, irrespective of the specific situations or the degree of economic profitability of each individual operation'.[74] The Court then had to consider 'the extent to which a restriction on competition or even the exclusion of

[71] Moral Soriano, 'Proporcionalidad y servicios de interés económico general', *Revista Española de Derecho Europeo* (2002) 387, at 396.

[72] Case C-320/91, *Corbeau* [1993] ECR I-2533. Its approach was confirmed in Case C-393/92, *Almelo* [1994] ECR I-1477.

[73] *Corbeau, supra* n. 72, para. 14 (emphasis added).

[74] *Ibid.*, para. 15.

all competition from other economic operators is *necessary* in order to allow the holder of the exclusive right to *perform its task of general interest and in particular to have the benefit of economically acceptable conditions*'.[75] For the Court, '[t]he starting point of such an examination must be the premise that the obligation on the part of the undertaking entrusted with that task to perform its services in conditions of economic equilibrium presupposes that it will be possible to offset less profitable sectors against the profitable sectors and hence justifies a restriction of competition from individual undertakings where the economically profitable sectors are concerned'.[76] '[T]o authorize individual undertakings to compete with the holder of the exclusive rights in the sectors of their choice corresponding to those rights would make it possible for them to concentrate on the economically profitable operations and to offer more advantageous tariffs than those adopted by the holders of the exclusive rights since, unlike the latter, they are not bound for economic reasons to offset losses in the unprofitable sectors against profits in the more profitable sectors.'[77] 'However,' the Court added, 'the exclusion of competition is not justified as regards specific services dissociable from the service of general interest which meet special needs of economic operators and which call for certain additional services not offered by the traditional postal service, such as collection from the senders' address, greater speed or reliability of distribution or the possibility of changing the destination in the course of transit, in so far as such specific services, by their nature and the conditions in which they are offered, such as the geographical area in which they are provided, do not compromise the economic equilibrium of the service of general economic interest performed by the holder of the exclusive right.'[78] The Court left it 'for the national court to consider whether the services at issue in the dispute before it meet those criteria'.[79]

In his Opinion in *Almelo*, Advocate General Darmon affirmed that *Corbeau*, instead of 'repeating the things which States are prohibited from doing in relation to the grant of exclusive rights, specifies what it is that they can do'. '[T]he competition rules may be disapplied not only where they make it impossible for the undertaking in question to perform its public service task but also where they jeopardize its financial stability.'[80] This opinion is shared by many commentators, who perceive this judgment as a major shift in the orientation of the case law, rendering it friendlier to services of general interest[81] and even giving priority to non-market values.[82]

Corbeau is an important development in the case law, but the conventional view could be mistaken or at least exaggerated. The judgment elaborates more extensively than previous judgments on the substance of Article 86(2), offers for the first time

[75] *Corbeau, supra* n. 72, para. 16 (emphasis added).

[76] *Ibid.*, para. 17.

[77] *Ibid.*, para. 18.

[78] *Ibid.*, para. 19.

[79] *Ibid.*, para. 20.

[80] *Almelo, supra* n. 72, paras. 144–146 of the Opinion.

[81] For example, Hamon, Note on *Almelo, L'actualité juridique—Droit administratif* (1994) 642.

[82] Moral Soriano, *supra* n. 71, at 412.

a definition of 'services of general economic interest' and its rhetoric may be more 'positive' than that of previous judgments. Nevertheless, its substance does not alter the balance between competition and services of general interest which was established in earlier cases. The fact that the Court emphasizes what Member States can do instead of what they cannot do does not mean that they are given carte blanche in this field. The keyword in the judgment is 'necessary': restrictions of competition or of other Treaty provisions should be necessary. And for all the 'positive' rhetoric of the judgment, the meaning of 'necessary' could be very restrictive, leading to a situation which merely 'transposes' in positive terms the negative test applied before *Corbeau*.[83] In addition, the allegedly more flexible application of Article 86(2) was matched by a more aggressive application of Article 86(1) together with Article 82, so that 'an exclusive right would automatically lead the beneficiary to abuse' a dominant position under Article 82.[84]

In any event, proportionality is not mentioned in *Corbeau*, even if it is generally seen as enshrining such a test for Article 86(2).[85] This is significant, as in 1993 the proportionality test of the Court was well developed and in his Opinion in *Corbeau* Advocate General Tesauro had argued in so many words for a strict application of that test.[86] The absence of any reference to proportionality in the judgment means that such a test was not the test applied by the Court. A proportionality test is clearly not applied in its strict versions, like the 'less restrictive option' test, since one may always find a less restrictive alternative than cross-subsidization, such as the compensation of the costs associated with public service obligations, which does not involve the total exclusion of competition in otherwise competitive activities. But perhaps *Corbeau* does not even apply a soft version of the proportionality test. A test of 'necessity' is not a test of proportionality proper, but only one of the elements thereof. One needs to add to the 'suitability' and 'necessity' of the measure a judgment on the appropriate intensity of the interference between two values or principles in order to have a proportionality test in any of its genuine forms.[87] In contrast, the test enshrined in *Corbeau* eschews that judgment on intensity or degree which is the very mark of genuine proportionality—especially in its strictest forms. In other words, Article 86(2) of the Treaty does not require that judicial authorities pass judgment on the appropriate degree of interference between competition and services of general interest, but simply on the objective necessity of the measure from the point of view of the provision of those services. And it is clear that a measure can be held to be objectively necessary to attain a certain objective even if there are other less restrictive alternatives that could have been used.

[83] See Kovar, *supra* n. 12, at 503.

[84] The so-called 'automatic abuse theory', in the words of Buendía Sierra, *supra* n. 9, at 296–298.

[85] *Ibid.*, at 297; see also Moral Soriano, 'How Proportionate Should Anti-Competitive State Intervention Be?', *ELR* (2003) 112, at 116.

[86] *Corbeau, supra* n. 72, para. 14 of the Opinion.

[87] See Alexy, 'On Balancing and Subsumption: A Structural Comparison', *Ratio Juris* (2003) 433, at 436–437.

What *Corbeau* adds are the ideas of 'economically acceptable conditions', 'economic equilibrium', and 'cross-subsidisation', which give hints for the application of the 'necessity' test. The Court also adds that 'dissociable services' should be opened to competition if that does not compromise the economic equilibrium of the undertaking in hand, something that runs in the face of the argument that *Corbeau* changes the balance in favour of services of general interest.

The national court may have had a hard time applying these principles. The ambiguity lies between paragraphs 18 and 19, which may cut in two different ways and mean, first, that it is possible to cross-subsidize, second, that some specific services should be open to competition, and, third, that this is not the case if the opening to competition of those specific services compromises the economic equilibrium of the undertaking. There is a principle, an exception and an exception to the exception, all three drafted in such a way that the national judge could have either convicted or acquitted Mr. Corbeau. Being so vague, the judgment could be used by both the partisans of competition and of public services. Being so balanced, the judgment leaves the case practically undecided.

Another thing to bear in mind that was not mentioned by the Court in the judgment is the network effect of 'small' openings to competition.[88] Taken together, very small intrusions in the profitable sectors of a public monopoly may hamper its economic equilibrium. The application of *Corbeau* may thus require an examination of the *general* effect that the opening of some specific services to competition would have on the economic equilibrium of the undertaking entrusted with the provision of services of general economic interest, not just of the effect that a single case such as that of Mr. Corbeau would have on it.[89]

In sum, the added value of *Corbeau* lies in a more sophisticated and cautious approach to Article 86(2). If we compare it with *Höfner*, it may strike us that the Court was extremely clear in the latter case and remained very vague in *Corbeau*. The reason was that *Höfner* was an easy case: demand was not satisfied and competition was tolerated. *Corbeau*, in contrast, was a hard case presenting difficult policy options: the *Höfner* rationale could have been thought to be enough to solve it in favour of Mr. Corbeau, who was offering specific services for which there was demand and no offer from the monopolist. But cross-subsidization and the equilibrium of the public service came into play and eschewed the simple economic (supply/demand) approach. This is not however to be seen as a change in favour of public services: the more sophisticated approach keeps the balance that we have found in previous cases, and also the idea that public authorities should have a margin in the way they organize the provision of services of general economic interest.

Corbeau constitutes the current state of the law with regard to the obstruction element in Article 86(2) of the Treaty. Two judgments confirm the interpretation of *Corbeau* that has been set out in this section.

[88] See Case C-234/89, *Delimitis* [1991] I-935.

[89] To this effect, see F. Blum and A. Logue, *State Monopolies under EC Law* (1998), at 89.

In *Commission* v *Netherlands*[90] the Court ruled on infringement proceedings launched by the Commission for a declaration that, by granting exclusive import rights for electricity intended for public distribution, the Netherlands had failed to fulfil its obligations under Articles 28 and 31 of the Treaty.[91] Once the exclusive rights had been held to be contrary to Article 31 the Court examined the application of Article 86(2).

The Commission had proposed a 'less restrictive alternative' to the Netherlands measure, arguing that that Member State had 'to establish [. . .] *that there were no other measures less restrictive of trade which would also allow fulfilment of the relevant public-service obligations*, such as in particular equalization of costs associated with public service obligations'.[92] The Commission thus took for granted that a strict proportionality test applied in the context of Article 86(2). The assessment of the Court starts by holding that, being 'a provision permitting derogation from the Treaty rules, Article 86(2) must be interpreted strictly'.[93] However, in the paragraphs that follow the Court is not so strict, setting out a simple necessity test instead of a proportionality test proper. The Court recalls that the aim of Article 86(2) is to '*reconcile* the Member States' interest in using certain undertakings, in particular in the public sector, as an instrument of economic or fiscal policy with the Community's interest in ensuring compliance with the rules on competition and the preservation of the unity of the common market'.[94] The key word here is 'reconcile', putting the emphasis on the balance between both aims, instead of giving priority to one over the other. Thus, the Court held that the Member States 'cannot be precluded, when defining the services of general economic interest which they entrust to certain undertakings, from taking into account of objectives pertaining to their national policy or from endeavouring to attain them by means of obligations and constraints which they impose on such undertakings'.[95] This constitutes an implicit recognition of the legitimacy and the margin of appreciation enjoyed by the Member States for the pursuance of non-competitive policies for reasons not linked to competition. Hence the test appears not to be as strict as the Commission would have it: 'It is not necessary that the survival of the undertaking itself be threatened.'[96] The Court most clearly rules out a 'less restrictive alternative' test when considering the burden of proof of the Member State: 'the burden of proof cannot be so extensive as to require the Member State, when setting out in detail the reasons for which, in the event of elimination of the

[90] Case C-157/94, *Commission* v *Netherlands* [1997] ECR I-5699.

[91] This was one of a series of infringement proceedings brought by the Commission on exclusive imports rights for electricity and gas. See also Case C-158/94, *Commission* v *Italy* [1997] ECR I-5789; Case C-159/94, *Commission* v *France* [1997] ECR I-5815.

[92] *Commission* v *Netherlands, supra* n. 90, para. 35 (emphasis added).

[93] *Ibid.*, para. 37.

[94] *Ibid.*, paras. 38–39 (emphasis added). Paragraph 39 comes from Case C-202/88, *France* v *Commission* [1991] ECR I-1223, para. 12.

[95] *Commission* v *Netherlands, supra* n. 90, para. 40.

[96] *Ibid.*, para. 43.

contested measures, the performance, under economically acceptable conditions, of the tasks of general economic interest which it has entrusted to an undertaking would, in its view, be jeopardized, to go even further and prove, positively, *that no other conceivable measure, which by definition would be hypothetical, could enable those tasks to be performed under the same conditions*'.[97] In my view, this holding clearly shows that a proportionality test is not being applied, for the comparison with other hypothetical measures is an essential feature of a genuine proportionality test.

The leading judgment in the *Albany* case also supports the analysis presented here. The textile undertaking proposed alternatives less restrictive of competition than the establishment of an obligatory pension fund, such as minimum requirements for pensions offered by insurance companies, without making affiliation to the fund compulsory.[98] The Court rejected that argument, emphasizing 'that, in view of the social function of supplementary pension schemes and the margin of appreciation enjoyed, according to settled case-law, by the Member States in organising their social security systems [. . .], it is incumbent on each Member State to consider whether, in view of the particular features of its national pension system, laying down minimum requirements would still enable it to ensure the level of pension which it seeks to guarantee in a sector by compulsory affiliation to a pension fund'.[99] Thus, the Member States are not bound to choose the alternative which is least restrictive of competition. They can choose from a number of policy options as long as they appear to be 'necessary' to achieve a legitimate result.

In spite of ambiguous language in certain decisions,[100] more recent judgments tend to confirm the analysis presented in this section.[101]

What lessons can be drawn from the case law?

A first general reflection is that Community lawyers tend to see proportionality as a flexible and rather indeterminate device that is hidden under every stone of the legal order—perhaps repeating normative habits learnt in various fields of

[97] *Commission* v *Netherlands, supra* n. 90, para. 58 (emphasis added).

[98] *Albany, supra* n. 42, para. 99.

[99] *Ibid.*, para. 122.

[100] For example, C-203/96, *Chemische Afvalstoffen Dusseldorf* [1998] ECR I-4075, para. 67: 'it is for the Netherlands Government [. . .] to show to the satisfaction of the national court that that objective cannot be achieved equally well by other means. Article [86](2) of the Treaty can thus apply only if it is shown that, without the contested measure, the undertaking in question would be unable to carry out the task assigned to it.' See also the Opinion of Advocate General Léger in *Wouters*, in which he argued that Article 86(2) includes both a 'necessity' and a 'proportionality' test: 'The proportionality test thus leads to establishing whether the undertaking's particular task might not be accomplished by measures less restrictive of competition. In other words, it requires the solution which is *the least detrimental to competition* to be chosen, having regard to the obligations and constraints borne by the undertaking' (Opinion of 10 July 2001, Case C-309/99, [2002] ECR I-1577, paras. 164–165, emphasis added; see also his Opinion of 25 May 2004, Case C-438/02, *Hanner*, pending, paras. 140–141).

[101] See *Glöckner, supra* n. 54 (in para. 58 the Court examines whether the cross-subsidization of emergency transport with the revenue of ordinary patient transport 'helps to cover the costs of providing the emergency transport service', but not whether cross-subsidization goes beyond what is necessary to cover the costs of the non-profitable sector or whether there are other alternatives less restrictive of competition). The *Altmark* judgment of 24 July 2003, *supra* n. 7, could also be seen as an example of

Community law—as if the principle of proportionality were a sort of trump or joker that could be played together with any other card that is found in the Treaty or even in Community legislation.[102] Nevertheless, proportionality may not always be available—at least in its strict versions—and, in any event, it is not manna for the resolution of legal problems.[103] Besides, it may be quite important to define it with a higher degree of precision and to distinguish between its various forms.

Proportionality, a useful technique of adjudication in particular fields, has both limits and perils. In its soft form (measures should be proportionate to their aims *and* not go beyond what is appropriate to achieve them), proportionality involves an effective power to constrain decision-makers. In what seems to me to be its strictest version (the *less* restrictive alternative test), it involves a power equivalent to the political power to decide. It is implicit in the maximizing/minimizing logic of the less restrictive alternative test that among the various options that are open to the decision-maker judicial authorities will ultimately point to one of them—the *least* restrictive of one of the values or protected goods in hand. In practice, this means that the judicial body may reduce to nil the margin of appreciation of decision-makers. And sometimes courts should not have that power, because they would be eschewing democratic processes and imposing delicate policy options of their own. Thus, the Court has followed a less strict approach in the field of services of general interest, in view of the delicate balance that has to be found between market and non-market considerations. Even if the case law has been rather pragmatic and has not expressly dealt with the problem of the level of scrutiny, it seems clear that the Court applies a test of 'objective necessity', which constitutes a middle ground between the most deferential 'manifest error' test and the soft proportionality test (a measure can indeed be objectively 'necessary' and still go beyond what is 'strictly' needed).

The test applied by the Court is a 'suitability' test with some added force from the 'necessity' element. Perhaps it should not be called a proportionality test if

the approach advocated here, as its third criterion (para. 92 of the judgment) reproduces the necessity test applied in the context of Article 86(2). See Wernicke, 'Die Wirtschaftsverfassung der Gemeinschaft zwischen gemeinwirtschaftlichen Diensten und Wettbewerb, oder: Wer hat Angst vor Art. 86 II EG?', *Europäische Zeitschrift für Wirtschaftsrecht* (2003) 481; and Acierno and Baquero Cruz, *supra* n. 7, at 185. Finally, in his Opinion in Joined Cases C-264/01, C-306/01, C-354/01 and C-355/01, *AOK Bundesverband*, of 22 May 2003, Advocate General Jacobs proposes to lower the baseline of scrutiny to measures which are 'manifestly disproportionate' with regard to their objective (paras. 93–101).

[102] See, for example, T. Tridimas, *The General Principles of EC Law* (1999), at 90 and 93 (proportionality 'permeates the whole of the Community legal system'; 'proportionality is a flexible principle which is used in different contexts to protect different interests and entails varying degrees of judicial scrutiny'). A similarly wide concept is to be found in N. Emiliou, *The Principle of Proportionality in European Law* (1996), Jans, 'Proportionality Revisited', *LIEI* (2000) 239, Schønberg, 'The Principle of Proportionality's Many Faces: A Comparative Study of Judicial Review in English, French and EU Law', *Justitia* (2000) 1, and de Búrca, 'The Principle of Proportionality and its Application in EC Law', *YEL* (1993) 105.

[103] The critique of the excesses of the principle of proportionality that is sketched in the following pages draws some inspiration from a well-known critique of 'balancing' in US constitutional law due to Aleinikoff, 'Constitutional Law in the Age of Balancing', *Yale Law Journal* (1987) 943.

we wish to preserve a precise meaning for such a test. The Court itself may have contributed to the current confusion that is due to the wide and flexible notion of proportionality which is applied in Community law.[104] However, legal certainty and the predictability of judicial decisions in Community law may need to be strengthened by a more precise definition of the proportionality principle and its limits, of its varieties, and of the fields and circumstances in which it applies.[105] Such a clarification may also be needed to allow for a more autonomous and predictable application of Community law not only by lower national courts[106] but also by the Court of First Instance and the eventual judicial panels that may be attached to it. In other words, it is essential to develop a clearer and more sophisticated theory and practice of the appropriate levels of judicial scrutiny in Community law.

The general critique of the uses and abuses of the proportionality principle and the elaboration of an alternative goes well beyond the scope of this chapter, which only attempts to clarify things in so far as Article 86(2) is concerned. In that context, the case law shows that a necessity test is applied. That test only involves two of the elements of a proportionality test: a legitimate aim and a measure objectively tailored to achieve that end. Therefore, the test applied by the Court only marginally gets into questions of degree, balancing and cost–benefit analysis—and it does not impose on the decision-maker the obligation to choose the option least restrictive of competition. The absence in the case law relating to Article 86(2) of an explicit reference to proportionality may be the clearer sign that the Court does not consider it to be the appropriate test in this context. In this manner, the Court has avoided giving a relative priority to competition over services of general economic interest. It regards both as having the same weight and tries to determine whether the decision-maker has reconciled them in an appropriate way. Proportionality, especially a strict version thereof, would give excessive weight to competition.

The situation under Article 86(2) may be compared to what we see in *Schmidberger*, in which the free movement of goods directly clashed with the fundamental right to assemble. The Court did not apply a proportionality test, but

[104] See, for example, Case C-491/01, *British American Tobacco* [2002] ECR I-11453, paras. 122-123 (referring to the 'proportionality' and the 'manifest inappropriateness' tests as if they were the same thing).

[105] See Schønberg, *supra* n. 102, at 43 ('the sort of test should be stated [. . .]. Detailed reasoning of this kind would reduce judicial discretion and thus help judges decide which of proportionality's many faces to turn to in future cases'). See, however, Bermann, 'Proportionality and Subsidiarity', in C. Barnard and J. Scott (eds.), *The Law of the Single European Market: Unpacking the Premises* (2002) 75, at 85 ('the Community courts need the freedom to intensify or relax the level of scrutiny with which they enforce [the principle of proportionality] as the cases come along. In point of fact, they will act in this fashion, whether we acknowledge their right to do so or not').

[106] A similar argument has been made, in the context of the free movement rules on goods and services, by Snell, 'True Proportionality and Free Movement of Goods and Services', *EBLR* (2000) 50, at 54.

assessed whether the public authorities had reached an adequate balance between the interests involved.[107]

This contrasts with certain decisions of the Commission that adopt a proportionality analysis, generally soft but sometimes the 'less restrictive alternative' sort of proportionality.[108] It may also contrast with the communications of the Commission on services of general economic interest, which usually take for granted that the principle of proportionality applies in this field.[109] And, finally, the Court of First Instance has sometimes interpreted Article 86(2) in a way that seems to give relative priority to competition over services of general interest.[110]

The test used by the Court in the field under consideration in this chapter is less ambitious and more straightforward than a genuinely strict test of proportionality, constituting a technique to assess whether regulatory measures connected to services of general interest are indeed in the general interest or whether they pursue private interests. To benefit from this more lenient necessity test, the public measure must be well articulated in the legal act that 'entrusts' the public service mission to an undertaking. If this is not the case, the undertaking will be subject to the competition rules. The necessity test is flexible enough to allow the Court to identify illegitimate uses of Article 86(2), while being less intrusive than that of proportionality. Besides, its application varies in relation to different Treaty rules, as in the same situation a restriction on competition may be necessary for the provision of the public service while a restriction on free movement may not be so. The test also allows the Court to preserve a margin of appreciation for public authorities and to respect the legitimacy of democratic processes and legislation.

Finally, the proposal of Buendía Sierra to apply a strict proportionality test if the general service obligations are new *or* if the Commission has intervened, and a softer test if the general service obligations already exist *and* the Commission has not acted[111] seems to me to be misguided. A single test should apply to all these

[107] Case C-112/00, *Schmidberger* [2003] ECR I-5659, para. 81: 'the interests involved must be weighed having regard to all the circumstances of the case in order to determine whether a fair balance was struck between those interests'.

[108] See Decision of the Commission 82/371/EEC of 17 December 1981 relating to a proceeding under Article 85 of the EEC Treaty (IV/29.995—Navewa-Anseau), OJ 1982 L 167/39, para. 66: 'A possible limitation of the application of the rules on competition can be envisaged only in the event that the undertaking concerned has no other technically and economically feasible means of performing its particular task.'

[109] See, for example, *Communication from the Commission: Services of General Interest in Europe* (*supra* n. 2, para. 23). In contrast, the *White Paper on Services of General Interest* of 12 May 2004 seems to take a more balanced approach and does not even mention proportionality: 'under the EC Treaty and subject to the conditions set out in Article 86(2), the effective performance of a general interest task prevails, in case of tension, over the application of Treaty rules' (*supra* n. 2, para. 3.2).

[110] See, for example, Case T-260/94, *Air Inter* [1997] II-997, para. 138: 'Since that condition [the obstruction to the performance of the service] must be interpreted strictly, it was not sufficient for such performance to be simply hindered or made more difficult.' See also, in relation to Article 86(3), Case T-17/96, *TF1* v *Commission* [1999] ECR II-1757, para. 50, *supra* n. 62.

[111] Buendía Sierra, book cited *supra* n. 64, at 334–336.

situations once it is clear that an undertaking has been entrusted with a task of general economic interest. There are no legal grounds and no convincing reasons for the application of a different degree of scrutiny to old and new obligations. Similarly, the idea that the Commission may, 'by virtue of the discretion it enjoys under paragraphs (2) and (3) of Article 86, strictly interpret the principle of proportionality',[112] presupposes that Article 86(2) may be interpreted differently by the Commission and by national or Community courts. It seems clear, however, that a constitutional provision such as Article 86(2) should have the same meaning for all the institutions concerned so long as it is not seen as a highly technical economic provision for the application of which the Commission is endowed with a specific expertise that courts do not have. I have argued that Article 86(2) is not such a provision, with the consequence that its interpretation should not vary depending on the institution applying it. One may wonder, however, whether the representation or non-representation of the interests of actors affected by a given measure in the decision-making process that led to its adoption may in some circumstances lead to a modulation of the level of scrutiny under Article 86(2), an issue to which we shall briefly return in section 6.

4. LEGISLATION ON SERVICES OF GENERAL ECONOMIC INTEREST: POWERS AND LIMITS

This section is devoted to two constitutional issues related to the legislation in this field: What is the extent and nature of the powers of the Commission under Article 86(3)? Which institution or institutions can legislate and on what basis?

The scope of the powers of the Commission pursuant to Article 86(3) has been defined in three main judgments.

In *France* v *Commission*, France, Italy, and the United Kingdom brought actions for a declaration that the transparency Directive was void.[113] This was the first Directive adopted by the Commission pursuant to Article 86(3). The Directive provided that the Member States had to keep available for five years information concerning public funds made available to public undertakings. The United Kingdom argued that 'Commission Directives are not of the same nature as those adopted by the Council. Whereas the latter may contain general legislative provisions which may, where appropriate, impose new obligations on Member States, the aim of the former is merely to deal with a specific situation in one or more Member States.'[114] The Court rejected this claim, highlighting that 'the limits of the powers conferred on the Commission by a specific provision of the Treaty are to be inferred

[112] Buendía Sierra, book cited *supra* n. 64, at 335.

[113] Commission Directive 80/723/EEC of 25 June 1980 on the transparency of financial relations between Member States and public undertakings (OJ 1980 L 195/35).

[114] Joined Cases 188 to 190/80, *France, Italy and United Kingdom* v *Commission* [1982] ECR 2545, para. 5.

not from a general principle, but from an interpretation of the particular wording of the provision in question, in this case Article [86], analysed in the light of its purpose and its place in the scheme of the Treaty'.[115]

Another argument was that the Directive could have been adopted by the Council pursuant to Article 89 of the Treaty, as a regulation for the application of the State aid rules, since the purpose of the Directive was to enable the Commission to ensure that the Member States respected the obligation to notify any plans to grant or alter State aid. This was also rejected by the Court: the power 'conferred upon the Commission by Article [86](3) [. . .] operates in a specific field of application and under conditions defined by reference to the particular objective of that article. It follows that the Commission's power to issue the contested directive depends on the needs inherent in its duty of surveillance provided for in Article [86] and that the possibility that rules might be laid down by the Council, by virtue of its general power under Article [89], containing provisions impinging upon the specific sphere of aids granted to public undertakings does not preclude the exercise of that power by the Commission.'[116]

The Court thus affirmed the powers of the Commission to enact such a measure pursuant to Article 86(3), implicitly highlighting the absence of a rigid separation of powers in the Community and accepting that the Treaty may exceptionally entrust important powers to the Commission.

In the second case, France had brought an action for the annulment of several provisions of a Directive on competition in the markets in telecommunications terminal equipment, the second Commission Directive based on Article 86(3).[117] The Directive established that Member States which had granted special or exclusive rights to undertakings for the importation, marketing, connection, bringing into service of telecommunications terminal equipment, and/or maintenance of such equipment were to ensure that those rights were withdrawn; Member States had to ensure that economic operators had the right to import, market, connect, bring into service, and maintain terminal equipment, subject to certain conditions; responsibility for drawing up specifications, monitoring their application, and granting type-approval had to be entrusted by the Member States to a body independent of public or private undertakings offering goods and/or services in the telecommunications sector; Member States were required to ensure that customers could terminate, with maximum notice of one year, leasing or maintenance contracts relating to terminal equipment which at the time when the contracts were concluded were subject to exclusive or special rights.

For Advocate General Tesauro, the Directive's aim was 'to lay down general, abstract rules for the sector ("define the obligations incumbent on the Member States"), and that exceeded the limits of Article [86](3) and fell within the

[115] *Ibid.*, para. 6.

[116] *Ibid.*, para. 14.

[117] Commission Directive 88/301/EEC of 16 May 1988 on competition in the markets in telecommunications terminal equipment (OJ 1988 L 131/73).

competence of the Council'. He saw the Directive as 'an essentially planning instrument', 'an anomalous anticipation of the legislative process'. He concluded that France's invocation of 'the principle that the institutions must act within the limits of their powers, and its reference to the balance between Community institutions, [were] [. . .] not unfounded. The adoption by the Commission of a legislative measure which, although intended to prevent infringements, amends the very basis for the presence of the State in a particular sector of the economy seems, in my view, to alter the balance between the institutions and therefore cannot be held by the Court to be lawful.'[118]

The Court did not follow the Opinion, and this could lead some to think that the judgment constitutes an affirmation of a legislative power for the Commission. Indeed, the Court held that, '[i]nasmuch as it makes it possible for the Commission to adopt directives, Article [86](3) of the Treaty empowers it to lay down general rules specifying the obligations arising from the Treaty which are binding on the Member States as regards the undertakings referred to in Article [86](1) and (2)'. 'Accordingly, the parties' pleas in law and arguments must be considered in the light of the question whether in this case the Commission has remained within the bounds of *the legislative power* thus conferred upon it by the Treaty.'[119]

In spite of this broad characterization of the powers of the Commission, the Court held that 'the supervisory power conferred on the Commission includes the possibility of specifying, pursuant to Article [86(3)], obligations arising under the Treaty. The extent of that power therefore depends on the scope of the rules with which compliance is to be ensured.'[120] This power can hardly be seen as legislative, since it does not entail the possibility of introducing new obligations but only of specifying obligations that already arise out of other Treaty provisions. The subject matter of the power of the Commission under this provision was said to be 'different from, and more specific than, that of the powers conferred on the Council by either Article [95] or Article [83]'.[121] The Court thus rejected the plea alleging lack of powers of the Commission.

The Court moved on to the plea concerning the misapplication by the Commission of several provisions of the Treaty. Again, this argument implies that in adopting the Directive the Commission was simply applying the Treaty. The prohibition of exclusive rights was upheld because the Commission was right to consider them incompatible with Article 28.[122] Insofar as special rights were concerned, the Directive was declared void, because it did not specify 'the type of rights which are actually involved and in what respect the existence of such rights is contrary to the various provisions of the Treaty'.[123] Thus, Article 2 of the Directive was declared invalid only in so far as it referred to special rights.

[118] *France* v *Commission, supra* n. 94, Opinion of Advocate General Tesauro, paras. 48, 54–55.

[119] *Ibid.*, paras. 14-15 (emphasis added).

[120] *Ibid.*, para. 21. See also para. 17.

[121] *Ibid.*, para. 25.

[122] *Ibid.*, paras. 31–44.

[123] *Ibid.*, para. 45.

Concerning the obligation to establish an independent body to draw up specifications and to grant type-approval, the Court held that it was justified, because 'a system of undistorted competition, as laid down in the Treaty, can be guaranteed only if equality of opportunity is secured as between the various economic operators'.[124] For the Court, an important aim of the competition rules is to guarantee an equality of opportunity between competitors. If specifications are drawn up and approvals are granted by an undertaking offering competing goods, there is no equality in the market. Thus, the obligation is upheld because the Commission has acted pursuant to the Treaty objective of a system of undistorted competition. This holding may have gone beyond the specification of obligations arising out of the Treaty, as the general provisions on the objectives of the Community do not create obligations.

The provision of the Directive on termination of leasing or maintenance contracts was declared void, because Article 86 'confers powers on the Commission only in relation to State measures [. . .]'. Therefore, Article 86 was not 'an appropriate basis for dealing with the obstacles to competition which are purportedly created by the long-term contracts referred to in the Directive'.[125] The validity of the rest of the Directive was upheld by the Court.

In *Spain and others* v *Commission*,[126] a new attack was launched on the powers of the Commission. The applicants asked the Court to annul a Commission Directive on competition in the markets for telecommunications services,[127] the third Directive adopted under Article 86(3). The Directive was similar to the telecommunication terminals Directive, establishing comparable obligations in the field of telecommunication services. The judgment upholds the validity of the Directive to the same extent and annuls similar provisions, but an important aspect is clarified. Responding to an argument of Belgium according to which the freedom to provide services was not as developed as the free movement of goods, so that the obligations imposed in the telecommunication terminals Directive would not be valid with regard to services, the Court held that '[s]ince Article [49] is thus, like Article [28], *a directly applicable provision*, the Commission was empowered, with a view to promoting the effective exercise of the freedom to provide services, to specify the obligations arising from that article without the need for any prior legislative action on the part of the Council'.[128] This puts an end to the ambiguity of *France* v *Commission*, which had resolved one of the issues by reference to the system of undistorted competition enshrined in Article 3 of the Treaty. This would perhaps go beyond the mere specification of obligations arising out of the Treaty, coming close to a genuine legislative power. But shortly afterwards the Court was

[124] *Ibid.*, para. 51.

[125] *Ibid.*, paras. 55 and 57.

[126] Joined Cases C-271/90, C-281/90 and C-289/90, *Spain, Belgium and Italy* v *Commission* [1992] ECR I-5833.

[127] Commission Directive 90/388/EEC of 28 June 1990 on competition in the markets for telecommunications services (OJ 1990 L 192/10).

[128] *Spain, Belgium and Italy* v *Commission, supra* n. 126, para. 21.

clear: in measures adopted under Article 86(3) the Commission can only specify obligations arising out of directly applicable Treaty provisions. Thus, the validity of the requirement of independence of the regulator established by the Directive is no longer founded on the system of undistorted competition of Article 3 of the Treaty, but on Article 82, a directly applicable provision.[129] The lack of independence of the regulator is in breach of Article 82, because of the conflict of interests that automatically ensues from its position as competitor and regulator. The judgment thus constitutes the final turn of the screw on the powers of the Commission under Article 86(3).

The conclusion to be drawn from these judgments is that the Commission's power under Article 86(3) is not a legislative power. Its usefulness as a policy-making tool is quite limited, as it does not allow the Commission to take policy options, and it adds little to the power of the Commission to bring before the Court infringement proceedings pursuant to Article 226 of the Treaty. Thus, Article 86(3) cannot be seen as a legal basis for *legislation* on services of general economic interest.

Although *France* v *Commission* refers to 'a legislative power', the reasoning of the Court and *Spain and Others* v *Commission* show that that power is so restricted that the Commission has to prove in each case that an infringement of directly applicable Treaty rules would result from the conduct it prohibits.[130] It appears, therefore, as a mass instrument to prevent or to bring an end to Treaty infringements. For Mattera, Directives adopted under Article 86(3) only constitute a sort of obligatory interpretive measure.[131] Indeed, the determination of the obligations of the Member States under directly effective Treaty provisions in the pre-litigation stage of Article 226 also involves an interpretation of those provisions.

The limits of the Commission's powers under Article 86(3) may explain why, after these judgments, that provision was only used to amend or recast the three existing Directives. The validity of the Directives was upheld, but the Commission lost the most important point of law, especially in the Spanish case.[132] As a consequence, the liberalization programmes fostered by the Commission had to be based on other legal bases providing for action on the part of the Parliament and Council. In the proposed legislation, the Commission invites the legislator to take options, sometimes hard policy options, and often it proposes those alternatives which are the least restrictive of competition that, as we have seen, are not mandated by Article 86(2), and cannot therefore be seen as specifications of obligations arising out of directly applicable Treaty provisions. Admittedly, the dividing line between policy options and administrative specifications is difficult to trace. But were the Commission to take decisions beyond the specification of Treaty provisions pursuant

[129] *Spain, Belgium and Italy* v *Commission, supra* n. 126, para. 22.

[130] See Mattera, 'L'arrêt "Terminaux de télécommunications" : interprétation et mise en œuvre des articles 30 à 36 et 90 du traité CEE', *RMUE* (1991) 245.

[131] *Ibid.*, at 246.

[132] One may even ask whether the transparency Directive would have passed the stricter test of *Spain and Others* v *Commission,* since it seems to create new obligations rather than just specifying obligations arising out of existing and directly applicable Treaty provisions.

to Article 86(3), one might expect that one or more Member States would attack those measures, and that the Court would trace and enforce the limits of the Commission's powers.

For Buendía Sierra, Article 86(3) remains of use as a weapon to be employed by the Commission when the legislative process stagnates, 'against excessive resistance to liberalization found in certain sectors'.[133] If this were the case, it would be an example of a misuse of political power and of a neo-liberal stand that could attract criticism from other equally legitimate views of law, politics and society. However, in view of its limitations, Article 86(3) cannot really serve as a weapon to advance the Commission's political agenda. Besides, the threat to withdraw a proposal would be a more credible and effective weapon in the hands of the Commission. Thus, the sole aspect of this provision that adds something to the powers that the Commission already has under Article 226 is its preventive use, which comes close to a sort of administrative interpretative regulation.

The powers of the Commission being so limited, legislation in this field is generally adopted by the Council with Parliament pursuant to the co-decision procedure of Article 251 of the Treaty (Article 95 on internal market measures or Article 71 on transport), and by the Council alone in the field of air and maritime transport (Article 80, paragraph 2). This raises two questions: Does the use of those legal bases result in measures that give precedence to the internal market and competition over the provision of services of general economic interest? Is there a need for a specific legal basis devoted to those services?

The use of Article 95 as a legal basis does not necessarily mean that the internal market will be given priority. The tobacco advertisement and the *British American Tobacco* judgments make clear that as long as a legislative measure genuinely has as its object the establishment and functioning of the internal market, 'actually contributing to the elimination of obstacles to the free movement of goods or to the freedom to provide services, or to the removal of distortions of competition', 'the Community legislature cannot be prevented from relying on [Article 95] on the ground that public health protection is a decisive factor in the choices to be made'.[134] This reasoning could be transposed to the field of services of general economic interest in spite of the fact that, unlike health, services of general interest are not mentioned in Article 95. Article 16 could give some support to the idea that legislation can be adopted pursuant to Article 95 that even gives priority to the choices regarding services of general interest over the internal market or competition objectives.[135] The final outcome will of course depend on the concrete measures adopted by the institutions, but it is clear that the legal basis most frequently used

[133] Buendía Sierra, *supra* n. 64, at 429.

[134] Case C-376/98, *Germany* v *Parliament and Council* [2000] ECR I-2247, paras. 84 and 88, and Case C-491/01, *British American Tobacco* [2002] ECR I-11453, paras. 60–62.

[135] In view of the flexibility of Article 95 of the Treaty, the actual impact of the inclusion of a specific legal basis on services of general economic interest in Article III-122 of the Treaty establishing a Constitution for Europe—if it comes into force—would be quite limited.

to legislate in this field does not impose a market bias. Such a bias may however arise as a consequence of the peculiar structure of the Community decision-making process.

5. LEGISLATION ON SERVICES OF GENERAL ECONOMIC INTEREST: SUBSTANCE

This is not the place to examine the ever-growing and ever-changing legislation on services of general economic interest, which covers fields such as electronic communications, transport, energy, and postal services.[136] Such an examination would be necessary to identify possible cases of regulatory capture or of a market bias in the legislation. This chapter simply describes its general traits and sketches a critique that would need to be tested and developed after a detailed examination of each sector.

The Directives adopted in those fields use the same concepts and deal with the same problems, being a legislative counterpart of Article 86(2). It is curious to observe that certain policy choices are presented as justified by the principle of proportionality.[137] The legislator thus opts for the alternative that is the least restrictive of competition, something which is not mandated by the constitutional framework, but which it may choose to do within the limits of Article 86(2). In other cases the legislation includes exceptions that recall or simply repeat the wording of Article 86(2). Thus, the problem of defining what is necessary for the provision of services of general interest is sometimes left unresolved by the legislator.[138]

The general aim of all these Directives and Regulations is that of a 'controlled and gradual opening up of markets towards full competition', which stands as the ultimate aim of the legislation.[139] The legislation generally establishes obligations concerning the opening of markets and competition. Undertakings operating in

[136] For a description of the legislation as it stood in 2000, see the *Communication from the Commission, supra* n. 2, at 16–23.

[137] See para. 9 of the preamble to Directive 2002/77/EC on competition in the markets for electronic communications networks and services (OJ 2002 L 249/21).

[138] See, for example, Article 7(1) of Directive 97/67/EC of the European Parliament and of the Council of 15 December 1997 on common rules for the development of the internal market of Community postal services and the improvement of quality of service (OJ 2003 L 15/14): 'To the extent necessary to ensure the maintenance of universal service, Member States may continue to reserve services to universal service provider(s). [. . .]'.

[139] See, for example, the preamble of Directive 2002/39/EC of the European Parliament and of the Council of 10 June 2002 amending Directive 97/67/EC with regard to the further opening to competition of Community postal services (OJ 2002 L 176/21, rec. 14): 'It is [. . .] appropriate to provide for a step-by-step approach to further market-opening, consisting of intermediate steps representing significant but controlled opening of the market, followed by a review and proposal confirming, if appropriate, the date of 2009 for *the full accomplishment of the internal market for postal services* or determining a relevant alternative step *towards it* in the light of the review results' (emphases added).

the sector or having exclusive or special rights must keep transparent accounts. The legislation also provides, to a variety of degrees, for the independence of the regulators.

An important notion found across the legislation is that of 'universal service'. The Commission defined it 'as the minimum set of services of specified quality to which all users and consumers have access in the light of specific national conditions at an affordable price'.[140] This concept is used throughout the legislation, although some measures simply refer to 'public service obligations'.[141] Universal service is meant to be an evolving concept: its contours may change in different sectors as the legislation is amended. Sometimes, but not always, universal service obligations are characterized as rights of end-users. The concept of universal service generally comes with the extremely vague notion of 'affordability of tariffs'. In the case of the postal service, for example, tariffs should no longer be uniform, but the 'Member States may decide that a uniform tariff should be applied throughout their national territory'.[142] Tariffs must be affordable, but the States may decide that they need not be uniform, which means that the concept of universal service could end up being narrower than that of service of general economic interest, as in *Corbeau* the uniformity of tariffs was part of the latter concept. Prices *must* be geared to costs, however, and customers should be able to conclude individual agreements with the universal service provider(s), even if a uniform tariff is established.

Most Directives foresee the possibility of establishing compensation funds to finance the universal service.[143] This is the preferred solution to the financial imbalance due to public service obligations, because it distorts competition less than cross-subsidies or equalization of the tariffs. However, the legislation does not impose it on the Member States. Finally, all these measures provide for an automatic system that binds the Commission to report periodically on their application and effects and, where appropriate, to submit proposals that move on towards 'full competition'.

The first general criticism to be made has to do with formal aspects of the legislation, which is poorly drafted and fragmented. The fragmentation is sometimes due to the 'packages' that are proposed by the Commission. As a result, antinomies and interpretive problems arise between the various elements of a single package. There is, besides, a lack of a general framework beyond Article 86(2). The proposals for a Charter of Services of General Interest and then for a framework Directive have been advanced as a way to overcome the liberal bent of the legislation. The draft Treaty establishing a Constitution for Europe has echoed this idea by amending the current text of Article 16 of the Treaty (Article III-122 of the Constitutional Treaty) to allow the legislator to enact a European law that would establish the

[140] *Communication, supra* n. 2, at 23.

[141] See Article 3 of Directive 2003/54/EC of the European Parliament and of the Council of 26 June 2003 concerning common rules for the internal market in electricity and repealing Directive 96/92/EC (OJ 2003 L 176/37).

[142] Article 12 of Directive 97/67/EC, *supra* n. 138.

[143] See, for example, Article 9(4) of Directive 97/67/EC, *supra* n. 138.

general principles governing legislation in the field. The Commission doubts whether such a legislative framework would have an added value.[144] In contrast, a resolution of the European Parliament has called—contrary to the motion and report of the Committee on Economic and Monetary Affairs—'for a legal framework to be drawn up under the codecision procedure', inviting the Commission to define its position in this regard.[145] The scepticism of the Commission may however be well founded: the framework legislation would have the same hierarchical rank as the other Directives and would not be able to perform its central role. Some sort of 'organic law' would be needed, with a status falling between that of the Treaty and the sectoral legislation, but such a source of law has not been provided for in the draft Constitutional Treaty. Finally, the framework legislation would probably share the same problems as the sectoral legislation, since it would be the result of the same decision-making process.

A second criticism would focus on the relentless march of the legislation towards full competition. Sometimes an amending Directive is adopted while a new proposal is already in the pipeline. As it has already been pointed out, the periodical review and update is provided for in the legislation itself. It is thus difficult to perceive its medium- and long-term effects. Sometimes it involves profound changes in the way services of general interest are provided, the effects of which may not be immediately visible. There is an acceleration of the legislative tempo which may not allow the actors to assess the consequences of changes in legislation.

Thirdly, the legislation is plagued with problems of interpretation that make it a potential nest of litigation. As we have seen, the open texture of Article 86(2) is sometimes reproduced in the legislation. This also means that the problems are referred back to the Court. It is for the Court to decide, as a general matter of institutional strategy, how to interpret the legislation. It will undoubtedly be tempted to have recourse to the traditional concepts of the Treaty, with which it feels comfortable, and transpose that case law to these Directives. In some cases it

[144] See the *Green Paper on Services of General Interest, supra* n. 2, at 13–14. In the *White Paper on Services of General Interest* of 12 May 2004, the Commission remains sceptical and declares that it 'will re-examine the feasibility of and the need for a framework law for services of general interest on the entry into force of the Constitutional Treaty' (*supra* n. 2, at 12).

[145] *Resolution on the Green Paper on Services of General Interest* (minutes of 14 January 2004, P5-TA-PROV(2004)0018, available online at http://www3.europeal.eu.int), paras. 5 and 6. The Parliament's resolution comes as a surprise as the report and motion on which it is based were very sceptical on the value of a general framework Directive and argued that it would 'undermine and confuse the sectoral liberalisation Directives previously adopted by Parliament and Council' (A5-0484/2003 of 17 December 2003, paras. 10 and 11). The final resolution appears to be much more balanced than the motion of the committee, most of which reads as a panegyric of the virtuous effects that competition has in different sectors (compare, for example, para. 7 in the resolution, absent in the motion, that recalls 'the problems encountered with liberalisation in certain sectors', considering it necessary to assess its social, territorial and other effects 'before initiating new phases of liberalisation', with para. 7 of the motion, absent in the Parliament's resolution, for which 'the liberalisation of key public services and the introduction of competition has been shown to deliver major benefits to consumers in terms of innovation, quality, choice and lower prices').

has already done so.[146] But it would perhaps be wiser for the Court not to follow such a route. The main objective of legislation is to translate the constitutional objectives and values in more precise ordinary law. This should be done according to the direction given by democratic politics and within the space of constitutionality defined by constitutional law, while providing for a higher degree of legal certainty. The Court should interpret legislation in the light of its specific objectives. Sometimes the strict version of the principle of proportionality is included in the legislation, and the margin left to the Member States will be reduced with respect to that of Article 86(2), but this is not always the case. When proportionality is not expressly included in the legislation it may be better not to use it and to adhere as far as possible to the wording and objectives of the legislation, unless it is challenged as incompatible with the Treaty. In this way, the Court would avoid working as a fine-tuning legislator. It would rather reinforce the decision-making process of the Community by showing the defects of legislative measures, and allow the legislator to correct them.

The fourth criticism has to do with the substance of the legislation. Going back to our central questions, some of the legislation in this field shows that the political institutions of the Community have opted to give a relative priority to competition over services of general interest. This is clear in that they try to introduce the maximum of competition compatible with the desirable level or services of general interest. Implicit is the assumption that services of general economic interest will always gain in quality through the introduction of competition, that the reduction or exclusion of limits to competition will always redound in better public services. This is also shown by the progressive character of liberalization, which has as its final aim the introduction of 'full competition'. It is clear, finally, in the political choices for the financing of the universal service: cross-subsidization, which involves the closure to competition of sectors of the economy, is limited or excluded. Funds or direct compensation are preferred, and their level should correspond to what is strictly necessary. This relative preference is also shown by the concept of universal service: the legislation aims at a maximum of competition but only guarantees a minimum service.

This could be problematic if the medium- and long-term social effects of the legislation prove not to be so 'virtuous'. Are there constitutional safeguards that would prevent such negative effects? If one sees Article 86(2) as having two edges, one in defence of competition and the other in defence of services of general interest, one may ask whether this minimum universal service could be reviewed and even held unconstitutional if it were manifestly insufficient. This social edge of Article 86(2) has so far been quite blunt, but it could be sharpened if affected litigants decided to read the law in a new light. Such review would be possible if the Community legislator were bound to respect the limits of Article 86(2). But is it?

[146] Case C-205/99, *Analir* [2001] I-1271, para. 70 (carrying out a proportionality analysis similar to that of the free movement rules instead of simply interpreting the provisions of a directive).

To answer this question one may first turn to the case law on the free movement rules. Even though they are generally thought to be addressed to the Member States, the Court has repeatedly held that the Community is bound by analogous principles: 'although it is true [. . .] that Articles [28 to 30] of the Treaty apply primarily to unilateral measures adopted by the Member States, the Community institutions themselves must also have due regard to freedom of trade within the Community, which is a fundamental principle of the common market'.[147] According to Peter Oliver, in the free movement field 'the Court has plotted a middle course: while setting bounds to the freedom enjoyed by the Community institutions in this regard, it has ensured that this freedom is greater than that permitted to the Member States in view of the special tasks which the Community itself is called upon to perform'.[148]

One may also look at the waste oil judgment of 1985, in which the Court emphasized that 'the principles of free movement of goods and freedom of competition, together with freedom of trade as a fundamental right, are general principles of Community law of which the Court ensures observance'. The Directive which was in question in that case, and presumably other pieces of Community legislation, 'should therefore be reviewed in the light of those principles'.[149]

Moreover, Article 86(2) itself does not exclude the European Community from its personal scope of application, and one may think of applying this provision directly to the Community institutions. The reference in Article 86(2) to 'undertakings entrusted with the operation of services of general economic interest' does not define its personal scope, and the Member States are also bound by it. That provision also refers to the 'rules of this Treaty' and it could be argued that, since Article 95 or other legal bases are rules of the Treaty, legislation adopted pursuant to them must respect, *inter alia*, the limits of Article 86(2). The 'application' of a legal basis is the adoption of legislation pursuant to it. Community legislation could thus be held unconstitutional if it obstructed the performance of the tasks assigned to undertakings entrusted with the operation of services of general economic interest or if it excluded competition and free movement when they would not obstruct such performance. If this argument were not accepted, one could still build an argument to the same effect based on general principles of Community law.

A different question is whether the Community legislator should have a wider margin of appreciation than the Member States, as is the case in the free movement field. At first sight it would seem that, since the margin of appreciation enjoyed by the Member States under Article 86(2) is already quite wide, the Community legislator should not have a wider margin. Besides, the position of the Community legislator with regard to services of general interest is not so different from that of national legislators to justify the application of a softer standard of review—at least

[147] Case 37/83, *REWE-Zentrale* [1984] ECR 1229.

[148] P. Oliver (assisted by M. Jarvis), *Free Movement of Goods in the European Community* (2003), at 73.

[149] Case 240/83, *ADBHU* [1985] 531, para. 9.

so long as the free movement rules are not applied together with Article 86(2). In the free movement field, in contrast, there may be important reasons related to the protection of commercial interests of other Member States that are not represented in the political process of one Member State—which may lead to protectionist measures taken by the latter—that could justify the application of a stricter standard of review to State measures than to Community measures, for the adoption of which all relevant interests are generally represented.[150]

In sum, it seems plausible that the Community legislator may also be bound by Article 86(2) or by similar principles. In view of this alternative 'social' use, Article 86(2) may have some bright future potential.

Whether Community legislation in this field is a threat to public services will have to be assessed with reference to the facts. The pursuit of 'full competition' as the most desirable of ends takes for granted that there is no trade-off between competition and services of general interest, including their social and territorial functions, that most public goods can and should presently be 'privatized', and that at any point of the possible 'policy-mixes' competition can only redound to the benefit of the provision of public services. Again, only medium- and long-term effects will tell if there is such a trade-off and how it was settled. It may well be that the liberalization process is beneficial for businesses and most individuals but not so for some individuals, leading to social and territorial exclusion.

Perhaps politics should be brought back into this delicate field, exorcising the idea of the 'inevitability', economic or legal, of the liberalization process, which has been taken by some institutional actors as a sort of dogma.[151] There is nothing inevitable in the liberalization process, which is the result of policy choices taken by the Community legislator that are not mandated by Article 86(2) and cannot be carried out by the Commission alone pursuant to Article 86(3). Nothing, constitutionally or practically, prevents the Community legislator from stopping short of full competition or even from retracing its steps if the results prove undesirable; nothing, perhaps, but the political process of the Community, which could be one of the causes of the relative priority given to competition.

The political process of the Community is characterized by a common trait of contemporary democratic politics: it tends to represent interests more than people, with the attendant danger that organized interests may end up weighing more than they should in strictly democratic terms. This danger may even be graver in the Community and one may actually argue that its decision-making process leads to some sort of structural or endemic capture, which is not the product of the malfunctioning of the mechanisms of representation and decision-making, but the natural result of deficient mechanisms. The main elements at the root of this

[150] See M. Poiares Maduro, *We the Court* (1998), at 174; Baquero Cruz, *supra* n. 3, at 132–133.

[151] See, for example, the opinion of the Economic and Social Committee on the further opening to competition of Community postal services (OJ 2001 C 116/99): 'While the ESC recognises *the inevitability of further liberalisation*, it is concerned that the process should be managed on a controlled basis with full regard to the interests of the various stakeholders' (emphasis added).

phenomenon of structural capture are well-known: the Commission's technocratic and 'apolitical' or 'neutral' character and its monopoly of initiative, the extraordinary legislative power of the executives and administrations of the Member States, unanimous or consensual decision-making or else an extremely high qualified majority that makes the option for the less common denominator the more likely to be chosen, the absence of a reserved domain for legislation, comitology, etc. In our particular field, most proposals of the Commission are tabled after extensive consultation with 'interested parties'. Organized interests, in particular business interests, seem to be even more effective at influencing the Community legislator at all levels than they are at influencing national legislators. And the unorganized individual may 'suffer in silence' as a result.[152]

In this connection, it is interesting to observe that in many sectors the liberalization process seems to have been designed to benefit the interests of businesses first and foremost and those of customers only as a consequence. In some cases, at the first stages of liberalization it only applies to undertakings. Take the example of the postal sector, where business correspondence amounts to roughly 90% of all correspondence. The opening up of this market will allow undertakings to negotiate cheaper prices with private companies and the reduction of the reserved sector may render cross-subsidies insufficient to finance universal service obligations and other public service obligations that the Member States may assume. The tariffs of the public service may still be affordable, but in the long run services of general interest may have to be financed with taxes or with higher tariffs and/or public service obligations may have to be reduced. The example of the postal Directive is significant, as it makes it quite clear that 'the application of a uniform tariff does not exclude *the right* of the universal service provider(s) to conclude individual agreements on prices with customers' and that 'tariffs must be transparent and non-discriminatory'.[153] This means that business making bulk use of postal services may pay less than individuals, because their services cost less. This is a *right* of the providers that will directly benefit the interests of business. Tariffs must otherwise be non-discriminatory, whereas uniform tariffs, which are not obligatory for the Member States under Article 12 of the Directive, clearly presuppose a degree of socially virtuous discrimination among users.

The central aim of such measures is to reduce the costs of undertakings, which may improve productivity, economic efficiency and growth—but at what price? As the costs of businesses diminish the benefits from profitable sectors shrink and tariffs paid by common customers may well be raised in order not to endanger the equilibrium of the postal service. Even if services of general economic interest become better and cheaper, legislation of this kind will probably damage the social and territorial policies pursued through the provision of services of general interest—policies which may not be pursued through other means—sacrificing

[152] In the words of M. Olson, *The Logic of Collective Action* (1965), at 165.

[153] Article 12 of Directive 97/67/EC, *supra* n. 138 (emphasis added).

them to an exclusively efficiency-oriented conception of competition. These are hardly neutral choices.

One could wonder, finally, whether this phenomenon of structural capture may justify the application of a stricter standard of judicial scrutiny under Article 86(2) in the context of eventual proceedings brought by undertakings or even individuals[154] against Community legislation that has the effect of obstructing the provision of services of general interest. Such proceedings are unlikely to arise, but they are not impossible. Undertakings entrusted with the task of providing services of general interest can invoke Article 86(2) in defence of their prerogatives. Individuals do not have a Community constitutional right to receive such services, to be sure, and it seems that Article 36 of the Charter of Fundamental Rights (Article II-96 of the Constitutional Treaty) would not change this situation, but Article 86(2), if interpreted along the lines proposed in this chapter, at least enshrines a directly effective[155] protected position not to have the services of general economic interest they receive obstructed by the application of the Treaty or of Community legislation. In any event, since process-based arguments of this sort seem to have little weight in Community law, if any such case ever reached the Court it is likely that its attitude would be very deferential towards the Community legislator. Moreover, although enhanced judicial intervention may be useful to correct isolated cases of malfunction of the political process, it would certainly be insufficient to counter the structural democratic problems of the European Union. Those problems can only be overcome through far-reaching constitutional changes that do not appear to be forthcoming.

CONCLUSION

My answers to the questions set out at the beginning of this chapter may already be clear in the mind of the reader, but let us repeat them: as interpreted by the Court of Justice, Community constitutional law does not give an absolute or a relative priority to competition over services of general economic interest—which are given an equivalent weight in a balanced relationship—nor does it compromise or prejudice the provision of those services. In contrast, Community legislation on services of general economic interest shows signs of a relative priority being given to competition over those services. Whether such priority will endanger the provision of those services will have to be assessed in view of its medium- and long-term effects. In the field of services of general interest, therefore, the market bias denounced by Scharpf is to be found in Community legislation rather than in the case law.

154 This eventual stricter standard of review would not be available to the Member States in so far as they are sufficiently represented in the decision-making process.

155 On the direct effect of Article 86(2), see *supra* n. 8.

This does not mean that the case law is unproblematic. Sometimes, as has been shown, it is quite 'thin' and ambiguous, leaving too wide a margin to national judges. In this field and also in other fields, an excessively 'thin' or 'poor' case law of the Court runs the risk of passing on the priority problem with insufficient guidance to precisely those national judges who sought guidance from it. National courts could then opt to give priority either to competition or to services of general interest, applying a strict proportionality instead of striking an adequate balance between both, and damaging that degree of uniformity in interpretation and application which is so essential to Community law. Or else they may give priority to services of general interest, disregarding competition as a secondary matter. The ideal case law should thus be balanced and stay away from a strict proportionality test, but it should be 'thick' in normative terms and reduce the margin left to national courts.

The problems with Community legislation in this field are more serious and no solution may presently be available. They go well beyond our topic, which is only an example of a more general problem. The peculiar structure of the European political process sometimes seems to lead to policy outcomes that may not be comparable to those of a traditional representative democracy. The solution to these difficulties would require a radical change in the structure of the European political process that would make it conform better to basic democratic principles. However, the poor outcome of the Convention and the attendant intergovernmental conference with regard to the democratic chapter suggest that the European Union is not yet ripe for such a change—or is it those representing its citizens who are not yet ripe? In fact, it would seem that this is not even perceived as a problem, and indeed that quite the opposite is true. As a result, it is not likely that we will soon witness the de-neutralization, de-'technocratization', and re-'politicization' of European politics that would be needed to change the market bias that seems to affect some of the legislation on services of general economic interest—and beyond—or at least to ensure that such a bias is the result of conscious political decisions adopted by the representatives of a majority of European citizens rather than the consequence of institutional and procedural constraints.

7

Social Europe and Experimentalist Governance: Towards a New Constitutional Compromise?

JONATHAN ZEITLIN

The European Union (EU) is once again at a crossroads, hesitating over the terms of a new constitutional compromise. To build an integrated continental market the Member States sacrificed some of their power to veto Union regulation. In return they got assurance that the regulatory choices submitted for their final approval would be shaped by a public-regarding process that filtered out proposals chiefly motivated by narrow self-interest. The 'classic' Community Method of EU policy-making, based on the agenda-setting role of the Commission and its exclusive powers of legislative initiative, provided that assurance. This compromise transformed the EU from an association of states into a single legal community whose integrity was ensured by the European Court of Justice (ECJ). Until now this community has worked well enough to assuage many of the most pressing concerns about its democratic legitimacy.

The potential new compromise regards 'Social Europe'. Faced with the urgent, politically imperative task of reconstructing, separately but harmoniously, their welfare states, the Member States would relax the power accorded them by the treaties and the Community Method to block EU intrusion into national systems of social protection. Again they would insist on institutionalization of a public-regarding process of agenda setting. This time that process would be embodied in new forms of experimentalist governance, epitomized by but not confined to the Open Method

This chapter draws on a joint paper with Charles Sabel of Columbia University Law School, 'Active Welfare, Experimental Governance, Pragmatic Constitutionalism: The New Transformation of Europe', available online at http://www2.law.columbia.edu/sable/papers.htm, as well as on my introduction and conclision to J. Zeitlin and P. Pochet, with L. Magnusson (eds.), *The Open Method of Coordination in Action: The European Employment and Social Inclusion Strategies* (2005). An earlier version was presented to an international conference organized by the Hellenic Presidency of the European Union on 'The Modernization of the European Social Model and EU Policies and Instruments', Ioannina, Greece, May 21–22 2003. I am grateful to Natalie Oldani for invaluable assistance in preparing the references.

of Coordination (OMC).[1] These permit exploratory learning within and among Member States by contrasting different problem-solving strategies, each informed by a particular idea of the good, with the aim of both improving local performance and creating frameworks for joint action at the Union level. Through the ramifications of experimental governance, this compromise could transform EU policy-making again, integrating it more fully into civil society. At the limit the compromise would help establish the EU as a new form of pragmatist democracy that sees problem solving and agonistic deliberation over ideals of the good as so indissolubly connected that effective learning becomes institutionalized in the continuing exploration of deep values.

The roots of this potential compromise are political and intellectual as well as administrative. Foremost among these has been the progressive shift in both national and EU debates away from the goal of a single Social Europe as a regulatory counterbalance to the single market in favour of an alternative approach based on connecting welfare diversity within the European Social Model through policy coordination and mutual learning.[2] This shift in the debate reflects in turn a number of surprising empirical findings and novel conceptual developments. One is the limited incidence of social dumping or regulatory races to the bottom, coupled with evidence of races to the top in some well-documented cases, which has made the EU appear less constitutionally hostile to market-correcting regulation than originally feared.[3] A second is the discovery that there is not one welfare state in Europe, but several welfare-state families: what Anton Hemerijck and Jos Berghman, following Fritz Scharpf, term 'legitimate diversity'.[4] Whatever their

[1] Other components of the new experimentalist governance in the EU include: the commitment to proportionality or framework legislation, comitology, networked administrative agencies, and transparency as a procedural safeguard. For a fuller discussion, see C. F. Sabel and J. Zeitlin, 'Active Welfare, Experimental Governance, Pragmatic Constitutionalism: The New Transformation of Europe', unpublished paper presented to the International Conference of the Hellenic Presidency of the European Union, 'The Modernization of the European Social Model and EU Policies and Instruments', Ioannina, Greece, May 21–22 2003.

[2] For a synthetic presentation of this shift, see T. Sakellaropolous and J. Berghman (eds.), *Connecting Welfare Diversity within the European Social Model* (2004).

[3] For the absence of 'social dumping' in the EU, see Guillén and Matsaganis, 'Testing the "Social Dumping" Hypothesis in Southern Europe: Welfare Policies in Greece and Spain during the Last 20 Years', 10 *JESP* (2000) 2. For 'races to the top' in occupational safety and environmental protection, see Eichner, 'Effective European Problem-Solving: Lessons from the Regulation of Occupational Safety and Environmental Protection' 4 *JEPP* (1997) 4; A. Héritier, *Policy-Making and Diversity in Europe: Escape from Deadlock* (1999), at ch. 5. For a summary of the 'achievements of Social Europe' in creating a binding set of rights through legislation and social dialogue agreements, see M. Ferrera, A. Hemerijck and M. Rhodes, *The Future of Social Europe: Recasting Work and Welfare in the New Economy*, (2000), at 73–76.

[4] Hemerijck and Berghman, 'The European Social Patrimony: Deepening Social Europe through Legitimate Diversity', in T. Sakellaropolous and J. Berghman (eds.), *Connecting Welfare Diversity within the European Social Model* (2004) 9; Scharpf, 'Legitimate Diversity: The New Challenge of European Integration', in T. Börzel and R. Chichowski (eds.), *The State of the European Union*, vol. 6, *Law, Politics, and Society* (2003) 79. This discovery originated with the seminal work of Gøsta

differences, moreover, members of each of these families have been struggling with similar challenges of adapting inherited institutions and programmes to changing employment patterns, household and family structures, demographic trends, and distributions of social risk—some countries more successfully than others. These same developments suggest that Europe might serve in a new way to enhance social protection in a period of increasing uncertainty by creating a forum for discussing and generalizing the results of the different national strategies of adjustment.[5]

1. THE OPEN METHOD OF COORDINATION: THEORETICAL PROMISE OF A NEW MODE OF EU GOVERNANCE

This is where the new governance comes in, above all the Open Method of Coordination. The OMC may be defined as an experimentalist approach to EU governance based on iterative benchmarking of national progress towards common European objectives and organized mutual learning.[6] Since its announcement as a new and broadly applicable governance instrument at the extraordinary Lisbon European socio-economic summit in March 2000, which drew on experience with the coordination of national economic and especially employment policies over the preceding decade, the OMC has been extended to cover an enormous range of policy fields. Beyond the Broad Economic Policy Guidelines (BEPG) introduced by the Treaty of Maastricht (1992), and the European Employment Strategy (EES) inaugurated by the Treaty of Amsterdam (1997), the OMC has become the central tool of EU social policy-making in the new millennium, with formal coordination processes launched for social inclusion and pensions over the period 2001 to 2003,

Esping-Andersen: G. Esping-Andersen, *The Three Worlds of Welfare Capitalism* (1990); G. Esping-Andersen (ed.), *Welfare States in Transition: National Adaptations in Global Economies* (1996); G. Esping-Andersen, *Social Foundations of Post-Industrial Economies* (1999) on the 'three worlds of welfare capitalism', even if subsequent analyses (e.g. Ferrera, 'The Four "Social Europes": Between Universalism and Selectivity', in M. Rhodes and Y. Mény (eds.), *The Future of European Welfare: A New Social Contract?* (1998) 79), have modified and extended his typology.

[5] See Ferrera and Hemerijck, 'Recalibrating Europe's Welfare Regimes', in J. Zeitlin and D. M. Trubek (eds.), *Governing Work and Welfare in a New Economy: European and American Experiments* (2003) 88; Hemerijck, 'The Self-Transformation of the European Social Model(s)', in G. Esping-Andersen, with D. Gallie, A. Hemerijck, and J. Myles (eds.), *Why We Need a New Welfare State* (2002) 173; Ferrera, Hemerijck, and Rhodes, *supra* n. 3; Zeitlin, 'Introduction: Governing Work and Welfare in a New Economy: European and American Experiments', in J. Zeitlin and D. M. Trubek (eds.), *Governing Work and Welfare in a New Economy: European and American Experiments* (2003) 1.

[6] Cf. the definition advanced by one of the OMC's founding fathers in the social policy field: 'Open coordination is a mutual feedback process of planning, examination, comparison and adjustment of the social policies of Member States, all of this on the basis of common objectives', Vandenbroucke, 'Foreword: Sustainable Social Justice and "Open Co-ordination" in Europe', in G. Esping-Andersen, with D. Gallie, A. Hemerijck, and J. Myles (eds.), *Why We Need a New Welfare State* (2002) viii.

and further proposals pending from the Commission and the Parliament for the application of this method to health and long-term care. As part of the 'Lisbon Strategy' aimed at turning the EU by 2010 into 'the most competitive and dynamic knowledge-based economy in the world capable of sustainable economic growth with more and better jobs and greater social cohesion', the March 2000 European Council authorized the extension of the OMC to a host of other policy areas, such as research/innovation, information society/eEurope, enterprise promotion, structural economic reform, and education and training. Since then, OMC-type processes and approaches have also been proposed by the Commission and other European bodies as mechanisms for monitoring and supplementing existing EU legislative instruments and authority in fields such as immigration and asylum, environmental protection, disability, occupational health and safety, and even fundamental rights, as well as in areas like youth policy where the Union has few if any legal powers.[7] In addition, following recommendations from the Commission's High Level Group on Industrial Relations, the European social partner organizations have drawn inspiration from the OMC for the monitoring and follow-up of

[7] For overviews of the scope and applications of the OMC across different policy areas, see Borrás and Jacobsson, 'The Open Method of Co-Ordination and New Governance Patterns in the EU', 11 *JEPP* (2004) 185; C. Radaelli, *The Open Method of Coordination: A New Governance Architecture for the European Union?* Sieps Report No. 1 (2003); de Búrca, 'The Constitutional Challenge of New Governance in the European Union', 28 *ELR* (2003) 814; European Convention Secretariat, *The Coordination of National Policies: The Open Method of Coordination. Note to the Members of Working Group on Economic Governance*, CONV WG VI WD 015, (2002); C. Romano, *La Méthode ouverte de coordination: Un nouveau mode de gouvernance?* (2002). On the OMC in research/innovation, immigration/asylum, and occupational health and safety respectively, see Kaiser and Prange, 'Managing Diversity in a System of Multi-Level Governance: The Open Method of Co-Ordination in Innovation Policy', 11 *JEPP* (2004) 249; Caviedes, 'The Open Method of Co-Ordination in Immigration Policy: A Tool for Prying Open Fortress Europe?', 11 *JEPP* (2004) 289; Smismans, 'Towards a New Community Strategy on Health and Safety at Work? Caught in the Institutional Web of Soft Procedures', 19 *International Journal of Comparative Labour Law and Industrial Relations* (2003) 1. For proposals that the OMC be used as a vehicle for the implementation of fundamental rights, see EU Network of Independent Experts in Fundamental Rights, *Report on the Situation of Fundamental Rights in the European Union and Its Members States in 2002* (2002); Bernard, 'A New Governance Approach to Economic, Social and Cultural Rights in the EU', in T. K. Hervey and J. Kenner (eds.), *Economic and Social Rights under the Charter of Fundamental Rights of the European Union* (2003) 247; de Schutter, 'The Implementation of Fundamental Rights through the Open Method of Coordination', in O. de Schutter and S. Deakin (eds.), *Social Rights and Market Forces: Is the Open Coordination of Employment and Social Policies the Future of Social Europe?* (forthcoming). A number of pre-existing European policy coordination processes have also been retrospectively interpreted as full or partial examples of the OMC *avant la lettre*, including the Cardiff Process for structural economic reforms, the Bologna Process for cooperation in European higher education, and the code of conduct against harmful tax competition: on these, in addition to the surveys cited above, see D. Foden and L. Magnusson (eds.), *Trade Unions and the Cardiff Process: Economic Reform in Europe* (2002); A. Hingel, *Education Policies and European Governance: Contribution to the Interservice Groups on European Governance* (2001); and Radaelli, 'The Code of Conduct against Harmful Tax Competition: Open Method of Coordination in Disguise?', 81 *Public Administration* (2003) 3, respectively.

non-binding framework agreements and guidelines at both cross-industry and sectoral levels.[8]

The OMC was defined by the Portuguese Presidency at Lisbon and afterwards in terms closely modeled on the EES as involving a specific ensemble of elements:

- 'Fixing guidelines for the Union combined with specific timetables for achieving the goals which they set in the short, medium and long term;
- establishing, where appropriate, quantitative and qualitative indicators and benchmarks against the best in the world and tailored to the needs of different Member States and sectors as a means of comparing best practices;
- translating these European guidelines into national and regional policies by setting specific targets and adopting measures, taking into account national and regional differences;
- periodic monitoring, evaluation and peer review organized as mutual learning processes.'[9]

But actual OMC processes as they have evolved since Lisbon vary considerably in their modalities and procedures, depending on the specific characteristics of the policy field in question, the Treaty basis of EU competence, and the willingness of the Member States to take joint action. Thus, for example, the Commission and the Council are empowered to issue joint recommendations to Member States on the implementation of the EES and the BEPG, but not on that of other OMC processes, while consultation of the European Parliament is formally required only in the case of the EES. Although most OMC processes are based on common European objectives, only the EES and BEPG involve detailed guidelines for their realization by Member States. Common European statistical indicators or benchmarks have been established for economic policy, structural reforms, employment, social inclusion, and education, but not yet for pensions or healthcare. The BEPG, backed by the Stability and Growth Pact, notoriously impose national ceilings on government deficits and public debt as a proportion of GDP; the EES has fixed European employment rate targets, disaggregated by age and gender, which some countries have translated into nationally specific objectives; and the Social Inclusion OMC calls upon Member States to set national targets for the reduction of relative income poverty.[10] Member States prepare National Action Plans (NAPs) for

[8] European Commission DG EMPL, *Report of the High Level Group on Industrial Relations and Change in the European Union* (2002). Agreements concluded so far have focused on the issues of teleworking and lifelong learning. For an overview of current developments, see European Commission DG EMPL, *Industrial Relations in Europe 2004* (2004).

[9] European Council, *Lisbon European Council Presidency Conclusions*, 23–24 March 2000, para. 37.

[10] The Barcelona European Council of 15–16 March 2002 also fixed national childcare and R&D investment/GDP targets for Member States as part of the EES and innovation policy OMC respectively, see European Council, *Barcelona European Council Presidency Conclusions*, 15–16 March 2002. The new employment guidelines, adopted in July 2003, include additional quantitative targets at national level for combating early school leaving and promoting participation in lifelong learning, see Council of the European Union, 'Council Decision of 22 July 2003 on Guidelines for the Employment Policies of the Member States', OJ L 197/13 5.8.2003.

employment and social inclusion, and National Progress Reports on structural economic reforms, but so far only more limited National Strategy Reports on pensions.[11] These national plans and reports are subjected to mutual surveillance and peer review by Member State representatives in the Employment Committee (EMCO), Social Protection Committee (SPC), and Economic Policy Committee (EPC) respectively, while active programmes for mutual learning through exchange of good practices (also confusingly termed 'peer review') have been organized within the framework of the EES and the Social Inclusion process. Other so-called OMC processes are more loosely structured, involving only selective elements of the broader method, such as scoreboards, peer evaluation, and exchange of good practices.[12] Hence as former Belgian Minister Frank Vandenbroucke, who played a key part in launching the social inclusion and pensions processes during his country's 2001 EU Presidency, has rightly observed: 'Open coordination is not some kind of fixed recipe that can applied to whichever issue,' but instead 'a kind of cookbook that contains various recipes, lighter and heavier ones.'[13]

Abstracting from such procedural variations, the OMC has been widely acclaimed as a theoretically promising governance instrument for EU policy-making in a number of crucial respects. As many commentators have emphasized, the OMC appears well suited for pursuing common European concerns while respecting legitimate national diversity because it commits Member States to work together in reaching joint goals and performance targets without seeking to homogenize their inherited policy regimes and institutional arrangements. Such capacity for

[11] Initially, these OMC processes also followed different timetables, with an annual cycle for the BEPG and EES, a biennial cycle for social inclusion, and a triennial cycle for pensions. But the EES and the BEPG have now been 'streamlined' and synchronized with one another on a triennial cycle, with guidelines fixed in the first year, followed by annual updates and implementation reports in years two and three. OMC processes in social inclusion and social protection (likely to include health and long-term care as well as pensions) are to be synchronized with this cycle of economic and employment policy coordination in 2006; see European Commission, *Communication from the Commission on Streamlining the Annual Economic and Employment Policy Co-ordination Cycles*, CPM (2002) 487 final, *Strengthening the Social Dimension of the Lisbon Strategy: Streamlining Open Coordination in the Field of Social Protection*, COM (2003) 61 final, *Modernising Social Protection for the Development of High-Quality, Accessible and Sustainable Health Care and Long-Term Care: Support for the National Strategies Using the 'Open Method of Coordination'*, COM (2004) 304 final; Social Protection Committee of the European Union, *Opinion of the Social Protection Committee on the Commission's Communication, Strengthening the Social Dimension of the Lisbon Strategy: Streamlining Open Coordination in the Field of Social Protection*, Council of the European Union 12909/03 (2003).

[12] These techniques are also used in policy coordination processes not formally designated as OMCs such as the code of conduct against harmful tax competition, or the peer evaluation mechanism for national arrangements in the fight against terrorism. On these, see respectively Radaelli, *supra* n. 7; Council of the European Union, 'Council Decision of 28 November Establishing a Mechanism in Evaluating the Legal Systems and their Implementation in the Fight Against Terrorism (2002/996/JHA)' OJ L 349/1-3 24.12.2002.

[13] Vandenbroucke, 'Open Co-Ordination on Pensions and the Future of Europe's Social Model', closing address to the conference 'Towards a New Architecture for Social Protection in Europe?', (Brussels, 19–20 October 2001); Vandenbroucke, *supra* n. 6.

reconciling European action with national diversity has become more vital than ever with the recent enlargement of the EU to include ten new Member States, which differ widely both from one another and from the original fifteen in their labour market institutions and social welfare regimes, as well as in their levels of economic development and rates of employment, unemployment, and income poverty.[14] In social policy more specifically, some leading proponents of the OMC have also hailed its potential as a cognitive and normative tool for defining and building consensus around a distinctive 'European' (or perhaps more accurately 'EU') 'Social Model' and policy paradigm based on shared values and objectives.[15] Insofar as the OMC systematically and continuously obliges Member States to pool information, compare themselves to one another, and reassess current policies and programmes in light of their relative performance, it likewise appears to be a promising mechanism for promoting experimental learning and deliberative problem solving across the EU. Diversity within Europe, on this view, should be regarded 'not as an obstacle to integration but rather as an asset [. . .] a natural laboratory for policy experimentation', which enhances opportunities for cross-national learning through comparison of different approaches to similar or related problems.[16] For each of these reasons, this method has rapidly become the governance instrument of choice for EU policy-making in complex, domestically sensitive areas where diversity among the Member States precludes harmonization but inaction is politically unacceptable, and where widespread strategic uncertainty recommends mutual learning at the national as well as the European level.

2. IS THE OMC LEGITIMATE? THREE CRITICAL QUESTIONS

Despite these theoretically promising features, however, a series of critical questions have been raised about the OMC's legitimacy as a new mode or instrument of EU governance.

A. Subsidiarity

One frequently raised concern about the OMC is that it violates the principle of subsidiarity by allowing the EU to encroach illegitimately into policy domains reserved by the Treaties to the Member States through the adoption of common European objectives and performance indicators, backed up by peer pressure.

[14] Hemerijck and Berghman, *supra* n. 4; B. Galgóczi, C. Lafoucrière, and L. Magnusson (eds.), *The Enlargement of Social Europe: The Role of the Social Partners in the European Employment Strategy* (2004).

[15] Vandenbroucke, *supra* n. 6; Ferrera, 'The European Social Model between "Hard" Constraints and "Soft" Coordination', unpublished paper presented to the conference on 'Social Models and EMU: Convergence? Co-existence? The Role of Economic and Social Actors' (Economic and Social Committee, Brussels, 18 November 2001); Ferrera, Matsaganis, and Sacchi, 'Open Coordination against Poverty: The New EU "Social Inclusion Process" ', 12 *JESP* (2002) 226.

[16] European Commission, *supra* n. 8, at 37; Cohen and Sabel, 'Sovereignty and Solidarity: EU and US', in J. Zeitlin and D. M. Trubek *supra* n. 5, at 368.

Understood properly, however, the OMC does not involve the subordination of one level of government to another, but rather a collaborative mode of governance in which each level contributes its distinctive expertise and resources to tackling common problems cutting across jurisdictions. In this sense, OMC should be seen as extending rather than infringing the principle of subsidiarity in EU policy-making. Such a view depends in turn on what one might call an 'experimentalist' interpretation of subsidiarity, advanced by Gráinne de Búrca and others, based on the theoretical incoherence and practical impossibility of reserving specific policy areas either to the Union or the Member States, as for example in the idea of a 'competence catalogue' demanded by the German Länder. The true meaning of subsidiarity, on this interpretation, is that the effectiveness of public action within the EU at different levels of governance and through different methods (including shared decision-making or application of a particular procedure such as the OMC) should itself be evaluated empirically in the light of practical experience in tackling the problem at hand.[17]

B. The 'Community Method'

A second widely voiced criticism is that the OMC's 'soft law' procedures represent a potential threat to the 'classic' Community Method of EU policy-making, based on binding legislation initiated by the Commission, enacted by the Council and the Parliament, and enforced by the Court of Justice. It has equally been considered a threat to the alternative method of EU social legislation, introduced by the Treaty of Maastricht, whereby European social partners negotiate framework agreements on issues proposed by the Commission, which are then approved as legally binding Council Directives, and implemented by the Member States either through transposition into domestic legislation or (more rarely) through encompassing collective agreements at national level. The assumption here is that the OMC's availability as a 'soft law' option may displace the use of 'hard law' instruments even where the EU already possesses legislative powers. Such concerns have led to demands by the Commission and others that the OMC should not be used when legislative action under the Community Method is possible.[18]

[17] For this 'experimentalist' interpretation of subsidiarity, see de Búrca, 'Reappraising Subsidiarity's Significance after Amsterdam', *Harvard Jean Monnet Working Paper* 7/99 (1999); de Búrca, *supra* n. 7; de Búrca and de Witte, 'The Delimitation of Powers between the EU and Its Member States', in A. Arnull and D. Wincott (eds.), *Accountability and Legitimacy in the European Union* (2002) 201.

[18] See for example, European Commission, *European Governance: A White Paper*, COM (2001) 428; Goetschy, 'The European Employment Strategy, Multi-Level Governance, and Policy Coordination', in J. Zeitlin and D. M. Trubek (eds.), *Governing Work and Welfare in a New Economy: European and American Experiments* (2003) 59; European Convention, *Final Report of Working Group XI on Social Europe*, CONV 516/1/03 REV 1 WG XI 9. As a number of authors have pointed out, the Community Method itself has evolved and diversified during the 1980s and 1990s in ways that do not fit well with the 'classic' model defended by the Commission's *White Paper on Governance*: see for example Scott and Trubek, 'Mind the Gap: Law and New Approaches to Governance in the European Union', 8 *ELJ* (2002) 1. Helen Wallace

But this objection seems both empirically and conceptually misplaced. Empirically, OMC processes have mainly been introduced or proposed in policy fields where EU Treaty powers are limited; where there is insufficient consensus among Member States to enact legally binding directives (e.g. immigration); or where there is too much national diversity for harmonization at European level to be a credible option (e.g. employment, social protection). Hence in these areas OMC processes cannot plausibly be regarded as a substitute for binding legislation through the 'classic' Community Method, but should be seen instead as an alternative to inaction.[19] Across an increasing range of policy fields, moreover, 'hard law' directives themselves increasingly tend to incorporate provisions for completion and periodic revision of standard-setting through 'soft law' OMC procedures, as in the regulation of industrial waste or occupational health and safety. Often, too, there is an integral continuity between the legally binding norms embodied in EU framework directives (whether enacted through the 'classic' Community Method of legislation or through the social dialogue procedure) and the 'soft' commitments of the EES guidelines, as in the regulation of part-time work or private pensions.[20] Hence the OMC can be seen as one element in a larger emergent system of experimental governance within the EU that blurs the distinction between 'hard' and 'soft' law, including growing reliance on framework directives, comitology, networked administrative agencies, and a commitment to transparency as a procedural safeguard.[21]

Within OMC processes, the common objectives play a pivotal role in linking EU policy-making upwards to the core values and goals of the Union (as set out in the Treaties and the Charter of Fundamental Rights) on the one hand, and downwards to more specific policy approaches and programmes pursued by the Member States

distinguishes five different modes of policy-making in the EU, among which the 'Community Method' is dominant only in certain sectors of activity: see Wallace, 'Analyzing and Explaining Policies', in H. Wallace and W. Wallace (eds.), *Policy-Making in the European Union* (2000) 65.

[19] For a development of this view in relation to European social policy, see Daly, 'The Possibility of an EU Social Policy: Lisbon and After', unpublished paper presented to the lecture series on 'Europeanization and Reform of National Welfare States', University of Wisconsin–Madison, 14 October 2004.

[20] For the example of industrial waste, see European Convention Secretariat, *The Coordination of National Policies, supra* n. 7; for occupational health and safety, see European Commission, *Adapting to Change in Work and Society: A New Community Strategy on Health and Safety at Work 2002–2006*, COM (2002) 0118 final. On the regulation of atypical forms of employment, see Davies and Freedland, 'The Role of EU Employment Law and Policy in the De-Marginalization of Part-Time Work: A Study in the Interaction between EU Regulation and Member State Regulation', in S. Sciarra, P. Davies, and M. Freedland (eds.), *Employment Policy and the Regulation of Part-Time Work in the European Union* (2004) 63; and Kilpatrick, 'Hard and Soft Law in EU Employment Regulation', paper presented to the European Union Studies Association Eighth Biennial International Conference, Nashville, 27–29 March 2003. On pensions, see Pochet, 'Pensions: The European Debate', in G. L. Clark and N. Whiteside (eds.), *Pension Security in the 21st Century* (2003) 44. For a general discussion of the hard law–soft law debate, see Trubek and Trubek, 'The Open Method of Coordination and the Debate over "Hard" and "Soft" Law', in J. Zeitlin and P. Pochet with L. Magnusson (eds.), *The Open Method of Coordination in Action: The European Employment and Social Inclusion Strategies* (2005) 83.

[21] For an elaboration of this argument, see Sabel and Zeitlin, *supra* n. 1.

on the other. Thus, for example, the annual employment guidelines begin by invoking the objective of 'promoting economic and social progress and a high level of employment' defined in Article 2 of the Treaty on European Union.[22] In defining accessibility along with quality and financial viability as long-term objectives of EU policy coordination in healthcare, the Commission and the Council likewise referred explicitly to the 'right of access to preventative health care and [. . .] medical treatment' proclaimed by the Charter of Fundamental Rights (Article 33).[23] In establishing an action programme to support the Social Inclusion OMC, similarly, the Council and the Parliament highlighted the right to protection against poverty and social exclusion enunciated by the Charter of Fundamental Rights and the European Social Charter.[24]

At a deeper level, the Community Method itself can be interpreted along the lines suggested by Paul Magnette and others as a deliberative agenda-setting mechanism through which the EU, despite its diversity, provides for public- or other-regarding decisions, where such regard means sufficiently responsive to the demands of Member States (and eventually citizens) to be accepted by them as legitimate. In Magnette's view, the Community Method embodies a constitutional requirement that EU institutions and Member States 'integrate *a priori* the *desiderata* of the others and take account of them in the formulation of their own preferences'.[25] One interpretation of the Community Method, favoured by the Commission, is that due regard for the interests of the others produces agreement on something approaching the Rousseauian general interest.[26] But on another reading, preferred by Magnette, the Community Method (or what he terms the 'Community Model') is a form of political cooperation characterized by a mixture rather than a separation of powers among EU institutions and the Member States, in which due regard for the others produces a permanent deliberative disequilibrium. This deliberative disequilibrium excludes selfish outcomes without necessarily producing outcomes that are transcendently public-regarding.[27] On both interpretations, however, deliberative agenda setting sufficiently reassures the Member States, and less immediately

[22] European Commission, *Strengthening the Implementation of the European Employment Strategy: Proposal for a Council Decision on Guidelines for the Employment Policies of the Member States: Recommendation for a Council Recommendation on the Implementation of Member State's Employment Policies*, COM (2004) 239 final.

[23] European Commission, *The Future of Health Care and Care for the Elderly: Guaranteeing Accessibility, Quality, and Financial Viability*, COM (2004) 304; and European Commission, *Modernising . . .*, *supra* n. 11, at 9.

[24] De Búrca, *supra* n. 7.

[25] P. Magnette, *L'Europe, l'État et la démocratie* (2000), at 251 (my translation).

[26] European Commission, *supra* n. 18, at 8.

[27] Magnette, *supra* n. 25, at 43–69, 75, 139–69, 203, 250–3. Magnette's colleague and collaborator Mario Telò, drawing on the work of Norberto Bobbio, has characterized the EU more generally as an instance of 'mixed government', which is currently being renewed through the OMC and the guiding role of the European Council within the Lisbon Strategy: see Telò, 'Introduction', in M. Telò (ed.), *Norberto Bobbio: L' État et la démocratie internationale: De l' histoire des idées à la science politique* (2001),

the citizens, that narrowly self-interested proposals will not be advanced for legislative approval. This reassurance in turn induces the Member States to relax veto powers whose exercise would paralyse decision-making in the EU. The Community Method can thus be seen as the constitutional precondition for the EU as a functioning polity.

Viewed in this way, the EU's emergent system of experimentalist governance, with the OMC at its centre, amounts to a renewal rather than a replacement of the Community Method. And the iterative, reciprocal exploration of the relationship between the Union's objectives and Member State policies through the OMC can be further understood as a new form of pragmatic constitutionalism, in which the meaning of common values (ends) is continuously redefined in light of collective experience with alternative means of pursuing them.[28]

C. Democracy

A third critical question about the OMC concerns its democratic character. Is the OMC part of the solution to the EU's democratic deficit or instead part of the problem? OMC processes, objectives, guidelines, and recommendations are formally authorized by Member State governments in the European Council and the sectoral formations of the Council of Ministers, and might thus be considered democratically legitimate from a narrowly intergovernmentalist perspective.[29] But most of the actual work of running OMC processes is done by unelected committees of national civil servants and Commission officials, whose decisions are rarely overturned or even discussed in the Council. The European Parliament has no direct decision-making or oversight role in OMC processes (though it does have a right to be consulted about the employment guidelines), while national parliaments are hardly involved in the preparation of National Action Plans even if they are formally consulted or informed in some Member States.[30]

Many proposals for increasing the OMC's legitimacy have focused on enhancing the role of the European and national parliaments in the process. But greater parliamentary involvement *per se* can hardly be regarded as a panacea, since there is already a substantial democratic deficit in this regard at the national level, where

at 43–45; Telò, 'Il metodo aperto di coordinamento: Dal Consiglio europeo di Lisbona al testo costituzionale', *Quaderni di rassegna sindacale* (2004) 1; cf. also J. L. Quermonne, *L'Europe en quête de légitimité* (2001), at ch. 4 on 'L'Invention de la méthode communautaire'.

[28] For further development of this argument, see Sabel and Zeitlin, *supra* n. 1.

[29] See for example Scharpf, 'Notes toward a Theory of Multilevel Governing in Europe', 21 *Scandinavian Political Studies* (2001) 1; Scharpf, 'The European Social Model: Coping with the Challenge of Diversity', 40 *JCMS* (2002) 4; Scharpf, *supra* n. 4.

[30] For critiques of this type, see Okma and Berghman, 'Coördination ouverte: entre science et politique?', 44 *Revue belge de sécurité sociale* (2002) 547; S. Smismans, 'EU Employment Policy: Decentralization or Centralization through the Open Method of Coordination?', *EUI Working Paper Law 2004/01* (2004); de la Porte and Nanz, 'The OMC: A Deliberative–Democratic Mode of Governance? The Case of Employment and Pensions', 11 *JEPP* (2004) 2.

legislatures have long experienced grave difficulties in exercising detailed control over policy-making and administration in complex, specialized fields such as employment and social protection.[31] Hence the OMC's democratic legitimacy must rest on an alternative basis: openness, transparency, and broad participation in public problem-solving activities, aimed at promoting mutual learning through coordinated monitoring of decentralized experimentation in pursuit of common goals. Of crucial importance here is broad participation in all phases of OMC processes not only by national administrations and the traditional social partner organizations representing business and labour, but also by other non-state and subnational actors with relevant interests and expertise, notably non-governmental organizations (NGOs) civil society organizations and local/regional authorities. Not only the legitimacy but also the effectiveness of OMC processes, on this view, depend on the participation of the widest possible range of stakeholders in policy formulation, implementation, monitoring, and evaluation at all levels (EU, national, subnational) in order to ensure the representation of diverse perspectives, tap the benefits of local knowledge, and hold public officials accountable for carrying out mutually agreed commitments. Transparency is no less vital, both as a procedural safeguard for European citizens' right to know the reasons behind public decision-making, and as a source of reliable information on which actors at different levels can draw to drive the policy coordination process forward.

Pushed to their logical conclusion, the application of these principles could transform the EU into a new form of pragmatist democracy, in which by directly engaging local administrative units and civil society actors as well as Member States in joint problem-solving through routine comparison of different practices, the Union deliberately raises and helps address doubts about apparently common-sense solutions and the meaning of fundamental values.[32] Both the European and national parliaments, on this view, could valuably participate in framing and debating OMC objectives and procedures, monitoring progress toward agreed goals, and revising the process in light of the results achieved. But this would involve a transformation of the conventional conception of parliaments' role in democratic polities as authoritative principals delegating detailed implementation of legislation to administrative agents, whose behaviour they seek to control through a combination of *ex ante* incentives and *ex post* sanctions. Effective participation by parliaments in OMC processes (as in the working of pragmatist or experimentalist democracies more generally) would require them to develop new roles in passing framework legislation embodying commitments to broad goals (like OMC objectives); establishing administrative infrastructures to stimulate decentralized experimentation about how best to achieve these goals, monitor the efforts of local units to improve their

[31] For recent reviews of this classic problem, see Dorf and Sabel, 'A Constitution of Democratic Experimentalism', 98 *Columbia Law Review* (1998) 2; Stewart, 'Administrative Law in the 21st Century', 78 *New York University Law Review* (2003) 437.

[32] For a fuller elaboration of this argument, see Sabel and Zeitlin, *supra* n. 1; Cohen and Sabel, *supra* n. 16.

performance against them, pool the resulting information, and set provisional standards in light of what they have learned; reviewing the results and revising the framework objectives and administrative procedures accordingly.[33]

As presently constituted, existing OMC processes in social and employment policy fall short of these ideals of transparency and broad participation. The deliberations of the EU Employment, Social Protection, and Economic Policy Committees take place behind closed doors and their internal debates are not open to public scrutiny, though all three committees have established open websites on which they post their formal opinions and reports.[34] At national level, too, NAP preparation has typically been dominated by bureaucratic insiders with close ties to European institutions, although a clear trend towards greater 'domestication' of the process has become visible over time in many countries. In most Member States, both media coverage and public awareness of OMC processes remain low, and have tended if anything to decline over time. Behind each of these limitations lies the fact that with few exceptions, NAPs are presented domestically as backward-looking activity reports to the EU and government documents 'owned' by the relevant ministries rather than as forward-looking action plans or strategic programming instruments subject to normal public scrutiny and debate by all stakeholders.[35]

But there are also encouraging signs of new participatory dynamics triggered by the OMC, especially in the Social Inclusion process, where 'mobilizing all the relevant bodies' in the fight against poverty and exclusion figures among its four core objectives. Thus in many EU Member States, as recent empirical research shows, the Social Inclusion process has stimulated the widespread development of new consultative bodies and structures to facilitate input from anti-poverty NGOs and local/regional authorities into the preparation and in some cases also the monitoring of their NAPs. At a European level, networks of social NGOs and local/regional authorities have likewise been extremely active in drawing domestic information upwards from their national affiliates, commenting critically on the NAPs and Joint Inclusion Reports, mobilizing pressure on EU institutions, diffusing

[33] For this view of the transformed roles of the legislature and administration in experimentalist democracies, see Sabel, 'Beyond Principal-Agent Governance: Experimentalist Organizations, Learning and Accountability', in E. Engelen and M. Sie Dhian Ho (eds.), *De Staat van de Democratie: Democratie voorbij de Staat* (2005) forthcoming.

[34] For a careful, well-informed, and balanced analysis of the operation of these committees, see Jacobsson and Vifell, 'Towards Deliberative Supranationalism? Analysing the Role of Committees in Soft Co-ordination', in I. Linsenmann, C. O. Meyer, and W. Wessels (eds.), *Economic Governance in the EU*, (2005) forthcoming.

[35] In addition to the chapters in J. Zeitlin, P. Pochet and L. Magnusson (eds.), *The Open Method of Coordination in Action: The European Employment and Social Inclusion Strategies* (2005), see also Meyer, 'Towards a Grand Débat Européen? Exploring the Europeanization of Socio-Economic Discourses in Selected Member States', in I. Linsenmann, C. O. Meyer, and W. Wessels (eds.), *EU Economic Governance: The Balance Sheet of Economic Policy Coordination* (2005) forthcoming; European Commission and Council of the European Union, *Joint Employment Report 2003–2004*, 7069/04, at 18.

European information downwards to their affiliates, and linking them together horizontally through conferences and round tables, often supported financially by the Commission and the Parliament. Even in the EES, where Member State governments have been more reluctant to open up the process to groups beyond the traditional social partners (whose cooperation is considered necessary for progress on labour market reforms in areas subject to collective bargaining), social NGOs and local/regional authorities have vigorously campaigned for the right to participate at both European and national levels, achieving significant advances in a number of countries. The Commission and the Parliament have actively supported these demands, especially those of the local and regional authorities, by pressing for changes to the Employment Guidelines and sponsoring innovative projects such as Local and Regional Action Plans (LAPs and RAPS), the development of territorially disaggregated indicators, and the creation of a European local development network and forum for information-sharing and exchange of good practices.[36]

A theoretically promising response to the limitations on transparency and participation in existing OMC processes would be to apply to their own procedures the key elements of the method itself: benchmarking, peer review, monitoring, evaluation, and iterative redesign. Thus for example Member States could be required to benchmark openness and participation within all OMC processes according to national laws, traditions, and practices, with due respect for the principle of subsidiarity.[37] The relative success of the Social Inclusion process in 'mobilizing all relevant bodies' testifies to the practical validity of this approach. So too do the Commission's proposals in the 2003 Employment Guidelines for 'the mobilization of all relevant actors [. . .] and main stakeholders', including civil society and local and regional authorities, along with the social partners and national parliaments.[38] In the event, these proposals were watered down by resistance from Member State representatives in the Employment Committee.[39] But enhancing participation of non-state and subnational actors in OMC processes remains a live and politically contested issue on the EU employment policy agenda, as for example through the recommendations of the 2003 Task Force chaired by Wim Kok, which called for consultation of civil society as well as the social partners in the preparation of the

[36] For a fuller analysis and supporting evidence, see Zeitlin, 'The Open Method of Coordination in Action: Theoretical Promise, Empirical Realities, Reform Strategy', in J. Zeitlin and P. Pochet with L. Magnusson (eds.), *The Open Method of Coordination in Action: The European Employment and Social Inclusion Strategies* (2005), § II.C.

[37] For elaboration of this approach, see *ibid.*, § III.C.

[38] European Commission, *Proposal for a Council Decision on Employment Policies of the Member States*, COM (2003) 176 final; cf. European Commission, *The Future of the European Employment Strategy (EES): A Strategy for Full Employment and Better Jobs for All*, COM (2003) 6 final.

[39] Member States insisted on deleting any reference to civil society, acknowledging only that: '1) Good governance and partnership are important issues for the implementation of the European Employment Strategy, while fully respecting national traditions and practices. 2) In accordance with national traditions, relevant parliamentary bodies as well as relevant actors in the field of employment at national and regional level have important contributions to make'; Council of the European Union, *supra* n. 10.

NAPs/empl and the creation of 'reform partnerships' involving local authorities alongside social partners and public agencies.[40] 'Ensuring effective implementation of reforms through better governance' was included at the Commission's insistence as one of four common recommendations to all Member States in the 2004 Joint Employment Package, and EMCO is developing indicators for benchmarking governance in the NAPs/empl.[41] More generally, the Commission has proposed that the emphasis on openness and the involvement of a wide range of actors (including NGOs and subnational authorities as well as social partners) in the Social Inclusion process 'could usefully be applied to the entire range of the future social protection process' under the new streamlined arrangements to be introduced in 2006, and this participatory approach is fully incorporated into its proposals for a new OMC process in health and elder care.[42]

3. IS OMC EFFECTIVE? AMBIGUITIES AND EMPIRICAL ASSESSMENT

Perhaps the most widespread criticism of the OMC concerns not its weak democratic legitimacy or potentially pernicious effects, but rather its alleged lack of substantive impact on the Member States. According to this view, the OMC in its present form amounts to little more than the European emperor's newest clothes, an exercise in symbolic politics where national governments repackage existing policies to demonstrate their apparent compliance with EU objectives.[43]

Despite the high political stakes involved, the debate surrounding the OMC is widely agreed to suffer from an empirical deficit. Many assessments of the OMC, including some that claim to conduct an 'in context' rather than 'in vitro' analysis of the method,[44] rely in practice on a very limited range of often outdated evidence, onto which they project their own theoretical and normative assumptions. Empirical analysis of the OMC is extremely challenging, for a series of interrelated reasons:

- The variety of distinct processes subsumed under the OMC rubric.
- The relative newness of most OMC processes.

[40] Employment Taskforce, *Jobs, Jobs, Jobs: Creating More Employment in Europe: Report of the Employment Taskforce Chaired by Wim Kok* (2003), at 56–58.

[41] European Commission, *supra* n. 22; EMCO Indicators Group, *Indicators Group Report to EMCO on Progress Made in the Field of Indicators to Monitor the Employment Guidelines*, EMCO/22/130704/EN (2004).

[42] European Commission, *Strengthening . . .*, *supra* n. 11; European Commission, *Modernising . . .*, *supra* n. 11.

[43] Chalmers and Lodge, 'The Open Method of Co-Ordination and the European Welfare State', *ESRC Centre for Analysis of Risk and Regulation Discussion Papers* 11 (London School of Economics, 2003); Radaelli, *supra* n. 7; Scharpf, *supra* n. 21; Scharpf, *supra* n. 4.

[44] E.g. Radaelli, *supra* n. 7, at 10, 50, 56; Chalmers and Lodge, *supra* n. 43.

- The horizontal and vertical complexity of OMC processes, which typically integrate multiple policy domains, and involve multiple levels of governance (EU, national, subnational) across fifteen (and now twenty-five) Member States.
- The methodological difficulties of assessing the causal impact of an iterative policy-making process based on collaboration between EU institutions and Member State governments without legally binding sanctions. Since Member State representatives continuously participate in the definition of objectives, guidelines, and indicators for OMC processes, which do not necessarily result in new legislation or justiciable obligations, standard approaches to assessing the domestic effects of 'Europeanization' based on 'goodness of fit', adaptational pressures, and compliance with EU law[45] cannot be directly applied. Member State governments may also have political reasons of their own for playing up or down the domestic influence of OMC processes in NAPs and evaluation reports. Hence statements about the sources of policy change in such official documents cannot be taken at face value but must be carefully contextualized and triangulated with other evidence.[46]

Despite these practical and methodological problems, there is now a very large body of material available on the empirical operation of OMC processes, particularly in the fields of employment and social policy. Such material includes not only numerous official reviews and reports,[47] but also a wide range of studies and assessments produced by European social partner organizations, NGOs, local and regional authority networks, EU agencies, think-tanks, academic research projects, and individual scholars.[48] The remainder of this section summarizes the conclusions

[45] E.g. M. G. Cowles, J. Caporaso, and T. Risse (eds.), *Transforming Europe: Europeanization and Domestic Change* (2001); K. Featherstone and C. Radaelli (eds.), *The Politics of Europeanization* (2003).

[46] For discussions of these methodological problems, see Zeitlin, Pochet, and Magnusson, *supra* n. 35; Büchs, 'Methodological and Conceptual Issues in Researching the Open Method of Coordination', in L. Hantrais (ed.), *Researching the European Social Model from a Comparative Perspective* (2003) 31; Barbier, 'Research on "Open Methods of Coordination" and National Social Policies: What Sociological Theories and Methods?', unpublished paper presented to the RC 19 International Conference, Paris, 2004; J. C. Barbier, *La Stratégie européenne pour l'emploi: genèse, coordination communautaire et diversité nationale*, report for the DARES, Ministère du travail, January 2004; López-Santana, ' "Unpacking" the Policy-Making Process: The European Employment Strategy and Europeanization', unpublished paper presented to the 14th International Conference of Europeanists, Chicago, 11–13 March 2004; Borrás and Greve, 'Concluding Remarks to Special Issue on "The Open Method of Co-ordination in the European Union": New Method or Just Cheap Talk?', 11 *JEPP* (2004) 329.

[47] The most significant of these are: the National Action Plans, Strategy Reports, and Joint Reviews for employment (1997–2003), social inclusion (2001, 2003), and pensions (2003); the national reports (often supported by independent research papers) and Commission transversal studies produced for the five-year impact assessment of the EES (2002); and the ongoing reports of the Commission's expert groups on Gender and Employment (EGGE) and Social Inclusion, all available on the DG EMPL website, http://europa.eu.int/comm/employment_social/index_en.html.

[48] A select bibliography of more than 140 books, papers, and reports, including links to relevant websites, is available at the University of Wisconsin–Madison's Online Research Forum on the Open Method of Coordination, http://eucenter.wisc.edu/OMC/index.htm.

of a comparative research project on the European Employment and Social Inclusion Strategies conducted by an international team of scholars, which focuses particularly on their operation and influence at national and subnational levels.[49]

A. Substantive Policy Change

Among the most widely attested findings of recent empirical work on the European Employment and Social Inclusion Strategies, both within and beyond our project, is that these OMC processes have raised the political salience and ambitions of employment and social inclusion policies at the national as well as the EU level. A second broadly supported finding is that these OMC processes have contributed to broad shifts in national policy orientation and thinking, involving the incorporation of EU concepts and categories into domestic debates. The most obvious examples of this cognitive influence of OMC on domestic policy orientations concern the shift of emphasis from reducing unemployment to raising employment rates as a core objective, from passive income support to activation services, and from a curative to a preventative approach to fighting unemployment. But many other key concepts associated with the EES and the Social Inclusion process have also entered or gained new prominence on the policy agendas of EU Member States, notably active ageing/avoiding early retirement, lifelong learning, gender mainstreaming, flexicurity (balancing flexibility with security), reconciling work and family life, an inclusive labour market, social exclusion as a multi-dimensional phenomenon beyond income poverty, and an integrated partnership approach to promoting employment, inclusion, and local development.[50]

Beyond these broad shifts in national policy thinking, there is also some evidence that these OMC processes have contributed to specific changes in individual Member States' policies. Such evidence is most abundant for the EES, which has been running considerably longer (seven rounds of NAPs and Joint Reports as against two for the Social Inclusion process), and has been subjected to more extensive research and evaluation. The most salient areas of influence on national policies concern the adoption of individual activation plans and a preventative approach to fighting unemployment, measures to close off pathways to early retirement and encourage lifelong learning, and the promotion of equal gender opportunities and

[49] Zeitlin, Pochet, and Magnusson, *supra* n. 35.

[50] In addition to *ibid.* on the EES see Jacobsson, 'Soft Regulation and the Subtle Transformation of States: The Case of EU Employment Policy', Stockholm, SCORE Stockholm Center for Organizational Research, 2002; Jacobsson, 'Between Deliberation and Discipline: Soft Governance in EU Employment Policy', in U. Mörth (ed.), *Soft Law in Governance and Regulation: An Interdisciplinary Analysis* (2005); European Commission, *Impact Evaluation of the European Employment Strategy: Technical Analysis Supporting (Taking Stock of Five Years of the EES)*, COM (2002) 416 final, at ch. 1; European Commission, *Taking Stock of Five Years of the European Employment Strategy*, COM (2002) 416 final, at 9–15. On the Social Inclusion process see Ferrera, Matsaganis, and Sacchi, *supra* n. 15; European Commission and Council of the European Union, *Joint Report by the Commission and the Council on Social Inclusion*, 7101/04, at 36–42.

gender mainstreaming, including efforts to reduce occupational segregation and pay gaps between men and women.[51]

Both in the case of broad cognitive shifts and of specific programmatic changes, however, identifying the precise causal impact of the EES and the Social Inclusion process on national policy-making raises difficult problems of interpretation. Thus changes in Member States' policy orientations, including enhanced attention to employment promotion and social inclusion, often preceded the launch of these OMC processes. In important respects, moreover, these OMC processes cannot be considered truly external to national policy-making, since Member States actively supported their initiation and continuously participate in the definition of objectives, guidelines, and indicators, into which they often seek to 'upload' their own domestic priorities and preferences. Not only have EU Member States actively participated in defining OMC goals and metrics, but they have also exercised considerable selectivity (both conscious and unconscious) in 'downloading' and inflecting European concepts and policy approaches in the fields of employment and social inclusion, as for example in the case of activation.[52]

Interpretation of the OMC's substantive policy impact is further complicated by the strategic behaviour of national governments in communicating with domestic publics on the one hand and EU institutions on the other.[53] Thus governments often use references to OMC processes as a source of legitimation and blame-sharing in order to advance their own domestic agenda, sometimes irrespective of their real influence on policy decisions. Conversely, governments may also consciously play down the influence of OMC processes in communicating with domestic audiences, especially in Member States or policy areas where the legitimacy of EU intervention is weak. Governments may likewise deliberately over- or understate the influence of OMC processes on domestic policy in reporting to the EU, depending on whether they want to burnish their credentials as 'good Europeans' by demonstrating consummate compliance with guidelines and recommendations, or instead to present themselves as defenders of subsidiarity and the national interest against Brussels.

[51] For a detailed presentation of the evidence, see Zeitlin, *supra* n. 36, § II.A. On gender equality and gender mainstreaming, see especially Rubery, 'Gender Mainstreaming and the OMC: Is the Open Method Too Open for Gender Equality Policy?', in J. Zeitlin and P. Pochet with L. Magnusson (eds.), *The Open Method of Coordination in Action: The European Employment and Social Inclusion Strategies* (2005) 391.

[52] On 'uploading' and 'downloading' between Member States and the EU, see Börzel, 'Pace-Setting, Foot-Dragging, and Fence-Sitting: Member State Responses to Europeanization', 40 *JCMS* (2002) 2. On the differential inflection of activation policies, see Barbier, 'The European Employment Strategy: A Channel for Activating Social Protection?', in J. Zeitlin and P. Pochet with L. Magnusson (eds.), *The Open Method of Coordination in Action: The European Employment and Social Inclusion Strategies* (2005) 417.

[53] For a subtle and insightful analysis of the Swedish case, see Vifell, 'Speaking with Forked Tongue—Swedish Employment Policy and European Guidelines: A Case of Europeanization through Soft Co-Ordination', paper presented to the Conference of Europeanists, Chicago, 11–13 March, 2004.

Hence both on substantive and methodological grounds, the relationship between OMC processes and Member State policies should be analysed as a two-way interaction rather than a one-way causal impact. The EES and the Social Inclusion process often operate as catalysts or 'selective amplifiers'[54] for national reform strategies, increasing the salience and urgency of particular issues and policy approaches, which may already have been familiar domestically, at least in certain quarters. But there is also hard evidence of the OMC's ability to challenge and expand the terms of national policy debate, especially in fields like gender equality and social inclusion.[55] Yet given the ongoing variations in national interpretation and implementation of European concepts and policy approaches, OMC processes in employment and social inclusion should be viewed less as mechanisms for producing 'cognitive harmonization'[56] than as means for the creation of a common language and categorical framework to discuss and evaluate different solutions to similar problems.

B. Procedural Shifts in Governance and Policy-Making Arrangements

More profound and more easily traceable than the OMC's influence on substantive policy changes within EU Member States has been its contribution to shifts in governance and policy-making arrangements, including administrative reorganization and institutional capacity-building, though here too there are many other causal factors. Nearly all accounts of OMC processes in action at a national level report that they have stimulated improvements in horizontal or cross-sectoral integration across formally separate but practically interdependent policy fields: labour market policy, unemployment benefits, social assistance, pensions, taxation, education/training, and local development in the case of the EES; housing, healthcare, justice, sport/leisure, and transport as well as the above in the case of social inclusion. A second major effect of the OMC has been to stimulate improvements in national statistical and steering capacities. Thus participation in the EES and the Social Inclusion process has pushed Member States to upgrade their policy monitoring and evaluation capabilities, as well as to harmonize national and European statistics. A third important influence of the EES and the Social Inclusion process has been to encourage the reinforcement of arrangements for vertical coordination among levels of governance. Such coordination has become both increasingly necessary and increasingly challenging as a result of the widespread decentralization of the

[54] Visser, 'The Open Method of Coordination as Selective Amplifier for National Reform Strategies: What the Netherlands Wants to Learn from Europe', in J. Zeitlin and P. Pochet with L. Magnusson (eds.), *The Open Method of Coordination in Action: The European Employment and Social Inclusion Strategies* (2005) 173.

[55] See also Jacobsson and Vifell, 'New Governance Structures in Employment Policy-Making? Taking Stock of the European Employment Strategy', in I. Linsenmann, C. Meyer, and W. Wessels (eds.), *Economic Governance in the EU* (2005) forthcoming.

[56] Palier, 'The Europeanisation of Welfare Reforms', unpublished paper presented to the Cost A15 Conference, Nantes, 20–22 May 2004.

public employment services and the devolution of welfare and employment policies in federal or federalizing polities. Sometimes this vertical coordination occurs through well-established institutional channels, while in others the NAP preparation process has led to the creation of new formal or informal mechanisms for cooperation and consultation between federal, regional, and in certain cases also local governments.[57]

C. Mutual Learning

Perhaps the most critical claim for the novelty of the OMC concerns its capacity to promote mutual learning among EU Member States. As in the case of substantive policy change, the strongest impact of the European Employment and Social Inclusion Strategies in this area has come through a series of indirect or higher-order effects, which are not always recognized as 'learning'. Thus both OMC processes, as Ferrera and Sacchi suggest, have stimulated cross-national learning through heuristic, capacity-building, and maieutic effects.[58]

In heuristic terms, as we have already seen, the EES and the Social Inclusion process have been rather successful in identifying common European challenges and promising policy approaches, which have in turn contributed to broad shifts in national policy thinking. Both OMC processes have likewise enhanced mutual awareness of policies, practices, and problems in other Member States, even if such knowledge has largely been concentrated in EU committees and the higher echelons of national administrations. Beyond the formal framework of the OMC itself, moreover, EU Member States show increasing interest in learning from one another in preparing their own domestic policy reforms.[59]

In terms of capacity-building, both the EES and the Social Inclusion process have given rise to the development of common European indicators and the creation of new data sources, such as the EU Statistics on Income and Living Conditions (EU-SILC). Despite continuing data limitations, moreover, they have also contributed to revisions and improvements in national social and employment statistics. In so doing, these OMC processes have stimulated cross-national debate and deliberation about the comparability, appropriateness, and significance of these indicators and the statistical data on which they are based, even if such discussions are largely confined to technical experts within the Employment and Social Protection Committees along with their academic interlocutors.[60]

[57] For details, see Zeitlin, *supra* n. 36, § II.B.

[58] Ferrera and Sacchi, 'The Open Method of Coordination and National Institutional Capabilities: The Italian Case', in J. Zeitlin and P. Pochet with L. Magnusson (eds.), *The Open Method of Coordination in Action: The European Employment and Social Inclusion Strategies* (2005) 137; Ferrera, Matsaganis, and Sacchi, *supra* n. 15.

[59] For specific examples, see Zeitlin, *supra* n. 36, § II.D.

[60] On the social inclusion indicators, see T. Atkinson, B. Cantillon, E. Marlier, and B. Nolan (eds.), *Social Indicators: The EU and Social Inclusion* (2002); Atkinson, Marlier, and Nolan, 'Indicators and Targets for Social Inclusion the European Union', 42 *JCMS* (2004) 1. For a critical discussion of the employment indicators, see Salais, 'La Politique des indicateurs: Du taux de chômage au taux d'emploi

In maieutic or reflexive terms, the EES and the Social Inclusion process have pushed EU Member States to rethink established approaches and practices as a result of comparisons with other countries on the one hand and of the obligation to re-examine and re-evaluate their own policies and performance on the other. These OMC processes have undoubtedly 'destabilize[d] existing understandings' and 'pressured policy-makers to give a second thought to existing policy choices in the light of new ideas and the agreed common framework, and to accept being compared to better performers'.[61] In some cases, such reflexive learning has involved making new connections between hitherto separate policy issues, such as pensions and lifelong learning or women's employment and childcare provision. In others, it has entailed recognizing that policies which seemed beneficial from one perspective can be harmful from another, such as early retirement as a palliative for unemployment created by industrial restructuring or high female employment in public social services as a source of occupational segregation and gender pay gaps.

At the same time, however, there are relatively few concrete cases at national level of direct or first-order policy learning from abroad about what works and what does not. Most of the examples of such direct learning cited in interviews and evaluation reports tend to focus on gender mainstreaming, the provision of personalized activation services, and the shift from a curative to a preventative approach to fighting unemployment.[62] Other examples of national policy learning tend to involve more problem recognition than adoption of foreign 'best practice' solutions, as for example with lifelong learning, gender segregation, and labour market integration of immigrants and ethnic minorities. Even where national policy-makers refer explicitly to other countries' practices and the influence of OMC processes, they typically borrow selectively and adapt foreign programmes to the peculiarities of their own domestic social, institutional, and political contexts.

The limited incidence of direct policy transfer, as Visser points outs, is a natural consequence of the OMC's 'contextualized benchmarking' approach, which unlike the 'decontextualized benchmarking' associated with the OECD Jobs Strategy, is more conducive to reflexive 'learning with others' than to 'adaptive mimicking' or what sociological institutionalists call 'mimetic isomorphism', which can easily

dans la stratégie européenne pour l'emploi (SEE)', in B. Zimmermann (ed.), *Action publique et sciences sociales* (2004) 287. Both the EMCO and SPC Indicators Groups regularly produce highly informative internal reports on their work. Those of the SPC are available on the Committee's website, http://europa.eu.int/comm/employment_social/social_protection_commitee/spc_indic_en.htm, whereas those of EMCO are regrettably unavailable to the general public at the present time.

[61] Trubek and Mosher, 'New Governance, Employment Policy, and the European Social Model', in J. Zeitlin and D. Trubek (eds.), *Governing Work and Welfare in a New Economy: European and American Experiments* (2003) at 46; Jacobsson and Vifell, *supra* n. 55.

[62] Some Member States such as France and Belgium with high levels of long-term unemployment still have significant reservations about the latter shift. See R. Salais, G. Raveaud and G. Mathieu, *L'Evaluation de l'impact de la Stratégie Européenne pour l'Emploi—Thème 10: Elaboration des politiques* (2002), at 13; DULBEA, *L'Evaluation d'impact de la stratégie européenne pour l'emploi en Belgique* (2002), at 6–7.

degenerate into uncritical trend following.[63] Such contextualized benchmarking as a mechanism for reflexive learning from others also fits well with the findings of comparative–historical research, which shows that foreign practices, whether in the economic or the political field, can rarely be successfully transferred from one social and institutional context to another without significant modification.[64] The need for such contextualization is explicitly recognized in OMC mutual learning programmes, which emphasize *in situ* explanation of 'good practices' by host country experts on the one hand and creative adaptation to different local conditions by visiting participants on the other.[65]

More problematic, however, is the limited evidence of reflexive learning from the results of OMC processes at EU level. According to the Commission's own analysis of the national Impact Evaluation reports, the EES did not do an especially good job during its first five years in identifying which types of active labour market policies or tax-benefit reforms were most effective under what circumstances, and revising the guidelines accordingly, despite all the political attention devoted to these issues, although the exercise itself generated a great deal of empirical material which could be used for that purpose.[66] Nor does the new EES agreed in 2003 fully incorporate the empirical findings of the Impact Evaluation in this regard, even if they do respond to the widely expressed demands of Member State governments and other participating actors for fewer, simpler, and more outcome-oriented guidelines.[67]

Even more strikingly, the Member States do not seem to have made much tangible progress in drawing on cross-national learning at the level of local practice about how best to integrate labour market activation with social inclusion, balance flexibility with security, or extend the scope of lifelong learning to a wider section

[63] Visser, *supra* n. 54; see also Hemerjick and Visser, 'Learning and Mimicking: How European Welfare States Reform', unpublished paper, University of Leiden and University of Amsterdam, June 2001; Hemerijck and Visser, 'Policy Learning in European Welfare States', unpublished paper, University of Leiden and University of Amsterdam, October 2003; P. J. DiMaggio and W. W. Powell (eds.), *The New Institutionalism in Organizational Analysis* (1991).

[64] Zeitlin, 'Introduction: Americanization and Its Limits: Reworking US Technology and Management in Post-War Europe and Japan', in J. Zeitlin and G. Herrigel (eds.), *Americanization and Its Limits: Reworking US Technology and Management in Post-War Europe and Japan* (2000) 1; Zeitlin, *supra* n. 5; R. Boyer, E. Charron, U. Jürgens, and S. Tolliday (eds.), *Between Imitation and Innovation: Transfer and Hybridization of Productive Models in the International Automobile Industry* (1998).

[65] Thus as a preliminary evaluation of the EES peer review programme reported: 'although Member States may not necessarily adopt the policies reviewed in an identical form, they are interested in adapting them to their own circumstances. In most cases, Member States have been inspired by their participation in the peer reviews to develop new initiatives or improve existing ones' European Commission DG EMPL, *Employment Strategy: Peer Review Programme 2002–2003*, Employment Committee, Ad Hoc Working Group/007/190901/EN, (2001), at 3; ÖSB/INBAS, *Evaluation of Peer Review Programme on Active Labour Market Policy 2000–2001* (2001).

[66] European Commission, *Impact Evaluation . . .*, *supra* n. 50, at chs. 3–4; cf. also Visser, *supra* n. 54; O'Donnell and Moss, 'Ireland: The Very Idea of an Open Method of Coordination', in J. Zeitlin and P. Pochet with L. Magnusson (eds.), *The Open Method of Coordination in Action: The European Employment and Social Inclusion Strategies* (2005) 311.

[67] European Commission, *The Future . . .*, *supra* n. 38; Council of the European Union, *supra* n. 10.

of the population.[68] The potential for such 'bottom-up' and 'horizontal' learning from local and regional experimentation is amply illustrated by reports of European networking conferences and innovative local employment projects mentioned earlier.[69] By stimulating the mobilization of non-state and subnational actors, moreover, the EES, and still more the Social Inclusion process, appear to be creating the conditions for such 'bottom-up' learning in many EU Member States even where national governments do not formally acknowledge this in their NAPs or Impact Evaluation reports.

What accounts for these limitations on mutual learning within OMC processes? Part of the problem stems from the ambivalent commitment to this objective on the part of the key actors themselves. Thus the failure to capitalize at a European level on opportunities for reflexive learning from practical experience with the implementation of activation and prevention policies reflects the primary focus within the Commission and EMCO on ensuring national compliance with the action targets in the guidelines, rather than on reviewing the recommended measures in light of accumulated evidence about their effectiveness. And the failure to take full account of the empirical findings of the Five-Year Evaluation in the redesign of the EES likewise reflects the predominance of political bargaining over the new guidelines between the Commission and the Member States, even if the negotiations within EMCO also appear to have been subject to a certain deliberative discipline.[70]

Other limitations on mutual learning, however, stem from more readily corrigible defects in OMC procedures and instruments. Thus, for example, there is broad agreement that the increasingly full agendas of EMCO and the SPC on the one hand and the very tight timetable for peer review of the NAPs on the other have crowded out opportunities for mutual learning among the participants. Although the EES peer review programme for the exchange of good practices is generally considered to have been more satisfactory, widespread criticisms have also been raised about its 'show and tell' character, whereby Member States nominate 'poster child' programmes, which are then selected through a 'beauty contest' for presentation to a restricted audience of national officials and experts from those countries that choose to participate.[71] These criticisms have been taken to heart by the members of EMCO and the SPC themselves, who have redesigned their peer review procedures and introduced new programmes to strengthen mutual learning, such as

[68] European Commission, *Impact Evaluation . . . , supra* n. 50, at chs. 5, 6, 8, 10

[69] See for example EAPN-EUROCITIES, *The EU Strategy for Social Inclusion: Making it Work at the Local Level*, Athens, 28 February–1 March 2003; European Commission DG EMPL, *Activity Report to EMCO Local Employment Development: 2001–2004* (2004), EMCO/14/220404/EN.

[70] Jobelius, 'Who Formulates the European Employment Guidelines? The OMC Between Deliberation and Power Games' paper presented to the Annual Conference of the ESPAnet, 'Changing European Societies: The Role for Social Policy', Copenhagen, 13–15 November 2003; Jacobsson and Vifell, *supra* n. 34; Vifell, *supra* n. 53.

[71] See for example C. de la Porte and P. Pochet, *The OMC Intertwined with the Debates on Governance, Democracy and Social Europe: Research on the Open Method of Co-Ordination and European Integration*, report prepared for Frank Vandenbroucke, Belgian Minister for Social Affairs and Pensions (2003); Jacobsson and Vifell, *supra* n. 34.

thematic review seminars and national follow-up activities open to a broader group of stakeholders, including social partners, independent policy experts, and possibly also local authorities and NGOs.[72] Another set of procedural limitations concern the indicators which are supposed to serve as crucial performance metrics within OMC processes, though here too many of the problems are widely recognized by the EU committees responsible for their administration, and corrective measures are already under way.[73]

A final set of procedural limitations on mutual learning within OMC processes concerns the barriers to participation and integration into domestic policy-making discussed in the previous section. Thus the paucity of 'bottom-up' cross-national learning within the EES identified by both the Five-Year Evaluation and the contributors to our comparative study is closely linked to the limited opportunities for participation by non-state and subnational actors in the process at all stages, from the definition of objectives, guidelines, and indicators, through the preparation, monitoring, and evaluation of the NAPs to the peer reviews and exchange of good practices. And the limited integration of both OMC processes into domestic policy-making, as we have likewise seen, inhibits the broad participation and public debate that is a necessary condition for experimental learning from local practice. Hence the best way to overcome these limitations, as argued earlier, would be reflexively to apply to the OMC's own procedures key elements of the method itself, such as benchmarking, peer review, monitoring, evaluation, and iterative redesign. Thus Member States could be required to benchmark, monitor, and review not only openness and participation within OMC processes, but also their mainstreaming and integration into domestic policy-making according to national laws, traditions, and practices, with full respect for the principle of subsidiarity. And as in the case of participation, social inclusion offers a partial model for the mainstreaming of OMC processes into domestic policy-making, whose extension to the EES and social protection more generally remains a live and contested issue on the EU agenda.[74]

4. THE CONVENTION AND SOCIAL EUROPE: NEW COMPROMISE OR ANTI-CLIMAX?

The Convention on the Future of Europe might have taken stock of the ongoing changes in the Community Method and incorporated the new compromise of experimentalist governance into the constitution of Europe. It might also have

[72] For the case of EMCO, see EMCO Ad Hoc Working Group, 'Future Focus and Format of the Cambridge Review Examination of the National Action Plans for Employment', EMCO/10/220404 (2004); European Commission DG EMPL, *Note to EMCO Ad Hoc Group Meeting 26.03.2004: Mutual Learning Programme on Employment Policies* (2004), EMCO/11/220404/EN. For a fuller discussion of ongoing and proposed reforms, see Zeitlin, *supra* n. 36, § III.D.

[73] For a full discussion and references, see *ibid.* §§ II.D, III.D.

[74] For an elaboration of this argument, see *ibid.*, § III.C.

helped to improve the legitimacy and effectiveness of experimentalist governance processes like the OMC by imposing procedural requirements for transparency and broad participation. In practice, it did neither. The achievement of the Convention was to have avoided any recourse to traditional forms of constitutionalism that might have fundamentally obstructed the innovations in EU governance. The Convention's failure was its inability to give due constitutional form to these innovations.

The debate over Social Europe at the Convention quickly stalemated in a way that reflected the limits of the traditional agendas of right and left in the EU. The right tried to keep Social Europe off the agenda altogether, while resisting any increase in the Union's social competences and powers. The left pressed for its historic goal of a single Social Europe, based on parity of the EU's social and economic objectives, together with extension of Union competences and qualified majority voting to all areas of social and employment policy. But the right could not prevent a broad front of Socialists and Christian Democrats from obtaining a Social Europe Working Group, while the group's internal deliberations quickly revealed the lack of broad support even within its own ranks for a single Social Europe. Nordic Social Democrats and British New Labourites joined with conservative liberals and Christian Democrats to oppose granting new competences or stronger powers for the EU in sensitive policy areas bearing directly on the core functions of national welfare states.[75]

This impasse could have been resolved in two distinct ways. One would have been for the Convention to do little or nothing, including little or no harm to innovative institutions, while simplifying the Treaties and tidying up constitutional loose ends. The alternative would have been formally to constitutionalize the new Community Method in a way that redefines the compromise between deliberative decision-making and relaxation of veto powers. Such a new compromise would involve two elements. The first is a substantial strengthening within the Constitutional Treaty of references to the EU's social values and objectives, which would place them on an equal footing with Union's economic goals. The second is the anchoring in the Treaty of new governance mechanisms such as the OMC, which enhance the Union's capacities to take effective action in pursuit of its social objectives.

The Convention and the Intergovernmental Conference (IGC) which followed made significant progress towards the first element of this new compromise. The Social Europe Working Group recommended adding a long list of items to the catalogue of values and objectives in Articles 2 and 3 of the draft Constitutional

[75] See European Convention, *Final Report of the Working Group VI on Economic Governance*, CONV 357/02 and European Convention, *supra* n. 18, along with the detailed working documents of both groups, available on the Convention website, http://european-convention.eu.int/doc_wg.asp?lang=EN. For useful commentary, see also the reports by Cécile Barbier of the Observatoire Social Européen in *Tomorrow Europe*, http://www.ciginfo.net/demain/en/default.htm, especially Nos. 11 ('Results of the First Working Groups', December 2002) and 12 ('European Convention: What About Social Europe?', February 2003).

Treaty. The Presidium, intent on keeping the opening 'constitutional' section of the revised Treaty to the barest essentials, proposed a much shorter and less expansive list of social values and objectives.[76] The final version included in the *Treaty Establishing a Constitution for Europe*, which incorporates numerous amendments, goes a long way towards achieving a new parity between the EU's social and economic goals. In particular, it declares that:

> The Union shall work for the sustainable development of Europe based on balanced economic growth, a highly competitive social market economy aiming at full employment and social progress, and a high level of protection and improvement of the quality of the environment [. . .]. It shall combat social exclusion and discrimination, and shall promote social justice and protection, equality between women and men, solidarity between generations and protection of the rights of the child. It shall promote economic, social and territorial cohesion, and solidarity among Member States [. . .].[77]

This strengthening of the EU's social values and objectives will be further reinforced by the incorporation into the Constitutional Treaty of the Charter of Fundamental Rights, and by the addition of a new 'horizontal' clause committing the Union to 'take into account' in defining and implementing all its substantive policies and actions 'requirements linked to the promotion of a high level of employment, the guarantee of adequate social protection, the fight against social exclusion, and a high level of education, training and protection of human health'.[78]

The fate of the other key element of the emergent compromise—constitutional anchoring of the OMC—is more ambiguous. The Social Europe Working Group endorsed the inclusion of the OMC in the draft constitutional treaty (as did three other Working Groups that considered the question) provided that, as one summary of its conclusions put it, 'the provision would not replace existing normative procedures or make the open method of coordination rigid in cases where there is no specific legislative method of procedure'.[79] These provisos reflected fears among

[76] CONV 516/1/03 REV 1, paras. 6–22; CONV 528/03, Arts. I-2, I-3.

[77] Intergovernmental Conference, *Treaty Establishing a Constitution for Europe* (2004), CIG 87/04, Art. I-3.

[78] *Ibid.*, Art. III-117. This latter clause, added by the Italian Presidency during the IGC negotiations, represents a partial response to demands by advocates of a stronger Social Europe for the inclusion of a 'horizontal clause on social values' in the first part of the Constitutional Treaty committing the Union 'to take into account in all the activities falling within its competence [. . .] the requirements related to achieving full employment and a high level of protection of human health, education and training, and to guaranteeing social protection and services of general interest which are accessible, financially viable, of high quality and organised on the basis of solidarity'. See Vandenbroucke, 'Intervention', presented to the Expert Hearing of Working Group 11 'Social Europe', European Convention, 21 January 2003; Vandenbroucke, 'The EU and Social Protection: What Should the Convention Propose?', *Max Planck Institute for the Study of Societies Working Paper 02/06* (2002); de Búrca, *supra* n. 7; Barbier, 'A Constitutional Treaty in Search of Its Authors', 23 *Tomorrow Europe* (2004) 8.

[79] Aoife Halligan, 'Convention Debates Social Europe', European Policy Center, http://www.theepc.net/home.asp (2003). For a comparison of the various Working Group recommendations, see de Búrca and Zeitlin, 'Constitutionalizing the Open Method of Coordination: What Should the Convention Propose?', *CEPS Policy Brief No. 31* (2003).

some members of the Working Group that constitutionalization of the OMC could undermine its flexibility and among others that it could subvert the use of the EU's existing Treaty powers to legislate in the social field. Hence a vocal minority within the Working Group and the wider Convention remained sceptical about the incorporation of the OMC into the draft constitutional treaty. The majority of the Social Europe Group insisted instead on specifying the scope and limits of the method, as well as the roles of different actors in the procedure, in ways that might have threatened its practical viability if enacted.[80]

These differences, as both political actors and academic commentators (including the present author) proposed at the time, could have been reconciled by a generic provision of the Constitutional Treaty defining only the fundamental aims and basic elements of the OMC; declaring that OMC processes be determined flexibly, subject to review by Parliament and other actors, unless specified otherwise by the Treaty; and disclaiming any intention to replace existing normative procedures by OMCs. To ensure the 'transparency and democratic character of the OMC', which the Social Europe Working Group likewise rightly deemed essential, this generic constitutional provision could also have included specific requirements for openness and broad participation of all relevant bodies and stakeholders (such as social partners, civil society organizations/NGOs, national parliaments, local and regional authorities) in accordance with national laws, traditions, and practices.[81]

In the event, however, the Convention Presidium itself deadlocked along similar lines to the Social Europe Working Group, reflecting a *de facto* alliance of opposites between defenders of the Member States' prerogatives against further intrusions by the EU on the one hand and those who feared dilution of the 'hard' *acquis communautaire* by soft law processes on the other. Hence the Presidium decided not to bring forward a proposal to incorporate the OMC into the Constitutional Treaty drafted by its Vice-President Giuliano Amato.[82] Instead, Article I-15 of the Constitutional Treaty gives the Union general powers to coordinate the economic,

[80] European Convention, *supra* n. 18, at paras. 37–45. See also the discussion of the Working Group debate in Trubek and Trubek, *supra* n. 20 and Tsakatika, 'The Open Method of Coordination in the European Convention: An Opportunity Lost?' in L. Dobson and A. Follesdal (eds.), *Political Theory and the European Constitution* (2004) 91.

[81] See de Búrca and Zeitlin, *supra* n. 79. For related proposals, see Vandenbroucke, 'Intervention', *supra* n. 78 and European Parliament 'Resolution on Analysis of the Open Coordination Procedure in the Field of Employment and Social Affairs, and Future Prospects', A5-0143/2003, 5 June 2003.

[82] Amato's proposal, reproduced in Telò, 'Il metodo aperto', *supra* n. 27, comprised the following three clauses that were to have been included in the first part of the draft Constitutional Treaty:

1. Where the Constitution excludes harmonization and does not specifically regulate coordination, the attainment of common European goals through national policies may be pursued by the open method of coordination, whenever the Member States so decide.
2. The open method of coordination shall be based on the definition of common guidelines or objectives with appropriate arrangements for periodic monitoring and evaluation. It may provide for timetables, indicators, benchmarking and exchange of best practices.

employment, and social policies of the Member States (with explicit reference to guidelines in the first two cases). In addition, Article I-17 allows the EU to take 'supporting, coordinating, or complementary action' in a series of other areas (industry; protection and improvement of human health; education, vocational training, youth, and sport; culture; civil protection) without harmonizing Member States' laws or regulations. Part III of the Constitutional Treaty then sets out specific procedures for the coordination of national policies in different areas, incorporating the existing Treaty provisions for the BEPG and the EES. But this part of the Constitutional Treaty also provides for the application of key features of the OMC in social policy, research and technological development, public health, and industry, without referring to it by name. In these areas, the Commission ('in close contact with the Member States') is charged with taking 'initiatives aimed at the establishment of guidelines and indicators, the organization and exchange of best practice, and the preparation of the necessary elements for periodic monitoring and evaluation', about which the European Parliament 'shall be kept fully informed' (Articles III-213, 250, 278, 279).[83]

Beyond the incongruity of referring covertly to what is supposed to be an *open* method of coordination, what difference, if any, will the failure to anchor it explicitly in the constitution make to the future of the OMC? There is no clear answer. Constitutional provisions undoubtedly matter in the EU, and the EES in particular has benefited from the added legitimacy conferred by its Treaty base in relation both to the Member States and to the BEPG. Explicit constitutional requirements

3. The European Council shall approve the definitions and adapt the method to match the specific needs of the particular policy area in which it wishes to promote coordination. At its request, the Commission shall support the process, by presenting proposals on guidelines and indicators, organizing the exchange of best practices and preparing the necessary elements for the periodic monitoring and evaluation. The European Parliament shall be kept fully informed.

Compared to current EU practice, this proposal would have narrowed the scope of the OMC by confining it to areas where harmonization is constitutionally excluded and made it more intergovernmental by depriving the Commission of the right to propose new OMC processes as well as the Member States.

[83] These provisions, which incorporate language from the final clause of Amato's proposed article, were added to the draft Constitutional Treaty at the last minute as a result of an intensive lobbying campaign orchestrated by Maria João Rodrigues, coordinator of the Lisbon Summit for the Portuguese presidency and the 'mother of the OMC': see Barbier, 'Final Amendments to the Constitution', 17 *Tomorrow Europe* (2003), at 3. The European Parliament has passed two resolutions calling for the OMC to be incorporated into the Constitutional Treaty and for an inter-institutional agreement with the Council and the Commission, 'laying down rules for governing the selection of policies for open coordination', together with 'a procedure for developing the open method of coordination into the Community Method', which could be formalized by the Intergovernmental Conference. See European Parliament, *supra* n. 81 and 'Resolution on the Application of the Open Method of Coordination', B5-0282/2003 (5 June 2003); C. Barbier, *From the Convention to the Next IGC* (2003), at 11–12. But the IGC did not reopen the compromise reached by the Convention on this subject. For a detailed and insightful analysis of the Convention debate on the constitutional status of the OMC and its outcome, see also de Búrca, *supra* n. 7.

for transparency and broad participation in OMC processes might also have helped to prevent Member State representatives in EMCO from watering down proposals by the Commission and the Parliament to enhance the role of non-state and subnational actors in the new Employment Guidelines for 2003–6, as discussed earlier.[84]

But other OMC processes which have a weaker Treaty base such as social inclusion have also taken off quite rapidly, eliciting broader participation from civil society at both national and European level. And if Member State governments find the OMC hard to live with, they seem to find it even harder to live without it. Increasing interdependence, strategic uncertainty, and ongoing pressures to 'do something' about urgent policy issues at a European level continually push Member States to expand the scope of the OMC and/or to apply closely related approaches based on mutual surveillance, peer evaluation, and exchange of good practices to new issue areas. Thus for example, despite fears of 'opening a box that can then never be closed' again by allowing EU-level discussion of national healthcare policies, Member States now seem ready to accept a fully fledged OMC process for health and elder care,[85] as well as to extend mutual learning and exchange of good practices to other domestically sensitive issues such as the provision of social services.[86] In other thorny areas such as the fight against terrorism and regulation of genetically modified crops, the Council and the Commission have likewise reached for OMC-style mechanisms such as guidelines, peer evaluation, recommendations, and exchange of best practices in order to coordinate national policies.[87]

The apparently staid Community Method has almost always run ahead not just of constitution making but also of constitutional theory in the EU. The ungainly but workable compromise reached by the Convention, which neither advances nor obstructs the EU's new experimentalist governance, offers little reason to think that the legal and constitutional hare will soon overtake the institutional tortoise.

[84] It may nonetheless be that European and national courts will use the strengthened commitments to transparency and participation in Arts. I-47 and I-50 of the Constitutional Treaty as grounds for reviewing the procedural conformity of OMC processes with these principles. But that possibility remains at present entirely speculative.

[85] Baeten, 'Health Care on the European Political Agenda', in C. Degryse and P. Pochet (eds.), *Social Developments in the European Union 2002* (2003) 169; European Commission, *Modernising Social Protection, supra* n. 11.

[86] This latter proposal was supported close to unanimously by national ministers at the Maastricht Informal Council on Employment and Social Affairs, 8–10 July 2004, according to remarks by Belgian officials at the first workshop on 'La Méthode Ouverte de Coordination (MOC) en matière des pensions et de l'intégration européenne', Office Nationale des Pensions, Brussels, 14 July 2004.

[87] Council of the European Union, *supra* n. 12; European Commission, *Commission Recommendation of 23 July 2003 on Guidelines for the Development of National Strategies and Best Practices to Ensure the Coexistence of Genetically Modified Crops with Conventional and Organic Farming*, (2003). I am grateful to Gráinne de Búrca for these references.

Index

Steam Generator Systems: Operational Reliability and Efficiency

Editor

Lucas Formann

scitus
academics

Steam Generator Systems: Operational Reliability and Efficiency
Edited by **Lucas Formann**

ISBN: 978-1-68117-615-4
Library of Congress Control Number: 2016946473

Printed in United States of America on Acid Free Paper

Preface

A steam generator, similar to a flash steam boiler, is a low water content boiler type. The normal construction can be like a spiral coil of a water tube, arranged as a single or possibly a monotube. Circulation is pumped under pressure once, like a forced circulation boiler. The high temperature could be generated by the combustion of a fuel including coal, oil, natural gas, municipal waste or perhaps biomass, a nuclear fission reactor and other sources. You will find an excellent variety of different types of steam generators ranging from small medical and domestic humidifiers to large steam generators used in conventional coal-fired power plants that generate about 3,500 kilograms of steam per megawatt hour of power generation. For a variety of applications, steam generators or perhaps boilers use heat to convert water to steam. Process heating and electricity generation are primary among these.

This book reveals latest information on operational reliability and efficiency of steam generators and related systems used in industrial environments. The book will appeal to students, engineers, practitioners, as well as researchers. We hope that the information presented in the book will be beneficial to all readers and that further research and development will be initiated with a view to a better future.

Table of Contents

Chapter 1

Feasibility Study of Solar Energy Steam Generator for Rural Electrification

Mouaaz Nahas[1], M. Sabry[2,3], Saud Al-Lehyani[2]

[1]Department of Electrical Engineering, College of Engineering and Islamic Architecture, Umm Al-Qura University, Makkah, KSA

[2]Department of Physics, College of Applied Sciences, Umm Al-Qura University, Makkah, KSA

[3]Solar Research Department, National Research Institute of Astronomy and Geophysics, Cairo, Egypt

ABSTRACT

In Middle East region, where there are plentiful amounts of solar radiation and great desert areas, solar energy can play a potential role in replacing conventional fuel-operated electricity generation methods with a cost-effective, sustainable solution. This paper presents a feasibility study of a low-cost solar energy steam generator for rural areas electrification. The proposed system is based on the use of trough concentrator which converts solar radiation into thermal energy in its focal line (where a receiver pipe is installed with a fluid flowing in its interior). The aim of the paper is to predict the feasibility and potential for steam generation using a stand-alone solar concentrator with a small dimension for domestic and small-scale electricity generation. The study presented here is based on modelling of the system to determine the points at which the system is expected to produce sufficient steam energy at the tube outlet to drive a steam engine for producing electricity. Results are presented in graphical forms to show the operating points and the effect of changing selected input parameters on the behavior of the system in order to set some limits (boundaries) for such parameters. Results show that among the three input design parameters selected, the tube diameter is the most dominant parameter that influences steam energy, then the tube length and finally the flow rate of the water passing through the tube. The results of this paper can provide a useful guideline for future simulation and/or physical implementation of the system.

KEYWORDS

Solar Radiation, Trough Concentrator, Radiation Intensity, Tube Diameter, Tube Length, Flow Rate, Steam Energy

1. INTRODUCTION

A continuously rising energy demand along with increasingly limited natural resources is challenging energy suppliers, industry as well as consumers to rethink how energy can be produced and used efficiently. Energy efficiency, smart energy use, and energy savings are keys to meet this challenge in a sustainable way [1] [2] .

State power grid systems supply electricity to the majority of the population living in state capitals and industrial centres [3] . It is highly uneconomical to extend the electrical power grid system into the sparsely populated regions. Hence, there are many small remote communities that need an independent source of electrical energy, especially in the Middle East region. These locations represent a significant potential for renewable energy applications. The importance of using renewable energy not only will be confined to meet the demands of remote sites, but also can contribute to the national grid, helping to meet the peak-load demand during the summer months [3] .

Renewable energy is becoming the focus of concern to both oil and non-oil producing countries. Nowadays, many countries around the world are keenly interested in taking an active part in the development of new technologies for exploiting and utilizing renewable sources of energy. The main motivation as to why renewable energy is given much attention is because of its contribution to reduce harmful emissions to the environment, especially carbon dioxide. There are rising concerns around the globe over the high oil and gas prices because of growing demand as well as the aspect to reserve oil for the next generation [4] . In countries located within the equatorial “Sun Belt” (where more solar radiation hits the earth than any other part of the globe), there is a massive amount of freely available solar energy which can be exploited. Besides receiving a lot of solar energy, desert countries in the Middle East have other competitive advantages when it comes to the potential of developing solar energy markets and technology. For instance, there can be lots of open lands, and more importantly, lots of sand which might contain a high percentage of silicon, the starting material for silicon solar “photovoltaic” (PV) cells and panels as well as semiconductor chips. Also, such countries have a relatively fast-growing young and educated population, many of whom are looking for good private sector jobs and careers (for further details, see [2]).

Middle East, Arabia and Gulf area present very high solar radiation potential especially Direct Normal Irradiance (DNI), i.e. the fraction of solar radiation which is not deviated by clouds, fumes or dust in the atmosphere and that reaches the Earth’s surface as a parallel beam [5] . The regional DNI map is shown in Figure 1. Clearly, DNI in such region is amongst the highest values in the world. Moreover, in this region, there are fewer restrictions in space available due to desert areas, while some of the rural areas have not been electrified yet or are under electrification with decentralized ways of connection. The large space combined with the abundant solar resources has made this region one of the promising areas for the installation of solar energy plants for providing electricity [6] .

Rural electrification is a global challenge in the developing countries especially those whose area is huge and has low population in scattered communities or tribes as is the case in most countries of the mentioned region. The socio-economic development processes revolve around suitable and sustainable power supply. In fact, it is the nucleus of operations and subsequently the engine of growth for all sectors of the economy. It also determines the living standard of the people and stops the immigration to urban areas as well [7] .

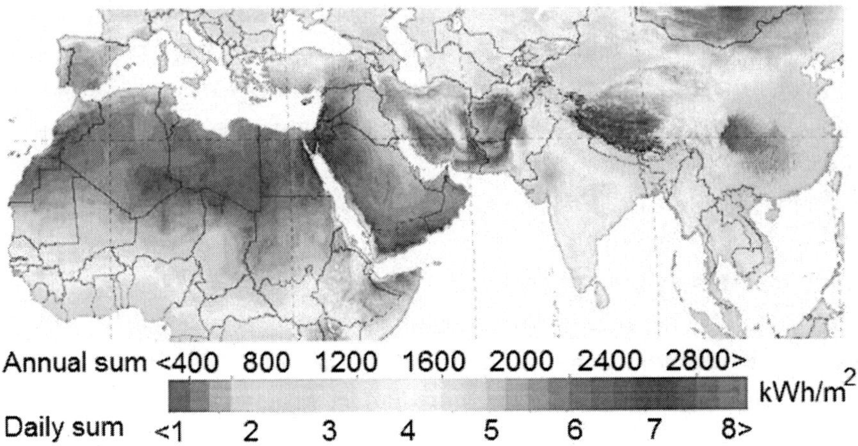

Figure 1. Solar radiation distribution over the Middle East, Arabia and gulf.

Amongst various renewable resources, solar energy could contribute in solving energy-deficiency problems like using electric-powered wells to obtain clean water for domestic use and/or some related activities in such rural communities and tribes.

Solar radiation incident could be concentrated using different imaging or nonimaging solar concentrators like Lenses, Parabolas, Troughs, etc. The only sunlight component that can be concentrated is the "Direct Normal Irradiance" (DNI) component—those rays which come directly from the sun without any scattering by dust or sands suspended in the sky. The other component, the diffuse solar radiation component cannot be concentrated because it occurs due to scattering by suspended particles in the sky. Increasing the percentage of direct solar radiation means that one can use solar concentrators effectively.

Concentrated sunlight has been used to perform useful tasks since long time ago. History mentions that the first one who used concentrated sunlight was Archimedes who used it on the invading Roman fleet and repelled them from Syracuse [8] . In 1866, Auguste Mouchout used a parabolic trough to produce steam for the first solar steam engine.

The first patent for a solar collector was obtained by the Italian Alessandro Battaglia in Genoa, Italy, in 1886. Over the following years, inventors such as John Ericsson and Frank Shuman developed concentrating solar-powered devices for irrigation, refrigeration, and locomotion. In 1913, Shuman finished a 55 HP parabolic solar thermal energy station in Meadi, Egypt for irrigation.

Giovanni Francia (1911-1980) designed and built the first concentrated-solar plant which entered into operation in Sant'Ilario, near Genoa, Italy in 1968. This plant had the architecture of today's concentrated-solar plants with a solar receiver in the centre of a field of solar collectors. The plant was able to produce 1 MW with superheated steam at 100 bar and 500 degrees Celsius [9] .

Different types of concentrators produce different peak temperatures and correspondingly varying thermodynamic efficiencies, due to differences in the way that they track the sun and focus light. New innovations in "Concentrated Solar Power" (CSP) technology are leading systems becoming increasingly more cost-effective.

CSP systems use mirrors or lenses to concentrate a large area of DNI onto a small area. Electrical power is produced when the concentrated light is converted into heat, which drives a steam turbine that is connected to an electrical power generator [10] .

The main focus of this paper is to study the feasibility of developing an electrical generator system based on the use of efficient solar concentrator.

The solar concentrator is mainly used for heating the fluid that will produce the steam (vapour) through the receiving of solar radiation. Our study will involve determining a particular set of concentrator parameters that can be used to design the sought system, keeping in mind that the system should be able to work efficiently in regions located near the equatorial (i.e. Middle East) as well as being simple, safe, portable, and cost-effective. Before determining the design parameters of our proposed concentrator-based system, it is important to understand its structure and how it works. This is carried out in the next section.

2. SOLAR ENERGY STEAM GENERATOR SYSTEM

This section describes—in brief—the proposed solar energy electrical generator system for which the feasibility study detailed in this paper is carried out. The proposed system idea is based on collecting solar energy by using solar concentrator which concentrates solar radiation on its focus by using a stationary nonimaging trough horizontal concentrator as shown in Figure 2.

Concentrators can absorb perpendicular incidence and scattered radiation in the received range causing the work temperature to reach 250°C or even higher. An example of trough solar concentrator is the Compound Parabolic Concentrator (CPC) having a pipe set in the focus as shown in Figure 3(a). Optical concentration ratio of a solar concentrator X_c is defined as [10] :

$$X_c = \frac{\text{Collector aperture width}}{\text{Receiver diameter}} \tag{1}$$

In the system proposed, a copper tube is situated exactly on the concentrator focus, which is heated by means of the concentrated solar radiation falling homogeneously over its external surface. The tube inlet is connected to a liquid reservoir, which passes through the tube till it reaches the tube outlet.

The liquid has to be chosen with a low boiling point such that when passing through the hot tube, its temperature increases till it reaches boiling point and converts to steam with relatively high pressure (hence speed) before reaching the tube outlet. Generated high pressure steam is then directed to a steam turbine, which rotates generating electricity for use in various applications (see Figure 3(b)).

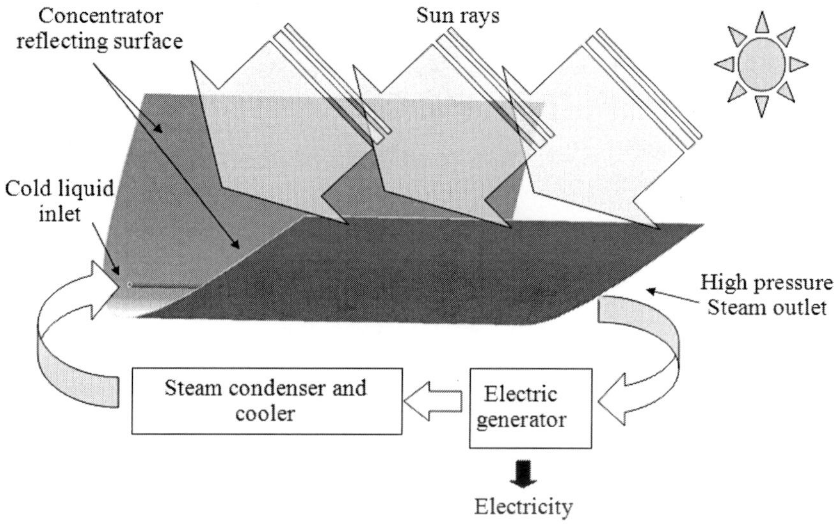

Figure 2. Flow diagram of the proposed system.

The study presented here is based on mathematical modelling of the system to determine the parameter values at which the system would produce sufficient amount of power (i.e. sufficient steam quantity which will rotate the turbine).

3. METHODOLOGY AND MATHEMATICAL MODELS

The study presented in this paper was carried out using MathCAD to develop mathematical models (equations) for calculating both energy absorbed by the water flowing in the tube and energy of the steam generated at the tube outlet to investigate the generated steam quantity and energy.

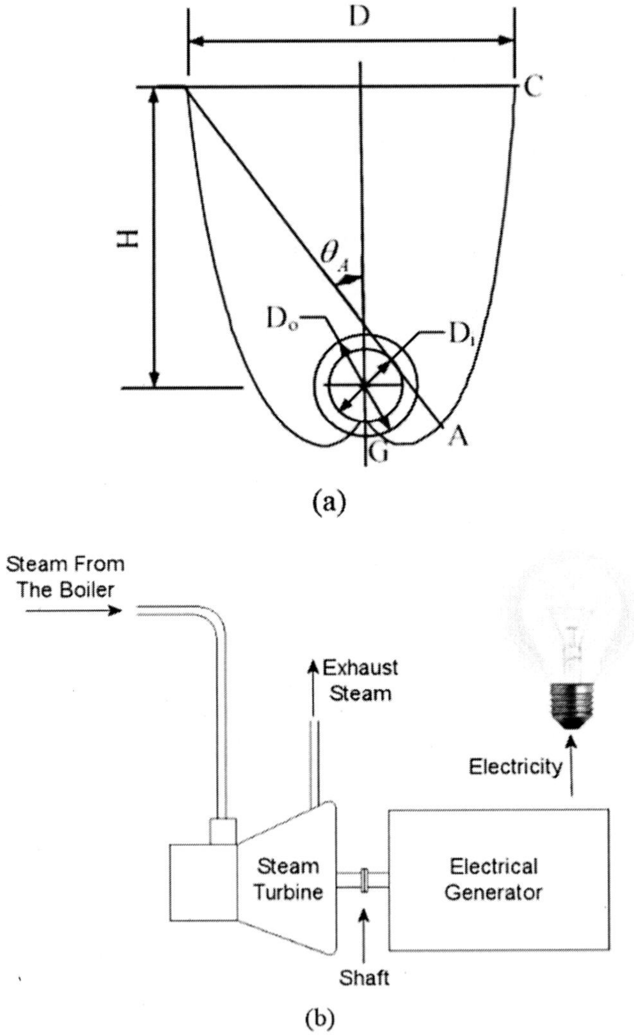

Figure 3. (a) Cross sectional view of a CPC; (b) Steam generator model.

The input parameters examined in this study are:

1) Incident solar radiation intensity.

2) Diameter of the tube (0.005, 0.01 and 0.015 m).

3) Length of the tube (1, 2, and 3 m).

4) Flow rate of water inside the tube (15, 10, and 7 kg/hr).

Then, various graphs were generated to define the points at which the system would operate effectively (i.e. points at which the system is expected to produce sufficient steam energy at the tube outlet to drive the steam engine). Graphs were also used to demonstrate the effect of changing each parameter on the behaviour of the system in order to set some limits (boundaries) for the input design parameters (more details are provided in Section 4).

In this section, we develop some equations to calculate the output steam energy in terms of the various input system parameters stated above.

The velocity of the water inside the tube is defined as the rate of flow of water over a specific area. Mathematically, the velocity vel is calculated in m/s as:

$$\mathrm{vel} = \frac{4\mathrm{FR}}{\pi d^2} \tag{2}$$

where FR is the flow rate in L/s and d is the diameter in m.

The energy absorbed by the water inside the tube E_{abs} is calculated as:

$$E_{\mathrm{abs}} = \mathrm{Rad}_{\mathrm{conc}} \cdot U_{\mathrm{area}} \cdot t_p \tag{3}$$

where $\mathrm{Rad}_{\mathrm{conc}}$ is the concentrated radiation in W/m^2, U_{area} is the unit side area in m^2, and t_p is the passage time of the water inside the tube; assuming that tube absorptivity is unity.

The energy of the steam generated at the tube outlet E_{steam} is calculated as:

$$E_{steam} = E_{abs} - (E_{boil} + E_{ltnl}) \tag{4}$$

where E_{boil} and E_{ltnt} are the boiling energy and latent energy of water (respectively).

Therefore, steam energy E_{steam} is calculated as:

$$E_{steam} = \pi^2 d^2 \cdot X_c \cdot \text{Int} \cdot \frac{\text{len}}{4\text{FR}} - \frac{\pi}{4} \cdot \rho \cdot d^2 \left(C_p \Delta T - E_{ltnt} \right) \tag{5}$$

where d is the tube diameter in m, Int is the intensity of incident radiation in W/m^2, FR is the flow rate in L/s, len is the tube length in m, ρ is the density of water in kg/m^3 and C_p is the specific heat capacity of water in J/kg · K. The collector aperture width is assumed to be a constant value of 1 m throughout this study.

Clearly from Equation (5), the steam energy is proportional to the square of the tube diameter, whereas its relation to the tube length and flow rate is directly proportional and inversely proportional (respectively). An intuitive schematic diagram showing the flow of calculations is demonstrated in Figure 4.

4. RESULTS

This section presents the results obtained in this study using graphical forms. The main aim of the presented graphs is to show the effect of various input parameters (i.e. tube length, tube diameter and flow rate) on the output of the system, namely the steam energy. The graphs are also used to determine the points at which the system is expected to produce sufficient steam energy at the tube outlet to drive a steam engine for producing electricity. From such graphs, it is possible to set some limits (boundaries) for the input parameters for practical implementation and/or simulation of the system.

We begin by showing the effect of tube diameter and tube length on the velocity and/or passage time of the water traveling in the tube. This is to begin to understand how such parameters will affect the energy of the steam produced at the tube outlet. Figure 5 shows the effect of tube diameter on the velocity and passage time of the water flowing in the tube for different flow rates. It is clear that as the tube diameter increases the velocity decreases and the passage time increases. Also, increasing flow rate results in increasing velocity and reducing passage time at each tube diameter.

Figure 6 shows the effect of tube diameter on the passage time of the water for different tube lengths. The figure clearly shows how the increase of tube length results in increasing the passage time at each tube diameter.

Figure 7 shows the effect of flow rate on the energy of steam generated for different tube. Clearly when flow rate increases, the energy of the produced steam decreases since the water does not spend enough time to heat up while traveling in the tube. Moreover, for different tube lengths, the steam energy will increase as the tube length increases at a given flow rate. This is simply because the water will travel for longer period of time in the tube and hence absorb more energy while traveling. The figure also shows the flow rate points above which the system will produce steam for the different tube lengths considered. For example, when using 1 m tube, only the three lowest flow rates will produce steam. As the tube length increases the steam will be produced with the higher flow rate values. For example, with 3 m tube, all flow rates considered here are expected to produce steam at the tube outlet. Note that the zero-line shown in the graph presents the threshold level above which the system is expected to produce steam and under which it will not produce any steam. This threshold value de pends on concentration ratio X_c, solar radiation intensity Int and rise in the inlet temperature ΔT. At this level, the absorbed energy is equal to the sum of boiling energy and latent energy of water, hence, the steam energy becomes zero; see Equation (4) above.

Figure 8 shows the effect of flow rate on the energy of steam generated for different tube diameters when the tube length is fixed to 1 m. Also here, it is clearly shown that as tube diameter increases, more energy will be produced from the system at a given flow rate. However, when increasing the tube diameter, steam energy grows faster than the case of increasing the tube length (compare with Figure 7). This is simply because the steam energy is squarely proportional to the tube diameter while it is directly proportional to the tube length, as in Equation (5). Moreover, it is clear that with all tube diameters considered, only flow rates below 0.004 kg/s will produce steam. Again this depends on the other operating conditions like tube length, incident radiation intensity and inlet temperature.

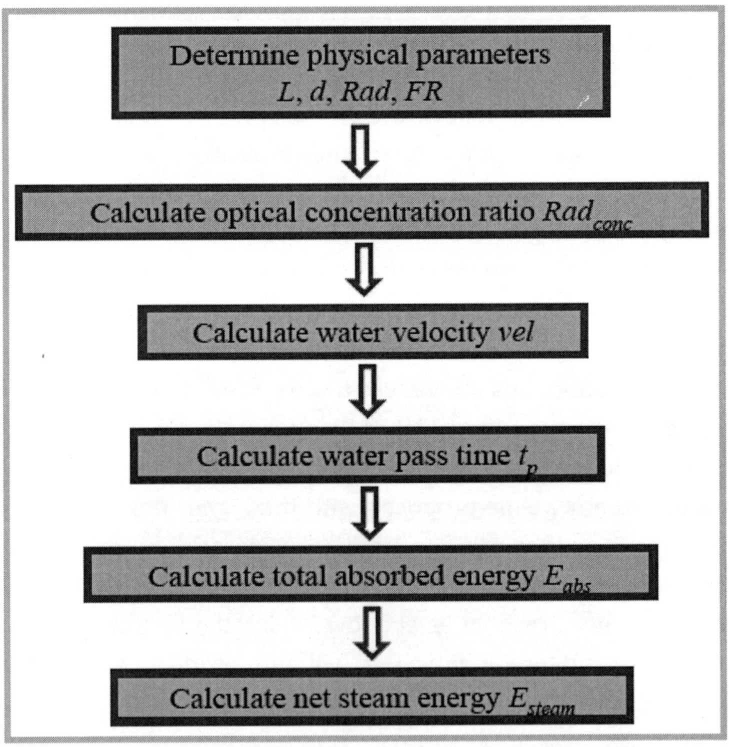

Figure 4. Intuitive schematic diagram.

Figure 9 shows the effect of radiation intensity on the energy of steam generated for different flow rates.

Here, the tube length and diameter are set to 1 and 0.005 m (respectively) with an inlet temperature of 30°C. Obviously, steam energy increases linearly as radiation intensity increases. Moreover, as flow rate decreases, steam can be produced by lower radiation intensity values. For example, using 7 kg/hr flow rate, the system will produce steam at all radiation intensities considered except at the lowest one (which is 100 W/m^2). Obviously, this is due to the low velocity and high passage time of the water inside the tube which makes it possible to convert into steam even with low radiation intensities. In contrast, for the 15 kg/hr flow rate (which is relatively high, resulting in high velocity and low passage time), the minimum radiation intensity needed to produce steam is 400 W/m^2. With lower intensity values, the water inside the tube will not absorb sufficient energy to convert into steam before reaching the tube outlet end.

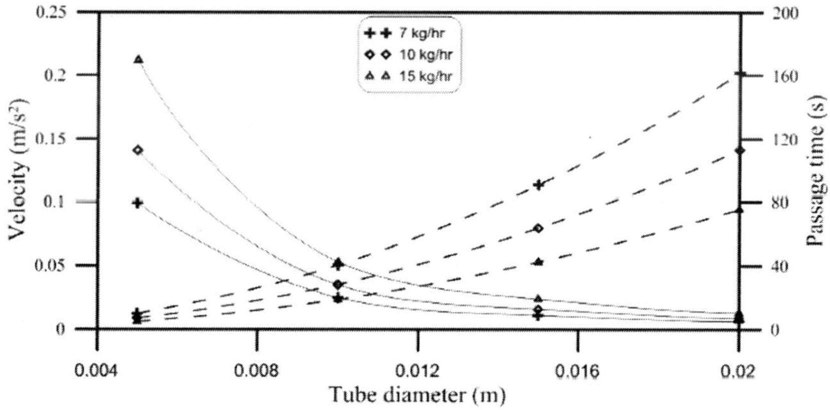

Figure 5. Effect of tube diameter on the velocity (solid) and passage time (dotted) for different flow rates.

Figure 10 shows the effect of radiation intensity on the energy of steam generated for different tube diameters. Here, tube length is set to 1 m and water flows with a rate of 15 kg/s. Again, steam energy increases linearly as radiation intensity increases. However, when increasing the tube diameter, steam energy grows faster than the case of increasing the flow rate (compare with Figure 9). Recall that the steam energy is squarely proportional to the tube diameter while it is inversely proportional to the flow rate, as in Equation (5). Also from the graph, with all tube diameters considered, the minimum radiation intensity needed to produce steam is 400 W/m^2 at the abovementioned operating conditions.

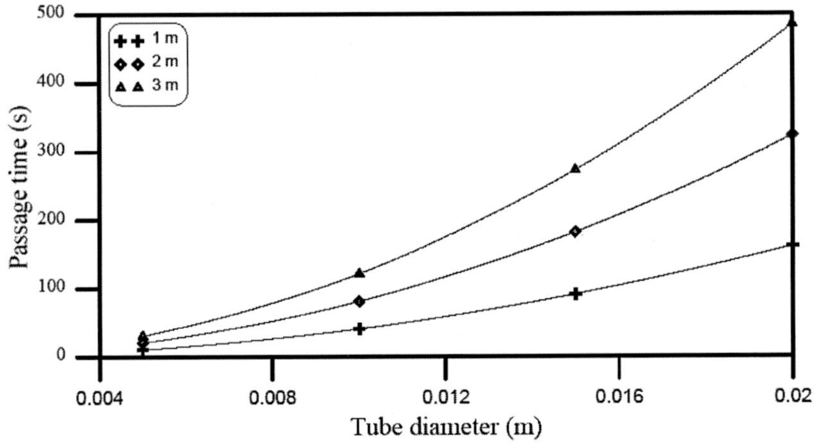

Figure 6. Effect of tube diameter on the passage time for different tube lengths.

To investigate the system's performance under realistic operating conditions, a daily profile of solar radiation intensity has been chosen along with ambient temperature. Then, steam generated from the different combinations of the abovementioned system parameters were calculated and compared.

Figure 11 shows the daily profile of radiation intensity and ambient (which is set equal to the inlet) temperature in a selected day in the concerned region.

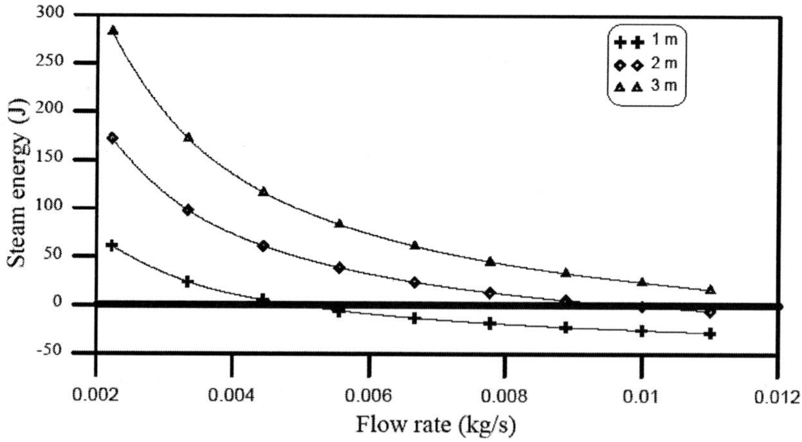

Figure 7. Effect of flow rate on the steam energy for different tube lengths.

Figure 12 to Figure 14 show the total accumulated steam energy for all input parameters considered in this study over that selected day from 8 am to 6 pm. The aim of these graphs is to investigate the effect weight of each parameter against the other parameters. More particularly,Figure 12 shows the total accumulated steam energy for all flow rates and tube diameters considered when fixing the tube length. Similarly, Figure 13shows the total accumulated steam energy for all tube lengths and tube diameters considered when fixing the flow rate, and Figure 14 shows the total accumulated steam energy for all tube lengths and flow rates considered when fixing the tube diameter.

The three graphs clearly show that the best steam quantity over the day is achieved with the largest tube diameter, largest tube length and lowest flow rate (and vice versa). However, by looking at the details, it can be noticed that:

1) For a given tube length, the effect of changing tube diameter overwhelms the effect of changing flow rate. Moreover, the total accumulated steam energy increases linearly with increasing the tube length.

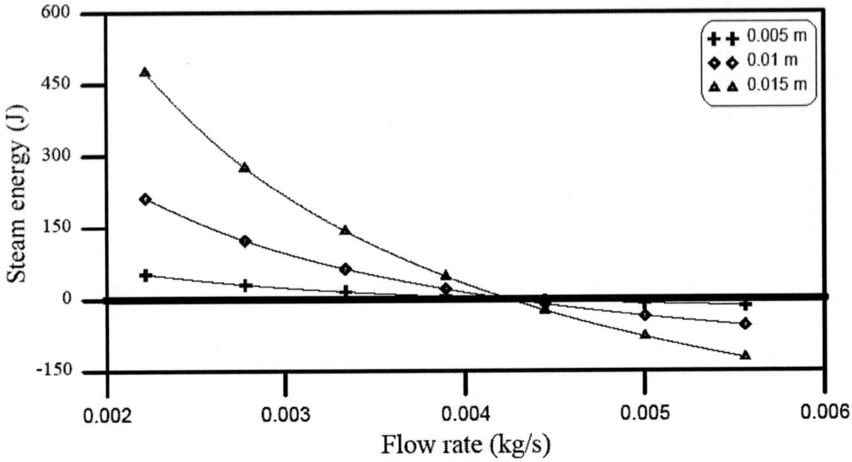

Figure 8. Effect of flow rate on the steam energy for different tube diameters.

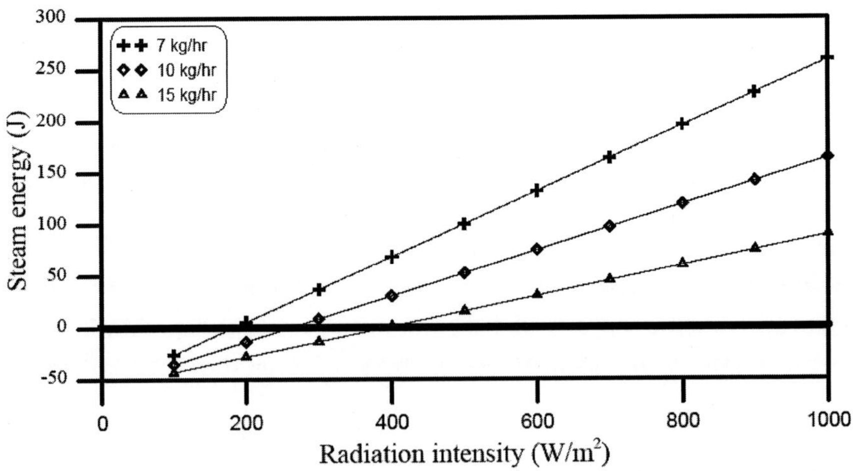

Figure 9. Effect of radiation intensity on the steam energy for different flow rates.

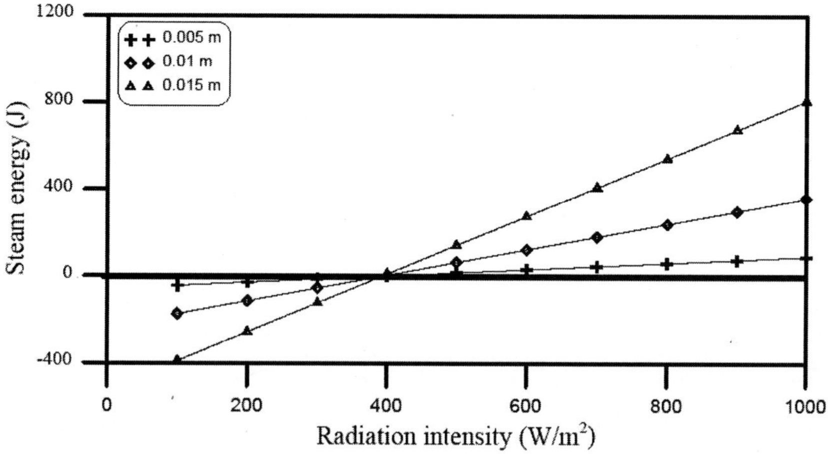

Figure 10. Effect of radiation intensity on the steam energy for different tube diameters.

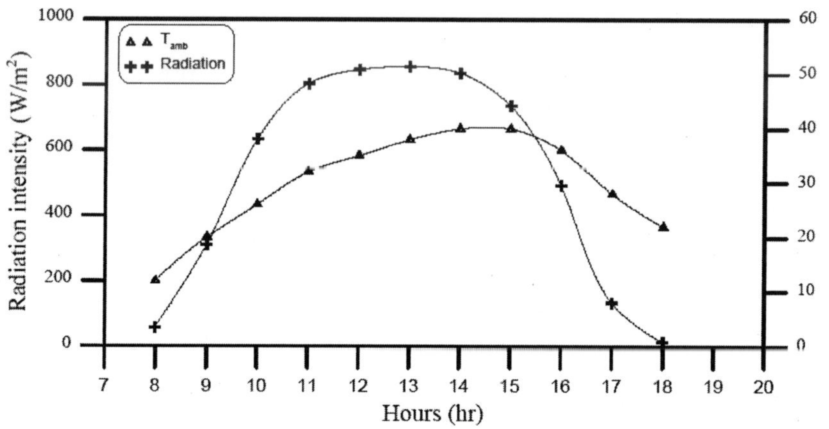

Figure 11. Daily profile of radiation intensity and inlet temperature.

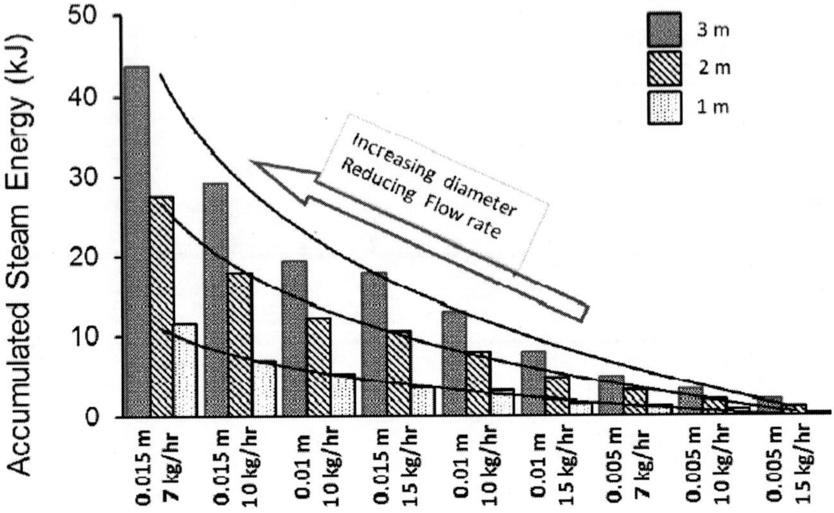

Figure 12. Accumulated steam energy for all flow rates and tube diameters considered when fixing the tube length.

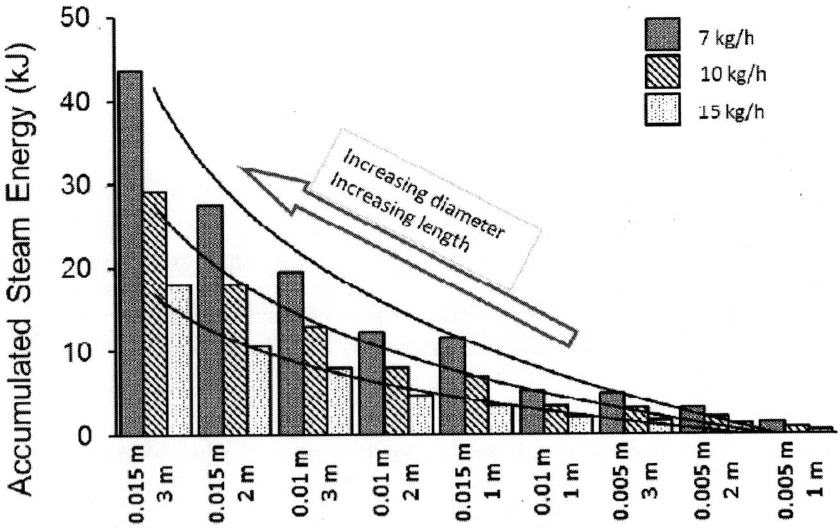

Figure 13. Accumulated steam energy for all tube lengths and tube diameters considered when fixing the flow rate.

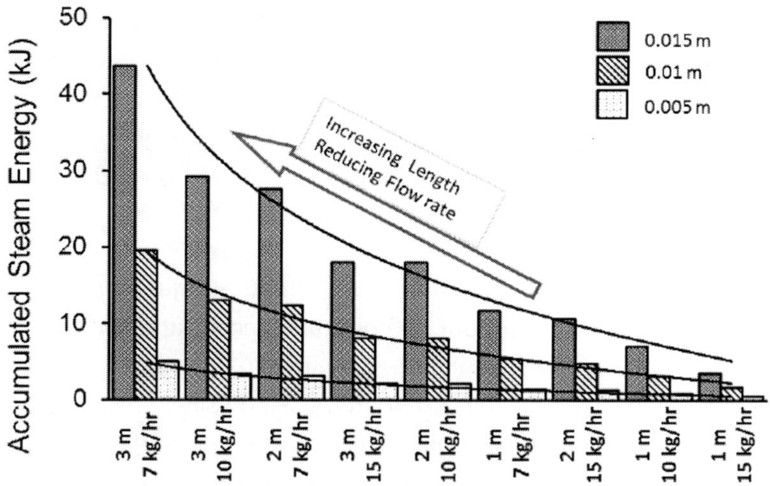

Figure 14. Accumulated steam energy for all tube lengths and flow rates considered when fixing the tube diameter.

2) For a given flow rate, the effect of changing tube diameter overwhelms the effect of changing tube length. Moreover, the total accumulated steam energy increases linearly with decreasing the flow rate.

3) For a given tube diameter, the effect of changing tube length overwhelms the effect of changing flow rate. However, the total accumulated steam energy increases nonlinearly (squarely) with increasing the tube diameter. It can also be noticed that with the very low tube diameters (such as the case of 0.005 m tube), total accumulated steam energy is not affected much by manipulating the other parameters.

5. CONCLUSIONS

The study outlined in this paper intended to investigate the feasibility of designing a small-size, stand-alone solar energy steam-based electric generator to use for domestic and small-scale electricity generation purposes. The proposed system was based on using nonimaging

"Compound Parabolic Concentrator" (CPC) in which a copper tube is placed on the concentrator focus and heated up by receiving homogeneous concentrated solar radiation on its external surface. A fluid (chosen here to be water) is injected in the hot tube that will pass through it— while being heated up—till it converts from liquid to steam before reaching the tube outlet end.

The study was based on developing mathematical equations to calculate the energy of the steam produced from the concentrator system in terms of four main parameters: radiation intensity, tube length, tube diameter and water flow rate. The three parameters—tube length, tube diameter and flow rate, were considered to be the main input design parameters of the system. Graphs were then presented mainly to show the effect of changing input design parameters on the quantity of steam generated at the tube outlet. In addition, graphs were also used to determine the values at which the system is expected to produce steam so as to set initial boundaries for the input design parameters for further design processes of the system.

Overall, the results obtained demonstrate that among the three input design parameters, tube diameter is the most dominant parameter that influences steam energy, then the tube length and finally the flow rate. This implies that for achieving better steam quantity the designer shall begin by increasing the tube diameter before increasing the tube length or reducing the flow rate at last. Such results can provide a guideline for simulating and/or implementing the system in practice.

It is worth noting that, in this study, the steam produced from the proposed system was only analyzed quantitatively since qualitative analysis cannot be performed by the approach considered in this study which is based on mathematical calculations. It is therefore suggested to conduct a computer simulation of the system using appropriate Computational Fluid Dynamics (CFD) simulation software. As such, the results presented here can be used effectively in the initial design (or modelling) phase of the system that is to be simulated.

ACKNOWLEDGEMENTS

Mouaaz Nahas, M. Sabry, Saud Al-Lehyani (Project ID 43305021) for the financial support.

REFERENCES

1. Rahman, F., Rehman, S. and Abdul-Majeed, M.A. (2012) Overview of Energy Storage Systems for Storing Electricity from Renewable Energy Sources in Saudi Arabia. Renewable and Sustainable Energy Reviews, 16, 274-283

2. Al-Ammar, E. and Al-Aotaibi, A. (2010) Feasibility Study of Establishing a pv Power Plant to Generate Electricity in Saudi Arabia, from Technical, Geographical, and Economical Viewpoints. International Conference on Renewable Energies and Power Quality (ICREPQ'10), Granada, 23-25 March 2010,

3. Said, S.A.M., El-Amin, I.M. and Al-Shehri, A.M. (2004) Renewable Energy Potentials in Saudi Arabia. Beirut regional Collaboration Workshop on Energy Efficiency and Renewable Energy Technology, American University of Beirut, Beirut, 76-82.

4. Alnatheer, O. (2006) Environmental Benefits of Energy Efficiency and Renewable Energy in Saudi Arabia's Electric Sector. Energy Policy, 34, 2-10.

5. Fernández-García, A., Zarza, E., Valenzuela, L. and Pérez, M. (2010) Parabolic-Trough Solar Collectors and Their Applications. Renewable and Sustainable Energy Reviews, 14, 1695-1721.

6. Tsikalakis, A., Tomtsi, T., Hatziargyriou, N.D., Poullikkas, A., Malamatenios, C., Giakoumelos, E., Jaouad, O.C., Chenak, A., Fayek, A., Matar, T. and Yasin, A. (2011) Review of Best Practices of Solar Electricity Resources Applications in Selected Middle East and North

Africa (MENA) Countries. Renewable and Sustainable Energy Reviews, 15, 2838-2849.

7. Afa, J.T. (2013) Problems of Rural Electrification in Bayelsa State. American Journal of Scientific and Industrial Research, 4, 214-220.

8. Africa, T.W. (1975) Archimedes through the Looking-Glass. The Classical World, 68, 305-308.

9. Butti, K. and Perlin, J. (1980) A Golden Thread: 2500 Years of Solar Architecture and Technology, Vol. 514. Cheshire Books, Palo Alto.

10. Rabl, A. (1976) Comparison of Solar Concentrators. Solar Energy, 18, 93-111.

Chapter 2

Modernization of Steam Turbine Heat Exchangers Under Operation at Russia Power Plants

A. Yu. Ryabchikov[1]

[1] "Turbines and Engines" department, Urals Federal University (UrFU), Yekaterinburg, Russia

1. INTRODUCTION

The authors' experience in the modernization of commercial heat exchangers in steam turbine units is discussed with the individual features of the operation of these heat exchangers at specific thermal power plants taken into account. The variety of conditions under which heat exchangers operate in specific engineering subsystems requires an individualized approach to the model solutions that have been developed for these systems modernizing. New tube systems for commercial heat exchangers have undergone industrial testing and are in successful operation at a wide range of thermal power plants.

2. RESEARCH PROBLEM FORMULATION

Extending the service life and increasing the operational efficiency and reliability of heat exchangers in steam turbine units at thermal power plants are of great current interest. Modernizing heat exchangers, operating at thermal power plants, involves less expense than replacing the entire heat exchanger and is mainly aimed at eliminating structural defects that have been identified. This is done both when worn out components are replaced and in the course of planned major overhauls, so that the efficiency and operational reliability of the heat exchangers and the steam turbine unit, as a whole, can be increased substantially.

The major engineering solutions for improvement of commercial heat exchangers in thermal power plants steam turbine units must, first of all, be directed at enhancing the efficiency and reliability of their tube systems, since they are the most subject to wear during operation. The choice of approaches and modern engineering solutions for heat exchangers improvement must meet a number of specifications including the following [1]:

- taking into consideration the specific operating conditions;
- raising the efficiency of heat exchanger while retaining reliability or increasing reliability while maintaining efficiency;
- improving or sustaining repairability and maintainability;
- meeting the standards and rules of the supervisory agency Rostekhnadzor.

The improvement of heat exchangers is a rather complicated system problem. A large number of factors at different levels which influence the efficiency and reliability of a heat exchanger should be taken into account, along with its relationship to the engineering subsystems of steam turbine unit of a thermal power plant. The choice of a modernization scheme involves solving a specific optimization problem where the target function or criterion determining the choice may be any of various characteristics, such as raising the thermal efficiency or the thermal capacity of heat exchanger, or increasing its operational reliability or repairability.

The approach determination for heat exchanger improvement can be divided structurally into three stages: a stage for analyzing the initial data, a stage of computations and accounting for a number of operational and design-engineering factors and a stage of technical and economic analysis and evaluation. One of the most important stages in the analysis is the use of computational methods which take most complete account of the features and behavior of the processes occurring in steam turbine heat exchangers. These methods are used to calculate separately heat transfer coefficients for two heat transfer media, while individual factors affecting the heat transfer are taken into account by introducing corrections to heat transfer coefficients base values. When estimating a choice of improvement method, each specific heat exchanger is considered as a component of a particular engineering subsystem of steam turbine (condensation unit, system for regenerative feed water heating, system of hot water heating, etc.) in which it is employed; here the effect of the proposed modernization scheme on other elements of the subsystem or on the turbine unit as a whole is evaluated.

When improvements are made in heat exchangers at thermal power plants under operating conditions, it is necessary to analyze and take into account a large number of factors and performance indicators, including the specific operating conditions. Most often it is possible to optimize only the basic (thermal and hydraulic) operating characteristics of heat exchanger, leaving the others at levels corresponding to commercial apparatuses.

3. SELECTION AND JUSTIFICATION OF TECHNICAL SOLUTIONS FOR HEAT EXCHANGER MODERNIZATION

Over many years the authors have proposed, tested and brought to realization a series of new, by now commercial, technical solutions for modernizing a large number of different heat exchangers for steam turbine units; these have provided satisfactory solutions of the problems arising during heat exchanger operation, such as [1—3]:

- retaining the external connector dimensions (through pipes and shells) of commercial equipment without change;
- estimation of the choice of material for tube systems and shell components (water chambers);
- use of high efficiency profiled tubes of different materials with optimal profiling parameters (Fig.1);
- optimization of the tube bundles configuration in heat exchangers (in some cases — the increase of heat transfer surface within the shell sizes of commercial heat exchangers);
- optimization of the intermediate partitions arrangement, the rise of tube system vibrational reliability by installing damper belts and clamps;
- employing of a high efficiency method for tubes to tube sheets fixing with the use of annular reliefs made in the tube sheet metal;
- efficient sealing of gaps between the intermediate partitions and the shell (for heat exchangers of "liquid — liquid" type);
- use of special protective coatings.

Retrofitting of the oil supply systems of turbine units is intended not only to recover indices characterizing their efficiency and environmental security but also to carry out measures that will improve their characteristics without significant financial and material outlays. These problems may be solved on the basis of technical considerations aimed primarily at oil coolers design.

Our analysis of the efficiency and in-service reliability of over 150 serially produced oil coolers, as well as the data of the Ural All-Russia Thermal Engineering Institute on the vulnerability to damage of oil coolers in service at steam-turbine units, has shown that the elements of these heat-exchangers most susceptible to damage are their tube bundles.

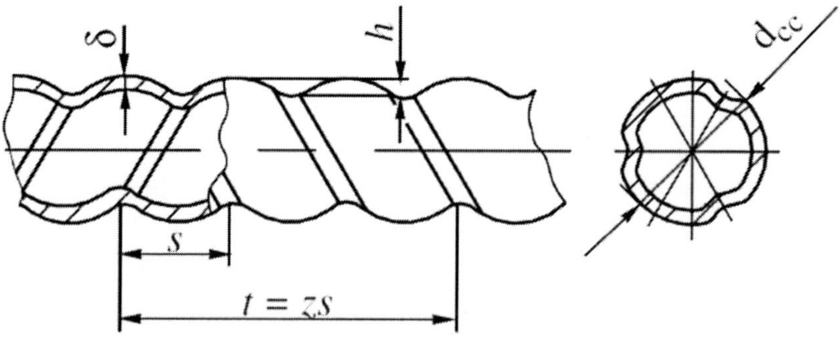

δ is the wall thickness, h is the groove depth, s is the pitch between neighboring grooves, z is the number of profiling threads, t is the thread rolling pitch, and d_{cc} is the circumferential diameter

Figure 1. External view and cross section of profiled twisted tube.

A summary of this data and also the results of tests on a number of apparatuses and experience with their operation under different conditions allowed us to formulate the main lines along which commercially produced oil coolers should be modernized. They are as follows:

- the selection of advanced materials for the elements of the construction;
- the use of heat exchange surfaces that augment heat transfer;
- the creation of optimized layouts for the tube bundles;
- the sealing of gaps in the oil space of the apparatuses;
- the improvement of the reliability of tubes fixing to the tube sheet;

- the protection of the tube sheets against corrosion.

Below, these lines will be considered in more detail.

When selecting the material for the structural elements of an oil cooler, several factors should be taken into account, such as the corrosiveness of the cooling water and the associated corrosion resistance of the heat-transfer tubes; the thermal and hydraulic characteristics of the tubes and their adhesive properties; the compatibility of different materials in one apparatus; the technological features of an assembly of apparatuses with the tubes made of the material selected; and also considerations of cost. The casing of the oil cooler and its parts are usually made of carbon-steel sheets and the tube sheets — of carbon-steel plates or from different types of brass. At most thermal power stations, tubes of brass L68 are installed in the oil coolers; this does not comply with present-day requirements. If a feasibility study is conducted and tubes of corrosion-resistant steels are used in the oil coolers, water chambers and tube sheets made of steels 12Cr18Ni10Ti or Cr23Ni17Mo2Ti can be manufactured. Lately stainless steel tubes are being installed more and more frequently in oil coolers. Considering the higher corrosiveness of the cooling water and the more stringent requirements for environmental safety of thermal power stations, in our opinion, the latter solution is more expedient.

When using stainless-steel tubes in oil coolers, one should bear in mind that the heating capacity of the apparatuses has decreased, because the thermal conductance of the steel is 6—7 times lower than that of brass.

Lately, the problem of using titanium alloy tubes in the tube bundles of heat exchangers has been widely discussed. Note that, notwithstanding the high corrosion-resistant and adhesive properties of titanium, several problems in its use still exist, such as protection of the “ferrous” metal of the tube sheets against electrochemical corrosion if it contacts the titanium and the insufficient resistance of titanium to friction wear and its corrosion instability in alkaline solutions with a $pH > 10$. Note also that the cost of titanium is higher than that of other materials.

The larger overall dimensions of oil coolers for high-power turbine installations required their developers and manufacturers to revise several basic concepts in the design of apparatuses associated, in particular, with the use of new heat exchange surfaces that augment the process of heat transfer, using variously profiled and finned tubes.

We know oil coolers that have tubes with spiral rolled finning, longitudinal welded finning, spiral wire mesh finning, and other kinds of finning. The comparatively new MP-165 and MP-330 oil coolers (for the K-300-240, K-500-240 and K-800-240 turbines manufactured by LMZ), with stainless steel tubes and cross fins manufactured by LMZ instead of the previously manufactured M-240 and M-540 oil coolers, are very efficient products. However, these new designs have, in our opinion, one shortcoming — comparatively low oil velocity, which is due to the non-optimal tube bundle layout in the apparatus.

4. SPECIAL FEATURES OF OPTIMIZATION CALCULATION TECHNIQUES FOR HEAT EXCHANGERS

Optimization of the tube bundle layout in heat exchangers, oil coolers included, is one of the most promising ways for improving them. It should be carried out on the basis of a comprehensive calculation of the thermal, hydrodynamic, and reliability characteristics of every given apparatus. The technique for such an optimization calculation has been worked out for oil coolers [4—7] both with plain and with twisted profiled tubes (TPT) that are used in power engineering (see Fig.1). It allows us to account for changes in the parameters of oil in different zones of the apparatus that have been selected downstream of the oil flow. One of the main factors determining the operating efficiency of oil coolers is the leakage of oil through the orifices in the intermediate partition plates and in gaps between the intermediate partition plates and the oil cooler shell. This factor is accounted for in another way.

The permeability of oil through an intermediate partition orifice in the oil cooler was studied at an experimental facility that simulated its geometrical, thermal, and physical performance parameters. The outside diameter of a working tube is 16 mm, the diameter of the orifice in an intermediate partition plate is 16.4 mm, and the thickness of a partition plate is 3 mm. In the experiments we used turbine oil UT30 with a temperature from 35 to 65 °C. The difference in the oil pressures on the partition plate ranged from 850 to 2910 Pa. All the experiments were carried out with the tube centered relative to the orifice in the intermediate partition plate.

Note that the well-known physical laws of liquid flow through an annular slot were confirmed in this study, and the quantitative and qualitative results allowed us to find more exact operating characteristics of oil coolers and to account for them in their designs. The oil flow rate through the annular slot increases as the oil temperature t*oil* rises and as the difference in pressure across the slot increases. The throughput capacity for the alternative with twisted profiled tubes (TPT) shown in Fig. 1 is considerably higher than that with an annular gap for a plain tube. In this connection, when designing and calculating oil coolers with TPT bundles and plain tubes, we should allow for a sufficiently high level of idle oil leakages through the annular gaps between the tubes and the orifices in the intermediate partition plates.

In contrast to existing methods, the more exact technique developed by us for calculations of oil coolers employs the zone-by-zone approach and accounts for changes in the oil parameters along the oil flow through the tube bundle (Fig. 2). In this case, the oil space of the oil cooler is divided by the partition plates into a number of zones: the input zone (I), the output zone (N), and intermediate zones (from I to N) in between. The heights of the zones correspond to the distances between the adjacent partition plates.

In every zone, the oil is separated into two or three flows: *Go* is the flow through the tube bundle; *GoI*= *Go* and *GoII* are the flow rates in zones I and II respectively; $G\delta_1^{I}$is the flow rate in the gap between the annular partition plate and the shell (see zone I in Figure 2); and $G\delta 2^{I}$ and $G\delta 3^{I}$ stand for flow rates in the gaps between the tube and the walls of the orifices in the intermediate partition plates, the annular and the disk ones, respectively.

Then the weighted mean temperature of the oil in every flow is calculated. Here, the oil flow rates *GoII*, $G\delta_1^{I}$, $G\delta_2^{I}$, and $G\delta_3^{I}$ were determined by an iterative calculation similar. In the course of the calculation, at a certain viscosity, the average oil flow rate through the tube bundle became negative. This meant that the oil did not reach the extreme tube rows; that is, the apparatuses have zones of stagnation. After making changes in the tube bundle layout, in particular, by decreasing the number of rows of tubes along the depth of the bundle, the thermal hydraulic calculation was repeated.

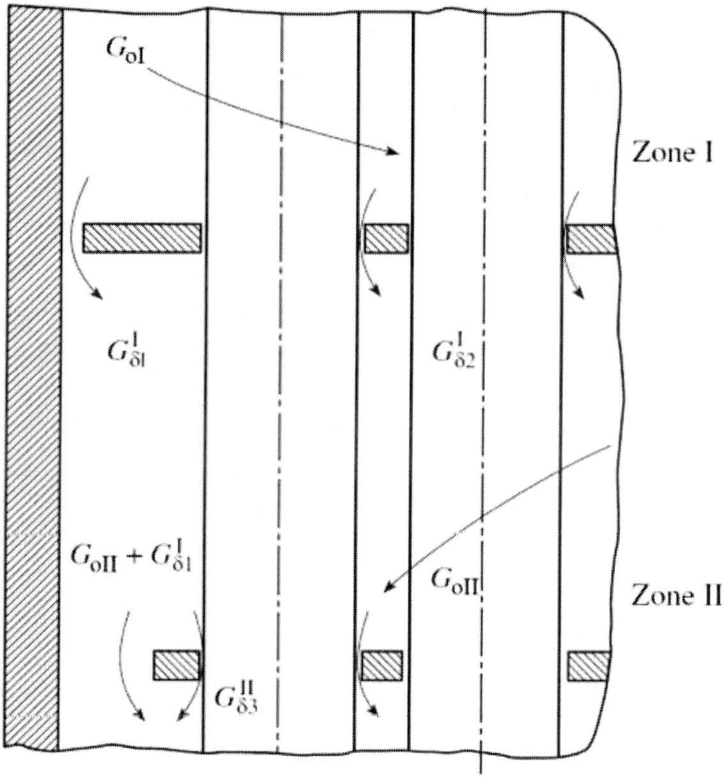

Figure 2. Scheme of oil flow in an element of a tube bundle of an oil cooler with partition plates of the "disc-ring" type and with unsealed gaps. δ_1, δ_2, δ_3 are the gaps between the shell and annular partition plate, in the orifices of the annular and disc partition plates; G_o is the oil flow rate through the tube bundle

Calculations executed in accordance with the above technique make it possible to optimize the layout of the tube bundles for the oil coolers and to determine such specifics as the number of rows of tubes that are removed from the center of the tube bundle; the distance between the tubes (the back pitch); the distance between the intermediate partition plates, that is, the number of passes for oil; and others.

5. METHODS OF HEAT EXCHANGER RELIABILITY IMPROVEMENT

It is known that one of the most important elements determining the operating reliability of an oil cooler is the joint attaching the tubes to the tube sheet. Operating experience with shell-and-tube apparatuses shows that mechanical flaring of tubes in the smooth orifices of the tube sheets (the usual way of attaching the tubes) does not ensure a reliable tightness of the joint. It depends on the following factors: the influence of heat cycles in different directions, the inherent and forced vibrations of the tubes in the bundle and in the apparatus as a whole, the corrosive effect of the cooling water, the natural aging of the material of tubes and tube sheets, etc. [1,2].

An improved tightness and reliability of the joint between the tubes and the tube sheets can be obtained by applying a new technology developed by the specialists of the St. Petersburg State Nautical Technical University. It amounts to flaring the tubes using annular reliefs on the metal in the orifices of the tube sheet, which are formed with the aid of a special tool (Fig. 3).

To find the optimal dimensions, shape, position, and mechanical characteristics of the annular reliefs, computational studies and experiments were conducted that gave the following results:

- in the area of the annular relief, the contact pressure increases considerably (by two to three times);

- the optimal shape of the relief from the standpoint of most complete imbedding into the tube surface is a triangle with a smooth transition from the base to the walls of the orifice (Fig. 3 a);
- the optimal height of the projection on the relief is in the range from 0.07 to 0.15 mm;
- the maximum increase in contact pressure is obtained when the hardness of the surface of the projection is higher by 30 to 35% on average than the hardness of the metal of the tube sheet;
- the annular relief should be located at a distance of at least 5 mm from the boundary of the zone where the tube is attached (flared) in the tube plate.

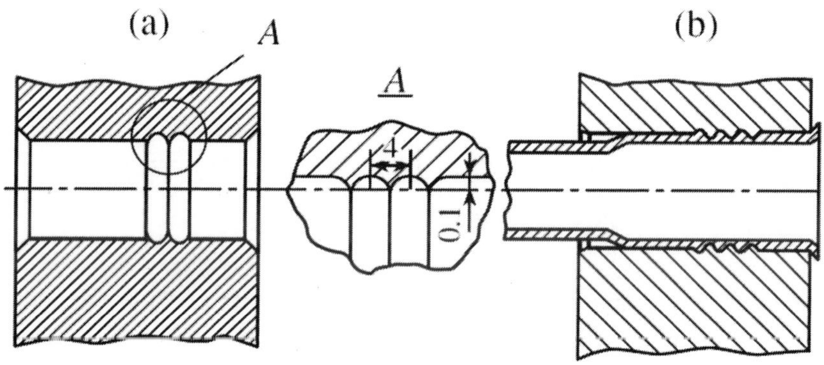

Figure 3. Method for attaching tubes to tube plates. (a) An orifice in the tube sheet with annular reliefs; (b) assembly of attachment of the tube to the tube plate after flaring

We checked the efficiency (reliability) of this technology of attachment on one-tube specimens, pilot modules, and a number of commercial apparatuses having tubes of different materials. On the basis of our investigations, we established that the given method provides a higher tightness than other previously known methods used in oil coolers do, and it is actually not inferior to the combined joint with flaring and welding. Nevertheless, note that the labor required by the proposed method is greater than with usual flaring by 25 to 30%. However, this may be justified.

It is known that the tube sheets of oil coolers can be protected against corrosion due to the cooling water in several ways:

- by rational choice of the material;
- by applying metal coatings and coatings based on paints, glass enamels, different resins, etc.

In oil coolers manufacturing, it is expedient to use corrosion-proof materials for the protection of the tube sheets or to apply metal coatings to them. In operation, the surface may be coated with an epoxy resin or minimum.

6. DISCUSSION OF MODERNIZATION RESULTS FOR POWER STATIONS HEAT EXCHANGERS

All the above considerations and advanced concepts on improvement of steam-turbine units oil coolers were the basis for modernizing a number of commercially produced oil coolers (MB-63-90; MB-40-60; MP-37; M-21; MOU-12; MO-11; MKh-4), which was done in accordance with our development works. The main measures in retrofitting the oil coolers were taken on the tube bundle, the element most vulnerable to damage in the apparatus. In doing this [1—3]:

- optimization of the layout of the tube bundle is carried out;
- the peripheral annular gap between the intermediate partition plates and the shell of the oil cooler is sealed with an oil-resistant rubber or Teflon plastic (Fig. 4);

- stainless steel twisted profiled tubes (see Fig. 1), whose profile parameters are selected to conform to special apparatuses and conditions of their operation, are employed;
- a new technology for attaching the tubes to the tube plates with annular reliefs is introduced (see above);
- the tube sheets are protected against corrosion.

As an example, in Fig. 5 we find the approximated results of comparative tests of an MP-37 oil cooler for a K-100-90 turbine in the Verkhnetagil district power station before and after retrofitting. From the figure we see that the oil outlet temperature of the retrofitted oil cooler is 0.5 to 2.5°C lower than that of a commercially produced oil cooler. Moreover, note that the operating efficiency of the commercially produced plain-tube apparatus conformed to the designed one. Similar results were obtained for other retrofitted oil coolers, as well.

Up to 10 years of operating experience with modernized oil coolers showed that they ensure the reliable service of the apparatuses without any reduction in their thermal efficiency. No remarks about them were received from the operating personnel.

By early 2000, the commercially produced oil coolers used in the lubrication systems of all LMZ K-800-240 turbines operating in the Russian Federation had worked out their service life and the question of replacing them arose. Although commercially produced M-540 oil coolers with wire-loop finning were available, replacement of the old oil coolers with these new ones turned to be inexpedient because the design of M-540 oil coolers had considerable shortcomings. The authors of this paper have developed a highly efficient and environmentally safe MB-270-330 shell-and-tube oil cooler with disk-ring partitions and propose for it to be used to replace commercially produced apparatuses. One specific feature relating to the operation of such heat exchangers with single-phase coolants is that the gaps in the structural members of the inter-tube space have an effect on the coefficients of heat transfer on the oil side.

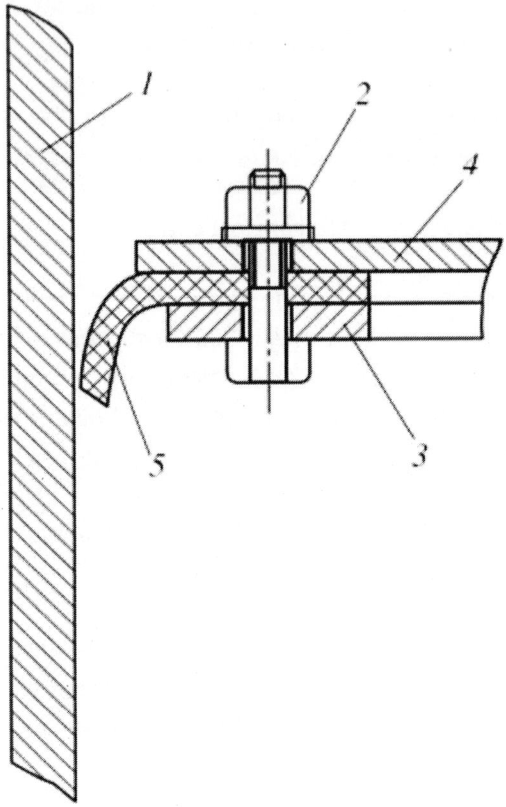

Figure 4. The seal between an annular partition plate and the shell of the oil cooler. (1) shell; (2) bolt with a nut; (3) clamping ring; (4) annular partition plate; (5) oil-resistant rubber (plasticized rubber)

Experience gained from modernization of oil coolers for 800-MW turbines has shown that stainless tubes should be used in oil coolers for bringing these apparatuses into compliance with the modern requirements for environmental safety of thermal power stations. In this case, in order to compensate for a lower heat conductivity coefficient of tubes (as compared with that in case of using tubes made of nonferrous alloys), it is recommended that smooth tubes be replaced by twisted profiled tubes (TPTs), which can be made of smooth ones by rolling a helical groove on their external surface. The corresponding protrusions will in this case appear on the inner surface of these tubes (see Fig. 1). The use of TPTs in oil coolers with disk-ring partitions is quite efficient, because it results not only in a smaller pressure drop on the oil side of the apparatus (as compared with its smooth-tube version), but also in a lower temperature of oil at the outlet.

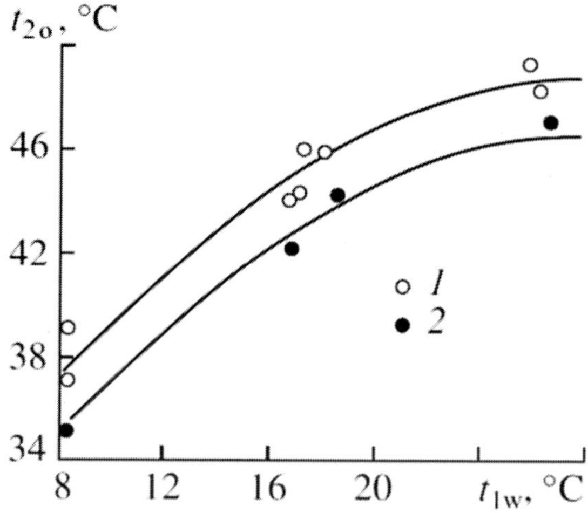

Figure 5. Curves of the oil outlet temperature of the MP-37 oil cooler as a function of the water inlet temperature at the Verkhnetagil district power station. (1) commercially produced oil cooler; (2) modernized oil cooler

The designs of modernized oil coolers must comply with often contradictory requirements that arise during operation of a thermal power station. This produces a need to carry out calculations of different design versions of oil coolers, which can be performed using zone-to-zone methods. Calculations according to these methods have shown that the number of passes on the oil side has the greatest influence on the thermal-hydraulic characteristics of an oil cooler.

The analysis also shows that there is no sense in sealing the gap in the intermediate partition in oil coolers of "disk-ring" partitions type. The gap between the shell and annular partition, however, should be sealed, because this measure helps improve the efficiency of an oil cooler and obtain lower temperature of oil at the apparatus outlet.

The results of calculations have also shown that the effect of tube material on the oil cooler characteristics is insignificant and that tubes made of Grade 08Cr18Ni10Ti stainless steel are more reliable under specific operating conditions. Changing the diameter of tubes (from 16 to 19 mm) results in that the heat- transfer area becomes 15—18% smaller, and it is hardly advisable. The transverse pitch between the tubes in the bundle is taken equal to 21 mm in the modernized version, which allowed us to obtain the required level of hydraulic resistance on the oil side.

Fig. 6 shows the results obtained from tests of the pilot MB- 270-330 oil coolers at the Perm district power station. It can be seen from the picture that the new oil cooler has better indicators compared with those of the commercially produced M-540 apparatus, which is manifested in a deeper cooling of oil (by 3°C).

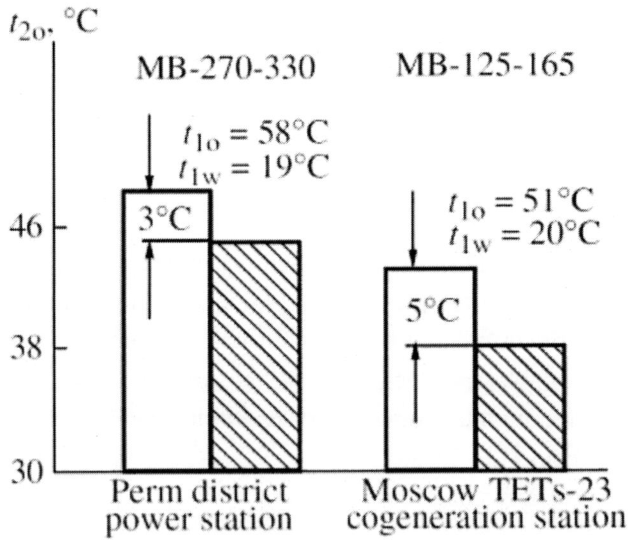

Figure 6. Results obtained from comparative tests of oil coolers. (□) Serially produced oil cooler and (▧) modernized oil cooler; t_{1o} and t_{2o} are the temperatures of oil at the inlet to the oil cooler and at the outlet from it, and t_{1w} is the temperature of water at the oil cooler inlet

Thirteen of the fifteen K-800-240 LMZ turbine units that are installed at Russian thermal power stations now are furnished with MB-270-330 oil coolers. Experience gained from long-term (up to 10 year) operation of the modernized oil coolers has confirmed the advisability of the design and engineering solutions used in these apparatuses that ensure their reliable and efficient operation.

Fig. 6 also shows the results obtained from tests of the MB-125-165 oil cooler that was developed by the authors of this paper and is installed in T-250/300-240 turbines of Ural Turbine Works production instead of the M-240 oil coolers with wire-loop finning that have worked out their service life. The main design and engineering solutions implemented in the MB-270-330 apparatus were used in the course of developing the MB-125-165 oil cooler. It follows from Figure 6 that the oil outlet temperature of the MB-125-165 cooler is 5°C lower than that in the commercially produced M-240 oil cooler. Fifteen MB-125-165 oil coolers have now been manufactured and installed at Russian thermal power stations.

In the following we discuss new designs for other heat exchangers that have been developed and carried out using the above proposed approaches and are well to be recommended for prolonged operation in thermal power plants. The scientific justification for these developments employs a set of theoretical and test stand (physical) studies.

The major problem In modernizing the PSV-315-14-23 hot water heater of KhTZ production K-300-240 turbine at the district heating system of the Reftinskaya State regional electric power plant (GRES) was to develop a design for the preheater which would compensate for the large thermal stresses which develop during startup and shutdown of the preheater while retaining the thermal capacity of the system. Here it was necessary to take into account the fact that during operation under the conditions at the Reftinskaya GRES the main water preheaters essentially operate without being contaminated and they are not cleaned.

This problem is solved by choosing a tube system for the heater (Fig. 7) made of 16/14 mm U-shaped tubes (material CuNi5Fe). The positions of the intermediate partitions are optimized and the bends in the pipes are wound with damping belts in order to reduce the danger of vibrational damage to the tube system. The design of the steam guard shield is changed; this increased the operational reliability of the peripheral sequences of tubes. The casing of the tube system of the heater has vertical and intermediate horizontal baffles whose design facilitates a reduction in the steam return flows alongside the tube bundle, thereby raising its thermal efficiency. The heat exchange surface of the preheater is increased to 335 m^2. A special method is used to fix the tubes to a tube sheet with orifices flared in advance (seeFig. 7).

The major problem in modernizing a VVT-100 heat exchanger intended for distillate cooling in the water cooling system for the generators of the LMZ K-800-240 turbines at the Perm GRES (Fig.8)was to increase the repairability of the heat exchanger while retaining its reliability and thermal capacity. The problem is stated this way because, after disassembly, repair, and reassembly, the gland seal in the VVT-100 heat exchanger is often not leakproof and, with time, the seals on the annular tube partitions are destroyed.

All components of the tube system of the modernized VVT-100M heat exchanger (profiled 16/14.4-mm-diam tubes, tube sheets, special casings) were made of corrosion resistant 08Cr18Ni10Ti (12Cr18Ni10Ti) alloy. The positions of the “disk-and-ring” partitions were determined taking the vibration characteristics of the tubes into account. Special casings which provided additional paths for the cooled distillate in the space between the tubes of the heat exchanger were installed in the upper and lower parts of the tube system to increase the heat transfer efficiency and segmented seals made of teflon tape were installed in the annular partitions to eliminate leakages alongside the tube bundle. A special method with pre-flaring of the orifices was used to fix the tubes in the tube sheets. The upper tube sheet has specially developed gland seals which make it possible to maintain a pressure of up to 2.5 MPa (25 kgf/cm^2) in tube space. This joint ensures leakproofing of the tube space of the heat exchanger when it is repeatedly assembled and disassembled (see Fig. 8.)

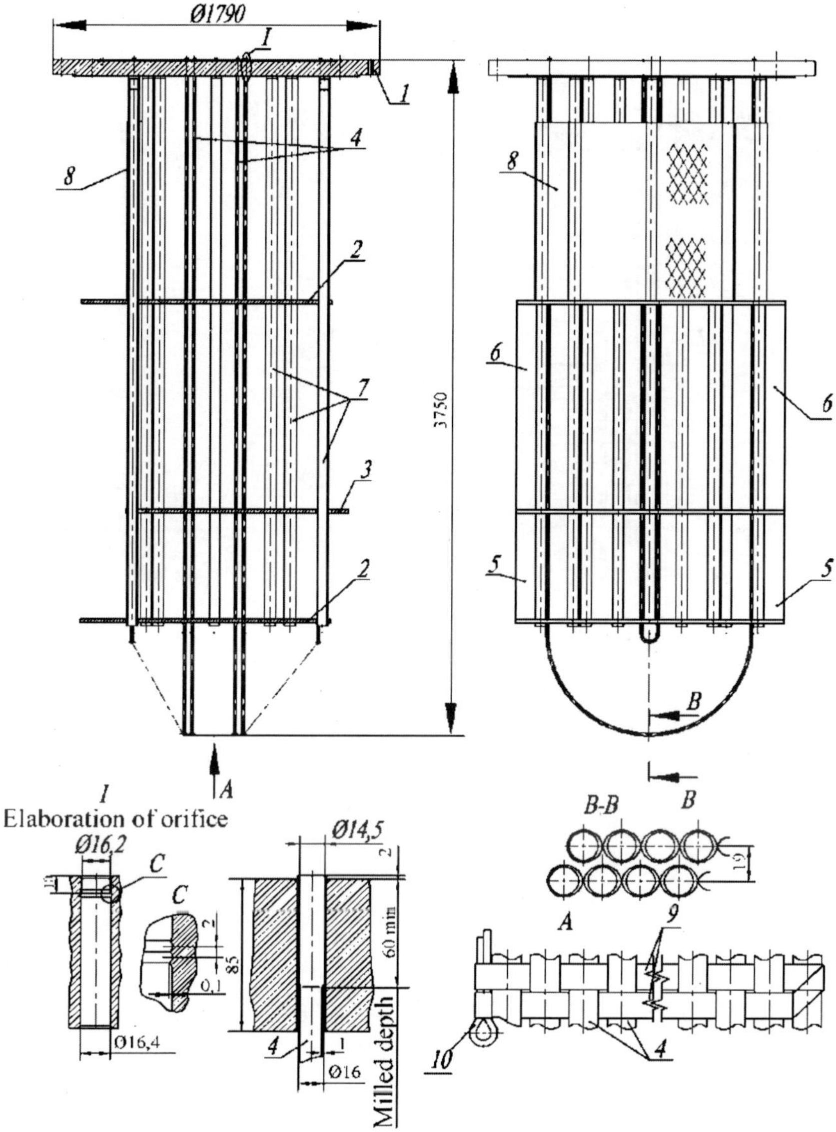

Figure 7. Modernized tube system for a type PSV-315M-14-23 hot water heater: 1 — tube sheet; 2, 3 — disk partitions; 4 — U- shaped heat exchanger tubes; 5, 6 — vertical baffles; 7 — frame tubes; 8 — steam guard shield; 9 — damping belt; 10 — cotter pin

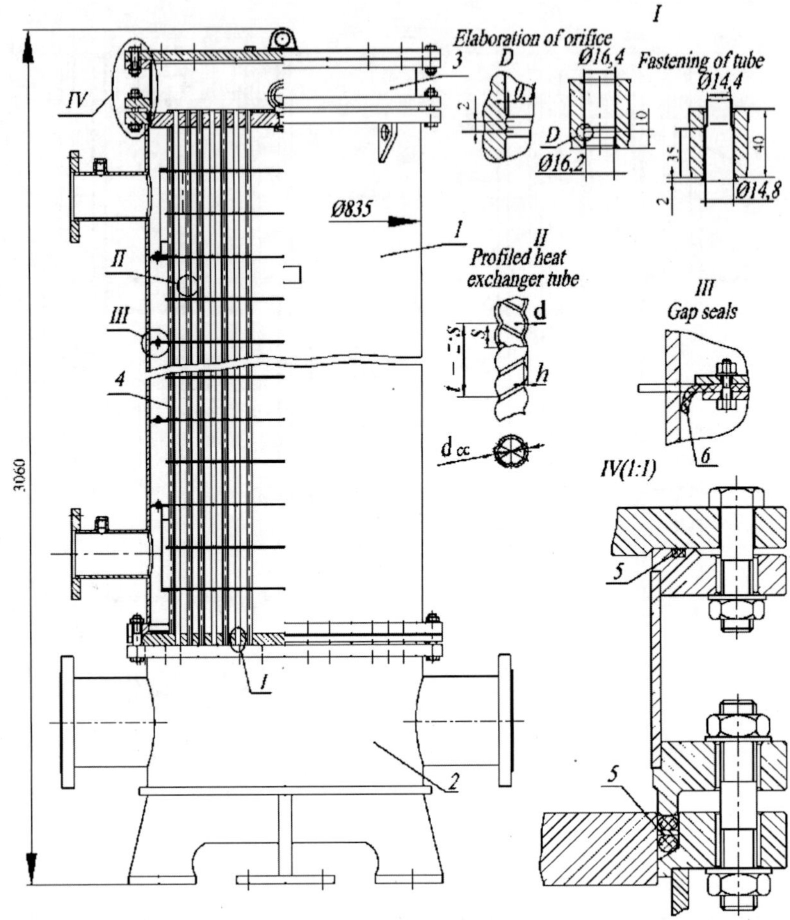

Figure 8. Modernized VVT-100M heat exchanger: 1 — shell; 2 — lower water chamber; 3 — upper water chamber; 4 — tube system; 5 — silicone ring; 6 — teflon seal

The upper water chamber of the heat exchanger has a removable lid for inspection and cleaning of the tubes without breaking the leaktightness of the tube space. For protection from corrosion the inner surfaces of the water chambers are coated with a special enamel.

The main task in modernizing the MB-190-250 oil cooler for the lubrication system of the KhTZ K-500-240 turbine at the Reftinskaya GRES (replacing a worn out unit) was to increase its repairability and reliability while retaining its thermal capacity.

The overall and connector sizes for the MB-190M-250 oil cooler (Fig. 9) are the same as those for the commercially manufactured MB-190-250 oil coolers. In the modernized oil cooler the major components of the water chambers, tube sheets and 16/14.4-mm-diam heat exchanger tubes are made of corrosion resistant 08Cr18Ni10Ti (12Cr18Ni10Ti) alloy. A special method was used for fixing the tubes to the tube sheets (see Fig. 9.) The system for arranging the "disk-and-ring" partitions and the configuration of the tube bundles were optimized taking the task of modernizing the oil cooler into account. (Plain tubes are installed in the oil cooler, since profiled tubes would lead to an unacceptable increase in the hydraulic resistance on the water side and to a limitation on the flow rate of cooling water in the unit.) In addition, special casings are installed in the upper and lower parts of the tube system to provide additional paths for the cooled oil in the tube space, while segmented seals made of teflon tape are mounted in the annular partitions in order to eliminate leakage along the tube bundle. The oil cooler was made more repairable by changing the design configuration for compensating the temperature expansion of the tube system relative to the shell. For this, the upper tube sheet has an elastic diaphragm (membrane) junction with the shell, while the upper water chamber has a removable cover for inspection and cleaning of the oil cooler tubes without breaking the leaktightness of the oil space. The surfaces of the covers and bottoms that are in contact with the cooling water are coated with a special anticorrosion coating.

Reconstruction of the main ÈP-3-25/75 ejectors coolers of the KhTZ K-300-240 turbine and the ÈP-3-50/150 ejectors coolers of the KhTZ K-500-240 turbine at the Reftinskaya GRÈS was carried out in connection with the end of the coolers' service lives and was related to a need to replace tubes made of CuNi5Fe alloy with tubes made of 08Cr18Ni10Ti stainless steel. The arrangement system for the tube partitions in the steam space of the cooler was optimized taking the change in the tube rigidity into account and the heat exchanger surface was increased as well. When the tubes were flared in the tube sheets a special method was used with the orifices pre-flaring. Profiled heat exchanger tubes were installed in the cooler.

The aim in reconstructing the tube bundles for the fire resistant liquid coolers in the regulatory system for LMZ K-300-240 turbines (Sredneural'sk GRES, Konakovo GRES — horizontal tube bundles) and LMZ K-800-240 turbines (Surgut GRES-2, Nizhnevartovsk GRES, Berezovskii GRES — vertical tube bundles) was to replace tube bundles that had gone past their service lifetimes, as well as to increase their thermal capacity and reliability.

The basic components of the cooler (profiled 16/14.4- mm-diam tubes, tube sheets, special casing) were made of corrosion resistant 08Cr18Ni10Ti (12Cr18Ni10Ti) steel. The configuration of the tube bundle is optimized on the basis of a set of thermal-hydraulic calculations. The thermal capacity of the cooler was raised by increasing its heat exchange surface beyond that of the commercial units. The tubes were flared in the tube sheets using special fixing method with the pre-flared orifices in the tube sheet.

Leakage of the fire resistant liquid off the tube bundle was eliminated by installing a special casing at the annular partitions which ensured that it was joined in a leakproof seal to the annular partitions to prevent the "idle" oil leakage.

Modernization was also carried out for water-to-water heat exchangers of OB-700-1 type deployed in a technological subsystem of Perm state district power station. Heat exchangers of OB-700-1 type are vertical shell-and-tube apparatuses of integral design and this considerably reduces the opportunities of diagnostics, maintenance and repair to be performed by operational personnel of state district power station.

Heat exchanger OB-700-1 is installed at Perm state district power station in the closed system of oil (or fire resistant liquid) cooling for K-800-240 turbines, so for the river Kama protection against oil pollution there is accomplished two-loop system of oil cooling. On passing through the oil coolers the cooling water is directed to two OB-700-1 heat exchangers where it is cooled by circulation water flowing inside the tubes.

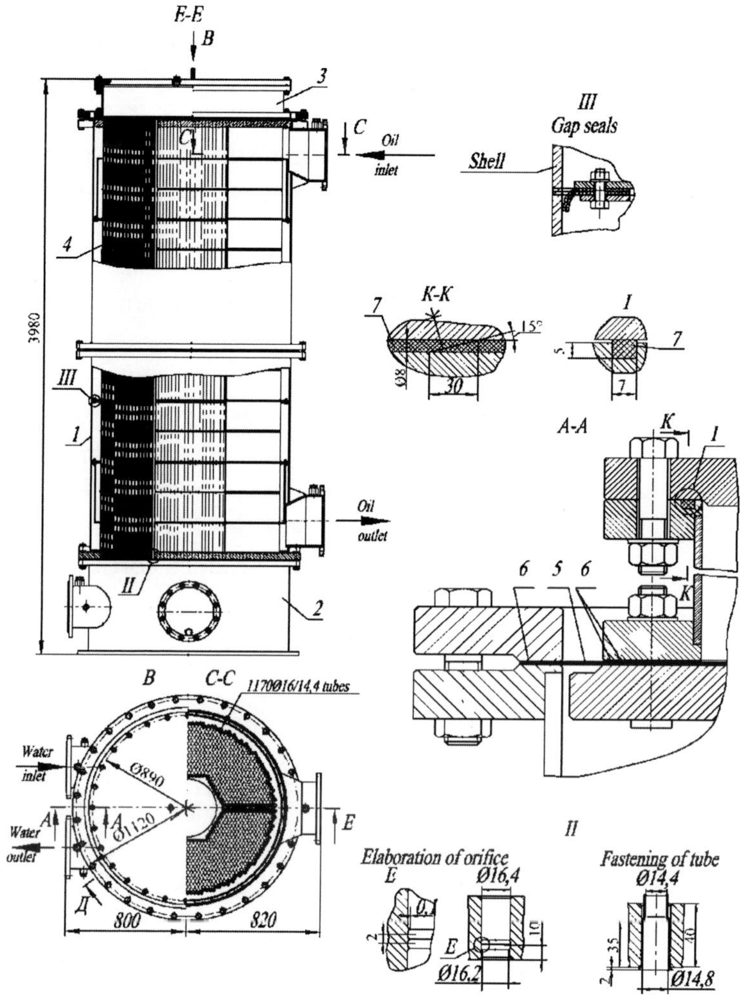

Figure 9. Modernized MB-190M-250 oil cooler: 1 — shell; 2 — lower water chamber; 3 — upper water chamber; 4 — tube system; 5 — diaphragm (membrane); 6 — oil resistant gasket; 7 — silicone ring

The analysis of operation regimes of said heat exchangers showed that during 20 years they were operated with smaller than recommended (nominal) rates of water flow. Because of strong pollution of outside tube surface and significant number of gagged tubes (up to 50%) the apparatuses have high intertube and inner tube hydraulic resistance. Besides significant corrosion deterioration is observed on tube plates.

According to technical project of Perm state district power station it was necessary when performing OB-700-1 modernization to meet the following basic requirements:

- to reduce surface pollution and lower its affect on thermal efficiency of heat exchangers;
- tube bundle should be disassembling to make it possible to disunite it from the shell provided that all the external connecting dimensions are left without changes;
- to raise the heat exchangers reliability and reduce corrosive affect of the cooling mediums;
- to provide an opportunity of hydraulic test of tube system to be carried out without removing it from the shell;
- to optimize heat exchangers thermal and hydraulic characteristics in order to minimize circulating water consumption.

To meet these challenges during modernization lots of optimizing calculations were carried out with reference to heat exchangers operating conditions at Perm state district power station.

At the concept phase of modernization project the calculations were performed of thermal, hydraulic and reliability characteristics for OB-700-1 heat exchangers. For all the apparatus elements operating under pressure 0.5 MPa durability and reliability characteristics were calculated according to actual normative and technical documentation. On the basis of thermal and hydraulic characteristics optimizing calculations and in order to reduce surface pollution an effective cross section of intertube space was increased due to tube bundle configuration change and to employing of intermediate partitions of «disk-and-ring» type. Also heat transfer surface was reduced from 896 m^2 to 480 m^2, demanded operational characteristics being unchanged. Tube system vibration characteristics calculation permitted to choose a number of its constructive parameters such as thickness of intermediate tube partitions, technological annular clearance between tube and tube sheet orifice, distance between intermediate tube sheets.

According to the design project developed by authors the tube system of modernized heat exchangers OB-700M (Fig. 10) employs intermediate tube partitions of «disk-and-ring» type, welded to frame tubes of tube bundle. Absence of leakage between intermediate tube partitions and cylindrical shell is provided by means of special sealing (Fig. 10).

During modernization of OB-700-1 type heat exchangers for Perm state district power station the following technical conceptions have also been accomplished:

- connecting and overall dimensions of the new (modernized) tube system make possible its installation into the existing cooler shell;

- tubes are made of copper-nickel alloy CuNi5Fe possessing high corrosion resistance. The anticorrosive covering is rendered on tube sheets and on internal surfaces of water chambers to increase their corrosion stability;

- for increasing of tube and tube sheet jointing tightness a special way is used employing reliefs rolled on a tube plate aperture surface;

- inward flange (item 5 in Fig. 10) is used which allows after bottom water chamber removal to carry out hydraulic test without tube system lifting out of the shell;

- for bottom water chamber as well as for inward flange sealing a silicon cord is employed enabling repeated disassembly of the chamber without replacement of sealing material;

- hatches of 500 mm in diameter are made in the top water chamber for tube sheets survey and cleaning.

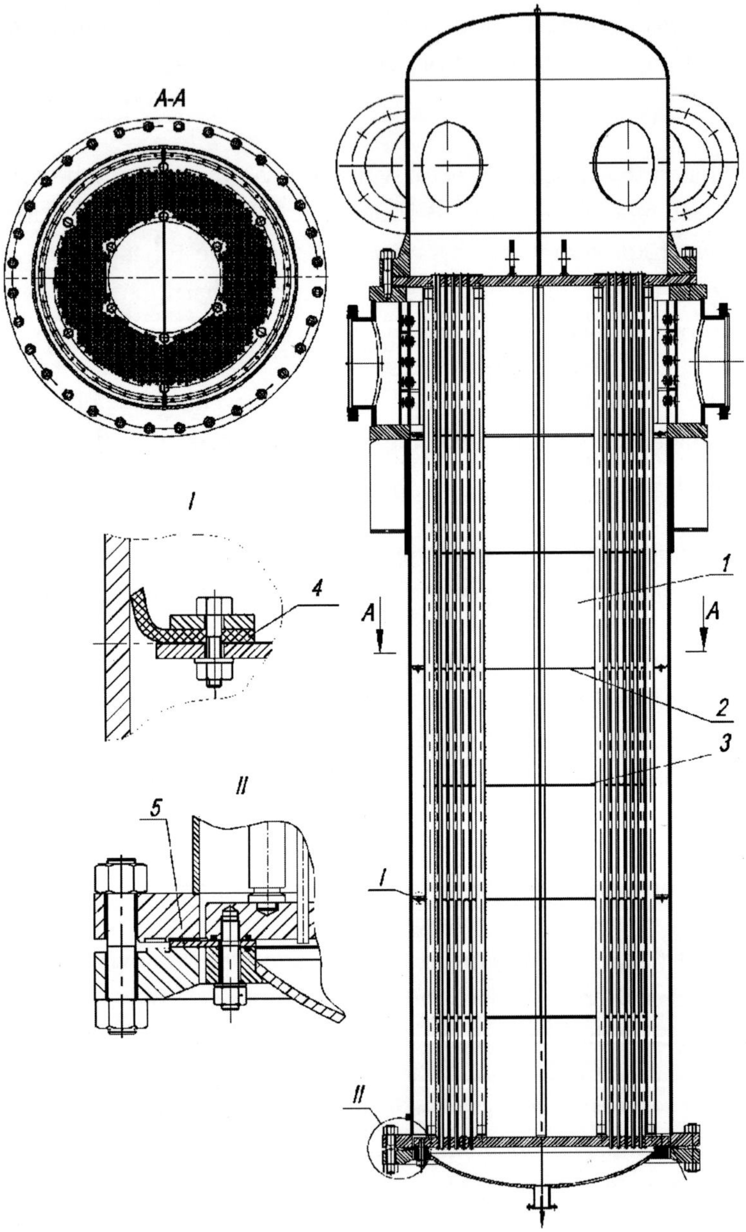

Figure 10. Heat exchanger OB-7OOM. 1 — tube system assembly, 2 — intermediate tube partition of «ring» type, 3 — intermediate tube partition of «disk» type, 4 — special sealing, 5 — inward flange

According to the described concept in 2005 modernization and advanced development were performed of two samples of OB-700M type heat exchangers. After the modernization some starting-up and adjustment tests on OB-700M heat exchangers were carried out at Perm state district power station. For this purpose the heat exchanger was equipped with measuring devices permitting complete thermal balance definition. During the tests the temperatures and flow rates were measured for cooling and cooled water as well. The maximal divergence of heat flow values did not exceed 9.2%.

Test results showed that modernized heat exchangers are capable to function effectively, i.e. to cool the water to temperature demanded by technological process.

The measured values of heat exchanging mediums temperatures are close to designed ones. Thus, for example, the difference between designed and measured water temperature does not exceed 0.6°C.

7. CONCLUSION

The article presents the results of selection and justification of a number of technical solutions for power station heat exchanger modernization. The calculation technique is laid down for oil coolers with TPTs. The results are shown of preproduction tests for the new heat exchangers as well as a number of advanced and refined designs of oil coolers and water heaters.

The heat exchangers of steam turbines modernized according to described concepts have undergone industrial tests and are in successful use at various thermal electric power plants of Russia. Prolonged (up to 20 years) operating experience for more than 500 developed and manufactured apparatuses has confirmed the validity of the technical solutions, as well as high efficiency and operational reliability of these heat exchangers.

REFERENCES

1. Ryabchikov, A.Yu., Aronson, K.E., Brodov, Yu.M., Khaet, S.I., Blinkov, S.N., Zhelonkin, N.V. "Modernization of Heat Exchangers in Steam Turbine Units Taking Features of Their Operation at Specific Thermal Power Plants into Account", 2010. Thermal Power Stations. № 3. p.p. 28—32.

2. Brodov, Yu.M., Aronson, K.E., Ryabchikov, A.Yu., Plotnikov. P.N., Bukhman, G.D. "Retrofitting of Oil Coolers for Steam-Turbine Installations". 1998. Thermal Engineering (English translation of Teploenergetika). № 12. p.p. 1012—1016.

3. Aronson, K.E., Brodov, Yu.M., Ryabchikov, A.Yu., Brezgin, V.I., Brezgin, D.V. "Experience Gained from Development of Modernized Oil Coolers for the Oil Supply Systems Used in 800-MW Turbines", 2009. Thermal Engineering (English translation of Teploenergetika). № 8. p.p. 636—643.

4. Brodov, Yu.M., Gal'perin, L.G., Savel'ev, R.Z., Ryabchikov, A.Yu., "Hydrodynamics and Heat Transfer in Film Condensation of Steam on Vertical Twisted Tubes," 1987. Thermal Engineering (English translation of Teploenergetika), 34 (7), pp. 382—385.

5. Berg, B.V., Aronson, K.E., Brodov, Yu.M., Ryabchikov, A.Yu. "Condensation of Steam in Transverse Flow to a Vertical Tube," 1988. Heat transfer. Soviet research, 20 (4), pp. 472—479.

6. Brodov, Yu.M., Aronson, K.E., Ryabchikov, A.Yu., "Heat Transfer with a Cross Flow of Steam Condensing on Vertical Tubes". 1989. Thermal Engineering (English translation of Teploenergetika), 36 (5), pp. 270—273.

7. Brodov, Yu.M., Aronson, K.E., Ryabchikov, A.Yu., Lokalov, G.A. "An experimental investigation of heat transfer for viscous liquid flowing over bundles of smooth and profiled tubes as applied to turbine unit oil coolers", 2008. Thermal Engineering (English translation of Teploenergetika), 55 (3), pp. 196—200.

Chapter 3

Performance Optimization of Dual Pressure Heat Recovery Steam Generator (HRSG) in the Tropical Rainforest

Sidum Adumene[1], Barinaadaa Thaddeus Lebele-Alawa[2]

[1]Department of Marine Engineering, Rivers State University of Science and Technology, Port Harcourt, Nigeria

[2]Department of Mechanical Engineering, Rivers State University of Science and Technology, Port Harcourt, Nigeria

ABSTRACT

This work evaluates the performance optimization of heat recovery steam generator system in Afam VI power plant, Rivers State. Nigeria. Steady state monitoring and direct collection of data from the plant was performed including logged data for a period of 12 months. The data were ana- lysed using various energy equations. Hysys software was used to model the temperature across the heating surfaces, and MATLAB software was used to determine the heat transfer coefficient, heat duties, steam flow, effectiveness of the HRSG. The optimization technique was carried out by varying the exhaust gas flow, exhaust gas temperature, steam pressure and the theoretical introduction of duct burner for supplementary firing. The results show that between 490°C and 526°C, the percentage increase in the overall heat absorbed in the HRSG is 37.39%. It also show that for an increase in the exhaust gas mass flow by 80 kg/s, the steam generation increase by 19.29% and 18.18% for the low and high pressure levels respectively. The overall result indicates an improvement in the HRSG energy efficiency and steam generation. As the exhaust gas mass flow and temperature increases, the steam generation and system effectiveness greatly improved under the various considerations, which satisfy the research objective.

KEYWORDS

HRSG, Effectiveness, Exhaust Gas Flow, Exhaust Gas Temperature, Steam Flow, Heat Duty

1. INTRODUCTION

Heat Recovery Steam Generator is the standard term used for a steam generator producing steam by cooling hot gases. Heat recovery system is obviously a very desirable energy source, since the product is available almost operating cost-free and increases the efficiency of the cycle in which it is placed, either for steam generation or for incremental power generation. Heat recovery steam generator can regain energy from waste-gas streams, such as incinerator gases, furnace effluents or most commonly the exhaust of a gas turbine.

In modern operation of heat transfer equipment such as heat recovery steam generator (HRSG), the exit gas temperature determines the amount of energy extracted from the flue gas stream of the gas turbine. This is an indication of the HRSG performance. Therefore, efforts are often made to lower the stack temperature as much as possible taken into consideration cost effectiveness and low temperature corrosion. The modifications of a single pressure HRSG to multi-pressures have also improve the energy efficiency of the heat recovery steam generator unit [1] . Heat recovery steam generators can be made up from a number of components, including evaporators, economizers, superheaters, reheater, integral deaerators and preheaters. Each of the heat transfer sections performs a specific task, and the one that is selected are generally dictated by the required steam conditions for process use or power generation, the type of power generation and/or the efficiency requirement, weighed against HRSG costs.

Heat recovery steam generator evaporator sections act to vaporize water and produce steam in one component. A bank of finned tubes is extended through the gas turbine's exhaust gas path from a steam drum (top) to a lower (mud) drum. The gas turbine is a very satisfactory means of producing mechanical power [2] [3] . Feed water is carefully supplied at the appropriate pressure to the upper drum below the water level, and circulates from the upper to lower drum, back to the upper drum by convection within the finned tube.

The economizers are serpentine finned-tube gas-to water heat exchangers, and add sensible heat (preheat) to the feed water, prior to its entry into the steam drum of the evaporator. Different heat transfer applications require different types of hardware and different configurations of heat transfer equipment [4] . In single pressure HRSG, the economizer will be located directly downstream (with respect to gas flow) of the evaporator section. In multi-pressure unit, the various economizer sections may be split, and be located in several locations both upstream and downstream of the evaporators. The superheater is a separate serpentine tube heat exchanger which is located upstream (with respect to gas flow) of the associated evaporator. This component adds sensible heat to the dry steam, superheating it beyond the saturation temperature.

In gas turbine heat recovery steam generator, its performance is dependent on the gas turbine exit temperature, inlet gas temperature, feed water temperature and steam pressure. The low exhaust gas temperature generates less steam on unit gas mass basis in the HRSG evaporator unit [5].

The HRSG is widely used equipment in various industries to which include process, power generation, and petroleum industry. The development of HRSG as a component part of the combined power cycle and cogeneration has improved power production and enhanced costs effectiveness within the sector. Energy and materials saving consideration, as well as economical consideration have stimulated the high demand for high efficient HRSG.

Meeting the growing requirement for cost-effective and undisturbed operation in today's economical environment drives power plants to reach for the best possible performance and higher availability. Power plants can no longer afford to operate without knowing the exact HRSG performances at all times or without taking immediate actions when problems occur. Even minor decreases in the HRSG efficiency and performance can cause significant financial and energy losses during the production phase of the plant. This called for several optimization techniques to maintain energy efficiency of the HRSG.

The hierarchical strategy implied for optimization of the whole combine-cycle power plant is as follows optimization of the gas turbine cycle, optimization of the operation parameters of the HRSG, and detailed optimization of the single heat exchanger section in the HRSG. One of the suggested ways to reach theoretically maximum efficiency is by increasing the turbine inlet temperature [6] . This requires a highly advanced cooling system to cool down the blades of the gas turbine. With existing technology levels, focus can be fixed on the HRSG, and its operating parameters to improve the efficiency of the combined-cycle plants. Optimization of the operating parameters of HRSG is the first step in the optimum design of the plants as stated in Franco and Russo [7] .

Reddy et al. [8] suggested a second law analysis of the heat recovery steam generator. This method is basically used to optimize and design various thermal units by minimizing the entropy generation in the unit. The operating parameters are non-dimensionalized, and an equation for the entropy generation number helps to study the effect of the dimensionless operating parameter.

Casarosa et al. [1] applied thermodynamic optimization technique which considered only the irreversibility due to temperature difference between hot and cold streams. Although this method did not apply any constraint on the cost of the HRSG, and on the surface area, it still gives a rough idea about the selection of operating parameters for the HRSG.

Ongiro et al. [6] developed mathematical models to simulate and study the performance of the HRSG. Subhramanyam et al. [9] considered the computational complexity of the HRSG and how it could be model. The proposed method calculates the velocity and temperature fields by discretisation and the solution of conservation equation derived for a HRSG of particular geometry and duty.

Dumont and Heyen [10] suggested a mathematical model for modeling and designing a once-through heat recovery steam generator. In a conventional boiler, each tube plays a well defined role like water preheating, vaporization and superheating. Empirical equations are readily available to predict the average heat transfer in each region which is not the case in a once through boiler. This increases the mathematical complexity as well as the number of equations to be solved for modeling these boilers.

The even increasing technology is the field of HRSG, as a potential option to improve the efficiency of the system. This necessitates having a numerical flow model with the capability to simulate combustion and the flow in the HRSG model, as well as the flexibility to simulate those for different designs with acceptable accuracy.

Valdes et al. [11] performed a thermo economic optimization of combined cycle gas turbine power plants using a genetic algorithm. They proposed two different objective functions; aimed at minimizing the cost of production per unit electricity and maximizing the annual cash flow.

Mohammad et al. [12] performed an exergetic and economic evaluation of the effect of HRSG configurations on the performance of combined cycle power plants. Their result showed that an increase in the number of pressure levels affects the exergy destruction rate in the HRSG.

Attala et al. [13] optimize a dual pressure level combined cycle gas turbine. They worked with a simulation program that included three models; the first simulates the cycle, the second evaluates the thermodynamic and thermo-economic parameters and the third is the optimization model.

Subrahmanyam et al. [9] discussed about the various factors affecting the HRSG design for achieving the highest combined cycle efficiency with cheaper, economical and competitive designs and with the highest requirement to meet the shorter deliveries.

Casarosa et al. [1] determine the operating parameters using both thermodynamic and thermo-economic function by analytical and numerical (mathematical) methods.

Reddy et al. [8] applied second law analysis for a waste heat recovery steam generator which consists of an economizer, an evaporator and a superheater. Introducing multiple pressure steam generation in the HRSG of a combined power plant improves the performance of the plant than that of a corresponding single pressure system

Bassily [14] modeled a dual and triple pressure reheat combined cycle with a preset for pinch points, the temperature difference for superheat approach, the steam turbine inlet temperature at steam turbine and the outlet without a dearator in steam bottoming cycle. Srinvivas [15] suggested an improved location for a deaerator in a triple pressure HRSG.

Mohagheghi and Shayegan [16] developed computer code to examine the competence for a variety of types of HRSG, from the thermodynamic optimization of the HRSG, they obtained a high rate of generating power in the steam cycle. Zhixin et al. [17] designed a condition of a single pressure waste heat recovery system when the temperature or flow rate of exhaust gas fluctuates; the results show that systems designed at the upper boundary of fluctuation range of exhaust gas could generate more power.

Manassaldi et al. [18] proposed a methodology which applied a mixed non linear program model to obtain the design according to their criteria; Net power maximization, the ratio between net power and material weight maximization, and the net heat transfer maximization.

Alus and Petrovic [19] performed an optimization of a triple pressure combined cycle gas turbine (CCGT). The objective of the optimization was to minimize the production cost of electricity in the CCGT power plant based on energetic and economic analysis. Ghazl et al. [20] carried out an optimization study to find the best design parameters (high and low degree pressures, steam mass flow rates, pinch point temperature difference and the duct burner fuel consumption flow rate) of a dual pressure combined cycle power. Total cost per unit of produced steam energy is defined as the objective function.

Vytla [21] performed a CFD modeling of the HRSG and its components using fluent. He focused on how CFD analysis can be used to assess the impact of the gas-side flow on the HRSG performance and identify design modification to improve the performance

In this work a sensitivity analysis and parametric modulation were carried out and the modeling of the HRSG using a computer program was created to produce the equation that can predict the functionality and optimization of the HRSG.

The study area is the Niger Delta area of Nigeria which lies between latitudes 4°N and 6°N, and longitude 5°E and 8°E. The vegetation of the area is equatorial rain forest. There are basically two seasons—the wet (April to September) and the dry (October to March). However, rain fall throughout the year. The mean annual rainfall in the area is between 200 mm in the North and 400 mm in the South of the region. The mean daily temperature of the region varies slightly from 27°C to 30°C all the year round. The maximum and minimum temperatures are 40°C and 20°C respectively. The relative humidity varies between a minimum of 70% and a maximum of 90% [22] [23].

2. MATERIAL AND METHODS

Data collected from the Afam VI HRSG was done by direct observation from the monitoring screen of the automated system called human machine interface (HMI), including data from log books and manufacturers manual as shown in Table 1 and Table 2. Such parameters include temperature of the flue gas, feed water pressure, mass flow rate, and ambient operating condition of the gas turbine. The Data obtained for this analysis are from the Afam VI power plant, Port Harcourt, Rivers State Nigeria. The design specification of the gas turbine and the dual heat recovery steam generator is shown below.

Technical Data of the Gas Turbine

Model: GT13E2

Power output (gross) 160 MW

Compressor pressure ratio 14.1

Mass flow rates (kg/s) 500

Efficiency (LHV), % 35.7

Heat Rate (kJ/kWh) 10,084

Isentropic Efficiency % 86

Natural Gas (LHV) 46798 kJ/kg

Combustor/burner Type Annular/EV

Nox (at 15%O_2, dy), ppmv <2

Technical Data of the HRSG

MCR (LP) 100 kg/s

S. H Steam Pressure 8 bar

S. H Steam Temperature 300°C

MCR (HP) 250 kg/s

S. H Steam Pressure 100 bar

S. H Steam Temperature 600°C

To predict the optimum performance of the HRSG, energy conservation principle is employed, hence the use of energy models to analyze the operating parameter of the HRSG is made. The total heat transfer may be related with its governing (operating) parameter. Hysys was used in simulating the temperature drop across the heating element in the HRSG, and MATLAB software was used to analysed the performance for optimization.

2.1. Heat Transfer Coefficients and Effectiveness Calculation Model

This method is based on heat transfer coefficients to obtain the heat transfer area for each heat exchanger in high and low pressure level of the dual pressure HRSG. The effectiveness of the heating surfaces in the HRSG is also calculated with Equations (3), (4).

The overall heat transfer coefficient U by the total heat exchange area is calculated as follows (Ahmadi et al., [24]):

$$UA_T = \frac{Q}{(f \cdot LMTD)};\ A_T = A_{hrsg} = \sum_{SH} A_{SH} + \sum_{EVA} A_{EVA} + \sum_{EC} A_{EC} \tag{1}$$

The logarithmic mean temperature difference is estimated from the following equation;

$$LMTD = \left[\frac{(T_{gi} - T_{we}) - (T_{ge} - T_{wi})}{\ln\left(\frac{T_{gi} - T_{we}}{T_{ge} - T_{wi}}\right)} \right] \tag{2}$$

Table 1. Average operating parameters of the HRSG.

Time	LP Section					HP Section					
	FW Pres. Bar	FW Flow, kg/s	Stm Pres. Bar	Stm Flow kg/s	Stm Temp, °C	FW Pres. Bar	FW Flow, kg/s	Stm Pres. Bar	Stm flow, kg/s	Stm Temp, °C	Stack Temp, °C
0:00	11	57	4.6	56	256	128	191	86	189	506	106
2:00	12	57	4.6	56	256	130	190	86	189	504	104
4:00	11	58	4.6	55	256	126	191	86	189	505	107
6:00	12	56	4.6	56	256	124	192	86	189	504	107
8:00	11	57	4.6	55	256	128	185	86	189	516	106
10:00	12	57	4.8	56	256	127	189	86	189	502	109
12:00	10	57	4.6	57	256	125	188	86	189	501	101
14:00	11	58	4.6	57	256	126	192	86	190	509	112
16:00	11	58	4.6	57	256	127	193	86	190	508	112
18:00	11	59	4.6	57	256	126	192	86	190	505	111
20:00	11	59	4.7	57	256	125	192	86	190	504	112
22:00	11	57	4.6	57	256	126	192	86	190	505	112

Table 2. Average operating parameters of the gas turbine.

Time	Amb. Temp, °C	Pres. Ratio, Bar	Amb Hum. %	Fuel gas flow, kg/s	Air mass flow, kg/s	Power factor	Exhaust Temp, °C	Exh. Mass flow, kg/s	Power output, MW
0:00	26.7	12.3	65	7.9	437.1	0.97	526	445	133
2:00	27.8	12.3	66	7.9	432.1	0.95	528	440	133
4:00	27.5	12.4	58	7.9	432.1	0.96	528	440	133
6:00	27.3	12.3	59	7.8	430.2	0.97	529	438	131
8:00	27.1	12.3	53	7.8	437.2	0.96	529	445	131
10:00	29.3	11.9	61	7.8	424.2	0.94	528	432	132
12:00	31.9	11.5	47	7.9	422.1	0.95	526	430	132
14:00	33.5	10.1	38	7.9	420.1	0.96	523	428	130
16:00	32.4	11.4	52	7.9	422.1	0.96	523	430	132
18:00	30.6	11.9	59	7.9	427.1	0.95	525	435	133
20:00	28.9	12.1	65	7.9	432.1	0.96	525	440	133

$$\varepsilon_{HRSG_{LP\ \text{components}}} = \frac{\text{Actual heat transfer rates}}{\text{Max. possible heat transfer rate}} = \frac{Q}{Q_{max}}$$
$$= \frac{m_s\left(h_{out} - h_{in}\right)LP}{m_g C_{pg}\left(T_{gin} - T_{gout}\right)} = \frac{m_s C_{pw}\left(T_{wout} - T_{win}\right)LP}{m_g C_{pg}\left(T_{gin} - T_{gout}\right)} \quad (3)$$

$$\varepsilon_{HRSG_{HP\ \text{components}}} = \frac{\text{Actual heat transfer rates}}{\text{Max. possible heat transfer rate}} = \frac{Q}{Q_{max}}$$
$$= \frac{m_s\left(h_{out} - h_{in}\right)HP}{m_g C_{pg}\left(T_{gin} - T_{gout}\right)} = \frac{m_s C_{pw}\left(T_{wout} - T_{win}\right)HP}{m_g C_{pg}\left(T_{gin} - T_{gout}\right)} \quad (4)$$

2.2. Heat Duty Calculation Model

The first step to simulate the HRSG performance is to balance the mass and energy transfer between the hot and cold streams (gas side and water/steam side) on different heat exchanger when the designed parameters (the flow rate, temperature, pressure of superheated steam and outlet temp of the exhaust gases, the heat duty) can be obtained (Ahmadi P. and Dincer I. [25]). The heat duty of the HRSG elements and the exhaust gas were modeled using the below energy equations.

Energy balance can be expressed as follows;

$$Q_T = \left[Q_{SH} + Q_{EVA} + Q_{EC}\right]_{HP} + \left[Q_{SH} + Q_{EVA} + Q_{EC}\right]_{LP} \quad (5)$$

$$\left(Q_{SH}\right)_{HP} = Q_{SH1_{HP}} + Q_{SH2_{HP}} + Q_{SH3_{HP}} \quad (6)$$

$$Q_{SH1_{HP}} = m_s = m_g C_{pg}\left(T_{g1} - T_{g2}\right) \quad (7)$$

$$Q_{SH2_{HP}} = m_s\left(h_{15} - h_{14}\right)_{HP} = m_g C_{pg}\left(T_{g2} - T_{g3}\right) \quad (8)$$

$$Q_{SH3_{HP}} = m_s \left(h_{14} - h_{13} \right)_{HP} = m_g C_{pg} \left(T_{g3} - T_{g4} \right) \tag{9}$$

$$\left(Q_{EVA} \right)_{HP} = m_s \left(h_{12} - h_{11} \right)_{HP} = m_g C_{pg} \left(T_{g4} - T_{g5} \right) \tag{10}$$

$$\left(Q_{EC} \right)_{HP} = Q_{EC1_{HP}} + Q_{EC2_{HP}} + Q_{EC3_{HP}} \tag{11}$$

$$Q_{EC1_{HP}} = m_w \left(h_{10} - h_9 \right)_{HP} = m_g C_{pg} \left(T_{g5} - T_{g6} \right) \tag{12}$$

$$Q_{EC2_{HP}} = m_w \left(h_9 - h_8 \right)_{HP} = m_g C_{pg} \left(T_{g6} - T_{g7} \right) \tag{13}$$

$$Q_{EC3_{HP}} = m_w \left(h_8 - h_7 \right)_{HP} = m_g C_{pg} \left(T_{g7} - T_{g8} \right) \tag{14}$$

$$\left(Q_{SH} \right)_{LP} = m_s \left(h_6 - h_5 \right)_{LP} = m_g C_{pg} \left(T_{g8} - T_{g9} \right) \tag{15}$$

$$\left(Q_{EVA} \right)_{LP} = m_s \left(h_4 - h_3 \right)_{LP} = m_g C_{pg} \left(T_{g9} - T_{g10} \right) \tag{16}$$

$$\left(Q_{EC} \right)_{LP} = m_w \left(h_2 - h_1 \right)_{LP} = m_g C_{pg} \left(T_{g10} - T_{g11} \right) \tag{17}$$

The temperature of the gas leaving the high pressure evaporator

$$T_{11} = T_{sHP} + T_{PP} \tag{18}$$

where T_s; is the saturation steam temperature at high pressure level.

Also the temperature of water into evaporator is $T_{11} = T_{sHP} - T_{AP}$

2.3. Steam Generation Calculation Model

$$m_{sHP} = \frac{m_g C_{pg} \left(T_{g1} - T_{g8}\right)}{\left(h_{ss} - h_s\right)_{HP}} \tag{19}$$

$$m_{sLP} = \frac{m_g C_{pg} \left(T_{g8} - T_{g11}\right)}{\left(h_{ss} - h_s\right)_{LP}} \tag{20}$$

3. RESULTS AND DISCUSSIONS

The result from the direct observation and measurement of the operating parameters of the HRSG, including data from the log book for the period under consideration are recorded in Table 1. These give detail of an average daily reading recorded from the human machine interface (HMI). The data include the feed water pressure, feed water temperature, feed water mass flow, steam pressure, steam temperature, stack temperature and steam mass flow for the low and high pressure levels, while Table 2 show the average operating data of the gas turbine plant for the period under consideration. The data measured include the ambient temperature, pressure, humidity, fuel gas flow rate, exhaust gas mass flow.

The Experiment platform was done through direct data monitoring on the human machine interface (HMI). See Appendix I for the experimental screen shot.

Hysys simulator was used to model the temperature gradient across the various heat exchanging units of the HRSG after several iterations. This gave the preliminary process of flow diagram, mass and energy balance at various gas turbine exhaust gas temperature and mass flow rate. For the normal operating mode; part load and base load, Tables 3-7 gives the heat exchange properties and performance detail.

A numerical method (MATLAB software) was also used to simulate the steam pressure, temperature, steam quality, effectiveness, and heat flux distribution for predicting the performance of the HRSG.

To calculate the performance of the heat exchangers in the HRSG in MATLAB, optimum performance was determined by sensitivity analyses of the varied parameters.

The optimum mode was modeled via sensitivity study by varying exhaust gas temperature and mass flow, steam pressure, steam flow from measurement.

Tables 3-7 show the results of the modeled equations using MATLAB program. The model gave the heat duty, log mean temperature difference, the heat transfer coefficient for the heating surfaces of the HRSG at exhaust gas temperature of 490˚C, 500˚C, 510˚C, 520˚C, and 526˚C respectively.

The results in Tables 3-7 were plotted as shown in Figures 1-3. The figures show the behavior of the heating elements in the HRSG. The heat duty of the element is plotted at different gas turbine exhaust gas temperature as shown in Figure 1. This give the various heat absorbed capacity of the heating surfaces of the HRSG. Figure 2 gave the heat exchange trend within the HRSG system, while Figure 3 show the plot of the total heat exchange at different exhaust gas temperature of the gas turbine.

Tables 8-11 show the results of the simulation for the exhaust gas temperature, HRSG effectiveness, steam generation analysis. The simulations were done by varying the parameters at various operating conditions. The modeled functions were the effectiveness at different steam pressure, effectiveness at different exhaust gas temperature, steam generation at different, exhaust gas flow and different steam pressure.

Figure 1, Figure 2 and Tables 3-7 show the absorbing capacity of the various heating element of the HRSG. The results give the amount of heat exchange in the superheater, economizer, and evaporator in both the low pressure and high pressure sections respectively. The plots show that HPSH2 had the highest heat exchange when the gas turbine exhaust gas temperature is 526˚C. At the exhaust gas temperature of 500˚C, the HPEVA had the highest heat exchange. The HPEVA give the same result when the exhaust gas temperature was at 520˚C and 490˚C reflectively. While when the exhaust gas temperature was 510˚C, the highest heat exchange occurred in the LPEVA.

Table 3. HRSG performance analysis at exhaust gas temperature of 490˚C.

Surface	Gas in ˚C	Gas out ˚C	Water/Steam in, ˚C	Water/Steam out, ˚C	Heat Duty KW	LMTD	UA KW/K
HP SH1	490	477	432	470	6824	24.97	317.82
HP SH2	477	461	400	432	8398	52.59	185.67
HP SH3	461	431	349	400	15740	70.98	257.84
HP EVA	431	360	336	349	37270	47.21	918.05
HP EC1	360	344	302	336	8399	32.17	303.63
HP EC2	344	314	278	302	15750	38.92	470.52
HP EC3	314	298	224	278	8399	52.71	185.19
LP SH	298	239	184	228	30970	62.2	578.98
LP EVA	239	182	115	184	29920	60.81	572.19
LP EC	183	129	80	115	27820	57.53	562.28

Table 4. HRSG performance analysis at exhaust gas temperature of 500˚C.

Surface	Gas in ˚C	Gas out ˚C	Water/Steam in, ˚C	Water/Steam out, ˚C	Heat Duty KW	LMTD	UA KW/K
HP SH1	500	460	370	450	20990	68.06	107.63
HP SH2	460	436	356	370	12590	84.9	172.43
HP SH3	436	390	330	356	24150	67.29	417.33
HP EVA	450	395	284	330	28350	49.33	668.31
HP EC1	390	336	254	284	20990	38.77	509.66
HP EC2	336	298	224	254	16790	41.97	465.19
HP EC3	298	264	200	224	14690	37.97	449.93
LP SH	264	236	150	194	24670	45.88	625.19
LP EVA	236	200	120	150	24150	46.41	605.05
LP EC	163	119	85	120	13120	38.32	398.07

Table 5. HRSG performance analysis at exhaust gas temperature of 510˚C.

Surface	Gas in ˚C	Gas out ˚C	Water/Steam in, ˚C	Water/Steam out, ˚C	Heat Duty KW	LMTD	UA KW/K
HP SH1	510	455	435	503	28871	12.38	271.1
HP SH2	455	439	406	435	8398.7	25.96	376.19
HP SH3	439	414	358	406	13123	43.49	350.86
HP EVA	414	388	336	358	13648	53.98	294.02
HP EC1	388	366	304	336	11548	56.85	236.18
HP EC2	366	314	266	304	27296	54.71	580.23
HP EC3	314	288	192	266	13648	69.25	229.17
LP SH	288	254	164	220	17847	78.49	264.41
LP EVA	254	170	136	164	44093	57.53	891.24
LP EC	170	120	90	132	26246	33.84	901.78

Table 6. HRSG performance analysis at exhaust gas temperature of 520˚C.

Surface	Gas in ˚C	Gas out ˚C	Water/Steam in, ˚C	Water/Steam out, ˚C	Heat Duty KW	LMTD	UA KW/K
HP SH1	520	482	449	504	19947	23.48	987.69
HP SH2	482	417	385	449	34120	32.49	1220.8
HP SH3	417	387	319	385	15748	47.76	383.41
HP EVA	387	326	256	319	32020	69	539.64
HP EC1	326	298	216	256	14698	75.84	225.35
HP EC2	298	282	178	216	28398	92.57	105.5
HP EC3	282	266	148	178	34199	44.2	110.48
LP SH	266	245	189	235	15223	42.28	418.71
LP EVA	245	180	118	189	34120	58.95	673.03
LP EC	180	131	70	118	25721	61.5	486.32

Table 7. HRSG performance analysis at exhaust gas temperature of 526˚C.

Surface	Gas in ˚C	Gas out ˚C	Water/Steam in, ˚C	Water/Steam out, ˚C	Heat Duty KW	LMTD	UA KW/K
HP SH1	526	500	460	490	13640	26.88	590.06
HP SH2	500	486	420	460	52489	51.92	162.35
HP SH3	486	450	375	420	18897	70.41	312.1
HP EVA	450	395	350	375	28871	58.72	571.63
HP EC1	395	340	294	330	28871	54.95	441.62
HP EC2	340	306	266	294	17847	42.93	483.4
HP EC3	306	285	189	266	11023	63.97	200.38
LP SH	285	250	180	240	18372	56.58	377.55
LP EVA	250	165	135	180	44618	64.87	799.76
LP EC	165	116	70	135	25721	57.98	515.86

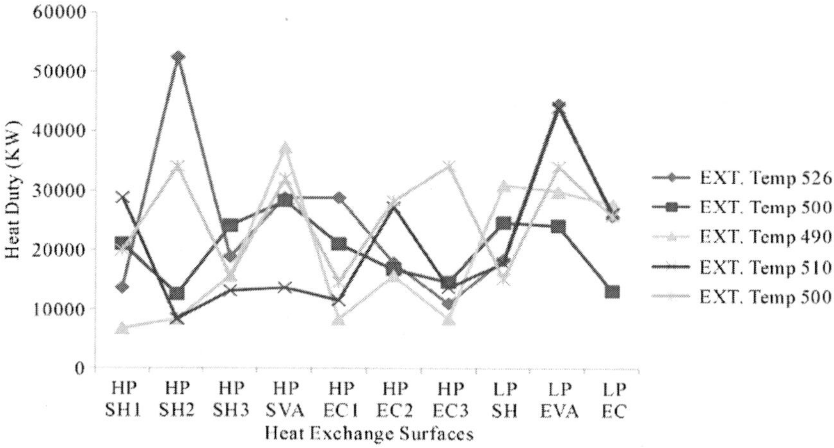

Figure 1. Absorbed heat distribution profile across the heating surfaces.

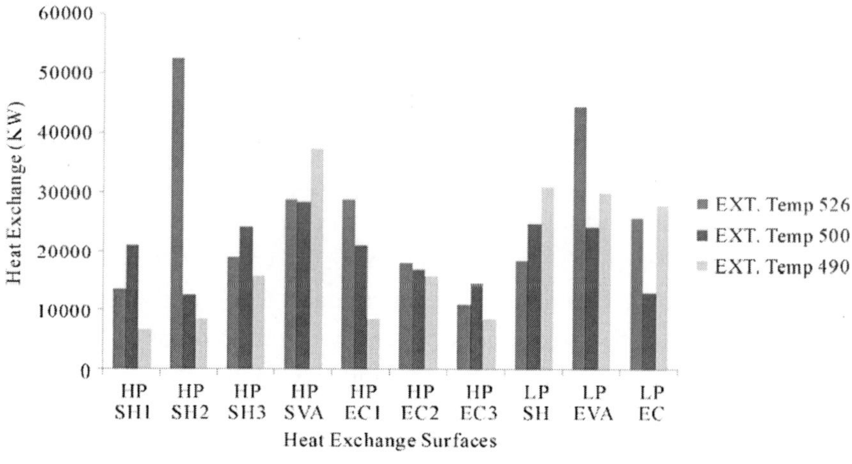

Figure 2. Absorbed heat across the heating element of the HRSG.

From Figure 3, the amount of heat absorbed increased as the exhaust gas increased. This shows that the temperature gradient of the exhaust gas of the gas turbine imparted greatly on the energy efficiency of the HRSG. The result shows that between 490°C and 526°C, the temperature difference was 36°C and there is a percentage increase in the heat absorbed of about 37.39%. This represents an increase in heat absorption of 1.04% for every 1°C increase in the gas turbine exhaust gas temperature at constant flow.

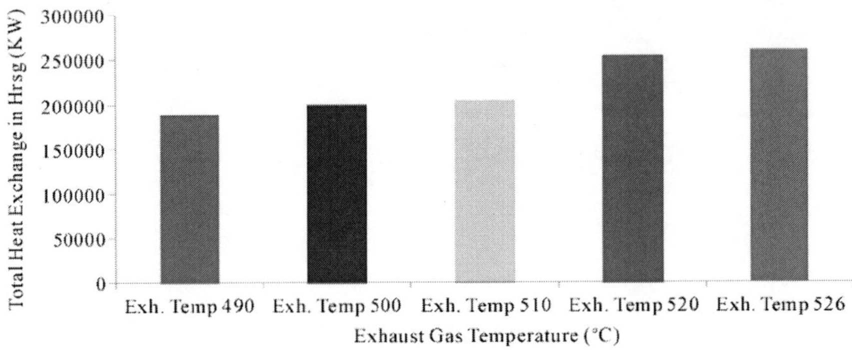

Figure 3. Total heat exchange in HRSG at different gas turbine exhaust temperature.

Table 11 and Figure 4, Figure 5, showed the steam generated by varying the steam pressure at constant steam temperature and exhaust gas mass flow for the LP and HP sections. The LP steam pressure variation was carried out at 256°C and 470 kg/s, while the HP was done at 510°C and 470 kg/s. The result show that as the steam pressure increased from 4 bar to 12 bar for the LP and 80 bar to 120 bar for the HP, there exist a percentage increase in the steam generation of about 0.21% and 0.07% for the LP and HP respectively. This analysis represent that for every 1°C increase in the steam pressure under the various consideration, the steam generation increased by 0.11% and 0.30% for the LP and HP section respectively.

It also shows the effectiveness of the HRSG LP and HP at different steam generation. The result indicated that for every 40 kg/s increase in the steam flow, the system effectiveness improved by about 13.3% in the LP section. The HP section shows that as the steam flow increased by 110 kg/s, the effectiveness of the system improved by 0.18%. The research indicated that the system effectiveness for the low pressure and high pressure level at different steam pressure. The result shows that as the steam pressure increased by 1bar, the effectiveness of the system decrease slightly by about 0.073%.

Table 8. Exhaust gas temp and turbine work at different pressure ratio.

Pressure Ratio	TIT avg. °C	Exh. Gas Temp °C	Turbine Work (MW)
11	970	579	210
12	970	568	216
13	970	559	221
14	970	550	225
15	970	543	229

Table 9. HRSG effectiveness at different exhaust gas temperature.

HRSG Heating Surfaces	Effectiveness			
	526°C	520°C	510°C	490°C
HPSH1	0.7135	0.7769	0.8072	0.9743
HPSH2	0.6727	0.8877	0.7963	0.5591
HPSH3	0.5454	0.9061	0.7973	0.6126
HPEVA	0.3364	0.647	0.3795	0.1841
HPEC1	0.4795	0.4848	0.5725	0.7887
HPEC2	0.5091	0.426	0.5113	0.4892
HPEC3	0.8854	0.3012	0.8161	0.8072
LPSH	0.252	0.2635	0.1992	0.1702
LPEVA	0.1726	0.2465	0.1046	0.2454
LPEC	0.2091	0.1924	0.2315	0.1729

Table 9 and Figure 6 showed the effectiveness of the heating surface at different gas turbine exhaust gas temperatures. It indicates that at 526°C, the HPSH1 show the highest effectiveness in heat exchange. At 520°C,

HPSH3 effectiveness was about 91%, while at 510˚C and 490˚C, HPSH1 gave about 80% and 97% respectively. This represents that the heat exchange efficiency could be optimum at higher exhaust gas temperature and higher mass flow.

Table 10. HRSG effectiveness at different steam pressure.

Steam Pressures bar		Effectiveness	
LP (250˚C)	HP (510˚C)	LP	HP
4	80	0.5397	0.3763
6	100	0.5389	0.3717
8	120	0.5373	0.3670
10	140	0.5356	0.3621
12	160	0.5339	0.3571

Table 11. Steam generation at different steam.

Pressure under constant Exh. Temp & Flow				
Steam Pressure, bar		Exh. Gas Mass Flow	Steam Flow, kg/s	
LP@256	HP@510		LP	HP
4	80	470	65.47	178.63
6	90	470	65.67	180.92
8	100	470	65.88	184.31
10	110	470	66.09	187.34
12	120	470	66.31	190.54

The results of the analysis were compared with the work of Mohammad et al. [12] and its show a similar trend in the temperature profile for both the gas-side and the water/steam side. Although Mohammad et al. [12] did not analysed the effectiveness of the heating surfaces and steam flow. Further comparison of simulated result was made with the work of Vytla [20] , where fluent was used to analysed the HRSG performance with 21 heating surfaces (heat Exchangers). The temperature profile of the gas-side of this work follows the trend with minimal variation.

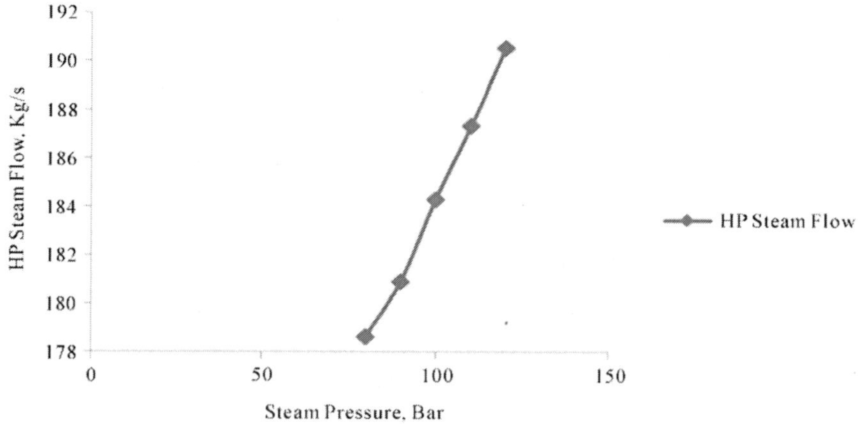

Figure 4. HP Steam generation at different steam pressure at constant exhaust gas flow.

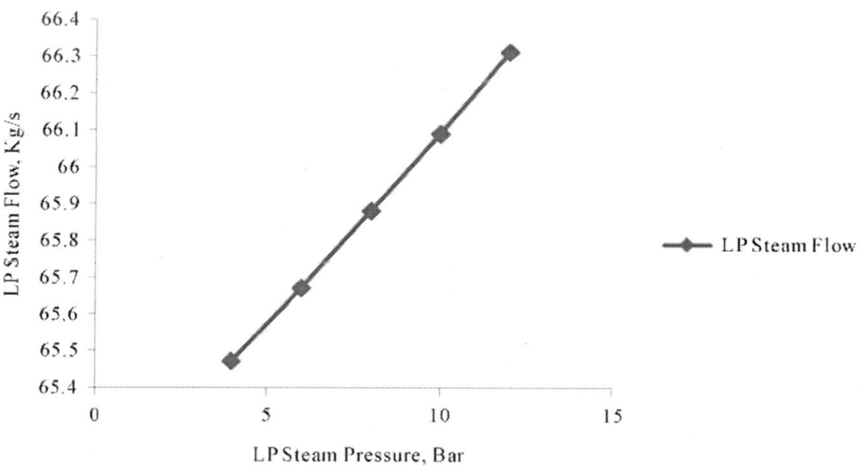

Figure 5. LP Steam generation at different steam pressure at constant exhaust gas flow.

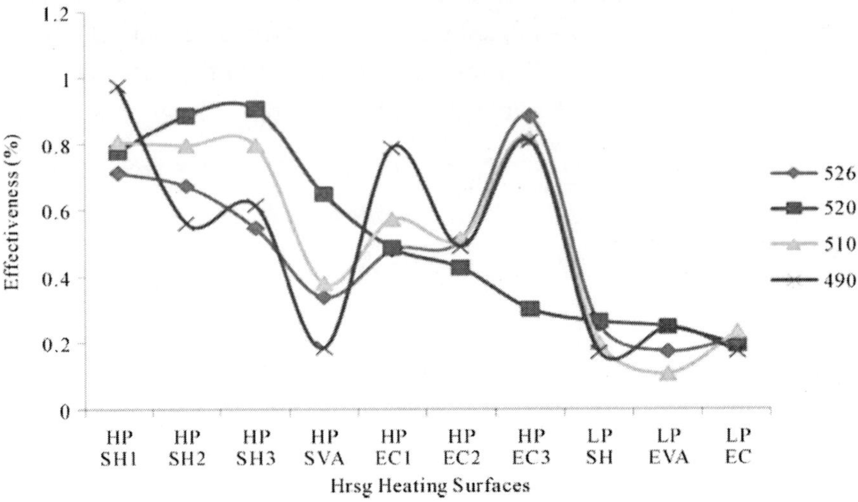

Figure 6. Effectiveness of the heating surfaces of the HRSG at different exhaust temperatures.

4. CONCLUSIONS

The work revealed the various parameters and energy based equations used in assessing the heat duty and effectiveness of the HRSG at various operating condition of the gas turbine exhaust in order to sustain its performance.

The sensitivity study carried out by varying the operating parameters, such as mass flow, steam pressure, exhaust gas temperature was analysed and the impact on the HRSG performance evaluated. The results for both the optimum mode and normal mode were compared. It provides a good improvement in the performance, especially in steam generation and heat exchange capacity. With this analysis, a predictive temperature distribution profile across the heating surfaces of the HRSG was established.

REFERENCES

1. Casarosa, F., Donatin, C. and Franco, A. (2004) Thermoeconomic Optimization of Heat Recovery Steam Generator Operating Parameters for Combined Plant. Energy, 29, 389-413.

2. Lebele-Alawa, B.T., Hart, H.T., Ogaji, S.O.T. and Probert, S.D. (2008) Rotor-Blades' Profile Influence on a Gas Turbine's Compressor Effectiveness. Applied Energy, 85, 494-505.

3. Lebele-Alawa, B.T. (2010) Axial Thrust Responses due to a Gas Turbine's Rotor Blade Distortions Journal of Engineering Physics and Thermophysics, 83, 991-994.

4. Lebele-Alawa, B.T. and Egwanwo, V. (2012) Numerical Analysis of the Heat Transfer in Heat Exchangers. International Journal of Applied Science and Technology, 2(4), 60-64.

5. Ganapathy, V. (2001) Optimize Energy Efficiency of the Heat Recovery Steam Generator. Power Engineering Article, 105. http://www.power-eng.com/articles/print/volume-

6. Ongiro, A., Ugursal, V.I., Al Taweel, A.M. and Walker, J.D. (1997) Modeling of Heat Recovery Steam Generator Performance. Applied Thermal Engineering, 16, 427-444.

7. Franco, A. and Russo, A. (2002) Combined Cycle Plant Efficiency Increase Based on the Optimization of Heat Recovery Steam Generator Operating Parameter. International Journal of Thermal Science, 41, 841-850.

8. Reddy, B.V., Ramkiran, G., Kumar, K.A. and Nag, P.K. (2002) Second Law Analysis of a Waste Heat Recovery Steam Generator. International Journal of Heat and Mass Transfer, 45, 1807-1814.

9. Subhramanyam, N., Rajaram, S. and Kamalnathan, N. (1995) HRSGs for Combined Cycle Power plants. Heat Recovery System & CHP, 15, 153-161.

10. Dumont, M.N. and Heyen, G. (2004) Mathematical Modeling and Design of an Advanced Once through Heat Recovery Steam Generator. Computers and Chemical Engineering, 28, 651-660.

11. Valdés, M., Durán, M.D. and Rovira, A. (2003) Thermoeconomic Optimist of Combined Cycle Gas Trubine Power Plants Using Genetic Algorithms. Applied Thermal Engineering, 23, 2168-2180.

12. Mohammad, T.M., Pouria, A., Abdolsaeid, G.K. and Mohammad, N.M.J. (2012) Exergetic and Economic Evaluation of the Effect of HRSG Configurations on the Performance of Combined Cycle Power Plants. Journal of Energy Conversion and Management, 58, 47-58.

13. Attala, L., Facchini, B. and Ferrara, B. (2001) Thermo Economic Optimization Method as Design Tool in Gas Steam Combined Plant Realisation. Energy Conversation and Management, 42, 2163-2172.

14. Bassily, A.M. (2007) Analysis and Cost Optimization of the Triple-Pressure Steam-Reheat Gas Reheat Gas-Recuperated Combined Power Cycle. International Journal of Energy Research, 32, 116-135.

15. Srinivas, T. (2009) Study of a Deaerator Location in Triple Pressure—Reheat Combined Power Cycle. Energy, 34, 1364-1371.

16. Mohagheghi, M. and Shayegan, J. (2009) Thermodynamic Optimization of Design Variable and Heat Exchanger Layout in HRSGs for CCGT, Using Genetic Algorithm. Applied Thermal Engineering, 29, 290-298.

17. Sun, Z.X., Gao, L., Wang, J.F. and Dai, Y.P. (2012) Dynamic Optimal Design of Power Generation System Utilizing Industrial Waste Heat Considering Parameter Fluctuations of Exhaust Gas. Energy, 44, 1035-1043.

18. Manassaldi, J.I. and Scenna, N.J. (2011) Optimal Synthesis and Design of Heat Recovery Steam Generation (HRSG) via Mathematical Programming. Energy, 36, 475-485.

19. Alus, M.M. and Petrovic, M.V. (2012) Optimization of Parameters for Heat Recovery Steam Generator (HRSG) in Combined Cycle Plants. Thermal Science, 16, 901-914.

20. Ghazi, M., Ahmadi, P., Stotoodeh, A.F. and Taherkhani, A. (2012) Modeling and Thermo-Economic Optimization of Heat Recovery Heat Exchanger Using a Multimodal Genetic Algorithm. Energy Conservation and Management, 58, 149-156.

21. Vytla, V.V.S.K. (2005) Thesis on CFD Modeling of Heat Recovery Steam Generator and Its Components Using Fluent. College of Engineering, University of Kentucky, Lexington.

22. Lebele-Alawa, B.T. and Asuo, J.M. (2011) Exergy Analysis of Kolo Creek Gas Turbine Plant. Canadian Journal of Mechanical Science and Engineering, 2, 172-184.

23. Lebele-Alawa, B.T. and Jo-Appah, V. (2015) Thermodynamic Performance Analysis of a Gas Turbine in an Equatorial Rain Forest Environment. Journal of Power and Energy Engineering, 3, 11-23.

24. Ahmadi, P., Hajadollahi, H. and Dincer, I. (2011) An Exergy-Based Multi-Objective Optimization of a Heat Recovery Steam Generator (HRSG) in a Combined Cycle Power Plant (CCPP) Using Evolutionary Algorithm. International Journal of Green Energy, 8, 44-64.

25. Ahmadi, P. and Dincer, I. (2011) Thermodynamic Analysis and Thermoeconomic Optimization of a Dual Pressure Combined Cycle Power Plant with a Supplementary Firing Unit. Energy Convers Manage, 52, 296-308.

Chapter 4

Energetic and Exergetic Analysis of Combined Cycle Power Plant: Part-1 Operation and Performance

Abdulrahman Almutairi [1,*], Pericles Pilidis [1] and Nawaf Al-Mutawa [2]

[1]Power and Propulsion Department, School of Aerospace, Transport and Manufacturing, Cranfield University, Cranfield, Bedfordshire MK43 0AL, UK

[2]Mechanical Engineering Department, College of Engineering and Petroleum, Kuwait University, Al Asimah, P.O. Box 5969 Safat 13060, Khalidiya 72301, Kuwait

ABSTRACT

Energetic and exergetic analyses are conducted using operating data for Sabiya, a combined cycle power plant (CCPP) with an advanced triple pressure reheat heat recovery steam generator (HRSG). Furthermore, a sensitivity analysis is carried out on the HRSG using a recent approach to differentiate between the sources of irreversibility. The proposed system was modelled using the IPSEpro software and further validated by the manufacturer's data. The performance of the Sabiya CCPP was examined for different climatic conditions, pressure ratios, pinch point temperatures, high-pressure steam, and condenser pressure values. The results confirmed that 60.9% of the total exergy destruction occurs in the combustion chamber, which constitutes the main source of irreversibilities within a system. The exergy destruction was significantly affected by both the pressure ratio and the high-pressure steam, where the relation between them was seen to be inversely proportional. The high-pressure stage contributes about 50% of the exergy destruction within the HRSG compared to other stages and the reheat system, due to the high temperature difference between the streams and the large number of components, which leads to high energy loss to the surroundings. Numerous possibilities for improving the CCPP's performance are introduced, based on the obtained results.

KEYWORDS

combined cycle; heat recovery steam generator (HRSG); reheat; exergy; destruction

1. INTRODUCTION

Power systems diagnosis is conducted, using thermal analysis tools, to determine the locations, magnitudes, and types of waste and losses within these systems. Identifying the sizes and locations of the deficiencies will assist in making modifications to improve the system. The primary analysis and assessment tools used in optimising the thermal energy systems are energy and exergy analyses [1,2]. Thermal energy systems have long been analysed and evaluated using energy tools; however, in the last two decades, exergy analysis has been increasingly used to evaluate and optimise the thermal system designs, for more efficient usage of energy resources. Currently, many researchers perform exergy and energy analysis simultaneously, to increase the value of the research, and provide a complete illustration of energy system characteristics.

Energy analysis, based on the first law of thermodynamics, cannot provide sufficient information about the degradation of energy during a process, or the quality of the various forms of energy. These limitations have been overcome by exergetic analysis, which is based on both the first and second law of thermodynamics. Exergy analysis allows the identification of irreversibility sources, or the inefficiencies in a thermal power system, to be revealed. Exergy within a thermal process is constantly consumed due to irreversibilities [2]. As energy analysis is unable to determine the irreversibilities within a thermal system, this successfully demonstrates the importance of exergy analysis, which allows for, and increases, the possibility of enhancing thermal systems, by using different modifications, to reduce the irreversibilities resulted from entropy generation [3,4].

In the current work, a CCPP, with triple pressure HRSG system, was investigated, due to their high energy conversion efficiency, which is necessary in order to delay the depletion of non-renewable resources, by reducing fossil fuel consumption, through utilising and recovering part of the waste energy from a gas turbine engine. From an environmental perspective, it reduces greenhouse gas emissions, and, thus, the changes in the climate decrease significantly. The environment is significantly affected by inefficiencies within the power system.

Many researchers, such as Kotas [5], Facchini *et al.* [6], Moran *et al.* [7], Rahim [8,9], Ersayin and Ozgener [10], Ameri *et al.* [11], Deng-Chern and Chuang [12] and Petrakopoulou *et al.* [13] have carried out exergy analyses on combined cycles power plants. Although numerous studies are available in the literature for CCPP, nevertheless none have explored a triple pressure reheat HRSG using a real set of data based on exergy analysis.

The aims of the present study are to analyse a very advanced CCPP, with a triple pressure reheat HRSG, using actual operating data from an energetic and exergetic perspective, which has not previously been considered in literature. Furthermore, the study aims to investigate an HRSG's performance, using recent methods, in order to distinguish between the sources of irreversibilities. Finally, in the context of the results, the study will introduce certain suggestions in order to improve plant performance.

2. SABIYA POWER PLANT SPECIFICATION

The Sabiya CCPP consists of three blocks. Each containing two GE gas turbine frame 9FAs, with two triple pressure reheat HRSGs, and one steam turbine. A typical block is illustrated in Figure 1. The plant's power output and efficiency is more than 2000 MW at local conditions, and 54.5%, respectively.

The exhaust gases' stream passes through 14 heat exchangers in each HRSG before it reaches the stack. The pressure and a temperature at the exit of stack are 101.325 kPa and 107 °C respectively. In the steam cycles there are three levels of steam pressures on each evaporator. Which are at 131.8, 28.78, and 5.208 bars. The steam inlet temperatures for the high pressure (HP) and intermediate pressure (IP) steam turbine are equal to 565 °C. They are identical and this is a consequence of the reheat effect. As seen in Figure 1, there are two high pressure superheaters (HP SH) as well as two reheaters (RH-1&2). Between both the two superheaters and reheaters there are two attemperators, which help to adjust the steam temperature. The intermediate pressure steam stream exits from the superheater (IP SH) and mixes with the reheat stream, before entering reheater-1. The low pressure superheater (LP SH) before entering the (LP) low pressure steam turbine mixes with the exit stream coming from the intermediate steam turbine. The low pressure stream expands to 0.1 bar, before entering the deaerating condenser, which is the more preferable equipment in the combined cycle power plant, rather than the separating one, due to its smaller size, which saves equipment space and is easy to deaerate makeup water. The steam condensate is then directed to the condensate pump, to convey the feed water to the low pressure economizer (LP EC). In the low pressure evaporator (LP EV), the flow is divided into three streams, based on the flow pressure, to continue the cycle. The operational data at different operating conditions was collected from the Ministry of Electricity and Water (MEW) and the plant manufacturer. This data includes the state of all streams and the power output at different ambient conditions and loads.

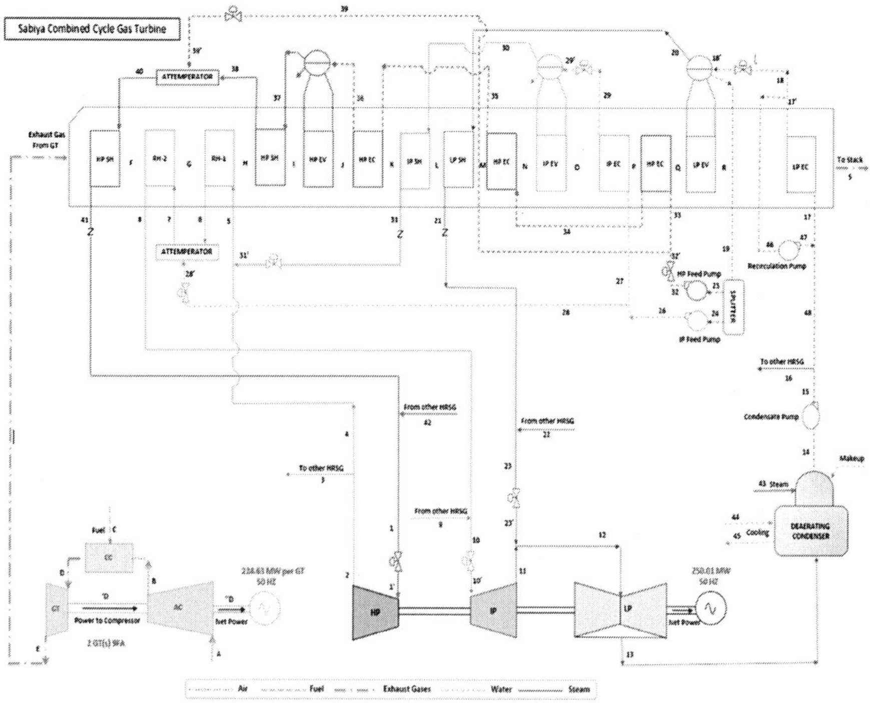

Figure 1. Schematic diagram for a Single Block of Sabiya Combined Cycle Power Plant [14].

3. PERFORMANCE ANALYSIS

The present study introduces a comparative energy and exergy analysis for Sabiya power plant. The analysis investigated the effects of different ambient temperatures, pressure ratios, pinch point temperatures, and condenser pressures. The following assumptions were made in modelling the gas turbine:

- The gas turbine model operated at a steady state.
- An ideal gas mixture concept is applied in both air and combustion products.
- Gas leakage is negligible.

- The kinetic and potential exergies of fluid streams are negligible.
- The combustion reaction is complete and N_2 is inert.
- Heat transfer from the combustor is 2% of the natural gas lower heating value (LHV)
- Natural gas is supplied to the system as fuel (the composition is given in Table 1).

Table 1. Molar fraction of the natural gas components.

Component	Molar Fraction (%)
Methane (CH_4)	93.34
Ethane (C_2H_6)	0.211
Propane (C_3H_8)	0.029
Nitrogen (N_2)	6.42

The fuel is provided to the combustor at high pressure with different mass flow rates, depending on the load variations and inlet temperature to the annular combustor. The air stream mass flow rate also varies, in the cold section, where the air composition is given in Table 2.

Table 2. Molar fraction of air.

Component	Molar Fraction (%)
Nitrogen (N_2)	77.48
Oxygen (O_2)	20.59
Water Vapour (H_2O)	1.9
Carbon dioxide (CO_2)	0.03

The air-to-fuel ratio (AFR) should always be higher than the stoichiometric air-to-fuel ratio, which means more air than theoretical air is used, and the mixture is called weak or lean. The stoichiometric air-to-fuel ratio represents the minimum amount of air required to achieve a complete burning of a given mass of fuel [1]. In reality, it is difficult to have a stoichiometric combustion system due to time limitations, air-fuel mixing and the presence of inert molecules, which obstruct the reaction between the active molecules. For these reasons, most combustion systems supply excess air in order to avoid the formation of smoke and carbon monoxide, and to achieve good, clean combustion.

3.1. Energy Analysis

The energy analysis is based on the first law of thermodynamics, which states that the exchange of energy for a system is the result of the applied work and heat transfer through that region. The first law of thermodynamics is based on two main concepts: (1) the energy cannot be destroyed; and (2) the energy can be transferred to other forms. In a thermal power plant, the energy is transferred from the chemical energy of the fuel to mechanical and/or electrical energies. The first law of thermodynamics in steady state form can be expressed as:

$$\dot{Q} - \dot{W} = \Delta H + \Delta Ke + \Delta Pe \quad (1)$$

The left-hand side of Equation (1) represents the net energy transfer by either heat and/or work, whereas the right-hand side shows the rate of change in enthalpy, kinetic and potential energies, respectively.

The combustion chamber performance is affected significantly by the plant operating conditions, which are based on the AFR variations. Molar analyses were performed in order to calculate the stoichiometric AFR, as elaborated by Bejan and Moran [1] and Moran *et al.* [7]. The molar analyses and energy balances for the proposed system components are derived, as illustrated in Appendix A.

3.2. Exergy Analysis

Exergy is the maximum amount of useful work that may be produced by a system in a reversible operation. Exergy consists of four components: physical, kinetic, potential and chemical. The general exergy balance of a system can be written as:

$$\dot{E}_x = \dot{E}_{ph} + \dot{E}_{ke} + \dot{E}_{pe} + \dot{E}_{ch} \tag{2}$$

The kinetic E˙ke and potential E˙pe exergies are related to ordered movement and to the elevation of particles, respectively. These forms of exergy, which do not function as substance or mixture, depend only on the mass and are fully convertible to work. There are no destruction or entropy generation terms in both types, and their equations are identical to potential and kinetic energies.

$$\dot{E}_{ke} = \frac{1}{2}\dot{m}V^2 \tag{3}$$

$$\dot{E}_{pe} = \dot{m}gz \tag{4}$$

The kinetic exergy is curial when exhaust gases directly interact with the environment at high velocity, where it is considered an exergy loss. Otherwise, in the present study, the kinetic and potential exergies are omitted due to insignificant effects in other locations.

Physical exergy is the maximum useful work that can be extracted from a unit mass of substance passing through a specified state (T_s, p_s) to the environmental or reference state (T_o, p_o) in purely physical processes. The physical exergy consists of two parts, mechanical and thermal exergy, and it is given by the expression:

$$\dot{E}_{ph} = \dot{m}[(h_s - h_o) - T_o\,(s_s - s_o)] \tag{5}$$

Once the specified temperature is equal to the reference temperature $T_s = T_o$ with the ideal gas relation, the Equation (5) becomes:

$$\dot{E}_{ph} = \dot{m}_e R T_o ln \frac{P_e}{P_o} \tag{6}$$

Chemical exergy represents the maximum useful energy that can be extracted while the flow moves from an environmental state to a dead state due to differences in concentration and molecular structure. In the environmental state, the system is mechanically and thermally at equilibrium state, but not chemically. The chemical exergy of a gas mixture can be calculated by:

$$\dot{E}_{ch} = \dot{n}\left[\sum y_k \bar{e}_k^{ch} + \overline{R}T_o \sum y_k \ln y_k\right] \tag{7}$$

where e¯chk is the molar chemical exergy for component k in the mixture, which can be selected from the standard chemical exergies table, as presented in [9]. The chemical exergy for fuel stream is given by:

$$\dot{E}_{ch} = \dot{n}\overline{LHV} \tag{8}$$

In all system components, the rate of exergy outlet is less than the rate at inlet due to exergy destruction and exergy loss. These quantities in steady state can be related by the following:

$$\dot{E}_i = \dot{E}_e + \dot{E}_d + \dot{E}_L \tag{9}$$

where E˙d and E˙L represent rates of exergy destruction and exergy loss, respectively. The exergy destruction during a process is proportional to entropy generation due to irreversibilities within each component in the process. There are many sources that cause irreversibilities, such as chemical reaction, mixing, friction, heat transfer driven by finite temperature difference, and non-quasi-equilibrium compression or expansion. The system inefficiencies can be measured from exergy destruction and exergy loss, as illustrated in Table 3, for all components.

Table 3. Exergy destruction rate and exergetic efficiency for different component at steady state [1].

Component	Exergy Destruction $\dot{E}_d$	Exergetic Efficiency η_{ex}
Compressor & Pump	$\dot{E}_e - \dot{E}_i$	$\frac{\dot{E}_e - \dot{E}_i}{\dot{W}_i}$
Gas & Steam Turbine	$\dot{E}_i - \dot{E}_e$	$\frac{\dot{W}_e}{\dot{E}_i - \dot{E}_e}$
Combustion Chamber	$\dot{E}_{i1} + \dot{E}_{i2} - \dot{E}_e$	$\frac{\dot{E}_e}{\dot{E}_{i1} + \dot{E}_{i2}}$
Heat Exchanger	$\dot{E}_{hi} + \dot{E}_{ce} - \dot{E}_{he} - \dot{E}_{ci}$	$\frac{\dot{E}_{he} + \dot{E}_{ci}}{\dot{E}_{hi} + \dot{E}_{ce}}$
Cycle components	$\sum \dot{E}_{d,k}$	$1 - \frac{\dot{E}_d + \dot{E}_L}{\dot{E}_f}$

The exergetic efficiency measures the performance of the thermal plant system from a thermodynamic prospective. The type of product and fuel are necessary to be defined because exergy analysis depends on the quality of energy. In the thermal plant system with single generation, thermal and exergetic efficiency are close to each other, whereas, in a multi-generation thermal plant system, the difference between them is obvious. The exergetic efficiency indicates how much can be extracted from the maximum available work, whereas thermal efficiency shows how much work output can be extracted from a specified input fuel. However, the exergetic efficiency is defined as the ratio of total exergy output to the total exergy input or the ratio of produced exergy to fuel exergy supplied to the system.

3.3. Waste Exergy in Heat Recovery Steam Generator (HRSG)

The HRSG consists of an economizer, an evaporator with a drum, and a superheater. In the economizer and the superheater, the phase does not change, whereas, in an evaporator, the latent heat dominates, by changing the phase of the water from liquid into the gaseous form (steam).

Exergy waste in thermal power systems is divided into two parts: exergy destruction, which is directly related to irreversibility within a system, and exergy loss, which is associated with the rejection of energy to the environment, at the end of the process. There are three forms of exergy waste across the heat exchanger, listed as follows:

- Exergy destroyed due to temperature difference between fluids.
- Exergy destroyed due to fluid friction as a result of movement along the pipes; and
- Energy release to the heat exchanger surroundings.

The waste exergy value of HRSG unit can be obtained based on the source of irreversibilities, using a new approach proposed by Paniagua *et al.* [15]. The waste exergy results from exergy destruction and exergy release to the environment, and can be calculated by:

$$\dot{E}_w = -\dot{Q}_{sur} + T_o\dot{S}_{\Delta T} + T_o\dot{S}_{\Delta P} \tag{10}$$

where E˙w and S˙ are the total wasted exergy and entropy generation respectively. Applying exergetic analysis into the HRSG or a heat exchanger is required to evaluate all three terms independently, which are highly affected by the temperature distribution inside each of the components in the HRSG. Thus, this shows some difficulty in calculation, as reported by Zunlong *et al.* [16].Theoretically, each term in Equation (9) can be developed as follows:

$$\dot{Q}_{sur} = \int d\dot{Q}_{surr}(1 - \frac{T_o}{T}) \tag{11}$$

$$\dot{S}_{\Delta T} = \int d\dot{Q}_{exch}(\frac{1}{T_c} - \frac{1}{T_h}) \tag{12}$$

$$\dot{S}_{\Delta P} = -\dot{m}_c \int_c \frac{v_c dP_c}{T_c} - \dot{m}_h \int_h \frac{v_h dP_h}{T_h} \tag{13}$$

where the subscripts c and h represent cold and hot fluid and v is the specific volume.

The proposed method is also known as the "black-box", which evaluates all sources of irreversibilities, from a thermodynamic perspective, at specified boundary conditions. The first step is to calculate the total wasted exergy, then obtain the temperature distribution in order to solve both the Equations (10) and (11). Finally, from Equation (9), the entropy generation due to pressure drop can be determined. There are a number of ways to solve the integral, using numerical integration. The Gaussian numerical integration was used in the analysis to simplify the calculations with more accurate results. More details about the proposed method and the Gaussian numerical integration are fully discussed in reference [15].

4. SIMULATION TOOLS

The proposed models in the current study have been modelled using a software package called IPSEpro (SimTech GmbH, Graz, Austria). This software is highly flexible for modelling and analysing processes in energy systems and in several other related areas. IPSEpro can perform heat balance calculations and simulates industrial processes. In general, the thermal process can be simulated and examined according to the specified thermodynamic properties. The Sabiya combined cycle power plant was validated with manufacturer's published data for different operating conditions and the results showed high compatibility with the proposed model.

5. RESULTS AND DISCUSSION

In this section, the results of energy and exergy analysis are presented for Sabiya CCPP at different ambient temperatures, pressure ratios, pinch point temperatures, condenser pressure and high pressure steam. A proper diagnosis leads to the identification of the sizes and locations of any deficiencies, which would assist in the modification or improvement of the plant, to reduce the environmental impact and energy costs and to achieve sustainable development, especially when fossil fuels are employed.

Similarly, analyses were performed at different operation conditions. The environmental state was selected at a temperature of 288 K, and an ambient pressure of 1.01 bar, for all streams. Table B-1 and Table B-2 in Appendix-B present the thermodynamic data, which include the exergy analysis at International Standards Organization (ISO) condition for the bottoming cycle and topping cycle and, respectively. Figure 1 illustrates two cycle streams at different states, with the topping cycle states (air and exhaust gases) indicated with letters, while the bottoming cycle states (steam) are represented by numbers.

Figure 2 shows the effect of ambient temperature variation on the exergetic efficiency, and the net power output per block in Sabiya CCPP. The rising ambient temperature leads to an increased exergy loss, which then leads to adverse effects on the system performance. The effect of ambient temperature is extended to the compressor's power consumption, which increases with high ambient temperatures, due to the increase in air density. Thus, the net power output will reduce as the ambient temperature rises. The exergetic efficiency and the net power output have the same trend, with ambient temperature variation, as they are inversely proportional with the ambient temperature.

The slope of the net power is higher than that of the exergetic efficiency, due to more power consumption in the compressor compared to energy saving as a result of increasing combustion chamber inlet temperature. The exergy destruction rates, for all Sabiya CCPP components at the ISO conditions, is shown in Figure 3. The greatest exergy destruction rate is shown at the combustion chamber, due to chemical reactions, mixing and large temperature differences, as confirmed by Kotas [5] and Ersayin and Ozgener [10].

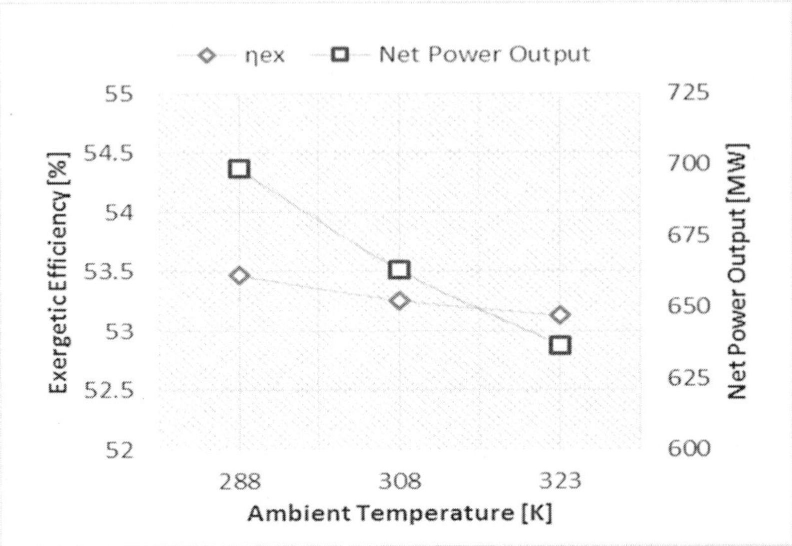

Figure 2. Exergetic efficiency and block net power output *verses* ambient temperatures.

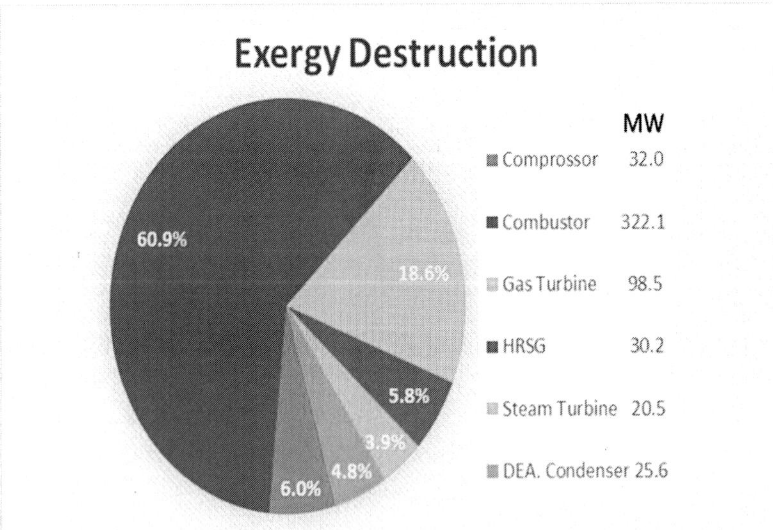

Figure 3. Exergy destruction rates for all components in Sabiya CCPP at ISO condition.

The gas turbine represents the second major source of irreversibility, as a result of high exergy input, temperature difference, expansion and friction. It is notable that the compressor has higher exergy destruction when compared to all bottoming cycle components. The HRSG represents the fourth source of irreversibility in the system, which may attribute to the temperature differences among the streams, friction and the heat dissipated to the surroundings. The fifth source of irreversibility occurs in deaerating condenser, due to the high energy loss to the coolant during the condensation process, in order to continue the cycle. The steam turbine constitutes the lowest source of irreversibility in the system. In spite of the fact that it occurs due to the same reasons as the gas turbine—due to the differences in the inlet temperature and the type of working fluid, which highly affect the heat capacity—the effect of reheat in HRSG leads to improve the steam turbine performance.

Figure 4 illustrates the exergetic efficiency and gas turbine exhaust gases temperature, against the pressure ratios for Sabiya CCPP. Numerous outcomes can be extracted from this figure. Initially, as the pressure ratio increases, the performance of the gas turbine improves—the reverse occurs for steam turbines—due to the substantial reduction in the exhaust gas temperatures. In spite of that, the whole plant's exergetic efficiency improves, because the reduction rate in the fuel consumption is higher than the steam turbine net power output. The reason behind that may be attributed to the result of the high inlet temperature in the combustion chamber for the former, and low gas turbine exhaust gases temperature, which significantly affects the steam capacity in the bottoming cycle and the steam turbine inlet temperature for the latter. The exhaust gas temperatures decrease as the pressure ratio increases at a constant power output due to the increase in the expansion ratio. The main constraint for increasing pressure ratio is the gas turbine exhaust temperature, which is confined by the HRSG configuration. The maximum exergetic efficiency is achievable at pressure ratio of 24.8, while, beyond that, the HRSG arrangement should be changed, due to low exhaust gases temperature. The Sabiya CCPP can be improved by using another gas turbine engine, with high pressure ratio, such as an industrial reheat gas turbine, in order to guarantee the high exhaust temperature, which will be more compatible with existing advanced HRSG.

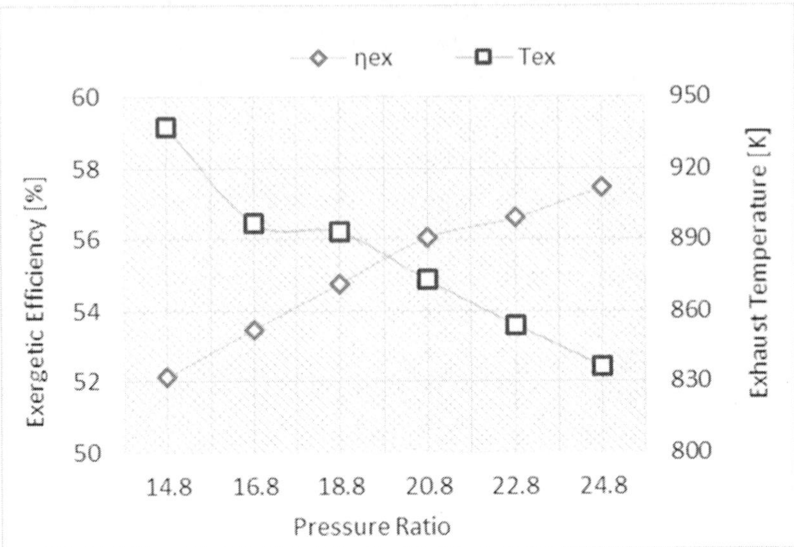

Figure 4. Exergetic efficiency and gas turbine exhaust gases temperature *versus* pressure ratios at ISO condition.

The relation between exergetic efficiency and condenser pressure is shown in Figure 5. Increasing the pressure in the condenser leads to creating an adverse effect in the performance, due to a reduction in the power output from the steam turbine. In addition, the temperature difference in the low pressure economizer is reduced, which is highly effective on heat transfer rate and increasing stack temperature. Adjusting condenser pressure significantly can have an effect on the plant performance and is highly recommended to sustain it at low level.

A triple-pressure reheat combined cycle consists of three levels of steam pressures at three different evaporators. The high pressure steam was investigated at different values, which are higher or lower than the design point at constant mass flow rate. It has significant influence on the CCPP performance, as illustrated in Figure 6. The relation between high pressure steam in HRSG, with exergetic efficiency, and block net power output is directly proportional. Increasing the pressure leads to reducing the latent heat of vaporisation, as well as the energy required to change the phase of water. Additionally, more power is produced due to an increase in the expansion range across the steam turbine with enthalpy. The exergetic efficiency increases, mainly due to the increase of net power output, which is interpreted by the trend similarity. The relation between steam pressure and plant performance is clear; therefore, high pressure is always preferable and is considered to be one of the important recommendations to achieve high plant efficiency.

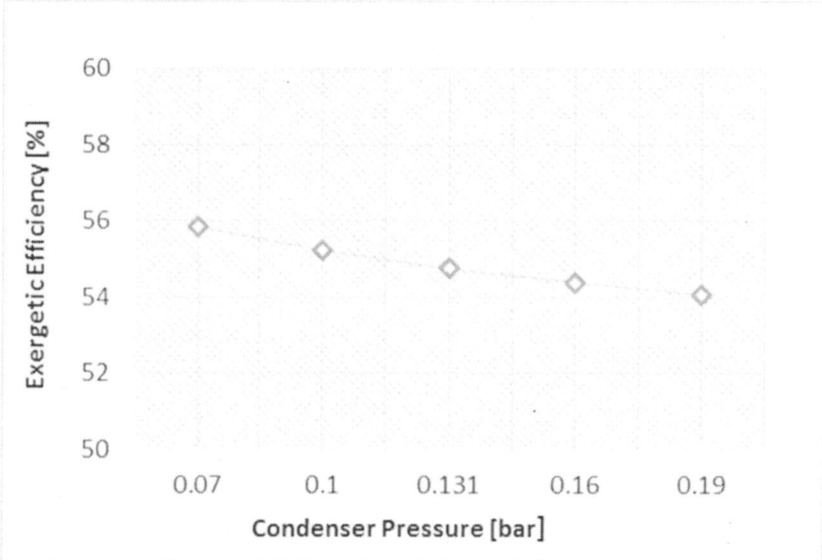

Figure 5. Exergetic efficiency *versus* condenser pressure at ISO condition.

Another significant parameter in plant performance is the pinch point of HRSG across three stages. The pinch point temperature is defined as the difference between the saturation temperature of the evaporator at specified pressure and the outlet exhaust gas temperature. From an operational perspective, adjusting the pinch point is achievable by changing the evaporator pressure, otherwise by modifying the HRSG design by changing the heat transfer area.

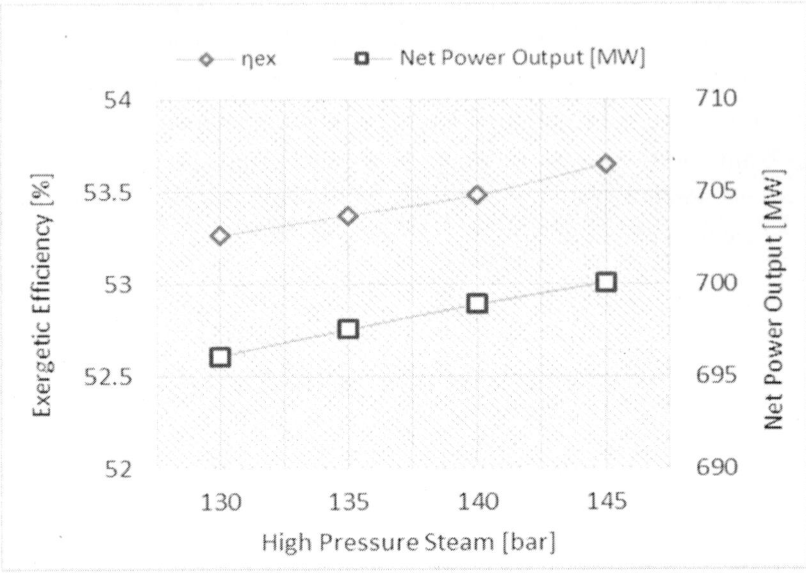

Figure 6. Exergetic efficiency and block net power output *versus* high pressure steam in HRSG.

The effect of HP pinch temperature on plant performance was investigated while keeping the IP and LP pinch temperatures at design values, as seen in Figure 7. It is noticed that, as HP pinch temperature reduces, the plant exergetic efficiency increases, due to the improvement of HRSG performance and the reduction of irreversibilities. The exergy destruction rate decreased as a result of improving the effectiveness of the evaporator and enhancement of the heat transfer rate between the two streams. The effect of HP pinch temperature and operating conditions are extremely dependent on HRSG configurations and the approach temperature, which represents the difference between the saturation temperature at the evaporator and water temperature, which exit from the economizer. The higher approach temperature at the same pinch temperature leads to a more efficient HRSG, and it increases the heat recovery. Thermodynamic and economical views must be taken into account, in order to achieve optimum HRSG design, that reflect on the plant's efficiency. In spite of the impact of the pinch and approach temperatures on thermal system performance, they are highly limited for existing systems in comparison to new plants. The HRSG configuration is considered to be a crucial factor in determining the behaviour of CCPP performance, specifically in the wasted heat recovery from the gas turbine.

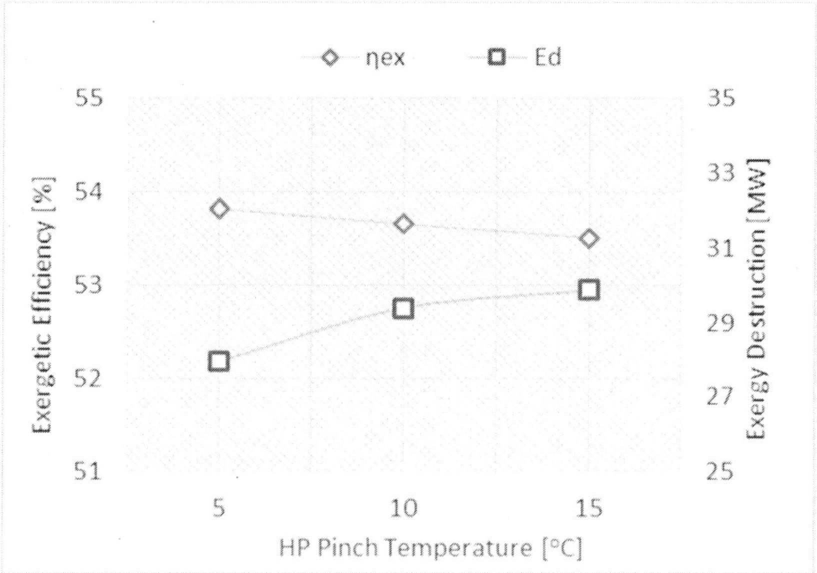

Figure 7. Exergetic efficiency and exergy destruction *versus* HP Pinch Temperature.

The exergetic analysis was performed on triple pressure reheat HRSG, using the new approach, in order to determine the sources of irreversibilities and exergy destruction per stage pressure. Figure 8 shows the exergy destruction for all HRSG stages. The exergy destruction at the high pressure stage [HP] achieves a high level, which is equivalent to all other stages. This is due to many reasons, such as the large number of components, high loss to the surroundings and high temperature difference between the streams. In contrast, the lowest level of exergy destruction occurs in the intermediate pressure stages [IP], as a result of the low heat loss, temperature differences between the streams, especially at superheater components, and mass flow rate. In the reheat section [RH] and low pressure stage [LP], the effect of the temperature difference is obvious.

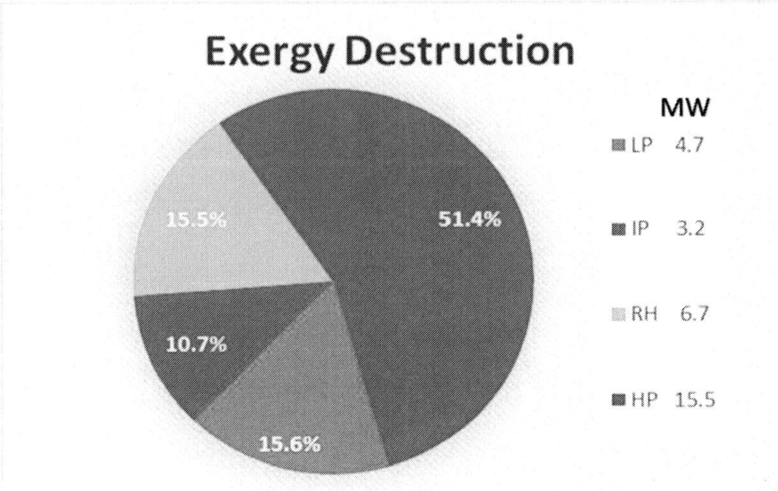

Figure 8. Exergy destruction for all HRSG stages at ISO condition.

The exergy destruction is significantly affected by the streams' pressures, and the relation between them is directly proportional. The overall exergy destruction of the HRSG, with the sources of irreversibilities, is illustrated in Figure 9. The highest source of irreversibilities caused from the temperature difference can be treated by preheating the cold stream, or adjusting the stream pressure. The second source comes from the heat loss to the surroundings, which mainly occurs due to a high temperature difference between the saturated temperature at the evaporator, and superheated steam at the inlet of steam turbine. The third source is related to the fluid friction, as a result of the movement along the pipes, and it appears in the form of pressure reduction. The order of exergy destruction is exactly identical to the previous literature [15], whereas, the level change is based on the HRSG configuration. However, knowing the sources of irreversibilities is considered to be useful information, in order to improve the component by eliminating, or limiting, the causes behind that.

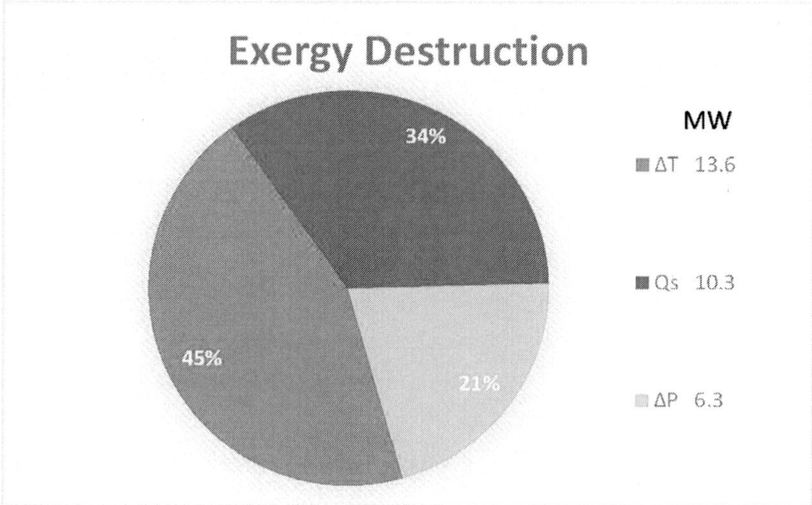

Figure 9. HRSG exergy destruction with different sources of Irreversibilities at ISO condition.

Finally, integrating Sabiya CCPP with low-grade heat source technologies, such as the organic Rankine cycle, absorption chiller and desalination plant, is highly recommended to improve plant efficiency. It is well known that an improvement in energy conversion level can be achieved by producing more useful types of energy from the same source of fuel. Low-grade heat source technologies will enhance plant performance without adding extra fuel in different forms. For example, this will:

- Produce more power by using the organic Rankine cycle.
- Improve the primary mover performance by cooling the intake area using an absorption chiller.
- Alternatively, save amount of energy consumed to cool the plant building.
- Save a considerable amount of the fuel required by the industrial boiler to operate the desalination system.

6. CONCLUSIONS

A detailed energetic and exergetic analysis of a 2000 MW CCPP has been carried out, based on a very advanced HRSG. The thermodynamic data were extracted from the CCPP model, developed by the IPSEpro software and validated with the manufacturer's published data, and it presented a high level of compatibility. The main conclusions that have been extracted from this study are listed below.

- The combustion chamber is the main source of irreversibility, with high exergy destruction attributable to three reasons: (i.) combined diffusion/fuel oxidation; (ii.) internal energy exchange–heat transfer; and (iii.) the mixing process.

- Inefficiency in the combustor can be reduced by improving the combustion process, adding an air preheater and reducing the air-to-fuel ratio.

- The steam turbine constitutes the lowest source of irreversibility as a result of the reheating system and the type of working fluid.

- The variation in ambient temperature has a significant effect on the CCPP's exergetic efficiency and net power output, and it is recommended to use a cooling system at the point of intake of the gas turbine engine in order to achieve high power output and exergetic efficiency.

- The reheat gas turbine engine, with a high-pressure ratio, will achieve substantial improvement in the CCPP due to a reduction in the fuel consumption, producing more power and maintaining the exhaust temperature at a high level, which is compatible with the triple pressure reheat HRSG.

- Adjusting the steam pressure at a high value and the condenser pressure at a low value can be proposed in order to improve the CCPP's efficiency.

- Regulating the HP pinch temperature at a low level will augment the CCPP's efficiency, while a high approach temperature is always preferable in order to recover more energy from the exhaust gases from the gas turbine.

- The temperature difference between the streams represents the major source of irreversibilities in the HRSG, and can be reduced either by preheating or adjusting the stream pressure.

- A large number of components in high pressure stream is not desirable, and can create an adverse effect on the performance, based on the optimum design criteria of the thermal system.

From the analysis conducted above, it can be concluded that there are abundant possibilities for improving the Sabiya CCPP, using the existing designs, by optimising the operating conditions. Improving the thermodynamic performance always has both economic and environmental implications, as will be published in the forthcoming second part of this study, using exergoeconomic and exergoenvironmental analysis of the same power plant.

ACKNOWLEDGMENTS

The authors wish to express their sincere thanks to the Ministry of Electricity and Water (MEW) in the state of Kuwait for its valuable support and assistance to the current work.

AUTHOR CONTRIBUTIONS

The authors have contributed equally in writing and revision of this manuscript.

CONFLICTS OF INTEREST

The authors declare no conflict of interest.

REFERENCES

1. Bejan, A.; Moran, M.J. *Thermal Design and Optimization*; John Wiley & Sons: Hoboken, NJ, USA, 1996.

2. Dincer, I.; Rosen, M.A. *Exergy: Energy, Environment and Sustainable Development*; Elsevier: Amsterdam, The Netherlands, 2012.

3. Aydin, H. Exergetic sustainability analysis of LM6000 gas turbine power plant with steam cycle. *Energy* **2013**, *57*, 766–774.

4. Tawney, R.K.; Ugolini, D.J.; Wengert, T.J.; Narula, R.G. Steam cycle selection considerations for combined cycleplant. In Proceedings of the Joint Power Generation Conference, Boston, MA, USA, 21–25 October 1990.

5. Kotas, T.J. *The Exergy Method of Thermal Plant Analysis*; Elsevier: Amsterdam, The Netherlands, 2013.

6. Facchini, B.; Fiaschi, D.; Manfrida, G. Exergy analysis of combined cycles using latest generation gas turbines. *J. Eng. Gas Turbines Power* **2000**, *122*, 233–238.

7. Moran, M.J.; Shapiro, H.N.; Boettner, D.D.; Bailey, M.B. *Fundamentals of Engineering Thermodynamics*; John Wiley & Sons: Hoboken, NJ, USA, 2010.

8. Rahim, M.A. Combined cycle power plant performance analyses based on the single-pressure and multipressure heat recovery steam generator. *J. Energy Eng.* **2011**, *138*, 136–145.

9. Rahim, M.A. Thermodynamic evaluation and parametric study of a combined cycle power plant: Application for Ankara City. *J. Energy Eng.* **2013**, *140*, 1–10.

10. Ersayin, E.; Ozgener, L. Performance analysis of combined cycle power plants: A case study. *Renew. Sustain. Energy Rev.***2015**, *43*, 832–842.

11. Ameri, M.; Ahmadi, P.; Khanmohammadi, S.H. Exergy analysis of a 420 MW combined cycle power plant. *Int. J. Energy Res.***2008**, *32*, 175–183.

12. Sue, D.-C.; Chuang, C.-C. Engineering design and exergy analyses for combustion gas turbine based power generation system.*Energy* **2004**, *29*, 1183–1205.

13. Petrakopoulou, F.; Tsatsaronis, G.; Morosuk, T.; Carassai, A. Conventional and advanced exergetic analyses applied to a combined cycle power plant. *Energy* **2012**, *41*, 146–152.

14. Ministry of Electricity and Water (MEW), State of Kuwait. Private Communication.

15. López Paniagua, I.; Rodríguez Martín, J.; González Fernandez, C.; Jiménez Alvaro, Á.; Nieto Carlier, R. A new simple method for estimating exergy destruction in heat exchangers. *Entropy* **2013**, *15*, 474–489.

16. Jin, Z.; Dong, Q.; Liu, M. Exergy study of fouling factors in heat exchanger networks. *J. Heat Transf.* **2010**, *132*, 011802.

Chapter 5

Model-Free Coordinated Control for MHTGR-Based Nuclear Steam Supply Systems

Zhe Dong [1,2]

[1]Institute of Nuclear and New Energy Technology (INET), Tsinghua University, Beijing 100084, China; Tel.: +86-10-6279-6425

[2]Collaborative Innovation Center of Advanced Nuclear Energy Technology of China, Beijing 100084, China

ABSTRACT

The modular high temperature gas-cooled reactor (MHTGR) is a typical small modular reactor (SMR) that offers simpler, standardized and safer modular design by being factory built, requiring smaller initial capital investment, and having a shorter construction period. Thanks to its small size, the MHTGRs could be beneficial in providing electric power to remote areas that are deficient in transmission or distribution and in generating local power for large population centers. Based on the multi-modular operation scheme, the inherent safety feature of the MHTGRs can be applicable to large nuclear plants of any desired power rating. The MHTGR-based nuclear steam supplying system (NSSS) is constituted by an MHTGR, a side-by-side arranged helical-coil once-through steam generator (OTSG) and some connecting pipes. Due to the side-by-side arrangement, there is a tight coupling effect between the MHTGR and OTSG. Moreover, there always exists the parameter perturbation of the NSSSs. Thus, it is meaningful to study the model-free coordinated control of MHTGR-based NSSSs for safe, stable, robust and efficient operation. In this paper, a new model-free coordinated control strategy that regulates the nuclear power, MHTGR outlet helium temperature and OTSG outlet overheated steam temperature by properly adjusting the control rod position, helium flowrate and feed-water flowrate is established for the MHTGR-based NSSSs. Sufficient conditions for the globally asymptotic closed-loop stability is given. Finally, numerical simulation results in the cases of large range power decrease and increase illustrate the satisfactory performance of this newly-developed model-free coordinated NSSS control law.

KEYWORDS

nuclear power plant; MHTGR; coordinated control; model-free; stability

1. INTRODUCTION

Small modular reactors (SMRs) are those nuclear fission reactors with electrical output power less than 300 MWe, and could be beneficial in providing electricity to the areas without transmission or distribution infrastructure in generating local power for a large population center and in being viable for specific applications such as heat sources for industrial complexes [1,2]. Due to the low power density and large heat capacity, some SMRs even have the inherent safety feature which is the most advanced feature of these SMR-based plants relative to those conventional nuclear plants and also prevents these SMRs from the hazards of core-melting, radiological release and loss of coolant accident (LOCA) [3,4]. Due to the ability of offering simpler, safer and standardized modular design by factory-building, less initial capital investment, and shorter construction period, SMRs have been viewed by International Atomic Energy Agency (IAEA) as a developing trend of nuclear energy. Through adopting multi-modular scheme, *i.e.*, multi-SMRs providing steam for one turbine/generator set, the inherent safety feature can be applicable to the large power plants of any desired power ratings. It is well known that the modular high temperature gas-cooled reactor (MHTGR, such as the HTR (High Temperature Reactor)-Module designed in Germany [5]), which uses helium as coolant and graphite as both moderator and structural materials, is a typical SMR with a strong inherent safety feature [6,7]. An MHTGR-based nuclear steam supplying system (NSSS) module composed of a one-zone pebble-bed MHTGR, a helical-coil once-through steam generator (OTSG) arranged side-by-side with the MHTGR and some connecting pipes is shown in Figure 1, which is one module of the under-constructed two-modular plant HTR-PM (Pebble-Bed Module) designed by Institute of Nuclear and New Energy Technology in Tsinghua University [8].

It is very clear that both the MHTGR and OTSG are complex nonlinear dynamic systems, and their dynamics are tightly coupled with each other. To improve both the steady and transient performance, it is necessary to develop coordinated control methods for the NSSS composed of the MHTGR and OTSG by considering the nonlinear dynamics. There are still very few results in the coordinated control of the reactor and steam generator. However, there have been some promising results in nonlinear control design methods for the reactors or the steam generators (SGs), which are helpful for developing coordinated control strategies. The sliding mode control (SMC) method is an effective approach to realize nonlinear control design for nuclear reactors. Shtessel gave a nonlinear power-level controller for space reactor TOPAZ II through the SMC method [9]. Due to the intrinsic chattering effect of the SMC, the recursive sliding mode control (RSMC) method was introduced by Huang, Edwards and Lee to solve the chattering problem and to improve the robustness. Based on the RSMC method, a fuzzy-adapted nonlinear power-level control law was designed for the advanced boiling water reactors (ABWR) [10]. The physics-based control (PBC) method is also an effective way to design nonlinear reactor control laws by retaining or strengthening stable subdynamics and by cancelling or suppressing unstable subdynamics, which has been applied to the load-following control design for the PWRs (Pressurized Water

Reactors) [11,12,13] and MHTGRs [14,15] recently. From the aspect of SG controller design, some advanced control approaches such as the model predictive control (MPC) [16], neurofuzzy [17] and feedback-dissipation [18] methods have all been applied to improve the regulation performance of SGs.

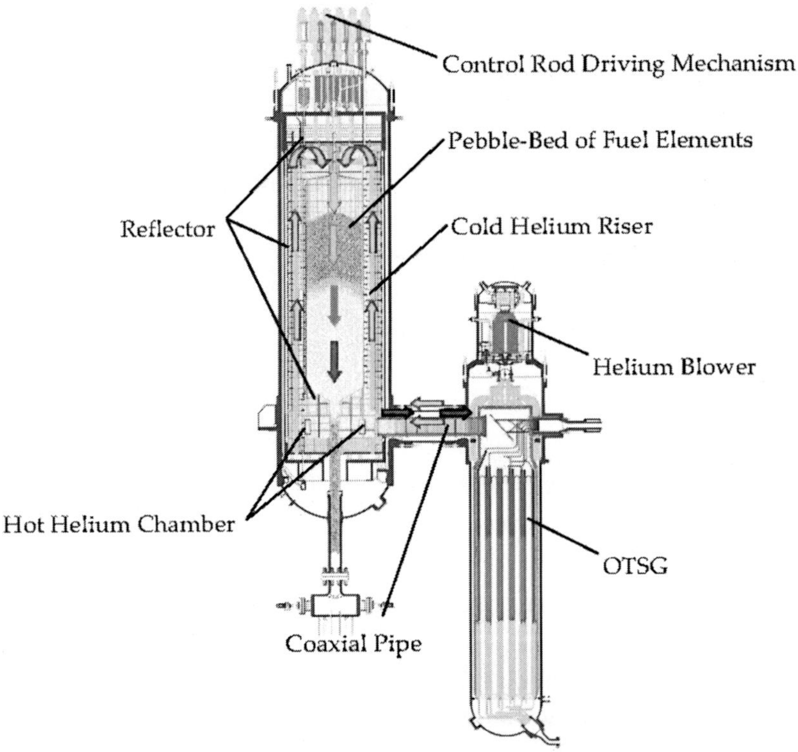

Figure 1. Schematic view of a modular high temperature gas-cooled reactor (MHTGR)-based nuclear steam supplying system (NSSS) module.

Although the above control strategies can provide large-scale closed-loop stability for the nuclear reactors or steam generators. However, these control laws have the drawback of heavy model-reliance. Some control laws needs the state prediction or observation directly based upon the reactor or SG models [9,10,11,12,14,15,16,17], and the control parameters also vary with the reactor or SG physical and thermal-hydraulic parameters [9,10,11,12,13,14,15,16,17,18], which leads to the difficulty in practically tuning and implementation. Therefore, it is necessary to develop model-free control methods to relieve the heavy model reliance of the designed control strategies. In the early 2000s, by applying the stable adaptive fuzzy control theory presented in [19], Marseguerra and Zio gave a model-free reactor control [20]. However, the fuzzy system of this model-free controller should be either suggested by experienced operators or trained online by measurement data, which is expensive especially for the newly-built reactors. Moreover, the fuzzy adaptive nonlinear control approach given in [19] is only suitable to those nonlinear systems in Brunovsky normalized form, which lose the prior knowledge about the structure of the plant dynamics given by both neutron kinetics and thermal-hydraulics. Thus, it is necessary and meaningful to study the model-free NSSS coordinated control design approach based on the inherent physical structure of the reactor and SG dynamics, which is not only for the freedom from the expression of dynamic model but also for insensitivity to the physical and thermal-hydraulic parameters. Actually, using inherent dynamical structure given by the energy or ectropy is a crucial way to design model-free control laws. For example, based upon the energy method, Rigatos gave a model-free controller of flexible-link robots [21], which is free from the dynamic model, and is also insensitive to the robot parameters. Thus, a physics-based control design method may also be an effective way to realize model-free coordinated control for MHTGR-based NSSSs.

Motivated by the necessity of developing model-free coordinated control method for NSSSs, a model free coordinated controller of the NSSS composed of one MHTGR and one OTSG are proposed through the physics-based approach in this paper. This NSSS coordinated control law has three key features: (a) there is no representation of any dynamic models for generating control input, state-observation or prediction; (b) the controller parameters are insensitive to the NSSS physical or thermal-hydraulic parameters; and (c) the closed-loop is globally asymptotically stable. Numerical simulation results in the cases of large range power increase and decrease illustrate the satisfactory regulating performance of this NSSS coordinated controller.

2. MODELING AND PROBLEM FORMULATION

In this section, the state-space model of the MHTGR-based NSSS for coordinate control design is firstly given, and then the theoretic problem to be solved in the following sections is formed.

From Figure 1, the MHTGR and OTSG in one NSSS are arranged side by side, and are connected with each other by a horizontal coaxial hot/cold gas duct. The cold helium enters the blower that mounted on the upper part of the OTSG, and is pressurized before flowing into the cold gas duct. It enters the channels inside the reflector from bottom to top for cooling the reflector, and then passes through the pebble-bed from top to bottom where it is heated to a very high temperature. The hot helium leaves the hot chamber inside the bottom reflector, and then flows into the OTSG primary side where it is cooled to be the cold helium by transferring its heat to the secondary water/steam flow. By adopting the point kinetics with one equivalent delayed neutron group and by considering the temperature feedback effect of the reactor core composed of the pebble-bed and reflector, the dynamic model for coordinated control design is:

$$\begin{cases} \Lambda \dot{n}_r = (\rho_r - \beta) n_r + \beta c_r + \alpha_R n_r (T_R - T_{R,m}), \\ \dot{c}_r = \lambda (n_r - c_r), \\ \mu_R \dot{T}_R = -\Omega_P (T_R - T_H) + P_0 n_r, \\ \mu_H \dot{T}_H = \Omega_P (T_R - T_H) - \Omega_S (T_H - T_S), \\ \mu_S \dot{T}_S = \Omega_S (T_H - T_S) - 2M_S (T_S - T_{Sin}), \\ \dot{\rho}_r = G_r v_r, \end{cases} \tag{1}$$

where the meaning of the variables are given in Nomenclature. Here, it is worthy to be noted that α_R is guaranteed to be negative by the physical design.

Define deviations of n_r, c_r, T_R, T_H, T_S, T_{Sin} and ρ_r from their equilibrium values, *i.e.*, n_{r0}, c_{r0}, T_{R0}, T_{H0}, T_{S0}, T_{Sin0} and ρ_{r0}, respectively, as $\delta n_r = n_r - n_{r0}$,

$\delta c_r = c_r - c_{r0}$, $\delta T_R = T_R - T_{R0}$, $\delta T_H = T_H - T_{H0}$, $\delta T_S = T_S - T_{S0}$, $\delta T_{Sin} = T_{Sin} - T_{Sin0}$, $\delta \rho_r = \rho_r - \rho_{r0}$. Since T_{Sin} is usually given by the environment, assume that:

$$\delta T_{\mathrm{Sin}} \equiv 0 \tag{2}$$

Because the helium flowrate can be adjusted by changing the main blower speed, it is not a loss of generality to assume that:

$$\delta \Omega_{\mathrm{S}} = \Omega_{\mathrm{S}} - \Omega_{\mathrm{S0}} = \kappa_{\mathrm{S}} \delta W_{\mathrm{P}} \tag{3}$$

where Ω_{S0} is the steady value of Ω_S, and δW_P is the variation of the primary helium flowrate relative to its steady value, and κ_S is a positive scalar.

Moreover, the feedwater flowrate can also be adjusted, and thus we assume that:

$$\delta M_{\mathrm{S}} = M_{\mathrm{S}} - M_{\mathrm{S0}} = C_{\mathrm{S}} \delta W_{\mathrm{S}} \tag{4}$$

where M_{S0} is the steady value of M_S, δW_S is the error of the feedwater flowrate relative to its steady value, and C_S is a positive scalar denoting the heat capacity of secondary coolant.

Define:

$$\mathbf{x} = \begin{bmatrix} x_1 & x_2 & x_3 & x_4 & x_5 \end{bmatrix}^{\mathrm{T}} = \begin{bmatrix} \delta n_{\mathrm{r}} & \delta c_{\mathrm{r}} & \delta T_{\mathrm{R}} & \delta T_{\mathrm{H}} & \delta T_{\mathrm{S}} \end{bmatrix}^{\mathrm{T}} \tag{5}$$

$$\xi = \delta z_{\mathrm{r}} = G_{\mathrm{r}}^{-1} \delta \rho_{\mathrm{r}} \tag{6}$$

$$\mathbf{u} = \begin{bmatrix} u_1 & u_2 & u_3 \end{bmatrix}^{\mathrm{T}} = \begin{bmatrix} v_{\mathrm{r}} & \delta W_{\mathrm{P}} & \delta W_{\mathrm{S}} \end{bmatrix}^{\mathrm{T}} \tag{7}$$

and

$$\mathbf{y} = \begin{bmatrix} x_1 & x_4 & x_5 \end{bmatrix}^{\mathrm{T}} \tag{8}$$

where $\boldsymbol{x}$ is called the NSSS state-vector, $\boldsymbol{u}$ is called the control input, $\boldsymbol{y}$ is the output that can be obtained by measurement, and δz_r is the total displacement of the control rods.

Then, nonlinear state-space model for coordinated control design can be written as:

$$\begin{cases} \dot{\mathbf{x}} = \mathbf{f}(\mathbf{x}) + \mathbf{g}_1(\mathbf{x})\xi + \mathbf{g}_2(\mathbf{x})u_2 + \mathbf{g}_3(\mathbf{x})u_3, \\ \dot{\xi} = u_1, \\ \mathbf{y} = \mathbf{h}(\mathbf{x}), \end{cases} \tag{9}$$

where

$$\mathbf{f}(\mathbf{x}) = \begin{bmatrix} -\Lambda^{-1}\beta(x_1 - x_2) + \Lambda^{-1}\alpha_R(n_{r0} + x_1)x_3 \\ \lambda(x_1 - x_2) \\ \mu_R^{-1}P_0x_1 - \mu_R^{-1}\Omega_P(x_3 - x_4) \\ \mu_H^{-1}\Omega_P(x_3 - x_4) - \mu_H^{-1}\Omega_{S0}(x_4 - x_5) \\ \mu_S^{-1}\Omega_{S0}(x_4 - x_5) - 2\mu_S^{-1}M_{S0}x_5 \end{bmatrix} \tag{10}$$

$$\mathbf{g}_1(\mathbf{x}) = \begin{bmatrix} \Lambda^{-1}G_r(n_{r0} + x_1) & \mathbf{O}_{1\times4} \end{bmatrix}^T \tag{11}$$

$$\mathbf{g}_2(\mathbf{x}) = \begin{bmatrix} \mathbf{O}_{1\times3} & -\mu_H^{-1}\kappa_S(T_H - T_S) & \mu_S^{-1}\kappa_S(T_H - T_S) \end{bmatrix}^T \tag{12}$$

$$\mathbf{g}_3(\mathbf{x}) = \begin{bmatrix} \mathbf{O}_{1\times4} & -2\mu_S^{-1}C_ST_S \end{bmatrix}^T \tag{13}$$

and

$$\mathbf{h}(\mathbf{x}) = \begin{bmatrix} x_1 & x_4 & x_5 \end{bmatrix}^T \tag{14}$$

From the MHTGR-based NSSS state-space model Equation (9), the theoretic problem to be solved in the next sections is summarized as:

Problem 1. How can a model-free control input $\boldsymbol{u}$ defined by:

$$\mathbf{u} = \begin{bmatrix} u_1 & u_2 & u_3 \end{bmatrix}^T \tag{15}$$

for nonlinear system Equation (9) be designed so that the closed-loop is globally asymptotically stable?

3. MODEL-FREE COORDINATED CONTROL DESIGN

The following Theorem 1, which is the main result of this paper, summarizes the design of model-free coordinated control input ***u*** for the MHTGR-based NSSS. The corresponding design process can be seen in the proof Theorem 1.

Theorem 1. *Consider nonlinear system Equation (9). The coordinated control given by:*

$$u_1 = -\left(k_{p11}x_1 + k_{d11}\dot{x}_1 + k_{p14}x_4 + k_{d14}\dot{x}_4 + k_{p15}x_5 + k_{d15}\dot{x}_5\right) \tag{16}$$

$$u_2 = \frac{\Omega_{S0}}{\kappa_S\left(T_H - T_S\right)}\left(k_{p24}x_4 - k_{p25}x_5\right) \tag{17}$$

and

$$u_3 = \frac{M_{S0}}{C_S T_S}k_{p35}x_5 \tag{18}$$

where feedback gains k_{p11}, k_{d11}, k_{p14}, k_{d14}, k_{p15}, k_{d15}, k_{p24}, k_{p25} and k_{p35} are all positive constants satisfying:

$$k_{d14} = (1-\eta_1)(\gamma_1+\gamma_2)\frac{|\alpha_R|\mu_H}{G_r\mu_R} \tag{19}$$

$$k_{d15} = (1-\eta_2)\left[\gamma_1 + \frac{\Omega_{S0}\left(1+k_{p25}\right)}{\Omega_{S0}\left(1+k_{p25}\right)+2M_{S0}\left(1+k_{p35}\right)}\gamma_2\right]\frac{|\alpha_R|\mu_S}{G_r\mu_R} \tag{20}$$

$$k_{p14} = \gamma_2\left(1+k_{p24}\right)\frac{2M_{S0}\left(1+k_{p35}\right)}{\Omega_{S0}\left(1+k_{p25}\right)+2M_{S0}\left(1+k_{p35}\right)}\frac{|\alpha_R|\Omega_{S0}}{G_r\mu_R} \tag{21}$$

and

$$k_{p15} = \gamma_1 \left(1 + k_{p35}\right) \frac{2\left|\alpha_R\right| M_{S0}}{G_r \mu_R} \tag{22}$$

respectively, and γ_i and η_i (i = 1, 2) are all given positive constants with $0 < \eta_i < 1$. Then, the closed-loop system formed by Equations (9) and (16)–(18) is globally asymptotically stable if:

$$k_{d11} > \frac{\left|\alpha_R\right| P_0}{G_r \Omega_P} \left(\gamma_1 + \gamma_2\right)^2 \left[1 + \frac{\eta_1 \mu_H}{4\mu_R} + \frac{\eta_2 \mu_S \left(1 + k_{p24}\right)}{4\mu_R \left(1 + k_{p25}\right)}\right] \tag{23}$$

$$k_{p24} > \frac{2\Omega_P}{\Omega_{S0}} \left(1 + \eta_1 \frac{\mu_H}{\mu_R}\right) - 1 \tag{24}$$

and

$$k_{p35} > \frac{\Omega_{S0}}{2M_{S0}} \left(1 + k_{p25} + \eta_2 \frac{\Omega_P \mu_S}{\Omega_{S0} \mu_R}\right) - 1 \tag{25}$$

Proof: See Appendix.

Remark 1. Define

$$\kappa_{p24} = \frac{\Omega_{S0}}{\kappa_S \left(T_H - T_S\right)} k_{p24} \tag{26}$$

$$\kappa_{p25} = \frac{\Omega_{S0}}{\kappa_S \left(T_H - T_S\right)} k_{p25} \tag{27}$$

and

$$\kappa_{p35} = \frac{M_{S0}}{C_S T_S} k_{p35} \tag{28}$$

From Equations (26)–(28), as well as inequalities Equations (24) and (25), we can easily obtain that both

$$\kappa_{p24} > \left[\frac{2\Omega_P}{\Omega_{S0}}\left(1+\eta_1\frac{\mu_H}{\mu_R}\right)-1\right]\frac{\Omega_{S0}}{\kappa_S\left(T_H-T_S\right)} \quad (29)$$

and

$$\kappa_{p35} > \left\{\frac{\Omega_{S0}}{2M_{S0}}\left[1+\frac{\kappa_S}{\Omega_{S0}}\kappa_{p25}\left(T_H-T_S\right)+\eta_2\frac{\Omega_P\mu_S}{\Omega_{S0}\mu_R}\right]-1\right\}\frac{\Omega_{S0}}{\kappa_S\left(T_H-T_S\right)} \quad (30)$$

should be satisfied for guaranteeing globally asymptotic closed-loop stability. Moreover, control input u_2 and u_3 can be certainly rewritten as:

$$u_2 = \kappa_{p24}x_4 - \kappa_{p25}x_5 \quad (31)$$

and

$$u_3 = \kappa_{p35}x_5 \quad (32)$$

respectively.

Remark 2. Since γ_i (i = 1, 2) are arbitrarily given positive constants, from Equations (21) and (22), it is clear that feedback gainsk_{p14} and k_{p15} can be arbitrary positive values. Moreover, since η_i (i = 1, 2) are arbitrary given constants satisfying $0 < \eta_i < 1$, from Equations (19) and (20), feedback gains k_{d14} and k_{d15} can be arbitrarily in the sets

$$\Pi_{d14} = \left\{\theta \in R \middle| \quad 0 < \theta < \left(\gamma_1+\gamma_2\right)\frac{|\alpha_R|\,\mu_H}{G_r\mu_R}\right\} \quad (33)$$

and

$$\Pi_{d15} = \left\{\theta \in R \middle| \quad 0 < \theta < \left[\gamma_1+\frac{\Omega_{S0}\left(1+k_{p25}\right)}{\Omega_{S0}\left(1+k_{p25}\right)+2M_{S0}\left(1+k_{p35}\right)}\gamma_2\right]\frac{|\alpha_R|\,\mu_S}{G_r\mu_R}\right\} \quad (34)$$

respectively. If constants γ_i and η_i (i = 1, 2) are given, then the values of feedback gains k_{p14}, k_{p15}, k_{d14} and k_{d15} are given. From Theorem 1, we can see that the globally asymptotic closed-loop stability can be guaranteed if inequalities Equations (23)–(25) are all well satisfied. Therefore, from

Equations (19)–(22) as well as inequalities Equations (23), (29) and (30), the values of feedback gainsk_{d11}, k_{d14}, k_{d15}, k_{p11}, k_{p14}, k_{p15}, κ_{p24}, κ_{p25}, κ_{p35} are all not directly determined by the NSSS physical and thermal parameters. Actually, the values of feedback gains k_{p11}, k_{p14}, k_{p15} and κ_{p35} can be arbitrarily given, and the values of feedback gains k_{d11}, k_{d14},k_{d15}, κ_{p24} and κ_{p25} can be chosen in the scopes determined by Equations (33), (34), (23), (29) and (30). Moreover, from the expressions of this newly-built coordinated control law composed of Equations (16), (31) and (32), there is no expressions about the dynamic model in this controller utilized for either state-prediction or control input generation. From the above discussion, MHTGR-based NSSS coordinated control given by Equations (16), (31) and (32) is model-free, which leads to easy implementation and tuning.

4. SIMULATION RESULTS WITH DISCUSSION

To show the feasibility and performance of the newly-built nonlinear adaptive coordinated control strategy given in Theorem 1, it is applied to the regulation of an NSSS of HTR-PM plant in this section.

The dynamic model of the MHTGR that is used for numerical simulation is the nodal model given in [22]. The OTSG model adopted the moving boundary model given in [23]. The code was developed based on VC++ [24], and this simulation was done by using this software. Actually, both the space-dependent reactor models given in [22,23] and point model Equation (1) can describe the NSSS dynamics. The former one gives a more detailed description and is more suitable for verification, and the later model is much simpler and is more suitable for control law design. The dynamic model of the second-loop system gives the feedwater temperature and pressure for the dynamic model of the NSSS. In the numerical verification, the simulation software adopts the software given in [24] which contains the dynamics models of the NSSS as well as the secondary-loop. Moreover, from the above Theorem 1 and Comment 1, the NSSS coordinated control law can be written as Equations (16)–(18), and can also take the form as Equations (16), (31) and (32). If the first form is adopted, then control gains

k_{p24} and k_{p35} should satisfy inequalities Equations (24) and (25). Moreover, if the second form is adopted, then control gains κ_{p24} and κ_{p35} should satisfy inequalities Equations (29) and (30). Here, the second form is adopted, and control gains are chosen as k_{d11} = 2.0, k_{p11} = 0.2, k_{d14} = 0.5, k_{p14} = 0.05, k_{d15} = 0.02, k_{p15} = 0.001, κ_{p24} = 0.5, κ_{p25} = 0.05 and κ_{p35} = 0.3 so that Equations (23), (29), (30), (33) and (34) are satisfied.

To illustrate the coordinate control performance, the following two case studies are done:

- Case A: Power-demand decreases from 100% to 50% RFP (Reactor Full Power) linearly in 10 min.

- Case B: Power-demand increases from 50% to 100% RFP linearly in 10 min.

Both cases A and B represent hard operations of the NHR. Dynamic responses of the relative nuclear power n_r, reactor outlet helium temperature T_{cout} and OTSG outlet steam temperature T_s as well as the control rod speed v_r, helium flowrate G_p and feedwater flowrate G_s generated by the newly-built coordinated controller in the above two cases are shown in Figure 2 and Figure 3, respectively. Here, the power-demand decrease starts at the 1000 s, and the power-demand increase starts at the 2000 s. The difference in the start-time of power-demand variation does not affect the verification result. Since the OTSG outlet steam temperature is constant (571 °C), and since the feed-water temperature of the OTSG is different at different power-levels, it is very clear that the feedwater flowrate in a 50% reactor full power-level (RFP) is not the 50% flowrate at 100% RFP.

Since the power-demand changes, the errors between the actual and referenced values of the relative nuclear power, reactor outlet helium temperature and OTSG outlet steam temperature become larger. These three errors make coordinated control law to drive the control rods, primary helium blower and feedwater pump to suppress these error signals. The system enters into a steady state when the supplied and demanded power balances with each other. From Figure 2 and Figure 3, it is clear that closed-loop stability can be well guaranteed by properly choosing the feedback gains k_{d11}, k_{d14}, k_{d15}, k_{p11}, k_{p14}, k_{p15}, κ_{p24}, κ_{p25} and κ_{p35} so that feedback gainsk_{d14} and k_{d15} are in the sets given by Equations (33) and (34), and inequalities Equations (23), (29) and (30) are satisfied. Thus, it is very clear that the numerical phenomena in this simulation fit well with the theoretic results. Finally, this newly-built model-free coordinated control for MHTGR-based NSSSs proposed in this paper has a simple form and can be easily implemented in the practical engineering.

Due to the HTR-PM plant still being under construction, we cannot verify the result in this paper by some real operating data in this stage. However, the obtained control parameters, *i.e.*, controller structures given by Equations (16), (31) and (32) as well as control gain scopes given by Equations (23), (29), (30), (33) and (34) have deep implications to the future realization of controlling the real HTR-PM nuclear system. Here, the implication lies in the following two aspects:

(1)Since the coordinated control law given by Equations (16), (31) and (32) has been proven to have the globally asymptotically stabilization performance, the coordinated control law of the real HTR-PM NSSS module should take the same form as Equations (16), (31) and (32) in the engineering.

(2)The control gains in the practical engineering should be chosen to satisfy conditions Equations (23), (29), (30), (33) and (34) generally. However, due to the mismatch between the real and designed NSSS parameters as well as that between the dynamic features of the real and designed actuators (such as the control rods, helium bowers and feedwater pumps), some experiments or tests should be given practically to verify that the overshoots and transition periods of the real response of key process variables meets the engineering requirements.

Furthermore, the parameters of the NSSS models for control design and simulation are given by physical and thermal-hydraulic design. It was verified that the model and software given in [22,23,24] can provide credible dynamical simulation for the HTR-PM plant. The theoretical and simulation results in this paper show at least that the coordinated control law determined by Equations (16), (31) and (32) can be implemented in the practical engineering. Verifying the results in this paper by the operating data of the HTR-PM plant will be very meaningful work in the future.

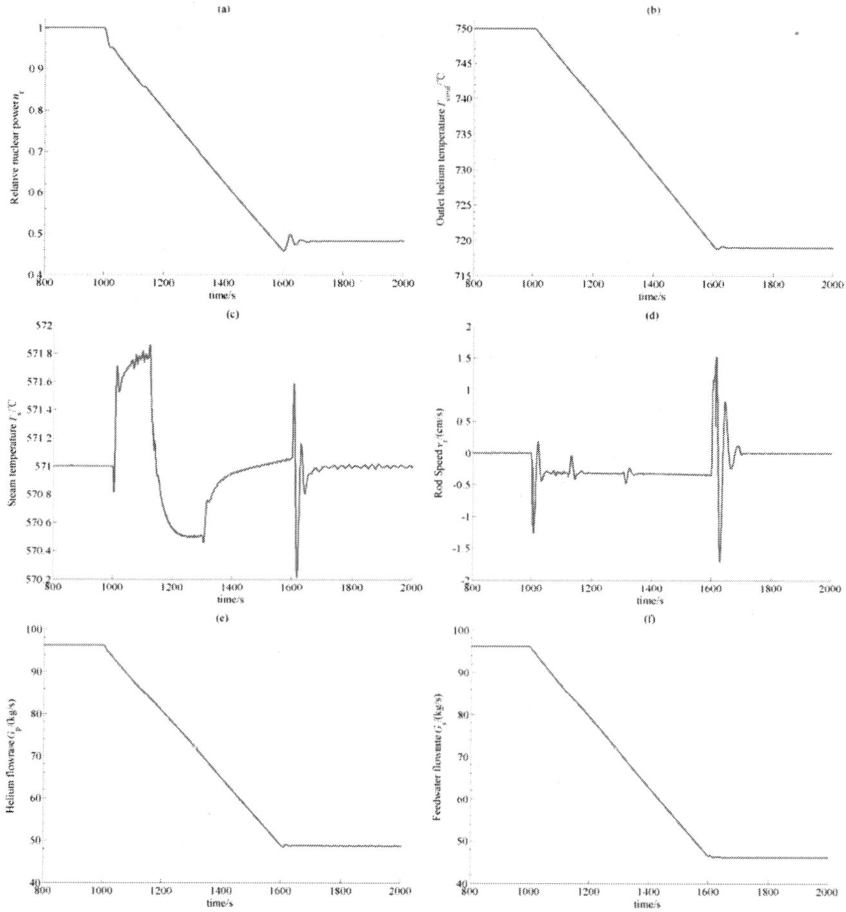

Figure 2. Simulation results in Case A: (**a**) Relative nuclear power; (**b**) Outlet helium temperature; (**c**) steam temperature; (**d**) Control rod speed signal; (**e**) Primary helium flowrate; (**f**) Feedwater flowrate.

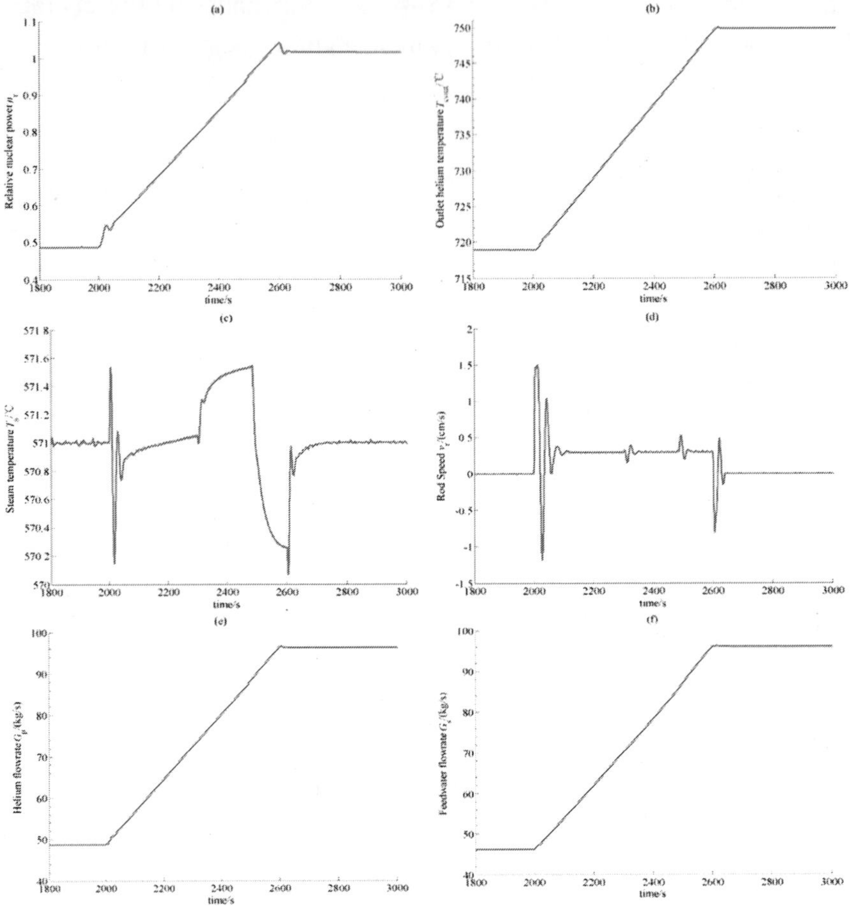

Figure 3. Simulation results in Case B: (**a**) Relative nuclear power; (**b**) Outlet helium temperature; (**c**) steam temperature; (**d**) Control rod speed signal; (**e**) Primary helium flowrate; and (**f**) Feedwater flowrate.

5. CONCLUSIONS

Due to the simpler, standardized, and safer modular design, SMRs have the virtues of being factory built, requiring smaller initial capital investment, and having shorter construction time. Because of its persistency of power supply, SMRs can be incorporated with new energy resources to build micro-grids and can also be used to build large-scale nuclear plants by the multi-modular scheme. Coordinated control of SMR-based NSSSs is meaningful to realize the load-following function of SMR-based nuclear plants. However, until now, there has still been very little work in the field of NSSS coordinated control. MHTGR is a typical SMR having the inherent safety features and economic competitive power, and has also been seen as a candidate for a next generation nuclear reactor. Coordinated control of MHTGR-based NSSSs is quite important in providing the stable and efficient operation for the MHTGR-based nuclear energy systems. In this paper, by considering the exterior disturbances, a model-free coordinated control law for the MHTGR-based NSSS is proposed, which does not contain any expressions of the NSSS dynamic model and is insensitive to the physical or thermal parameters. The sufficient conditions for guaranteeing globally asymptotic closed-loop stability are given. Numerical simulation results show the satisfactory regulation performance of this newly-built model-free coordinated controller. Due to its simplicity, this control law can be very easily implemented in those digital control system platforms.

Moreover, the MHTGR-based NSSS is quite different from the PWR-based NSSS. As stated in Section 1 of this paper, the MHTGR-based NSSS consists of a modular high temperature gas-cooled reactor (MHTGR), a helical-coil once-through steam-generator (OTSG), primary helium blower and some connecting pipes. However, the PWR-based NSSS usually consists of a pressurized water reactor (PWR), a U-tube steam-generator (UTSG), primary feed-water pump and some pipes. The main difference of the dynamics of the MHTGR and that of the PWR is determined by the reactivity effect of the coolant. For the MHTGR, the coolant is helium, which is transparent to the fission reaction and has NO reactivity feedback effect on the neutron kinetics. For the PWR, the coolant is the pressurized water, which is also utilized as the moderator and does have reactivity feedback effect on the neutron kinetics. The difference in the reactor dynamics is only the first difference between the MHTGR and PWR based NSSSs. The second difference is that the MHTGR-based NSSS adopts the helical-coil OTSG, and the PWR-based NSSS adopts the UTSG. Since natural circulation in the UTSG exists, its dynamic behavior is quite different from that of the OTSG. Therefore, the dynamic behavior of the PWR-based NSSS cannot be described by model Equation (1) in this paper, and the coordinated control proposed in this paper for the MHTGR-based NSSS cannot be directly applied to the other types of NSSSs such as the PWR-based NSSS. However, the key idea of control design approach in this paper, *i.e.*, the physics-based control design approach is helpful to realize the coordinated control laws for other types of NSSSs.

ACKNOWLEDGMENTS

The author would like to thank the anonymous reviewers for the constructive comments. Moreover, the author would like to gratefully acknowledge the contributions of Xiaojin Huang for the valuable discussions with him and the positive suggestions from him.

CONFLICTS OF INTEREST

The author declares no conflict of interest. The founding sponsors had no role in the design of the study; in the collection, analyses, or interpretation of data; in the writing of the manuscript, and in the decision to publish the results.

REFERENCES

1. Vujić, J.; Bergmann, R.M.; Škoda, R.; Miletić, M. Small modular reactors: Simpler, safer, cheaper? *Energy* **2012**, *45*, 288–295.

2. Rowinski, M.K.; White, T.J.; Zhao, J. Small and medium sized reactors (SMR): A review of technology. *Renew. Sustain. Energy Rev.* **2015**, *44*, 643–656.

3. Reutler, H.; Lohnert, G.H. The modular high-temperature reactor. *Nucl. Technol.* **1983**, *62*, 22–30.

4. Reutler, H.; Lohnert, G.H. Advantages of going modular in HTRs. *Nucl. Eng. Des.* **1984**, *78*, 129–136.

5. Lohnert, G.H. Technical design features and essential safety-related properties of the HTR-MODULE. *Nucl. Eng. Des.* **1990**,*121*, 259–275.

6. Lanning, D.D. Modularized high-temperature gas-cooled reactor systems. *Nucl. Technol.* **1989**, *88*, 139–156.

7. Wu, Z.; Lin, D.; Zhong, D. The design features of the HTR-10. *Nucl. Eng. Des.* **2002**, *218*, 25–32.

8. Zhang, Z.; Wu, Z.; Wang, D.; Xu, Y.; Sun, Y.; Li, F.; Dong, Y. Current status and technical description of Chinese 2 × 250 MWth HTR-PM demonstration plant. *Nucl. Eng. Des.* **2009**, *239*, 2265–2274.

9. Shtessel, Y.B. Sliding mode control of the space nuclear reactor system. *IEEE Trans. Aerosp. Electron. Syst.* **1998**, *34*, 579–589.

10. Huang, Z.; Edwards, R.M.; Lee, K.Y. Fuzzy-adapted recursive sliding-mode controller design for a nuclear power plant control.*IEEE Trans. Nucl. Sci.* **2004**, *51*, 256–266.

11. Dong, Z. Nonlinear state-feedback dissipation power level control for nuclear reactors. *IEEE Trans. Nucl. Sci.* **2011**, *58*, 241–257.

12. Dong, Z. Nonlinear dynamic output-feedback power-level control for PWRs: A shifted-ectropy based design approach. *Prog. Nucl. Sci.* **2013**, *68*, 223–234.

13. Dong, Z. PD power-level control design for PWRs: A physically-based approach. *IEEE Trans. Nucl. Sci.* **2013**, *60*, 3889–3898.

14. Dong, Z. Dynamic output feedback power-level control for the MHTGR based on iterative damping assignment. *Energies* **2012**,*5*, 1782–1815.

15. Dong, Z. Physically-based power-level control for modular high temperature gas-cooled reactors. *IEEE Trans. Nucl. Sci.* **2012**,*59*, 2531–2549.

16. Na, M.G.; Shim, Y.R.; Lee, Y.J. Design of an adaptive predictive controller for steam generator. *IEEE Trans. Nucl. Sci.* **2003**,*50*, 186–193.

17. Munasinghe, S.R.; Kim, M.-S.; Lee, J.-J. Adaptive neurofuzzy controller to regulate UTSG water level in nuclear plants. *IEEE Trans. Nucl. Sci.* **2005**, *52*, 421–429.

18. Dong, Z.; Huang, X.; Zhang, L. Saturated output feedback dissipation steam temperature control for the OTSG of MHTGRs.*IEEE Trans. Nucl. Sci.* **2011**, *58*, 1277–1289.

19. Wang, L.-X. Stable adaptive fuzzy control of nonlinear systems. *IEEE Trans. Fuzzy Syst.* **1993**, *1*, 146–155.

20. Marseguerra, M.; Zio, E. Model-free fuzzy tracking control of a nuclear reactor. *Ann. Nucl. Energy* **2003**, *30*, 953–981.

21. Rigatos, G.G. Model-based and model-free control of flexible-link robots: A comparison between representative methods. *Appl. Math. Model.* **2009**, *33*, 3906–3925.

22. Dong, Z.; Huang, X.; Zhang, L. A nodal dynamic model for control system design and simulation of an MHTGR core. *Nucl. Eng. Des.* **2010**, *240*, 1251–1261.

23. Dong, Z. A Differential-algebraic model for the once-through steam generator of MHTGR-based multi- modular nuclear plants.*Math. Probl. Eng.* **2015**, *2015*, 370101.

24. Dong, Z.; Huang, X. Real-time simulation platform for the design and verification of the operation strategy of the HTR-PM. In Proceedings of the 21th International Conference on Nuclear Engineering, Chengdu, China, 29 July–2 August 2013.

Chapter 6

An experimental result on flaw sizing of steam generator tube at nuclear power plants using ultrasonic testing

Byungsik Yoon*{ , Yongsik Kim and Seunghan Yang

NDE Technology Group, KHNP Central Research Institute, 70, 1312 Gil, Yuseongdaero, Yuseong-gu, Daejeon 305–343, Korea

ABSTRACT

A steam generator at a nuclear power plant consists of thousands of thin tubes, and is a highly important component in operation. Also, steam generator tubes play a critical role in maintaining pressure boundaries of the primary and secondary sides, and can be easily damaged due to operation conditions caused by high temperature and pressure. Therefore, considerable amount of efforts are being committed to evaluating structural integrity of steam generators during in-service inspection. Eddy current testing is the commonly used inspection technique to evaluate a steam generator tube's integrity, but it has limitations in accurately sizing flaws due to the nature of the technique which determines size based on the entire volume of a flaw. In this study, experiments were performed by using ultrasonic testing instead of eddy current testing for the inspection of steam generator tubes to detect various kinds of flaws and to see if the detected flaws can be sized accurately. Consequently, the ultrasonic testing technique could detect various types of flaw, and the flaw sizing results were reliable in length and depth.

KEYWORDS

nuclear power plant, steam generator, ultrasonic testing, eddy current testing, flaw sizing, in-service inspection

1. INTRODUCTION

Steam generator tubes at a nuclear power plant are a pressure boundary between the primary side where radioactive materials exist and the secondary side's pressure boundary, which is not contaminated by radioactive materials. A steam generator tube is an important element of a nuclear power plant that can influence entire safety of the plant. More specifically, if a steam generator tube is damaged, radioactive materials on the primary side may leak, leading to a serious accident. In other words, damage or rapture involving a steam generator tube is closely related to the life and output power of a nuclear power plant. So far, several items have been known causing damage to a steam generator tube, and of these, damage to primary water stress corrosion cracking (PWSCC) taking place at the inner diameter, which is the primary side, and outer diameter stress corrosion cracking (ODSCC) at the outer diameter, which is the secondary side account for 60% of all flaws, taking up the biggest portion 1. In addition to the aforementioned, steam generators are damaged in various ways including fretting and other fatigue crack, wear, denting and pitting due to its high-temperature and pressure operational conditions. The most frequent damage occurring at steam generator tubes of nuclear power plants in Korea is caused by PWSCC in the primary side and wear. In particular, PWSCC happens when the inner tube is cracked, and the depth of a crack increases toward the outer side alongside the wall thickness. Here, cracks can be divided into those in the axial direction where the length of a crack grows in the direction of a tube's length, and those in the circumferential direction where the length of a crack grows along the circumference of a tube. Both types of cracking at nuclear power plants in Korea have been reported 2. In general, inspection of steam generator tubes during in-service inspection of nuclear power plants is currently performed by eddy current testing. While eddy current testing have advantages such as fast inspection speed and convenience, but it is difficult to evaluate accurate sizes of flaw length or depth with this method, because the sizing estimation based on signal amplitude is affected by the flaw's entire volume due to the nature of eddy current testing. Steam generator tube inspection using ultrasonic testing began as part of efforts to develop various inspection methods in order to meet inspection requirements specified by “PWR Steam Generator Examination Guideline” introduced by Electric Power Research Institute (EPRI) of the US in 1981 3. L. Gay performed studies on steam generator tube inspection and applicability by using a rotational ultrasonic transducer 4, whereas Kenefick studied a steam generator tube testing method using phase array testing 5–7. More recently, studies and efforts are underway to apply array-type eddy current testing in order to overcome limitations of the existing eddy current testing technique.

In this study, volumetric examination was performed on tube thickness using an array-type ultrasonic transducer with five high-frequency, focused ultrasonic transducers placed within the tube of steam generator in order to measure the size of a flaw precisely when it is detected primarily through eddy current testing. The purpose of this experiment is to see if various flaws can be detected, and to verify accuracy of ultrasonic testing for steam generator tubes at nuclear power plants by confirming flaw sizing accuracy experimentally through ultrasonic testing.

2. ULTRASONIC TRANSDUCER MODELING

2.1. Configuration of ultrasonic transducer

In addition to cracking-related flaws such as stress corrosion crack (SCC), various other flaws such as wear, bulge, and dent are found in a steam generator tube. Such flaws are generated in a steam generator tube's axial or circumferential direction and thus have various orientations. Therefore, inspection in all directions must be performed in consideration of this characteristic.

Used in this experiment is an array-type ultrasonic transducer consisting of one 0° normal transducer to check thickness change and wear of steam generator tubes, two 45° shear wave transducers for flaw detection in the axial direction, and two 45° shear wave transducers for flaw detection in the circumferential direction. Beam orientation and array of each transducer is shown in Figure 1.

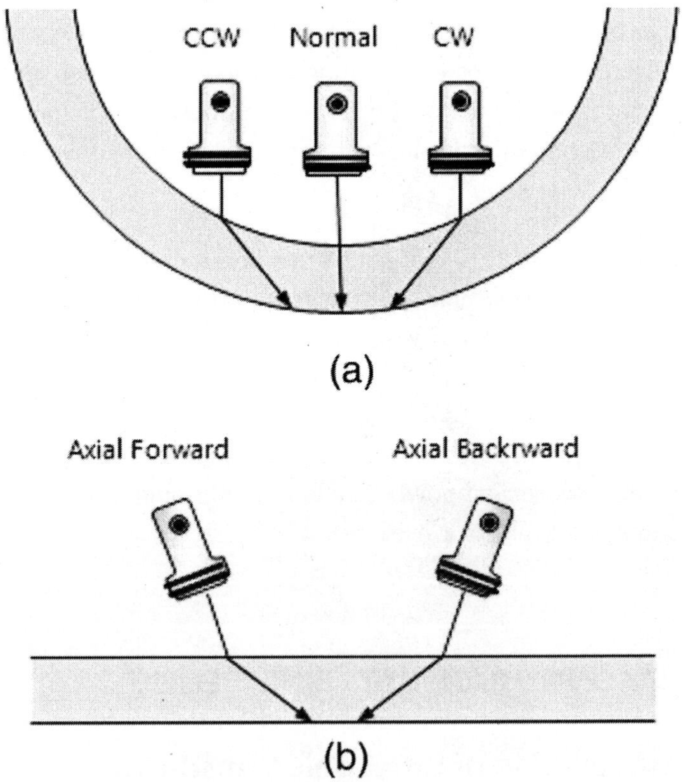

Figure 1. Ultrasonic beam orientations to detect axial and circumferential oriented flaws. (a) Transducer configuration for wall loss and axial crack. (b) Transducer configuration for circumferential crack.

2.2. Ultrasonic modeling

Each ultrasonic beam to be arrayed inside the array-type ultrasonic transducer body, which will be inserted into steam generator tubes, should be designed so that they are focused on half way between the inner and outer diameters in order to enhance the transducer's ability to detect flaws occurring on the steam generator tube. High ultrasonic frequency must be applied in order to raise sensitivity for micro-cracks. Also, because ultrasonic transducer to be used in experiments is inserted inside steam generator tubes, it is necessary to analyze ultrasonic beam's propagation characteristics that may occur in a curvature shape. Therefore, a modeling for ultrasonic sound field is necessary to determine various characteristics of such ultrasonic transducers and to evaluate propagation characteristics of ultrasonic beams.

Ultrasonic field was calculated by using three-dimensional modeling in consideration of the actual shape of steam generator tubes. The modeling condition of the tube inside is water filled and the outside condition of tube is air. The Kirchhoff approximate solution was applied to the modeling, and the shear wave speed of the steam generator tube upon modeling was 3020 m/s. In addition, it was assumed that inside the tube was in water condition and outside the tube was in air condition. Figure 2 shows the results of modeling using a normal 0° transducer. As shown in the modeling results in Figure 2, beam focus of the ultrasonic beam generated from the transducer with 15 MHz frequency was realized in the middle of inner and outer diameters of the tube.

Figure 3 is the modeling result of the CW (clock wise) and CCW (counter-clock wise) transducer which was designed to detect flaws in the axial direction. As shown in the outcomes of C-scan and B-scan, ultrasonic beam was focused in the middle of the tube.

Figure 4 is the modeling result of a beam moving 45° forward and backward to detect flaws in the circumferential direction.

As can be seen from the modeling result, each ultrasonic beam was focused in the middle of the tube thickness. The distance between the transducer and the specimen's inner diameter, as well as the shape of focus lens of the ultrasonic transducer was determined based on the modeling result.

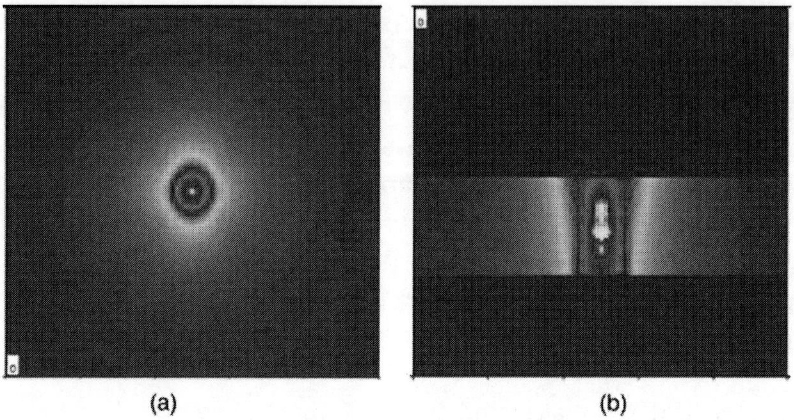

Figure 2. The modeling result of normal beam sound field focused at middle of tube thickness. (a) C-scan image. (b) B-scan image.

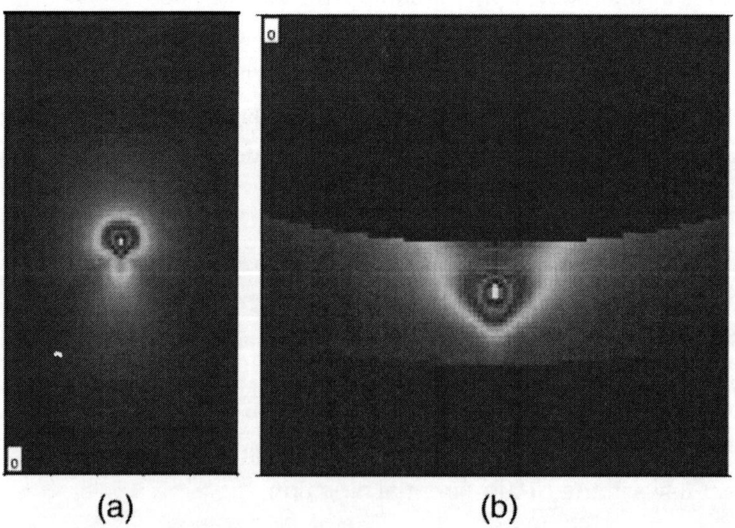

Figure 3. The modeling result of CCW and CW beam sound field focused at middle of tube thickness. (a) C-scan image. (b) B-scan image.

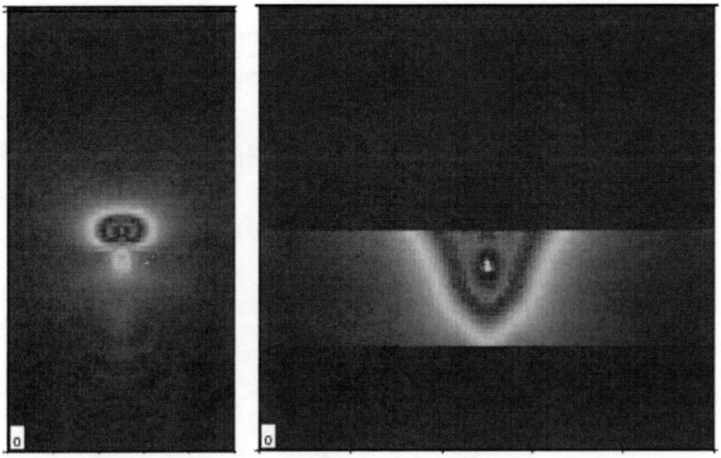

(a) (b)

Figure 4. The modeling result of backward and forward beam sound field focused at middle of thickness. (a) C-scan image. (b) B-scan image.

2.3. Ultrasonic transducer assembly design

Using the modeling result, an array-type ultrasonic transducer having five transducers arrayed in a cylindrical body with 16 mm diameter was manufactured, which was to be inserted inside the steam generator tube. Figure 5 shows the shape of the array-type ultrasonic transducer designed based on the modeling result and the manufactured transducer.

Table 1 outlines ultrasonic characteristics of each ultrasonic transducer designed to be arrayed.

3. SPECIMEN AND EXPERIMENTAL METHOD

3.1. Specimen

For this study, an experiment was performed on steam generator tubes at Uljin Nuclear Power Plant Units 1 and 2, which are known to experience

PWSCC and ODSCC flaws. The steam generator tubes at the Uljin Nuclear Power Plant Units 1 and 2 are Framatom-type nuclear reactors whose outer diameter is 22.22 mm and are 1.27 mm thick with relatively larger diameter than Westinghouse or CE reactor steam generator tubes. The tube specifications are shown in Table 2.

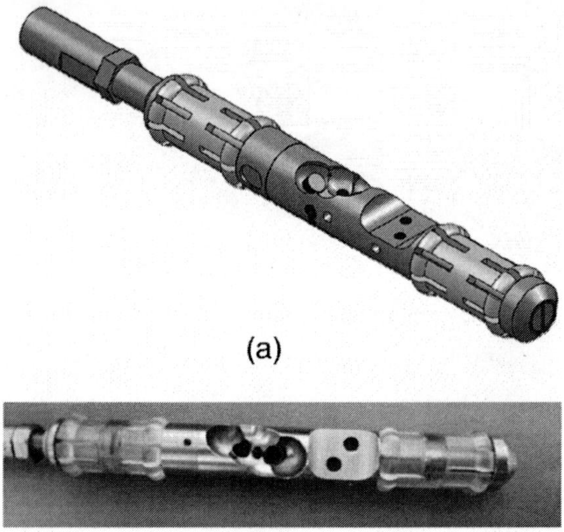

(a)

(b)

Figure 5. Ultrasonic transducer for steam generator tube inspection designed based on the modeling result. (a) Modeling result. (b) Manufactured multi-array ultrasonic assembly.

Table 1. Ultrasonic characteristic measurement of each element (at 6 dB).

Ch. no	Focal distance (mm)	Beam diameter (mm)	Depth of field (mm)	Center frequency (MHz)
0°	10	0.51	11.6	14.7
45°DN	14.1	0.36	6.4	14.1
45°UP	13.8	0.33	6.7	13.8
45°CW	15.5	0.30	6.2	15.5
45°CCW	14.7	0.30	6.7	14.7

Table 2. Dimensional specification of steam generator tube specimen.

Material	Diameter	Thickness
Inconel 600	22.22 mm	1.27 mm

For this study, a tube specimen with fabricated electric discharge machining (EDM) notch was manufactured in order to perform an experiment to detect flaws. To simulate flaws with various orientations, flaws in the axial and circumferential directions were fabricated at various depths. Figure 6 shows specifications and shape of the notch specimen devised for this experiment.

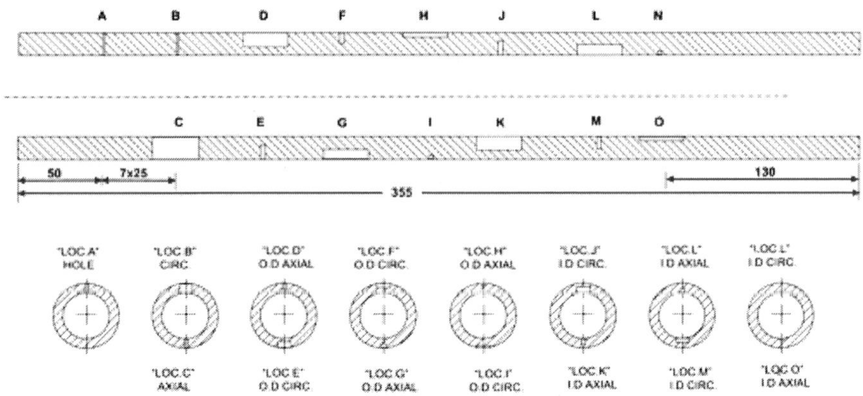

Figure 6. Test tube drawing for the steam generator ultrasonic testing experiment with artificial flaws (unit : mm).

Table 3 and Figure 6 show detailed dimension including location and orientation of each flaw.

Table 3. Detail dimensions of EDM flaws embedded in steam generator tube.

No.	Location	Flaw Orient.	Depth		Width (mm)	Length (mm)
			(mm)	(%)		
#A	N/A	Hole	1.27	100	1.69	1.69
#B	N/A	Circ.	1.27	100	0.14	9.54
#C	N/A	Axial	1.27	100	0.14	9.53
#D	OD	Axial	0.762	60	0.15	9.54
#E	OD	Circ.	0.762	60	0.15	9.54
#F	OD	Circ.	0.508	40	0.14	9.53
#G	OD	Axial	0.508	40	0.14	9.52
#H	OD	Axial	0.254	20	0.14	9.51
#I	OD	Circ.	0.254	20	0.14	9.51
#J	ID	Circ.	0.762	60	0.15	9.54
#K	ID	Axial	0.762	60	0.15	9.54
#L	ID	Axial	0.508	40	0.14	9.53
#M	ID	Circ.	0.508	40	0.14	9.52
#N	ID	Circ.	0.254	20	0.14	9.52
#O	ID	Axial	0.254	20	0.14	9.52

3.2. Composition of the experimental apparatus

The steam generator tube testing system can be largely divided into two parts, an ultrasonic system and a vertical work bench. The schematic diagram of an ultrasonic system is shown in Figure 7.

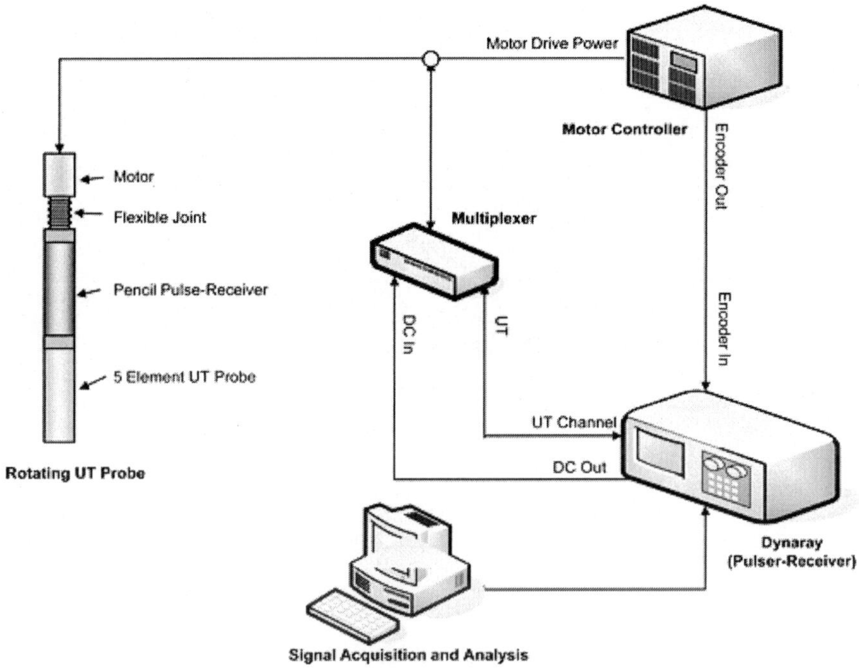

Figure 7. The schematic diagram of ultrasonic experiment system.

ZETEC's Dynaray was used for the ultrasonic system's pulse-receiver, and a multiplex was installed between the pulse-receiver and the transducer so that five transducers can transmit and receive signals through a single cable, thereby minimizing the diameter of the cable to be embedded into the tube. A dual-axial control was used to allow the transducer body to rotate 360° and to move toward the axial direction of the tube.

The vertical work bench is devised so that it can fix the steam generator tube and insert and transport the rotating ultrasonic transducer vertically into the tube. Its composition is shown in Figure 8. The transducer was used to obtain data at 90°/s of rotation speed in the circumferential direction and at 0.125 mm/s of axially travelling speed.

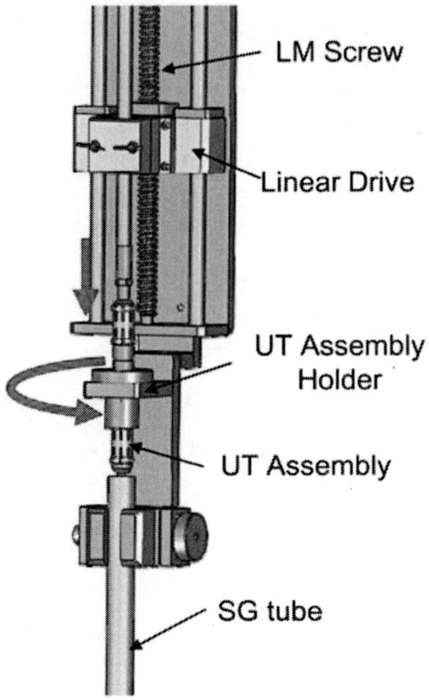

Figure 8. Experimental apparatus for linear driving of rotating ultrasonic probe.

4. RESULTS AND DISCUSSIONS

The ultrasonic testing experiment was carried out for detection and quantitative sizing of fabricated flaws in the steam generator tube, and as a result, all of the 15 artificial EDM flaws were detected. Figure 9 represents C-Scan signals of flaws detected from the 0° normal transducer. In Figure 9, the horizontal direction is the circumferential angle of the tube, whereas the vertical direction represents the axial direction of the tube. As shown in the figure, all 15 flaws were detected, and the geometrical orientation of the flaws could be visibly confirmed. The length and width of the flaws could be measured by using the test results of the 0° transducer.

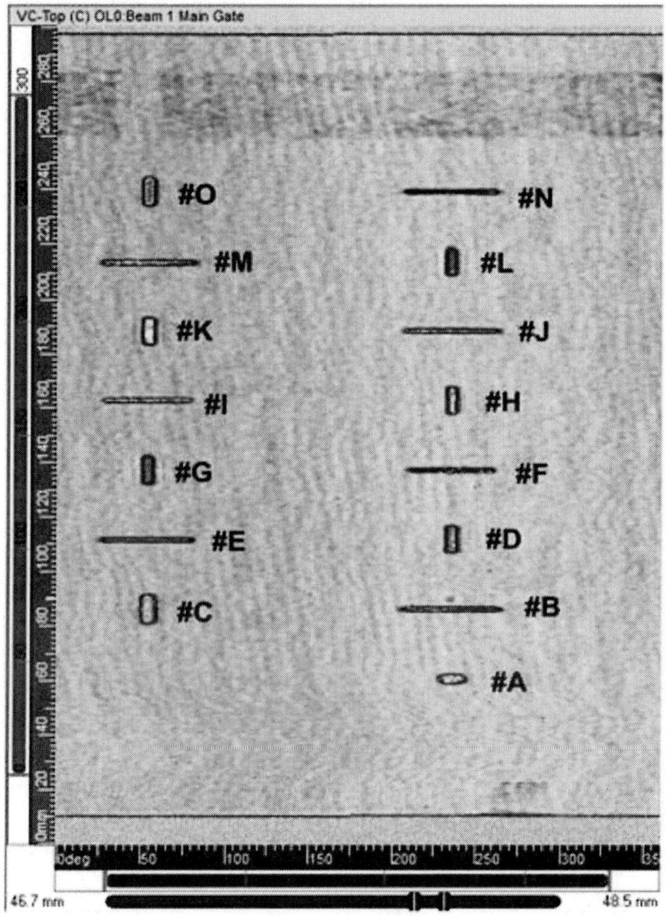

Figure 9. The experimental result showing C-Scan image from 0° degree transducer signal.

In addition to the 0° normal transducer used in this experiment, all flaws were detected with four 45° shear wave transducers and 0° normal transducers. Figure 10 shows signals as a result of the CW transducer experiment, which was used to detect axial flaws. All axial flaws, i.e. #C, #D, #G, #H, #K, #L, and #O and hole #A with 100% penetration were confirmed. Circumferential flaws having depth greater than 40% of tube thickness and located on tube inside #J and #M were detected but have low amplitude. Figure 11 shows signals detected by the backward transducer whose ultrasonic beam propagates toward the tube's axial direction designed to detect circumferential flaws. As a result of the experiment, all the circumferential flaws #B, #E, #F, #I, #J, #M, and #N were detected. Axial flaws having depth greater than 20% tube thickness and located on tube inside #K, #L, and #O were found. Also, the deepest depth flaw #C located on tube outside is detected.

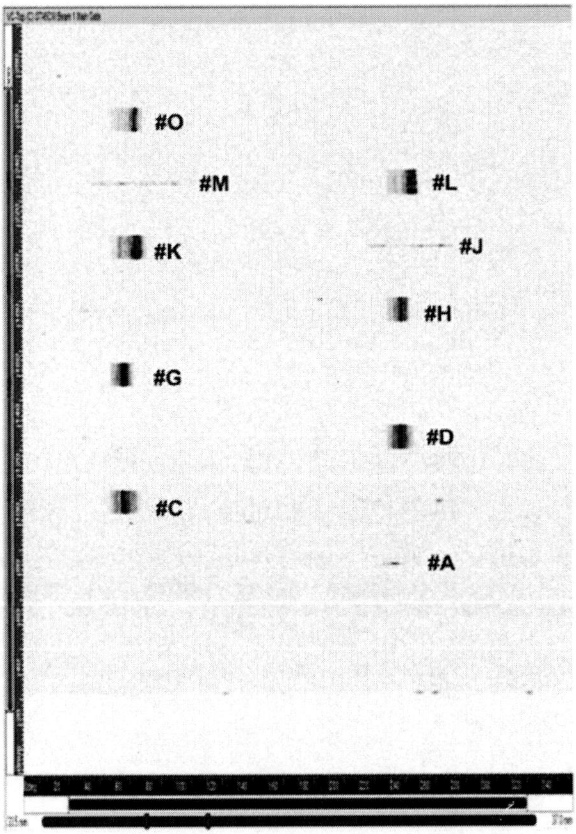

Figure 10. C-Scan signals of flaws detected by using CW transducer.

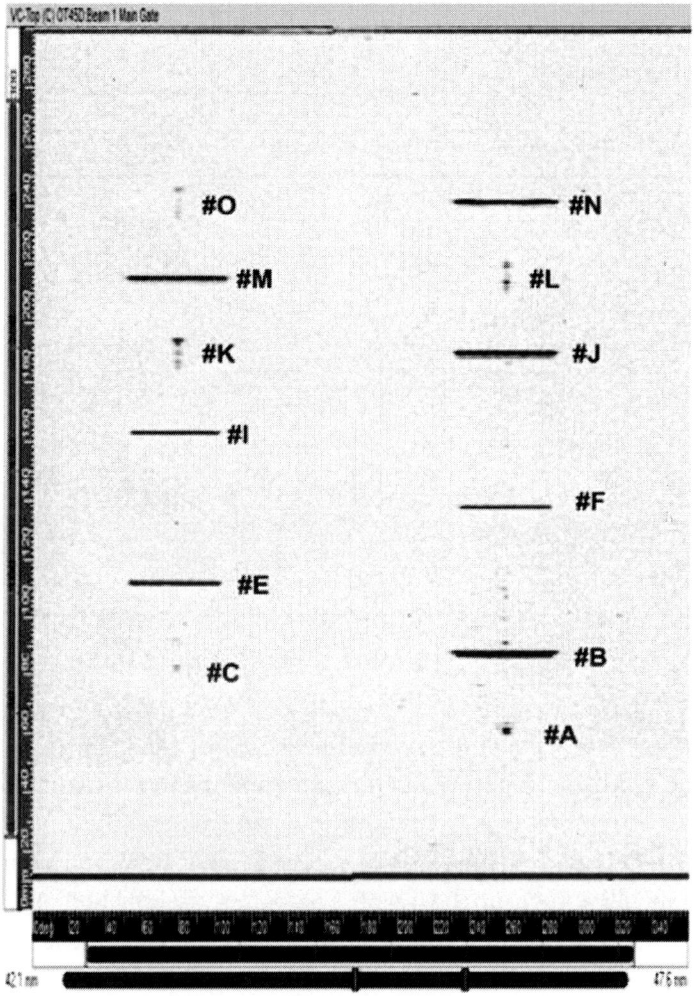

Figure 11. C-Scan signals of flaws detected by using backward transducer.

The length sizing of artificial flaws of the experimental tube was performed, and from the highest amplitude of the flaw to the point where the signal went down to the level of 6 dB was evaluated as the length and width of the flaw, and the tip-diffraction technique using diffracted ultrasonic signals at the top of the flaw was employed as the basic depth evaluation technique. Table 4 shows sizing results of ultrasonic signals for all EDM notches used in the experiment.

Table 4. Sizing results of detected flaws.

No.	Location	Flaw orient.	Depth (mm)	Width (mm)	Length (mm)
#A	N/A	Hole	1.27	1.70	1.70
#B	N/A	Circ.	1.26	0.80	9.80
#C	N/A	Axial	1.27	0.74	9.50
#D	OD	Axial	0.79	0.80	9.10
#E	OD	Circ.	0.76	0.77	9.80
#F	OD	Circ.	0.58	0.65	9.70
#G	OD	Axial	0.55	0.70	9.50
#H	OD	Axial	0.3	0.57	10.0
#I	OD	Circ.	0.35	0.70	10.2
#J	ID	Circ.	0.7	0.67	10.0
#K	ID	Axial	0.86	0.60	10.0
#L	ID	Axial	0.5	0.68	9.50
#M	ID	Circ.	0.58	0.71	10.0
#N	ID	Circ.	0.3	0.77	10.3
#O	ID	Axial	0.28	0.55	10.1

Figure 12 is a graph showing the difference between the length, width, and depth of the notches measured in this experiment and the actual size of the flaws. The horizontal axis is for flaw numbers whereas the vertical axis denotes the error between actual size and the size measured in this experiment. As shown in the graph, the notch's width had the greatest error and the length had a smaller error compared to the width, and the depth had the most accurate result. Length measurement result shows that the biggest error is 0.78 mm, and root mean square error (RMSE) for the measured length of all the flaws was calculated to be 0.42 mm.

Root mean square error was calculated by using the equation below:

$$\mathrm{RMSE} = \sqrt{\frac{\sum_{i=1}^{n}(m_i - t_i)^2}{n}}$$

Here, m_i = length or depth of the flaw measured in the experiment; t_i = length or depth of the actual flaw; n = the number of measured flaws.

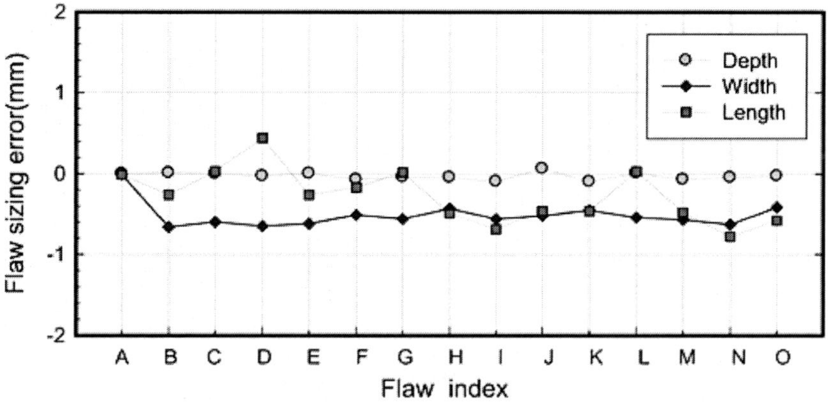

Figure 12. Comparison of measured flaw size errors based on flaw length, width and depth for each flaws.

Root mean square error of the measurement result for the flaw's width was 0.66 mm. It was analyzed that, although minimization of the ultrasonic beam's focus can be attempted by using a focused ultrasonic transducer, the 0.12 mm EDM notch width was relatively over-evaluated due to the notch's relatively small width as well as overlapping of the ultrasonic beam at both corners, which are the starting points of the notch width. The RMSE value for the depth of evaluated flaw has the smallest error, 0.05 mm, and it was confirmed that the results measured with the tip-diffraction method was quite accurate.

5. CONCLUSIONS

In order to measure various flaws occurring at steam generator tubes at a nuclear power plant accurately and quantitatively, an array-type ultrasonic transducer with orientation was designed. From the experiment, the following conclusions could be drawn:

1) An ultrasonic transducer for inspection of steam generator tubes at nuclear power plants was designed through ultrasonic modeling, and

an array-type ultrasonic transducer was manufactured based on the modeling results.

2) By using the manufactured ultrasonic transducer, various types of artificial flaws fabricated inside and outside of steam generator tubes could be detected.

3) It was possible to detect all fabricated flaws at the inner and outer diameters, and length measurement for all detected flaws was performed with RMS error of 0.42 mm.

4) Flaws having depth from 20% of the steam generator tube thickness to 100% penetration holes were measured and accurate results with RMS error of 0.05 mm could be obtained.

5) Consequently, the size of artificial flaws could be measured very accurately by using an array-type ultrasonic transducer in steam generator tubes of nuclear power plants. Thus, this inspection technique, once applied to nuclear power plants, is expected to enhance reliability of steam generator inspection.

REFERENCES

1. Choi, M.S and Hur, D.H. 2002. Signal characteristics of eddy current test for intergranular attack of steam generator tubes. *J. Korean Soc Nondestruct. Test*, 22: 198–199.

2. Choi, M.S. and Hur, D.H. 2001. Evaluation of eddy current signals from the inner wall axial cracks of steam generator tubes.*J. Korean Soc Nondestruct. Test*, 21: 501–509.

3. Behravesh, M. and Henry, G. 2002. *Pressurized Water Reactor Steam Generator Examination Guidelines, Revision 6* Charlotte, NC, USA TR-1003138, EPRI NDE Center,

4. Gay, L. and Bourgogne, R. Steam Generator Tubes: Crack Sizing by Ultrasonic Inspection Using a Rotating Multi-Transducers Probe. *Proceedings of the 7th European Conference on Non-Destructive Testing*. May26–29. pp.26–29. Copenhagen, Denmark

5. Kenefick, S. and Henry, G. 1999. *Field Implementation of Ultrasonic Crack Tip Diffraction Sizing Techniques in Steam Generator Tubing at Comanche Peak Steam Station, TE-114508, pp* 1–2. Charlotte, NC, USA EPRI NDE Center

6. Kenefick, S. Recent Applications of Ultrasonic Examination of Steam Generator Tubes. *2nd International Conference on NDE in Relation to Structural Integrity for Nuclear and Pressurized Components*. May24–26. pp.3–5. New Orleans, Louisiana, USA

7. Kenefick, S. and Henry, G. 1999. *Phased Array Ultrasonic Inspection of Steam Generator* Charlotte, NC, USA TE-114394, EPRI NDE Center

Chapter 7

Simulation of a Standalone, Portable Steam Generator Driven by a Solar Concentrator

Mohamed Sabry [1,2,*], Mouaaz Nahas [3] and Saud H. Al-Lehyani [1]

[1]Physics Department, College of Applied Sciences, Umm Al-Qura University, Makkah 21955, Saudi Arabia

[2]Solar Research Department, National Research Institute of Astronomy and Geophysics, Cairo 11421, Egypt

[3]Electrical Engineering Department, College of Engineering and Islamic Architecture, Umm Al-Qura University, Makkah 21955, Saudi Arabia

ABSTRACT

Solar energy is a good solution for energy-deficiency problems, especially in regions such as rural areas in the Middle East that have not been electrified yet or are under electrification. In this paper, with the aid of a Computational Fluid Dynamics simulation, we propose a system that comprises a trough solar concentrator and a pipe—with flowing water—that is set in the concentrator focus. The aim of this work is to investigate the feasibility of generating steam from such a system as well as analyzing the generated steam quantitatively and qualitatively. Effects of variation of solar radiation intensity, ambient temperature, water flow rate and pipe diameter on the quantity and quality of the generated steam have been investigated. The results show that a quantity of about 130 kg of steam could be generated per day with a 0.01 m diameter with 0.0042 kg/s flowing water, although qualitatively, a narrower pipe achieves better performance than a wider one. About 74 kg of daily accumulated steam mass with a temperature >423 K could be achieved for a 0.005 m diameter tube compared to about 50 kg for the 0.01 m diameter tube. Steam quality factor is higher at all flow rates for the 0.005 m diameter tube compared to that of 0.01 m.

KEYWORDS

solar energy; steam generation; Computational Fluid Dynamics (CFD) simulation

1. INTRODUCTION

Current high electricity loads require appropriate and adequate power generation. However, it is well known that conventional power generation by means of fossil fuels is a major cause of environmental pollution [1]. Any comparison of solar energy and conventional generation is unfair if it does not include the indirect costs of conventional energy, which are defined by factors such as its environmental and health impacts [2]. Solar Thermal Power Plants (STPP) are expected to share the energy production scenario with conventional energy generation technologies like fossil and nuclear [3].

The Middle East, Arabia and the Gulf countries have very high solar radiation potential, especially for direct solar radiation or Direct Normal Irradiance (DNI), *i.e.*, the fraction of solar radiation which is not deviated by clouds, fumes or dust in the atmosphere and that reaches the Earth's surface as a parallel beam [4]. The regional DNI map is shown in Figure 1. The large area combined with the abundant solar resources has made this region one of the most promising areas for the installation of solar energy plants for providing electricity [5]. Rural electrification is a global challenge in developing countries, especially those whose area is huge and have a low population in scattered communities or tribes as is the case in most countries of the mentioned region. It also determines the living standard of the people and as well stops the immigration to urban areas [6].

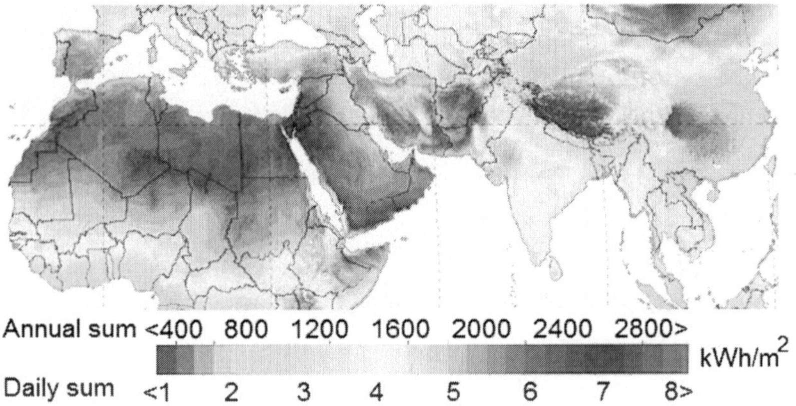

Figure 1. Solar radiation distribution over the Middle East, Arabia and Gulf region.

Concentration of solar radiation becomes necessary when high temperatures are desired. The concentration ratio is defined as [7]:

$$C = \frac{Aperture\ area}{Absorber\ area} \quad (1)$$

Solar concentrators work perfectly at locations where DNI dominates. Electrical power is produced when the concentrated light is converted into heat, which drives a steam turbine that is connected to an electrical power generator [8].

Solar radiation is converted into thermal energy in the focus zone of solar thermal concentrating systems. A receiver tube is installed in the focal line with a fluid flowing inside it that absorbs concentrated solar energy from the tube walls and raises its enthalpy. The collector is provided with a one-axis solar tracking system to ensure that the solar beam falls parallel to its axis. Using evacuated tubular absorbers is one of the foremost technologies currently used in solar thermal electric power generation plants [9].

Previous research work has investigated the thermal performance of parabolic trough collectors for operation with synthetic oil and water as the working fluids. Also, a model of thermal losses from the collector has been developed to predict the performance of the collector with any working fluid. The effects of absorber emissivity and internal working fluid convection effects are evaluated in [9]. The collector thermal loss when using synthetic oil as the working fluid was estimated to be higher than when using water.

A modelling program called PTCDES was used in the past to predict the quantity of steam produced by the system [10]. The values of solar radiation and ambient air temperature used in this modelled performance of the system were 500 W/m^2 and 30 °C, respectively.

A Computational Fluid Dynamics (CFD) model has been generated using same software used in this work applied to a North–South oriented solar collectors' loop, composed of 11 parabolic-trough collector units connected in series, with a total length of 500 m. The experimental test facility is located at the Plataforma Solar de Almería, Spain. The research concluded that the model shows a very good performance and the results presented support the applicability of CFD modeling to study dynamics of direct steam generation in parabolic-trough solar collectors [11].

A parabolic solar concentrator prototype has been built by other researchers [12,13]. Temperatures above 200 °C and pressures up to 12 kg/cm^2 could be achieved experimentally. Higher temperature and pressure could have been achieved, but errors associated with the shape of the parabolic surface existed [12,13].

In this work, we propose a standalone portable system comprising a parabolic trough concentrator and a pipe—with flowing water—set in the concentrator's focus as shown in Figure 2. As the water flows inside the pipe, the concentrated solar energy is absorbed and steam is generated at the pipe outlet which will in turn drive a steam turbine to generate electricity.

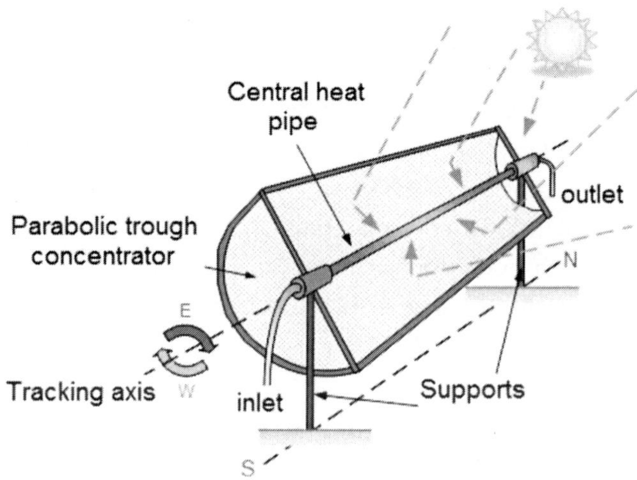

Figure 2. Flow diagram of the proposed system [14].

Understanding of the dynamic behavior of the direct steam generation process is essential for proper operation and output optimization of this type of proposed standalone solar plant. Accurate CFD modeling can lead to clear determination of the optimal operating point in the design of such a system, allowing us to identify critical process conditions that may lead to anticipated failures like two-phase flow phenomena occurring in the proposed system.

The aim of the work is to investigate the capability of steam generation using a 1 meter portable parabolic solar concentrator that could operate in remote areas. The study approach is to perform a CFD simulation of water flowing inside the pipe with the relevant physical conditions applied to it like solar radiation intensity, ambient temperature, tube diameter and water flow rate, in order to investigate the quantity and quality of the generated steam.

2. CFD SIMULATION APPROACH

Since the outer tube is completely isolated from the inner tube, radiative and conductive heat losses from the outer surface of the inner (metallic) tube are neglected. Rather an overall loss from the inner tube of about 20% is assumed [15]. Radiative and conductive heat transfer losses from the whole system are considered when we discuss a specific design of a system with known dimensions and materials. Detailed analysis of the heat transfer to water through the evacuated tube is calculated by employing a finite volume algorithm using STAR CCM, a commercially available CFD package that has been tested [16] and proven good capability for solving such problems. The flowing water has only been taken into consideration in the simulation process with heat loss of about 20% of the incident concentrated solar radiation. Mesh has been built for the 1 m length water using multilayer polyhedral cells as shown in Figure 3.

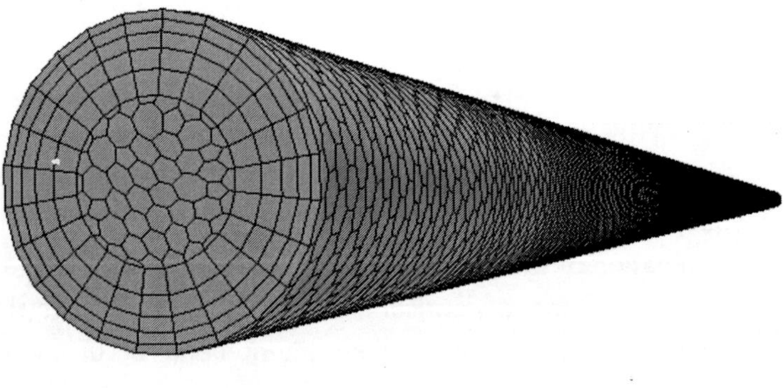

Figure 3. Polyhedral meshing of the water inside the tube.

In order to make sure that simulation results are independent of the mesh, a grid sensitivity study with different base-size and growth-rate meshes has been performed applying the physical parameters and boundary conditions listed in Table 1. Two mesh dimensions have been applied to the tube and resulted in the same solution features as listed in Table 2. A reduction of the base mesh size from 0.01 m to 0.003 m with a simultaneous increase of number of prism layers has resulted in an increase of the number of volume mesh cells from 156,356 to 233,441. As listed in the Table, a small variation of average outlet temperature (from 479 K in the first set of mesh settings to 486 K in the second mesh) has been found. However, no variations have been observed in the average outlet steam fraction as will be discussed later. The coarser mesh model "Mesh 1" was then adopted, as a good compromise between reasonable grid-independence of the solution and computation time.

A three-dimensional, steady state multiphase fluid model with turbulent flow has been used in the CFD simulation process. In more detail, a single continuity equation (Equation (2)) is solved for a fluid having a mixture of liquid and gas phases, where each distinct phase has its own set of conservation equations.

Phases are considered to be mixed on length scales smaller than the length scales to resolve, and coexist everywhere in the flow domain. The volume fraction is the portion of a volume that a phase occupies [16,17,18].

Table 1. Dimensions and material of the proposed system.

Part	Dimensions
Parabolic trough	Length: 1 m
	Aperture: 1.6 m
	Optical collection efficiency: 64% [10]
Evacuated tube	Length: 1 m
	Inner tube material: steel
	Outer tube material: evacuated glass
	Collection efficiency: 80% [15]
	Inner tube diameter: 0.005 m, 0.01 m
Flowing liquid	Material: Water
	Flow rate (kg/h): 0.0019, 0.0022, 0.0025, 0.0028, 0.0031 and 0.0042

Table 2. Mesh specifications used in grid sensitivity test.

	Cell base size	No. of prism layers	No. of mesh cells	Ave. outlet temperature (K)	Ave. outlet steam fraction (%)
Mesh 1	0.01 m	5	156356	479	0.98
Mesh 2	0.0030 m	7	233441	486	0.98

$$\frac{\partial}{\partial t}(\alpha_i \rho_i) + \nabla.(\alpha_i \rho_i v_i) = \sum_{i \neq j} (m_{ij} - m_{ji}) + S_i^{\alpha} \tag{2}$$

In addition, the volume fractions must satisfy Equation (3):

$$\sum_i \alpha_i = 1 \tag{3}$$

In these simulations the realizable two-layer turbulence model [17] was used. In this model, C_μ, a critical coefficient of the model, is expressed as a function of mean flow and turbulence properties, rather than assumed to be constant as in the standard model. This allows the model to satisfy certain mathematical constraints of the normal stresses consistent with the physics of turbulence (realizability), which are also consistent with experimental observations in boundary layers. The realizable model is substantially better than the standard model and is implemented in STAR-CCM with a two layer approach, which enables it to be used with fine meshes that resolve the viscous sub-layer. The turbulent viscosity μ_t is expressed as [16,17]:

$$\mu_t = \frac{\rho C_\mu k^2}{\varepsilon} \tag{4}$$

where C_μ is a coefficient given by $C_\mu = \frac{1}{A_0 + A_s U^{(*)} \frac{k}{\varepsilon}}$, ρ is the density; $U(*)$ is a function of strain rate tensor and vorticity tensor; A_0whose value is taken as 4.0; while A_s is taken as [17,18]:

$$A_s = \sqrt{6} \cos \emptyset \tag{5}$$

$$\emptyset = \frac{1}{3}\cos^{-1}\sqrt{6}W \qquad (6)$$

Hourly profiles of direct solar radiation of two selected clear-sky days, representing summer and winter, respectively, along with their ambient temperature values, have been considered, as shown in Figure 4. The location considered in this paper is Makkah, Saudi Arabia (21.4167° N, 39.8167° E), where the authors reside. These temperature values are used as inputs to the simulation process to calculate the net thermal energy gain of the system. The water inlet's temperature is assumed as the ambient temperature. Wind speed data was not available for the chosen location, so rather a total loss has been considered.

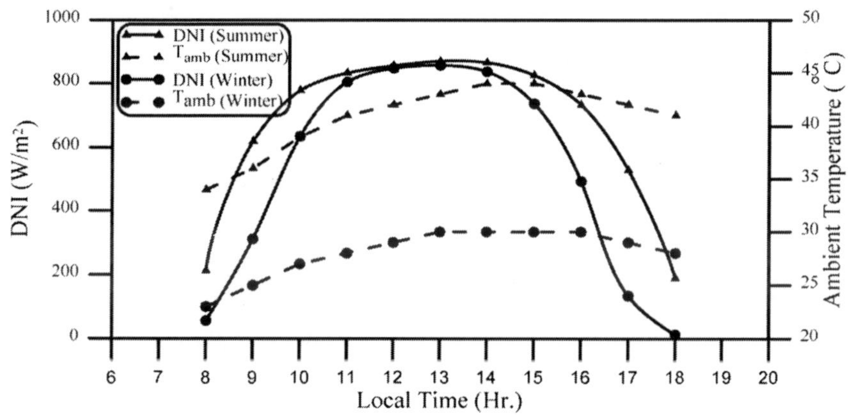

Figure 4. Hourly direct solar radiation and ambient temperature profiles for two typical days in summer and winter.

3. SIMULATION RESULTS

Data collected from the CFD simulation are in the form of temperature, volume fractions of water and steam, and velocity of flow of the fluid components at almost every point inside the tube. Figure 5 shows some simulation results for a 0.01 m diameter tube with flow rate of 15 kg/h (or

0.0042 kg/s) at noon time in a typical summer day. Figure 5a shows temperature distribution of a water-steam mixture at the tube outlet, while Figure 5b shows the volume fraction of steam generated relative to water at the outlet. Both graphs show that water temperature, hence steam volume fraction at the water-tube interface, is higher than that in the middle of the tube. This is because the water and steam layers are in contact with the hot metallic tube. In contrary, the lowest temperature, and hence the lowest steam volume fraction is shown in the middle of the water tube as it receives less energy. Both graphs also show that both temperature and steam volume fraction are higher on the upper half of the tube outlet than that of the lower half. This is due to the fact that water density reduces with increasing temperature, so higher temperature water and steam rise on top of the colder ones. This is also clear in Figure 5c which shows the volume fraction of steam at a cross sectional plane across the tube length. Figure 5c is intentionally drawn not to scale, *i.e.*, the ratio of tube length to its diameter has been distorted to show the buildup of steam during its passage across the tube.

In the next section, quantitative and qualitative analysis of steam emerging from the outlet will be carried out. A comparison between two systems having diameters of 0.005 m and 0.01 m, respectively, is performed. Changing tube diameter is responsible for changing the absorber area according to Equation (1), and hence the concentration ratio and flow speed inside the tube are changed. A set of six flow rates have been tested, namely 7, 8, 9, 10, 11 and 15 kg/h (corresponding to 0.0019, 0.0022, 0.0025, 0.0028, 0.0031 and 0.0042 kg/s, respectively) and the water-steam has been investigated qualitatively and quantitatively at the tube exit.

4. SYSTEM PERFORMANCE

As discussed above, the system is proposed to operate under ambient temperature and DNI in two selected days in summer and winter, respectively, as shown in Figure 4. The simulation is performed for each hour by inputting the ambient temperature and DNI values to the model and assuming the water inlet has a temperature equal to the ambient temperature at that hour. Simulations have been performed for the flow rates mentioned above. Average temperature profiles of the water/steam mixture at the outlet of the 0.005 m diameter pipe in summer are calculated and shown in Figure 6. As expected, increasing the flow rate resulted in a reduction of the average temperature of the outlet mixture. A similar behavior ocurrs for the daily profile of the 0.005 m diameter pipe in winter with a lower average outlet temperature as shown in Figure 7 (in comparison with that of Figure 6). In both graphs, the average steam temperature is directly proportional to both the solar radiation intensity and ambient temperature as shown in Figure 4 and Figure 11and as will be discussed below.

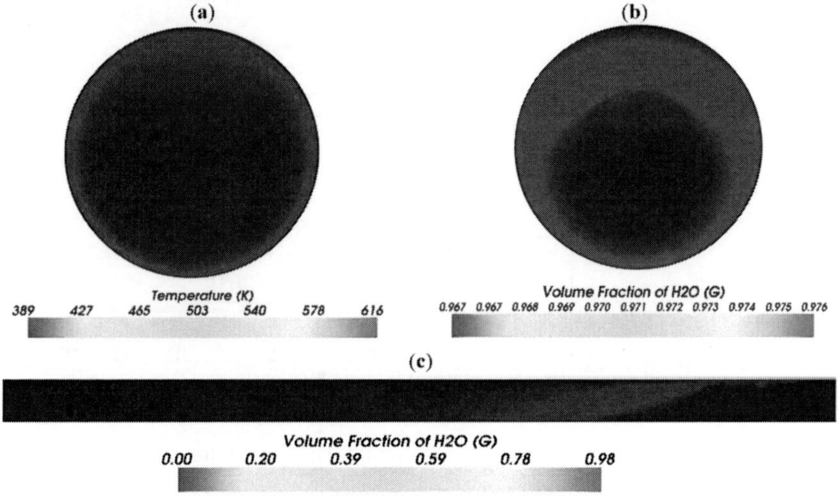

Figure 5. Steam outlet (**a**) temperature distribution; (**b**) volume fraction and (**c**) volume fraction at a cross sectional plane across the tube axis (not to scale) for a 0.01 m diameter tube with flow rate of 15 kg/h (0.0042 kg/s) at noon in summer.

Rate of steam generated is then investigated by evaluating the mass of water that has been converted into steam again for the 0.005 m diameter pipe in summer and winter, which are shown in Figure 8 and Figure 9, respectively. These graphs show that a saturation of steam generation is established on either side of noontime with a rate of generation proportional to the inlet flow rate. Rate of generated steam in winter shown in Figure 9 has a narrower profile width as compared to that of Figure 8. This is due to the lower values of both DNI and water inlet temperature in winter than in summer (this is obviously due to the later sunrise and earlier sunset times in winter as compared to summer days; also ambient temperature in summer day is much higher than that of winter day).

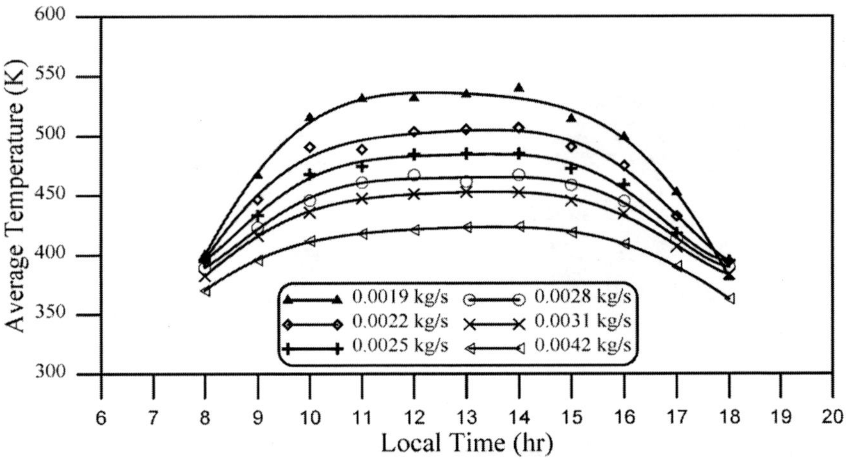

Figure 6. Daily profile of average output temperature for a 0.005 m diameter tube on a typical summer day.

Average outlet temperature and generated steam mass rate are higher in summer than those of winter for the 0.01 m diameter pipe because both the solar radiation intensity and ambient temperature are higher in summer than that in winter. Average outlet temperature has been graphed against incident solar radiation in Figure 10.

A nonlinear increase of temperature is due to the effect of increasing ambient temperature along with increasing solar radiation. The outlet temperatures increase above the inlet at noon for the two tube diameters under investigation in the proposed summer day as a function of water flow rate is shown in Figure 11.

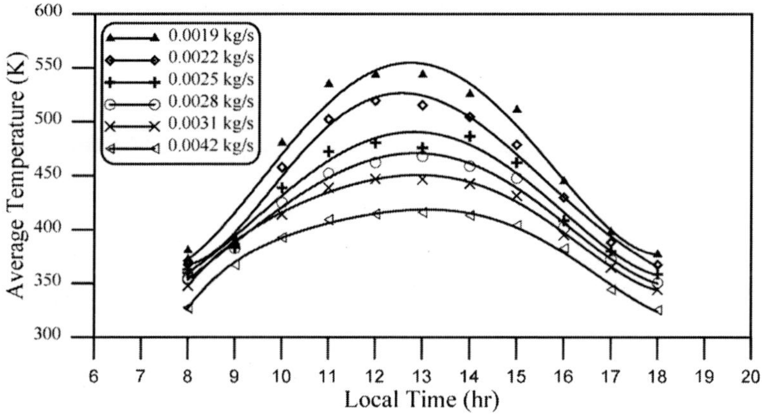

Figure 7. Daily profile of average output temperature for a 0.005 m diameter tube on a typical winter day.

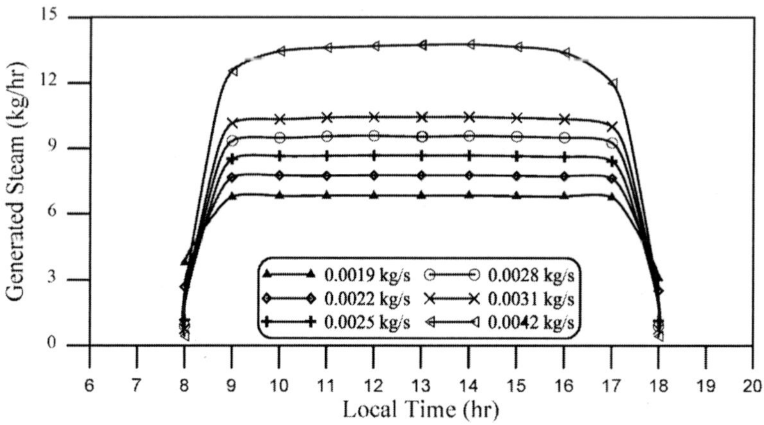

Figure 8. Daily profile of rate of generated steam mass for a 0.005 m diameter tube in a summer day.

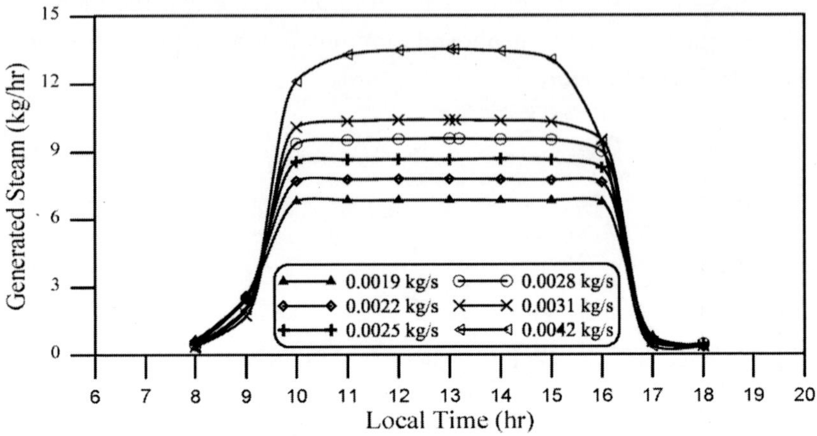

Figure 9. Daily profile of rate of generated steam mass for a 0.005 m diameter tube in a winter day.

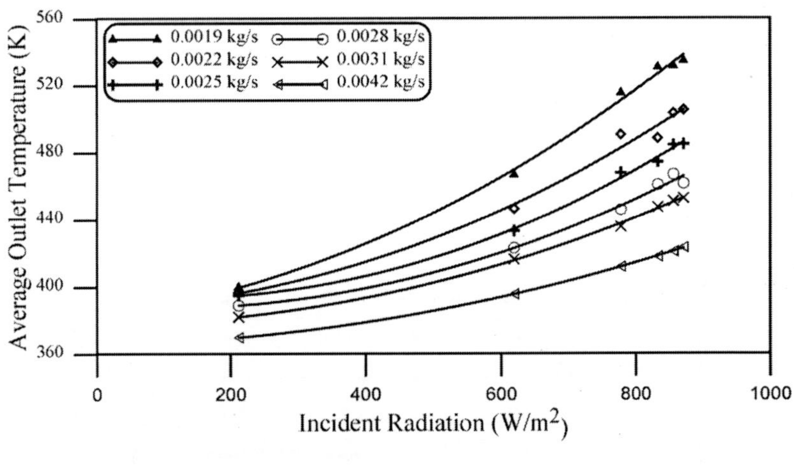

Figure 10. Average outlet temperature with increasing incident solar radiation for the 0.005 m tube in summer.

Increasing flow rate shows an asymptotic reduction of the average outlet temperature for both tubes as clearly shown in the figure. The narrower tube has an average outlet temperature increase of about 220 K at a flow rate of 0.0019 kg/s, corresponding to an increase of about 165 K at the same flow rate. Both tubes have nearly the same average outlet steam temperature increase of about 105 K at a flow rate of 0.0042 kg/s. This is because of the reduction in the passage time of water flowing inside the tube as a result of increasing water flow rate and hence water speed that is shown in Figure 12. This graph represents calculations of both passage time and speed of water upon entering the inlet based on the values of tube diameter, length and the flow rate of water inside the tube. These calculations are valid only for water phase inside the tube. Once water in the liquid phase changes to steam phase, its volume increases greatly, hence, its speed and passage time will vary greatly depending on the location of steam inside the tube.

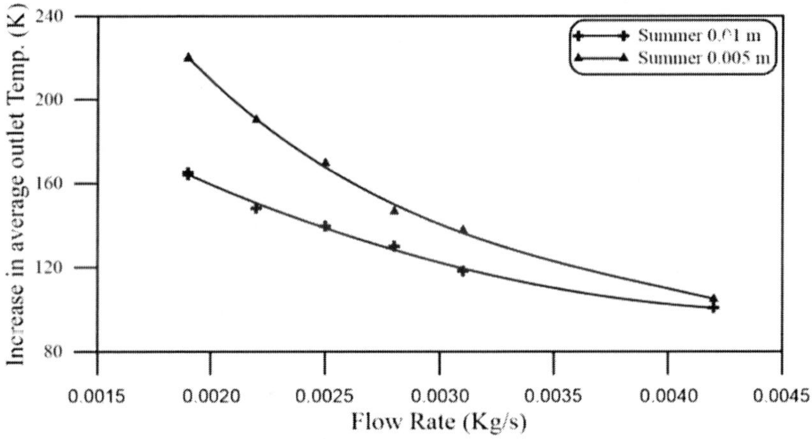

Figure 11. Increase in the average outlet temperature for the 0.005 m and 0.01 m tubes on a summer day.

Generated steam fraction at noon time has been extracted from the simulation data, which expresses the mass of seam generated to water mass at the pipe outlet. This is graphed as a function of inlet flow rate for two tube diameters of 0.01 m and 0.005 m, respectively, in the proposed summer day as shown in Figure 13. The wider the tube, the higher the steam fraction in spite of the average outlet temperature (cf. Figure 11). This is because with a narrower diameter, the average temperature is affected by the temperature of the water near the outer tube surface which can be very high. On the other hand, the tube with the wider diameter has better distribution of heat at the outlet surface, hence, produces more steam.

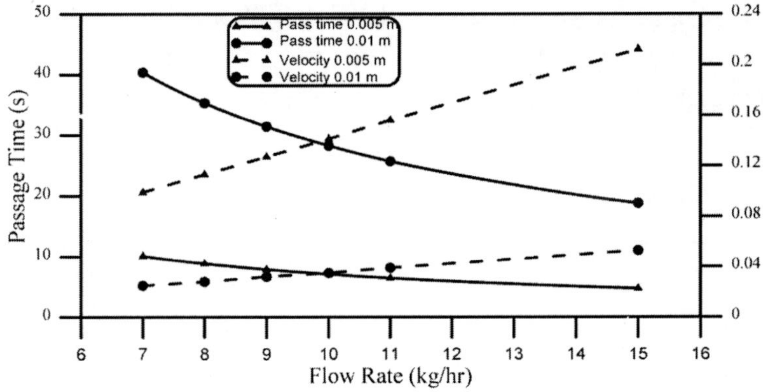

Figure 12. Passage time and velocity of water inside the 0.005 m and 0.01 m diameter tubes.

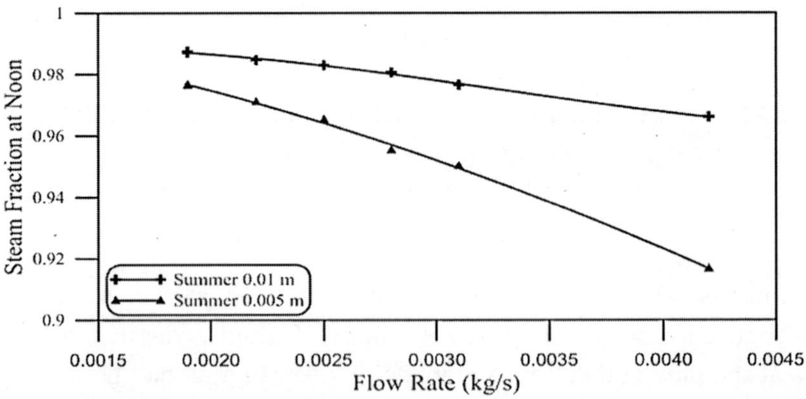

Figure 13. Steam fraction at noon for the 0.005 m and 0.01 m tubes on a summer day.

Figure 14 shows the daily accumulated steam mass in kg as a function of water flow rate for the two proposed diameters and their performance in winter and summer, respectively. Simulations show that for achieving a higher accumulated steam mass, the choice of the pipe diameter depends mainly on the intensity of solar radiation. In this figure, the 0.005 m diameter pipe generates a higher steam mass on a summer day than the 0.01 m diameter pipe on a winter day in spite of its narrower diameter. The 0.005 m diameter pipe's performance is the lowest in winter days.

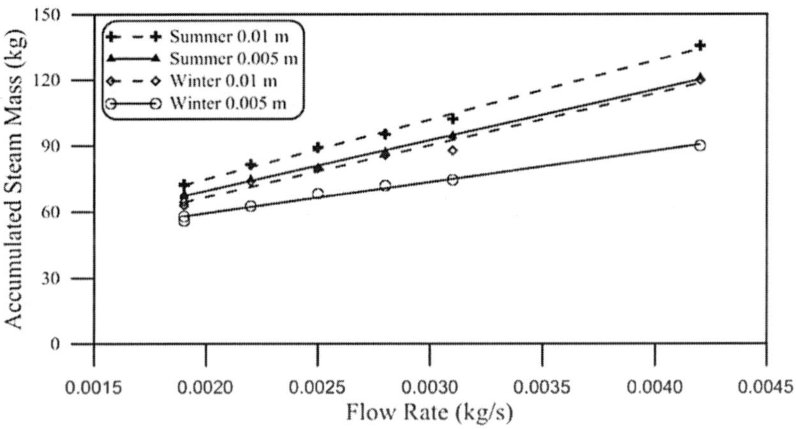

Figure 14. Accumulated steam mass over the day for the 0.005 m and 0.01 m tubes in winter and summer, respectively.

Qualitative analysis of the system performance depends on the structure of the output. In many cases, superheating is required to get a better steam temperature. This may be done by exposing the steam to additional solar energy for better steam quality. To study the quality of the steam generated, analysis of the outlet profiles of steam temperature has been performed to investigate the accumulated steam whose temperature is over 423 K as shown in Figure 15 for the two proposed pipe diameters in winter and summer, respectively. The narrower tube showed better performance in terms of steam quality in both winter and summer, with an optimal flow rate of 0.0028 kg/s. On the contrary, the wider pipe showed a performance that is inversely proportional to the water flow rate. This is reflected inFigure 16 which shows the steam quality factor for the two proposed pipe diameters in both winter and summer respectively as a function of water flow rate. Steam quality factor is calculated by Equation (7):

$$Steam\ quality\ factor = \frac{Daily\ accumulated\ steam\ mass\ with\ temperature > 423K}{Total\ daily\ accumulated\ steam\ mass} \quad (7)$$

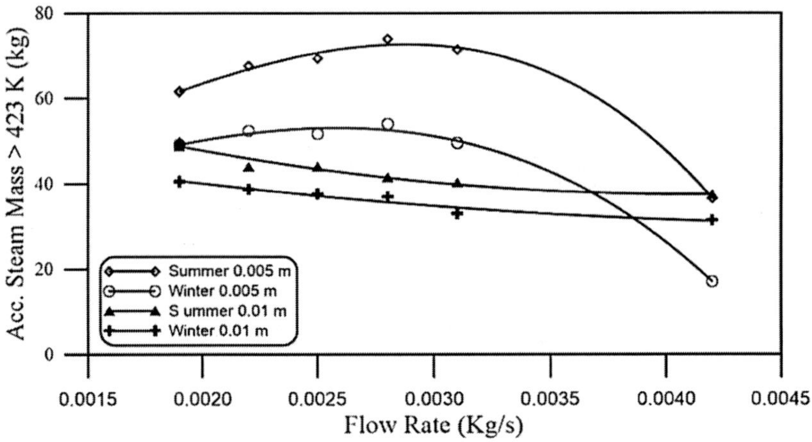

Figure 15. Accumulated steam whose temperature is over 423 K for 0.005 m and 0.01 m tubes in winter and summer, respectively.

In some cases, high steam temperature is required for industrial purposes for example. Overheating may be used for achieving such high temperatures. For system optimization or for specific steam temperature demands, steam quality factor at that temperature may be calculated in order to investigate the performance at that specific temperature and determine the tube length for overheating process.

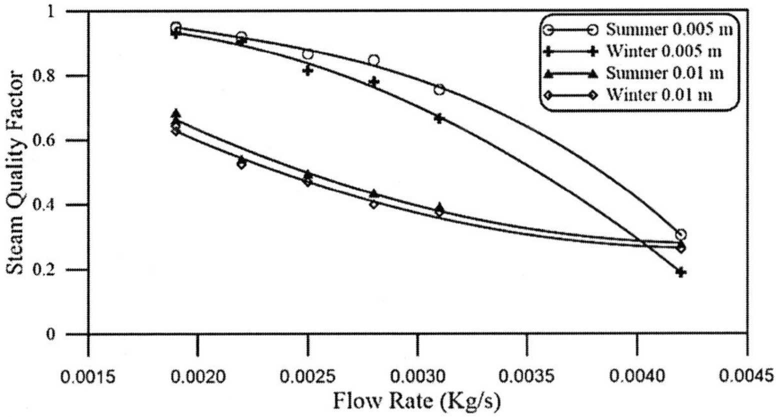

Figure 16. Steam quality factor for the 0.005 m and 0.01 m tubes in winter and summer.

5. CONCLUSIONS

In this paper, analysis of steam generated from a water pipe exposed to concentrated solar radiation has been performed. Steam is generated from two proposed pipes with diameters of 0.005 m and 0.01 m, respectively, containing water flowing with different flow rates. As expected, increasing water flow rate reduced the average outlet temperature because of the reduction in the residence time of the water flowing inside the pipe. Quantitatively, an average increase of outlet temperature was about 220 K and 165 K for pipe diameters of 0.005 m and 0.01 m, respectively, at a flow rate of 0.0019 kg/s in summer. On the contrary, it was found that steam fraction was higher for the 0.01 m diameter pipe than that of the 0.005 m one for all flow rates. On the other hand, overheated steam was generated from the narrower pipes regardless of the solar radiation intensity, and it decreased with increasing water flow rate. A qualitative investigation shows that daily accumulated steam mass whose outlet temperature >423 K for the 0.005 m tube was maximum (about 74 kg/day and 53 kg/day in summer and winter respectively, both at a flow rate of 0.0028 kg/s) compared to that of the 0.01 m tube (about 50 kg/day and 40 kg/day in summer and winter, respectively, both at a flow rate of 0.0019 kg/s). Steam quality calculations show that the 0.005 m tube should be chosen if a high quality steam is desired. Otherwise, the 0.01 m diameter tube should be selected if a higher quantity of steam is required regardless of its quality.

ACKNOWLEDGMENTS

The authors would like to thank the Institute of Scientific Research and Revival of Islamic Heritage at Umm Al-Qura University (Project ID 43305021) for the financial support.

AUTHOR CONTRIBUTIONS

All authors contributed equally to this work. In particular, M. Sabry mainly worked on the modeling of the system and contributed to the simulation and the literature review. Mouaaz Nahas contributed to the simulation and the literature review. Saud H. Al-Lehyani gave technical support and conceptual advice. All authors worked on results analysis and writing of the manuscript.

REFERENCES

1. Almasoud, A.H.; Gandayh, H.M. Future of solar energy in Saudi Arabia. *J. King Saud Univ. Eng. Sci.* **2014**.

2. Gandayh, H. Appraisal of prospective schemes in solar energy applications. Master's Thesis, King Abdulaziz University, Jeddah, Saudi Arabia, 2012.

3. Rovira, A.; Montes, M.J.; Varela, F.; Gil, M. Comparison of heat transfer fluid and direct steam generation technologies for integrated solar combined cycles. *Appl. Therm. Eng.* **2013**, *52*, 264–274.

4. Fernández-García, A.; Zarza, E.; Valenzuela, L.; Pérez, M. Parabolic-trough solar collectors and their applications. *Renew. Sustain. Energy Rev.* **2010**, *14*, 1695–1721.

5. Tsikalakis, A.; Tomtsi, T.; Hatziargyriou, N.D.; Poullikkas, A.; Malamatenios, C.; Giakoumelos, E.; Jaouad, O.C.; Chenak, A.; Fayek, A.; Matar, T.; *et al.* Review of best practices of solar electricity resources applications in selected Middle East and North Africa (MENA) countries. *Renew. Sustain. Energy Rev.* **2011**, *15*, 2838–2849.

6. Afa, J.T. Problems of rural electrification in bayelsa state. *Am. J. Sci. Indus. Res.* **2013**, *4*, 214–220.

7. Jaramillo, O.A.; Venegas-Reyes, E.; Aguilar, J.O.; Castrejón-García, R.; Sosa-Montemayor, F. Parabolic trough concentrators for low enthalpy processes. *Renew. Energy* **2013**, *60*, 529–539.

8. Sunshine to Petrol. Available online: http://energy.sandia.gov/energy/renewable-energy/solar-energy/sunshine-to-petrol (accessed on 20 April 2015).

9. Odeh, S.D.; Morrison, G.L.; Behnia, M. Modelling of parabolic through direct steam generation solar collectors. *Sol. Energy***1998**, *62*, 395–406.

10. Kalogirou, S.; Lloyd, S.; Ward, J. Modelling, optimization and performance evaluation of a parabolic trough solar collector steam generation system. *Sol. Energy* **1997**, *60*, 49–59.

11. Lobón, D.H.; Valenzuela, L.; Baglietto, E. Modeling the dynamics of the multiphase fluid in the parabolic-trough solar steam generating systems. *Energy Convers. Manag.* **2014**, *78*, 393–404.

12. Escobar-Romero, J.F.M.; Vázquez y Montiel, S.; Granados-Agustín, F.; Cruz-Martínez, V.M.; Rodríguez-Rivera, E.; Martínez-Yáñez, L. Building a parabolic solar concentrator prototype. *J. Phys. Conf. Ser.* **2011**, *274*, 012104.

13. Fernández-García, A.; Rojas, E.; Pérez, M.; Silva, R.; Hernández-Escobedo, Q.; Manzano-Agugliaro, F. A parabolic-trough collector for cleaner industrial process heat. *J. Clean Prod.* **2015**, *89*, 272–285.

14. A parabolic trough reflector increases the suns energy. Alternative Energy Tutorials. Available online: http://www.alternative-energy-tutorials.com/solar-hot-water/parabolic-trough-reflector.html (accessed on 20 April 2015).

15. Ma, L.; Lu, Z.; Zhang, J.; Liang, R. Thermal performance analysis of the glass evacuated tube solar collector with U-tube.*Build. Environ.* **2010**, *45*, 1959–1967.

16. Sabry, M.; Eames, P.C.; Singh, H.; Wu, Y. Smart windows: Thermal modelling and evaluation. *Sol. Energy* **2014**, *103*, 200–209.

17. Shih, T.H.; Liou, W.W.; Shabbir, A.; Yang, Z.; Zhu, J. *A New k-epsilon Eddy Viscosity Model for High Reynolds Number Turbulent Flows: Model Development and Validation*; NASA-TM-106721; NASA Technical Reports Server: Cleveland, OH, USA; 1; August; 1994.

18. Shih, T.H.; Liou, W.W.; Shabbir, A.; Yang, Z.; Zhu, J. A new k-ε eddy viscosity model for high reynolds number turbulent flows.*Computers Fluids* **1995**, *24*, 227–238.

Chapter 8

Calculation of Efficiencies of a Ship Power Plant Operating with Waste Heat Recovery through Combined Heat and Power Production

Mirko Grljušić [1,2,*], Vladimir Medica [3,†] and Gojmir Radica [1,†]

[1] Faculty of Electrical Engineering, Mechanical Engineering and Naval Architecture, University of Split, Rudjera Boškovića 32, 21000 Split, Croatia

[2] GM TURBO d.o.o., Vukovarska 58, 21000 Split, Croatia

[3] Faculty of Engineering, University of Rijeka, Vukovarska 58, 51000 Rijeka, Croatia

ABSTRACT

The aim of this research was to investigate the possibility of a combined heat & power (CHP) plant, using the waste heat from a Suezmax-size oil tanker's main engine, to meet all heating and electricity requirements during navigation. After considering various configurations, a standard propulsion engine operating at maximum efficiency, combined with a supercritical Organic Rankine cycle (ORC) system, was selected to supply the auxiliary power, using R245fa or R123 as the working fluid. The system analysis showed that such a plant can meet all heat and electrical power requirements at full load, with the need to burn only a small amount of supplementary fuel in a heat recovery steam generator (HRSG) when the main engine operates at part load. Therefore, it is possible to increase the overall thermal efficiency of the ship's power plant by more than 5% when the main engine operates at 65% or more of its specified maximum continuous rating (*SMCR*).

KEYWORDS

ship power plant; waste heat recovery; combined heat and power production; Organic Rankine Cycle (ORC); ship power plant efficiency; waste heat efficiency

1. INTRODUCTION

Low speed two-stroke turbocharged diesel engines are the most commonly used marine propulsion engines today. These engines are the most efficient, exhibiting 50% efficiency, with the remaining 50% of the energy released from fuel combustion being dispelled to the atmosphere as waste heat.

The potential uses of waste heat and other forms of low temperature energy have been investigated for decades, but its use to generate power by means of ORC systems is a relatively recent notion. Such systems are similar to conventional steam power plants in their configuration. By the use of organic working fluids instead of steam, it is possible to increase the plant efficiency and reduce its cost when recovering power from heat sources at temperatures below 500 °C.

When cooling water is available, Aly [1] estimated that the heat recovered from diesel engine exhaust gases can be used to obtain an additional 15% to 16% increase in the total power output. The uses for exhaust gas heat, taken into account by Shu *et al.* [2], are turbocharger/power, fresh water obtained by using multiple effect distillation or multi-stage flash desalination technology, electric/power obtained from a Rankine cycle system and air conditioning and ice-making obtained by means of sorption refrigeration. They estimated that 2150 kW can be generated using the exhaust gas from a turbocharged diesel engine of 69,900 kW power output to raise the steam in a dual pressure system with a multi stage turbine. Heat is also recovered from the jacket cooling water and scavenging air cooler to preheat feed water before it enters the boiler. This could be raised to 4000 kW if part of the exhaust gases bypasses the turbocharger. The best result was achieved with an additional power turbine using bypass exhaust gases to generate a total of 5610 kWe. This increased the overall plant thermal efficiency by 8.03%. Butcher and Reddy [3] carried out a second law analysis of the influence of the gas composition, specific heat and pinch point temperature on the performance of a Heat Recovery Steam Generator (HRSG). They found that the performance of the power generation system is very sensitive to the gas composition. The pinch point (PP) is a dominant parameter and should be selected carefully. Wang *et al.* [4] revealed that R11, R141b, R113 and R123 exhibit slightly better thermodynamic performance than other fluids, while R245fa and R245ca are the most suitable ones (R11 and R113 have been completely banned since 2005). In this work, which is a continuation of work presented in [5], a new method for waste heat recovery (WHR) was investigated to decrease the fuel consumption and emissions of ship propulsion systems.

2. WHR SYSTEM MODELING

A study was made to determine whether a CHP system could be developed to obtain the entire auxiliary power and heating requirements for the ship, during navigation, from its waste heat. This was based on the use of an ORC WHR system, using R245fa and the R123 as working fluids. The analysis was based on the use of steady flow thermodynamic equations. These are applicable for all operating conditions, other than those encountered during extremely heavy seas, bad weather conditions or when maneuvering. The thermodynamic properties of air, exhaust gases, fuel, water and the working fluids were all obtained using version 9 of the National Institute of Standards and Technology (NIST) Refprop program [6]. The cogeneration system was analyzed as a thermodynamic flow process, and presented schematically with *h-s* and *T-s* diagrams.

Suezmax-sized oil tankers were considered for this study, with 18,660 kW@91rpm at *SMCR*, which equals 100% Nominal Maximum Continuous Rating (*NMCR*). In such a tanker, the auxiliary power is normally obtained from a 912 kWe diesel genset.

The heavy fuel oil (HFO) and lube oil (LO) have to be heated before separation. This is done for the HFO in a feeder/booster module, the HFO tanks (service tanks, settling tanks, storage tanks), and the low grade sulfur (LGS) HFO tank. In addition, seasonal heating must be provided for the crew. The steam required for these and any other ship heating requirements is generated in a boiler. A common design is for a composite boiler consisting of an oil-fired section and an exhaust gas section, both placed in a common shell. During navigation, the exhaust gas heat from the main engine is utilized as the heat source for these functions. In port, when the main engine is shut down, the oil fired section takes over to produce steam. The following assumptions were made in these calculations:

Table 1. Heat consumption during navigation for fuel, lube oil and hot water heating.

Steam heat consumers	Consumed energy $\dot{Q}$ (kW)	Max. temperature (°C)
ME/AE FO module	196	from 110 °C to 145 °C
HFO storage tanks	160	45 °C
Others	320	max 98 °C

The steam heat consumer classified as others includes heating of the HFO, DO, LO and hot water for crew requirements, up to a maximum temperature of 98 °C. In this work, the heating of the crew living space was neglected for ISO Standard Conditions. Hence, as shown in Table 1, the total heat requirement during navigation is 676 kW.

Although previous calculations [5] showed that it was not necessary to use heat from the jacket cooling water, in this study, the heat from the main engine jacket cooling water was included as well as that from the scavenged air and the exhaust gases. The initial data refer to the standard ambient reference conditions according to ISO 3046 [7]. The engine data; specific fuel consumption, temperature and mass flow rate of the exhaust gases, jacket cooling water and scavenged air were acquired from the MAN engine room dimensioning software [8] for the 6S70MC-C7-T1 engine. These values are not constant. The only constant value used is the information on exhaust emissions obtained from the MAN data for a similar engine. The composition of the exhaust gas was calculated using an in house zero-dimensional model. The propulsion engine model depicting the main input and output variables is shown in Figure 1.

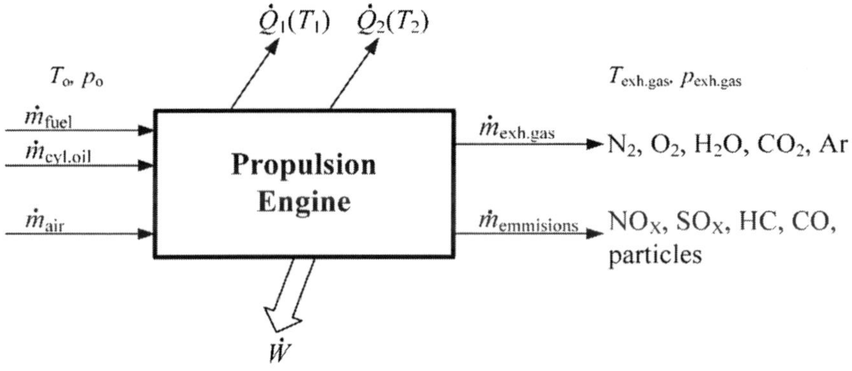

Figure 1. The propulsion engine model depicting main input and output substances and energy flows.

It was assumed that the fluid flow through the propulsion engine is steady. The observer position is stationary with respect to the control volume surrounding the drive motor, which, in this case, is the ship's propulsion engine.

The first law of thermodynamics can be expressed as the conservation of energy in the control volume. Disregarding changes in potential and kinetic energy, the following can be expressed as:

$$\dot{Q} - \dot{W} = (\sum_{i} \dot{m}_i \cdot h_i)_{out} - (\sum_{i} \dot{m}_i \cdot h_i)_{in} \tag{1}$$

where Q˙ is the total heat inflow; W˙ the shaft work outflow and m˙i and hi are the mass flow rates and specific enthalpies of the individual flow substances.

Although the scavenged air consumption was taken from MAN B&W CEAS_ERD at ISO standard conditions, the composition of the air was calculated by NIST using our initial values. The fuel composition for MDO and cylinder oil composition were also taken into account. The heat input from the fuel is expressed in terms of its Lower Calorific Value while the fuel and air mass flow rates must meet the following relation:

$$\dot{W} = \dot{m}_{fuel} \cdot Q_{LCVp} - (\dot{m}_{air} + \dot{m}_{fuel}) \cdot c_{p,\, exh\, gas}(T_{exh\, gas} - T_0) + \dot{Q} \tag{2}$$

2.1. Working Fluid and Cycle Selection

The exhaust gas temperatures for the assumed diesel engine vary from 230 °C to 250 °C [8], while Larsen *et al.* [9] suggested that for heat sources of more than 240 °C the most efficient is the supercritical ORC cycle. A similar conclusion was reached by Gao *et al.* [10]. In addition to the temperature and mass flow rate of exhaust gases [8] for the main engine load from 25% to 100% *SMCR*, other data are provided including mass flow rate and pressure of turbocharged air, temperature before and after the air cooler, the scavenge air cooler heat, jacket water cooler heat and main lubrication oil heat. Accordingly, a supercritical cycle was assumed for this study, with the R245fa as the working fluid with an optimal maximum pressure of 4.5 MPa. This is in very good correlation with the work of Gao *et al.* [10].

Table 2. Properties of R123, R245fa and R245ca [6].

Property	R123	R245fa	R245ca
Chemical/structural formula	$C_2HCl_2F_3$	$CHF_2CH_2CF_3$	$CHF_2 CF_2CH_2F$
Molecular mass kg/kmol	152.93	134.05	134.05
Boiling point at 1.0133 bar	27.82 °C	15.140 °C	25.133 °C
Density kg/m^3 at 1.0133 bar	(L) 1,456.6 (V) 6.4717	(L) 1,364.9 (V) 5.9619	(L) 1,386.0 (V) 5.7371
Enthalpy kJ/kg at 1.0133 bar	(L) 228.03 (V) 398.22	(L) 219.51 (V) 415.55	(L) 232.82 (V) 433.78
Critical point °C/bar	183.68 / 36.618	154.01/36.51	174.42/39.25
Atmospheric Life Time (ALT)	1.3 y	7.6 y	6.2y
Ozone Depletion Potential (ODP)	0.02	0	0
GWP	77	1030	693
ASHRAE safety group	B1	B1	n.a.

As an alternative to the R245fa, R123 was also considered and some of its properties are shown in Table 3, together with the properties of the R245ca. A *T-s diagram* of the most commonly used or considered fluids for the power recovery systems from low grade heat is shown in Figure 2.

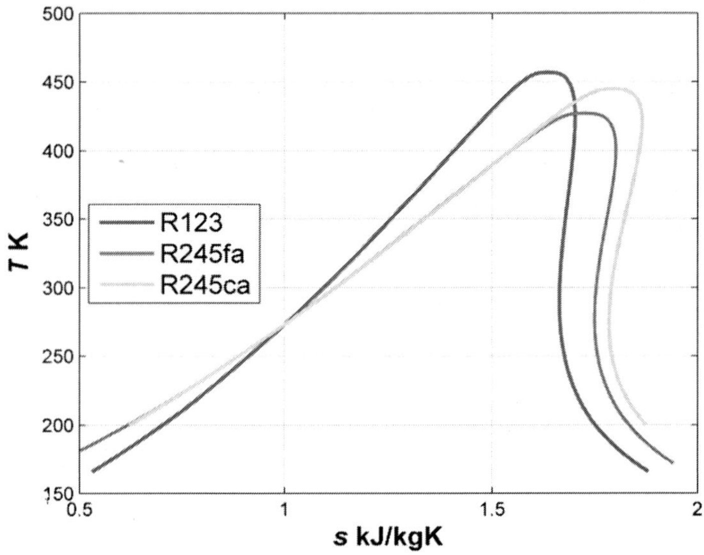

Figure 2. *T-s* diagram of the selected working fluids based on [6].

Organic fluids such as R245fa, R245ca and R123 are recognized as very convenient fluids for the use in organic Rankine cycles. Fluids R245fa and R245ca are dry fluids, and R123 can be considered as an isentropic fluid, even though it is a dry fluid.

The main advantage of operating at a supercritical pressure is that the continuously increasing temperature during heat input results in a better match with the heat source and hence produces a higher thermal efficiency. Currently, turbines with power outputs ranging from a few kW up to 3 MW are used as expanders in ORC processes and these achieve adiabatic efficiencies of approximately 85% in turbines of over 0.5 MW output [11,12].

According to [13,14], the advantages of organic fluid turbines are their high adiabatic efficiencies, the low mechanical stress on the turbine due to the low blade speed, no blade erosion due to the absence of moisture during expansion, while the low turbine rotational speed enables direct coupling to the generator, and a longer service life compared to steam turbines. Additionally, organic working fluids enable higher cycle efficiencies to be obtained compared to steam, due to a better temperature matching in the heating process.

In this case it was assumed that the boiler functions through direct heating of the working fluid by the exhaust gases from the main ship engine without an intermediate thermal loop. The CHP plant with R245fa as the working fluid is shown in Figure 3, and with R123 as the working fluid in Figure 4.

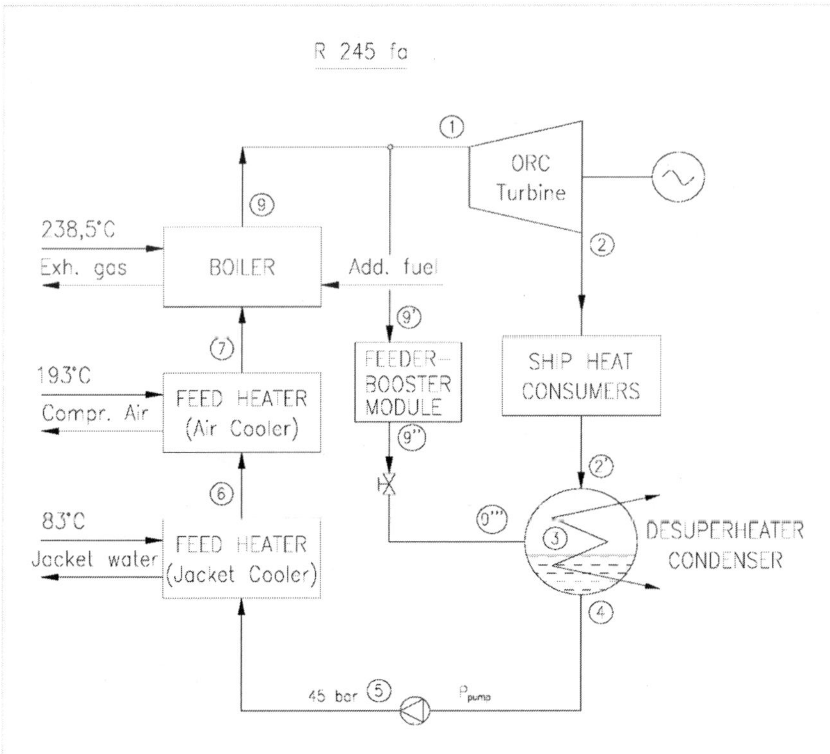

Figure 3. Schematic diagram of the CHP plant with R245fa fluid [5,15].

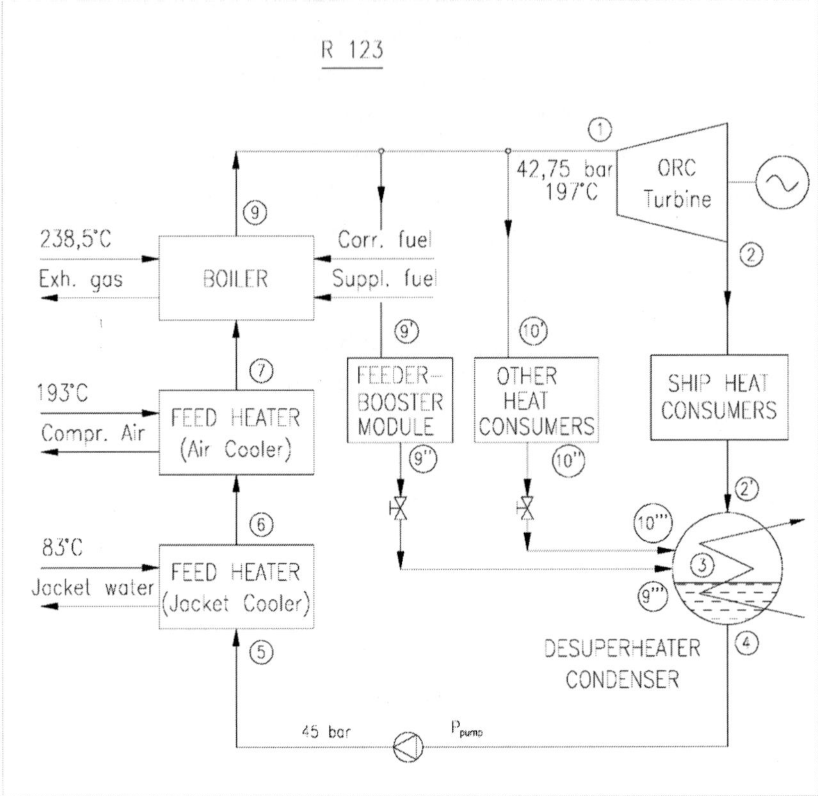

Figure 4. Schematic diagram of CHP plant with R123 fluid PP15 [15].

2.2. Thermodynamic Analysis of the WHR Plant and the Calculation for a Vapor Turbine using R245fa and R123 as Working Fluids for Full Electrical Power

All the displayed computations were performed, assuming the ISO standard conditions. The losses in fluid pressure were not considered except those between the boiler and the turbine. The computations for the auxiliary engine were made using HFO. In the Emission Control Area (ECA), the standard HFO is not acceptable; LGS HFO, marine DO or natural gas is used. In the ECA, a 0.10% sulfur limit came into effect on 1st January 2015. This means that low grade sulfur marine gas oil (LGSMGO) or natural gas must be used as a ship's fuel. As these fuels are more expensive (especially LGSMGO) than the HFO, the potential financial savings, from waste heat recovery, are thereby increased [16]. When using fuel with LGS, the exhaust gas temperature can fall below 145 °C. As already explained, direct coupling of the turbine to the generator was assumed and therefore, as shown in Figure 5, no gearbox was considered in the calculations.

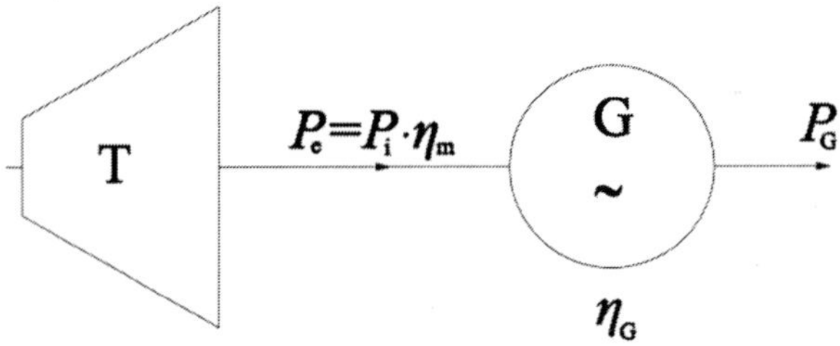

Figure 5. Turbine genset for electricity production during ship sails.

The *T-s* diagram of the CHP plant with a turbine and the R245fa as the working fluid is shown in Figure 6 and R123 as the working fluid is shown in Figure 7.

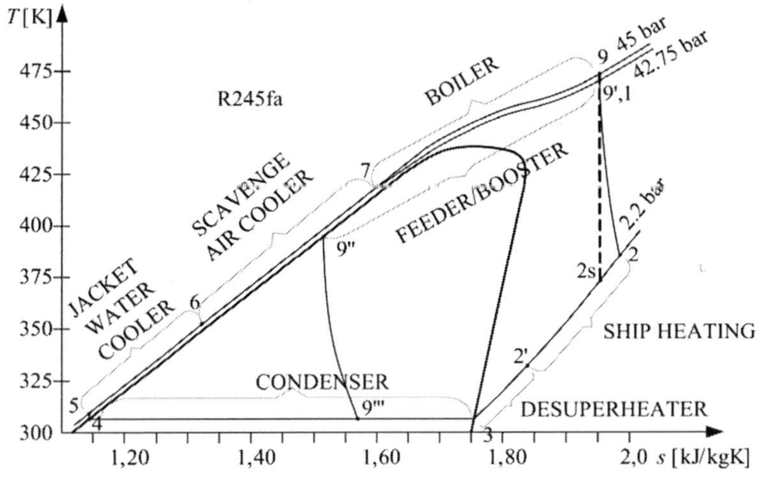

Figure 6. *T-s* diagram for the ORC CHP Plant with R245fa fluid [5,15].

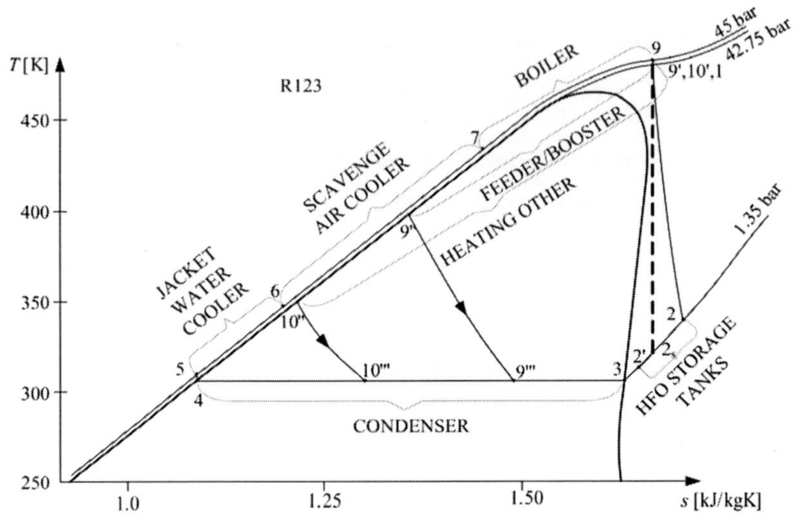

Figure 7. *T-s* diagram for ORC CHP Plant with R123 fluid [15].

Before starting with the calculations it was necessary to assume values for some parameters, as shown in Table 3.

In accordance with the similar designs/power, η_m and η_G were selected. The internal turbine power and the internal efficiency are as follows:

$$P_i = \frac{P_G}{\eta_m \cdot \eta_{GB} \cdot \eta_G} \tag{3}$$

$$\eta_i = \frac{P_i}{P_{i,s}} = \frac{h_{01} - h_{02}}{h_{01} - h'_{02s}} \tag{4}$$

$$\eta_i = \eta_{TS} = \frac{h_{01} - h_{02}}{h_{01} - h_{2s}} = \frac{h_{01} - h_{02}}{h_{01} - (h_{02s} - c_{2s}^2 / 2)} \tag{5}$$

Table 3. Major assumptions for the thermodynamic analysis.

Parameter	Unit	Value
Turbine Isentropic Efficiency, $\eta_i = \eta_{TS}$	–	0.85
Turbine mechanical efficiency, η_m	–	0.96
Gearbox efficiency, η_{GB}	–	1.00
Generator efficiency, η_G	–	0.95
Pump isentropic efficiency, η_p	–	0.85
Pump mechanical efficiency, η_{pm}	–	0.8
Heat lost in the heat exchanger, hl	%	1
Heat lost in the HRSG, hl	%	2
Combustion efficiency of supplement fuel, η_b	–	0.99
HFO Lower heating value, Q_{LHVp}	kJ/kg	40,210
Minimum exhaust gas temperature at HRSG outlet, T	°C	145
Pinch Point (PP)	°C	15
Working fluid pressure loss from HRGS to turbine, p_{loss}	%	5
Working fluid temperature loss from HRGS to turbine, T_{loss}	°C	3
Power factor, cosφ	–	0.8
Full electric power during navigation for Diesel genset, P_G	kW	912
Standard electric power during navigation for Diesel genset, P_G	kW	620
Power plant working hours per year, $t_{h/y}$	h/y	5,796.2

The small difference in enthalpies and the power target justify the considerable amount of fluid in this cycle. However, the fluid outlet state (T_2, p_2) has still a large specific volume. Therefore, fluid outlet speeds of c_2 = 40 to 60 m/s should be used. The outlet diameter of the pipeline towards the condenser can be estimated using the continuity equation:

$$\frac{D\rho}{Dt} = -\rho(\nabla\vec{c}) \tag{6}$$

In macroscopic form and control volume (V_c):

$$\left(\frac{\mathrm{d}m}{\mathrm{d}t}\right)_{Vc} = \dot{m}_{\text{in}} - \dot{m}_{\text{out}} \tag{7}$$

For steady state one dimensional flow:

$$\dot{m}_2 \cdot v_2 = A_2 \cdot c_2 \tag{8}$$

Equation (4) shows that:

$$h_{02} = h_{01} - \eta_i (h_{01} - h_{2s}) \tag{9}$$

$$p_{02} = p_2 + \bar{\rho} \frac{c_2^2}{2} \tag{10}$$

Furthermore, the following are applicable:

$$h_2 = h_{02} - \frac{c_2^2}{2} \tag{11}$$

$$h_{02s} = h_{2s} + \frac{c_{2s}^2}{2} \tag{12}$$

$$P_i = \dot{m}_{\mathrm{ORC,turbine}} \cdot (h_{01} - h_{02}) \tag{13}$$

Because the temperature of the R245fa working fluid is 108.02 °C, after expansion in the turbine, the heat rejected from the working fluid, prior to condensation, can be used for all heating needs on the ship except for heating the HFO in the feeder/booster module before injection. To heat the HFO in the feeder/booster module, it is necessary to heat an additional amount of the working fluid in the HRSG. This additional working fluid is extracted before the turbine and transferred to the HFO heaters. For the R245fa fluid, the procedure is explained in ref [5]. When using the R123 working fluid, the situation is different. The R123 working fluid after expansion in the turbine has a low temperature, 54.3 °C, and thus it is possible to heat HFO storage tanks only. All other heatings require heating an additional amount of the R123 fluid in the HRSG. Therefore, it is not only necessary to heat an additional amount of R123 for heating the HFO in the feeder-booster module (196 kW), it is also necessary to heat all other heat consumers (320 kW) with an additional amount of the R123 in the HRSG.

The HFO storage tanks (160 kW) are heated with working fluid after exiting the turbine.

The required heat power for the booster module is the same for both working fluids:

$$\dot{Q}_{\mathrm{ORC,booster}} = \frac{\dot{Q}_{\mathrm{HFO,booster}}}{(1-\mathrm{hl})} \tag{14}$$

where *hl* is the percentage of heat lost in the heat exchanger. Hence,

$$\dot{Q}_{\mathrm{ORC,booster}} = \dot{m}_{\mathrm{ORC,booster}} \cdot (h_{9'} - h_{9''}) \tag{15}$$

The working fluid (Figure 4 and Figure 5) enters the fuel module at 197 °C and leaves it at 120 °C (Table 5), which is 10 °C higher than the initial temperature of the heated HFO. For the given temperatures and for p9′ = 0.95·p9= 42.75 bar, the enthalpies $h_{9'}$ and$h_{9''}$ can be obtained. Because the working fluid is throttled after heating the HFO inside the fuel module, $p_{2'''}$ = p_2 and $h_{9''}$ = $h_{9'''}$.

For the R123 working fluid, other heat consumers require 320 kW, and another amount of working fluid is heated at 45 bar up to 200 °C. This fluid heats HFO/DO and LO before separators, service and settling tanks, and water for the crew demands. The maximum heating temperature is 98 °C. After heating other consumers, R123 fluid is at state 10′′. After throttling to 10′′′, the fluid flows to the condenser. The feed ORC fluid from the condenser at the state point 4 is pumped up to 45 bar, reaching the state point 5.

The feed-pump power is as follows:

$$P_{\mathrm{pump}} = \frac{\dot{m}_{\mathrm{ORC,t}} \cdot v_4 (p_5 - p_4)}{\eta_{\mathrm{mp}} \cdot \eta_{\mathrm{pump}}} \tag{16}$$

Compared to the water-based process, the ORC requires a much larger feed pump due to the considerably larger mass flow rate of the organic fluid.

The computation is repeated to calculate the power required for the generator and turbine:

$$P_{G1} = P_G + P_{pump} \tag{17}$$

$$P_i = \frac{P_{G1}}{\eta_m \cdot \eta_{GB} \cdot \eta_G} \tag{18}$$

The computation was repeated to check the pump power and mass flow rate of the working fluid. The total mass flow rate of the working fluid is as follows:

$$\dot{m}_{ORC,t} = \dot{m}_{ORC,other} + \dot{m}_{ORC,booster} = \dot{m}_{ORC,turbine} + \dot{m}_{ORC,booster} \quad \text{for R245fa} \tag{19}$$

$$\dot{m}_{ORC,t} = \dot{m}_{ORC,other} + \dot{m}_{ORC,storage\ tanks} + \dot{m}_{ORC,booster} = \dot{m}_{ORC,other} + \dot{m}_{ORC,turbine} + \dot{m}_{ORC,booster} \quad \text{for R123} \tag{20}$$

The computation was repeated with the new generator and the turbine power using Equations (13) and (20).

After the condenser, the working fluid is pumped to 45 bar and the first heating is in the jacket water cooler. It is assumed that $T_{ORC,6}$ = 75 °C. At the iteration start, it is assumed that the jacket water outlet temperature is $T_{jacket,2}$ = 59.0 °C.

After being heated with the hot water from the cylinder jacket, the working fluid flows to the two-stage scavenged air heat exchanger. If the fluids do not change phase, the following is true:

$$\dot{Q}_h = \dot{m}_h \cdot \overline{c}_{p,h} \cdot \Delta T_h = \dot{m}_{air} \cdot \overline{c}_{p,air} \cdot (T_{air,1} - T_{air,2}) \tag{21}$$

$$\dot{Q}_c = \dot{m}_c \cdot \overline{c}_{p,c} \cdot \Delta T_c = \dot{Q}_{ORC} = \dot{m}_{ORC} \cdot \overline{c}_{p,ORC} \cdot (T_{ORC,7} - T_{ORC,6}) \tag{22}$$

The heat lost in the heat exchanger air/organic fluid depends on cooling through insulation only, totaling approximately 1% with normal insulation design:

$$\Delta T_{\text{air}} = \frac{\dot{Q}_{\text{air}}}{\dot{m}_{\text{air}} \cdot \bar{c}_{\text{p,air}}} \tag{23}$$

In the boiler, the working fluid should be heated from 150 °C to 200 °C at 45 bar (assuming that no working fluid pressure is lost through the boiler):

$$\dot{Q}_{\text{ORC,boiler}} = \dot{m}_{\text{ORC}} \cdot (h_{9,\text{ORC}} - h_{7,\text{ORC}}) \tag{24}$$

$$\dot{E}_{\text{exh.gas,need}} = \frac{\dot{Q}_{\text{ORC,boiler}}}{(1-\text{hl})} \tag{25}$$

According to [3], the heat lost in the HRSG is typically 2%–3%. The pinch point is assumed to be 15 °C while the minimal temperature at the boiler outlet is 145 °C because at temperatures below 145 °C, sulfuric acid may form/by condensation. Therefore:

$$T_{\text{exh.gas,2}} = T_{\text{ORC,7}} + 15\,°\text{C} \tag{26}$$

Since the working fluid at high main engine loads can heat easily with scavenged air to 150 °C, it is necessary to keep the exhaust gases temperature at the HRSG outlet at least 15 °C higher, in that range the exhaust gas temperature should be 165 °C. The exhaust gas energy disposal can be calculated by Equation (27):

$$\dot{E}_{\text{exh.gas,disposal}} = \dot{m}_{\text{exh.gas}} \cdot c_{\text{p,gas,12}} \cdot (T_{\text{exh.gas,1}} - T_{\text{exh.gas,2}}) = \dot{m}_{\text{exh.gas}} \cdot (h_{\text{exh.gas,1}} - h_{\text{exh.gas,2}}) \tag{27}$$

The surplus/shortage of energy in the exhaust gases totals the following:

E˙exh.gas,surplus/shortage=E˙exh.gas,disposal−E˙exh.gas,need

$$\dot{E}_{\text{exh.gas,surplus/shortage}} = \dot{E}_{\text{exh.gas,disposal}} - \dot{E}_{\text{exh.gas,need}} \tag{28}$$

In order to produce 912 kW/1012.5 kW/1038.9 kW of electrical energy, supplemental fuel is required for the exhaust gas boiler at some engine loads:

$$\dot{E}_{\text{supp.fuel}} = \dot{E}_{\text{exh.gas,shortage}} = \dot{m}_{\text{supp.fuel}} \cdot Q_{\text{LHVp}} \cdot \eta_{\text{b}} \tag{29}$$

When using R123 as a working fluid it is also necessary to burn the corrected supplemental fuel at full electrical power to keep the pinch point 15 °C at certain main engine loads. Therefore:

$$\dot{E}_{\text{supp.fuel CORR}} = \dot{E}_{\text{exh.gas,shortage}} + \dot{E}_{\text{fuel CORR}} \tag{30}$$

One of the tasks of this work is the calculation of the fuel consumption during an auxiliary Diesel genset acceptance test:

$$P_{\text{G,t}} = 1140\ \text{kVA} \tag{31}$$

$$P_{\text{G}} = P_{\text{G,t}} \cdot \cos\varphi = 912\ \text{kW} \tag{32}$$

$$P_{\text{AE}} = \frac{P_{\text{G}}}{\eta_{\text{m}} \cdot \eta_{\text{G}}} \tag{33}$$

$$\dot{m}_{\text{D2}} = P_{\text{AE}} \cdot b_{\text{e}} \tag{34}$$

According to the manufacturer’s instructions, 5% higher fuel consumption in the auxiliary engine is allowed during service:

$$\dot{m}_{\text{D2,service}} = \dot{m}_{\text{D2}} \cdot 1.05 \tag{35}$$

$$\dot{E}_{\text{D2}} = \dot{m}_{\text{D2}} \cdot Q_{\text{LHV,D2}} \tag{36}$$

$$\dot{m}_{\mathrm{HFO}} = \dot{E}_{\mathrm{HFO}} / Q_{\mathrm{LHV,HFO}} \tag{37}$$

The fuel saving at 100% *SMCR* is as follows:

$$\Delta\dot{m}_{\mathrm{HFO}} = \dot{m}_{\mathrm{HFO,serviceAE}} - \dot{m}_{\mathrm{suppl.\ fuel}} \tag{38}$$

$$\Delta\dot{m}_{\mathrm{HFO,day}} = \dot{m}_{\mathrm{HFO}} \cdot 24 \tag{39}$$

The pinch point of 15 °C is selected. The temperature difference, through the exhaust gas boiler at the main engine loads is varying from 50% to 100% and the working fluid parameters from state 7 to state 9 have to be calculated:

$$\dot{Q}_{\mathrm{ORC}} = \sum_{i=1}^{10} \dot{Q}_{i,\mathrm{ORC}} = \dot{m}_{\mathrm{ORC}} \cdot \sum_{i=1}^{10} \overline{T}_{i,\mathrm{ORC}} \cdot \Delta s \tag{40}$$

$$\dot{Q}_{\mathrm{ORC}} = \dot{m}_{\mathrm{ORC}} \cdot (h_9 - h_7) \tag{41}$$

$$\Delta h_{\mathrm{i,ORC}} = (h_9 - h_7) / 10 \tag{42}$$

$$\dot{E}_{\mathrm{gas,need}} = \frac{\dot{Q}_{\mathrm{ORC,boiler}}}{(1 - \mathrm{hl})} \tag{43}$$

2.3. Calculation for a Vapor Turbine Using the Organic Fluids for Standard Electrical Power

The computation for organic fluid was repeated for the standard electrical power (620 kWe). The same equations and assumptions were used, the regenerative ORC and the heat production for ship demands remain unchanged, and the turbine genset running on organic working fluid is identical to that previously used. Therefore, the turbo genset was used, as shown in the *T-s* diagrams and inFigure 6 and Figure 7. The mechanical efficiency of the turbine and the generator will be the same as in the previous computation.

The internal turbine power is:

$$P_{i} = \frac{P_{G}}{\eta_{m} \cdot \eta_{GB} \cdot \eta_{G}} \tag{44}$$

The utilization boiler parameters are the same as at full electrical power. Pressure and heat losses are identical to the previous ones.

The internal turbine efficiency using the R245fa or the R123 working fluid is 85% and the expansion finishes at the superheated region p2=2.2 bar at Tconden=36.125 °c for the R245fa, and for the R123 at superheated region p2=1.3507 bar at Tconden=36.0 °c.

The ship heating requirements are the same as at full electrical power. For the heating of working fluid the heat from jacket water, scavenged air and exhaust gases are used.

The calculation shows that at these conditions the exhaust gas energy is sufficient from 60% to 100% of *SMCR*. Only below 60%*SMCR* of the main engine load, it is necessary to burn a small amount of the supplemental fuel in the utilization boiler to cover all ship power and heat demands.

2.4. Definitions of Efficiencies

The thermal efficiency of the organic CHP cycle is defined as follows:

$$\eta_{CHP,th} = \frac{\text{work \& heat output to ship consumers}}{\text{total heat input by organic fluid}} \tag{45}$$

$$\eta_{CHP,th} = \frac{P_{el.} + \dot{Q}_{heat\ output}}{(\dot{Q}_{ORC,exh.\ gas} + \dot{Q}_{ORC,air} + \dot{Q}_{ORC,jacket\ w.})} \tag{46}$$

The efficiency of the heat-exchange system, which transfers the heat from the heat source, in this case waste heat to the organic fluid, is defined as follows:

$$\eta_{HEx} = \frac{\dot{Q}_{ORC,t}}{\dot{E}_{waste\ heat,t}} = \frac{\dot{Q}_{ORC.exh.gas} + \dot{Q}_{ORC,air} + \dot{Q}_{ORC,jacket\ w.}}{\dot{E}_{exh.\ gas} + \dot{E}_{air} + \dot{E}_{jacket\ w.}} \tag{47}$$

The efficiency of the cogeneration system or waste heat cogeneration efficiency can be defined as follows:

$$\eta_{CHP,system} = \eta_{CHP,th} \cdot \eta_{HEx} = \text{WHR } \mathit{Efficiency} = \frac{\text{work \& heat output}}{\text{total waste heat input}} \tag{48}$$

$$\eta_{CHP,system} = \text{WHR } \mathit{Efficiency} = \frac{P_{el.} + \dot{Q}_{heat\ output}}{(\dot{E}_{exh.\ gas} + \dot{E}_{air} + \dot{E}_{jacket})} \tag{49}$$

In the analyzed ship power system, the waste heat is not always sufficient for the production of the necessary work and the heat demanded. In some ranges of main engine loads it is necessary to burn supplemental fuel (sometimes adding corrected fuel) to keep necessary PP in the HRSG, and the above equation becomes:

$$\eta_{CHP,system} = \text{WHR } \mathit{Efficiency} = \frac{P_{el.} + \dot{Q}_{heat\ out}}{(\dot{E}_{exh.\ gas} + \dot{E}_{air} + \dot{E}_{jacket}) + \dot{E}_{suppl.\ fuel}} = \frac{P_{el.} + \dot{Q}_{heat\ out}}{\dot{E}_{exh.\ gas\ need} + \dot{E}_{air} + \dot{E}_{jacket}} \tag{50}$$

In the case when heating on board is not considered, (even though it is performed), the above equation becomes the efficiency in electrical power production from the waste heat:

$$\eta_{P,el} = \frac{P_{el.}}{(\dot{E}_{exh.\ gas} + \dot{E}_{air} + \dot{E}_{jacket}) + \dot{E}_{suppl.\ fuel}} = \frac{P_{el.}}{\dot{E}_{exh.\ gas\ need} + \dot{E}_{air} + \dot{E}_{jacket}} \tag{51}$$

At this point it is necessary to emphasize that the calculation was done in such a way that the main engine waste heat was used only in the amount which is needed for ship electrical (and heat) consumption during navigation. The surplus of waste heat energy, especially at high main engine loads, is not used in this calculation; therefore this surplus energy is lost in a chimney.

At some main engine loads it is necessary to burn supplemental fuel in the HRSG. Therefore, the defined efficiency is not “clear” waste heat efficiency. As an alternative, it is possible to move E˙suppl. fuel from denominator to numerator but with the negative sign.

The total efficiency of the analyzed ship thermal power plant is as follows:

$$\eta_{\text{CHP,ship total}} = \frac{\text{ship total work \& heat output}}{\text{total heat input}} = \frac{P_b + P_{el.} + \dot{Q}_{\text{heat output}}}{\dot{E}_{\text{fuel ME}} + \dot{E}_{\text{suppl. fuel + CORR}}} \tag{52}$$

$$\eta_{\text{P,ship}} = \frac{\text{ship total work}}{\text{total heat input}} = \frac{P_b + P_{el.}}{\dot{E}_{\text{fuel ME}} + \dot{E}_{\text{suppl. fuel + CORR}}} \tag{53}$$

It is important to notice that this efficiency could be higher if the total waste heat energy would be used for the production of electrical power. This surplus electrical power could be used to gain propulsion power through the propeller shaft generator.

The gain in the total efficiency of the analyzed ship thermal CHP plant compared to the efficiency of the conventional main engine is:

$$\text{Gain\%} = \left(\frac{\eta_{\text{CHP,ship total}}}{\eta_{\text{ME}}} - 1\right) \cdot 100\% \quad \text{(el. power \& heat)} \tag{54}$$

$$\text{Gain\%} = \left(\frac{\eta_{\text{P,ship}}}{\eta_{\text{ME}}} - 1\right) \cdot 100\% \quad \text{(el. power only)} \tag{55}$$

3. RESULTS

The fuel consumption of the auxiliary diesel genset during navigation depends on the ship demand. This research accounts for two possible network loads: full electrical power and standard electrical power. Therefore, it is assumed that the ship heat consumption is always the same at ISO standard conditions, while electrical power consumption could be full electrical power consumption or standard electrical power consumption. The calculated electrical power using organic RC instead of Diesel genset is shown in Table 4.

Table 4. Calculated ship electrical power using ORC.

Parameter	Unit	Value
Full electric power during navigation for the R245fa, P_{G1}	kW	1012.5
Standard electric power during navigation for the R245fa, P_{G1}	kW	690.1
Full electric power during navigation for the R123, P_{G1}	kW	1038.9
Standard electric power during navigation for the R123, P_{G1}	kW	711.5

Although the ORC technology has been developed and introduced in shore-based industrial plants for a few decades (geothermal energy, solar energy, biomass, waste heat, *etc.*), the available literature and results useful for comparison are scarce. The results related to full electrical power consumption during navigation are presented in Table 5, Table 6, Table 7, Table 8 and Table 9. Table 5shows the working fluid states before and after the feeder/booster module.

The working fluid calculation results before and after the turbine are shown in Table 6. The data for the working fluid after the turbine and before heating are presented in Table 7.

The data for the working fluid after the feed pump and after heating with jacket water, scavenged air and exhaust gases are presented in Table 8.

Table 5. State points of working fluid R123; HFO feeder/booster heating and other heating.

State Point in the Diagram	9	9'	9''	9'''	10'	10''	10'''
Pressure, p (bar)	45	42.75	42.75	1.3507	42.75	42.75	1.3507
Temperature, T (°C)	200	197	120	36.00	197	80.0	36.00
Density, ρ (kg/m³)	475.03	434.49	1,206.5	15.291	434.49	1,331.6	29.341
Specific enthalpy, h (kJ/kg)	461.73	462.96	328.48	328.48	462.96	283.93	283.93
Specific entropy, s (kJ/kg K)	1.6813	1.6850	1.3790	1.4227	1.6850	1.2596	1.2786
Vapour mass flow, $\dot{m}$ (kg/s)	28.409	1.4721	1.4721	1.4721	1.8054	1.8054	1.8054

Table 6. R123 vapor state points before and after turbine; repeated calculation.

State Point in the diagram	9	01	02s	02	2s	2
Pressure, p (bar)	45	42.75	1.4531	1.4531	1.3507	1.3507
Temperature, T (°C)	200	197	47.08	56.32	45.03	54.3
Density, ρ (kg/m³)	475.03	434.49	8.7833	8.4918	8.1947	7.9220
Saturation temperature, T_{sat} (°C)	–	–	38.16	38.16	36.00	36.00
Specific enthalpy vapor, h (kJ/kg)	461.73	462.96	410.89	417.64	409.64	416.39
Specific entropy, s (kJ/kg K)	1.6813	1.6850	1.6851	1.7059	1.6850	1.7059
Vapor quality, x (kg/kg)	–	–	Superh. *	Superh.	Superh.	Superh.
Vapor mass flow from turbine, $\dot{m}$ (kg/s)	–	25.132	25.132	25.132	25.132	25.132
Total condensate mass flow, $\dot{m}$ (kg/s)	28.409	–	–	–	–	–

Table 7. R123 state points after the turbine and before heating; repeated calculation.

State point in the diagram	2	2s	3	4	5
Pressure, p bar	1.3507	1.3507	1.3507	1.3507	45
Temperature, T °C	54.3	45.03	36.00	36.00	37.63
Specific enthalpy vapor/liquid, h kJ/kg	416.39	409.64	403.14	236.44	239.47
Specific entropy, s kJ/kg K	1.7059	1.6850	1.6642	1.1250	1.1250
Density ρ kg/m³	7.9220	8.1947	8.4829	1,435.4	1,445.0
R123 mass flow, $\dot{m}$ kg/s	25.132	25.132	25.132	28.409	28.409

The converged jacket water, scavenged air and exhaust gases data (state points) before and after cooling of the working fluid, and after iterations are displayed in Table 9.

Table 8. R123 state points at heating; repeated calculation.

State point in the diagram	6	7	9
Pressure, p (bar)	45	45	45
Temperature, T (°C)	75	150	200
Specific enthalpy vapor/liquid, h (kJ/kg)	278.60	364.48	461.73
Specific entropy, s (kJ/kg K)	1.2439	1.4667	1.6813
Density ρ (kg/m^3)	1,346.7	1.089.9	475.03
R123 mass flow, $\dot{m}$ (kg/s)	28.409	28.409	28.409

Table 9. Jacket water, scavenged air and exhaust gases state points after iteration.

Parameter	Jacket water		Scavenged air		Exhaust gases	
State point	in	out	in	out	in	out
Pressure, p (bar)	2.5	2.5	3.79	3.79	1.03	1.015
Temperature, T (°C)	83.535	58.818	193.0	142.09	238.5	183.08
Specific enthalpy, h (kJ/kg)	350.01	246.43	483.55	431.23	599.75	541.01
Density ρ (kg/m^3)	969.62	983.86	2.8178	3.1642	0.6996	0.7732
Mass flow rate $\dot{m}$ (kg/s)	10.8395	10.8395	47.111	47.111	48.0	48.0

The surplus or shortage of exhaust gas energy, and necessary supplemental HFO at full electrical power are shown in Figure 8 and Figure 9.

The surplus or shortage of exhaust gas energy, and necessary supplemental HFO energy at standard electrical power are shown inFigure 10 and Figure 11.

Exhaust gas energy need for full and standard electrical power and heat are shown in Figure 12 and Figure 13.

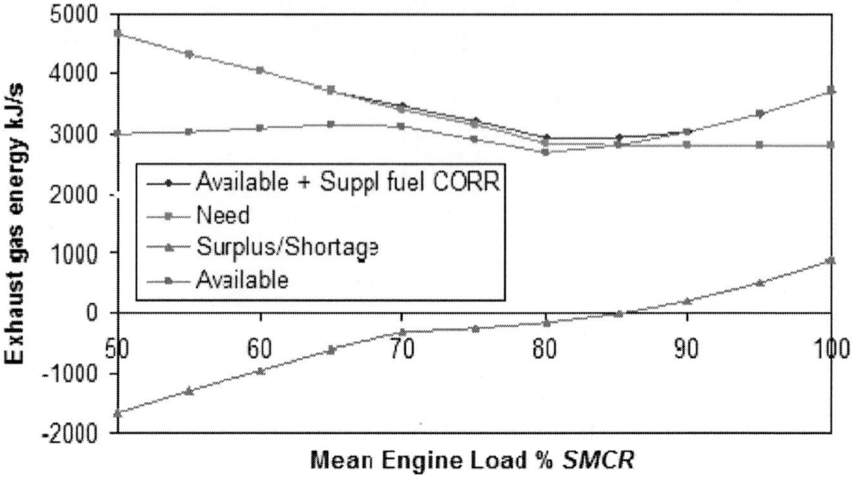

Figure 8. Exhaust gas energy and supplemental HFO at full electrical power for the R123 fluid.

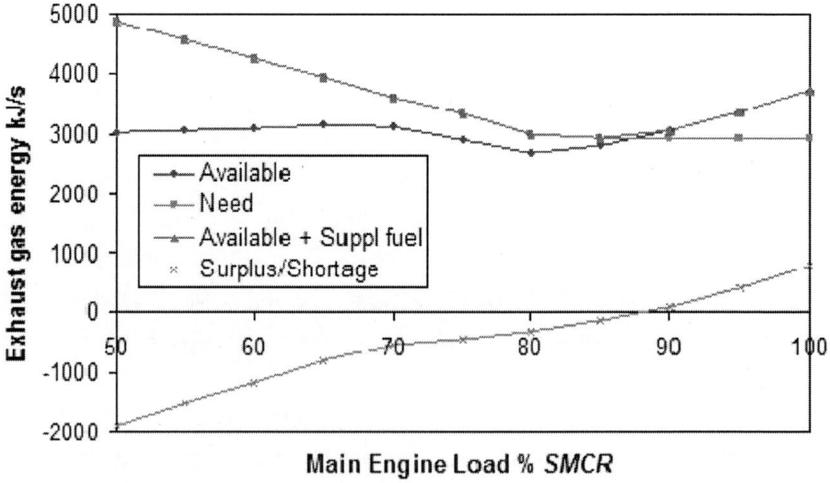

Figure 9. Exhaust gas energy and supplemental HFO at full electrical power for the R245fa fluid.

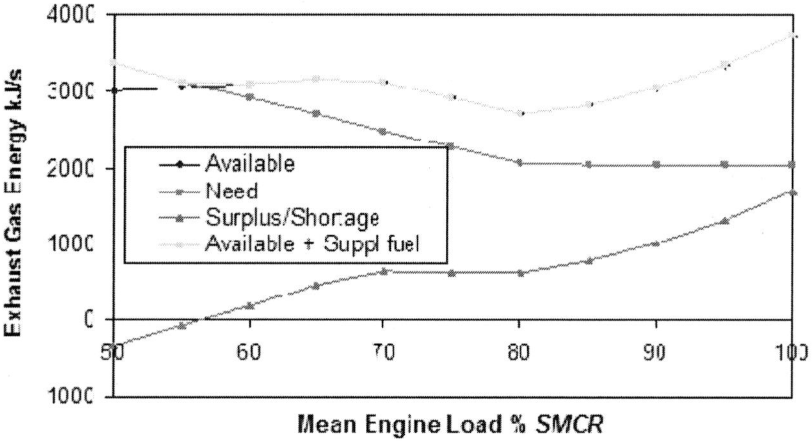

Figure 10. Exhaust gas energy and supplemental HFO energy at standard electrical power and heat for the R123 fluid.

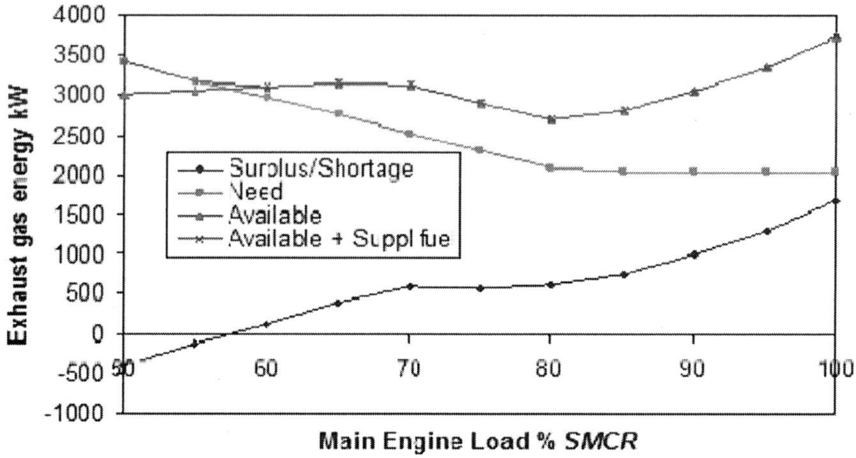

Figure 11. Exhaust gas energy and supplemental HFO energy at standard electrical power and heat for the R245fa fluid.

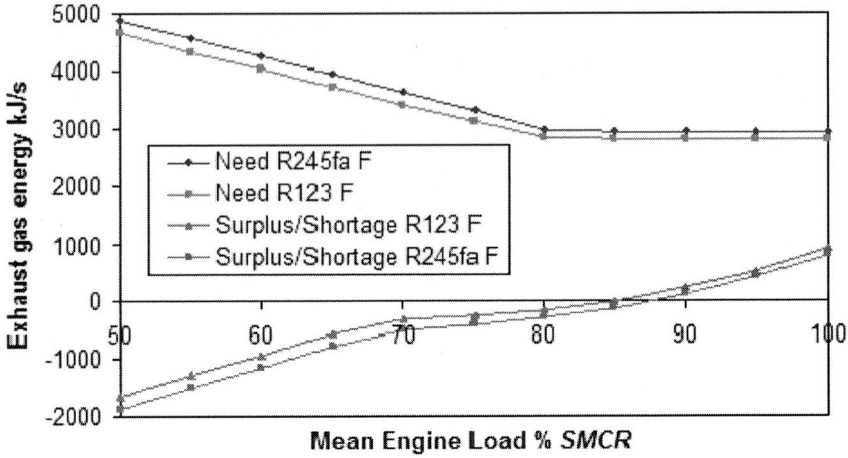

Figure 12. Exhaust gas energy need and surplus/shortage of energy at full electrical power and heat.

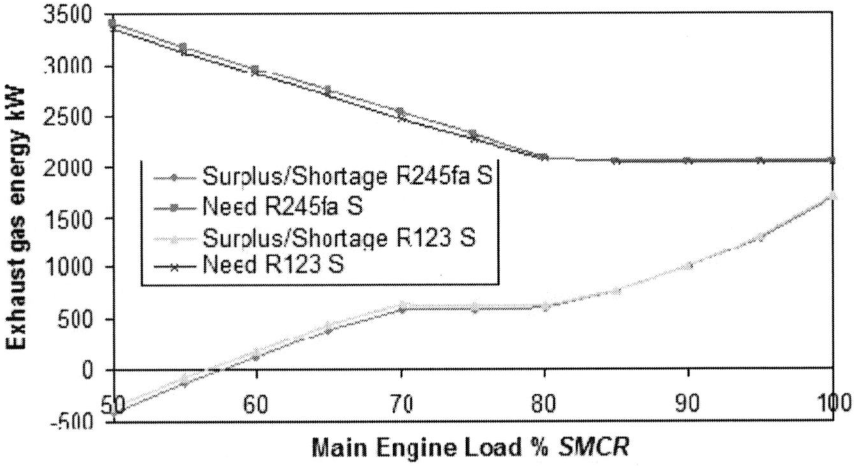

Figure 13. Exhaust gas energy need and surplus/shortage of energy at standard electrical power and heat.

The supercritical single pressure vapor system utilizes the exhaust gas heat; see the process diagrams in Figure 3 and Figure 4, *T-s*diagrams in Figure 6 and Figure 7, and the corresponding temperature/heat transmission diagrams in Figure 14 and Figure 15. The check of the temperature difference between the exhaust gases and the working fluids was performed carefully taking into account that the PP should be at 15 ºC. In [17] in Figure 10 the graphs show the influence of the PP on the boiler heat transfer surface and steam production. The lower the PP, the larger is the heat transfer surface, the more efficient is the exhaust gas boiler, and the higher is the gas pressure loss across the boiler. The verification of the temperature difference through the exhaust gas boiler at main engine loads from 50% to 100% *SMCR* is shown in Figure 14 for R123 working fluid. For the R245fa the temperature difference is shown in Figure 15.

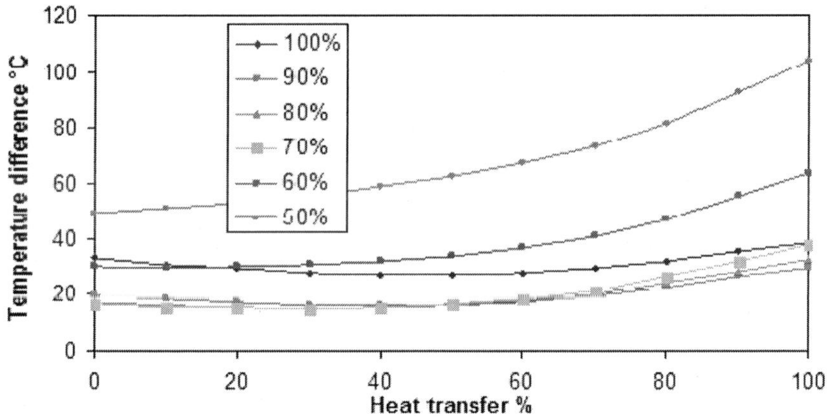

Figure 14. Temperature difference in the exhaust gas boiler with the organic working fluid R123 at full electrical power and the main engine loads from 50% to 100% *SMCR*.

The efficiencies of main engine waste heat recovery are shown in Figure 16 and Figure 17. Figure 16 shows the $\eta_{CHP,system}$ *i.e.*, the efficiency in the conversion of main engine waste heat to ship electricity and heat. Figure 17 displays $\eta_{P,el}$ *i.e.*, the efficiency in conversion of main engine waste heat to ship electricity.

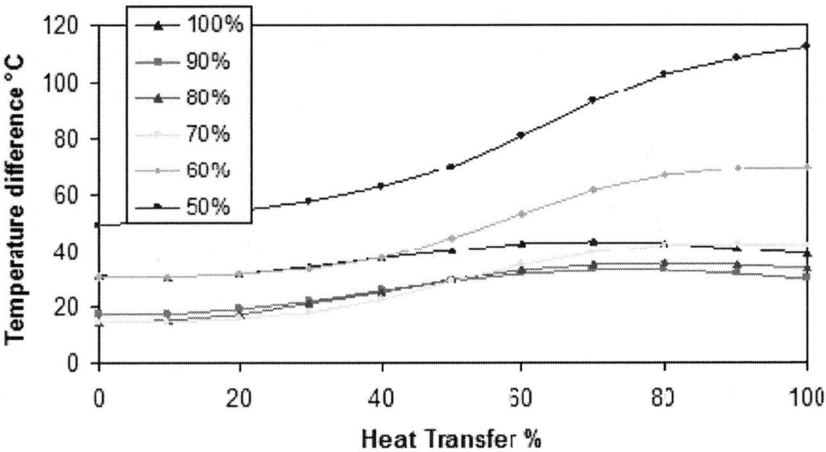

Figure 15. Temperature difference in the exhaust gas boiler with the organic working fluid R245fa at full electrical power and the main engine loads from 50% to 100% *SMCR*.

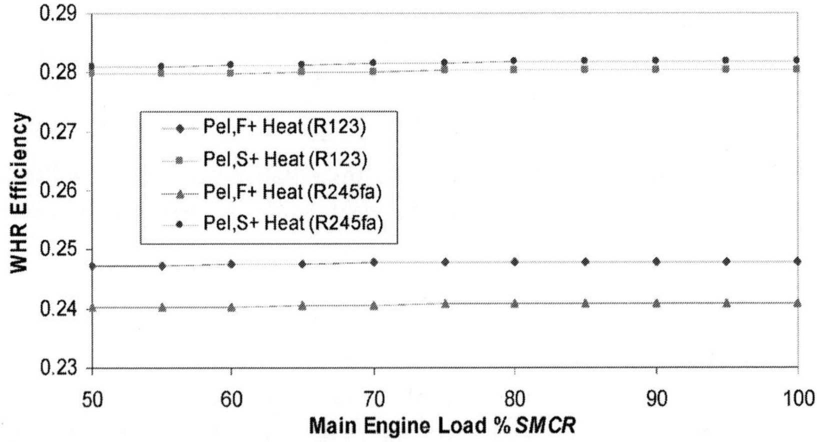

Figure 16. WHR Efficiency with organic fluids—$\eta_{CHP,system}$ (electrical power and heat).

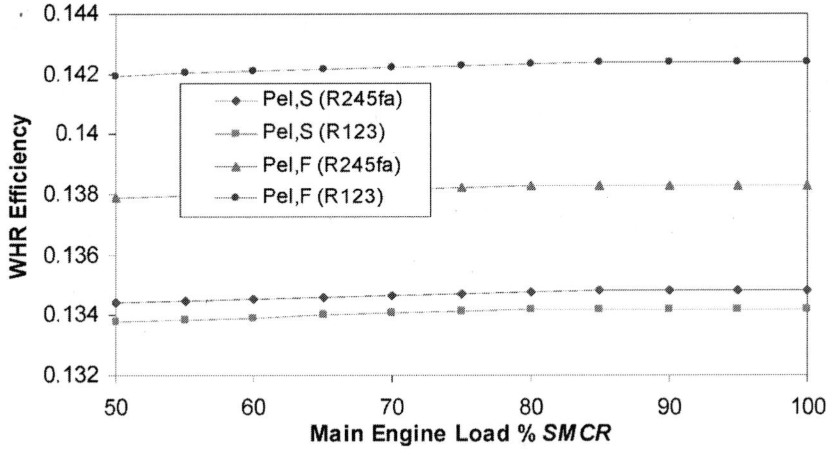

Figure 17. WHR Efficiency with organic fluids—$\eta_{P,el}$ (electrical power only).

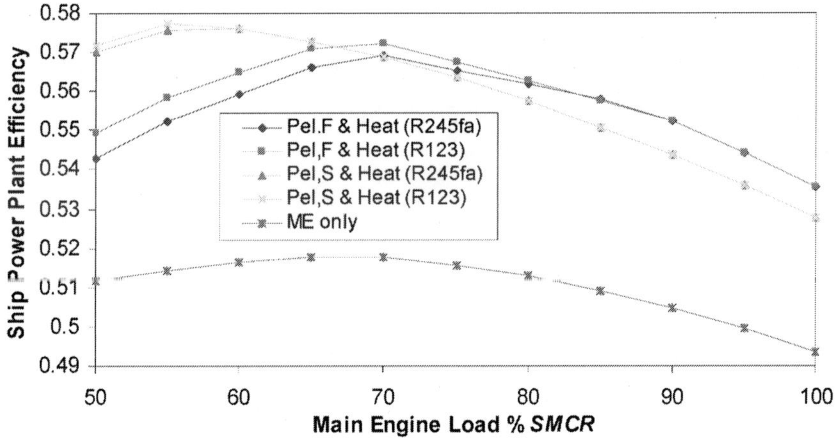

Figure 18. Ship Power Plant Efficiency with organic fluids—$\eta_{CHP,ship\ total}$ (power and heat).

Figure 19 presents a similar situation as Figure 18 but neglecting heat used for onboard heating. The results are similar, however, the values are lower.

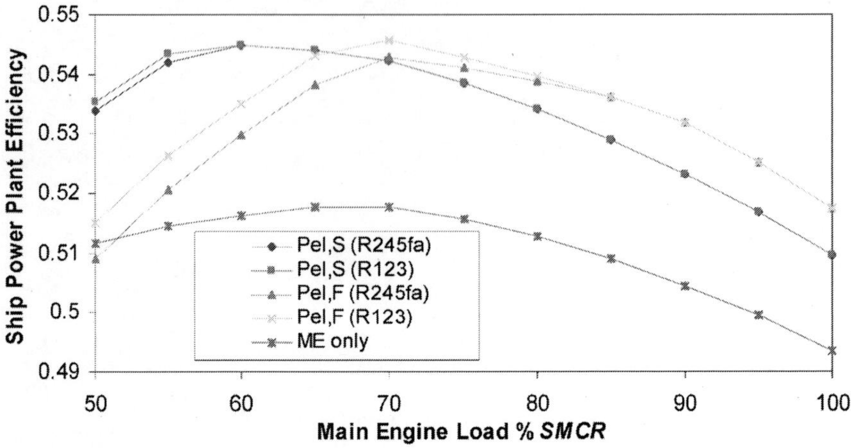

Figure 19. Ship Power Plant Efficiency with organic fluids—$\eta_{P,ship}$ (power only).

Figure 20 shows the gain in the ship power efficiencies when heat and power (main engine and electrical power) efficiencies are compared to the conventional main engine efficiency.

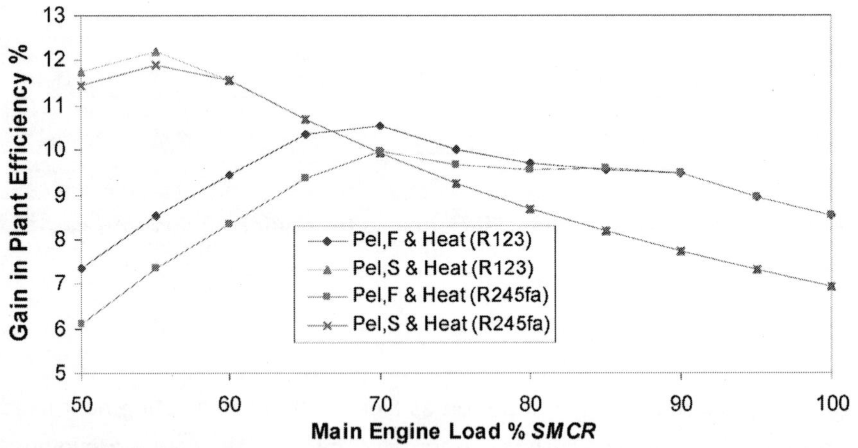

Figure 20. Gain in Ship Power Plant Efficiency with organic fluids—heat and electrical power.

Figure 21 shows the gain in the ship power efficiencies when power (main engine and electrical power) efficiencies, are compared to the conventional main engine efficiency.

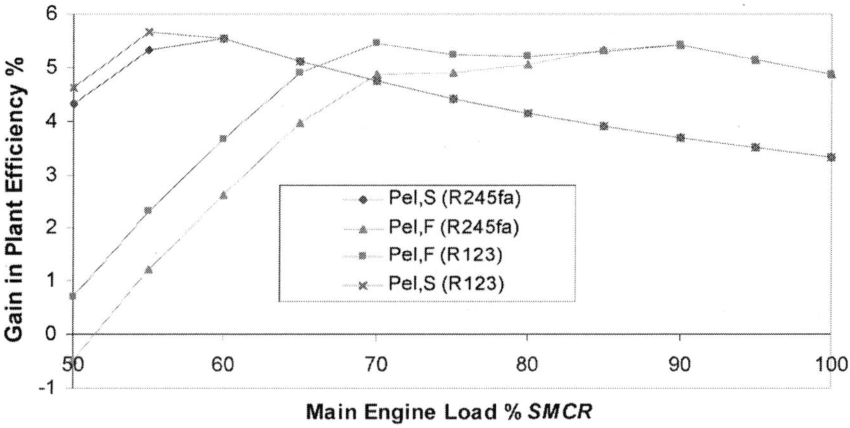

Figure 21. Gain in Ship Power Plant Efficiency with organic fluids—electrical power only.

4. DISCUSSION

Because the process containing organic fluids R245fa or R123 has a much larger mass flow rate, the required feed pump power is considerably higher compared to a steam cycle. Therefore, the full electrical power necessary for the R245fa cycle is 1,012.5 kWe instead of 912 kWe, and 690.1 kWe instead of 620 kWe for standard electrical power. For the R123 cycle, the necessary full electrical power is 1,038.9 kWe instead of 912 kWe, and 711.5 kWe instead of 620 kWe for standard electrical power.

The surplus of exhaust gas energy at full electrical load using R245fa organic fluid appears to be over 88% *SMCR*, and over 85%*SMCR* with R123 organic fluid. It is necessary to burn supplemental fuel when R123 fluid is used, in case when the exhaust gas energy is too low. In the region of 65%

to 90% *SMCR* it is also necessary to burn a small amount of corrective fuel to keep the PP at 15 °C.

The surplus exhaust gas energy for the R123 and R245fa fluids at standard electrical power starts over 56% *SMCR*. A considerable exhaust gas energy surplus is from 65% to 80%, and significant from 85% to 100% *SMCR*.

At full electrical power demand (Figure 12), the need for exhaust gas energy is lower for the R123 than for the R245fa fluid. The same is at standard electrical power demand (Figure 13), but the difference is smaller. Figure 13 shows that the surplus of the exhaust gas energy is high for both working fluids if the ship electrical demand is standard. The expansion in the turbine with the R123 fluid takes place until 1.35 bar and 54.3 °C, which is more favorable compared to the R245fa fluid. At the same inlet parameters to the turbine and lower output parameters from the turbine, the R123 fluid has a more efficient Rankine cycle. Additionally, the maximum inlet temperature for the R245fa fluid is 200 °C (by Gao *et al.* [10] the max inlet temperature is 227 °C), while the R123 due to the thermal stability allows a higher inlet temperature. The advantage of the organic Rankine cycle with the R123 fluid is even higher.

The WHR efficiency for production of heat and electricity $\eta_{CHP,system}$ is higher for standard electrical power than for full electrical power (see Figure 16). The highest WHR efficiency for the R245fa fluid is 28.18% and it is lower for the R123 fluid amounting to 28.05%. At full electrical power and heat, $\eta_{CHP,system}$ is higher for the R123 working fluid and equals 24.79% compared to 24.1% for the R245fa fluid. At standard electrical power the exhaust gas energy is high enough over nearly a complete working range of the main engine, and there is no need to burn supplemental fuel. At full electrical power, below 90% *SMCR* it is necessary to burn supplemental fuel, but $\eta_{CHP,system}$ is also high.

Figure 17 presents the same situation as Figure 16, but in this case the heat consumed on board is not taken into consideration. Figure 17 presents only the produced electrical power from the main engine waste heat. In this case the highest $\eta_{P,el}$ has full electricity production by the R123 working fluid and amounts over 14.23%. $\eta_{P,el}$ at full electrical power with the R245fa working fluid achieves 13.83%. These results could be partially compared to the results of Larsen *et al.* [9] in Table 5 for SI process and R245fa fluid. Their η_{th} = 17%, but in our calculation the surplus of the exhaust gas energy is lost in the chimney. The values of $\eta_{P,el}$ at standard electrical load amount to 13.48% for the R245fa fluid, and 13.42% for the R123 fluid. The reason for such a low efficiency is a high amount of the exhaust gas energy exiting unused the atmosphere (see Figure 13). Karellas and Schuster [18] presented the system with internal combustion engine and ORC with R245fa working fluid. The heat source (thermal oil) reached the temperature of about 240 °C. For the supercritical ORC process η_{system} = 12.72% was achieved, which is close to our results ranging from 13.4% to 13.8%. Vescovo [19] states: "Customized ORC systems are employed to recover heat from lower temperature heat sources (below 250 °C) and refrigerant-based working fluids (non-flammable, non-corrosive, with low toxicity) are used in these systems. These plants are typically used for low temperature liquid flow heat recovery, and electrical efficiencies vary widely, depending upon the heat source temperatures and other specific conditions, ranging from 8% to 18%."

Figure 18 shows the ship power plant efficiency, $\eta_{CHP,ship\ total}$, in production of propulsion power, heat and electricity on board. For conventional ship design, the main engine efficiency η_{ME} is over 51% from 50% to 80% *SMCR*. With additional heat and power production from waste heat, the highest $\eta_{CHP,ship\ total}$ efficiency is at 70% *SMCR* and reaches 57.2% for the R123 fluid, and 56.9 % for the R245fa fluid. In the complete service range (from 60 to 85% SMCR) $\eta_{CHP,ship\ total}$ is high. When producing standard electrical power, $\eta_{CHP,ship\ total}$ is even higher and equals 57.72% at low main engine loads up to 70% *SMCR*. Due to the waste heat lost through the chimney, $\eta_{CHP,ship\ total}$ decreases at higher main engine loads.

Figure 19 shows the efficiency of the ship's power plant using the waste heat of the main engine. For full electrical load maximum efficiency $\eta_{P,ship}$ is achieved at 70% *SMCR* and amounts to 54.58% for R123 fluid, and 54.28% for R245fa fluid. In a standard electrical load $\eta_{P,ship}$ is slightly smaller and identical for both fluids. The reason of this is that over 60% *SMCR* there is a considerable excess heat in the exhaust gases that are lost in the chimney.

The company MAN B&W Diesel A/S in [20] for 12K98ME/MC engine in Thermo Efficiency System (TES) version operating at ISO ambient reference conditions and at 100% *SMCR* (68,640 kW@94 rpm) obtained total power output efficiency of 54.2%. The waste heat energy was recovered in the steam turbine. Schmid of Wärtsilä [21] showed similar results for 12RT-flex96C engine where the overall efficiency of 54.9% was obtained using the WHR by steam turbine and power turbine. In our work with organic fluids, such efficiency was obtained at 70% *SMCR* (Fig 19) where the lost exhaust gas energy is not taken into account. In this work a large amount of exhaust gas energy is lost, especially at higher main engine loads.

The gain in the plant efficiencies are shown in Figure 20 and Figure 21. In Figure 20 the gain ranges from 9.44% at 60% *SMCR* up to 10.55% at 70% *SMCR* for the R123 fluid. This gain is high up to 90% *SMCR* and equals 9.46%. The gain with R245fa fluid is lower. In the case of standard electrical power the gain is high at low main engine loads and exceeds over 12%, but decreases at higher main engine loads due to the loss of exhaust gas energy.

When the gain is considered not taking into account the ship heat consumption (Figure 21), the R123 has again better values in full and standard electricity production. During full electrical load, this gain equals approximately 5% in the range from 65 to 100% *SMCR*. Ahnger [22] states that the organic Rankine cycle products of today give 8%–10% additional power—even for small engines. Those are much higher values than shown in Figure 21. But, at full electrical load and especially at standard electrical load, a great amount of exhaust gas energy is lost through the chimney, instead to be used in the ORC ship power plant. Such calculations have not been performed in this paper.

A partial model validation can be performed by comparing the results obtained by Larsen *et al.* [9] and the ones obtained in the real-life WHR systems built by Dresser Rand, Mitsubishi Heavy Industries Ltd, Shinko Ind. Ltd and Siemens. MAN B&W [23] recommends an ORC plant for a propulsion engine power below 15,000 kW, whereas for 15,000 kW to 25,000 kW the power gas turbine or superheated steam turbine cycle is recommended.

5. CONCLUSIONS

The application of the supercritical ORC during the production of electrical energy and heat, using waste heat energy from the main engine jacket water, scavenged air and exhaust gases has been explored in this work. A CHP plant with R245fa or R123 fluid using supercritical ORC meets all the demands for electrical energy and heat while burning only a small amount of supplemental fuel in the HRSG.

This paper deals with the savings in fuel consumption for the WHR CHP plant using organic fluids. The comparison was made: (i) with conventional low speed two stroke propulsion engines, (ii) with TES developed by MAN B&W and WHR Plant developed by Wärtsilä, and, (iii) with similar organic Rankine plants.

Using the ORC for electricity production, the ship power plant efficiency rises significantly compared to the conventional main engine. During the standard electrical load a great amount of surplus exhaust gas energy is lost through the chimney. This lost gas energy can be converted to electrical energy and transferred to the propeller shaft. That would additionally increase the ship power plant efficiency.

The comparison with MAN and Wärtsilä waste heat recovery systems showed similar results. However, the MAN and Wärtsilä systems are not applicable for such small engines as shown in this work. The comparison with similar organic RC plants provided results which are in good correlation, but the work which should take into account the exhaust gas energy lost in a chimney would give the right answer.

To enhance the cogeneration efficiency, the maximum temperature of the applied organic fluid should be increased in order to increase the turbine outlet temperature and improve the quality of the heat consumed on board. The R123 fluid provides better results compared to R245fa, therefore, its usage should be taken into consideration after 2020/2030.

This analysis has revealed the possible savings in fuel consumption when using the supercritical ORC CHP for low temperature WHR in ship propulsion plants. Concurrently, the lower fuel consumption reduces greenhouse gas emissions and their environmental impact.

ACKNOWLEDGMENTS

This work was sponsored by the Ministry of Science, Education and Sports of the Republic of Croatia. The authors would like to thank Professor Ian K. Smith from City University, London for his helpful suggestions and useful technical information.

REFERENCES

1. Aly, S.E. Diesel engine waste heat power cycle. *Appl. Energy* **1987**, *29*, 179–189.

2. Shu, G.; Liang, Y.; Wei, H.; Tian, H.; Zhao, J.; Liu, L. A review of waste heat recovery on two-stroke IC engine abroad ships.*Renew. Sustain. Energy Rev.* **2013**, *19*, 385–401.

3. Butcher, C.J.; Reddy, B.V. Second law analysis of a waste heat recovery based power generation system. *Int. J Heat Mass Transf.* **2007**, *50*, 2355–2363.

4. Wang, E.H.; Zang, H.G.; Fan, B.Y.; Ouyang, M.G.; Zhao, Y.; Mu, Q.H. Study of working fluid selection of organic rankine cycle (ORC) for engine waste heat recovery. *Energy* **2011**, *36*, 3406–3418.

5. Grljušić, M.; Medica, V.; Račić, N. Thermodynamic analysis of a ship power plant operating with waste heat recovery through combined heat and power production. *Energies* **2014**, *7*, 7368–7394.

6. *NIST Standard Reference Database 23: Reference Fluid Thermodynamic and Transport Properties-REFPROP*; Version 9.0. National Institute of Standards and Technology: Gaithersburg, MD, USA, 2010.

7. *Reciprocating Internal Combustion Engines—Performance—Part 1: Declarations of Power, Fuel and Lubricating Oil Consumptions, and Test Methods—Additional Requirements for Engines for General Use*; International Organization for Standardization (ISO): Geneva, Switzerland, 2002; ISO3046-1:2002.

8. MAN Diesel and Turbo, Marine/Low Speed/CEAS-ERD Engine Room Dimensioning, Main Engine Room Data, 6S70MC-C7.1-TI. Available online: http://apps.mandieselturbo.com/ceas/client/erd.aspx (accessed on 9 November 2014).

9. Larsen, U.; Pierobon, L.; Haglind, F.; Gabrielli, C. Design and optimisation of organic rankine cycles for waste heat recovery in marine applications using the principles of natural selection. *Energy* **2013**, *30*, 1–10.

10. Gao, H.; Liu, C.; He, C.; Xu, X.; Wu, S.; Li, Y. Performance analysis and working fluid selection of a supercritical organic rankine cycle for low grade waste heat recovery. *Energies* **2012**, *5*, 3233–3247.

11. Bini, R.; Manciana, E. Organic rankine cycle turbogenerators for combined heat and power production from biomass. In Proceedings of 3rd Munich Discussion Meeting Energy Conversion from Biomass Fuels Current Trends and Future Systems, Munich, Germany, 22–23 October 1996.

12. Duvia, A.; Bini, R.; Spanring, H.; Portenkirchner, K. Application of ORC Units in the MDF and Particleboard Sector—General Considerations and Overview of the Experiences of the First ORC Plant in this industry installed at MDF Hallien. Available online: http://www.turboden.eu/en/public/downloads/Application_of_ORC_units_in_the_MDF_and_particleboard_sector.pdf(accessed on 10 March 2014).

13. Bini, R.; di Prima, M.; Guercio, A. Organic Rankine Cycle (ORC) in Biomass Plants: An Overview on Different Applications. Available online: http://www.turboden.eu/en/public/downloads/10A02943_paper_marco.pdf (accessed on 20 July 2014).

14. Rentizelas, A.; Karellas, S.; Kakaras, E.; Tatsiopoulos, I. Comparative techno-economic analysis of ORC and gasification for bioenergy applications. *Energy Convers. Manag.* **2009**, *50*, 674–681.

15. Grljušić, M. Thermodynamic Analysis and Optimisation of Marine Low Speed Propulsion Diesel Engine Operating with Waste Heat Recovery. Ph.D. Thesis, University of Rijeka, Rijeka, Croatia, 10 September 2012.

16. Bunkerworld Fuel Prices. Available online: http://www. bunkerworld. com/prices/ (accessed on 25 July 2014).

17. MAN Diesel and Turbo. Soot Deposits and Fires in Exhaust Gas Boiler. Available online: http://www.mandieselturbo.com/files/news/ filesof 11026/5510-0065-01ppr_low.pdf (accessed on 10 April 2014).

18. Karellas, S.; Schuster, A. Supercritical fluid parameters in Organic Rankine Cycle applications. *Int. J. Thermodyn.* **2008**, *11*, 101–108.

19. Vescovo, R. ORC recovering industrial heat—Power generation from waste energy streams. Available online: http://www. cospp.com/ articles/print/volume-10/issue-2/features/orc-recovering-industrial-heat-power-generation-from-waste-energy-streams.html (accessed on 5 February 2015).

20. *Thermo Efficiency System (TES)—for Reduction of Fuel Consumption and CO2 Emission*; MAN B&W Diesel A/S: Copenhagen, Denmark, October 2014. Available online: http://marine.man.eu/docs/ libraries provider6/technical-papers/thermo-efficiency-system.pdf?sfvrsn=22 (accessed on 1 February 2015).

21. Schmid, H. *Less Emission through Waste Heat Recovery*; Wärtsilä Corporation: Helsinki, Finland; April; 2004.

22. Ahnger, A. ECC with internal combustion engines. Wärtsilä Technical Journal in detail, Issue No. 2. 2007, pp. 4–6. Available online: http://www.indetailmagazine.com/en/ (accessed on 1 February 2015).

23. MAN Diesel and Turbo. Waste Heat Recovery System for Reduction of Fuel Consumption, Emissions and EEDI. Available online: http://www.mandieselturbo.com/files/news/filesof17740/5510-0136-00pp_low.pdf (accessed on 10 April 2014).

Chapter 9

Air/steam flow and steam wetness dependence on acoustic resonance in safety relief valves

Keita Okuyama*, **Akinori Tamura and Shiro Takahashi**

Hitachi Research Laboratory, 7-1-1, Omika-cho, Hitachi-shi,
Ibaraki 319-1221, Japan

ABSTRACT

Many experimental studies related to the flow-induced acoustic resonance closed side branches have been reported. However, few studies have reported on the effects of air/steam flow and steam wetness dependence on fluctuating pressure amplitude. Therefore, we investigated the effect of air/steam flow and steam wetness dependence on fluctuating pressure amplitude by conducting a high temperature and high pressure tests at the Hitachi Utility Steam Test Leading Facility (HUSTLE). The test section consisted of a main pipe and a side branch. The side branch was mounted on the long straight main pipe. Fluctuating pressures at the end face of the side branches were measured. The following two results were obtained; the first is that the air/steam flow had little effect on the fluctuating pressure amplitude normalized by dynamic pressure and frequency normalized by the resonance frequency; the second is that under the acoustic resonance (St = 0.41) and non-resonance (St = 0.55) conditions, fluctuating pressure and frequency changed little with steam wetness. The steam wetness during the boiling water reactor operation was less than 0.1%; thus, there was no effect of steam wetness on the acoustic pressure amplitude and the frequency under this operating condition.

KEYWORDS

boiling water reactor, fluid flow, pressure wave, resonance

1. INTRODUCTION

Extended power uprates (EPUs) have been implemented or are under consideration at several nuclear power plant facilities to improve plant efficiency. In EPU conditions, the boiling water reactor (BWR) in the Quad Cities Unit 2 experienced a significant increase in steam moisture in the main steam lines (MSLs) [1]. Inspection of a steam dryer showed that it was likely damaged by high cycle fatigue due to the flow-induced acoustic resonance at 17% EPU. The principal cause of the dryer failure was thought to be flow-induced acoustic resonance at the side branches of the safety relief valves (SRVs) in the MSLs. Fluctuating pressure was generated in the SRV side branches and propagated from the SRVs to the dryer through the MSLs and generated in the dryer loading, as shown in **Figure 1** .

Figure 2 shows the mechanism of flow-induced acoustic resonance, which is known as the cavity tone phenomena. The shear layer departed leading edge of the cavity is unstable and generates periodic vortices that excite acoustic standing waves in the cavity [2]. If these acoustic waves are reflected at the end face of the side branch, the oscillations on the shear layer will be enhanced. If this process is regenerative, large coherent vortices on the shear layer will develop and a highly intense fluctuating pressure will occur in the cavity [3].

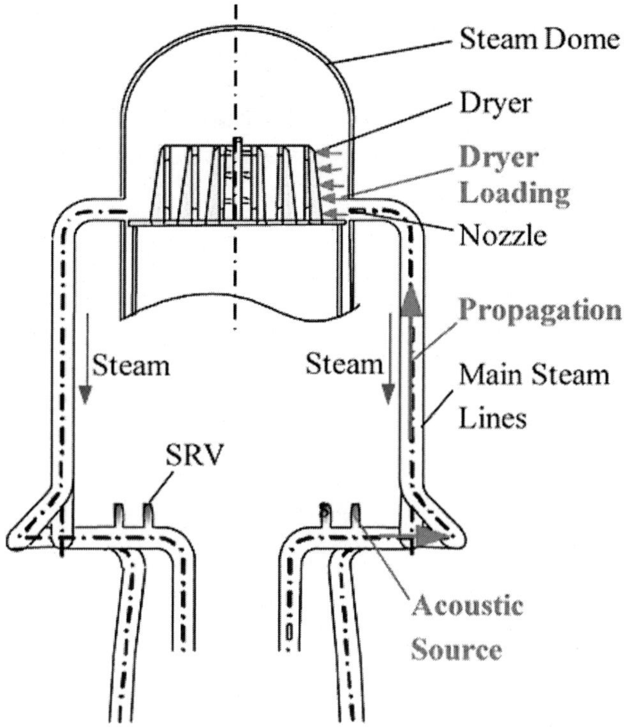

Figure 1 BWR steam dome, dryer, and MSLs

Many experimental studies [4–10] related to the flow-induced acoustic resonance of closed side branches have been reported. Jungowski et al. [4] investigated the effect of the diameter ratio on the Strouhal number and the amplitude of the acoustic wave. Bruggeman et al. [5] proposed a theoretical model for the acoustic sources responsible for the flow-induced acoustic resonance in a piping system with closed side branches. Ziada and Buhlmann [6] demonstrated that side branches in close proximity are particularly susceptible to resonance. Kriesels et al. [7] studied the detailed behavior of the flow in a piping system with two opposite closed side branches of equal length in a cross configuration. Visualization of flow-induced acoustic resonance was also studied by Okuyama [2], Ziada [3], Dequand et al. [8], and Li et al. [9]. Knott [10] investigated the effect of edge shape of T-junction on fluctuating pressure. However, few studies have reported on the effects of air/steam flow and steam wetness on fluctuating pressure amplitude. For this study, we carried out high temperature and high pressure tests to investigate the effect of air/steam flow on fluctuating pressure. We also investigate the dependence of steam wetness on fluctuating pressure with changing steam wetness.

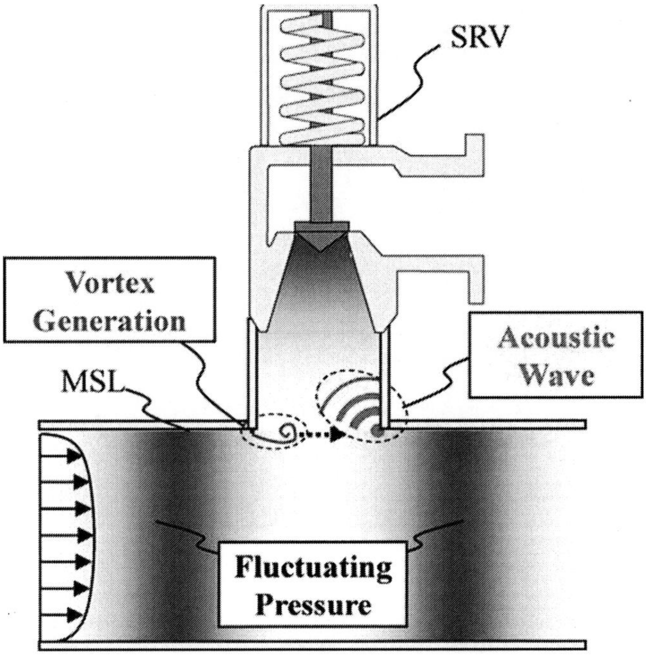

Figure 2 Flow-induced acoustic resonance at the SRV side branch

2. EXPERIMENT

2.1. Experimental apparatus

We conducted the experiment at the Hitachi Utility Steam Test Leading Facility (HUSTLE). A schematic view of this facility is shown in **Figure 3** . Superheated steam was supplied to the test section by the steam compressor. Steam passing through the test section returned the steam loop via a mist trap placed downstream of the test section. Details of the test section are shown in **Figure 4** . The test section consisted of a main pipe and side branch. The single side branch was mounted on the long straight main pipe. The T-junctions had a sharp edge. All the cross sections of the main pipe and side branch were circular. Silencers were installed upstream and downstream from the test section to reduce the noise coming from the compressor and pressure regulating valve. We measured fluctuating pressures at the end face of the side branches for 20 seconds using pressure sensors mounted on the top of the side branches. The sampling rate and the averaging number were 20 kHz and 360,000, respectively. A series of experiments was performed by changing the flow velocity of the main pipe flow. Each test was conducted three times under the same condition and the accuracy of the fluctuating pressure measurements was higher than 5%. The flow velocity of the main pipe was determined by measuring the pressure, temperature, and mass flow rate of the main pipe. In the steam flow test, we regulated the steam wetness by spraying water at room temperature into upstream of the test section. The distance between spraying point and test section was 200 *D* (*D* is the inner diameter of the main pipe (m)), thus there had been little effect on velocity distribution of main flow. We measured the size distribution of fine droplets using an optical probe based on the multi-wavelength light extinction [11]. The sampling rate and the averaging number were 5 Hz and 10, respectively. The steam wetness (*y*) was calculated according to its definition as follows:

$$y = \frac{V \cdot \rho_w}{V \cdot \rho_w + (1 - V)\rho_v} \approx \frac{V \cdot \rho_w}{V \cdot \rho_w + \rho_v}, \qquad (1)$$

where ρ_w and ρ_v are specific densities of saturated water and steam (m^3/kg), respectively. *V* is the water volume in per unit volume (-) as follows [12]:

$$V = \int \frac{\pi}{6} x^3 N(x)\, dx, \qquad (2)$$

where *x* is the diameter of droplet and *N*(*x*) is the size distribution of fine droplets. To estimate the measuring errors of the probe, colloid concentration of standard latex particles (mean diameter; 102 ± 3 nm) solution was measured with the probe. The experimental deviation of particle diameter was less than 14%. By converting to wetness at 3 MPa, the accuracy of wetness was higher than 0.07%.

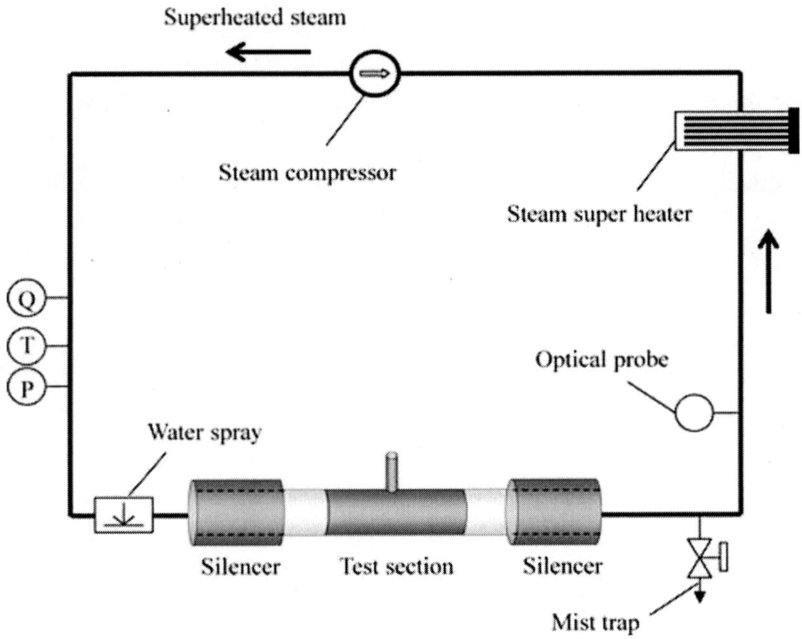

Figure 3 Experimental apparatus

2.2. Test conditions

A highly intense fluctuating pressure in the cavity was induced by the interaction between vortex generation and acoustic waves; thus, the dominant factors of this phenomenon were the Reynolds number (Re), Strouhal number (St), and Mach number (*M*), as expressed below,

$$\mathrm{St} = f\frac{d}{U} \tag{3}$$

$$M = \frac{U}{a} \tag{4}$$

$$\mathrm{Re} = \frac{Ud}{\nu}, \qquad (5)$$

where *f* is the resonance frequency (Hz), *d* is the inner diameter of the side branch (m), *U* is the flow velocity of the main pipe flow (m/s), *a* is the sound speed (m/s), and ν is the dynamic viscosity (m^2/s).

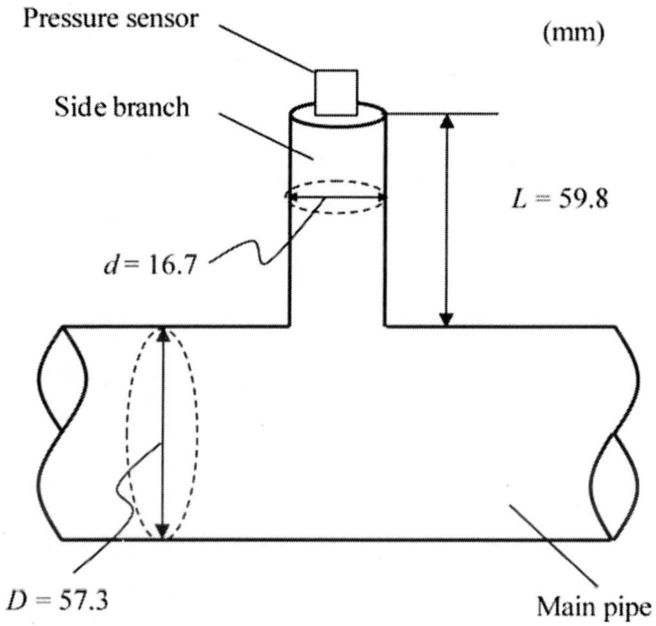

Figure 4 Details of test sections

We first evaluated the effect of air/steam flow on fluctuating pressure by conducting an air/steam flow test under almost same dominant factors, as shown in **Table 1** .Then, we evaluated the dependence of steam wetness on fluctuating pressure by changing the steam wetness without changing the above dominant factors, as shown in **Table 2** .

Table 1 Experimental conditions and dominant factors for evaluation of air/steam difference on fluctuating pressure

Item	Unit	Air test	Steam test
Fluid	–	Air	Steam
Pressure	MPa	0.65	3
Temperature	°C	230	240
Velocity	m/s	43–72	32–78
Density	kg/m^3	4.5	15
St	–	0.38–0.63	0.40–0.98
M	–	0.10–0.16	0.06–0.16
Re	–	$4.2–7.0 \times 10^5$	$1.6–3.9 \times 10^6$

3. RESULTS AND DISCUSSION

3.1. Effect of air/steam flow on peak fluctuating pressure

We measured fluctuating pressures at the end face of the side branches using pressure sensors mounted on the top of the side branch. To analyze this fluctuating pressure in detail, we calculated the power spectrum density (PSD), as shown in**Figure 5** . The PSD was normalized by the root mean square of the dynamic pressure of the main pipe flow. The horizontal axis shows the sound frequency normalized by the resonance frequency (f_n) of the first mode (n = 1) as expressed in Equation (6),

$$f_n = \frac{a(2n-1)}{4(L+L_e)} \quad n = 1, 2, 3, \ldots, \tag{6}$$

where L is the length of the side branches (m) and L_e is the end correction (m) [10]. An outstanding high peak was observed at the resonance frequency of the first mode (f_1 = 1910 Hz); therefore, this peak was clarified as the flow-induced acoustic sound. The effect of flow velocity, i.e., St, on peak pressure amplitude is shown in **Figure 6** . The root mean square of peak fluctuating pressure was normalized by the dynamic pressure of the main pipe flow. In the steam test, the pressure amplitude changed cyclically with changing St. Significantly high fluctuating pressure was generated at St = 0.4 and 0.8, and fluctuating pressure was small when St was 0.6. This tendency of steam flow agreed with that of air flow.

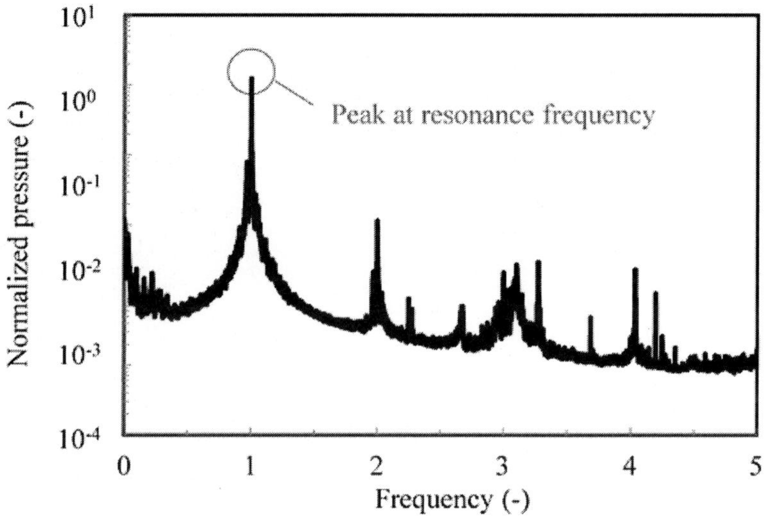

Figure 5 PSD of fluctuating pressure (dry steam, 3.0 MPa, St = 0.40, M = 0.16, Re = 3.9 × 10^6)

The effect of St on the frequency of peak pressure amplitude is shown in **Figure 7** . The ordinate shows the acoustic frequency normalized by the resonance frequency of the first mode, as shown in Equation (6). When St – 0.4 and 0.8, which resulted in the detection of high fluctuating pressure in Figure 6, the acoustic frequency was almost identical to the resonance frequency of the first mode. At St = 0.4–0.6 and St = 0.7–1.0 regions, the higher the St, the lower the acoustic frequency. In this case, flow velocity was low; thus, the periodic vortices generated at the lead edge of the cavity took a long time to drift toward the bottom edge of the cavity. Thus, the lower the frequency of vortex, the lower the frequency of fluctuating pressure. We inferred the existence of two resonant modes; single vortex mode at St = 0.4 and double vortices mode at St = 0.8. These modes changed at St = 0.6; thus, acoustic frequency shifted drastically. A similar trend was reported in a previous paper [3].

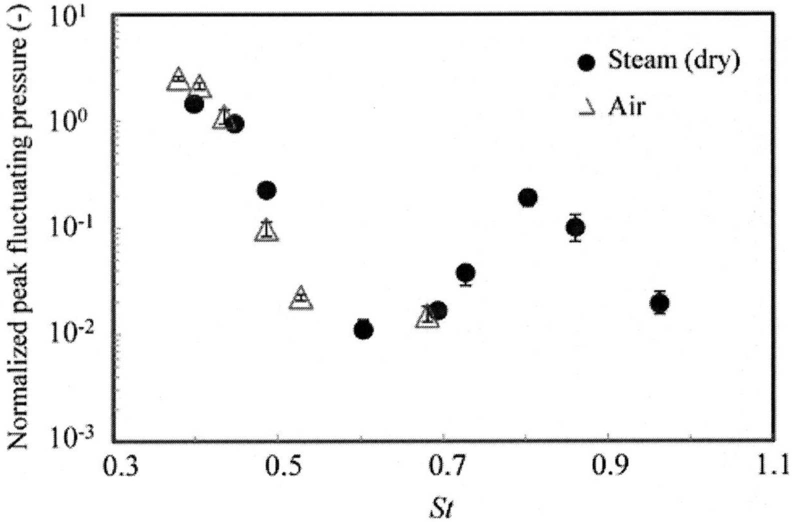

Figure 6 Effect of St on peak fluctuating pressures

Table 2 Experimental conditions and dominant factors for evaluation of steam wetness on fluctuating pressure

Item	Unit	Condition
Fluid	–	Steam
Pressure	MPa	7
Temperature	°C	286
Velocity	m/s	50, 76
Density	kg/m^3	37
Wetness	%	0–0.13
St	–	0.41, 0.55
M	–	0.10, 0.15
Re	–	5.6×10^6, 8.4×10^6

The tendency of fluctuating pressure amplitude and frequency of steam flow agreed with that of air flow; thus, air/steam flow has little effects on fluctuating pressure amplitude normalized by dynamic pressure and frequency normalized by resonance frequency.

3.2. Dependence of steam wetness on fluctuating pressure

We measured the size distribution of fine droplets using an optical probe based on the multi-wavelength light extinction, as shown in **Figure 8** . The steam wetness was calculated using Equations (1)–(3). Fluctuating pressure amplitude and frequency with changing steam wetness are shown in **Figures 9** and **10** , respectively. The horizontal axis shows steam wetness. Pressure and frequency were normalized by the dynamic pressure of the main pipe flow and resonance frequency of the first mode, respectively. Fluctuating pressure and frequency changed little with steam wetness. The frequency of fluctuating pressure depends on sound speed, thus sound speed may change little with steam wetness in this experiment. Mach number, which is one of the dominant factors of the flow-induced acoustic resonance, also did not change with steam wetness. Therefore, it seemed that steam wetness has little effect on propagating acoustic waves on the cavity and fluctuating pressure amplitude. Uchiyama reported that the fluctuating pressure decreases when the steam wetness is more than several percentages [13]. He indicated that the cause of pressure drop may be the liquid–vapor phase change. In our experiment, steam wetness was 1 order of magnitude less than that in the previous study; thus, steam wetness has no effect on propagating acoustic waves and fluctuating pressure amplitude.

The steam wetness during the BWR operation was less than 0.1%; thus, there was little effect of steam wetness on acoustic pressure amplitude and frequency under this operating condition.

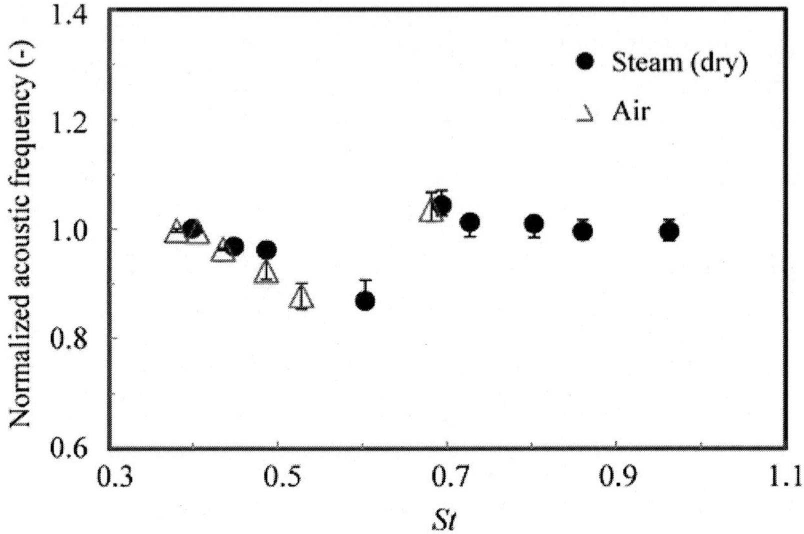

Figure 7. Effect of St on frequency of peak pressure amplitude

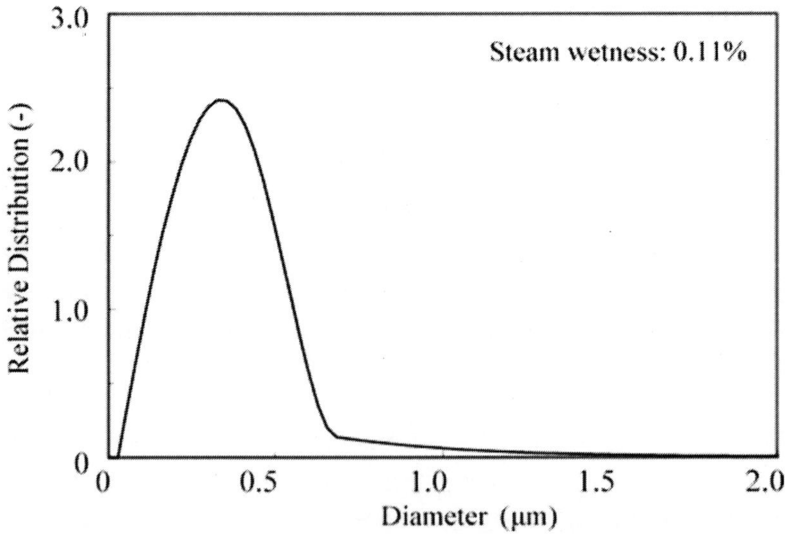

Figure 8 The size distribution of fine droplets (steam, 7.0 MPa, St = 0.41, M = 0.15, Re = 8.4×10^6)

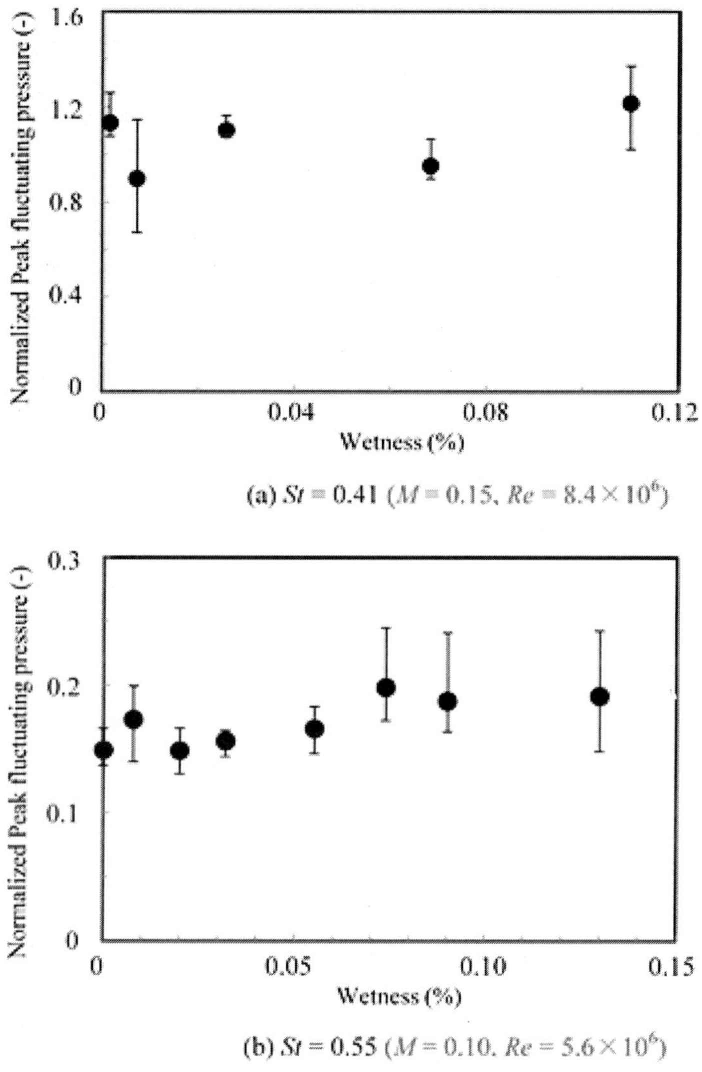

Figure 9 Fluctuating pressure amplitude with changing steam wetness

4. CONCLUSION

We investigated the effect of air/steam flow and steam wetness on fluctuating pressure. We conducted high temperature and high pressure tests at HUSTLE. The test section consisted of a main pipe and side branch.

The single side branch was mounted on the long straight main pipe. Fluctuating pressures at the end face of the side branches were measured using pressure sensors mounted on the top of the side branches. Our observations are summarized as follows.

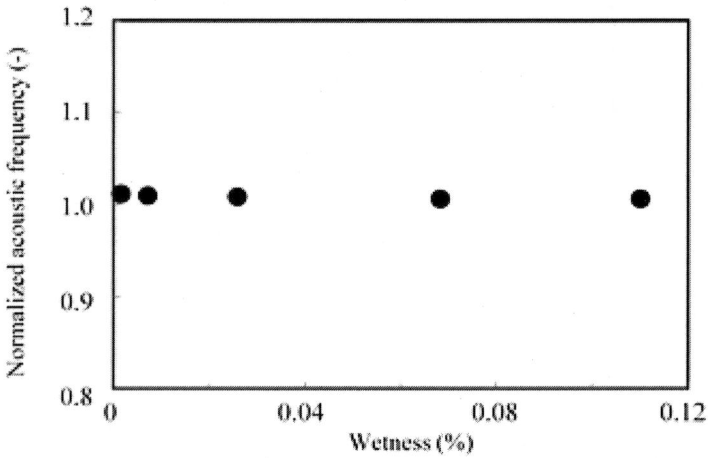

(a) $St = 0.41$ ($M = 0.15$, $Re = 8.4 \times 10^6$)

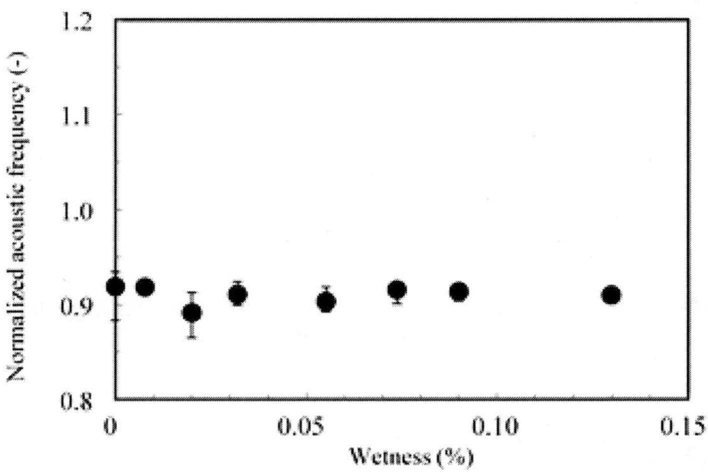

(b) $St = 0.55$ ($M = 0.10$, $Re = 5.6 \times 10^6$)

Figure 10 Fluctuating pressure frequency with changing steam wetness

1) The tendency of fluctuating pressure amplitude and frequency of steam flow agreed with that of air flow; thus, the air/steam flow had little effect on fluctuating pressure amplitude normalized by dynamic pressure and frequency normalized by resonance frequency.

2) Under acoustic resonance (St = 0.41) and non-resonance (St = 0.55) conditions, fluctuating pressure and frequency change little with steam wetness. The steam wetness during the BWR operation was less than 0.1%; thus, there was no effect of steam wetness on acoustic pressure amplitude and frequency under this operating condition.

REFERENCES

1. DeBoo, G and Gesior, R. 2006. Quad Cities Unit 2 main steam line acoustic source identification and load reduction. 14th International Conference on Nuclear Engineering(ICONE14). Jul 17–202006, Miami, FL.

2. Okuyama, K, Takahashi, S, Tamura, A, Nishida, K, Ohtsuka, M and Tsubaki, M. 2009. Flow visualization of acoustic resonance for safety relief valves in power uprated BWRs. 17th International Conference on Nuclear Engineering (ICONE17). Jul 12–162009. Brussels, , Belgium

3. Ziada, S. 1994. A flow visualization study of flow-acoustic coupling at the mouth of a resonant side-branch. *J Fluid Struct*, 8: 391–416.

4. Jungowski, W M, Botros, K K and Studzinski, W. 1989. Cylindrical side-branch as tone generator.. *J Sound Vib.*, 802: 265–285.

5. Bruggeman, J C, Hirschberg, A, Dongen, M EH, Wijnands, A PJ and Gorter, J. 1991. Self-sustained aeroacoustic pulsations in gas transport systems: experimental study of the influence of closed side branches. *J Sound Vib.*, 150: 371–393.

6. Ziada, S and Buhlmann, E T. 1992. Self-excited resonances of two side-branches in close proximity. *J Fluid Struct*, 6: 583–601.

7. Kriesels, P C, Peters, M CAM, Hirschberg, A, Wijnands, A PJ, Iafrati, A, Riccardi, G, Piva, R and Bruggeman, J C. 1995. High amplitude vortex-induced pulsations in a gas transport system. *J Sound Vib.*, 184: 343–368.

8. Dequand, S, Hulshoff, S J and Hirshberg, A. 2003. Self sustained oscillations in a closed side branch system. *J Sound Vib.*, 265: 359–386.

9. Li, Y, Someya, S and Okamoto, K. 2008. A visualization study of flow-induced acoustic resonance in a branched pipe. 6th Japan-Korea Symposium on Nuclear Thermal Hydraulics and Safety (NTHAS6). Nov 24–272008, Okinawa, Japan.

10. Knotts, B D and Selamet, A. 2003. Suppression of flow-acoustic coupling in sidebranch ducts by interface modification. *J Acoust Soc.*, 265: 1025–1045.

11. Hesler, S H, Maurer, R H and Shuster, L H. 1998. Optical probe for measurement of steam wetness fraction in LP turbines.ASME International Joint Power Generating Conference. 1998, New York, NY. pp.213–219.

12. Cai, X, Ning, T, Niu, F, Wu, G and Song, Y. 2009. Investigation of wet steam flow in a 300 MW direct air-cooling steam turbine - part 1: measurement principles, probe, and wetness. *J Power Energy*, 223: 625–634.

13. Uchiyama, Y and Morita, R. “Evaluation of acoustic resonance at branch section in main steam line (Part 1), Effects of steam wetness on acoustic resonance”. In *Central Research Institute of Electric Power Industry Research*, Japan: Central Research Institute of Electric Power Industry. (no. L10009). Japanese

Chapter 10

Dynamic Modeling of the Solar Field in Parabolic Trough Solar Power Plants

Lourdes A. Barcia [1,*], Rogelio Peón Menéndez [2], Juan Á. Martínez Esteban [3], Miguel A. José Prieto [3], Juan A. Martín Ramos[3], F. Javier de Cos Juez [4] and Antonio Nevado Reviriego [5]

[1]Normagrup Technology S.A. Llanera 33420, Asturias, Spain

[2]Grupo TSK, Gijón 33203, Asturias, Spain

[3]Department of Electrical Engineering, University of Oviedo, Gijón 33203, Asturias, Spain

[4]Department of Explotation and Prospection of Mining, University of Oviedo, Asturias 33004, Spain

[5]Department of Electrical, Electronics and Control Engineering, National Distance Education University, Madrid 28040, Spain

ABSTRACT

Parabolic trough solar power plants use a thermal fluid to transfer thermal energy from solar radiation to a water-steam Rankine cycle in order to drive a turbine that, coupled to an electrical generator, produces electricity. These plants have a heat transfer fluid (HTF) system with the necessary elements to transform solar radiation into heat and to transfer that thermal energy to the water-steam exchangers. In order to get the best possible performance in the Rankine cycle and, hence, in the thermal plant, it is necessary that the thermal fluid reach its maximum temperature when leaving the solar field (SF). Also, it is mandatory that the thermal fluid does not exceed the maximum operating temperature of the HTF, above which it degrades. It must be noted that the optimal temperature of the thermal fluid is difficult to obtain, since solar radiation can change abruptly from one moment to another. The aim of this document is to provide a model of an HTF system that can be used to optimize the control of the temperature of the fluid without interfering with the normal operation of the plant. The results obtained with this model will be contrasted with those obtained in a real plant.

KEYWORDS

thermal power plant; heat transfer fluid (HTF); process modeling

1. INTRODUCTION

Solar radiation can be exploited in several ways. While photovoltaic (PV) systems use luminous solar radiation to produce electricity, thermoelectric solar plants use thermal radiation. There are different technologies that take advantage of the solar thermal energy. They can be classified depending on the temperatures they can reach. In [1], differences between these technologies are shown. Parabolic trough collector (PTC) technology is one of the most mature and, for that reason, the most implanted one worldwide. They use a heat transfer fluid (HTF) that flows inside several absorber pipes placed in the focal axis of a set of mirrors. These mirrors focus the solar radiation over the pipes in such a way that the HTF absorbs the thermal energy of the sun.

Although some of the older concentrated solar power (CSP) plants do not have any sort of thermal energy storage, the fact is that during the last years several installations with a thermal energy storage (TES) system have appeared, as well as papers dealing with different methods to store thermal energy and with how to control such storage [1,2,3,4,5,6].

Figure 1 shows a schematic of a solar thermal power plant of PTCs with a TES system. This thermoelectric solar plant works basically like a conventional thermal one. It consists of a generator steam train that, thanks to the contribution of thermal energy, turns liquid water into steam. This steam drives a turbine coupled to an electric generator that produces electricity.

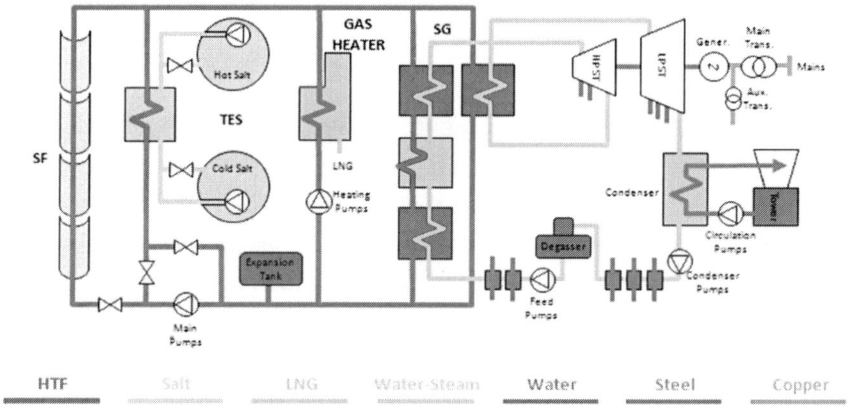

Figure 1. Schematic of a parabolic trough collector (PTC) solar thermoelectric plant.

In order for these plants to be able to use solar thermal radiation, they have a subsystem named solar field (SF). This system absorbs the solar radiation, extracts its thermal energy and transports it to the rest of the subsystems, such as the steam generator (SG) and the TES. A HTF crosses the SF absorbing thermal energy from the sun and transferring it to the rest of the plant.

The main objective is to achieve as high a fluid temperature as possible at the output of the SF, but without exceeding the maximum operating temperature of the fluid. The purpose of the control of the heating process is to define a set point temperature and guarantee that, if the temperature at the output of the SF tends to rise above that set point, the control causes the mass flow of the fluid to rise and*vice versa*. In order to optimize this control system, an accurate model of the process to be controlled is required, since the power plant will not stop production so that different control strategies can be tested. The goal of this paper is to produce a simple yet accurate version of such a model.

2. RESULTS AND DISCUSSION

2.1. Description of the Solar Field (SF)

In order to adequately model the thermal-fluid heating process, it is mandatory to understand the main elements of the HTF system. This system contains several solar collector assemblies (SCA), Figure 2 formed by solar collector elements (SCE), Figure 3. Each SCE has mirrors (28 mirrors in Figure 3) as well as absorber pipes arranged in such a way that the SCE is parabolic-trough shaped and the pipes are placed in its focal axis.

Depending on the solar thermal plant, the SCA may have six, eight or 12 SCEs. The dynamic model developed in this paper is based on the HTF system of the PTC solar plant “La Africana”, located in Cordoba, Spain. In the SF of “La Africana”, each SCE has three absorber tubes arranged in series and each SCA is formed by 12 SCEs.

SCAs are arranged in series forming loops. These loops can be U-shaped or W-shaped. In the model described, U-shaped loops with four SCAs each are considered.

Figure 2. Solar collector assembly (SCA).

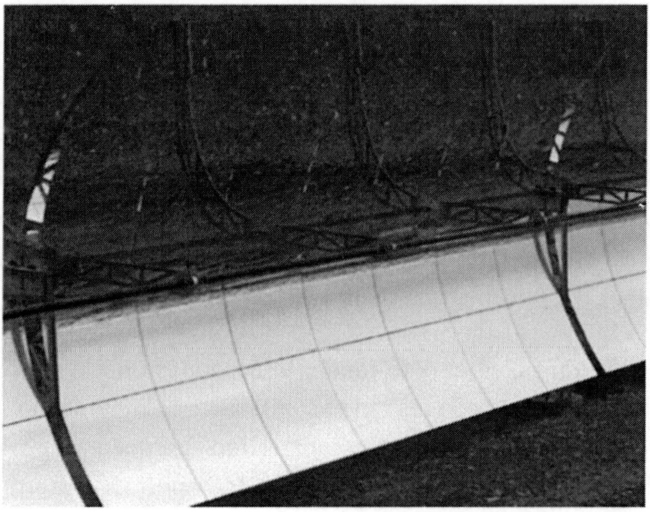

Figure 3. Solar collector element (SCE) with 28 mirrors and three absorber pipes.

The beginning of the loop is linked to a large diameter pipe (cold header) that contains cold HTF (HTF that has not been heated by the solar radiation yet). The end of the loop is linked to another large diameter pipe (hot header) in such a way that, once the fluid coming out of the loops has been heated, it is transported to the steam generator system (SGS) and/or the TES system, depending on the operation mode. Figure 4 shows one of these loops.

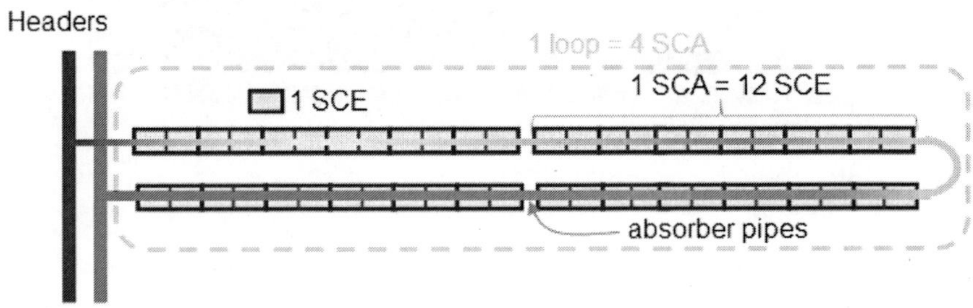

Figure 4. U-Shaped loop in PTC solar plants.

The elements included in the HTF system, also referred to as SF, modeled in this paper has 168 loops with 4 SCA per loop. Each SCA consists on 12 SCE that contains 3 absorber pipes. Therefore, this HTF systems has 24.192 absorber pipes transporting the fluid.

The most important elements to take into account in the modeling of this process are the absorber pipes, shown in Figure 5 They are in charge of absorbing the solar radiation and turning it into thermal energy. Thanks to the fluid that flows through them, they also transport that thermal energy to the rest of the plant where needed.

They consist of two concentric pipes. The inner one is metallic with a blue film to minimize radiation thermal losses, whereas the outer pipe is made of glass. Vacuum is created between them in order to avoid convention and conduction thermal losses. Figure 6shows the main parts of an absorber pipe.

Figure 5. Headers.

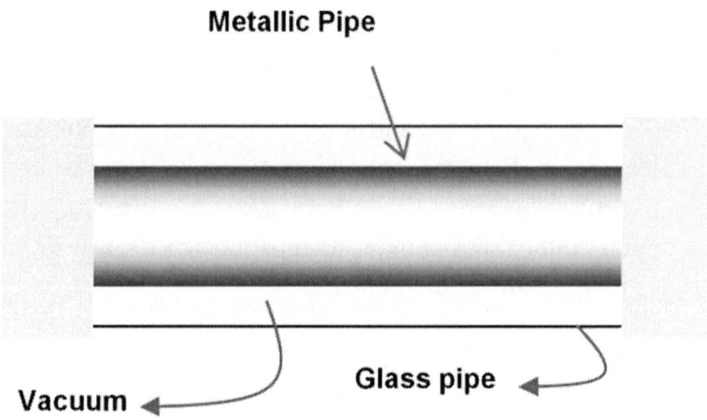

Figure 6. Absorber pipe.

2.2. Description of the Heat Transfer Fluid (HTF)-Heating Process

The solar radiation is reflected by the mirrors over the absorber pipes, thus heating the HTF. A comparative study of the different thermal fluids most currently used in PTC power plants (oil, molten salt and water steam) is presented in [7]. The authors conclude that direct steam generation is more efficient than the other two. In spite of that, and although other alternatives are being studied [8,9,10,11,12,13,14], most of the PTC plants use some sort of synthetic oil, mainly due to its lower freezing point (around 12 °C) when compared to other HTFs.

According to the literature, there are different kinds of fluids that have been or are being analyzed to be used as HTF. One of them is molten salt. Taking into account that they are used to store thermal energy in the TES, it would be relatively easy to use it also in the SF. The main problem is its high freezing point (around 140 °C). Due to the small internal diameter of the absorber pipes, having part of the molten salts freeze would cause blockages that could cause the pipes to break. Other installations use direct steam generators (DGS) instead, in which water acts as HTF. The main advantages of this technology are its lower thermal losses and, therefore, its higher cycle efficiency. Its drawbacks are the higher pressures required and the more complex control needed. These drawbacks are also present in installations that use gas and air as HTF. Two new research lines are emerging nowadays: nanofluids and ionic fluids. The first one consists of adding metallic nanoparticles or carbon nanotubes in order to improve its optical and thermal properties. Ionic fluids are very promising. They are formed by joining anions and cations so that they can result in billions of different ionic fluids for multiple applications.

Using synthetic oil as HTF also has drawbacks, the main one being its maximum operation temperature, which is around only 400 °C in the best-case scenario. This critical point can be easily exceeded when direct solar irradiation (DNI) is high. Given that solar radiation is a phenomenon that can vary widely in a short space of time, a good regulation method is necessary. This method should allow the oil to leave the SF with the highest possible temperature while, at the same time, preventing the oil from exceeding its maximum operating point.

To meet this goal, the control method varies the mass flow of the fluid in such a way that, if the oil temperature exceeds a given set point (393 °C in the case considered), the mass flow will increase. Thus, the time the fluid stays in the SF will be shorter and its temperature will drop. Similarly, if the oil temperature is below the set point, the mass flow must be reduced. Table 1 and Table 2 show all the variables (perturbations, input, output and control variables) involved in the HTF-heating process:

Table 1. Input, output and control variables of the HTF-heating process.

Variable	Acronym	Description
Input	THTFc	Heat transfer fluid (HTF) temperature at the input of the solar field (SF) (°C)
Output	THTFh	HTF temperature at the output of the SF (°C)
Control	$\dot{m}_{HTF}$	HTF mass flow (kg/s)

Table 2. Perturbations of the HTF-heating process.

Perturbations	Description
Direct solar irradiation (DNI)	Direct normal irradiation (W/m^2)
φ	Angle of incidence (°)
Tamb	Ambient temperature (°C)

Figure 7 shows the block diagram that represents the process described above.

The goal of this work is to obtain a simple, accurate and dynamic model that allows designers to optimize the control of this process.

2.3. Modeling of the HTF-Heating Process

Several models of different parts of the PTC thermoelectric plants have been developed in the last years. In [15], a mathematical model is described that compares the quasi-dynamic test (QDT) and the steady-state test (SST) in five different types of collectors. In [16], the authors present a dynamic model for the collector field and a steady-state model for the power plant; this paper is based on a real PTC solar plant and the whole plant has been mathematically modeled. In [17] models for different geometries and insulation materials with different thicknesses have been carried out in order to select the best one for high temperature processes; in this paper, all the models are numerically compared and, hence, absolute values are not provided. A paper written by one of the main manufacturers of solar absorber pipes [18] explains all the thermal exchanges between the different parts or elements that form a pipe; this paper is a good starting point to develop the dynamic model of the HTF-heating process. In reference [19], the authors established a computational fluid dynamics (CFD) model to calculate the temperature profile on the wall of the absorber tubes of DSG plants. The authors of [20] compare three different models of absorber pipes: a one- and a two-dimensional analytical model and a three-dimensional one using finite-element techniques.

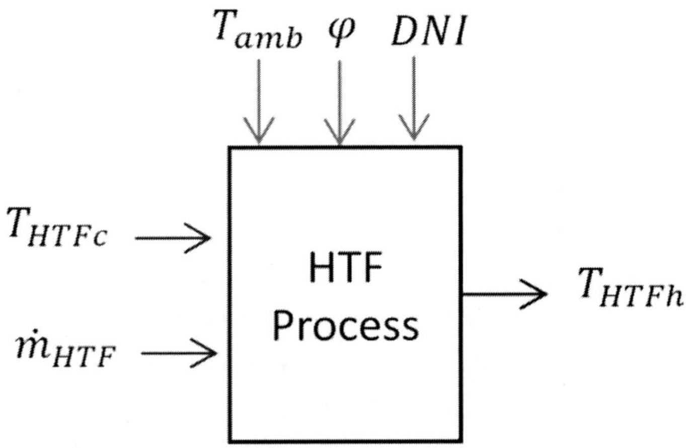

Figure 7. Heat transfer fluid (HTF)-heating process model.

It must be said that most of these references model the absorber pipes in order to determine the gradient of temperature between their elements, but they are not used as a dynamic model susceptible of being used in the control of the HTF-heating process.

To model the HTF-heating process, some simplifications of the SF must be carried out, namely, the 168 loops have been modeled as four serial-connected unitary blocks. Each unitary block contains 168 parallel-connected SCAs. This configuration is shown in Figure 8.

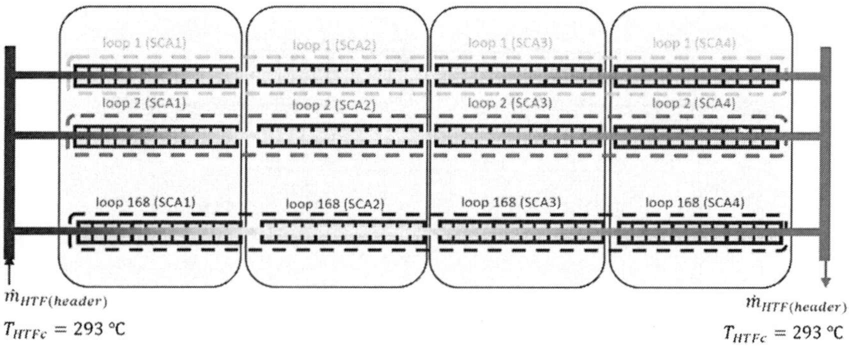

Figure 8. Loop simplification.

Similarly, the headers are modeled as four serial-connected blocks, each containing a quarter of the total amount of HTF. Figure 9shows the block diagram of the SF to be used in the modeling of the HTF-heating process, and Figure 10 shows the blocks used to model the loops described above.

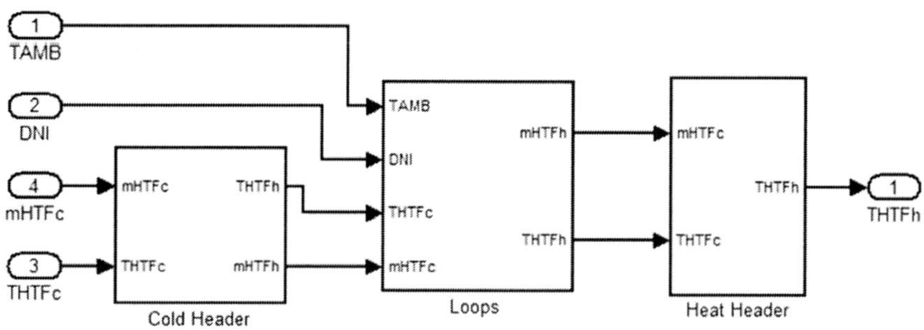

Figure 9. Solar field (SF) model.

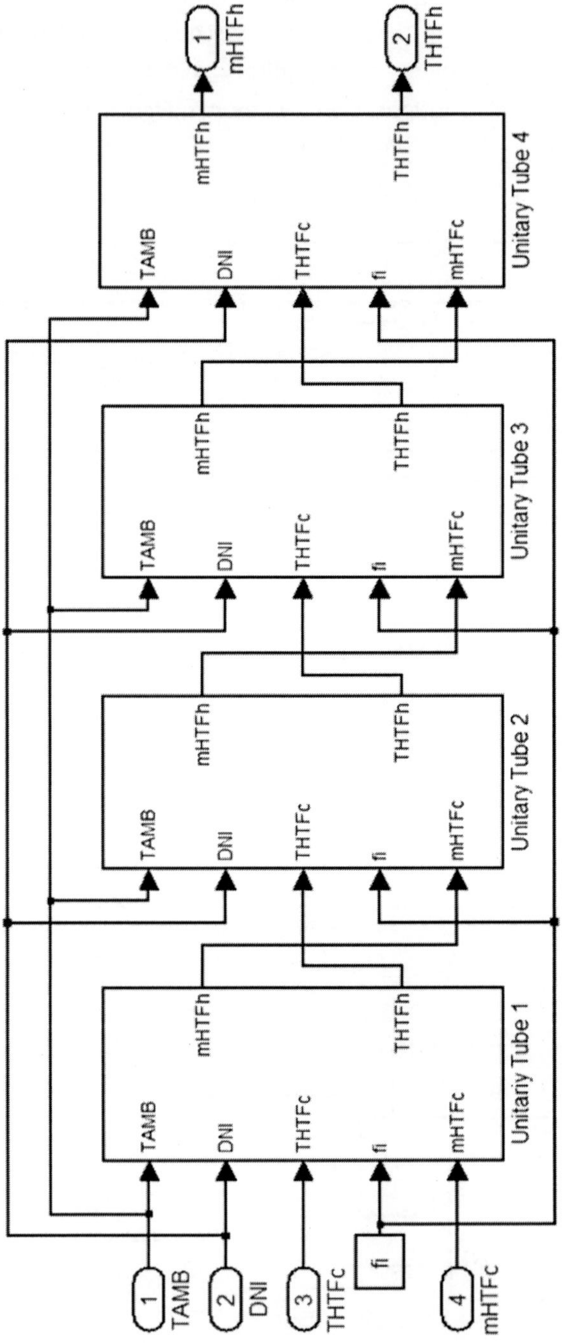

Figure 10. Loops model.

These Simulink blocks can be easily used for modeling larger or smaller SFs by respectively adding or removing unitary tubes.

Energy transfer from solar radiation to the fluid takes place inside the unitary tubes as well as inside the headers. For that reason, all the equations related to mass and energy conservation principles should be included in those blocks.

The conservation energy principle provides the following equations:

$$\dot{E}_{\text{input}} = \dot{E}_{\text{output}} \tag{1}$$

Energy can be transferred as work, heat and mass:

$$\dot{Q}_{\text{in}} + \dot{W}_{\text{in}} + (\dot{m} \cdot e)_{\text{in}} = \dot{Q}_{\text{out}} + \dot{W}_{\text{out}} + (\dot{m} \cdot e)_{\text{out}} \tag{2}$$

where Q˙ is the absorbed or released heat, W˙ is the work done by the HTF and e is the energy transported per unit mass of a moving fluid, whose expression is given by Equation (3):

$$e = h + \frac{1}{2}V^2 + gz \tag{3}$$

Finally, assuming that in the absorber pipes kinetic and gravitational energies are negligible and that, due to the mass conservation principle in the control volume considered in the process, input and output mass flows are similar, Equation (2) is simplified as indicated in Equation (4):

$$h(t) = \int_0^t \frac{\dot{m}_{\text{HTF}} \cdot (h_i - h_o) + \dot{Q}_{\text{gain}}}{\rho_{\text{HTF}} \cdot v_c} \cdot dt \tag{4}$$

where Q˙gain is the heat that the HTF absorbs from the solar radiation once all the losses due to thermal transfer from the fluid to the environment have been taken into account.

The net heat transferred from the HTF to other subsystems of the solar plant is the result of the total heat absorbed by the fluid minus the thermal losses due to radiation, convection and conduction from the fluid to the air around it.

The heat absorbed by the fluid depends on geometric, optical and thermal factors. Firstly, not all the solar radiation that reaches the mirrors (Q˙capt) is reflected over the absorber tubes and then absorbed by the fluid, due to phenomena such as shadows, angle of incidence far from the optimal 90°, dirty mirrors, non-optimal reflectivity and transmissivity, etc. This results in the heat that reaches the fluid being reduced by the efficiency of the SCA (ηSCA). Additionally, of all the heat reaching the fluid, some is lost in unwanted thermal transfers (Q˙thloss):

$$\dot{Q}_{gain} = \dot{Q}_{capt} \cdot \eta_{SCA} - \dot{Q}_{thloss} \qquad (5)$$

All these phenomena have been modeled in a Simulink block (Figure 11) called Q˙gain.

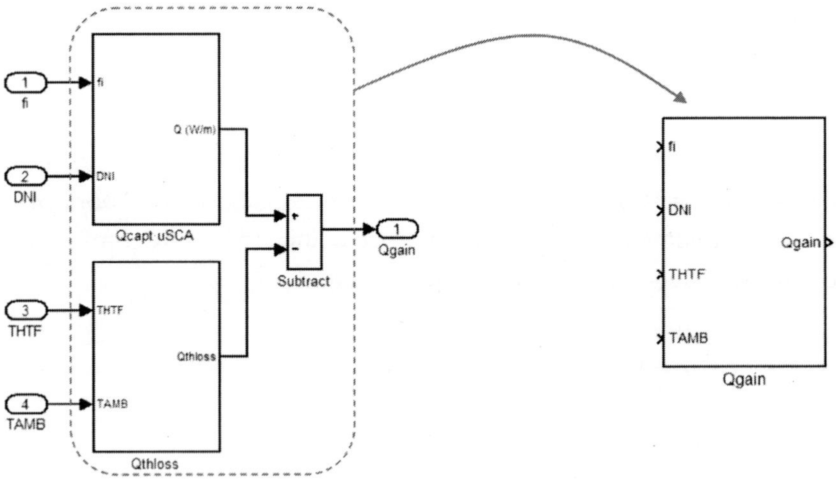

Figure 11. Simulink block model to calculate Q˙gain.

Figure 12 shows all the thermal exchanges involved in the different parts of the SCE (mirrors, absorber tube, HTF) with the environment. Some of those losses are negligible when compared to others [15,16,17]. This is the case of conduction and convection losses between the outer wall of the metallic tube and the inner wall of the glass cover (thanks to the vacuum created between them), or of conduction thermal losses produced in the walls of the tubes to mention a few.

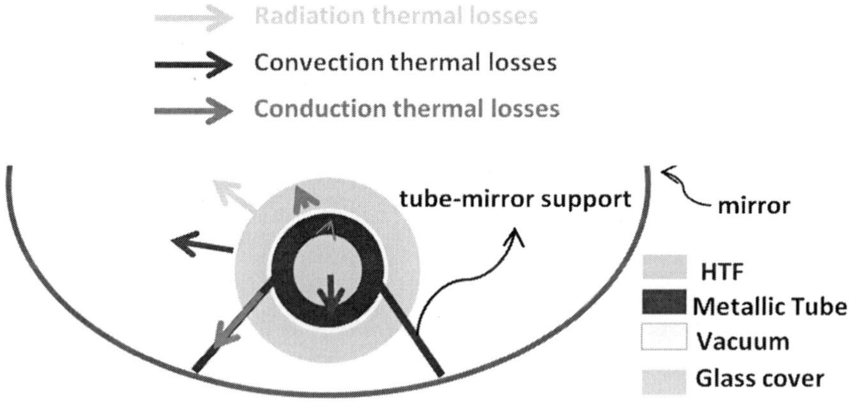

Figure 12. Thermal exchanges between solar collector elements (SCE) and surround ambient.

Figure 13 shows the Simulink blocks used to model all those thermal losses, which are included in the Q˙thloss block of Figure 11.

Several equations are included in these blocks:

$$\dot{Q}_{\mathrm{radGLASS-AMB}} = \varepsilon_{\mathrm{CUB}} \cdot \sigma \cdot Ae_{\mathrm{GLASS}} \cdot \left(T^4_{\mathrm{GLASS}} - T^4_{\mathrm{AMB}} \right) \tag{6}$$

where Q˙radGLASS–AMB represents the radiation thermal losses per meter (W/m) from the outer wall of the absorber pipe glass cover to the environment, εGLASS is the emissivity coefficient of the external surface of the glass cover, σ is the Stefan-Boltzmann constant ($W/m^2 \cdot C^4$), AeGLASS is the external surface of the absorber pipe glass cover per unit length (m^2/m) and TGLASS and TAMB are, respectively, the glass cover and the ambient temperatures (°C):

$$\dot{Q}_{convGLASS-AMB} = h_{GLASS-AMB} \cdot Ae_{GLASS} \cdot (T_{GLASS} - T_{AMB}) \tag{7}$$

where Q˙convGLASS–AMB represents the convection thermal losses per meter (W/m) from the outer wall of the absorber pipe glass cover to the surround ambientand hGLASS–AMB is the convection coefficient between the external surface of the glass cover and the surround ambient. This coefficient is highly dependent on wind speed and can be calculated as:

$$h_{GLASS-AMB} = \frac{Nu_{AMB}}{De_{GLASS}} \cdot K_{AMB} \tag{8}$$

In Equation (8), NuAMB is the dimensionless Nusselt number, DeGLASS is the outer diameter of the glass cover and KAMB is the thermal conductivity of the air.

To calculate the Nusselt number, Hilpert equation for forced convection flow is used:

$$Nu_{AMB} = C \cdot Re^{m} \cdot Pr^{1/3} \tag{9}$$

where *Re* is the dimensionless Reynolds number and parameters, *C* and *m* depend on the value of the Reynolds number. Pr is the dimensionless Prandtl number of the air, the value of which is around 0.7.

Finally, the dimensionless Reynolds number of the air over the outer wall of the glass cover is calculated from Equation (10):

$$Re = \frac{V_{air} \cdot De_{GLASS} \cdot \rho_{air}}{\mu_{air}} \tag{10}$$

where Vair, ρair, μair are the air speed, density and dynamic viscosity respectively.

Equation (11) is used to calculate thermal radiation transference from the outer surface of the metallic pipe to the inner wall of the glass cover Q˙radMET−CUB:

$$\dot{Q}_{\mathrm{radMET-GLASS}} = \frac{\sigma\cdot Ae_{\mathrm{MET}}\cdot(T^4_{\mathrm{MET}} - T^4_{\mathrm{GLASS}})}{\frac{1}{\varepsilon_{\mathrm{MET}}} + \frac{1-\varepsilon_{\mathrm{GLASS}}}{\varepsilon_{\mathrm{GLASS}}}\cdot\left(\frac{De_{\mathrm{MET}}}{Di_{\mathrm{GLASS}}}\right)} \qquad (11)$$

where AeMET is the external surface of the metalic pipe per unit length (m^2/m) and TMET and TGLASS are, respectively, the metallic pipe and the glass cover temperatures (°C).

Once all the blocks have been defined and all the equations have been included, the dynamic model of the HTF heating process is obtained. Figure 14 shows the Simulink diagram that includes all the blocks and equations described above. Inside that block there are the four unitary tubes that contain the time-dependent Equation (4) as well as the block Q˙gain described in Figure 11. In this way, the fluid temperature varies along the path as do all the temperature-dependent variables (enthalpy, fluid density, *etc.*).

3. EXPERIMENTAL SECTION

To validate the already developed model, the control strategy usually applied in thermoelectric solar plants was implemented. Due to the complexity of a PTC solar plant and the amount of subsystems included in it, there are many controllers to regulate different outputs: mirrors position (in order to have the lowest possible optical losses), temperature and flow rate in the TES system (in order to have as much storage as possible during the molten salt charge process and the highest energy transference to the fluid in the discharging mode [1]) and so on. To cope with all this, solar plants must have a distributed control system (DCS) [21] that receives field signals (such as ambient temperature, HTF temperature, incident angle, the

DNI, *etc.*) and sends them to the appropriate controller, which generates the adequate actions in each case.

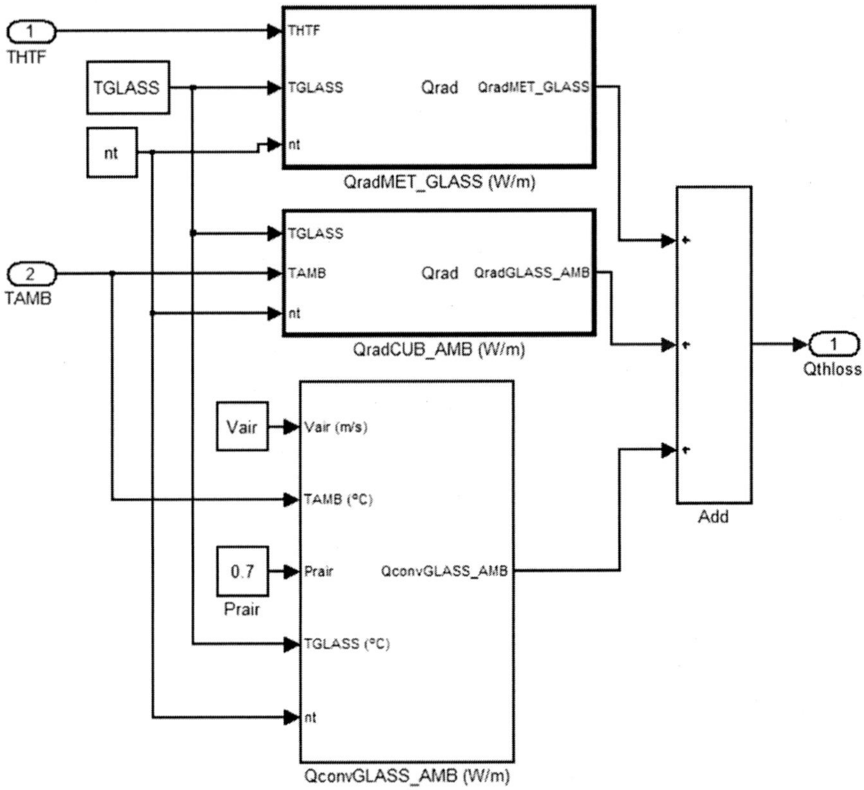

Figure 13. Thermal losses blocks.

The control of the HTF heating is typically performed in either of two different ways. Some plants have a semiautomatic proportional-integral-derivative (PID) regulator that relies on an operator observing the output variables of the process, mainly the HTF temperature, and changing the mass flow input set point to make this output temperature be constant despite the perturbations. Once the mass flow input set point has been fixed by the operator, internal PID regulators will operate the pumps to achieve that set point. This semiautomatic method has two drawbacks: in addition to its accuracy depending on the operator's experience, it is carried out by steps.Figure 15 shows a diagram of the regulator.

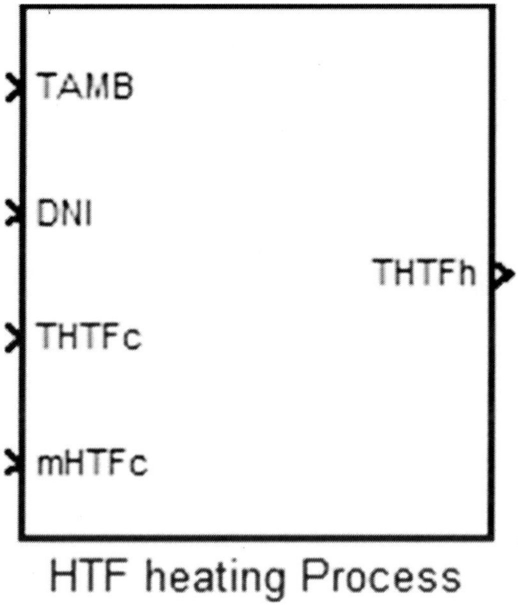

Figure 14. HTF heating process.

More modern plants have substituted the operator by an external PID regulator in such a way that this new controller is the one that determines the HTF mass flow to achieve as a result of a comparison between the real temperature of the HTF at the output of the SF (THTFh) and the set point of the fluid temperature at the output of the SF, previously fixed (SPTHTFh). Figure 16 shows the PID automatic control.

Figure 17 shows how the dynamic model of the heating process was linked to a model of a PID regulator using also Matlab and Simulink. Different perturbations where introduced in the input variables (Tamb, DNI and THTFc) and the performance of the system was analyzed.

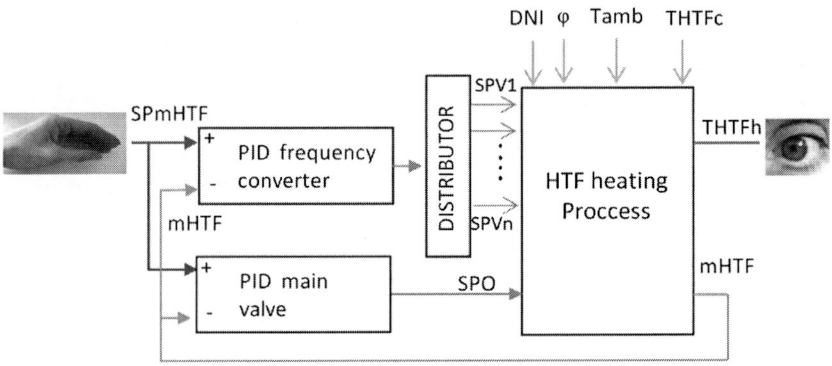

Figure 15. Semiautomatic control of the HTF-heating process.

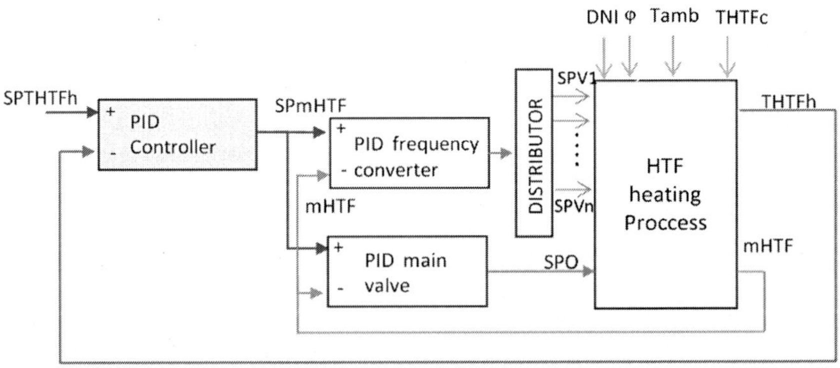

Figure 16. Proportional-integral-derivative (PID) automatic control of the HTF-heating process.

Figure 18 shows the response of the process to a sharp step perturbation in the DNI. This sort of perturbations may occur, for example, when multiple clouds suddenly disappear.

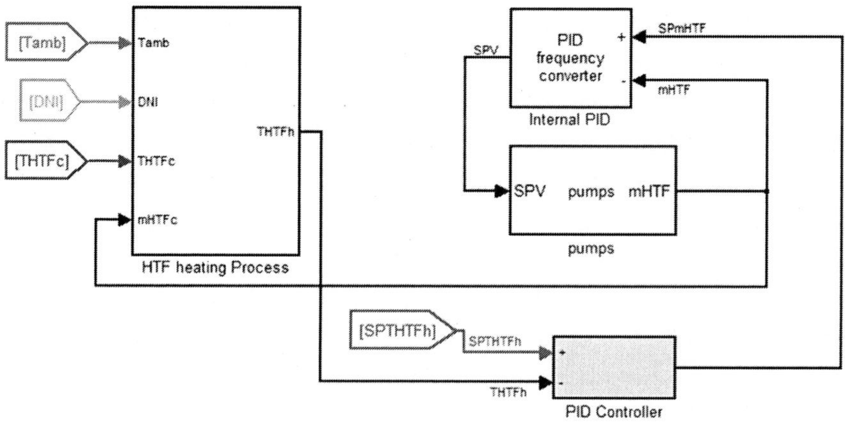

Figure 17. MatLab-Simulink model of the PID control for the HTF-heating process.

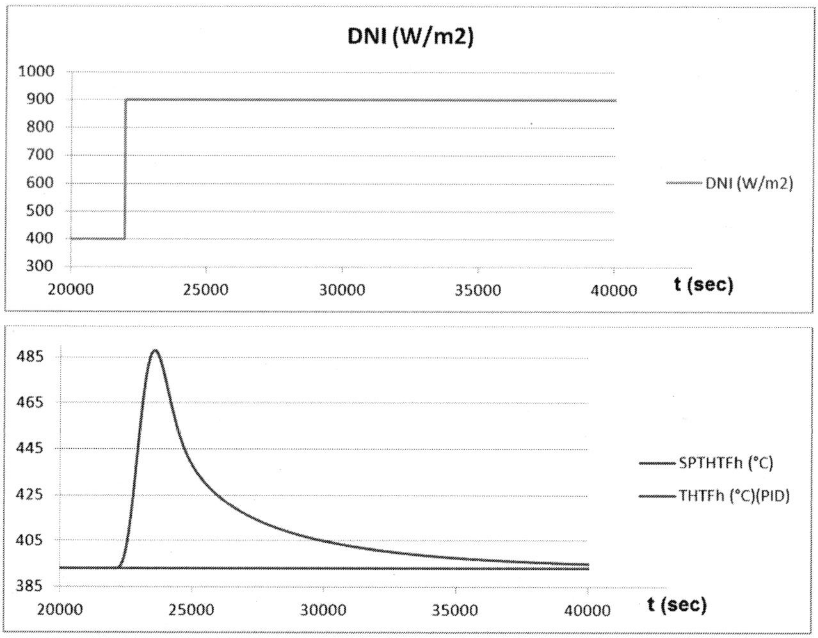

Figure 18. PID controller response to a sharp step in direct solar irradiation (DNI).

It is possible to see that the behavior of the PID when there is a sharp variation in the solar radiation is far from optimal, and a very high temperature can be reached, which would result in faster fluid degradation. Besides, the settling time is also high so any intent to reduce the high peak, will give rise to an even slower settling time. The slow response to a rapid and sharp change in an input variable as the DNI can be explained by the amount of time the oil stays in the SF, which gives rise to thermal inertia. One of the effects of this inertia is transport delay; a variation of temperature at the inlet of the pipe is not reflected at the output until sometime later. The other effect of thermal inertia is similar to a filtering. At a constant flow rate, a step of radiation produces a variation in the temperature at the loop output that looks like a pure delay stage with respect to the variation of radiation.

In the collectors that gather and mix the oil from the loops, the HTF of each loop has a different delay depending on their distance to the power block (also called power island), which is normally located in the center or north of the SF. The overall effect is that a step in the solar radiation results in a delay plus an additional filtering effect in such a way that the global response to that step is a pure delay followed by a second-order overdamped response.

Once the steady state has been established, the average error between the set point and the real temperature is below 1 °C.

The model was also subjected to values of the input variables extracted from an actual plant called "La Africana" situated in Cordoba, Spain. These values were taken in different years and seasons: September 2010, April 2011 and July 2013 and they were extracted from the DCS. The response of the model developed in this paper, to those input variables can be seen in Figure 19, Figure 20 and Figure 21.

In these figures, horizontal axis represents the time in seconds and the vertical axis shows the true representation of the absolute values of the different variables.

Figure 19 shows that, when variations in the input variables are not sharp, the PID response does not involve high peak temperatures.Table 3 shows the error average value (μ) and the error standard deviation (σ) calculated for all the values obtained during 5 h.

Table 3. Numerical results of simulation with PID (September 2010).

Control Strategy	Input Values	$e = SPTHTF_h - THTF_h$	
		μ	σ
Proportional-integral-derivative (PID) controller	September 2010	−1.92	3.27

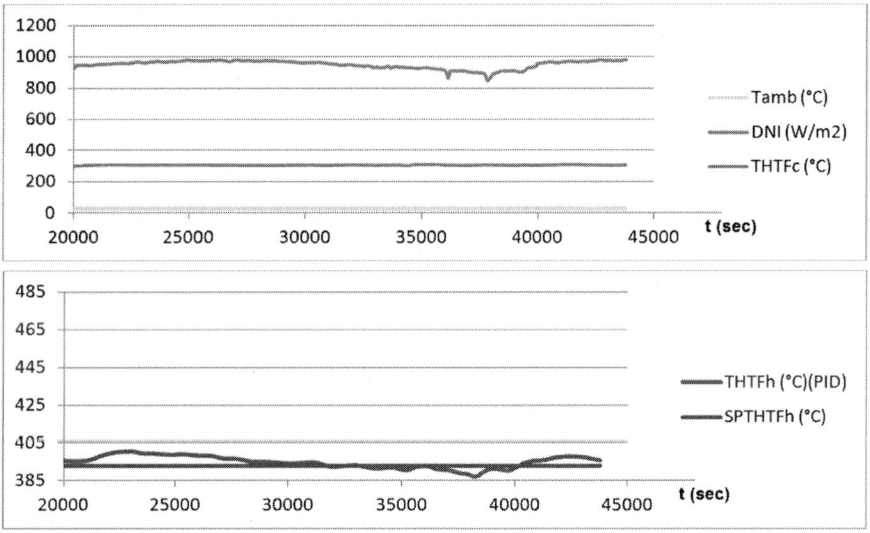

Figure 19. PID controller response to September 2010 values.

When solar radiation falls below a certain value, however, the PID controller is not able to provide rapid response and temperature deviates greatly from its set point, as can be seen in Figure 20. This is also confirmed by the value of the standard deviation in Table 4.

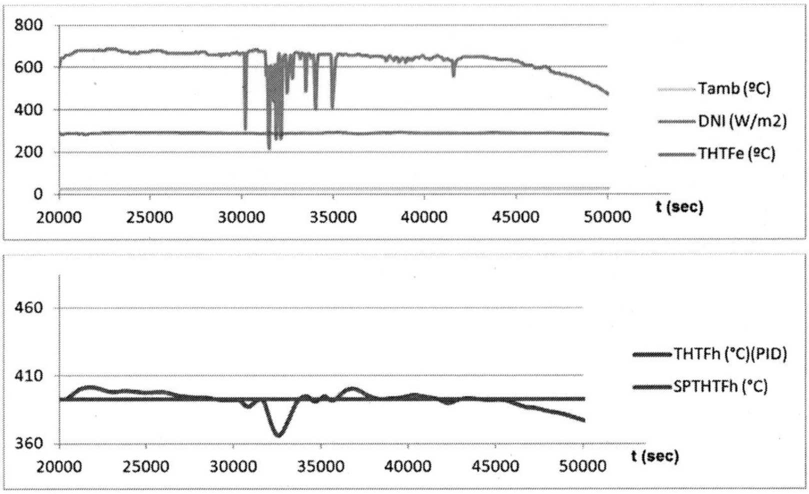

Figure 20. PID controller response to April 2011 values.

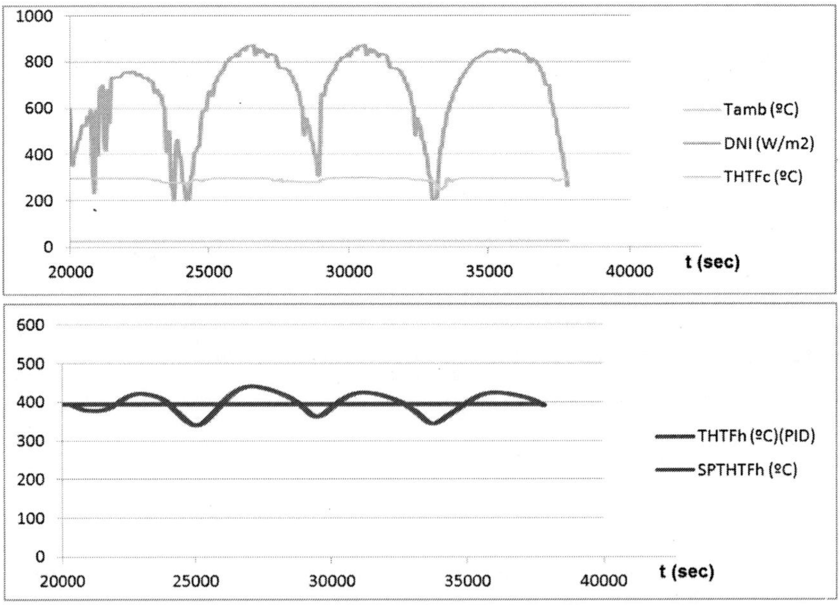

Figure 21. PID controller response to July 2013 values.

Table 4. Numerical results of simulation with PID (April 2011).

Control Strategy	Input Values	$e = SPTHTF_h - THTF_h$	
		μ	σ
PID controller	April 2011	6.35	15.11

If the set of values corresponding to a DNI under 500 W/m^2 are removed, the error and standard deviation values are shown in Table 5.

Table 5. Numerical results of simulation with PID (April 2011).

Control Strategy	Input Values	$e = SPTHTF_h - THTF_h$	
		μ	σ
PID controller	April 2011	−3.20	12.04

Figure 21 shows the PID response when there are quick and sharp changes in the solar direct normal irradiation. Even though the PID succeeds in following these variations, the oscillation is high and the standard deviation is large, as indicated in Table 6.

Table 6. Numerical results of simulation with PID (July 2013).

Control Strategy	Input Values	$e = SPTHTF_h - THTF_h$	
		μ	σ
PID controller	July 2013	−4.06	25.90

Looking at the PID response for different values of the input variables (some of which have been obtained from an actual thermal power plant), it can be shown that this controller has an adequate behavior when those input variables do not vary suddenly. However, it has a very slow response to quick variations; therefore this control method should be improved if the global efficiency of these plants has to be optimized.

The goal of this paper, however, is not determining what the best control strategy is, but rather defining a model of the SF that can be later used to optimize such strategies. In this regard, it must be said the results obtained with the model presented match those measured in the actual plant under similar conditions.

4. CONCLUSIONS

A dynamic model of the HTF heating process as it flows through the SF has been developed. The use of Simulink has allowed a model of the process to be obtained that is very visual and easy to follow. Besides, since it has been built from the simplest blocks to the more complicated ones, it can also be used to model the fluid heating process of other solar plants with different sizes by just adding or removing unitary tubes (see Figure 10).

Some of the fluid properties such as density, thermal conductivity, specific heat, *etc.* have been included as temperature dependent equations that can be easily changed so that the model can be also used in solar plants where the HTF is not synthetic oil (as in the case considered) but water steam, molten-salt, *etc.*

Looking at Figure 18, Figure 19, Figure 20 and Figure 21 it is possible to see that, even though a PID controller might be suitable when there are no rapid changes in environment conditions, its response is slow when a sharp change is produced. The developed model is able to identify this situation and can therefore be used to test other algorithms of control, such as predictive ones, adaptative, and so on, to optimize the behavior of the HTF temperature controller without interfering in the operation of the plant, *i.e.* using just simulations. Once the regulator has been selected, it can be implemented in the real plant.

ACKNOWLEDGMENTS

This work has been subsidized through the Plan of Science, Technology and Innovation of the Principality of Asturias, (Ref: FC-15-GRUPIN14-122).

AUTHOR CONTRIBUTIONS

This paper is part of the Ph.D Thesis of Lourdes Álvarez Barcia, who has therefore carried out most of the work presented here. Juan Á. Martínez and F. Javier de Cos were the supervisors of this work, Rogelio Peón had a relevant contribution with his extensive knowledge about the operation of thermoelectric solar plants, whereas Miguel A. José, Juan A. Martín and Antonio Reviriego assisted Lourdes Álvarez with Simulink simulations and regulation topics.

CONFLICTS OF INTEREST

The authors declare no conflict of interest.

REFERENCES

1. Peón Menéndez, R.; Martínez, J.A.; Prieto, M.J.; Barcia, L.Á.; Martín Sánchez, J.M. A Novel Modeling of Molten-Salt Heat Storage Systems in Thermal Solar Power Plants. *Energies* **2014**, *7*, 6721–6740.

2. Barlev, D.; Vidu, R.; Stroeve, P. Innovation in concentrated solar power. *Sol. Energy Mater. Sol. Cells* **2011**, *95*, 2703–2725.

3. Kuravi, S.; Trahan, J.; Goswami, D.Y.; Rahman, M.M.; Stefanakos, E.K. Thermal energy storage technologies and systems for concentrating solar power plants. *Prog. Energy Combust. Sci.* **2013**, *39*, 285–319.

4. Kenisarin, M.M. High-temperature phase change materials for thermal energy storage. *Renew. Sustain. Energy Rev.* **2010**, *14*, 955–970.

5. Gil, A.; Medrano, M.; Martorell, I.; Lazaro, A.; Dolado, P.; Zalba, B.; Cabeza, L.F. State of the art on high temperature thermal energy storage for power generation. Part 1—Concepts, materials and modellization. *Renew. Sustain. Energy Rev.* **2010**, *14*, 31–55.

6. Medrano, M.; Gil, A.; Martorell, I.; Potau, X.; Cabeza, L.F. State of the art on high-temperature thermal energy storage for power generation. Part 2—Case studies. *Renew. Sustain. Energy Rev.* **2010**, *14*, 56–72.

7. Montes, M.J.; Abánades, A.; Martínez-Val, J.M. Thermofluidynamic Model and Comparative Analysis of Parabolic Trough Collectors Using Oil, Water/Steam, or Molten Salt as Heat Transfer Fluids. *J. Sol. Energy Eng.* **2010**, *132*.

8. Montes, M.J.; Abanades, A.; Martinez-Val, J.M.; Valdes, M. Solar multiple optimization for a solar-only thermal power plant, using oil as heat transfer fluid in the parabolic trough collectors. *Sol. Energy* **2009**, *83*, 2165–2176.

9. Lopez-Gonzalez, D.; Valverde, J.L.; Sanchez, P.; Sanchez-Silva, L. Characterization of different heat transfer fluids and degradation study by using a pilot plant device operating at real conditions. *Energy* **2013**, *54*, 240–250.

10. Feldhoff, J.F.; Schimtz, K.; Eck, M.; Schnatbaum-Laumann, L.; Ortiz-Vives, F.; Laing, D.; Schulte-Fischedick, J. Comparative system analysis of direct steam generation and synthetic oil parabolic trough power plants with integrated thermal storage. *Sol. Energy* **2012**, *86*, 520–530.

11. Haddad, Z.; Abid, C.; Oztop, H.F.; Mataoui, A. A review on how the researchers prepare their nanofluids. *Int. J. Therm. Sci.***2014**, *76*, 168–189.

12. Flamant, G.; Gauthier, D.; Benoit, H.; Sans, J.L.; Boissiere, B.; Ansart, R.; Hemati, M. A new heat transfer fluid for concentrating solar systems: Particle flow in tubes. *Energy Procedia* **2014**, *49*, 617–626.

13. Ghadimi, A.; Saidur, R.; Metselaar, H.S.C. A review of nanofluid stability properties and characterization in stationary conditions. *Int. J. Heat Mass Transf.* **2011**, *54*, 4051–4068.

14. Alguacil, M.; Prieto, C.; Rodriguez, A.; Lohr, J. Direct steam generation in parabolic trough collectors. *Energy Procedia* **2014**,*49*, 21–29.

15. Osório, T.; Carvalho, M.J. Testing of solar thermal collectors under transient conditions. *Energy Procedia* **2012**, *30*, 1344–1353.

16. Thorsen, S.; Blair, N.; Mitchell, J.A.; Beckman, W.A. Automatic Control of a 30 MWe SEGS VI parabolic trough plant. *Sol. Energy* **2004**, *76*, 187–193.

17. Roldán, M.; Cañadas, I.; Casas, J.L.; Zarza, E. Thermal analysis and design of a solar prototype for high-temperature processes. *Int. J. Heat Mass Transf.* **2013**, *56*, 309–318.

18. Burkholder, F.; Kutscher, C. *Heat Loss Testing of Schott's 2008 PTR70 Parabolic Trough Receiver*; National Renewable Energy Laboratory: Golden, CO, USA, 2009.

19. Roldán, M.; Valenzuela, L.; Zarza, E. Thermal analysis of solar receiver pipes with superheated steam. *Appl. Energy* **2013**, *103*, 73–84.

20. Eck, M.; Feldhoff, J.F.; Uhlig, R. Thermal Modelling and Simulation of Parabolic Trough Receiver Tubes. In Proceedings of the 4th International Conference of Energy Sustainability, Phoenix, AZ, USA, 17–22 May 2010; pp. 659–666.

21. Bong-Kuk, L.; Yong-Hak, S. The integrated monitoring and control system for the combined cycle power plant. In Proceedings of the International Conference on Control, Automation and Systems, Seoul, Korea, 14–17 October 2008; pp. 1479–1483.

Chapter 11

Renewable municipal solid waste pathways for energy generation and sustainable development in the Nigerian context

Olaleye M Amoo[1*] and Richard Layi Fagbenle[2]

[1]Stevens Institute of Technology, Hoboken, NJ 07030, USA.

[2] Mechanical Engineering, Obafemi Awolowo University, Ile-Ife, Osun State, Nigeria.

ABSTRACT

The continued concerns over energy prices, increase in population, and climate change issues have led towards a need for alternative and new energy sources. Municipal solid waste (MSW) is generally accepted as a renewable energy resource. This research study presents a techno-economic assessment potential to utilize the energy obtainable from MSW for the generation of electrical power. The assessment was carried out for energy generation by thermochemical (incineration or combustion) and biochemical (landfilling and anaerobic digestion) processes and based on the available data from seven selected municipalities. Due to the broad scope of this topic, life cycle impact of waste management, social acceptance, policy aspects, and emission reduction or fossil fuel offset are not considered and are not part of the assessment. Results presented in tabular form indicate, for example, that the price of steam generated by a fluidized steam generator is in the range of US$0.018/kWh $_t$ (Lagos) to US$0.044/kWh (Nsukka) and compares favorably with the typical cost of steam at US$0.015/kWh. Electrical power generation using a combined heat and power plant provides electricity at a cost that is in the range of US$0.017/kWh $_e$ (Lagos) to US$0.040/kWh $_e$ (Nsukka) and also compares well with the typical cost of electricity in Nigeria at US$0.14/kWh $_e$(as of 2012).

KEYWORDS

Municipal solid waste, Combustion, Energy, Electricity, Environment, Economics, Nigeria

1. BACKGROUND

Nations are today faced with an overwhelming social problem of processing and disposal of municipal solid waste (MSW). With increasing population growth, rapid urbanization, rising levels of affluence, and resource scarcity, waste-to-energy (WTE) is reestablishing itself as an attractive technology option to promote low carbon growth among other renewable energy technologies. WTE is a proven process that provides electricity and steam generation in a sustainable way.

Nigeria is the most populated nation in Africa. With a 2011 population estimate of 162.4 million, growing annually at an estimated rate of 3% [1] and generating 0.55 to 0.58 kg of municipal solid waste per person per day [2], Nigeria can be said to be equally experiencing significant waste-related environmental problems. These problems can be said to have begun in the period when Nigeria gained independence, became rapidly urbanized, and thus generated more solid waste than nature can absorb or that Nigeria can efficiently dispose. MSW is produced daily all over the world, and it is a renewable energy resource with the potential to produce energy via WTE plants while also reducing the volume of waste. WTE can address the twin issues of land use and pollution from landfills and the well-established environmental perils of fossil fuels known as greenhouse gas emissions (GHG). Figure 1 shows the map of Nigeria showing Abuja, the capital.

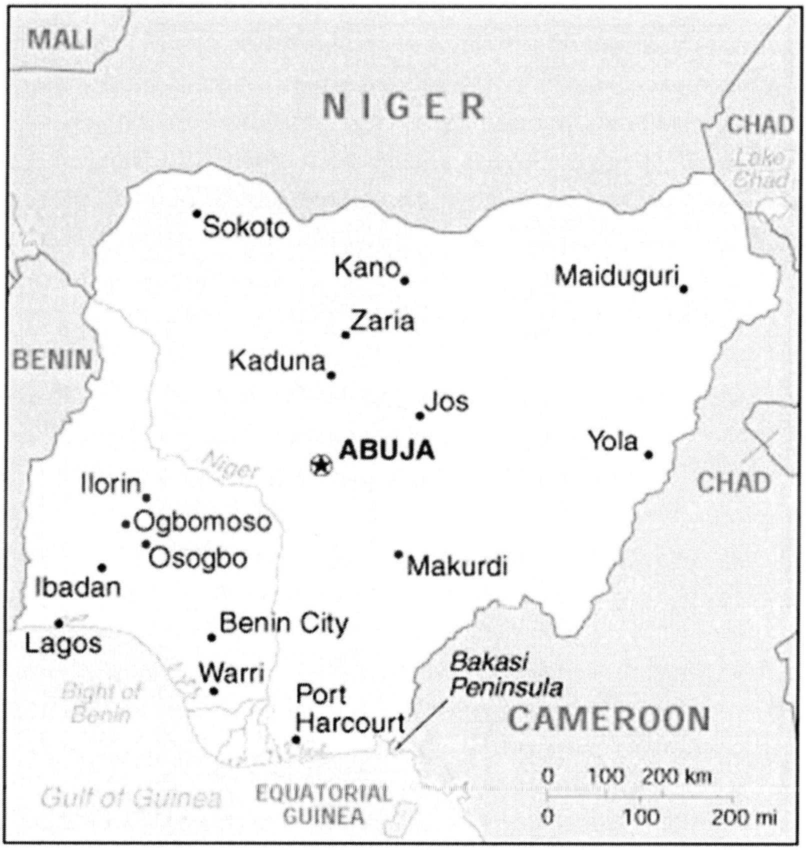

Figure 1. Map of Nigeria.

Rapid urbanization, oil spills, and loss of arable land have created several environmental problems in Nigeria [3]. Among these environmental problems are sheet and gully erosion, coastal and marine erosion and land subsidence, flooding, drought and desertification, oil pollution, urban decay and squatter settlements, industrial pollution and waste, municipal solid waste, biodegradable petrochemical products, concrete jungles or cities, loss of fauna and flora, and climatic change [4].

MSW can be regarded as 'useless' , unwanted, and discarded materials that resulted from society's normal or routine daily activities and, in general, may be in solid, liquid, or gaseous form [5]. It is often accompanied by commercial waste, whether solid or semisolid. It also comes in the form of food wastes, paper, cardboard, plastics, textiles, leather, wood, glass, and other household items. In most industrialized nations, from the time wastes are generated, they go through a solid waste chain, consisting of waste handling and separation; storage and processing at source; collection, separation, processing, and transformation of solid wastes; transfer and transport; energy generation; and disposal. This is however not the case in Nigeria or most developing countries. In many parts of the developing world, solid waste disposal is done through dumping and burning without control [6]. These practices pollute land, water, and air. Although these practices are illegal and their consequences recognized and felt in Nigeria, they persist in both urban and rural areas because of weak law enforcement regimen and limited public sector financial resources. A sustainable solution to this gigantic problem, which affects every populace, is through more efficient solid waste management. The generation of energy from MSW (though largely dependent on MSW composition) has the propensity to reduce greenhouse gas emissions, to generate renewable energy, and to provide energy diversity while also ensuring safe, hygienic, and reliable disposal practices.

The volume of waste generated in the world today is enormous. This volume of waste generated is to some degree due to inefficiencies (e.g., in usage, sorting, and processing) and, in principle, might be reduced [7]. As of 2011, the world generated an estimated two billion tons of MSW, and this number is expected to grow much higher [8]. MSW is a renewable form of energy that includes both commercial and residential wastes generated in municipalities. The US Environmental Pollution Agency (USEPA) goes further to classify MSW as a source of clean energy. From a sustainable development perspective, the focus is on reduction of waste, followed by recycling, both of which are advantageous in terms of reducing greenhouse gas emissions. Several analysis done using the USEPA models show that WTE avoids 36 million tons of greenhouse gases yearly [9]. However, not all wastes are recyclable, and as such, an energy recovery method becomes essential.

The interest in the practical applications of WTE dates back to several decades. WTE is hardly a new or novel idea. What is however new is the confluence of factors that have increased the attractiveness of WTE. These factors include rising oil prices, urban air pollution, energy supply security, reduction in foreign oil imports, carbon dioxide (CO_2) emissions, and climate change. These considerations are not confined to a single nation or part of the world and thus render the concept of WTE as abundantly and equitably available to humanity. Energy recovery through WTE can be defined as a waste treatment process that allows for the generation of energy in the form of electricity or heat from wastes that would have otherwise been disposed off in landfills [7–13]. It involves the use of modern combustion technologies for the recovery of energy from a mix of MSW. Today, more than 800 thermal WTE plants currently operate in nearly 40 countries around the globe [14]. WTE systems will treat at least 261 million tons of waste annually by 2022, with a total estimated output of 283 TWh of electricity and heat generation, which increased from 221 TWh in 2010. Under a more optimistic scenario, WTE will potentially treat 396 million tons of MSW a year, producing 429 TWh of power [14]. The global market for thermal and biological WTE technologies will reach about US$6.2 billion in 2012 and grow to about US$29.2 billion by 2022, according to forecasts by Cleantech market intelligence [14], while under an optimistic scenario, market value could reach US$80.6 billion by 2022. WTE facilities are integrated into broader waste management practices and policies with the goal of reducing the use of landfills. Although combustion technologies continue to lead the market, advanced thermal treatment technology deployments such as pyrolysis are expected to pick up as diminishing landfill capacity improves WTE economics. The utilization of biological technologies is also expected to increase worldwide.

It is imperative for every nation to find environmentally benign methods related to sound management of MSW for sustainable development. The energy potential of MSW is contained in materials that are either biogenic or anthropogenic in origin [15]. Biogenic materials are those that include paper, food, and yard wastes and are considered to be renewable. Anthropogenic materials, on the other hand, are those that include plastics which are derived from fossil fuels and are not sustainable. Several methods exist to analytically determine the biogenic and anthropogenic fractions of energy-generating components of MSW. Unlike some other renewable energy resources such as tidal, solar, and wind, MSW is always available. Benefits of WTE include waste volume reduction, sanitation and detoxification, stabilization, and energy recovery. The technologies that exist to produce energy from wastes are anaerobic digestion, combustion, gasification, and landfill gas to energy.

WTE has been well proven in Europe, where energy and solid waste policies have evolved from the Kyoto protocol [16] GHG reduction goals, to include renewable energy (RE) and decreased waste emissions from landfills [16]. This has been invariably good in advancing the state of technology for waste management and conversion to energy such that it is an integral component of solid waste management in Europe. About 18 European Union countries engage in thermally treating 58 million tons of wastes in WTE plants to produce energy annually [17]. As such, RE aspects of solid waste management policies work well together with waste reduction policies.

2. WASTE MANAGEMENT PRACTICES IN NIGERIA

2.1 Waste management practices then and now

The collection and disposal of solid waste in Nigeria were controllable and not a problem before the country's independence in 1960. Before the 1960s, the population was low and not concentrated in urban areas, and people lived in traditional ways [18]. Previous studies described the major cities of Nigeria, such as Ibadan, Calabar, and Port Harcourt, as clean and beautiful. However, when the country gained independence from the colonial masters and oil was subsequently discovered, migration from rural areas to urban areas increased as a result of people wanting to live more comfortably. Nigeria began importing many varieties of foods and luxury goods with consequent increase in solid wastes. Plastics and polythene produced negligible waste in 1971. Today, they make up a large part of the refuse. Empty beverage cans are found littered in every corner of the road. In fact, consumption patterns have dramatically changed since the 1960s and 1970s. For example, according to Paris-based magazine *Jeane Afrique*, Nigerians consumed 593,000 bottles of champagne in 2010, 50% more than the richer rival nation of South Africa - possibly due to the population effect with Nigeria being at least three times larger in population than South Africa.

Solid waste is now a troubling problem to both the government and the public [18]. As with many other nations, solid waste generation in Nigeria is a function of the population, its industrialization level, socioeconomic status, and dominant commercial activities [18]. Some of the factors, which influence the generation and stockpiling of solid waste, are the lack of modern waste disposal technology; the lack of facility to separate the waste at source; the effectiveness of existing solid waste management policy and its enforcement, environmental education, and awareness; and the income status. The indiscriminate dumping of secondhand electronic gadgets has also contributed to the waste disposal problem [18]. Waste storage and collection are the responsibility of state environmental agencies, private companies, or both. The wastes collected are dumped together, that is, unsegregated, indicating a lack of awareness of their nature and compatibility with one another. The populace also burns their refuse in open dump sites, e.g., documents, rags, and tires, often without sanitary or environmental control. This attracts scavengers at the dumps where they gather plastic cans and bottles, glass, and other recyclables mainly for sale to other secondhand goods markets. More than 50% of the people's wastes are highly decaying food surpluses, and more than 15% are plastic wastes. Wastes are generally recycled by the informal sector while scavengers scan for usable items, as described earlier [19].

The solid waste problem is acutely felt in Lagos State because it is the most populated city and among the most industrialized in sub-Saharan Africa. In 1995 alone, it produced approximately four million tons of solid wastes.

The long history of the waste problem in Lagos goes back to the transfer of waste management from the local governments to the state. Policies kept on changing, leading to management lag. The wastes are generally not treated but moved to landfill sites where they are openly burned. The two incineration plants in Lagos are capable of treating wastes with less than 20% water, but they have never been used as the state's wastes contain 30% to 40% water. Lagos is currently undertaking efforts to generate revenue from waste management [20, 21].

2.2 A brief on waste management policies in Nigeria

Intervention by the Federal Ministry of Environment has been in the form of a revised policy on environment in 1999 and the National Agenda 21 published also in 1999 [19]. These measures complemented existing guidelines and standards for environmental pollution, the waste management regulation of 1991, the Environmental Impact Assessment Decree number 86 of 1992, and an environmental edit of 1997. However, as earlier mentioned, nature's way of absorbing waste and human efforts combined have been surpassed by the enormity of the problem and its impact on the environment. Every material or product goes through a long cycle, consisting of activities, which produce greenhouse gas emissions. These are through energy consumption, methane emissions, and carbon storage. The current state of waste management in Nigeria is clearly a picture of neglect and failure in the enforcement of solid waste management policies. The effects of this neglect include unnecessarily lost resources, increased adverse impact on biological processes, disruption of infrastructure, greater risks of flooding and distribution of vermin and pests, and the deterioration of air quality.

2.3 Waste-to-energy technologies and opportunities for Nigeria

Technologies for WTE production have been rapidly evolving and changing communities and countries [20] yielding dual benefits from effective solid waste management practices. Not only will WTE deliver useful energy that is needed in many countries, but it will also aid to dispose of MSW effectively and safely. A community or country's solid waste management goals and objectives, the environmental impact, and production and consumption patterns will help determine if WTE production technology is appropriate for that community or country [20]. For example, with current government interest and the necessary investment, over the coming years, Lagos State is expected to generate revenue from better waste management, which would be beneficial to remote and rural areas of the state overall [21].

The main categories of waste to energy technologies are (1) physical technologies which process waste to produce fuel (i.e., refuse-derived fuel or solid-recovered fuel), (2) thermal technologies which can produce heat, fuel oil, or syngas from both organic and inorganic wastes, and (3) biological technologies whereby bacterial fermentation is used to digest organic wastes to produce useful fuel. These can be further elaborated as gasification (pyrolysis - thermal and plasma-arc types), anaerobic digestion, and combustion. Gasification of waste involves thermochemical conversion reactions, which will induce gases under high temperature and low concentration of pure oxygen or air. Methane is produced and can be applied to run an internal combustion engine to generate electricity. Gasification can reduce waste by 70% to 80% while preserving the land area.

Anaerobic digestion is a biochemical conversion process, which produces fuel for energy through an enclosure called a *digester*. It is currently used in both developed and developing countries to treat both wet and dry biomass resources and to convert MSW and other wastes and residues. It has been successfully used to generate electricity for rural and remote areas of developing countries.

Combustion or incineration consists of burning the whole mass of waste in an incinerator. Incineration of MSW can drastically reduce the volume of MSW by up to 80% to 90%. The process releases gaseous pollutants such that a pollution control system needs to be set up along with it. This technology operates at 800°C to 1,000°C. It is also important to note that it is however not as popular as gasification.

Since WTE would be a relatively new concept in Nigeria, the populace would need effective public awareness and sensitization programs and campaigns. The government, for its part, must establish partnership with the organized private sector entities for the needed investments [20–24]. With the exception of recent progress on waste issues in Lagos State, issues related to sound MSW management such as recycling programs, waste reduction, and waste disposal have not been adequately addressed in Nigeria. Investigation of the potential contribution of such underutilized fuels like MSW to the energy mix in a sustainable way while minimizing GHG emissions currently produced from landfilling, open dumps, and open burning of solid wastes is a worthwhile undertaking in a developing country like Nigeria.

3. METHODS

3.1 Materials and methodology for the estimation of the potential

We begin this work by estimating the calorific value in MSW for selected municipalities in Nigeria based on available data from the literature. The calorific value is derived from the MSW weight distribution (wt.% for as-received MSW on a wet basis) that was obtained from [25–31]. The MSW was categorized as food waste or vegetables as well as putrescibles, paper, plastics, metals, textile or rubber, and inert or miscellaneous. The calorific values in the MSW collected for Lagos, Port Harcourt, Abuja, Ibadan, Kano, Makurdi, and Nsukka are estimated from their respective MSW data. We consider three ways of handling MSW which have been mentioned earlier. Solid waste is not recycled or composted and is hence disposed to the MSW collection system. It is assumed that plastics, metals, and glass will be recycled with a high degree of success and will not be introduced into a landfill, an incinerator, or an anaerobic digester. From the known moisture and ash content, the dry percentage weight (wt.%) for each category of the MSW was determined.

3.2 Calorific value by thermochemical conversion or direct combustion

The calorific value has been determined using a universal correlation for the process where MSW is incinerated. Two processes - using grate furnace and fluidized furnace steam generators - were considered to convert chemical energy to thermal energy (steam). Conventional Rankine cycle and combined heat and power (CHP) plant were considered to convert chemical energy to electrical energy. The thermal energy (steam generation) or electrical energy generated was calculated using assumed conversion efficiencies for the processes. In the first instance, calorific value was determined for the following categories: vegetables and putrescible or food waste, paper, textiles, and plastics. Glass and metals with zero or negligible free carbon content were not included in the calculation of the calorific value. It is also assumed that these materials will eventually be recycled and will not enter the MSW stream meant for recovering its calorific value through some process. The inputs that are necessary to determine the calorific value, that is, the high heating value (HHV; in MJ/kg dry MSW), are the mass of MSW collected, weight percentage on a dry and ash-free basis, ash content from a proximate analysis, and the ultimate analysis.

Two correlations were used, both of which depend on the knowledge of ash content determined by a proximate analysis and the elemental compositions of carbon, hydrogen, nitrogen, oxygen, sulfur, phosphorous, and chlorine obtained from an ultimate analysis. The unified correlations used were presented by Channiwala and Parikh [32] and has been found to estimate the calorific value (HHV) of a variety of MSW with acceptable accuracy. Another correlation by Grabosky and Bain, used for comparison, has been found to have 1.5% accuracy in the predicted calorific value for biomass [32]. The MSW collected in most cities is predominated by biomass contribution. The calculated HHV was then converted to low heating value (LHV in MJ/kg dry MSW) using Equation 1:

$$\text{LHV (MJ/kg)} = \text{HHV (MJ/kg)} - (9 \times \%\text{H} + \%\text{H}_2\text{O}) \times 2.44\ \text{MJ/kg}, \quad (1)$$

where %H and $\%H_2O$ are the weight percentages of atomic hydrogen and water, respectively. HHV and LHV per unit mass were converted to calorific value potential per month using the following equation:

$$\text{LHV or HHV (MJ/month)} = \text{LHV or HHV (MJ/kg dry mass)} \times \text{dry mass (kg/month)}. \quad (2)$$

3.3 Landfill methane generation

The second scenario that was considered is where the organic wastes (food and yard waste, wood, and textiles) [25–31] are sent to (a landfill) and undergo a biodegradation process. In order to calculate methane generation potential (L_O) from the landfill, decomposable organic carbon (%DOC) on a dry mass basis was determined for the categories of MSW mentioned earlier. Furthermore, the calculation assumes that only putrescible and other organic wastes are discarded in the landfill. The net quantity of the methane generation potential from the landfill (combusted in an internal combustion engine) may be lower due to some of the methane not collected (i.e., flared or emitted as GHG). The %DOC was calculated as follows:

$$\%\text{DOC} = (\%\text{C}_{\text{textile}} \times \%\text{W}_{\text{textile}}) + (\%\text{C}_{\text{gardenwaste}} \times \%\text{W}_{\text{gardenwaste}}) + (\%\text{C}_{\text{foodwaste}} \times \%\text{W}_{\text{foodwaste}}) + (\%\text{C}_{\text{wood}} \times \%\text{W}_{\text{wood}}), \quad (3)$$

where %C is the carbon percentage on a dry mass basis obtained from an ultimate analysis of the specific category of MSW. The calculated %DOC is converted to a fraction and is used in the equation below. The quantity %W is the weight percent of the category of MSW that is considered. Mass of methane potentially generated in a month ($M_{methane}$ (Gg/month)) is calculated as follows [30]:

$$M_{methane}(Gg/month) = MSW_T \times MSW_F \times MCF \times DOC \times DOCF \times F \times \left(\frac{16}{12} - R\right) \times 1 - O_x, \quad (4)$$

where MSW_T is the total MSW generated and collected (Gg/month), MSW_F is the fraction of MSW that is collected and disposed in the landfill (taken to be 0.74), MCF is the methane correction factor (taken to be 0.4 for a shallow unmanaged landfill), DOC_F is the fraction of DOC converted to landfill gas by decomposition, $F$is the fraction of methane (by volume) in the landfill gas, set at a default value of 0.5, and R is the amount of methane recovered and is set to zero. This enables the calculation of the maximum methane generation potential, i.e., the amount that will be potentially emitted as GHG, O_x is the oxidation factor, taken as zero, which implies that the biodegradation takes place strictly anaerobically, and the ratio (16:12) is the mass ratio of 1 g mol methane for each gram mole of carbon. The value of DOC_F was determined as follows:

$$DOC_F = (0.014 \times T(°C)) + 0.28 \quad (5)$$

An average temperature T of 28°C was assumed for the municipalities considered. It should be pointed out that this calculation determines the methane generation potential only. The fraction out of the generated total that is not recovered is what is lost to the atmosphere as a GHG emission. The calculated mass of methane potentially generated ($M_{methane}$) per month can be converted to methane generation potential, L_O:

$$L_o(m^3/Gg\ MSW) = \frac{(M_{methane}(kg))/0.717(kg/m^3)}{MSW_T(Gg/month)} \quad (6)$$

or reported as gravimetric ratio ($Gg_{methane}/Gg_{MSW}$).

These calculations do not determine the time dependence of methane generation potential and the effect on the methane generation potential as more MSW is added to an operating landfill over its lifetime. However, the calculated L_O has been used to determine the methane generated over the lifetime of a landfill and is presented in the next section that discusses the economics of energy generation using the landfill methane that is generated.

3.4 Economic analysis of landfill methane generation

It is assumed that the organic part of the MSW will be sorted and that 74% of MSW_F collected will be discarded in the landfill [33]. We consider a situation where the landfill already exists or existing ones will be improved and that they are shallow and poorly managed with a MCF of 0.4. The electrical energy generated by combustion of methane was calculated using a LHV of methane of 37.2 MJ/Nm^3.

The economic analysis assumes the following: (1) The landfill will be operational in 2013. (2) The landfill will collect MSW at the same level as mentioned for 30 years at the end of which it will be shut down; after the shutdown, the landfill will no longer accept any MSW. (3) However, the landfill will continue to produce methane. The landfill will be monitored, and with the inherent methane collected for the next 30 years, (4) only 50% (by volume) of the methane that is produced is captured by the recovery system. Remainder is emitted and constitutes a greenhouse gas emission, (5) the capital investment is assumed to be financed for 30 years at the rate of 9%, (6) the operating costs are not financed, (7) methane will be combusted in an internal combustion engine that is coupled to an electric generator with a thermal efficiency of 0.33 [34] and (8) the plant is operational for 7,488 h/year, and (9) tipping fees collected from the municipality or other revenue streams are not considered. In this sense, the costs calculated below for the cost of electricity is the minimum pricing at which electricity can be sold to the consumer or to the grid; (10) for the direct gas use scenario, the monetary value for greenhouse gas offset is set at US$0 per tonne of carbon equivalent. In other words, no credit is allowed for the offset of greenhouse gas emissions. Capital investment and operating costs only include investment on the landfill and gas handling. The costs associated with the internal combustion engine plant are excluded, and (11) 'direct gas' is assumed to be purified and compressed to

344,737.5 Pa (or 50 psi) and piped to a customer 8 km (or five miles) away [35] for direct use. The costs calculated are for a gas that is predominantly methane. The capital investment includes the investment made in developing/improving the landfill and in establishing the ICE power plant. The purpose of the economic analysis is to determine the specific unit price of electrical energy obtainable from methane combustion in an ICE-driven power generation plant.

LandGEM a software developed by the USEPA [36, 37] was used to determine the amount of methane generated from 2013 till 2073, for a period of 60 years. The program requires the following for an input and proceeds as described in the Equation 7: (1) amount of MSW added to the landfill each year (M_i), (2) values for maximum methane generation potential L_O (in m^3/Mg MSW) were used from Table 1, (3) fraction of methane in the landfill gas 50%, with the other 50% being predominantly CO_2, (4) a MCF value of 0.4, and (5) reaction rate constant (k) of 0.05/year. This can be represented as

$$V_{CH_4}(\mathrm{m^3/year}) = \sum_{i=1}^{n} \sum_{j=0.1}^{1} kL_o \left(\frac{M_i}{10}\right) e^{-kt_{ij}}. \quad (7)$$

Table 1. Methane generation potential in selected municipalities and the corresponding degradable organic carbon

Location	%DOC	L_O (m^3/Mg MSW)
Lagos	32.36	63.09
Port Harcourt	17.84	22.29
Abuja	26.26	48.56
Ibadan	32.24	59.62
Kano	23.75	35.62
Makurdi	25.32	41.14
Nsukka	27.32	50.54

V_{CH4} is the volume of methane generated (m^3/year) in the year of calculation, i is a 1-year time increment, n is year of calculation, that is, initial year of waste acceptance. The value of n changes from 0 to 30 based on the assumption that the landfill is operational for 30 years, k is the reaction rate constant, j is a 0.1-year time increment, L_o is the potential methane generation capacity (m^3/Mg), M_i is the mass of waste accepted in the i th year (Mg), and t_{ij} is the age of j th section of waste mass M_i accepted in the i th year.

3.5 Anaerobic digestion of MSW

The anaerobic digestion (AD) process has been around for a long time and has found varied success [38]. There is a renewed effort to improve this process and recognize its full potential to handle the biodegradable organic matter (yard, kitchen, and agricultural waste) and combustible organic fraction (paper, wood) in a municipal solid waste. There is a variety of anaerobic digestion processes, but the general reaction block diagram of the process consists of the following:

1) Waste sorting (to separate plastics, glass, and metals) and shredding

2) Feeding system and retention in an anaerobic bioreactor in the presence of microorganisms that promote acidogenesis and methanogenesis [39]. (This reaction occurs under well-controlled temperature, pH, elemental ratio, and feed dilution with water.)

3) Biogas removal from bioreactor and purification (removing carbon dioxide and ammonia from the product methane stream)

4) Methane gas handling for the distribution or feeding system into a single- or dual-fuel engine plant

The degradation of organic matter in a municipal solid waste in an anaerobic-controlled environment of a digester serves as a responsible way to handle municipal solid waste [38]. In order to calculate the methane generation potential, the elemental compositions of C, H, N, and O that are available from an ultimate analysis of various organic fractions of an MSW were used as suggested by Parkin and Owen [40]. The authors suggest that for an organic compound with the composition $C_nH_aO_bN_c$, the amount of methane generated by anaerobic digestion, where water is used as a reactant, proceeds as per the reaction:

$$C_nH_aO_bN_c + \left[n-\frac{a}{4}-\frac{b}{2}+3\frac{c}{4}\right]H_2O\left[\frac{n}{2}-\frac{a}{8}+\frac{b}{4}+3\frac{c}{8}\right]CO_2\left[\frac{n}{2}+\frac{a}{8}-\frac{b}{4}-3\frac{c}{8}\right]CH_4 + cNH_3. \quad (8)$$

Anaerobic digestion tends to be a preferred method, over landfilling, for handling the organic content of municipal solid waste. The organic content consists of vegetative matter, food waste, and agricultural wastes. The advantage of anaerobic digestion over landfilling is its high decomposition potential and production of biogas, which is predominantly methane and compost as a final product [40]. The methane generation potential is calculated using the mass fraction (on a dry mass MSW basis) of elemental C, H, O, and N obtained from the ultimate analysis for each of the following categories indicated by index *I*: vegetables and putrescibles, paper, and textiles. The mass fraction is converted to gram moles of the elementsn_C, n_H, n_O, and n_N from which the maximum potential for methane generation is calculated as

$$\frac{(n_{CH_4})_i}{\text{kg MSW}} = \left(\frac{n_C}{2}+\frac{n_H}{2}+\frac{n_O}{2}+\frac{n_N}{2}\right)_i, \quad (9)$$

The total number of moles of methane generated is the sum of the number of moles of methane generated from each of the categories of waste that is considered and represented as

$$n_{CH_4}(\text{g moles } CH_4/\text{kg MSW}) = \sum_i (n_{CH_4})_i. \quad (10)$$

Equation 10 is then converted to the actual mass or volume of the methane generated for a given dry mass or as-received mass of municipal solid waste.

3.6 Economic analysis of methane generation in an AD process

Among the several AD processes, the Valorga process is the one that is widely used and, as of May 2010, had a combined installed methane production capacity of 263 million cubic meters [39]. Hence, the economic analysis was based on the Valorga design. Typical biogas generation capacity for this plant is in the range of 80 to 160 Nm^3/Mg MSW and typical methane fraction in the biogas is 0.6. *While performing the economic analysis, an average methane production of 72 m^3 /Mg MSW was used.* This number is much lower than the calculated potential presented in Table 2.

The economic analysis assumes the following:

- Methane constitutes about 60% (by volume) of the biogas produced.
- An average biogas production of 120 Nm^3/Mg MSW and specifically an average methane production of 72 m^3/Mg MSW. Using a calorific value for methane of 37.2 MJ/Nm^3, this translates to a specific energy of 707 MJ/Mg MSW.
- Methane will be combusted in an internal combustion engine that is coupled to an electric generator with a thermal efficiency (η_e) of 0.26. This efficiency is lower than the value of 0.33 assumed for a methane landfill plant as the AD process uses some of the gas and electricity produced for its operation.
- The capital investment is assumed to be financed for 20 years at the rate of 9%.
- The operating costs are not financed.
- The plant is operational for 7,488 h/year or for 24 h/day for 26 days/month.

Table 2. Calculated methane production potential (m ^{3}/Mg MSW) via an AD process for various locations in Nigeria

Location	MSW generated (Mg/month)	VGF (wet basis) (Mg/month)	Calculated potential (m^3 CH_4/Mg MSW)
Lagos	3.71×10^5	3.04×10^5	296
Port Harcourt	1.81×10^5	9.07×10^4	168
Abuja	2.78×10^4	1.94×10^4	257
Ibadan	1.35×10^5	1.16×10^5	313
Kano	1.57×10^5	9.41×10^4	231
Makurdi	2.42×10^4	1.62×10^4	247
Nsukka	1.19×10^4	8.68×10^3	266

VGF: Vegetables, Garden and Fruit waste.

- Tipping fees collected from the municipality or other revenue streams are not considered. In this sense the costs calculated below for the cost of electricity or the cost of methane is the minimum pricing at which electricity or gas can be sold to the consumer.

The capital costs were then estimated using a power law based on capacity ratios as given below:

$$\text{AD plant}/C_{\text{cpl}} = C_{\text{cpl}_{\text{reference}}} \left(\frac{M_{\text{MSW}}\,(\text{tonnes/year})}{\text{Capacity}_{\text{reference}}} \right)^{0.6}, \tag{11}$$

$$\text{ICE power plant}/C_{\text{cpp}} = C_{\text{cpp}_{\text{reference}}} \left(\frac{\text{Nominal power generation capacity}}{\text{Power generation capacity}_{\text{reference}}} \right)^{0.6} \tag{12}$$

The reference ICE power plant was identified for cost comparison based on the nominal power generation capacity expected for the AD plants being considered. The capital costs and operating costs for the reference AD and the power plant are given in Table 3. The nominal generation capacity was carried out as shown in Equation 13:

$$\text{Plant capacity}\,(\text{W},\ \text{MW}_e) = \frac{120\,(\text{Nm}^3\ \text{biogas/Mg MSW}) \times M_{\text{MSW}}\,(\text{Mg/month}) \times Q_{\text{CH}_4}\,(\text{MJ/m}^3) \times \eta e \times 0.6\ \text{Nm}^3\ \text{methane/Nm}^3\ \text{biogas}}{26\ \text{days/month} \times 24\ \text{h/day} \times 3,600\ \text{s/h}} \tag{13}$$

where Q_{CH4} is the calorific value of methane and taken to be 37.2 MJ/m^3 and η_e is the thermal-to-electrical efficiency of methane gas-powered ICE plant and taken to be 0.26.

The typical capital cost (US\$/kW$_e$) ranges from US\$1,100 to US\$1,300 for a co-firing biogas power plant to US\$3,000 to US\$4,000 for a gasification and CHP plant. The reference capital costs used here (US\$1,200/kW$_e$) compares to the capital cost of a co-firing plant.

The unit cost of electricity is calculated as follows:

$$C_{\$/\text{kWh}_e} = \frac{\left[(\text{CO}_{\text{AD}} + \text{CC}_{\text{pp}}) - \text{PMT}\left(\frac{9.9\%}{12},\ 30 \times 12, \text{CC}_{\text{AD}} + \text{CC}_{\text{pp}}\right) \right]}{E(\text{kWh}_e/\text{year})}, \tag{14}$$

Table 3. Plant capacity, capital, and annual operating costs for reference AD and ICE power plants

Cost		Value
Reference AD plant (Valorga at Tillburg)	Capacity capital cost $\left(C_{cpl_{reference}}\right)$	52,000 VGF tonnes/year
		US$17,500,000
	Annual operating cost	US$800,000/year (labor)
		US$ 800,000/year (supply/maintenance)
Reference ICE power plant (generating capacity 5 MW_e)	Capital cost $\left(C_{cpp_{reference}}\right)$	US$6,000,000
	Operating cost	US$657,000

where CO_{AD} and CC_{pp} are respectively the annual operating cost for the AD and power plant. CC_{AD} and CC_{pp} are the respective capital cost for the AD and power plant. *E* is the electrical energy generated per year using the methane separated from the biogas and is calculated using Equation 15:

$$E_{\mathrm{kWh}_e/\mathrm{year}} = \frac{M_{\mathrm{MSW}}(\mathrm{Mg/year}) \times 120\ \mathrm{m^3\ biogas/Mg\ MSW} \times 0.6\ \mathrm{m^3\ CH_4/m^3\ biogas} \times 37.2\ \mathrm{MJ/m^3\ CH_4} \times \eta_e}{3.6\ \mathrm{MJ/kWh}_e}. \tag{15}$$

where η_e (0.26) is the thermal-to-electrical energy efficiency. The unit cost of gas is calculated as

$$C_{\$/\mathrm{m^3\ CH_4}} = \frac{\left[\mathrm{CO_{AD}} - \mathrm{PMT}\left(\frac{9\%}{12},\ 20 \times 12,\ \mathrm{CC_{AD}}\right)\right]}{V(\mathrm{m^3\ CH_4/year})} \tag{16}$$

$$V(\mathrm{m^3\ CH_4/year}) = M_{\mathrm{MSW}}(\mathrm{Mg/year}) \times 120\ \mathrm{m^3\ biogas/Mg\ MSW} \times 0.6\ \mathrm{m^3\ CH_4/m^3\ biogas}. \tag{17}$$

3.7 Incineration and combined heat and power

The 'fuel' or waste can be incinerated in a grate furnace or a fluidized furnace. Detailed engineering analysis is required to determine which furnace design is the optimal choice. The calorific value of the fuel is converted to electrical energy or thermal energy or both in a CHP plant. The reference plant used is shown in Table 4. The electrical (E_e) or thermal energy (E_{th}) generated by each of the energy conversion mechanisms was derived from the calorific value as follows:

$$E_{\mathrm{th}}\ or\ E_e(\mathrm{MJ/Mg\ MSW}) = \eta(\mathrm{LHV}(\mathrm{MJ/Mg\ MSW})), \tag{18}$$

where $\eta = E_e/\mathrm{LHV}$ for a thermal power plant and also $\eta = E_{th}/\mathrm{LHV}$ for a steam generation boiler (E_{th} is ≥ the enthalpy change between the liquid water and steam at a specified temperature and pressure).

Table 4. Parameters of the reference MSW incineration plant (capacity, capital investment, and operating costs)

Reference plant size (tonnes/day)	Capital investment ($Ccp_{reference}$) (US$)	Annual operating cost (reference) (US$)	Operating cost/capital investment
62,500	21.3 million	6.76 million	0.32
703,000	212.7 million	41.4 million	0.19

For a CHP plant, two efficiencies may be defined - electrical efficiency and thermal efficiency. Also relevant to determining the total energy generation is the steam-to-power ratio. For the CHP process, the total energy generated (E_{th} + E_e) per megagram MSW is presented below. The preliminary calculations assume the use of four different options:

- Grate furnace boiler/steam generator - Thermal efficiency = 0.4.
- Fluidized bed steam generator - Thermal efficiency = 0.85.
- Rankine cycle-based thermal power plant with fluidized bed furnace - Overall efficiency = 0.35.
- The CHP plant electrical efficiency is taken as 0.27, and thermal efficiency is taken as 0.64, while for the overall efficiency, we use 0.88 with a power to heat ratio of 0.42 [41].

3.8 Economic analysis of MSW incineration

The economic analysis of MSW incineration proceeds in two different ways:

1. Given the selling price of energy (heat or electrical power), what does it cost (capital investment C_{cp} and operating costs C_o) the company to generate energy at that cost? In this case, the energy sold is revenue. This

approach assumes that electrical energy is sold at US$35/MWh and thermal energy (steam) is sold at US$15/MWh.

2. Given the costs of capital investment and operating costs, what should be the price of energy to the consumer, i.e., determine the unit cost estimate?

3.9 Baseline capital costs and operating costs

Baseline costs were determined from an article by the ASME committee [42]. This article evaluates the cost of incinerating wastes with or without polymer polyvinylchloride and across incineration plants that are categorized as small (200 metric tons (MT)/day), medium (800 MT/day), and large (2250 MT/day). The small- and medium-sized plants had two incinerator lines each, while the large plant had three incinerator lines. The plants are equipped with air pollution control devices (APCD) and continuous emission monitoring systems (CEM) and use dry lime injectors, fabric filters, and/or spray drying for air pollution control. The small plants were designed to produce steam, while the medium- and large-sized plants generate electricity. The capital investment costs and operating costs for the reference plants were averaged for each size classification, and the average costs were used in the calculations. The capital cost includes the cost of the incinerator plant and cost of APCD and CEM facilities. The plant is assumed to operate for 7,488 h/year. The annual operating cost includes both direct and indirect operating costs. The amount of MSW collected per month was compared to the plant size in the baseline that was the closest. The actual fixed capital cost (C_{cp}) for the plants were estimated by applying the power factor formula to the plant capacity ratio as shown [43]:

$$C_{cp} = C_{cp\ reference}\left(\frac{(M_{MSW}(\text{tonnes/year}))_{actual}}{(M_{MSW}(\text{tonnes/year}))_{reference}}\right)^{0.7}, \qquad (19)$$

where M_{MSW} is the mass of MSW collected annually and $C_{cpreference}$ is the known capital investment for the reference plant. The operating cost was assumed to be the same fraction of the capital cost for both the reference plant and the actual plant. The reference capital investment and operating costs were assumed to be the same for a plant of a given MSW handling capacity for a thermal power plant, a fluidized or grate boiler steam generator, and a CHP plant. It was assumed that the cost of capital included the yearly repayment of the borrowed capital investment and the interest on the borrowing (at 9% per annum for 30 years). The PMT function in Microsoft Excel was used to calculate the yearly payments (US$/year) on the borrowed capital. The PMT function returns a number with a negative sign implying that it is a cost for the plant operator or company. If the funds to meet the operating costs are not borrowed, then there is no cost involved in acquiring the operating capital. When the generated heat (E_{th} in MWh/year) and electric power (E_e in MWh/year) are sold at US$15/MWh and US$35/MWh, respectively, the net annual cost factor (C_F in US$/Mg MSW) may be calculated as

$$C_F = \frac{C_O - \mathrm{PMT}\left(\frac{9\%}{12},\ 30\times 12,\ C_{cp}\right) - \left[(E_{th}\times \mathrm{US15/MWh}) + (E_e \times \mathrm{US35/MWh})\right]}{\mathrm{Mg\ MSW}}. \quad (20)$$

It should be noted that the tipping fee collected by the incinerator facility is not included in the revenue stream. Hence, the cost factor is positive in most instances, except for a CHP plant in Lagos. A positive cost factor implies that the expense exceeds the revenue. The positive cost factor thus indicates the additional revenue that must be generated through tipping fee and subsidies that must be secured. Alternately, one may determine the specific unit price of energy (C in US$/kWh) as shown in Equation 21:

$$C(\mathrm{US/kWh}) = \frac{\left(C_O - \mathrm{PMT}\left(\frac{9\%}{12},\ 30\times 12,\ C_{cp}\right)\right)}{M_{MSW}(\mathrm{Mg/year})\times E(\mathrm{kWh/Mg})}, \quad (21)$$

where E is the annual energy generation per metric ton MSW. The specific energy costs are in US$/kWh $_e$ for a thermal plant and in US$/kWh$_{th}$ for fluidized and grate furnace plants. The CHP plant generates both steam and electricity, with a power-to-heat ratio of 0.42, and the specific energy cost is the average of both thermal and electrical energies.

3.10 Landfill gas and ICE power plant scaling: the reference data

In order to estimate the capital cost of a landfill (C_{cpl}) and the relevant operating costs, reference cost information was established based on two USEPA reports [35,44]. The capital cost for establishing a landfill is scaled as per a power law based on the capacity of the landfill over its lifetime (known as *the amount of waste in place* (WIP)). The landfill used as a reference consisted of gas handling and flare systems and has a total WIP of one million metric tons [35]. As per USEPA classification, these landfills range from very large (>15 million metric tons (MMT)) to medium (>5 MMT) in size. The landfill that is used as a reference is located in Munster, IN, USA. The LandGEM program was executed to determine the volume of methane generated per year. Using that information, the average electrical energy produced (in MW) over the 60-year period was calculated. This provided an estimate of the nominal power generation capacity of the plant to be installed onsite. The capital investment cost for the actual plant (C_{cpl} and C_{cpp}) was then scaled based on the power generation capacity as per a power law relation as given Equations 22 and 23.

$$\text{Landfill}/C_{cpl} = C_{cpl.reference} \times \left(\frac{M_{MSW}(\text{tonnes/year}) \times 12\ \text{months/year} \times 30\,\text{years}}{\text{Capacity}_{reference}}\right)^{0.6}. \qquad (22)$$

$$\text{Power plant}/C_{cpp} = C_{ccp.reference} \times \left(\frac{\text{Nominal power generation capacity}}{\text{Power generation capacity}_{reference}}\right)^{0.6}. \qquad (23)$$

The annual operating cost for the landfill is scaled as a power of 0.6 based on the mass of MSW handled per year. The annual operating cost of the ICE power plant is assumed to be a fixed percentage (9.9%) of the capital cost of the ICE power plant. This assumption is justified when the estimated costs are presented below. The continuous power generation capacity is determined based on methane generated for a given year. The methane production rate is assumed to be constant and that only 50% of the methane that is generated is captured and utilized (the recovery factor of 0.5 in Equation 24). The plant is assumed to operate for 7,488 h/year.

$$\text{Power generation, year } i\,(W_i, \text{MW}_e) = \frac{V_{\text{CH}_4}(\text{m}^3/\text{year}) \times Q_{\text{CH}_4}(\text{MJ/m}^3) \times \eta_e \times 0.5}{7,488 \text{ h/year} \times 360 \text{ s/h}}, \tag{24}$$

$$\text{Nominal power generation}\,(\text{MW}_e) = \frac{\Sigma_{i=1}^{60} W_i}{60}. \tag{25}$$

The nominal size of the plant is the average of the power generation capacity averaged over the 60 operating years of the plant. The capital cost is determined based on this nominal plant capacity:

$$E_{\text{avg}}\ (\text{GWh}_e/\text{year}) = \left[\left(\frac{\frac{\Sigma_i^{60}(V_{\text{CH}_4})_i(\text{m}^3/\text{year}) \times 0.5 \times Q_{\text{CH}_4}\ (\text{MJ/m}^3) \times \eta_e}{60}}{1,000 \text{ MJ/GJ} \times 3,600 \text{ GJ/GWh}}\right)\right]. \tag{26}$$

The unit-specific cost of electricity generated (C_e) after suitable unit conversions is calculated from Equation 27:

$$\text{Cost}\ (\text{s/kWh}_e) = \frac{[(C_{\text{ol}} + C_{\text{op}}) - \text{PMT}(\frac{9\%}{12},\ 30 \times 12,\ C_{\text{cpl}} + C_{\text{cpp}})]}{E_{\text{avg}}\ (\text{kWh}_e/\text{year}).} \tag{27}$$

where C_{ol} is the operating cost of the landfill and C_{op} is the operating cost of the power plant. E_{avg} is the average electrical energy generated over a 60-year period. The direct use, the landfill methane, *as a fuel for combustion in household or commercial applications is considered as well*. The capital cost includes the costs associated with the development and operation of the landfill, collecting, flaring, compressing, handling, purification, and piping of the landfill gas. The ICE power plant costs are excluded as there is no power generation on site.

Table 5 gives the pertinent information for the reference landfill capital and operating costs as well as the costs for direct gas plant. The capital cost of the landfill and direct gas plant are scaled as a power of 0.6 of the ratio of the WIP amount, as specified in Equation 13. The annual operating cost for the landfill is scaled as a power of 0.6 based on the mass of MSW handled per year [42]. The landfill that is used as a reference is located in Munster, IN, USA. Equation 7 gives the annual methane production rate which is averaged over 60 years to give $\bar{V}_{CH4}$. The unit-specific cost of methane recovered (C_{gas}) for use is calculated as

$$C_{\mathrm{gas}}\ (\mathrm{US/MJ}) = \frac{\left[\left(C_{\mathrm{ol}} + C_{o,\mathrm{gas}}\right) - \mathrm{PMT}\left(\frac{9\%}{12},\ 30\times 12,\ C_{\mathrm{cpl}} + C_{\mathrm{op,gas}}\right)\right]}{\frac{\left[\bar{V}_{\mathrm{CH_4}} \times 0.5\ \left(\mathrm{m^3/year}\right)\right]}{Q_{\mathrm{CH_4}}\ \left(\mathrm{MJ/m^3}\right)}} \tag{28}$$

Table 6 gives the capital and operating costs for the reference landfill and ICE power plant.

3.11 Waste composition of the selected municipalities and assumptions

The calorific value of the MSW collected in each city was calculated for vegetable and yard waste, paper, and textiles only. It was assumed that plastics, bottles, and metals will be captured by a recycle system and excluded from incineration.

3.12 Lagos

The MSW collected in Lagos has significant food waste and putrescible content (68 w/o on an as-received basis). Papers make the next major category. The moisture and ash contents in the MSW are not explicitly known. Hence, typical values were used for the moisture content taken from [45]. The ash content used was obtained [28] as determined for MSW collected in Port Harcourt.

Table 5. Capital and operating cost information for a reference landfill and direct gas plants

Cost		Value
Reference landfill	Capacity (WP)	1 million MT
	Capital cost $\left(C_{cpl_{reference}}\right)$	US$700,000
	Mass MSW received per year	8,000 metric tonnes/year
	Annual operating cost (C_{ol})	US$196,647/year (collection)
		US$765,761/year (sort and dispose)
Reference direct gas plant	Capacity (WP)	1 million MT
	Capital cost $\left(C_{cpgas_{reference}}\right)$	US$1,639,000
	Annual operating cost (C_{ogas})	US$136,000

Table 6. Capital and operating cost information for a reference landfill and ICE power plants

Cost		Value
Reference landfill	Capacity	1 million metric tonnes
	Capital cost $\left(C_{cpl_{reference}}\right)$	US$700,000
	Mass MSW received per year	8,000 metric tonnes/year
	Annual operating cost	US$196,647/year (collection)
		US$765,761/year (sort and dispose)
Reference ICE power plants	Generation capacity	5 MW_e
		3 MW_e
		2 MW_e
		1.5 MW_e
		1 MW_e
	Capital cost $\left(C_{cpp_{reference}}\right)$	US$6,000,000
		US$3,957,000
		US$2,517,000
		US$1,927,000
		US$1,322,000
	Operating cost	US$657,000
		US$394,000
		US$263,000
		US$197,000
		US$131,000

3.13 Port Harcourt

The MSW data and the proximate and ultimate analysis data for Port Harcourt are very comprehensive as reported by [28]. Published ash and moisture contents were used to arrive at the ash- and moisture-free elemental ultimate analysis. These values were used in the correlations to arrive at the calorific value for MSW. It is interesting to note that the moisture content is very high in the food waste and wood waste categories at 65.2 and 19.2 w/o. The mass distribution of food waste is low (29.2 w/o); on the other hand, the combined mass distribution from plastics, glass, and metal waste is significant at nearly 41 w/o.

3.14 Abuja

The MSW distribution in Abuja is dominated by food wastes that contribute 55 w/o. The ash content and ultimate analysis were obtained from a report prepared by the Center for People and Environment prepared for USEPA [46]. This report particularly considered the landfill methane generation potential in Ibadan and Abuja, Nigeria. The moisture content was assumed to be the same as in Lagos [43]. The ash content used was obtained from [28], determined for MSW collected in Port Harcourt.

3.15 Ibadan

The MSW distribution in Abuja is dominated by food wastes that contribute 64.9 w/o. The ash content and ultimate analysis were obtained from a report prepared by the Center for People and Environment prepared for USEPA [46]. The moisture content was assumed to be the same as in Lagos [45]. The ash content used was obtained from [28], determined for MSW collected in Port Harcourt. The total mass of the MSW collected per month was not available; hence, representative values published in the literature were used for Ibadan [29].

3.16 Kano

MSW collected in Kano has a low contribution from food wastes (38 w/o). Papers contributed as high as 15 w/o, and glass and plastics contributed a combined 22 w/o; these are materials that can potentially be recycled or their usage reduced. The moisture content was assumed to be the same as in Lagos [45]. The ash content used was obtained from [28], determined for MSW collected in Pt. Harcourt.

3.17 Makurdi

Makurdi has a significant amount of vegetable waste (52 w/o). The moisture content was assumed to be the same as in Lagos [45]. The ash content used was obtained from [28], determined for MSW collected in Port Harcourt.

3.18 Nsukka

Municipal waste collected in Nsukka has a significant amount of vegetable and paper waste. It also contains significant quantity of metals and plastics that can be recycled and not introduced into the MSW stream.

4. RESULTS AND DISCUSSION

4.1 Landfill methane generation

The methane generation potential was calculated as described earlier. These calculations determine the methane generation potential from the landfill. The results are summarized in Table 1.

The calculated methane generation potential (in m^3 methane/Mg MSW) is lower than the typical range of about 50 to 100 kg methane per tonne MSW (70 to 140 m^3 methane per Mg MSW) for a landfill methane generation estimated by the International Energy Agency (IEA) [47]. The difference could be attributed to the fact that the IEA estimate is based on landfill methane plants operated in developed countries where the degradable carbon content may be higher. Furthermore, the landfill WIP at the end of 30 years for the various cities in Nigeria ranges from approximately 133 million metric tonnes (MMT) for Lagos to 4.3 MMT for Nsukka.

Table 7 gives the summary of the monthly MSW collection and the cost (not the net cost) per tonne of MSW handled. This is the cost incurred at the landfill for collection and sorting operations and does not include the cost associated with electricity generation or direct gas use. The costs of electricity and direct landfill methane are also presented. The daily MSW collection rate ranges from 12,350 to 400 tonnes/day for the selected municipalities. These numbers are derived from the data that was provided. USEPA guidelines for full cost accounting data state that in this range of daily MSW collection rates, the net cost per ton of MSW handled ranges from less than about \$36/ton (at 1,500 tons/day) to about \$85/ton (at 400 tons/day). The numbers estimated reveal the same trend but are slightly lower because the cost of capital to establish the landfill is not included. The calculations also assume that the MSW in a place like Lagos goes to a single appropriately sized large landfill. The EPA estimates consider a landfill with 1,500 tonnes/day for the highest daily capacity. The landfill rule was promulgated in the USA as a part of the Clean Air Act of 1996. According to this rule, future landfills, with the size larger than 2.5 MMT and volume greater than 2.5 million m^3, will have to install features that would either collect or flare the landfill gas. The USEPA report has determined the economics of electricity generated from direct gas use of the landfill methane [37]. For landfills that are not subject to the landfill rule and whose range in size is from 50,000 to 11,000,000 MT, the break-even gas price was calculated. For these landfills, electricity generation was not considered feasible. The break-even gas price is the price of gas at which the project results in US\$0 NPV (net present value) at the end of the 15-year life of the project. For the landfill project to be viable, the WIP must be greater than or equal to the break-even WIP. The results are summarized in Table 8.

Table 7. Specific cost of electricity and direct landfill methane for the selected municipalities

Location	Waste collection (tonnes/month)	Operating cost of landfill (US$/tonne)	Total CH_4 recovered in 60 years (m^3)	Nominal power (MW_e)	Price of electricity (US$/$KWh_e$)	Price of gas (US$/GJ CH_4)
Lagos	370,556	9.60	2.88×10^9	21.6	0.29	27.60
Port Harcourt	181,450	13.40	3.33×10^8	2.5	1.56	152.00
Abuja	27,795	22.00	1.56×10^8	1.2	1.08	108.00
Ibadan	135,391	14.40	1.86×10^9	13.9	0.25	23.40
Kano	156,676	13.50	5.53×10^8	4.1	0.88	84.60
Makurdi	24,242	28.60	1.06×10^8	0.8	1.47	144.00
Nsukka	12,000	37.90	6.99×10^7	0.5	1.47	145.00

Table 8. Break-even landfill direct gas price and landfill WIP

Size of landfill WIP (break-even WIP)	Break-even price (US$/GJ CH_4)
50,000 MT	52.00
500,000 MT	6.38
1,000,000 MT	2.04
11,000,000 MT	1.28

Comparing the estimated price of electricity for Nigerian towns to the USEPA projections, the price of landfill gas electricity for Nigeria is nearly a factor of 5 higher at best. The market price of natural gas is about US$2.74 per one million British thermal units (MMBtu), and the average industrial gas methane price is about US$3.42 per MMBtu. The cost of coal mine gas is also in the same range, about US$2.53 per MMBtu. For a landfill generating electricity to be viable, the break-even WIP is 2.9 MMT and the price of electricity would be US$0.04/kWh$_e$. For a landfill that produces gas for direct use, the price of gas is about US$2.74 per MMBtu (US$2.59/GJ) for a break-even landfill with a WIP of about 1 MMT. Both these projections assume US$0/TCE, i.e., no extra value for the offset of greenhouse gas emission, and do show incremental emission reductions. This renders the cost of landfill direct gas scenario to nearly 17 to 20 times higher for the municipalities considered. A significant reason for the higher estimate for Nigeria is because the calculations assume a minimally managed landfill with gas collection in place but only capturing 50% of the generated methane. This same factor contributes to the higher estimate for the price of gas. In addition, for a given landfill, the capital investments and operating costs appear to be much higher for a direct gas plant versus an ICE power plant. The extra cost comes from the cost of compression that is about 344,737.5 Pa and piping gas to the consumer from the plant. It must be emphasized that this is an estimate that does not take into account any revenue-generating stream such as tipping fee or garbage collection fee.

4.2 Anaerobic digestion

The methane is combusted in an ICE power plant or can be sold as a direct gas at higher pressures transported through a pipe network. The volume of methane generated by anaerobic digestion for each location that was considered is given in Table 2.

It may be noted that the cost of methane generated through anaerobic digestion is much cheaper than landfill methane. The price of the low pressure gas compares very closely with the average cost of natural gas (US$2.59/GJ) as presented in Table 9. When the product gas has to be sold as direct gas to the consumer, it may have to be purified, compressed, and transported through pipes to the consumer. Thus, a factor of 15% has been added to the price of low-pressure product gas to arrive at the price of direct gas. The percentage increase in price is the same as what was estimated to deliver landfill methane for direct gas use. The price of the direct gas obtained through anaerobic digestion is very much competitive with the price of natural gas. In the scenario where methane is generated using an AD process, the methane is subsequently combusted in an ICE power plant or is sold as direct gas at higher pressures, transported through a pipe network. The price of methane is competitive with the market price of natural gas at about US$2.74 per MMBtu, and the average industrial methane gas price is about US$3.42 per MMBtu for most of the selected municipalities except perhaps Nsukka. In addition and as an added benefit, the AD process produces compost that has use in agricultural practices.

4.3 Incineration or combustion

Table 10 shows the potential for energy generation (E_e in MJ_e) or thermal (E_{th} in MJ_t) by incinerating the *organic part* of the MSW. It is true that at the end of incinerating the MSW or combusting the methane gas, CO_2 will be produced. On the one hand, it is less potent than methane, and it is hoped that local environmental regulations will regulate the CO_2 emissions as well.

Table 9. Specific cost estimate for electricity and gas produced by AD of MSW for various locations in Nigeria

Location	Nominal capacity of power plant (MW_e)	Cost of electricity (US$/$kWh_e$)	Cost of low-pressure gas (US$/GJ CH_4)	Cost of direct gas (US$/GJ CH_4)
Lagos	117	0.0209	0.89	1.27
Port Harcourt	57	0.0239	0.8	1.25
Abuja	9	0.0560	2.28	3.24
Ibadan	43	0.0317	1.37	1.94
Kano	49	0.0268	1.04	1.48
Makurdi	8	0.0584	2.35	3.35
Nsukka	4	0.0792	3.28	4.66

Table 10. Energy generation potential by incinerating MSW in Nigeria

Location	Calorific value (LHV) (MJ/Mg)	Electrical or thermal energy generated			
		Thermal power plant (MJ_e/Mg MSW)	Fluidized bed steam generator (MJ_t/Mg MSW)	Grate incinerator boiler (MJ_t/Mg MSW)	CHP (MJ/Mg MSW)
Lagos	1.18×10^4	4,141	9,937	4,732	10,766
Port Harcourt	6.76×10^3	2,367	5,680	2,705	6,153
Abuja	1.04×10^4	3,650	8,761	4,172	9,491
Ibadan	1.27×10^4	4,436	10,647	5,070	11,534
Kano	9.49×10^3	3,320	7,968	3,794	8,632
Makurdi	1.00×10^4	3,514	8,433	4,016	9,136
Nsukka	1.08×10^4	3,787	9,088	4,328	9,845

The World Bank has determined that for the viability of a WTE project, a minimum LHV of MSW of 6,000 MJ/Mg throughout the season and an annual average of 7,000 MJ/Mg are required [48]. As the calorific value estimates are revealed earlier in Table 3, incineration appears to be *technically* viable in the selected municipalities, except in Port Harcourt. It is clear that the cost factor for incinerating a ton of waste in a grate furnace steam generator is high. In [48], it was also noted that the net cost factor for treating a tonne (Mg) of MSW in an incinerator ranges between US$10 and US$100/Mg with an average cost factor of about US$50/Mg. The cost factor for a CHP-WTE plant is at or below the average cost factor. It may be noted that a fluidized bed steam generator and a thermal power plant have similar cost factors. The specific cost of electrical power generated using CHP compares well with the price of electrical power at US$0.14/$kWh_e$. The price of steam generated using a fluidized steam generator also compares favorably with the average price of steam at about US$0.015/$kWh_t$ as shown in Table 11. The International Energy Agency has reviewed the economic and environmental benefits of a CHP technology based on the installed and projected capacity in G8+5 countries. The report calls for increased adaptation of the CHP technology and projects about 19% reduction in CO_2 emissions in 2030 in comparison with projected emissions from fossil fuel-based power generation without a combined heat cycle [49]. The method and approach presented in this work are very much comparable to that reported in [46] and thus provide credence to the accuracies of the present results.

5. IMPLICATIONS AND RECOMMENDATIONS

The effectiveness of the proposed technologies of this study can be described as follows:

- Propensity to reduce landfill dumping and large amounts of land area designated as dump sites. Such lands can be used for other purposes while incineration of waste can produce a much needed energy and reduce the volume of waste by as much as 90%.

Table 11. Cost factor and specific unit price of energy generated by various processes using MSW as fuel

Location	Thermal plant		Fluidized steam generator		Grate furnace generator		CHP	
	CF	C	CF	C	CF	C	CF	C
	US$/Mg	US$/kWh	US$/Mg	US$/kWh	US$/Mg	US$/kWh	US$/Mg	US$/kWh
Lagos	10.4	0.044	9.3	0.018	31.0	0.039	−11.9	0.017
Port Harcourt	39.8	0.095	39.1	0.040	51.5	0.084	27.0	0.037
Abuja	49.9	0.084	48.9	0.035	68.0	0.074	30.0	0.032
Ibadan	25.4	0.056	24.2	0.023	47.4	0.049	1.50	0.021
Kano	33.3	0.071	32.4	0.030	49.8	0.062	15.4	0.027
Makurdi	54.8	0.091	53.8	0.038	72.2	0.080	35.8	0.035
Nsukka	73.0	0.104	72.0	0.044	91.8	0.091	52.6	0.040

- Propensity to reduce dependence on fossil fuels. The advanced technologies of WTE can produce fuel that does not require mining or drilling for non-renewable fossil fuel resources.

- Capacity to offset GHG emissions and pollution caused by burning fossil fuels, and

- Production of clean energy since WTE technologies have significantly advanced as a function of policy measures such as the Kyoto Protocol [16].

Furthermore, the technologies analyzed in this study have been well demonstrated and employed in varying capacities [17]. Electricity generation from MSW is highly feasible in Nigeria considering the population factor and the subsequent large amounts of waste generated which are not effectively managed. Another rationale for exploring underutilized fuels like MSW is for minimizing GHG emissions currently produced by open dumping. WTE is a reasonable and sustainable MSW management strategy in terms of weight and volume reduction coupled with energy recovery, and it is recommended that this should be vigorously explored.

Regulatory and policy measures to promote WTE technologies and market penetration should be established by federal, state, and local governments. Such measures should have clear strategies for implementation and enforcement. Likewise, the weak and almost non-existent financial instruments need to be strengthened and broadened to attract the necessary private sector investments for the adoptions of MSW management via WTE technologies.

Future studies should consider (1) feasibility studies of other municipalities in Nigeria; (2) life cycle assessment of waste disposal options; (3) emissions aspects, carbon offsets, and fossil fuel displaced; and (4) policy and social aspects.

6. CONCLUSIONS

WTE in Nigeria can be developed as an important integrated waste management strategy while simultaneously producing energy, can displace fossil fuels and can reduce pollutant emissions. The operational reliability of WTE systems will be improved over time as more systems are commissioned and operated at a commercial level. WTE should be recognized as part of a future, balanced mix of energy technologies and policies. The location of WTE plants in order to consolidate MSW from various locations to achieve economies of scale will be important. In addition, waste composition is highly unlikely to remain stable, and changes in waste policies and population habits can contribute to waste composition changes which would also affect the performance of WTE plants. Waste having high calorific value will result in more energy recovery. As more societies in the world increasingly adopt the reduce, reuse and recycle strategies, the amount of MSW collected would reduce significantly. While the authors in [50–53] have equally estimated in one capacity or the other the potential for energy generation from other renewable energy sources such as biomass, corn cob, and animal waste for Nigeria, they however did not consider the economics of the potential. Technical and economic assessments of three waste treatment methodologies have been reported in this study. The calorific value and methane generation potential for MSW generated in various towns in Nigeria has been determined. From the estimates of the calorific value and the methane generation potential, the technical feasibility of power generation and/or direct (methane) gas availability has been determined. Within the study, it appears that incineration (particularly a CHP) or anaerobic digestion may be more economical. The costs for power produced by incineration and AD compare very well with what it is in developed countries.

This study has not addressed the emission aspects and carbon offset arguments of the three MSW management approaches considered here. A compelling argument is self-evident if we consider what happens to MSW today in developing countries that are also energy hungry. Currently, MSW is discarded in most developing nations in a landfill. These landfills are undeveloped swath of land that pollutes the environment. Methane and

CO_2 are produced in the landfill, often without any means for methane capture and recovery. Given this scenario, the direct benefits of offsetting methane emission are compelling. It is true that at the end of incinerating the MSW or combusting the methane gas, CO_2 will be produced. On the one hand, it is less potent than methane, and it is hoped that local environmental regulations will regulate carbon dioxide emissions as well. Within the stated study limitations, the following were found:

- An incinerator plant based on CHP or a fluidized combustion technology is a viable option for Lagos, Ibadan, and Kano.

- The viability of landfill methane generation may not be excluded, but it requires further analysis, specifically determining the capital cost with better specificity and methane recovery benefits of a landfill with a MCF of 0.7 and a methane recovery greater than 50%. Landfills tend to take up vital land resource, and such lands cannot be put to any other use for years. This may act as a reason against adopting landfill as a MSW management strategy.

- Anaerobic digestion certainly appears to be a promising and viable MSW management strategy for Nigeria. The price of gas or electricity produced is competitive with fuel currently used and electricity generated through other fossil fuel means.

- The economic performance of the different waste management options is sensitive to their capital costs and this would depend on plant scale, suppliers and local area logistics. As such, there are some inevitable and inherent uncertainties in the estimated values.

This work serves as a preliminary assessment aimed at identifying which MSW management option would be technically and economically viable. The benefits of energy recovery from waste fuels are such that any nation's waste management policy should embrace energy recovery irrespective of the individual local strategic preferences.

ACKNOWLEDGEMENTS

The authors wish to acknowledge the anonymous reviewers for their recommendations to improve the paper. We appreciate the numerous individuals who have contributed in one capacity or the other towards the successful completion of this publication.

COMPETING INTERESTS

The author(s) declare that they have no competing interests.

AUTHORS' CONTRIBUTIONS

OMA conceived the problem and drafted the manuscript. RLF supervised and approved the draft. All authors read and approved the final manuscript.

REFERENCES

1. UN Department of Economic and Social Affairs (UNDESA): *Population Division*. (2012). http://www.un.org/esa/population/unpop.htm (2012). Accessed 1 Dec 2012

2. Babayemi JO, Dauda KT: *Evaluation of solid waste generation, categories and disposal options in developing countries: a case study of Nigeria*. (2009). http://www.bioline.org.br/pdf?ja09042 (2009). Accessed 23 June 2013

3. Central Intelligence Agency: *Nigeria*. (2012). https://www.cia.gov/library/publications/the-world-factbook/geos/ni.html (2012). Accessed 25 Nov 2012

4. Adeyinka MA, *et al.*: *Environmental statistics: situation in Federal Republic of Nigeria*. Dakar Senegal: Workshop on Environmental Statistics; 2005.

5. Fagbenle LR: The solid waste problem in Ibadan municipality: a 1980 case study. *Polytechnic J.* 1982, 1: 56–81.

6. Couth R, Toris C: Carbon emissions reduction strategies in Africa from improved waste management: a review. *Waste Manag.* 2010, 30: 2336–2346.

7. Castaldi MJ, Themelis NJ: The case for increasing the global capacity for waste to energy (WTE). *Waste Biomass Valor.* 2010, 1: 91–105.

8. Pike Research: *Global waste to energy market to reach 29.2 billion by 2022*. (2012). http://www.pikeresearch.com/newsroom/global-waste-to-energy-market-to-reach-29–2-billion-by-2022 (2012). Accessed 25 Nov 2012

9. United States Environmental Protection Agency (USEPA) (2012). http://www.epa.gov/cleanenergy/energy-and-you/affect/municipal-sw.html (2012). Accessed: 25 Oct 2012

10. Ciglotti V: Biomass and waste as sustainable resources. In *Fuel Cells in the Waste to Energy Chain: Green Energy Technology*. Edited by: McPhail SJ, Ciglotti V, Moreno A. London: Springer-Verlag; 2012:23–44.CrossRef

11. Kim MH, Song HB, Song Y, Jeong IT, Kim JK: Evaluation of food waste disposal options in terms of global warming and energy recovery: Korea. *Int. J. Energy Environ. Eng.* 2013, 4: 1.

12. Pandyaswargo A, Onoda H, Nagata K: Energy recovery potential and life cycle impact assessment of municipal solid waste management technologies in Asian countries using ELP model. *Int. J. Energy Environ. Eng.* 2012, 3: 28.

13. Eddine B, Salah M: Solid waste as renewable source of energy: current and future possibility in Algeria. *Int. J. Energy Environ. Eng.* 2012, 3: 17.

14. Environmental and Energy Study Institute: *Reconsidering municipal solid waste as a renewable energy feedstock*. (2009). Accessed 30 Oct 2012 http://www.seas.columbia.edu/earth/wtert/sofos/eesi_msw_issuebrief_072109.pdf (2009). Accessed 30 Oct 2012

15. Pytlar TS: *Inclusion of municipal solid waste as a renewable energy source*. (2009). http://www.swananys.org/pdf/MunicipalSolidWasteEnergyJune09.pdf (2009). Accessed 25 Nov 2012

16. Steiner CG: Kyoto protocol-compliant waste-to-renewable energy with zero air, water and solids pollution. *Bull Energy Efficiency.* 2004, 5(3):12–14.

17. *Confederation of European waste-to-energy plants*. (2012). http://www.cewep.eu (2012). Accessed 25 Sept 2012

18. Sridhar MKC, Bammeke AO, Ademola Omishakin M: A study on the

19. Babayemi JO, Dauda KT: Evaluation of solid waste generation, categories and disposal options in developing countries: a case study of Nigeria. *J Appl Sci Environ Manage.* 2009, 13: 3.

20. Solomon UU: *The state of solid waste management in Nigeria: waste management*. (2009). http://www.elsevier.com/locate/wasman (2009). Accessed: 5 June 2012

21. Punch News: *Lagos to earn income from waste*. (2012). http://www.punchng.com/business/homes-property/lagos-to-earn-income-from-waste-management/ (2012). Accessed 25 Nov 2012

22. Christian, EI: *Potential impacts of climate change on solid waste management in Nigeria*. (2010). http://www.earthzine.org/2010/10/04/potential-impacts-of-climate-change-on-solid-waste-management-in-nigeria/ (2010). Accessed 15 May 2012

23. Miranda ML, Hale B: Waste not, want not: the private and social costs of waste-to-energy production. *Energ Pol.* 1997, 25(6):587–600.

24. Mokhtar AS: Renewable power generation opportunity from municipal solid waste: a case study of Lagos Metropolis (Nigeria). *J Energy Technol Policy.*2012, 2(2):1–14.

25. Nagebu AB: An analysis of municipal solid waste in Kano metropolis, Nigeria.*J. Hum. Ecol.* 2010, 31(2):111–119.

26. Imam A, Mohammed B, Wilson DC, Cheeseman CR: Solid waste management in Abuja, Nigeria. *Waste Mgmt.* 2008, 28: 468–472.

27. Olanrewaju OO, Ilemobade AA: Waste to wealth: a case study of the Ondo State Integrated waste recycling and treatment project, Nigeria. *European J Social Scie.* 2009, 8(1):7–16.

28. Igoni AH, Ayotamuno MJ, Ogaji SOT, Probert SD: Municipal solid-waste in Port Harcourt, Nigeria. *Appl Energy.* 2007, 84(6):664–670.

29. Ogwueleka TC: Municipal solid waste characteristics and management in Nigeria. *Int J Environ Health Sci Eng.* 2009, 6(3):173–180.

30. Sha'Ato R, Aboho SY, Oketunde FO, Eneji IS, Unazi G, Agwa S: Survey of solid waste generation and composition in a rapidly growing urban area in central Nigeria. *Waste Mgmt.* 2007, 27: 352–358.

31. Oresanya O Paper presented at the 47th Annual International Conference of the Nigerian Mining and Geosciences Society (NMGS). In *Integrated waste management shifting the paradigm*. Minna; 2011:6–11.

32. Parikh PP, Channiwala SA: A unified correlation for estimating HHV of solid, liquid and gaseous fuels. *Fuel.* 2002, 81(8):1051–1063.

33. Kumar S, Gaikwad SA, Shekdar AV, Kshirsagar PS, Singh RN: Estimation method for national methane emission from solid waste landfills. *Atmos Environ.* 2004, 38: 3481–3487.

34. USEPA: *Landfill Methane Opportunities Program*. http://EPA.gov/lmop . Accessed 15 May 2013

35. EPA: *US methane emissions 1990–2020: inventories, projections, and opportunities for reductions. EPA 430-R-99–013 report*. Washington, DC: EPA; 1999.

36. Alexander A, Burklin C, Singleton A: *Landfill gas emissions model (LandGEM) version 3.02 user's guide*. Philadelphia: Office of Research and Development, USEPA; 2005.

37. USEPA: *USEPA technology transfer network: clean air technology center*. (2005). http://www.epa.gov/ttncatc1/products.html (2005). Accessed 20 May 2013

38. Verma S: *Anaerobic digestion of biodegradable organics in municipal solid wastes*. (2002). http://www.seas.columbia.edu/earth/vermathesis.pdf(2002). Accessed 18 May 2012

39. Arsova L (2010). http://www.seas.columbia.edu/earth/research_associates/CVs/arsova.pdf (2010). Accessed 20 May 2012

40. Owen GF, Parkin WP: Fundamentals of anaerobic digestion of wastewater sludges. *J Environ Eng.* 1986, 112(5):867–920.

41. Kirjavainen M, Sipila K, Alakangas E, Savola T, Salomon M: *Small-scale biomass CHP technologies situation in Finland, Denmark and Sweden: OPET report 12*. Espoo: VTT Processes and Finnish District Heating Association; 2004.

42. ASME: *An evaluation of the cost of incinerating wastes containing PVC*. (2012). http://files.asme.org/Committees/K&C/TCOB/BRTD/EEW/24116.pdf (2012). Accessed 10 June 2012

43. Peters MS, Timmerhaus KD: *Plant Design and Economics for Chemical Engineers*. New York: McGraw-Hill Book Company; 1980.

44. EPA: *Full cost accounting in action: case studies of six solid waste management agencies. EPA 530-R-95–041 report*. Washington, DC: EPA; 2007.

45. Salami L, *et al.*: *Int Jour Appl Sci Tech.*. 2011, 1(3):47–52.

46. Center for People and Environment: *Landfill recovery and use in Nigeria. Report prepared for the Methane-to-Markets program of the US Environmental Protection Agency*. https://www.globalmethane.org/Data/347_Landfill.Recovery.and.Use.in.Nigeria(LFGE)Final.Report.pdf (2011). Accessed 3 Sept 2013

47. IEA: *IEA Energy Technology Essentials*. Paris: IEA; 2007.

48. World Bank: *Municipal solid waste incineration: World Bank technical guidance report*. Washington, DC: World Bank; 1999.

49. Kerr T: *Combined Heat and Power*. Paris: International Energy Agency; 2007.

50. Suberu MY, Mokhtar AS, Bashir N: Potential capability of corn cob residue for small power generation in rural Nigeria. *ARPN J Eng Appl Sci.* 2012, 7: 1037–1046.

51. Mohammed YS, Mokhtar AS, Bashir N: Renewable power generation opportunity from municipal solid waste in Lagos metropolis (Nigeria). *J Energy Tech Policies.* 2012, 2: 1–14.

52. Mohammed YS, Bashir N, Mustafa MW: Biogenic waste methane emissions and methane optimization for bioelectricity in Nigeria. *Renew Sustain Energy Rev.* 2013, 25: 643–654.

53. Mohammed YS, Mustafa MW, Bashir N, Mokhtar AS: Renewable energy resources for distributed power generation in Nigeria: a review of the potential. *Renew Sustain Energy Rev.* 2013, 22: 257–268.

Index